Lecture Notes in Computer Science 10650

More information about this series at http://www.springer.com/series/7409

Heinrich C. Mayr · Giancarlo Guizzardi
Hui Ma · Oscar Pastor (Eds.)

Conceptual Modeling

36th International Conference, ER 2017
Valencia, Spain, November 6–9, 2017
Proceedings

Springer

Editors
Heinrich C. Mayr
University of Klagenfurt
Klagenfurt
Austria

Hui Ma
Victoria University of Wellington
Wellington
New Zealand

Giancarlo Guizzardi
Free University of Bozen-Bolzano
Bozen-Bolzano
Italy

Oscar Pastor
Valencia University of Technology
Valencia
Spain

ISSN 0302-9743 ISSN 1611-3349 (electronic)
Lecture Notes in Computer Science
ISBN 978-3-319-69903-5 ISBN 978-3-319-69904-2 (eBook)
https://doi.org/10.1007/978-3-319-69904-2

Library of Congress Control Number: 2017957732

LNCS Sublibrary: SL3 – Information Systems and Applications, incl. Internet/Web, and HCI

Printed on acid-free paper

This Springer imprint is published by Springer Nature
The registered company is Springer International Publishing AG
The registered company address is: Gewerbestrasse 11, 6330 Cham, Switzerland

Preface

The International Conference on Conceptual Modeling (ER) is the leading global forum for current research on conceptual modeling (CM) and trendsetting CM applications. The topics of interest span the entire spectrum of CM: theoretical and ontological foundation, methods and tools for developing and communicating conceptual models and meta models, techniques for transforming conceptual models into effective implementations, and the impact of CM techniques on databases, business strategies, and information systems development. The ER conference series has been held at a variety of superb locations, rotating in successive years between Europe, the Asia-Pacific region, and the Americas, and attracting an international community of scholars.

This volume contains the research and technical papers comprising the main program of ER 2017 in its 36th conference edition held during November 6–9, 2017, in the beautiful city of Valencia, Spain. More than 450 researchers from all over the world followed our call for papers and submitted 153 papers about their latest research results. Each paper was carefully reviewed by at least three members of the Program Committee, which consisted of renowned scientists from more than 40 nations. Finally, 28 papers, i.e., about 18%, were selected as full papers to be presented at the conference and to be included in this volume. An additional 10 submissions were accepted as short papers. The quality of these 38 papers is a tribute to the authors and also to the reviewers who guided any necessary improvements.

Focal points of these papers are: (1) CM and ontologies in the context of requirements analysis, business processes, and other domains; (2) foundations of CM, for example, regarding multi-level modeling; (3) CM methodology with a broad spectrum of innovative answers to interesting research questions; (4) ontologies; and (5) model efficiency.

This volume would not have materialized without the support of many people. First, we are very grateful to all the authors for their continuous commitment and intensive work. Second, we would like to thank the Program Committee members and additional reviewers for providing timely and in-depth assessments. Furthermore, we thank all the people and sponsors who helped in the organization of ER 2017. Without all that effort there would have been no substance for this volume and no success for ER 2017. Last but not least, we are greatly indebted to the five invited speakers, Prof. Lois Delcambre (USA), Prof. Josef Mitterer (Austria), Prof. Antoni Olivé (Spain), Francisco Garcia-Moran (Spain), and Prof. Yair Wand (Canada), for accepting our invitation to address this conference.

September 2017

Heinrich C. Mayr
Giancarlo Guizzardi
Hui Ma
Oscar Pastor

Organization

Program Committee

Jacky Akoka	CNAM and TEM, France
Raian Ali	Bournemouth University, UK
Joao Paulo Almeida	Federal University of Espirito Santo, Brazil
Yuan An	Drexel University, USA
Joao Araujo	Universidade Nova de Lisboa, Portugal
Alessandro Artale	Free University of Bolzano-Bozen, Italy
Claudia P. Ayala	Technical University of Catalunya, Spain
Fatma Başak Aydemir	Utrecht University, The Netherlands
Doo-Hwan Bae	KAIST, South Korea
Fernanda Araujo Baiao	UNIRIO, Brazil
Zhifeng Bao	RMIT University, Australia
Judith Barrios Albornoz	University of Los Andes, Colombia
Ladjel Bellatreche	LIAS/ENSMA, France
Nelly Bencomo	Aston University, UK
Kawtar Benghazi	Universidad de Granada, Spain
Sandro Bimonte	IRSTEA, France
Mokrane Bouzeghoub	UVSQ/CNRS, France
Shawn Bowers	Gonzaga University, USA
Stephane Bressan	National University of Singapore
Cristina Cabanillas	Wirtschaftsuniversität Wien, Austria
Diego Calvanese	Free University of Bozen-Bolzano, Italy
Maria Luiza Campos	Federal University of Rio de Janeiro, Brazil
Luca Cernuzzi	Universidad Católica, Asunción, Paraguay
Vinay Chaudhri	Independent Researcher, USA
Roger Chiang	AIS, USA
Suphamit Chittayasothorn	King Mongkut's Institute of Technology Ladkrabang, Thailand
Dickson K.W. Chiu	The University of Hong Kong, SAR China
Byron Choi	Hong Kong Baptist University, SAR China
Isabelle Comyn-Wattiau	ESSEC Business School, France
Nelly Condori-Fernández	Universidade da Coruña, Spain
Dolors Costal	Universitat Politècnica de Catalunya, Spain
Alfredo Cuzzocrea	ICAR-CNR and University of Calabria, Italy
Fabiano Dalpiaz	Utrecht University, The Netherlands
Karen Davis	Miami University, USA
Valeria De Antonellis	University of Brescia, Italy
Sergio De Cesare	Brunel University, UK
Jose Luis de La Vara	Carlos III University of Madrid, Spain

José Palazzo M. de Oliveira	Federal University of Rio Grande do Sul, Brazil
Adela Del Río Ortega	University of Seville, Spain
Lois Delcambre	Portland State University, USA
Gill Dobbie	University of Auckland, New Zealand
Johann Eder	Alpen-Adria-Universität Klagenfurt, Austria
Vadim Ermolayev	Zaporizhzhya National University, Ukraine
M.J. Escalona	University of Seville, Spain
Sergio Espana Cubillo	Universiteit Utrecht, The Netherlands
Ricardo A. Falbo	Federal University of Esprito Santo, Brazil
Hans-Georg Fill	University of Bamberg, Germany
Xavier Franch	Universitat Politècnica de Catalunya, Spain
Enrico Franconi	Free University of Bozen-Bolzano, Italy
Ulrich Frank	Universität Duisburg-Essen, Germany
Agnès Front	LIG, SIGMA, Grenoble University, France
Frederik Gailly	Ghent University, Belgium
Aldo Gangemi	Université Paris 13 and CNR-ISTC, France
Faiez Gargouri	Institut Supérieur d'Informatique et de Multimédia de Sfax, Tunisia
Aurona Gerber	CAIR, University of Pretoria, South Africa
Sepideh Ghanavati	Texas Tech University, USA
Mohamed Gharzouli	Constantine 2 University, Algeria
Aditya Ghose	University of Wollongong, Australia
Giovanni Giachetti	Universidad Tecnológica de Chile INACAP, Chile
Paolo Giorgini	University of Trento, Italy
Cesar Gonzalez-Perez	Incipit, CSIC, Spain
Jeff Gray	University of Alabama, USA
Georg Grossmann	University of South Australia
Nicola Guarino	ISTC-CNR, Italy
Esther Guerra	Universidad Autónoma de Madrid, Spain
Giancarlo Guizzardi	Federal University of Espirito Santo (UFES), Brazil; Free University of Bozen-Bolzano, Italy
Sven Hartmann	Clausthal University of Technology, Germany
Martin Henkel	Stockholm University, Sweden
Arantza Illarramendi	Basque Country University, Spain
Matthias Jarke	RWTH Aachen University, Germany
Manfred Jeusfeld	University of Skövde, Sweden
Ivan Jureta	University of Namur, Belgium
Gerti Kappel	TU Wien, Austria
Dimitris Karagiannis	University of Vienna, Austria
Kamalakar Karlapalem	CDE, IIIT Hyderabad, India
David Kensche	SAP, Germany
Vijay Khatri	Indiana University, USA
Dimitris Kiritsis	EPFL, Switzerland
Agnes Koschmider	Karlsruhe Institute of Technology, Germany
Hasan Koç	Universität Rostock, Germany

Mong Li Lee	National University of Singapore
Moonkun Lee	Chonbuk National University, South Korea
Julio Cesar Leite	PUC-Rio, Brazil
Guoliang Li	Tsinghua University, China
Stephen Liddle	Brigham Young University, USA
Tok Wang Ling	National University of Singapore
Sebastian Link	University of Auckland, New Zealand
Pericles Loucopoulos	University of Manchester, UK
Hui Ma	Victoria University of Wellington, New Zealand
Wolfgang Maass	Saarland University, Germany
Patricia Martin-Rodilla	Institute of Heritage Sciences Spanish National Research Council, Spain
Paloma Martínez Fernández	Universidad Carlos III de Madrid, Spain
Beatriz Marín	Universidad Diego Portales, Chile
Heinrich C. Mayr	Alpen-Adria-Universität Klagenfurt, Austria
Raul Mazo	Paris 1-Sorbonne University, France
Vitaly Mezhuyev	University Malaysia Pahang, Malaysia
Judith Michael	Alpen-Adria-Universität Klagenfurt, Austria
Zoltan Micskei	Budapest University of Technology and Economics, Hungary
Lourdes Moreno	Universidad Carlos III de Madrid, Spain
Haralambos Mouratidis	University of Brighton, UK
John Mylopoulos	University of Toronto, Canada
Wilfred Ng	HKUST, SAR China
Selmin Nurcan	Université de Paris 1, France
Antoni Olivé	Universitat Politècnica de Catalunya, Spain
Andreas L Opdahl	University of Bergen, Norway
Jinsoo Park	Seoul National University, South Korea
Jeffrey Parsons	Memorial University of Newfoundland, Canada
Chris Partridge	Brunel University, BORO Solutions, UK
Oscar Pastor	Universitat Politecnica de Valencia, Spain
Barbara Pernici	Politecnico di Milano, Italy
Geert Poels	Ghent University, Belgium
Henderik Proper	Public Research Centre Henri Tudor, Luxembourg
Ricardo Rafael Quintero Meza	Instituto Tecnológico de Culiacán, Mexico
Christoph Quix	Fraunhofer FIT, Germany
Jolita Ralyté	University of Geneva, Switzerland
Sudha Ram	University of Arizona, USA
Suwanna Rasmequan	Burapha University, Thailand
Iris Reinhartz-Berger	University of Haifa, Israel
Manuel Resinas	University of Seville, Spain
Daniel Riesco	National University of San Luis, Argentina
Stefanie Rinderle-Ma	University of Vienna, Austria
Stefano Rizzi	University of Bologna, Italy

Genaina Rodrigues	University of Brasilia, Brazil
Colette Rolland	Université Paris 1, France
Raul Ruggia	University of the Republic, Uruguay
Marcela Ruiz	Utrecht University, The Netherlands
Antonio Ruiz-Cortés	University of Seville, Spain
Keun Ho Ryu	Chungbuk National University, South Korea
Sourav S Bhowmick	Nanyang Technological University, Singapore
Motoshi Saeki	Tokyo Institute of Technology, Japan
Melike Sah	Trinity College Dublin, Ireland
Camille Salinesi	CRI, Université de Paris 1 Panthéon-Sorbonne, France
Kurt Sandkuhl	University of Rostock, Germany
Flavia Santoro	NP2Tec/UNIRIO, Brazil
Klaus-Dieter Schewe	Software Competence Center Hagenberg, Germany
Daniel Schwabe	PUC-Rio, Brazil
Vladimir A. Shekhovtsov	Alpen-Adria-Universität Klagenfurt, Austria
Peretz Shoval	Ben-Gurion University, Israel
Samira Si-Said Cherfi	CEDRIC, Conservatoire National des Arts et Métiers, France
Guttorm Sindre	NTNU, Norway
Monique Snoeck	K.U. Leuven, Belgium
Pnina Soffer	University of Haifa, Israel
Il-Yeol Song	Drexel University, USA
Veda Storey	GSU, USA
Stefan Strecker	University of Hagen, Germany
Arnon Sturm	Ben-Gurion University, Israel
David Taniar	Monash University, Australia
Ernest Teniente	Universitat Politècnica de Catalunya, Spain
James Terwilliger	Microsoft Corporation
Bernhard Thalheim	Christian Albrechts Universität Kiel, Germany
Victoria Torres	Universidad Politecnica de Valencia, Spain
Juan-Carlos Trujillo	University of Alicante, Spain
Jose Turull-Torres	Universidad Nacional de La Matanza, Argentina, and Massey University, New Zealand
Panos Vassiliadis	University of Ioannina, Greece
Tanja E.J. Vos	Open Universiteit, The Netherlands
Gerd Wagner	Brandenburg University of Technology at Cottbus, Germany
Barbara Weber	Universität Innsbruck, Austria
Claudia Werner	UFRJ, Brazil
Roel Wieringa	University of Twente, The Netherlands
Manuel Wimmer	Vienna University of Technology, Austria
Carson Woo	University of British Columbia, Canada
Robert Wrembel	Poznan University of Technology, Poland
Huayu Wu	Institute for Infocomm Research, Singapore

Hwan-Seung Yong	Ewha Womans University, South Korea
Eric Yu	University of Toronto, Canada
Yanchun Zhang	Victoria University, Australia
Iyad Zikra	Stockholm University, Sweden

Additional Reviewers

Abdelahad, Corina
Artale, Alessandro
Asprino, Luigi
Baek, Youngmin
Bianchini, Devis
Borges, Marcos R.S.
Bork, Dominik
Böhmer, Kristof
Calvanese, Diego
Chu, Lisa
Chuah, Seong Ping
Corman, Julien
Estrada Torres, Irene Bedilia
Feltus, Christophe
Fernandes, Filipe
Fernandez, Pablo
García, José María
Huemer, Christian
Kaczmarek, Monika
Khodabandelou, Ghazaleh
Khouri, Selma
Koh, Judice
Köpke, Julius
Mazak, Alexandra
Melchiori, Michele
Nalchigar, Soroosh
Noguera, Manuel
Oriol, Xavier
Ouhammou, Yassine
Panach Navarrete, Jose Ignacio
Piras, Luca
Pittl, Benedikt
Prince Sales, Tiago
Razo-Zapata, Iván S.
Russo, Alessandro
Sangat, Prajwol
Shin, Donghwan
Silveira, Denis
Souza, Vitor E. Silva
Stertz, Florian
Troya, Javier
Unger, Moshe
Walch, Michael
Wally, Bernhard
Winter, Karolin
Wolny, Sabine

Sponsors

Main Organizers

Invited Talks

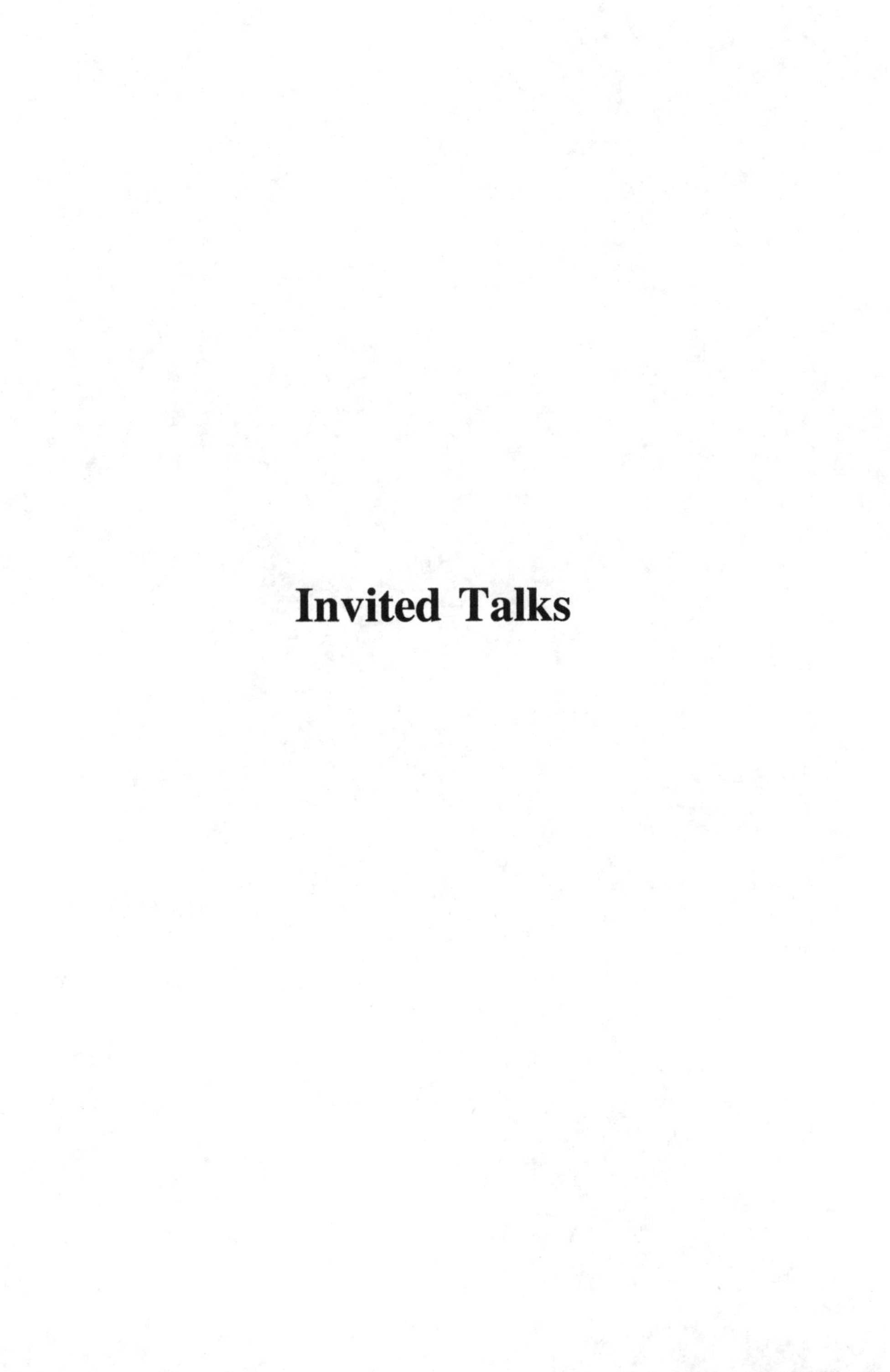

Conceptual Modeling? When We are Awash in Information?

Lois Delcambre

Computer Science Department,
Portland State University
lmd@pdx.edu

Abstract. We challenge the traditional who/what/why of conceptual modeling of information in a world where structured data is ubiquitous.

Who (defines conceptual models?) Analysts? Developers? Ontology specialists? All of the above. But non-traditional users such as scientists, journalists, educators, and almost anyone with data to share are being empowered to define their own information with easy to use data storage and web management systems.

What (is being modeled?) A database as part of an information system or software system? Information that supports a business process? Definitely. But some users define their structured information directly – for display and processing.

Why (is a conceptual model defined?) To describe information and processing of an information system or a software system? To promote collaboration and communication? To increase understanding of a domain? To document a system? Certainly. But let's consider the goals of people who define and publish their own structured information directly; perhaps we can use a conceptual model to offer them useful functionality for their information (e.g., for browsing, mapping, calculations).

We suggest that domain users are doing conceptual modeling. And we believe that they can relate their conceptual model to a domain model when they are enticed by sophisticated information widgets that can select, display, and process their information. We also highlight a problem that has been present since conceptual models (or database schemas) were first created: information of interest to a user might be present in the "data" (such as "Oregon" being part of someone's address) or in the "schema" such as "Oregon" or "California" being attribute names (for a sport fishing registry). Finally, we show that users (who understand their own information) can perform schema integration, including complex operations such as pivot and unpivot, when guided with examples (of the widgets) using sample data.

Conceptual Modeling: Philosophical Considerations

Josef Mitterer

Alpen-Adria-Universität Klagenfurt
josef.mitterer@aau.at

Abstract. The underlying philosophies of Conceptual Modeling vary between Critical Realism and Ontological Constructivism and fit into the philosophical panorama: *There are distinctions and therefore we make them* (Realism) — *We make distinctions and therefore they are* (Idealism/Constructivism).

The presupposition of dichotomies between language and world, description and object, between what we talk and what we talk about, helps to freeze, dogmatize and fundamentalize the *status quo* into a "real" world and "its" representations.

Claims of representing the real world remain irrelevant as long as consensus prevails. When conflicts arise, the world and other potential decision criteria in a beyond of discourse stay mute: the criteria fail and the opposing parties get into a stalemate… In a recent conversation the ontologist Barry Smith said on how he would deal with competing ontologies: "I try to win."

Proposing an alternative philosophy of change requires a shift in the vocabulary and in the direction of discourse: Instead of advocating a dichotomy between a fixed/independent world and privileged representations, a philosophy of change favors relations between *so far* and *from now on*. The object of a description relates to the description of the object like the description *so far* to the description *from now on*. Every description of the object changes the object into a new object of further descriptions.

Philosophical ontologists try to transcend the "here and now" into the past and future. I opt for transparence rather than transcendence. The world, the reality is nothing but the present state of things.

IT Professionals and Conceptual Modeling

Francisco Garcia Moran

European Commission, BECH C3/631, Luxembourg
francisco.garcia-moran@ec.europa.eu

Abstract. IT professionals, explicitly or implicitly, develop conceptual models when trying to produce a high level description of the fundamental principles and the main functionalities of the "systems" (understood in the most general way: Enterprise Architecture, Infrastructure Blueprints, Information Systems, Database Systems, etc.) they want to implement. They do it because they want

1. enhance the understanding of the "users",
2. facilitate the dialogue among system's stakeholders,
3. provide system designers with an input to produce system specifications at different levels, and
4. document the system for future reference and collaboration activities.

There are several relevant questions to IT practitioners about the use of conceptual modelling that the author will try to cover in his presentation on his more than 40 years of professional experience in the public sector as well as his conversations with hundreds of IT professionals in the public and private sectors:

1. Why "conceptual modeling" is considered by many IT professionals as "too theoretical" or "too heavy"?
2. Which are the barriers and facilitators for its more formal adoption?
3. Is there a contradiction between "being agile" (for instance using agile development methodologies like Scrum) and the formal use of conceptual models?
4. What can be done about it?

The author will try to illustrate the answer to some of the above mentioned questions based on the results on an informal survey filled in by many of his contacts in public and private sectors.

Classification and Science

Yair Wand

Sauder School of Business, The University of British Columbia,
Vancouver, BC, Canada
yair.wand@ubc.ca

Abstract. Classifying phenomena is deeply intertwined with cognition and human information processing. Therefore, identifying classes is a central aspect of information technology (IT). Choosing a "good" set of classes is both theoretically and practically important. Two cognitive principles underlie the cognitive approach to classification. First, classes encapsulate inferences about the properties of their instances – in other words, knowing a category can "tell" us more about an instance that required to identify the category it belongs to. Second, collections of classes should provide economy of storage. This leads to a view of classes as carriers of domain knowledge in the form of inferences about situations, which is more than "containers" for information.

We discuss how this view can be used to model scientific theories. We explain how the principles can be used to guide the choice of collections of classes. We show how the approach can be used in scientific discourse by applying it to one of the most well-known areas of physics – the electromagnetic equations as developed originally by Maxwell. The example shows how the classification based approach can be generally applied to scientific problems and that it has two advantages. First, it can provide a simpler and more informative account of the sample phenomena. Second, the classification principles can lead to questions to be asked to help resolve differences between observations and predictions. This means that the resolution of problems can be framed in terms of changes to classification structures, and to principles suggesting how such changes might occur.

Contents

Conceptual Modeling and Requirements

Foundations

Ontologies

The Universal Ontology: A Vision for Conceptual Modeling and the Semantic Web (Invited Paper)

Antoni Olivé(✉)

Department of Service and Information System Engineering, Universitat Politècnica de Catalunya – Barcelona Tech, Barcelona, Catalonia
antoni.olive@upc.edu

Abstract. This paper puts forward a vision of a universal ontology (UO) aiming at solving, or at least greatly alleviating, the semantic integration problem in the field of conceptual modeling and the understandability problem in the field of the semantic web. So far it has been assumed that the UO is not feasible in practice, but we think that it is time to revisit that assumption in the light of the current state-of-the-art. This paper aims to be a step in this direction. We try to make an initial proposal of a feasible UO. We present the scope of the UO, the kinds of its concepts, and the elements that could comprise the specification of each concept. We propose a modular structure for the UO consisting of four levels. We argue that the UO needs a complete set of concept composition operators, and we sketch three of them. We also tackle a few issues related to the feasibility of the UO, which we think that they could be surmountable. Finally, we discuss the desirability of the UO, and we explain why we conjecture that there are already organizations that have the knowledge and resources needed to develop it, and that might have an interest in its development in the near future.

Keywords: Conceptual modeling · Semantic web · Conceptual schemas · Ontologies · Universal ontology

1 Introduction

This paper puts forward a vision of a universal ontology aiming at solving, or at least greatly alleviating, two important problems in the fields of conceptual modeling and the semantic web.

As a first approximation, by universal ontology (UO) we mean the formal specification of all the concepts that we use and share. This includes the concepts of general use, those that are particular to the existing disciplines, and those specific to any kind of human or organizational activity. The UO specifies the concepts that apply to objects, to their relationships, and to the actions or events involving those objects.

The UO could be a radical solution to at least two important problems. One of them is the problem of the semantic integration of information in the fields of information systems and databases. The problem arises when two or more systems whose

H.C. Mayr et al. (Eds.): ER 2017, LNCS 10650, pp. 1–17, 2017.
https://doi.org/10.1007/978-3-319-69904-2_1

As an example, consider the concept whose name in English is *dog*. Its identifier could be *Q144*. It would be defined as an entity type. The concept has one or more names in each natural language. The definition would be an expression in each natural language. *Q144* is involved in several *IsA* relationships, such as (in English) *Dog IsA Animal*. An analytical constraint could be that the sets of instances of *Dog* and *Cat* are disjoint. The concept *Dog* may be defined as an instance of *Species* (*Dog InstanceOf Species*), where *Species* is a meta entity type.

There is a large set of similar properties that are instantiated in many facts. These are the attributes whose name is the name of an entity or data type. Almost all names of entity and data types can be in some context the name of an attribute of some subject. This observation leads us to propose to make in the UO the "*assumption of implicit attributes*", by which we mean that for each entity or data type defined in the UO there is an implicit attribute property with the same name. The domain of the property is the top-level entity type (such as *Entity*) and its range is the corresponding entity or data type. For example, if *Seller* is the name (in some language) of an entity type, then we assume that there is an implicit attribute whose name (in the same language) is *seller*, domain *Entity* and range *Seller*.

The assumption of the implicit properties is of practical importance because it may save a great deal of effort in the definition of the UO. As an example, the great majority of the properties defined in schema.org[2] would be implicit in the UO, because their name would coincide with those of entity and data types, or could be composed from them, as will be explained in Sect. 4.

We note that in schema.org (and in many other ontologies) the definition of a property includes its domain and range, which may be different from that assigned by the above assumption. However, this might not be important in the proposed UO, since its envisaged objective does not include the control of the validity of facts nor the reasoning from facts.

3 The Structure of the UO

The UO is huge; therefore, in order to be manageable, it must be modularized [15]. We distinguish four levels of concepts, and we group the concepts at the same level into a module [16]. The levels are: Conceptual Model, Foundational, General, and Domain. Each of these levels is briefly described below. If we arrange vertically the levels, and populate each level, the result can be seen as a pyramid, which we call the UO pyramid (Fig. 1).

There must be an organization that has an overall responsibility for the UO. We call UO regulator to this organization. Other regulators would have a responsibility for specific parts of the UO. In the description that follows we will indicate the role of each regulator in each level.

---

[2] http://schema.org/.

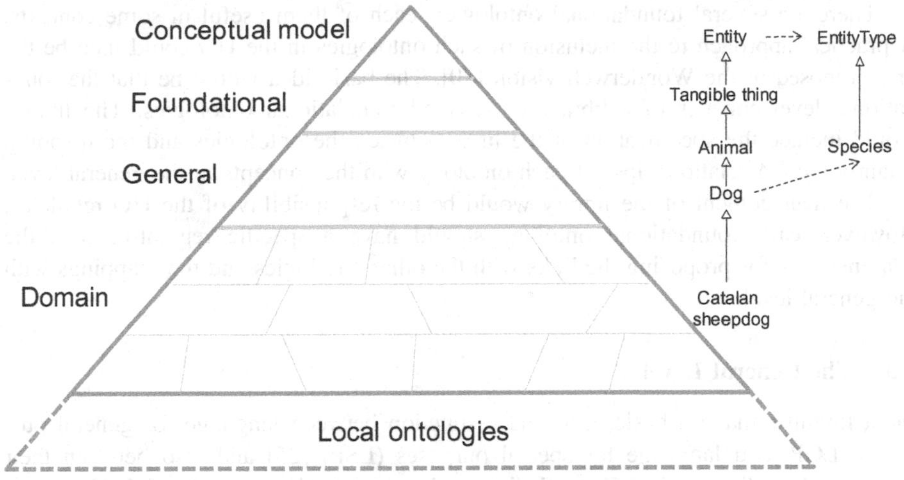

Fig. 1. The levels of the UO pyramid

3.1 The Conceptual Model Level

The conceptual model (or ontology model) level comprises the meta types and the direct or indirect supertypes of all the concepts in the UO [17, 18]. The concepts at this level are used to define the rest of the UO. Figure 1 shows two example concepts at this level, that we have called *Entity* and *EntityType*, with an *InstanceOf* relationship between them. *Entity* would be the supertype of all entity types, while *EntityType* would be the supertype of all meta entity types.

Each conceptual/ontology model (such as, for example, UML, ER, RDFS or OWL) includes the concepts needed for this level of the UO. For example, in RDFS the concepts would be *Class*, *Resource*, *Datatype*, *Literal*, *Property*, etc. [19]. In any case, the number of concepts at this level is very small.

Based on the existing conceptual/ontology models, it should not be difficult to reach an agreement on the concepts to be included in the proposed UO. The concepts at this level should be under the responsibility of the UO regulator.

3.2 The Foundational Level

The foundational level, which is also small in size, includes abstract concepts that have been proposed in the foundational ontologies [20, 21], such as DOLCE [22] or UFO [23, 24]. The concepts at this level cannot be directly instantiated to publish facts and, therefore, they are not essential in the proposed UO. However, they may be useful for clarifying the semantics of other concepts, for defining only once knowledge that is common to several concepts, and for reasoning purposes. As an example, UFO makes a fundamental distinction between individuals that are *Endurant* and *Event*. Another example is the concept *TangibleThing*, a subtype of *Entity*, shown in Fig. 1. In general, the definitions and constraints of these concepts are "inherited" by all the concepts that are defined as their direct or indirect subtypes.

There are several foundational ontologies, each of them useful in some contexts. A practical approach to the inclusion of such ontologies in the UO could then be the one proposed in the Wonderweb vision [20]. The basic idea would be that the foundational level consists of a library of selected foundational ontologies. The library would include the specification of the links between the ontologies and the mapping (mainly the *IsA* relationships) of each ontology with the concepts in the general level.

The management of the library would be the responsibility of the UO regulator. However, each foundational ontology should have a specific regulator, with the responsibility for proposing the links with the other ontologies and the mappings with the general level.

3.3 The General Level

Most linguists make a basic, informal distinction between language for general purposes (LGP) and language for special purposes (LSP) [25] and also between their corresponding dictionaries. General dictionaries contain those words of the language which are of general use, representing various spheres of life and presenting a complete picture of the general language. They are meant for the general user of the language. Special dictionaries either cover a specific part of the vocabulary or are prepared with some definite purpose [26].

Going from words to concepts, it seems natural to stablish a similar basic, informal distinction between concepts for general purposes and concepts for special purposes. We can then include the former in the general level of the UO pyramid and the latter in the domain level. In the example of Fig. 1, there are three concepts in the general level: *Animal*, *Dog* and *Species*, with *Dog IsA Animal* and *Dog InstanceOf Species*.

The concepts at the general level are subtypes or instance of concepts at the conceptual model level, and, possibly, of concepts at the foundational level.

There are several ontologies that could provide an excellent basis from which to build the general level of the UO. Among them, we mention here WordNet [27], SUMO [7], CYC [28], and BabelNet [29]. For the purposes of illustration, in the following we will assume WordNet.

WordNet defines noun, verb and adjective synsets that may be the source of the entity types and properties of the UO. WordNet 3.0 comprises over 80,000 noun synsets (concepts), which include most (if not all) entity types that have a name in the English LGP. By the application of the assumption of implicit attributes, there would also be an implicit attribute for each entity type. There are already “wordnets” in many languages [30], which include links to the English WordNet.

WordNet comprises also over 13,000 verb synsets, which include most (if not all) properties that have a name in verb form in the English LGP.

Finally, WordNet comprises also over 18,000 adjective synsets, most of which can be considered as Boolean properties. For example, the adjective synset *local#2*, with the gloss “of or belonging to or characteristic of a particular locality or neighborhood”, could be considered as a Boolean datatype property, with its own identifier and English name “is local”.

In order to guarantee the consistency of the general level, its creation and evolution should be under the responsibility of the UO regulator.

3.4 The Domain Level

In the UO pyramid, the domain level contains the concepts for special purposes corresponding to the LSP. Therefore, this level contains all existing domain ontologies. Since there are many domain ontologies, some of which very big, the domain level includes in total several millions of concepts. Achieving a satisfactory arrangement of these ontologies is the main technical challenge of the UO. Figure 1 shows an example of concept at this level, *CatalanSheepdog,* which is a subtype of the concept *Dog* at the general level.

The concepts at the domain level are subtypes or instance of concepts at the general level, and, possibly, of concepts at the foundational level.

An ontology can be a part of the domain level of the UO if its mappings with the rest of the UO are defined. There are two kinds of mappings: vertical and horizontal. The vertical mappings define the correspondences between that ontology and the concepts at the general level. The horizontal mappings define the correspondences between that ontology and the other ontologies at the domain level.

In both mappings, a correspondence is a relationship between two concepts. In general, it can be an equivalence (the concepts are the same), an *IsA* (a concept is a subtype of the other) or a disjointness (no entity -or property- can be an instance of both concepts) [31]. Equivalent concepts are considered the same and, therefore, the equivalence correspondences are ignored.

The mappings must preserve the completeness of the UO [12, 32, 33]. In our context, this implies that the two following conditions are satisfied at any time:

"1. Let C_1 and C_2 be two concepts in the UO. If in the real-world the instances of C_1 must necessarily be also instances of C_2, then in the UO there must be a direct or indirect subtype correspondence between C_1 and C_2."
"2. Let C_1 and C_2 be two concepts in the UO. If in the real-world the instances of C_1 cannot be also instances of C_2, then in the UO there must be a direct or indirect disjointness correspondence between C_1 and C_2."

Satisfaction of the first condition guarantees, among other things, that users querying the instances of C_2 will get also the instances of C_1 even if users are unaware of the existence of C_1 in the UO. Satisfaction of the second condition is mandatory in an open world assumption of the UO.

Each domain ontology should be under the control of a specific regulator. To include a new ontology in the domain level, its regulator should provide the vertical mappings with the concepts at the general level. The UO regulator should review and approve those mappings before the "official" adoption of the new ontology within the UO.

The new ontology may overlap with one or more ontologies already existing in the domain level. Therefore, it is necessary to discover those ontologies and to define the corresponding mappings. The discovery of the set of potentially overlapping ontologies can be automated to a great extent by using the previous vertical mappings [34]. For each potentially overlapping ontology, it will be necessary to define the correspondences with the new ontology. Ideally, this should be done by the regulators of both ontologies. Existing or future matching systems should be of great help in determining both the potentially overlapping ontologies and their correspondences [31, 35]. A recent example of the use of matching systems for automatically determining the mappings between ontologies is described in [36].

3.5 Local Concepts

Local concepts are specializations of concepts defined in the UO, but that are not part of it. Local concepts are not intended to be generally shared. Through time, a local concept may evolve and become part of the appropriate level of the UO.

There will always be a strong need of local concepts. However, many of them could be defined as a composition of other concepts already defined in the UO. If there were a mechanism for defining and using compound concepts that would not require their inclusion in the UO, the need of local concepts could be significantly decreased. We deal with this in the next section.

4 Concept Composition

The UO described above specifies only a limited (even if very large) number of concepts. However, it is a fact that using an appropriate set of composition operators we could compose a limitless number of concepts from them. We call *core* UO the explicitly defined ontology, and *extended* UO the set of concepts that could be composed from the core. The *full* UO would then be the union of the core and extended parts.

The concepts of the extended UO could be used in the publication and query of facts, markup of web pages, conceptual schemas, database schemas, and similar places, like those of the core UO. The crucial point is that such use would be done without the explicit inclusion of the composed concepts in the core UO. Composed concepts are defined when and where used.

There is an insightful parallelism between the UO and a human language. Human languages are usually described as consisting of two parts: a *lexicon*, a catalogue of a limited number of words, and a *grammar*, a system of rules which allow for the combination of those words into a limitless number of sentences. Applying this parallelism, the lexicon would be the core UO, the grammar the set of composition operators, and the sentences the full UO.

It is surprising that concept composition, as indicated above, has been used so little in the conceptual modeling and semantic web fields, especially if one takes into account that some of the languages used in those fields (such as OCL and OWL) allow the definition of compound concepts.

One of the few exceptions is SNOMED CT [37], which is a controlled vocabulary for the clinical domain. SNOMED CT provides a mechanism that enables clinical phrases (facts) to be represented, even when a single SNOMED CT concept does not capture the required level of detail. This is important as it enables a wide range of clinical meanings to be captured in a record, without requiring the terminology to include a separate concept for every detailed combination of ideas that may potentially need to be recorded.

We believe that the UO could achieve its intended objective only if there is a powerful set of composition operators that allows defining and using the concepts in the extended UO. In rest of this section, we sketch only three of these operators: two inspired in compound nouns (Sect. 4.1) and one based on aggregate functions (Sect. 4.2).

4.1 Compound Nouns

Word compounding is a mechanism we use to generate a limitless number of words from an existing, limited, lexicon. Word compounding has been widely studied in linguistics [38]. Similarly, concept combination is a mechanism we use to generate a limitless number of concepts from a limited number of existing ones. Concept combination has been studied in cognitive psychology and cognitive science [39].

In linguistics, a compound consists of the concatenation of two or more words. A compound may be of any syntactic category, but in this paper we will only deal with compounds that are nouns that correspond to entity types (such as *lodging business*). From a morphological point of view, English noun compounds can be open (as in *lodging business*), hyphenated (as in *world-beater*) and closed (as in *sheepdog*) [40].

There exist several different classes of noun compounds. In this section we will focus on the endocentric compounds, which are the most frequent in English [41]. An endocentric compound noun *W* consists of a head *H*, which is a noun, and a modifier *M*. The noun *W* is more specific than *H*, and therefore it holds that *W IsA H* [36]. In English, the modifier *M* is normally a noun, an adjective or a verb, as illustrated by the following examples from schema.org:

- Noun: *Flight reservation*, *Government organization*, *Tourist attraction*.
- Adjective: *Financial product*, *Local business*, *Medical organization*.
- Verb: *Sell action*, *Send action*, *Receive action*.

Based on this, in the following we propose two concept composition operators of entity types.

Entity-Property Composition. The entity-property compound is analogous to the above adjective-noun compound. Let E_i be an entity type and let P_j be a datatype property whose range is *Boolean*, and such that E_i is in the domain of P_j. Then we denote by $EP(E_i, P_j)$ the compound entity type whose instances are the instances of E_i for which P_j is true.

As an example, consider the entity type that corresponds to a local business. This type is not defined in WordNet, but we could define it as an *EP* composition from two concepts defined in it: the noun synset *business#1* and the adjective synset *local#2*. The noun synset *business#1* corresponds to an entity type, while the adjective synset *local#2* would corresponds to a *Boolean* property. Then, *EP*(*business#1*,*local#2*) would be the compound entity type whose instances are the instances of *business#1* for which *local#2* is true.

Note that the *EP* operator is language independent. We do not suggest here a user-friendly notation for compound concepts. The point that we want to make here is that the expression $EP(E_i,P_j)$ (or some equivalent notation or name, see below) can be used like any other entity type of the core UO, even if it is not explicitly defined in it.

The expression $EP(E_i,P_j)$ would be the identifier and the default name of the compound concept. In general, however, these names are not user friendly. A better option could be the use of naming functions. There could be a naming function F_C for each composition operator C, such that $F_C(C_{exp},L)$ gives a name of the concept obtained by the expression C_{exp} using the operator C in language L. For example, F_{EP}*(EP(business#1, local#2),English)* could give the name "Local business".

From the definition it follows that $EP(E_i,P_j)$ *IsA* E_i. On the other hand, if P_j and P_k are two properties such that P_j *IsA* P_k then it follows that $EP(E_i, P_j)$ *IsA* $EP(E_i,P_k)$.

In large ontologies there are many compound concepts that could be defined using *EP* compositions from noun and adjective synsets included in WordNet. A prominent example may be Microsoft Concept Graph (MCG), which contains above five million concepts, most of which named with a compound [42]. In MCG there are over 1.3 million concepts that could be defined by means of the *EP* operator, using over ten thousand adjective synsets.

Entity-Property-Entity Composition. Let E_1 and E_2 be entity types, and let P_j be an entity property such that E_1 is in the domain of P_j and E_2 is in the range of P_j. Then, we denote by $EPE(E_1,P_j,E_2)$ the entity type whose instances are the instances of E_1 for which the value of P_j includes instances of E_2 [39, 41].

As an illustration, consider the following examples, involving noun and verb synsets of WordNet:

- *Toy store* can be defined as *EPE(store#1,sell#1,toy#1)*. Then, an instance of that compound concept is a store that sells toys.
- *Dog magazine* can be defined as *EPE(magazine#1,deal#1,dog#1)*. Then, an instance of that compound is a magazine that deals with dogs.
- *Flu virus* can be defined as *EPE(virus#1,cause#1,flu#1)*. Then, an instance of that compound is a virus that causes flu.

From this definition it follows that $EPE(E_1,P_j,E_2)$ *IsA* E_1. Furthermore, if P_j and P_k are two properties such that P_j *IsA* P_k then $EPE(E_1,P_j,E_2)$ *IsA* $EPE(E_1,P_k,E_2)$. Finally, if E_2 *IsA* E_3, then it follows that $EPE(E_1,P_j,E_2)$ *IsA* $EPE(E_1,P_j,E_3)$. For example, *EPE (magazine#1,deal#1,dog#1) IsA EPE(magazine#1,deal#1,domestic animal#1)*.

The analogous construct in linguistics is the noun-noun compound. However, there is an important difference: in natural language, the property that connects the two nouns of a noun-noun compound is not specified. This fact leads to ambiguities in some cases. We do not suggest here any example of naming function for this operator.

In MCG, there are over three million compound concepts that could be defined using *EPE* compositions from noun synsets defined in WordNet. The number of noun synsets that would be used is over thirty thousand.

4.2 Count Composition

A very large set of frequently used properties give the result of aggregate functions [43]. For example, the datatype property that gives the number of employees of a company. It is practically impossible to define all those properties in the core UO, but they can be easily defined when needed by means of composition operators. In the following we sketch the operator corresponding to the count function. Others could be defined similarly.

Let P_j be a property with domain E_1 and range E_2. Then we denote by *Count*(P_j) the datatype property with domain E_1 and range *Integer* that gives the number of instances of type E_2 that are related through P_j to an instance of E_1.

For example, assuming the implicit attribute corresponding to the WordNet noun synset *employee#1*, the operator *Count*(*employee#1*) is the datatype property that gives the number of employees of a given instance of its domain. The domain of *Count* (*employee#1*) would be *Entity*, and the range *Integer*.

Count(*employee#1*) (or an equivalent notation) would be the identifier and the default name of the datatype property. A better name could be obtained by the corresponding naming function F_{Count}, which in this case could give, for example, F_{Count}(*Count*(*employee#1*), *English*) = "number of employees".

5 Feasibility and Desirability of the UO

Once we have analyzed a possible basic structure of the UO and shown how it could be extended by means of the composition operators, in this section we tackle the issues of the feasibility and desirability of the UO.

5.1 Feasibility

Terminology. Some authors point out that "different communities of practice use the same terms with quite different meanings" [13], which can be a problem for the references to the concepts of the UO. This is the well-known problem of homonymy and/or polysemy in natural languages. In the proposed UO, each concept has a unique identifier, which is used in the publication of facts. Each concept has also a name and a set of synonyms in each language, which can be used in the external references to the concept. As in, for example, WordNet, the name and synonyms may not be unique, but people should be able to solve ambiguities by means of the definition of the concept or its composition expression.

Agreement. Some authors think that it would be very difficult to reach an agreement on the UO because it is very large and diverse. The following excerpts are representative of these views:

- "Although some may think the solution is to come up with a single context for the whole world… in reality this is extremely difficult for any complex organization" [44]
- "… people will always disagree about what terms to use and how to define them, a global ontology will always be seen as flawed" [13]
- "It is of course unrealistic to hope that there will be an agreement on one or even a small set of ontologies" [45]

- "Enforcing one centralized global ontology… is impractical to develop an ontology with consent from the user community at large" [54]
- "A single huge ontology of everything is difficult to accomplish, as the effort of getting consensus on it becomes unimaginable" [46].

Our general response to these views is that the proposed UO would not be built from scratch, but it would integrate existing concepts and ontologies. The concepts to be included in the UO are not new; they have been already agreed, defined, and are currently used by people and organizations. In the following, we detail this response for each UO level.

Technically, it should not be difficult to agree on the conceptual model level. The ambition of the proposed UO is quite limited, and therefore a subset of the existing conceptual/ontology models would suffice.

In the foundational level, several foundational ontologies could coexist. We have shown that there is no need to select only one of them. The only requirement is that each ontology includes the mappings to the other ontologies in the same level, and with the general level. The addition of foundational ontologies can be done incrementally.

The concepts to be included in the general level have already been specified in several places, notably in WordNet and in similar ontologies. The names of these concepts in many languages are known. There are satisfactory definitions of most of them, and their *IsA* relationships are known in most cases. It is safe to say that there exists already a substantial agreement on the concepts of the general level among their users.

The domain level would include all public domain ontologies. There are many, but the concepts of each of them have been already defined and agreed by their regulators. The problem may be the definition of the mappings of these ontologies with the general level and with the other ones in the same level. As we have mentioned in Sect. 3.4, this is the main technical challenge of the UO. The addition of domain ontologies can be done incrementally.

Management. Some authors argue that the management of the UO would be very difficult: "A huge, central ontology would be unmanageable" [47]; "Even if initial agreement were reached, there are many maintenance issues to be faced" [13].

The management of the UO may be difficult, but some of the management approaches that have been applied to successfully build similar artifacts could be appropriate for a UO with a modular structure. Besides the large ontologies, examples of such artifacts may be the open source projects [48], the Oxford English Dictionary (over 600,000 words[3]), the Encyclopedia Britannica, or UMLS (over 3.4 million concepts[4]). Of particular interest could be the approach taken in the development of schema.org [49].

Redundancy and Usability. There are a few problems in the UO that are also present in the natural language field. In principle, techniques developed in this field for dealing with those problems could be adapted in the UO context. Among those problems, we

3 http://www.oed.com/.

4 https://www.nlm.nih.gov/research/umls/knowledge_sources/metathesaurus/release/statistics.html.

mention here construct redundancy [50] and usability [51]. Ideally, there should be little redundancy in the core UO, but it is likely to have more in the extended UO, because sometimes the same concept can be expressed by means of several combinations of composition operators. A similar problem in natural language is that a concept may have several compound names.

On the other hand, there may be usability problems, because in a large ontology it may be difficult to find the most appropriate concept for a particular situation. A similar problem occurs with the lexicons.

5.2 Desirability

Some authors have expressed in the past the view that a global ontology would be desirable. The following excerpts are representative of these views:

- "some may think the solution is to come up with a single context for the whole world" [44]
- "In theory, a good solution to this problem would be to adopt a single global vocabulary that is widely accepted and embraced by everyone in the organization" [13]
- "one centralized global ontology prevents semantic heterogeneity since no more ontology exists and everyone is using the same ontology" [54]
- "for the semantic web to be a success, would it be nice, or almost necessary, that we could have just one single ontology, which actually covers all the common things in life?" [9].

We certainly agree that the UO is (highly) desirable but, of course, we must take into account its cost. Some authors have indicated that "the creation and maintenance of such an ontology is usually prohibitively expensive" [54]. Socio-economic factors dictate reality, and therefore the obvious question is "Who will develop the common ontologies and will they invest the effort and then allow them to be used for free?" [52].

It is not possible to give a precise answer to that question. However, we believe that there are currently already organizations that might have in the near future an interest in the UO and the resources needed to develop it. We mention two of them here. The first are standard organizations that have experience in the development of large standards, and have a means to get the resources needed. One of these organizations could be the World Wide Web Consortium (W3C), which is the main international standards organization for the web. For W3C, the UO would be a natural continuation of the many standard ontologies and languages that have developed so far. On the other hand, it could not be difficult for W3C to get the resources from its member organizations.

Search engine companies, which already have the knowledge and experience in building large knowledge graphs, might also be interested in the development of the UO. A clear indication of this is schema.org. It was built with the collaboration of the major search engines Bing, Google, and Yahoo (later joined by Yandex). Schema.org was launched in 2011 with 297 classes and 187 relations, and since then its size and adoption level have been increasing continuously [49]. Both webmasters and search engines have a strong interest in the schema.org markup. The former can publish the contents of their websites in a way that is understood also by the search engines. The latter can provide much better results to the search requests. The interest might be so high that "the question often comes up whether schema.org is an end-all solution for defining terminology for the Semantic Web" [53].

6 Conclusions

We have put forward a vision of a universal ontology (UO) aiming at solving, or at least greatly alleviating, the semantic integration problem in the field of conceptual modeling, and the understandability problem in the field of the semantic web. The semantic integration problem arises when two or more systems, whose conceptual schemas have been developed independently, need to exchange messages or share information. The understandability problem arises when the structured data published in datasets or in webpages cannot be understood by its full target audience (people and machines).

So far, it has been widely accepted that the UO would be a solution for those problems, but, at the same time, it has been assumed that it is not feasible in practice. In this paper, we have challenged that assumption. We have argued that in the current state-of-the-art it could be feasible to build a UO that solves those problems to a great extent. We have made an initial proposal of a UO able to achieve a limited objective, but useful for the (big) problems intended to solve.

We have explained the kinds of concepts that could be defined in the UO, and the minimum specification we propose of each concept. We have proposed also a modular structure for the UO, with four levels. We have also shown that the UO needs a powerful mechanism for concept composition, which we have sketched.

We have tackled a few issues related to the feasibility of the UO, such as terminology, agreement and management, and we have shown that although they are important, there are solid reasons to think that they are currently surmountable. Finally, we have discussed the desirability of the UO, and we have shown that there are already organizations that might have in the near future an interest in the UO, and the knowledge and resources needed to develop it.

Acknowledgments. The author is greatly indebted to his colleagues Albert Abelló, Jordi Cabot, Ernest Teniente, and Toni Urpí for their comments to earlier drafts of this paper. This work has been partially supported by the Ministerio de Economía y Competitividad, under project TIN2014-52938-C2-2-R.

References

1. Batini, C., Ceri, S., Navathe, S.: Conceptual Database Design: An Entity-Relationship Approach. Benjamin-Cummings Publishing Company Inc., Redwood City (1992)
2. Doan, A., Halevy, A., Ives, Z.: Principles of Data Integration. Morgan Kaufmann, Burlington (2012)
3. van Harmelen, F.: Ontology mapping: a way out of the medical tower of babel? In: Miksch, S., Hunter, J., Keravnou, E.T. (eds.) AIME 2005. LNCS, vol. 3581, pp. 3–6. Springer, Heidelberg (2005). doi:10.1007/11527770_1

4. Heath, T., Bizer, C.: Linked Data: Evolving the Web into a Global Data Space. Synthesis Lectures on the Semantic Web: Theory and Technology, 1st edn., vol. 1, no. 1, pp. 1–136. Morgan & Claypool (2011)
5. Park, J., Ram, S.: Information systems interoperability: what lies beneath? ACM Trans. Inf. Syst. **22**(4), 595–632 (2004)
6. Uschold, M., Grüninger, M.: Ontologies and semantics for seamless connectivity. SIGMOD Rec. **33**(4), 58–64 (2004)
7. Pease, A., Niles, I., Li, J.: The suggested upper merged ontology: a large ontology for the semantic web. In: Proceedings of AAAI-2002 Workshop on Ontologies and the Semantic Web (2002)
8. Allemang, D., Hendler, J.A.: Semantic Web for the Working Ontologist - Effective Modeling in RDFS and OWL, 2nd edn. Morgan Kaufmann, Burlington (2011)
9. Yu, L.: A Developer's Guide to the Semantic Web. Springer, Heidelberg (2014). doi:10.1007/978-3-662-43796-4
10. Gruninger, M., Fox, M.S.: Methodology for the design and evaluation of ontologies. In: Proceedings of Workshop on Basic Ontological Issues in Knowledge Sharing, IJCAI 1995 (1995)
11. Noy, N.F., McGuinness, D.L.: Ontology Development 101: A Guide to Creating Your First Ontology. Stanford University (2001)
12. Olivé, A.: Conceptual Modeling of Information Systems. Springer, Berlin (2007). doi:10.1007/978-3-540-39390-0
13. Uschold, M.: Creating, integrating and maintaining local and global ontologies. In: Proceedings of First Workshop on Ontology Learning OL 2000 in Conjunction with the 14th European Conference on Artificial Intelligence ECAI 2000 (2000)
14. Aguilera, D., Gómez, C., Olivé, A.: A complete set of guidelines for naming UML conceptual schema elements. Data Knowl. Eng. **88**, 60–74 (2013)
15. Spaccapietra, S. (coordinator): Report on Modularization of Ontologies. Technical report, Knowledge Web Deliverable D2.1.3.1 (2005)
16. Roussey, C., Pinet, F., Kang, M.A., Corcho, O.: An introduction to ontologies and ontology engineering. In: Falquet, G., et al. (eds.) Ontologies in Urban Development Projects. Advanced Information and Knowledge Processing, vol. 1, pp. 9–38. Springer, London (2011). doi:10.1007/978-0-85729-724-2_2
17. Mylopoulos, J., Borgida, A., Jarke, M., Koubarakis, M.: Telos: representing knowledge about information systems. ACM Trans. Inf. Syst. **8**(4), 325–362 (1990)
18. de Carvalho, V.A., Almeida, J.P.A., Fonseca, C.M., Guizzardi, G.: Multi-level ontology-based conceptual modeling. Data Knowl. Eng. **109**, 3–24 (2017)
19. Brickley, D., Guha, R.V.: RDF Schema 1.1. W3C Recommendation (2014). http://www.w3.org/TR/rdf-schema/
20. Masolo, C., Borgo, S., Gangemi, A., Guarino, N., Oltramari, A.: WonderWeb Deliverable D18, Ontology Library (final). ICT Project (2003)
21. Pastor, O.: Conceptual modeling of life: beyond the homo sapiens. In: Comyn-Wattiau, I., Tanaka, K., Song, I.-Y., Yamamoto, S., Saeki, M. (eds.) ER 2016. LNCS, vol. 9974, pp. 18–31. Springer, Cham (2016). doi:10.1007/978-3-319-46397-1_2
22. Gangemi, A., Guarino, N., Masolo, C., Oltramari, A.: Sweetening WORDNET with DOLCE. AI Mag. **24**(3), 13–24 (2003)
23. Guizzardi, G., Wagner, G., de Almeida Falbo, R., Guizzardi, R.S.S., Almeida, J.P.A.: Towards ontological foundations for the conceptual modeling of events. In: Ng, W., Storey, V.C., Trujillo, J.C. (eds.) ER 2013. LNCS, vol. 8217, pp. 327–341. Springer, Heidelberg (2013). doi:10.1007/978-3-642-41924-9_27

24. Guizzardi, G., Wagner, G., Almeida, J.P.A., Guizzardi, R.S.: Towards ontological foundations for conceptual modeling: the unified foundational ontology (UFO) story. Appl. Ontol. **10**(3–4), 259–271 (2015)
25. Bergenholtz, H., Tarp, S. (eds.): Manual of Specialised Lexicography. The Preparation of Specialised Dictionaries. John Benjamins Publishing Company, Amsterdam (1995)
26. Singh, R.A.: An introduction to lexicography. Central Institute of Indian Languages (1982)
27. Fellbaum, C. (ed.): WordNet: An Electronic Lexical Database. MIT Press, Cambridge (1998)
28. Lenat, D.B.: CYC: a large-scale investment in knowledge infrastructure. Commun. ACM **38** (11), 32–38 (1995)
29. Navigli, R., Ponzetto, S.P.: BabelNet: the automatic construction, evaluation and application of a wide-coverage multilingual semantic network. Artif. Intell. **193**, 217–250 (2012)
30. Global Wordnet Association. http://globalwordnet.org/wordnets-in-the-world/
31. Shvaiko, P., Euzenat, J.: Ontology matching: state of the art and future challenges. IEEE Trans. Knowl. Data Eng. **25**(1), 158–176 (2013)
32. Lindland, O.I., Sindre, G., Sølvberg, A.: Understanding quality in conceptual modeling. IEEE Softw. **11**, 42–49 (1994)
33. Gómez-Pérez, A.: Evaluation of ontologies. Int. J. Intell. Syst. **16**(3), 391–409 (2001)
34. Noy, N.F.: Ontology mapping. In: Handbook on Ontologies, pp. 573–590 (2009)
35. Choi, N., Han, H., Song, I.: A survey on ontology mapping. SIGMOD Rec. **35**, 34–41 (2006)
36. Arnold, P., Rahm, E.: Enriching ontology mappings with semantic relations. Data Knowl. Eng. **93**, 1–18 (2014)
37. SNOMED International. SNOMED CT Starter Guide (2017). http://snomed.org/sg
38. Lieber, R., Stekauer, P. (eds.): The Oxford Handbook of Compounding. Oxford University Press, Oxford (2011)
39. Murphy, G.L.: The Big Book of Concepts. MIT Press, Cambridge (2004)
40. Wikipedia. https://en.wikipedia.org/wiki/English_compound
41. Nakov, P., Hearst, M.A.: Semantic interpretation of noun compounds using verbal and other paraphrases. TSLP **10**(3), 13:1–13:51 (2013)
42. Microsoft. https://concept.research.microsoft.com/
43. Cabot, J., Mazón, J.-N., Pardillo, J., Trujillo, J.: Specifying aggregation functions in multidimensional models with OCL. In: ER 2010, pp. 419–432 (2010)
44. Madnick, S.E.: Are we moving toward an information superhighway or a tower of babel? The challenge of large-scale semantic heterogeneity. In: ICDE 1996, pp. 2–8 (1996)
45. Noy, N.F.: Semantic integration: a survey of ontology-based approaches. SIGMOD Rec. **33** (4), 65–70 (2004)
46. Berners-Lee, T., Kagal, L.: The fractal nature of the semantic web. AI Mag. **29**(3), 29–34 (2008)
47. Herman, I.: State of the Semantic Web. Norway (2007). https://www.w3.org/2007/Talks/0424-Stavanger-IH/Slides.pdf
48. Mockus, A., Fielding, R.T., Herbsleb, J.D.: Two case studies of open source software development: apache and Mozilla. ACM Trans. Softw. Eng. Methodol. **11**(3), 309–346 (2002)
49. Guha, R.V., Brickley, D., Macbeth, S.: Schema.org: evolution of structured data on the web. Comm. ACM **59**(2), 44–51 (2016)
50. Burton-Jones, A., Wand, Y., Weber, R.: Guidelines for empirical evaluations of conceptual modeling grammars. J. AIS **10**, 1 (2009)
51. Conesa, J., Storey, V.C., Sugumaran, V.: Usability of upper level ontologies: the case of ResearchCyc. Data Knowl. Eng. **69**(4), 343–356 (2010)

52. Kashyap, V., Bussler, C., Moran, M.: The Semantic Web. Semantics for Data and Services on the Web. Springer, Heidelberg (2008). doi:10.1007/978-3-540-76452-6
53. Mika, P.: On Schema.org and why it matters for the web. IEEE Internet Comput. **19**(4), 52–55 (2015)
54. Ding, L., Kolari, P., Ding, Z., Avancha, S., Finin, T., Anupam Joshi, A.: Using ontologies in the semantic web: a survey. In: Sharman, R., Kishore, R., Ramesh, R. (eds.) Ontologies. Springer, Boston (2007). doi:10.1007/978-0-387-37022-4_4

Conceptual Modeling Methodology

CE-SIB: A Modelling Method Plug-in for Managing Standards in Enterprise Architectures

Christoph Moser[1(✉)], Robert Andrei Buchmann[2], Wilfrid Utz[1], and Dimitris Karagiannis[1]

[1] Knowledge Engineering Research Group, University of Vienna, Vienna, Austria
{cmoser,wilfrid,dk}@dke.univie.ac.at
[2] Business Informatics Research Center, Babeş-Bolyai University, Cluj-Napoca, Romania
robert.buchmann@econ.ubbcluj.ro

Abstract. In Enterprise Architecture (EA) Management, adoption of standards brings essential benefits pertaining to compatibility and repeatability but also raises governance challenges. EA frameworks recommend placing architecture artifacts under strict governance to control technological diversity towards reduced costs of operation or business-IT alignment; however, they do not provide methodological guidance on how to support decision-making for standards management. Business process management, model-driven software engineering or IT service management do address such challenges, but fall short in covering all relevant architectural layers. Driven by industry experience, this paper proposes a modelling method plug-in ("function block") to support a model-based integration of practices for standards compliance management and their relevant model bases. It also aims for generality, as the proposal is pluggable through "semantic docking points" to arbitrary EA frameworks. A prototypical implementation in the form of a modelling tool is discussed as an expository instantiation, as well as basis for evaluation and learned lessons.

Keywords: TOGAF standards information base · Enterprise Architecture Management · Standardization · Compliance Evaluation · Metamodelling

1 Introduction

To overcome challenges pertaining to infrastructure heterogeneity and complexity management, Enterprise Architecture (EA) practitioners (see e.g., [1, 7]) and frameworks (see e.g., [13, 30, 35]) advocate the adoption and governance of standards. Generally, standards may be defined at any level of the organization: standard business processes, standard applications, standard technologies etc.; their relevance and alignment within EA must be assessed and governed, considering the management practices already in place.

For example, TOGAF [35] recommends the alignment of EA management activities with Portfolio, Solution Development or Operations Management methods but

H.C. Mayr et al. (Eds.): ER 2017, LNCS 10650, pp. 21–35, 2017.
https://doi.org/10.1007/978-3-319-69904-2_2

falls short in providing guidance on how to integrate the key information artifacts produced and exchanged within these management practices. With a focus on standards management, TOGAF recommends a collection of technical specifications within a "Standards Information Base" (SIB), as a reference for architecture conformance. Implementing a system to "ensure compliance with internal and external standards and regulatory obligations" is considered a key aspect of effective EA governance [7].

The work at hand is motivated by compliance requirements in industry cases. The contribution, labelled with the acronym **CE-SIB** (Compliance Evaluation for Standards Information Bases), is a *modelling method function block* that can extend EA frameworks with a model-based dashboard for defining, aligning and communicating organizational standards. It is designed to be pluggable to arbitrary model-driven management practices, both to their model bases and underlying modelling methods. This means that it provides extensions to all the building blocks of a modelling method and its deployment relies on existing methodologies for agile customization of modelling tools – e.g., the Agile Modelling Method Engineering methodology [22] - and its technological enablers (the ADOxx metamodelling platform [24]). However, the proposal will be abstracted in order to inspire adoption for other frameworks.

The remainder of the paper is organized as follows: Sect. 2 generalizes the problem statement from industry experience and contrasts the approach against related works. Section 3 uses a minimal yet representative example as an explanatory starting point, then it generalizes the CE-SIB building blocks with respect to the generic notion of a *modelling method*. Section 4 discusses an expository instantiation in the form of a modelling prototype. The paper closes with a summative SWOT evaluation.

2 Problem Statement and Background

2.1 Problem Statement

The SIB catalogue proposed by TOGAF [7, 36] holds descriptions of technology products and their versions (e.g., "Apache 2.4") and interoperability standards (e.g., "Web Service Definition Language 2.0") to be used as requirements for procurement. However, TOGAF does not explain (i) how the standards collude conceptually with the TOGAF meta-model; (ii) how architecture development and governance processes should ensure architecture compliance; (iii) what viewpoints should support the depiction and communication of standards compliance; and (iv) how evaluation can be ensured by model-based mechanisms or algorithms.

All these are pragmatic requirements identified in TOGAF-driven industry cases (in banking and public administration sectors) that motivated the work at hand. The major stakeholders in these cases were the technology/solution architects and the operations managers. Their commonly employed tools were Excel (for standards description), Visio and Powerpoint (for communication) with no semantic integration between contents, between standards and architecture elements, and no on-demand reporting mechanisms. To overcome limitations, a model-driven solution is hereby proposed for better maintainability of SIBs and technology portfolios.

EA frameworks like TOGAF [35], FEAF [13] and PEAF [30] propose architecture principles such as “Control Technical Diversity”, “Interoperability”, “Common Use of Applications”, and “Reuse” to govern the selection and implementation of IT solutions; however, they also do not explicitly recommend how governance could be exerted through these principles. The work at hand aims to fill this gap with a Design Science artifact – the CE-SIB *modelling method function block* providing extensions to all building blocks of a modelling method.

2.2 Related Works

Other examples of Standard Information Bases are SAGA, the governmental interoperability framework of the German federal administration, and comparable frameworks like EIF (the European Interoperability Framework) or NISP (NATO Interoperability Standards Profiles) (see [4] for an overview). Like TOGAF’s SIB, their main contribution is to recommend a catalogue of IT standards, with no explicit methodical support on how to monitor these standards and their involvement in other EA layers.

Besides the set of standards catalogued within a SIB, there is also a set of characteristics, namely “qualities” that apply across all architecture building blocks [7]: maintainability, security, reliability and efficiency. According to TOGAF, some of these qualities are easier to describe in the form of “standards” [7], rather than “metrics”. Buckl et al. [9] present an evaluation function using metrics based on probabilistic relations models (PRM), using the quality “availability” for illustration purposes. In contrast, the contribution at hand focuses on the description of required standards as semantically rich modelling objects whose alignment to requirements (or compliance, if we take the internal perspective) is quantified and color-coded in a model-based dashboard based on specific comparison assessment mechanisms.

In [8], an approach for controlling and measuring the degree of standardization of an IT landscape, utilizing fuzzy logic concepts and a basic metamodel for representing the IT landscape, are introduced. The approach allows the calculation of the compliance degree of service categories. In contrast, CE-SIB focuses on standardization degrees of architecture artifacts; however, the approach in [8] can be combined with the foundation provided by CE-SIB: it delivers those artifacts (within a service category) to be recommended as a standard.

The proposal may also be understood as having a more general scope than the EA monitoring approach proposed by [26] in the form of Archimate extensions. At the same time, it instantiates the “embrace pragmatics” theory developed by [6], as the proposal is motivated by case-based requirements of altering standard modelling methods to achieve a pragmatic goal – here, governance of standards adoption. Consequently, the work is also related to [17], which introduced its own notion of “method integration” by placing emphasis on socio-technical implications, whereas our proposal focuses on semantic and functional aspects (some aspects pertaining to the involved collaborative work will be discussed in Sect. 3.3).

3 Design Decisions

3.1 CE-SIB: A Design Science Artifact

EA is typically regarded as a holistic approach which serves as an "umbrella" for specialized management practices (see e.g. [5, 21, 34, 35]). EA Management viewpoints can be anchored in model-driven software engineering (MDSE), business process management (BPM), business planning methods (see e.g. [27] for IT-based scorecards), project portfolio management (see e.g. [10]) and IT service management (see e.g. [11] for integrating ITILs configuration management process with EA practices). In a complex environment with an extensive modelling culture, these viewpoints are supported by different modelling notations and languages (see [2]).

CE-SIB aims to be reusable and pluggable to any of these approaches (and their hybridizations), therefore it extends the *modelling method* building blocks defined by Karagiannis and Kühn [25]. As discussed in [37], a *modelling method function block* has the same components as modelling methods:

- A *modelling language* comprising a modelling notation and a metamodel that defines the language grammar and vocabulary. CE-SIB defines a metamodel fragment (see Sect. 3.2) for "semantic docking" to modelling methods that support the above mentioned management practices. The integration itself relies on the Agile Modelling Method Engineering methodology [22] which facilitates the agile tailoring of modelling methods/tools in response to pragmatic requirements (e.g., those derived from the problem statement in Sect. 2.1);
- A *modelling procedure* comprising the required processes for creating and maintaining a model base. CE-SIB defines a socio-technical procedure for monitoring the standards compliance of architecture building blocks, aiming to replace legacy procedures with a diagrammatic model analysis environment (see Sect. 3.3);
- Model-based *mechanisms/algorithms*: CE-SIB defines quantitative evaluation mechanisms for standards compliance criteria (see Sect. 3.4).

3.2 The CE-SIB Language Fragment: Semantic Docking

The CE-SIB metamodel relies on *semantic docking points* that can be identified in EA-supporting modelling languages or in language hybridizations (e.g., between models expressing EAM, BPM, MDSE, business planning or service management viewpoints). To ensure understandability, we will focus on a simplified yet representative example derived from experience with two viewpoints expressed through two popular modelling languages - Archimate and UML.

A "semantic docking point" is a recurring pattern identified in TOGAF as follows: TOGAF defines a *building block* as "a package of functionality defined to meet the business needs across an organization" [7] and differentiates between: (i) *Architecture Building Blocks* (ABBs) representing the required architecture capabilities (functional view); and (ii) *Solution Building Blocks* (SBBs) representing the concrete components that will be used to implement required capabilities – e.g. concrete application components and technology products. TOGAFs Architecture Development Method cycle refines ABBs into one or more SBBs (see [35], phase G).

An example is Archimate's recommendation to refine *application components* and application interfaces (both ABBs, mapped to "application co-operation" viewpoints and "infrastructure usage" viewpoints) into "UML components" (SBBs mapped on modular parts of a software system). Figure 1 shows an implementation and deployment viewpoint including the used application components, further refined in the corresponding UML (specification level) deployment diagram. The application components (an Archimate concept, here acting as ABB) are refined into technical artifacts which in turn are deployed on nodes (UML concepts, here acting as SBBs). In a modelling tool, this "refinement" will manifest in the form of a machine-readable relation (e.g., visual connectors or hyperlinks across models) subjected to constraints (e.g., domain, range, cardinality etc.) and possibly enriched with its own attributes (input for mechanisms and algorithms). In the same figure, at metamodel level the ABB-to-SBB relation forms the *semantic docking point* for the CE-SIB language block.

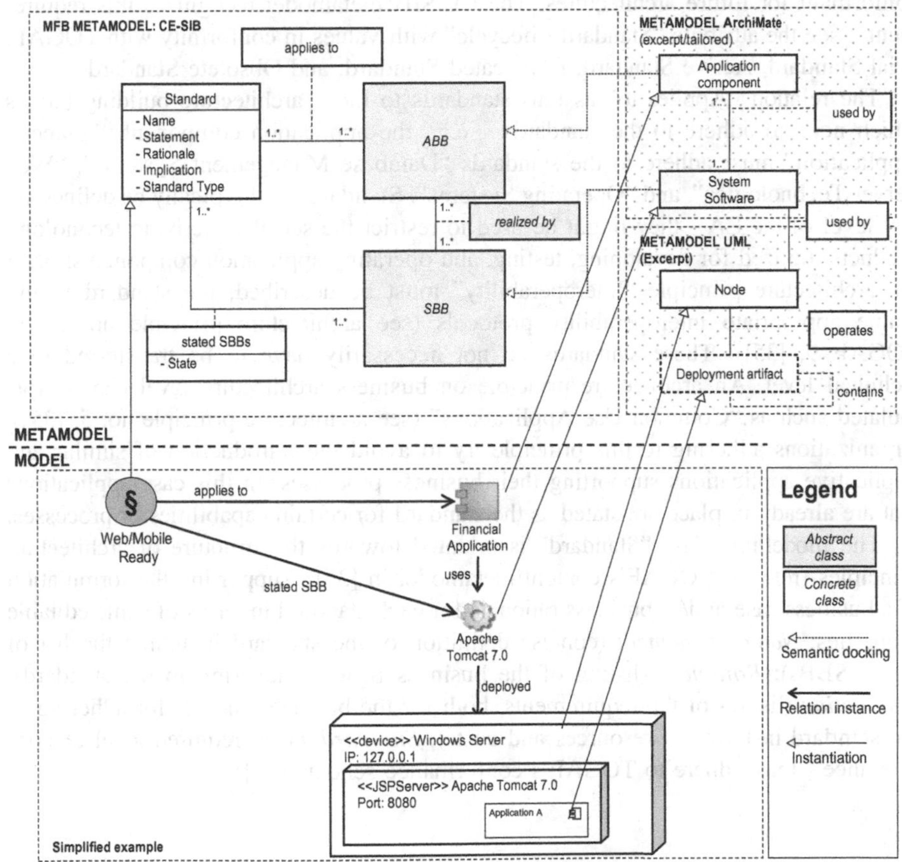

Fig. 1. CE-SIB metamodel block "plugged" to an Archimate-UML hybrid method.

Other examples of docking points to which this may be generalized are: the refinement of data objects into UML classes/objects, the refinement of business processes into UML activity diagrams, the refinement of Archimate nodes into UML nodes (see [3] for a more detailed discussion). In this particular example, CE-SIB enriches the Archimate-to-UML semantic docking point with a modelling concept "Standard" and two semantically-rich relations, namely "Stated SBB" and "Applies to".

The relation "Stated SBBs" specifies all valid and standard-conforming architecture elements specified by a certain standard. Contrasting from TOGAF, in CE-SIB the Standard Information Base is not only a list of SBBs serving as standards. A bundle of SBBs can be assigned to the "Standard" plus qualities such as "Statement" and "Rationale". An example instance for this could relate to "Web Application Server Technologies": the standard might specify the set of concrete web server technologies (SBBs such as Apache Tomcat 7.0, Java Glassfish 4.1) as the technology components (i.e., nodes) an organization's application components can use. These SBBs have their own lifecycle and pass through a series of status in the context of a standard. A status is defined via the attribute "State" of the relation class "Stated SBBs"; while an SBB might be stated as an active standard for the as-is architecture it might be non-conformant for future architectures. The CE-SIB metamodel recognizes this requirement – see the attribute "Standard Lifecycle" with values in conformity with TOGAF: Trial Standard, Active Standard, Deprecated Standard, and Obsolete Standard.

The relation "Applies to" assigns standards to those architecture building blocks which need to adhere to the standards – e.g., the application component "Financial Application" must adhere to the standards "Database Management Systems", "Web Server Technologies", and "Operating Systems". Standards will typically be defined on any level of the EA - they might be used to restrict the set of underlying technology products, utilized for developing, testing, and operating application components; or, if the architecture principle "Interoperability" must be described, the standard would define appropriate interoperability protocols (see architecture principle no. 21 in TOGAF 9, [35]). These standards do not necessarily have to be transferred to a technical level. An architecture principle on business architecture level can be formulated such as "Common Use Applications" (see architecture principle no. 5, [35]). Organizations adhering to this principle try to avoid the introduction of similar and duplicative applications supporting their business processes. In this case applications that are already in place are stated as the standard for certain capabilities or processes.

The modelling class "Standard" is oriented towards the structure of architecture principles (refer to TOGAF's content metamodel in [35]), supporting the formulation of a business case and/or business rationale for each standard in terms of some editable properties: *Name; Statement* (concise definition of the standard including the list of stated SBBs); *Rationale* (listing of the business benefits adhering to the standard); *Implication* (listing of the requirements, both for the business and IT, for adhering to the standard in terms of resources and costs); *Standard Type* (required level of conformance - may adhere to TOGAF's conformance schema [35]).

3.3 The CE-SIB Procedure: Managing Standards Compliance

Since it is a method function block, CE-SIB also defines its application procedure steps to be assimilated by in-place management practices:

Step 1. Adopt and maintain standards. In this step the set "STD" of standards is formulated (i.e., their attributes relevant for EA standards management are described) and promoted within the organization. Standards must be derived from the organizations strategy – i.e., architecture principles [7, 33] and business goals. This is a collaborative effort between subject matter experts and a cross-organizational architecture board to oversee the quality and the strategic/tactical impact of the standards. Each standard is described based on the presented metamodel. Let S be the set of SBBs stated by a standard – i.e., the set of architecture artifacts assigned to a standard via the relation class "Stated SBB", and U be the set of solution building blocks an ABB uses (i.e. is implemented on). The predicate "uses" is represented in the metamodel through the "Realized by" relation assigning SBBs to ABBs, with a variety of possible implementation-level manifestations in a modelling tool (e.g., visual connectors, hyperlinks). Figure 2 illustrates a Standard (Web Application), an ABB (Financial Application), and the sets S and U of solution building blocks (SBBs) - ensured by the standard and used by the ABB, respectively.

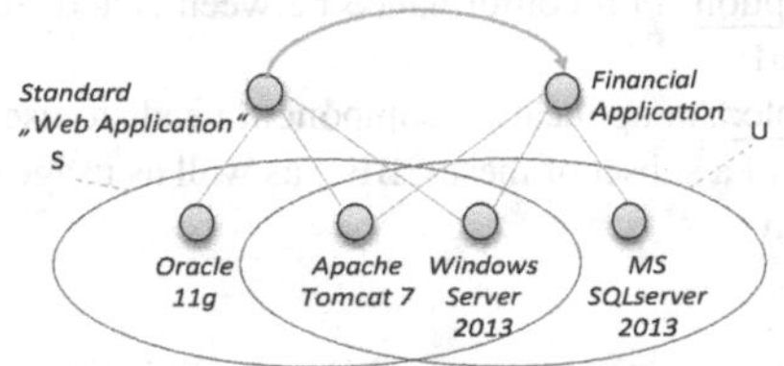

Fig. 2. Example of comparison assessment

The financial application ABB runs on the following SBBs: Apache Tomcat 7.0, Windows Server 2013 and MS SQLserver 2013. The standard "Web Application" assigned to the financial application states the following SBBs: Oracle 11 g, Apache Tomcat 7.0, and Windows Server 2013. The usage of MS SQLserver 2013 is not in conformance with the standard. In order to identify the relevant SBBs (in Fig. 1 the artifacts of modelling class "node") CE-SIB provides mechanisms for evaluating the graph "Application Component > Artifact > Node" and the degree of compliance relative to the compliance types in Table 1.

Step 2. Weigh standards. The defined standards are weighted according to their importance for the organization. Like the weighing of architecture principles (proposed in [23]) each standard is weighted from 1 (minor importance) to 5 (high importance), i.e., $\omega(std) \in \{1, 2, 3, 4, 5\}$.

Step 3. Stipulate SBBs and set lifecycles. Subject matter experts continuously define SBBs best supporting a standard, ensuring that only valid, up-to-date and available SBBs are postulated by the standards. In case of technology standards, non-functional

Table 1. Types of standards compliance

Type	Explanation
Non-conformant	Fulfilment Requirements: $S \cap U = \emptyset$ Description: SBBs which are explicitly not allowed to be used by an ABB Example: No application component shall be implemented on a certain technology component (e.g. technology products which reached end-of-life and vendor-support is not guaranteed anymore)
Compliant	Fulfilment Requirements: $U \subseteq S$ Description: A number of SBBs are endorsed by the standard – at least one of these SBBs must be used Example: A standard "Web Server Technologies" states "Apache 2.4" and "IIS 10" as technology components an application component can be implemented on
Conformant	Fulfilment Requirements: $U \supseteq S$ Description: All stated SBBs are to be used by an ABB, but the ABB might use additional solution building blocks (not stated by the standard) Example: The standard "Allowed Web Application Technologies" might state SBBs such as "Apache Tomcat" and "Unix". Hence, a web application shall use both of these SBBs, however, the developing team has the freedom to use any further technology components
Fully compliant	Fulfilment Requirements: $S = U$ Description: Full conformance between stated SBBs and used SBBs is required Example: An application component needs to use exactly the stated SBBs. Usage of a subset of these SBBs, as well as usage of additional SBBs is not allowed

requirements such as costs, functionality, usability, reliability, supportability [12] need to be considered. A more sophisticated approach is discussed in [8], where categories of services are standardized.

Typically, the owner of the standard will assign appropriate SBBs, by scanning the market for new appropriate (versions of) SBBs. Valuable information sources for technical infrastructures are the mentioned SIBs (SAGA, EIF, NISP, also see [4] for an overview), official vendor support policies like the "Oracle Lifetime Support Policy" (see [28]) as well as existing service level agreements concluded with suppliers. Criteria such as information on internal skills for the support and maintenance of the SBBs are also considered. Based on this information one of the status "Trial Standard", "Active Standard", "Deprecated Standard", or "Obsolete Standard" is assigned: $status(sbb, std) \in \{trial, active, deprecated, obsolete\}$.

Step 4. Define atomic scoring values. Each type of lifecycle state (trial, active, deprecated, obsolete) is assigned to ratings on a scale as recommended in [23]: *r(active) := 1, r(trial) := 2, r(deprecated) := 3 and r(obsolete) := 5*. An ABB receives a (desired) low standardization degree (SD), if it primarily uses active SBBs. The scoring can be adapted as required by the EA board when deploying the method.

Step 5. Assess compliance. Compliance levels can be calculated from the perspective of the standards (i.e., the compliance level of a concrete standard along the entire EA) as well as from the perspective of the ABBs (i.e., the compliance level of an ABB along the set of standards it must adhere to). In order to calculate the standardization degree $SD(a, std)$ of an ABB *abb* in the context of a standard *std* (and vice versa) we decompose the set of SBB in the subsets indicated by Fig. 3:

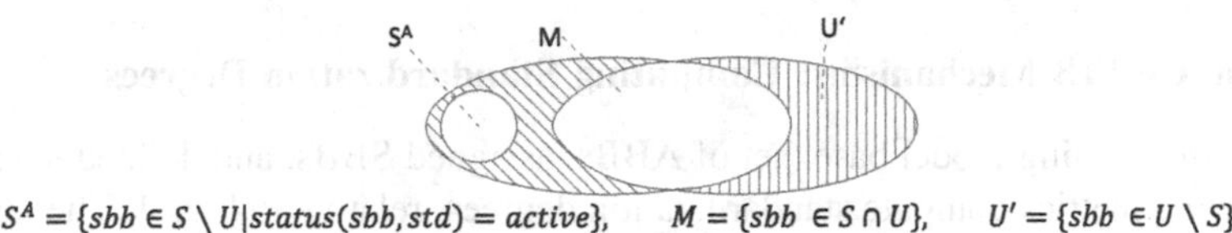

S^A
M
U'
S^A = {sbb ∈ S \ U|status(sbb, std) = active},
M = {sbb ∈ S ∩ U},
U' = {sbb ∈ U \ S}

Fig. 3. Decomposing the SBB set

S^A is the set of SBBs scored "active" but not used by the *abb*. *M* is the set of SBBs stated by the standard and at the same time used by the *abb* independent of their scoring in context of the standard. *U'* is the set of SBBs used by the *abb* but not stated by the standard. Based on these subsets the standardization degree (SD) of an ABB can be calculated for each type of standard (conformant, compliant etc.). Take the running example of the financial application and the standard "Web Application" (see Fig. 2):

$$S^A = \{Oracle\,11g\},\ M = \{Appache\,2.4,\ Windows\,Server\,2013\},\ U' = \{\,SQLserver\,2013\}$$

Depending on the type of standard, the weighing of the applied standards, the status of the used SBBs, and the applied atomic scoring values, the standardization degree per standard and per ABB can be calculated. Depending on the type of standard, usage of Oracle 11 g instead of MS SQLserver 2013 might lead to a bad rating of the standardization degree. The standardization degree calculations are performed by model-based assessment mechanisms to be detailed in Sect. 3.4.

Step 6. Address exceptions. Goodhue et al. [18] consider standards without governance to be useless. Peterson [29] discusses the necessity of the institutionalization of monitoring processes in terms of diagnosing IT governance effectiveness and value contribution. CE-SIB recognizes these requirements and proposes evaluating the standardization degree on an ongoing basis. In cases of non-compliance, change requests to improve the architecture need to be raised. However, Gartner [16] rates over-standardization, as one of the worst practices in EAM. Hence, in cases of identified non-compliance, mechanisms for interim conformance are provided. These are exceptions that must be corrected within a granted lifespan of the exception. The CE-SIB method allows exceptions for the tuple of an ABB and its used SBBs, in case of non-compliant SBBs (e.g., SBBs in state "obsolete"). CE-SIB reflects exceptions by neutralizing bad ratings via exceptions. Thus, the value *r(obsolete) := 5* for non-compliant SBBs is mitigated by subtraction of the value 4 (see next section).

Step 7. Create viewpoints for decision support. As the CE-SIB method is meant to be framework-agnostic, no concrete viewpoints are stipulated - graph-based diagrams (with nodes and edges), matrices etc. can be used. Current deployments have been coupled with the CE-HM (Compliance Evaluation Featuring Heat Maps) mechanisms introduced in [23], which enables color-coding mechanisms ("heatmaps") in arbitrary modelling notations, while also propagating such visual cues to superordinated levels of the EA (e.g., superordinated business processes, business capabilities).

3.4 The CE-SIB Mechanisms: Computing Standardization Degrees

Based on the existing model base (set of ABBs, assigned SBBs, and defined standards) the following metrics compute standardization degrees, relative to Fig. 4. The numbers depicted within the subsets present the ratings of SBBs in context of the particular type of standard (fully conformant, conformant, compliant etc.).

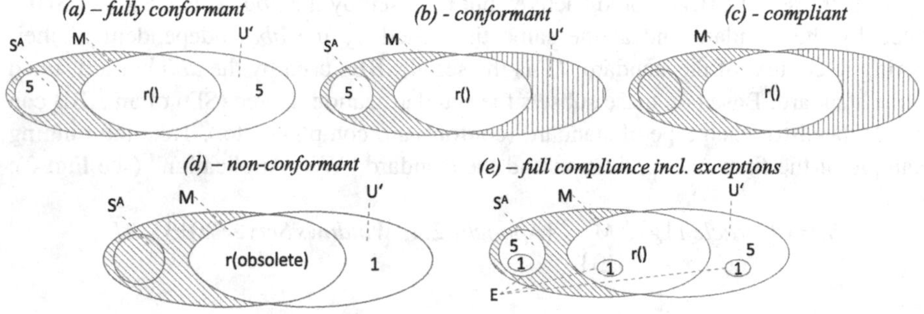

Fig. 4. Sets and scores for different compliance types

The formulas for degrees are marked with the corresponding letters from the figures:

$$SD_{fully}(abb, std) := \frac{\sum_{sbb \in M} r(status(sbb, std)) + 5 \times |S^A| + 5 \times |U'|}{|M| + |S^A| + |U'|} \quad \text{(a)}$$

$$SD_{conformant}(abb, std) := \frac{\sum_{sbb \in M} r(status(sbb, std)) + 5 \times |S^A|}{|M| + |S^A|} \quad \text{(b)}$$

$$SD_{compliant}(abb, std) := \begin{cases} \frac{\sum_{sbb \in M} r(status(sbb, std))}{|M|}, if\ |M| > 0 \\ 5, else \end{cases} \quad \text{(c)}$$

$$SD_{non\text{-}conf}(abb, std) := \frac{\sum_{sbb \in M} r(status(sbb, std)) + |U'|}{|M| + |U'|} \quad \text{(d)}$$

Note, that in case of required non-conformance all stated SBBs will be scored r(obsolete) as usage of any of the stated SBBs should be avoided. All other used SBBs are scored with a value of 1.

From the viewpoint of an ABB *abb*, the standardization degree *SD(abb)* of the ABB is the weighted average of the standardization degrees of the tuples of the ABB and its assigned standard, i.e.:

$$SD(abb) := \frac{\sum_{i \in STD} SD(abb, std_i) \times \omega(std_i)}{\sum_{i \in STD} \omega(std_i)}$$

where *STD* is the set of standards assigned to an ABB.

From the viewpoint of a standard *std*, the standardization degree *SD(std)* is the average of the standardization degrees of the tuples of the standard and the ABBs it applies to:

$$SD(std) := \frac{\sum_{j \in \mathrm{ABB}} SD(abb_j, std)}{|\mathrm{ABB}|}$$

Situation (e) in Fig. 4 illustrates how exceptions are considered for a standard requiring full-compliance (E is the set of obsolete SBBs with granted exceptions):

$$SD_{fully,ex}(abb, std) := SD_{fully}(abb, std) - \frac{|\mathrm{E}| \times 4}{|\mathrm{M}| + |\mathrm{S}^A| + |\mathrm{U}'|} \quad \text{(e)}$$

4 Implementation and Evaluation

The proof-of-concept depicted in Fig. 5 was implemented on the metamodelling platform ADOxx - made available as part of the Agile Modelling Method Engineering framework [22] by the Open Models Initiative Laboratory [24]. It integrates a hybrid of

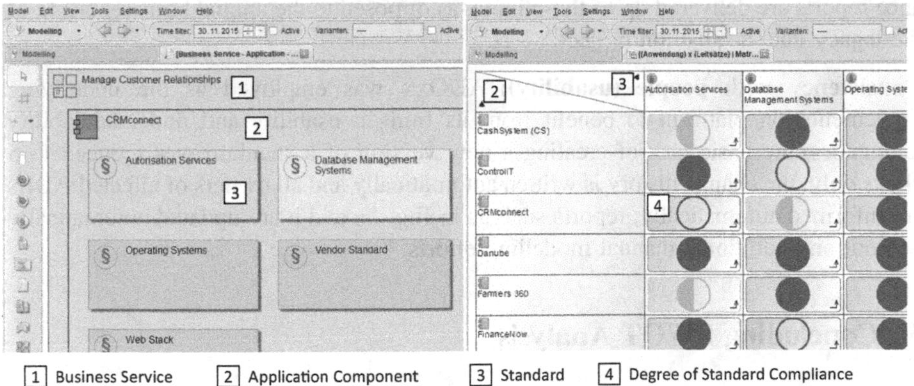

Fig. 5. Exemplary viewpoints: (a) compliance clustermap, (b) compliance matrix

Archimate viewpoints and a subset of UML (namely class/object diagrams, component diagrams, and deployment diagrams) extended with the CE-SIB plug-in, following Shneiderman's visualization "mantra" overview first, zoom and filter, and details on demand [32]. Figure 5a and b exemplarily depict two viewpoints. The clustermap (Fig. 5a) is an EA viewpoint recommended by [14] for communicating standards conformity and exceptions. In Fig. 5a the worst score is propagated to the "higher" levels (from application components to superordinate business processes). Within the application components the relevant standards are depicted. This viewpoint is intended to give an "overview first" on weak spots within the EA.

The matrix view in Fig. 5b is recommended by TOGAF [35] to communicate relationships between architecture artifacts, giving insight to scorings of ABBs in context of the assigned standards. On the x-axis standards such as "Authorization Services" and "Database Management Systems" are depicted. Based on the discussed thresholds and metrics matrix cells are color-coded.

As the CE-SIB method block was introduced here as a Design Science artifact, it can be subjected to the wide tableaux of evaluation criteria surveyed by [31]. The current implementation was driven by requirements from industrial cases (a banking institution and an organization from the public administration sector) therefore certain criteria gained priority:

Generality: CE-SIB is reusable for any semantic "docking points" (as defined in Sect. 3.2) identified between arbitrary metamodels. This relies on the Agile Modelling Method Engineering framework [22] - the key enabler for agilely plugging the CE-SIB block to existing modelling method implementations (where relevant concepts can fulfill the ABB and SBB roles).

Consistency with organization (fit with organization requirements): The implementation was tailored for the mentioned industrial cases to replace legacy Excel-based methods and to support already in place model-based management practices. The generality factor mentioned above ensures that similar requirements from organizations of different domain-specificity may be agilely satisfied. By building on the existing model base, efforts for maintaining the SIB could be dramatically reduced by approximately 70% (based on stakeholder feedback). Additionally, standards compliance reports are delivered up-to-the-minute, as opposed to the annual basis reporting of the legacy data acquisition project.

Consistency with people (usability): ADOxx was employed as the underlying implementation platform to benefit from its built-in usability and understandability facilitators: the basic task of creating a new version of a standard was reduced to 5 clicks only; the change history is written automatically and all owners of affected ABBs are informed automatically; reports such as in Fig. 5a and b are updated automatically without any additional manual modelling efforts.

5 Concluding SWOT Analysis

A SWOT evaluation summarizing the key learned lessons was derived from hands-on experience with the implementation and interviews with key stakeholders in their respective organizations.

Strengths: CE-SIB allows nonambiguous definition and communication of standards and can be integrated in commonly used EA frameworks. Adherence to these standards becomes measureable. In the course of the evaluation it was shown that usage of the method and communication of standards compliance degrees (based on modelling viewpoints) lead to comprehensible results. Understandability and acceptance were assessed through qualitative interviews with major EA stakeholders, where the proposal was deployed in modelling tools agilely extended through the Agile Modelling Method Engineering methodology.

Weaknesses: One major restriction of CE-SIB is that it requires a model-based system engineering (MBSE, see [15]) approach to EA management (in contrast to a traditional document-based approach). Thus the EA documentation must be available as a diagrammatic model base, with models depicting different EA facets under an overarching metamodel (for which CE-SIB acts as integrator).

Opportunities: Standards are defined from the point of view of different domains and organizational units and different standards may be conflicting in their statements regarding SBBs. Providing means to uncover these inconsistencies will add another valuable feature to CE-SIB. The strict focus on the MBSE can be relaxed by applying data integration and clearance mechanisms from the fields of business analytics as discussed in [19]. For this, future work will focus on a Data Integration and Cleansing Environment (DICE) (see [20]) implemented on the same metamodelling platform.

Threats: The stakeholder involvement has shown that the definition of standards throughout an organization requires strong negotiating skills, persuasiveness, and political savviness. The main touch points, contrasted to TOGAFs ADM the phases B-D (where the architectures are designed), phase E (where the best solution is chosen), and H (evaluation) have to be clearly defined. Currently CE-SIB does not address these touch-points in detail. Evaluation results clearly show that more detailed guidance on implementing the CE-SIB procedures in the organization is required.

Acknowledgment. The work of Dr. Robert Buchmann is supported by the Romanian National Research Authority through UEFISCDI, under grant agreement PN-III-P2-2.1-PED-2016-1140.

References

1. Accenture: Architecture frameworks for client/server and netcentric computing. In: Myerson, J.M. (eds.) Enterprise Systems Integration, pp. 39–78 (2002)
2. Anaby-Tavor, A., et al.: An empirical study of enterprise conceptual modeling. In: Laender, A.H.F., Castano, S., Dayal, U., Casati, F., de Oliveira, J.P.M. (eds.) ER 2009. LNCS, vol. 5829, pp. 55–69. Springer, Heidelberg (2009). doi:10.1007/978-3-642-04840-1_7
3. Armstrong, C., et al.: Using the ArchiMate Language with UML (2013). http://cdn2.hubspot.net/hub/183807/file-1805596253-pdf/site/media/downloads/W134.pdf?t=1418385713847
4. Beauftragte der Bundesregierung für Informationstechnik (BfIT): SAGA-Modul Grundlagen Version de.bund 5.1.0 (2011)

5. Bernard, S.A.: An Introduction to Enterprise Architecture. AuthorHouse, Bloomington (2012)
6. Bjeković, M., Proper, H.A., Sottet, J.-S.: Embracing pragmatics. In: Yu, E., Dobbie, G., Jarke, M., Purao, S. (eds.) ER 2014. LNCS, vol. 8824, pp. 431–444. Springer, Cham (2014). doi:10.1007/978-3-319-12206-9_37
7. Boh, W.F., Yellin, D.: Using enterprise architecture standards in managing information technology. J. Manag. Inf. Syst. **23**(3), 163–207 (2006)
8. Brückmann, M., et al.: Evaluating enterprise architecture management initiatives-how to measure and control the degree of standardization of an IT landscape. In: Mendling, J., Rinderle-Ma, S., Esswein, W. (eds.) EMISA, pp. 155–168 (2009)
9. Buckl, S., et al.: A pattern based approach for constructing enterprise architecture management information models. In: Wirtschaftinformatik Proceedings 2007, p. 65 (2007)
10. Colombo, A., et al.: The use of a meta-model to support multi-project process measurement. In: 15th Asia-Pacific Software Engineering Conference, APSEC 2008, pp. 503–510. IEEE (2008)
11. Correia, A., e Abreu, F.B.: Integrating IT service management within the enterprise architecture. In: Fourth International Conference on Software Engineering Advances, ICSEA 2009, pp. 553–558. IEEE (2009)
12. CIO Council: A Practical Guide to Federal Enterprise Architecture, Version 1.0 (2001)
13. CIO Council: Federal Enterprise Architecture Framework, Version 1.0 (1999)
14. Ernst, A.M.: Enterprise architecture management patterns. In: Proceedings of the 15th Conference on Pattern Languages of Programs, pp. 7:1–7:20. ACM, New York (2008)
15. Fisher, A., et al.: 3.1. 1 model lifecycle management for MBSE. In: INCOSE International Symposium, pp. 207–229. Wiley Online Library (2014)
16. Gartner: Thirteen worst enterprise architecture practices, Report No. G00164424 (2009)
17. Goldkuhl, G., Lind, M., Seigerroth, U.: Method integration: the need for a learning perspective. IEE Proc.-Softw. **145**(4), 113–118 (1998)
18. Goodhue, D.L., et al.: The impact of data integration on the costs and benefits of information systems. MIS Q. **16**(3), 293–311 (1992)
19. Grossmann, W.: A conceptual approach for data integration in business analytics. Int. J Softw. Inform. **4**, 53–67 (2010)
20. Grossmann, W., Moser, C.: Big data—integration and cleansing environment for business analytics with DICE. In: Karagiannis, D., Mayr, H., Mylopoulos, J. (eds.) Domain-Specific Conceptual Modeling, pp. 103–123. Springer, Cham (2016). doi:10.1007/978-3-319-39417-6_5
21. Hanschke, I.: Strategic IT Management: A Toolkit for Enterprise Architecture Management. Springer Science & Business Media, Heidelberg (2009). doi:10.1007/978-3-642-05034-3
22. Karagiannis, D.: Agile modeling method engineering. In: Proceedings of the 19th Panhellenic Conference on Informatics, pp. 5–10. ACM, New York (2015)
23. Karagiannis, D., Moser, C., Mostashari, A.: Compliance evaluation featuring heat maps (CE-HM): a meta-modeling-based approach. In: Ralyté, J., Franch, X., Brinkkemper, S., Wrycza, S. (eds.) CAiSE 2012. LNCS, vol. 7328, pp. 414–428. Springer, Heidelberg (2012). doi:10.1007/978-3-642-31095-9_27
24. Karagiannis, D., Buchmann, R.A., Burzynski, P., Reimer, U., Walch, M.: Fundamental conceptual modeling languages in OMiLAB. In: Karagiannis, D., Mayr, H., Mylopoulos, J. (eds.) Domain-Specific Conceptual Modeling, pp. 3–30. Springer, Cham (2016). doi:10.1007/978-3-319-39417-6_1
25. Karagiannis, D., Kühn, H.: Metamodelling platforms. In: EC-Web, p. 182 (2002)

26. Lara, P., Sánchez, M., Villalobos, J.: Bridging the IT and OT worlds using an extensible modeling language. In: Comyn-Wattiau, I., Tanaka, K., Song, I.-Y., Yamamoto, S., Saeki, M. (eds.) ER 2016. LNCS, vol. 9974, pp. 122–129. Springer, Cham (2016). doi:10.1007/978-3-319-46397-1_10
27. Lichka, C., et al.: IT-based balanced scorecard. In: WISU Wirtschaftinformatik, p. 31 (2002)
28. Oracle: Oracle Lifetime Support Policy: Oracle and Sun System Software (2012). http://www.oracle.com/us/support/library/lifetime-support-hardware.pdf
29. Peterson, R.: Crafting information technology governance. Inf. Syst. Manag. **21**(4), 7–22 (2004)
30. Pragmatic EA Ltd.: Pragmatic EA Framework Version 2.0 (2010)
31. Prat, N., et al.: Artifact evaluation in information systems design-science research-a holistic view. In: PACIS 2014 Proceedings - Pacific Asia Conference on Information Systems, p. 23 (2014)
32. Shneiderman, B.: The eyes have it: a task by data type taxonomy for information visualizations. In: Proceedings of IEEE Symposium on Visual Languages, pp. 336–343. IEEE (1996)
33. Stelzer, D.: Enterprise architecture principles: literature review and research directions. In: Dan, A., Gittler, F., Toumani, F. (eds.) ICSOC/ServiceWave-2009. LNCS, vol. 6275, pp. 12–21. Springer, Heidelberg (2010). doi:10.1007/978-3-642-16132-2_2
34. The Open Group: ArchiMate 3.0 Specification (2016)
35. The Open Group: TOGAF Version 9.1 (2011)
36. Varnus, J., Panaich, N.: TOGAF 9 enterprise architecture survey results. In: 23rd Enterprise Architecture Practitioners Conference (2009)
37. Zivkovic, S., et al.: Facilitate modelling using method integration: an approach using mappings and integration rules. In: ECIS 2007 Proceedings, pp. 2038–2049 (2007)

A Catalogue of Reusable Context Model Elements Based on the *i** Framework

Karina Abad[1], Wilson Pérez[1(✉)], Juan Pablo Carvallo[2], and Xavier Franch[3]

[1] University of Cuenca, Cuenca, Ecuador
{karina.abadr,wilson.perez}@ucuenca.edu.ec
[2] University of Azuay, Cuenca, Ecuador
jpcarvallo@uazuay.edu.ec
[3] Universitat Politècnica de Catalunya, Barcelona, Spain
franch@essi.upc.edu

Abstract. The definition of the context of a system is one of the most relevant activities in the early phases of information systems engineering. It allows system engineers to narrow the system scope, by defining well established system boundaries. In practice, outlining a system context model is complex and cumbersome. In order to support context modeling, in this paper we propose a catalogue of context model elements expressed in *i**, which can be reused as building blocks in the construction of context models for new systems. We describe the process used for the identification of a set of actors and dependencies recurrently appearing in several academic and industrial cases, and the process to store them into a catalogue of reusable *i** context dependencies.

Keywords: Goal-oriented model · Model reuse · iStar framework · Context model

1 Introduction

The definition of the context of a system is one of the most relevant activities in the early phases of information system engineering [1]. It allows system engineers to narrow the system scope, by defining well established boundaries in relation to the actors placed in its context (organizations, people, cyber-technical systems, etc.) and the interactions (processes) that it must support to communicate with them. The definition of system context requires at least four facets to be considered [1]:

- **Use**: the kind of users that will interact with the system and their abilities and limitations (physical or mental).
- **Object**: the system-to-be and its functional coverage.
- **System**: the platform, protocols and technologies required to run and support system operation.
- **Development**: standards and tools used to drive system construction.

In practice, modeling a system context is complex and cumbersome. It requires continuous and fluid communication among system designers, stakeholders and

H.C. Mayr et al. (Eds.): ER 2017, LNCS 10650, pp. 36–49, 2017.
https://doi.org/10.1007/978-3-319-69904-2_3

managers visualizing and defining business strategy, but also notations and tools required to support and document their interaction and agreements in the form of a Context Model (CM).

In order to support this process, in the last few years we have been intensively using the *i** framework [2] to model system contexts, and proposed the DHARMA [3] method to discover the system architecture departing from these models. The application of DHARMA in a good dozen of cases led us to propose some patterns aiming at improving CM construction [4], by reusing some elements that repeatedly appeared in several of these cases. Although these patterns proved to be useful in practice [4], after conducting over 36 academic and industrial experiences, we concluded that, due to the creative nature of both managers and organizations, even in the same industry, the patterns tend to structure and behave in very dissimilar ways, making their application highly difficult. These cases also proved that that reuse of more atomic sets of elements was not only feasible, but also a way to more efficiently construct CM [5].

In this paper, we present a catalogue of reusable CM elements expressed in *i** to be used as building blocks in the construction of CM for new systems. We describe the process used to identify a set actors and related dependencies, which frequently occurred in these cases, and the process to store them into a catalogue of reusable *i** context dependencies. Dependencies can be independently reused as atomic patterns or together, in subsets of dependencies selected in relation to labels assigned to actors. These subsets of dependencies structure larger "dynamically constructed" patterns or CM chunks, which can be parametrized in relation to the specific domain.

The rest of the paper is structured as follows. Section 2 presents the background, including the DHARMA method, and some related work on pattern-based reuse. Section 3 shows the process followed for the catalogue construction. Section 4 summarizes the contents of the final catalogue. Section 5 shows how the catalogue can be used to automatize the construction of CM. Finally, Sect. 6 presents some conclusions and future work.

2 Background and Related Work

2.1 The DHARMA Method

The DHARMA (Discovering Hybrid ARchitectures by Modelling Actors) method [3] aims at the definition of enterprise architectures using the *i** framework [2], which allows representing, modeling and reasoning about socio-technical systems through graphical models based on a set of modeling constructs. DHARMA relies upon two concepts defined by Porter [6]: (1) the model of market forces designed to reason about potential available strategies and how to make them profitable and helpful in the analysis of the influences of market forces; and (2) a value chain that includes primary and support activities. The process consists in four activities (see Fig. 1). Activity 1 models the enterprise context; the organization and its strategy are carefully analyzed, to identify its role inside the context, making evident the Context Actors (CA) and the Organizational Areas (OA) structuring the organization. *i** SD models are built and used to support reasoning and represent results from this activity. Activity 2 places a system-to-be into the organization and analyzes the impact that it has over the elements in the CM. Strategic dependencies identified in the previous activity (internal and context), are inspected to determine which of them may be totally or partially satisfied by system. In Activity 3, dependencies included in the CM are analyzed and decomposed into a hierarchy of goals required to satisfy them. The goals represent the services that the system must provide, to support interaction with CA and OA activities. An *i** SR diagram for the system is built. Finally, Activity 4 is used to identify the generic architecture of the system (system actors that structure the system, the services - goals- that must be covered by each of them and the relationships among them).

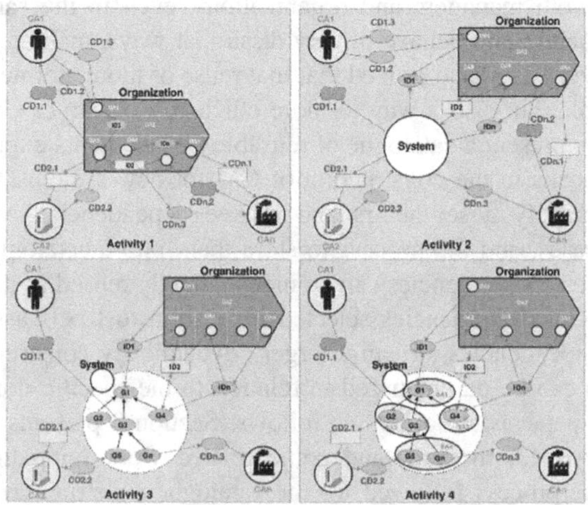

Fig. 1. The DHARMA method

2.2 Related Work on Reuse Through Patterns

The reuse of requirements through patterns has been proposed and used broadly in the field of requirements engineering [7]. Most of them focus on non-functional requirements (NFR) as in [8, 9], where a set of defined patterns is presented; these patterns aim to capture and reuse some specific aspects linked to data security. The PABRE framework [10] makes use of patterns in order to define requirements expressed in natural language. The catalogue used by PABRE was grounded on real software requirement documents and applies to both functional requirements and NFRs.

In the *i** community, we find several approaches too. In [11] an evaluation was carried out around the application of patterns over *i** models, trying to find out if those patterns improve CM construction, finding that their application allow to define elements with a broader coverage. Nevertheless, their construction requires a deep understanding and effort; therefore, in this work it was not possible to demonstrate that their application decreases the complexity of the construction of CM. With a similar aim of exploring pattern application, in [4] we proposed a set of patterns based in the Porter's model and some strategies, specifically the CRM strategy, and we formulated patterns for this strategy, which are formally described and oriented to industrial applicability. In [12], we have proposed a first approach for reusing elements through a catalogue of CM elements and showed how to automate the construction of *i** SD based-CM, starting the construction of CM from a solid base instead of departing from scratch.

In this work, we aim to provide guidance in early phases of the Enterprise Engineering process, providing artifacts to bridge communication gaps among technical Enterprise Engineering staff and administrative staff, starting from previous works and improving them. In relation to [10], our contribution is focused in the exclusive use of the *i** notation instead of natural language (which provides an adequate level of abstraction for modeling CM). We improved the catalogue of common elements presented in [12] to include more CM to the analysis, this paper presents the process to construct such catalogue; we also introduce and show the use of parametric actors and dependencies.

3 Catalogue Construction

In this section, we present the process performed to construct the catalogue of CM elements. The process starts with the data collection, then we analyze separately actors and dependencies. Due to the large number of CM elements, each analysis was performed in many steps, as explained below.

3.1 Data Collection

The models upon which we based this analysis were constructed by university students in their final grade project, acting as junior consultants in 36 organizations. The students were trained in the construction of CM, specifically in the *i** notation and the DHARMA method, according to the scope, objectives and activities proposed in such method. Since DHARMA is relatively new in the context of its application, we consider usable the CM constructed by the students according to the study carried out in [13], where the authors concluded that the performance observed in students and professionals is similar when the approach is new. The models were created for the organizations through formal agreements among them and the University of Cuenca. In the study, 27 organizations were small sized, 6 medium sized and 3 large sized. This distribution largely corresponds with the reality of the country where the studies were conducted, whose industrial network is composed by small companies as majority (97, 94%) [14]. The organizations were classified according to NACE Rev2's domains [15] identifying: 12 manufacturing, 16 wholesales, 2 human health, 4 education, 1 transportation and 1 financial.

In each organization, the modelling process started with the construction of CM and finished with the identification of the system architecture required to support its operation. The junior consultants worked in pairs in order to complete each DHARMA activity. To perform Activity 1 of the DHARMA method, an interview with the interlocutor assigned by each organization was conducted; its objective was to get information enough as to allow the identification of actors inside and outside the organization, and to discover the relations among them. The junior consultants performed the process manually and the final product of this activity was a set of *i** diagrams and its tabular representation according to DHARMA. Each group was able to identify around 31 actors and 58 dependencies per organization in average, with a maximum of 50 actors and 113 dependencies and a minimum of 17 actors and 20 dependencies.

3.2 Actors Analysis

The analysis of actors started by considering two generic groups as defined by Porter [6], namely: 8 external context actors (*Suppliers, Consumers, Strategic Partners, Distributors, Financial Institutions, Regulatory Agencies, Control Agencies and Competitors*) and 9 internal context actors (*Inbound Logistics, Operations, Outbound Logistics, Marketing and Sales, Services, Infrastructure, Human Resources Management, Technology Development and Procurement*). To define the catalogue of actors extending this initial group, we followed a three-step process, described below.

First, the 36 CM were integrated into a single data space, where each actor in a CM was classified as one of the 8 external or 9 internal context actors enumerated above (see results in Table 1).

A total of 1109 actors were found, from which 886 are external and 223 are internal. The most common types of actors are *Suppliers* and *Customers* with a 38.89% appearance rate. On the other hand, the least common actor is *Services*, included only in 5 organizational models.

Second, we proceeded to unify all the actors duplicated in the models, so that we obtained a set of instances for each internal and external actor. Table 2 shows an excerpt of actors identified as *Supplier* instances and their occurrences in the 36 organizations. We can see instances like *Basic services supplier*, *Technology supplier*, etc. Summarizing, from the 886 external actors, only 203 were unique instances and from the 223 internal actors, only 77 were unique instances.

Third, after getting the instances, we realized that some of them had common characteristics, being able to group them into categories, obtaining a hierarchical structure; the categories are called dimensions and are composed by the specific instances found in the previous step. As an example, consider actors categorized under the *Supplier* generic actor, which defines three dimensions (see Table 3): *Type* (Goods, Hardware, Basic services, Technology, etc.); *Volume* (Wholesaler and Retailer); and *Location* (Local, International and National).

3.3 Dependencies Analysis

The analysis of dependencies was focused on their description and type in order to define a catalogue of dependencies. This process was performed in two steps, as described below.

First, similarly to actors' identification, the CM corresponding to the 36 organizations were integrated into a single data space and the dependencies of each organization were analyzed based on their type (goal, softgoals, resources and tasks). Results are shown in Table 4. A total of 2095 dependencies were found (1351 dependencies related to external actors and 744 dependencies related to internal actors);

Table 1. Actors identified per organization. Organization size (S – Small, M – Medium and L - Large). Domain classification (M - Manufacturing, E - Education, T - Transportation, H - Human Health, W - Wholesale and F - Financial activities)

Organization			External Context Actor									Internal Context Actor									
Id	Size	Domain	Suppliers	Consumers	Control Agencies	Regulatory Agencies	Distributors	Strategic Partners	Competitors	Financial Institutions	**Total**	Inbound logistics	Outbound logistics	Operations	Services	Firm Infrastructure	Technological development	Procurement	Human Resource	Marketing and sales	**Total**
Org1	S	M	9	3	7	3	0	0	0	0	22	1	1	1	0	1	0	1	1	1	7
Org2	S	M	5	3	7	3	1	2	3	0	24	1	0	1	0	1	0	0	1	2	6
Org3	S	M	3	5	7	5	2	3	0	1	26	1	1	1	0	0	0	0	0	1	4
Org4	S	M	8	5	6	3	2	1	0	1	26	1	1	1	1	0	1	0	1	2	8
Org5	S	W	6	7	2	3	1	2	1	1	23	0	0	0	0	0	0	0	0	0	0
Org6	S	W	5	6	2	2	1	1	0	1	18	1	1	1	1	0	0	0	0	1	5
Org7	S	W	4	7	3	2	1	0	1	0	18	1	1	0	0	0	0	0	1	2	5
Org8	S	E	4	4	3	2	1	2	0	1	17	0	0	0	0	0	0	0	0	0	0
Org9	S	W	6	7	4	3	2	1	2	2	27	1	1	1	1	0	0	0	1	2	7
Org10	S	W	3	5	4	4	0	0	0	0	16	1	0	0	0	1	1	0	0	1	4
Org11	S	W	10	12	7	3	4	3	2	3	44	1	0	1	0	2	0	0	1	1	6
Org12	S	W	4	3	2	1	2	0	0	1	13	1	1	1	1	0	0	0	1	2	7
Org13	S	M	3	6	5	2	3	0	3	2	24	1	0	1	0	1	0	0	0	1	4
Org14	S	W	8	5	6	3	2	1	0	1	26	1	0	1	0	2	0	0	0	1	5
Org15	M	W	8	9	7	3	3	4	2	2	38	1	1	0	0	2	0	1	1	3	9
Org16	M	W	7	5	6	3	2	1	0	0	24	2	1	0	0	2	0	2	0	3	10
Org17	S	W	7	5	3	4	2	2	1	1	25	0	0	1	0	2	0	2	1	1	7
Org18	S	M	5	7	2	2	1	1	1	1	20	1	1	1	0	0	0	0	1	2	6
Org19	S	W	9	3	7	3	0	0	0	0	22	0	0	0	0	1	0	1	0	1	3
Org20	S	W	8	5	6	3	2	1	0	1	26	1	1	1	0	1	0	0	1	2	7
Org21	M	E	9	8	6	3	4	4	2	2	38	0	0	0	0	2	3	0	0	0	5
Org22	S	F	8	3	7	3	0	0	0	1	22	0	0	1	0	3	1	0	1	2	8
Org23	S	W	6	5	5	2	3	0	3	1	25	1	0	2	0	1	1	0	1	1	7
Org24	S	W	8	3	7	3	0	0	0	0	21	0	0	1	0	1	0	0	0	1	3
Org25	S	M	7	5	6	3	3	4	2	2	32	1	0	1	0	2	0	0	1	1	6
Org26	S	E	5	6	2	3	1	2	1	1	21	0	0	3	0	1	0	0	0	2	6
Org27	L	M	7	7	5	3	4	4	2	1	33	1	1	1	0	4	0	1	1	1	10
Org28	S	E	9	8	6	3	4	4	2	2	38	0	0	3	0	1	0	0	1	0	5
Org29	S	M	6	6	2	2	1	0	1	0	18	1	1	8	0	2	0	0	1	1	14
Org30	S	M	8	5	6	3	2	1	0	1	26	1	1	2	0	1	0	0	1	2	8
Org31	S	W	5	4	2	1	2	0	1	1	16	1	0	0	0	4	1	0	1	0	7
Org32	M	M	8	3	7	3	0	0	0	0	21	1	0	0	0	3	0	0	0	0	4
Org33	M	H	5	4	2	1	2	0	0	0	14	1	0	3	0	0	0	0	0	1	5
Org34	M	H	7	7	5	3	4	4	2	1	33	1	0	2	1	2	1	1	1	4	13
Org35	L	M	6	7	6	3	2	1	1	0	26	2	0	2	0	3	1	1	1	2	12
Org36	L	T	8	5	6	3	0	0	1	0	23	0	0	0	0	0	0	0	0	0	0
Total			234	198	176	99	64	49	34	32	**886**	28	14	42	5	46	10	10	21	47	**223**

from them, 862 dependencies are goals, 537 softgoals, 619 resources and 77 tasks. The scarce use of task dependencies is probably due to their high level of prescriptiveness, which is something that does not match well with the activity of context modeling.

Table 2. Excerpt of actors identified and their occurrence in the 36 cases conducted

Generic Actor	Actor	Org1	Org2	Org3	Org4	Org5	Org6	Org7	Org8	Org9	Org10	Org11	Org12	Org13	Org14	Org15	Org16	Org17	Org18	Org19	Org20	Org21	Org22	Org23	Org24	Org25	Org26	Org27	Org28	Org29	Org30	Org31	Org32	Org33	Org34	Org35	Org36	Total	Percentage
Supplier	Hardware																			X									X						X			3	8%
	Basic services									X	X	X	X		X		X	X				X		X				X	X	X	X						X	14	39%
	Technology						X																															1	3%
	Transport								X			X				X																						3	8%
	Wholesale										X																											1	3%
	Local	X			X	X				X		X		X							X																	7	19%
	National				X	X		X		X				X	X						X															X	X	9	25%
	International							X		X					X		X				X										X					X		7	19%

Table 3. Dimensions found for the *Supplier* generic actor.

Generic actor	Dimension	Actor instances
Supplier	Type	Goods
		Hardware
		Basic services
		Technology
		…
		Transport
	Volume	Wholesaler
		Retailer
	Location	Local
		National
		International

Table 4. Dependencies identified per organization

Type	Org1	Org2	Org3	Org4	Org5	Org6	Org7	Org8	Org9	Org10	Org11	Org12	Org13	Org14	Org15	Org16	Org17	Org18	Org19	Org20	Org21	Org22	Org23	Org24	Org25	Org26	Org27	Org28	Org29	Org30	Org31	Org32	Org33	Org34	Org35	Org36	Total
Goal	16	31	22	36	15	39	26	19	39	14	29	25	15	29	29	32	16	14	16	9	40	30	28	29	17	24	46	20	30	28	13	16	10	9	15	36	**862**
Softgoal	11	10	9	19	11	12	2	4	18	6	15	22	8	19	23	15	10	21	11	9	19	18	21	17	13	14	32	22	23	33	4	7	7	10	22	20	**537**
Resource	18	12	0	26	10	10	2	13	22	5	15	18	14	25	22	32	16	24	13	11	21	11	24	39	15	27	32	12	21	35	8	5	3	14	26	18	**619**
Task	0	0	0	1	0	2	0	0	7	2	0	2	4	2	4	6	0	0	1	2	1	4	3	1	1	7	3	1	7	8	1	0	0	0	5	2	**77**
Total	45	53	31	82	36	63	30	36	86	27	59	67	41	75	78	85	42	59	41	31	81	63	76	86	46	72	113	55	81	104	26	28	20	33	68	76	**2095**

Second, we proceeded to group the 2095 dependencies with their respective generic actors. In this step, the duplicated dependencies were omitted, finding 994 dependencies (408 dependencies linked to external actors and 586 to internal actors). Summing up, from the 862 goal dependencies identified in the previous step (Table 4), 449 are unique instances; from the 537 softgoals, 249 are unique instances; from the 619 resources, 254 are unique instances; and from the 77 tasks, 42 are unique instances.

3.4 Synonyms in Actors and Dependencies

During the data analysis, we found some actors and dependencies representing the same entity or idea but written differently, that is, synonyms. An example is the occurrence of two actors, *Final client* and *Final customer,* in two different organizations; for dependencies, consider the dependencies *Timely delivery* and *On-time delivery* found in two different organizations. In summary, we found 13 synonyms in external actors, 51 in dependencies linked to external actors, 32 synonyms in internal actors and 86 in dependencies linked to internal actors. For dependencies, 68 were goals, 48 softgoals and 21 resources. To simplify the catalogue, we decided to create a section focused in those findings. The main idea is that in later stages, through the use of semantic technologies, analyze the actors and dependencies entered by the user as part of a CM and inform him that a similar actor or dependency has been previously defined with different words (if that is the case), and let him decide which of them is the best option.

Figure 2 shows graphically how the total number of actors and dependencies shrank little by little after each step described in Sects. 3.2 and 3.3, including the results of synonyms, obtaining a total of 235 actors, from them 190 are external context actors and 45 internal context actors. Additionally, 857 dependencies were identified (381 goals, 201 softgoals, 233 resources and 42 tasks).

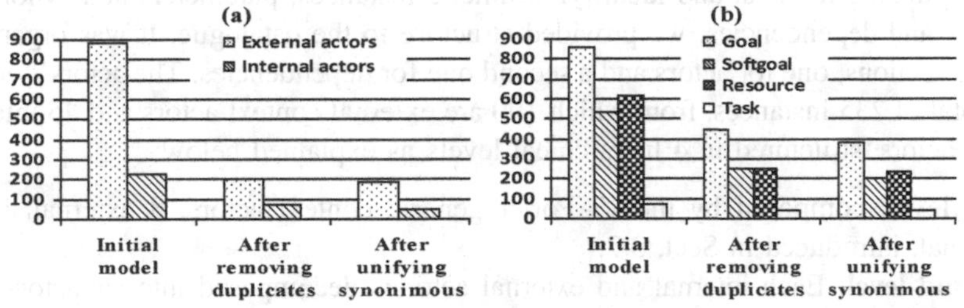

Fig. 2. Number of elements shrunk on each step. (a) Actors, (b) Dependencies

3.5 Parametric Actors and Dependencies

Even after the consolidation of actors and dependencies as explained in the previous subsections, we found groups of actors or dependencies identified in different organizations but all those sharing similar characteristics. To make explicit this similarity and also to make the catalogue more compact, we incorporated parameters to the definition of actors and dependencies. As an example of parametric actors, consider an organization where the actor *Primary Students* has been identified, and a second organization where the actor *High School Students* emerged, both of them with similar relationships in their respective organization. That allowed us to group them in one category, with the possibility to parametrize them, that is, the parametric actor is defined as *<type-of-student> Students*, where the parameter *<type-of-student>* can be instantiated as *Primary* or *High school*. Other possible case of parametrization can be found with actors sharing characteristics as the sector, but differing in the industry, it means, the parametric actor could be *Supplier of <services>* and the tag *<services>* can be parametrized as *basic services, telecommunications, security,* etc.

The same occurs in dependencies. For instance, let's consider the dependency *<Products> acquired*; the parameter *<Products>* can be replaced by *furniture, clothes, equipment, etc.,* according to the industry of the depender or dependee. Sometimes, parametric dependencies can be associated to parametric actors, for example, the parametric actor *Supplier of <services>* (mentioned in the paragraph above) is associated to the parametric dependency *<Specific documents>*, if the actor is instantiated as *Supplier of transport services*, the dependency has to be instantiated as *Waybill* or if the actor is *Supplier of medical services*, the dependency has to be instantiated as *Medical record*.

A total of 41 actors in the catalogue were identified as parametric (22 external and 19 internal) and 63 dependencies (35 dependencies linked to external actors and 28 to internal actors), where 25 are goals, 6 softgoals, 28 resources and 4 tasks.

4 The Catalogue of Context Model Elements

After organizing the data and identifying unique instances, parameters and synonyms of actors and dependencies, we provided structure to the catalogue. It was organized into two sections, one for actors and a second one for dependencies. The actors' section has a total of 235 instances, from which 190 are external context actors and 45 internal context actors, structured in 4 hierarchical levels as explained below:

- **Fist level:** composed by the 17 Porter generic context actors, 8 external and 9 internal, introduced in Sect. 3.2.
- **Second level**: Each internal and external actor is decomposed into subactors (defined as "Dimensions" in Table 3). From them, 17 are dimensions of external context actors, and 7 are dimensions of internal context actors.
- **Third level**: Contains a total of 39 instances on external context actors and 9 instances on internal context actors (see column "Actor instances" in Table 3).
- **Fourth level**: This level contains the parameters that can be used as instances of parametric actors defined in the third level and has 190 external context actors and 45 internal context actors.

From the point of view of the dependencies, the catalogue contains a total of 857 dependencies, from which 381 are goals (126 dependencies linked to external actors and 255 to internal actors); 201 softgoals (107 dependencies linked to external actors and 94 to internal actors); 233 resources (109 dependencies linked to external actors and 124 to internal actors); and 42 tasks (15 dependencies linked to external actors and 27 to internal actors).

Table 5. Catalogue excerpt

Generic actor	Dimension	Actor instances	Dependency	Type	Direction
Customer	Frecuency or volume	Potential	Widespread promotions	Goal	>
			Promotional samples	Resource	<
		New	Membership card provided	Goal	>
			Special introduction prices provided	Softgoal	>
			Membership card	Resource	>
			Personal information registered	Goal	<
		Important	VIP benefits granted	Goal	>
			Personalized attention	Softgoal	>
			VIP card	Resource	>
			Important high volume order placed	Goal	<
	Distribution channel	Wholesaler	Product availability guaranteed	Goal	<
			Product distribution agreement signed	Softgoal	<
			Increase sales through the distribution chain	Softgoal	<
			Product distribution agreement	Resource	<
			Product distribution chain achieved	Softgoal	>
		Retailer	Restocking in small quantities provided	Goal	>
			Approach consumers through a specific location	Softgoal	<
			Increase sales through individual stores	Softgoal	<
		Specificmarket segment	Specialized customer service infrastructure	Softgoal	>
			Trained stuff for specific needs	Softgoal	>
			Specific documents	Resource	>
	Payment method	Credit	Deferred payments	Goal	>
			Credit flexibility	Softgoal	>
			Acceptance of various credit cards	Softgoal	>
			Voucher	Resource	>
			Warranty documents	Resource	<
		Cash	Cash rebates	Goal	>
			Money	Resource	<
Supplier	Type	Goods	Health service obtained	Goal	>
		Services	Home service	Goal	>
	Volume	Wholesaler	Large purchase orders	Goal	>
		Retailer	Restocking in small quantities provided	Goal	<
	Location	Local	Cash payment discounts	Goal	>
		National	Deferred payments	Goal	>
		International			

The catalogue (currently in Spanish only) can be accessed at a given URL address[1]. Table 5 shows an excerpt of the catalogue, presenting the dimension, actors and dependencies identified for the *Customer* and *Supplier* actors.

5 Catalogue Use

In this section, we show a use case were the catalogue of CM elements was applied, the example shows how the catalogue was applied over a small organization which included some of the elements listed in the catalogue (see Sect. 5.1) and Sect. 5.2 shows some statistics about the reusability level achieved when applying the catalogue.

5.1 Use Case

To validate the catalogue, we proceeded to model a small organization of the academic sector that develops scientific, professional and technical activities. The modeling process was performed in 4 phases, where, each phase was modeled using the catalogue:

1. *Identification of Internal Actors:* We performed an interview with the manager of the organization, asking him to check the internal actors from the catalogue that represent departmental areas in the organization. This step exposes all the actors inside the organization.
2. *Identification of External Actors:* Each internal actor identified in Step 1 was interviewed and asked to identify the external actors from the catalogue with which it interacts in a daily basis.
3. *Establishing dependencies between Actors:* Once identified both, external and internal actors, we checked the dependencies from the catalogue that included each pair of actors, obtaining a set of dependencies validated by the internal actor being interviewed.
4. *Constructing the i* diagrams:* we generated a set of *i** diagrams that included actors and dependencies identified for the organization. The *i** diagrams resulting were validated with the manager of the organization.

The results obtained in this use case contain a total of 39 actors (33 external and 6 internal context actors) and 185 dependencies (101 goals, 34 softgoals, 44 resources, and 6 tasks). In each phase were identified new elements (actors and dependencies), this elements were added to the catalogue. Regarding actors, 33 out of 39 are included in the catalogue (30 external and 3 internal) and 6 actors were identified during the interviews (3 external and 3 internal). Regarding dependencies, 176 out of 185 dependencies were included in the catalogue (97 goals, 34 softgoals, 42 resources and 3 tasks) and 9 dependencies were identified during the interviews (4 goals, 2 resources and 3 tasks). Figure 3 show the catalogue usage statistics.

[1] https://www.dropbox.com/sh/7jnwsv7vqwwhnv8/AADqaiHx_vDj-gi6mk_5pg_Ca?dl=0.

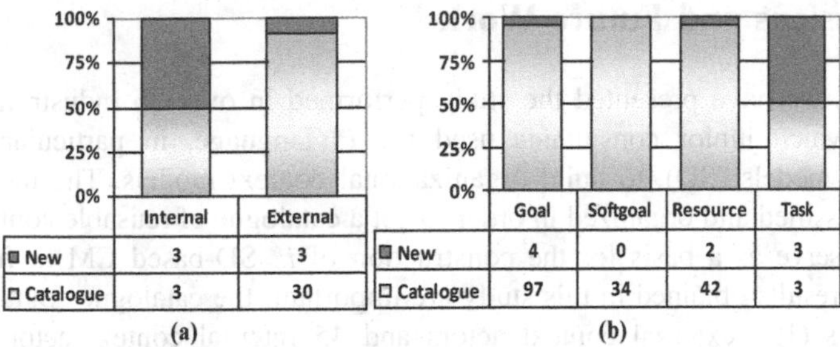

Fig. 3. Use of the catalogue

The use of the catalogue in this use case facilitated the identification of actors and dependencies through the reuse of elements already identified, where the consultants selected the elements of the catalogue that matched those of the organization. In this way, it allowed to streamline and create stable models taking advantage of the knowledge base, compared to the time it would take to model from scratch.

5.2 Reusability

As stated by Porter [6], organizations share common elements in their context (e.g. external actors derived from the model of market forces and internal actors derived from the value chain) it can be considered as fact that some activities performed by these actors share commonalities, this is the reason why we have decided to analyze many academic and industrial cases. The analysis leads us to confirm our beliefs, many global activities were the same among different organizations. However, as we drilled down to more specific industry segments, more specific elements started to emerge, which, at some point, required an exhaustive analysis about including them or not in the catalogue, at the end, we decided to create parametric actors and dependencies. Although the construction of the catalogue was very laborious, the final result is satisfactory since after making a first use (explained in previous section) we noticed that its application helps to create CM with the following characteristics:

1. Due to the wide range of industry segments of the organizations analyzed in this work, we consider that the catalogue is representative, almost complete, and the consultant can select elements from a wide variety of possibilities.
2. As actors and dependencies are categorized and include definitions of type, it is easier for the consultants to clarify concepts regarding to types and hierarchies.
3. When performing the interview with the responsible of each organization area, the consultant will have a solid knowledge base that will help him to understand the organizational context without starting from scratch and reusing elements identified in the catalogue.

6 Conclusions and Future Work

In this work, we have presented the study performed in over 36 industrial IS architectural in which junior consultants used the *i** language, in particular Strategic Dependency models (SD), to build organizational context models. The models were analyzed, classified and organized in order to get a catalogue of reusable context model elements to serve as a basis for the construction of *i** SD-based CM in future case studies. The results obtained in this study are important; the catalogue contains a total of 235 actors (190 external context actors and 45 internal context actor) and 857 dependencies (381 are dependencies of type goal, 201 are dependencies of type softgoal, 233 dependencies of type resource, and 42 dependencies of type task). Also, we validated the catalogue through its application in a small organization, finding that most of the elements included in the final CM (>80%) are contained in our catalogue.

Work in progress includes the further refinement of the existing catalogue; we plan to conduct a similar study focused on *i** SR models, which are used in later phases of the DHARMA method, analyzing goal decomposition, means-end links, etc. Also, it is worth mentioning that we have created an ontology network [16] to add semantics to our catalogue and we also have developed a tool to support the application of the catalogue [17]; the tool makes easier the application of the catalogue, filtering its elements and generating *i** models automatically; nevertheless, we aim to improve the ontology and the tool to support the construction of CM avoiding synonyms in actors and dependencies.

References

1. Pohl, K.: Requirements Engineering: Fundamentals, Principles, and Techniques. Springer, Heidelberg (2010)
2. Yu, E.: Modelling strategic relationships for process reengineering. Ph.D. thesis, University of Toronto, Department of Computer Science, Canada (1995)
3. Carvallo, J.P., Franch, X.: Descubriendo la arquitectura de sistemas de software híbridos: un enfoque basado en Modelos i*. In: WER (2009)
4. Carvallo, J.P., Franch, X.: Building strategic enterprise context models with i*: a pattern-based approach. In: Aier, S., Ekstedt, M., Matthes, F., Proper, E., Sanz, Jorge L. (eds.) PRET/TEAR -2012. LNBIP, vol. 131, pp. 40–59. Springer, Heidelberg (2012). doi:10.1007/978-3-642-34163-2_3
5. Abad, K., Pérez, W., Carvallo, J.P., Franch, X.: i* in practice: identifying frequent problems in its application. In: ACM SAC (2017)
6. Porter, M.: Competitive Strategy. Free Press, New York (1980)
7. Withall, S.J.: Software Requirement Patterns. Microsoft Press (2007)
8. Supakkul, S., Hill, T., Chung, L.: An NFR pattern approach to dealing with NFR. In: RE (2010)
9. Ruiz-López, T., Garrido, J., Supakkul, S., Chung, L.: A pattern approach to dealing with NFRs in ubiquitous systems. In: CEUR-WS (2013)
10. Renault, S., Méndez, O., Franch, X., Quer, C.: Constructing and using software requirement patterns. In: RCIS (2009)

11. Strohmaier, M., Horkoff, J., Yu, E., Aranda, J., Easterbrook, S.: Can patterns improve i* modeling? Two exploratory studies. In: Paech, B., Rolland, C. (eds.) REFSQ 2008. LNCS, vol. 5025, pp. 153–167. Springer, Heidelberg (2008). doi:10.1007/978-3-540-69062-7_16
12. Abad, K., Carvallo, J.P., Peña, C.: iStar in practice: on the identification of reusable SD context models elements. In: iStar (2015)
13. Salman, I., Misirli, A.T., Juristo, N.: Are students representatives of professionals in software engineering experiments? In: ICSE (2015)
14. Instituto Nacional de Estadísticas y Censos. Ecuador en cifras. http://aplicaciones2.ecuadorencifras.gob.ec/dashboard2/pagina3.php
15. Office for Official Publications of the European Communities. NACE Rev 2. Statistical classification of economic activities in the European Community (2008)
16. Pérez, W., Abad, K., Carvallo, J.P., Espinoza, M., Saquicela, V.: Ontología DHARMA para la construcción de Arquitectura de Sistemas Empresariales. Revista Maskana **7**, 177–185 (2016)
17. Abad, K., Pérez W., Carvallo, J.P.: Managing i*-based reusable context models elements through a semantic repository. In: iStar (2016)

Modelling Processes with Time-Dependent Control Structures

Horst Pichler, Johann Eder(✉), and Margareta Ciglic

Department of Informatics-Systems, Alpen-Adria Universität Klagenfurt, Klagenfurt, Austria
{horst.pichler,johann.eder,margareta.ciglic}@aau.at
http://isys.uni-klu.ac.at

Abstract. The modeling of processes with temporal constraints suffers from a mismatch between more procedural process models and more declarative formulations of temporal constraints. We propose the introduction of temporal conditions in the formulation of conditional constructs, in particular XOR-splits and loops to give process designers explicit control over the temporal behaviour of the processes they model. We define syntax and semantics of temporal splits and temporal loops and propose the notion of controllability for defining the (temporal) correctness of process definitions with temporal control structures.

1 Introduction

Compliance to temporal constraints like deadlines, reaction times, process durations rank among the most important quality measures [1,10] for (business) process management. To speed up processes, decrease the number of deadline violations, and pro-active avoidance of temporal constraint violations should therefore be among the major objectives in this field. Since the late 1990s a lot of research was devoted to modeling temporal constraints and checking correctness of temporally constrained process definitions. But what is the current situation? We have elaborate concepts for expressing temporal constraints in a declarative way [2,6,13] and checking correctness of process definitions with temporal constraints according to the notion of (dynamic) controllability is already well established for acyclic workflows [4,6,8,12].

However, the current situation has shortcomings: (i) the separation of concerns between mismatching proscriptive control structures and declarative temporal constraints, (ii) missing temporal control of loops, and (iii) constructs for addressing temporal aspects in process enactment systems are mostly too low level (timer events, exception handling) and needs to be raised to the level of conceptual modeling of processes.

Within process models a designer is typically confronted with a mix of proscriptive and declarative elements. This is hardly avoidable as some temporal constraints are preferably defined in form of declarative constraints. But consider the following example "if the process is late (more than 100 time units old) proof reading and layout improvement are rather done in parallel than in

H.C. Mayr et al. (Eds.): ER 2017, LNCS 10650, pp. 50–58, 2017.
https://doi.org/10.1007/978-3-319-69904-2_4

sequence" or "repeat resubmission of the paper as often as you like until the deadline". Current processes modelling languages do not allow to easily and directly express these scenarios. We argue that a better support for explicitly influencing the time-dependent run-time behaviour of processes would make designing processes with temporal aspects much more intuitive.

In this paper we propose improvements for this situation in form of explicit temporal control structures together with an apparatus for supporting process modeling and checking of process definitions. In particular, we propose the use of temporal conditions such as "elapsed time $\leq$ constant" in xor-gateways and loops, complemented by algorithms for design time checking of the temporal properties of process definitions: checking correctness and controllability of the process definition, computing minimum and maximum duration of processes, computation of schedules in form of execution intervals for process execution to respect all temporal constraints, and the identification of flaws in process models.

Caveat: In this paper we focus on the proposed temporal control structures and on controllability. The present approach, however, extends naturally to the inclusion of other temporal constraints.

2 Temporal Control Structures

The extended BPMN-notation in Fig. 1 shows a simplified critical support and maintenance process of Machine Inc., a company that builds, installs, and maintains machines. The process was specifically designed for customers with a service level agreement that obligates Machines Inc. to limit each problem-related downtime of their machines to 120 ($\delta = 120$) h, or, otherwise, face severe penalty payments.

The process is started by the customer or by specific error codes reported online by the machine's diagnostic component. It begins with activity *A:Problem Analysis* based on error description and diagnostic log data which may last between 10 and 20 h.

Depending on the outcome of A either *B:Reconfiguration and Software Update* for problems that can be solved rather fast on-line by support personal or programmers, or *C:Repair Task* for severe problems that require more time and a repair team on-site (journey to site included). The duration of diamond-shaped control nodes is assumed to be [0, 0].

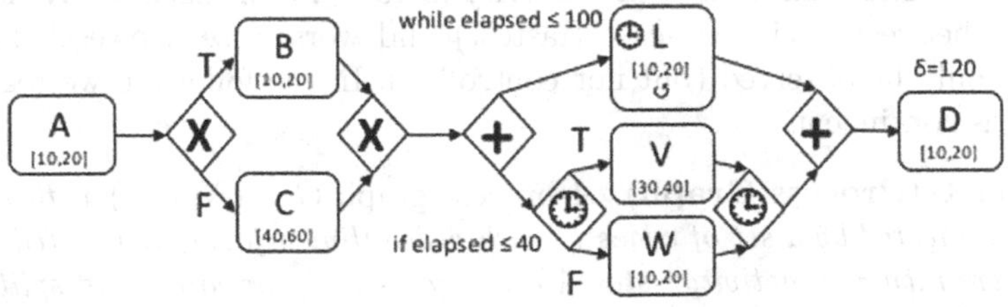

Fig. 1. Process graph with temporal controls

Machine Inc. reduces future problems and down times by applying thorough tests and machine maintenance whenever possible. Thus, subsequently two quality assurance measures are taken in two parallel branches (after node +).

The upper parallel branch executes as many *L:Automated Diagnostic Test Suites* as possible, where each test suite will run between 10 and 20 h. We propose **temporal loops** to express this kind of temporal behavior, represented as an activity augmented with a loop-icon and a clock-icon. It repeatedly executes L while $elapsed \leq 100$ h, stating that L will start another iteration if the elapsed time is less or equal 100 (L may represent a sub-process).

The lower parallel branch is dedicated to on-site maintenance, which will either be *V:Regular Service* or a *W:Quick Service* if the process is late. To represent behavior we propose the **temporal xor-split**, represented by a diamond augmented with a clock-icon, which exclusively chooses one out of two paths as follows: if $elapsed \leq 40$ h then V else W, which means that a slow process will save time by choosing W (quick service) instead of V (regular service).

Finally, when quality assurance is done, the process is concluded by *D:Review, Monitored Operation and Clearance.*

Based on this temporal information and the control flow semantics it is possible to calculate (implicit) temporal properties of process models and to compute schedules for the correct execution of processes. In the following sections we introduce temporal control structures in process definitions, formally define the semantics of the new constructs and develop an algorithm for checking the controllability of processes with temporal control structures.

3 Process Model with Temporal Control Structures

We use a simple workflow process metamodel, which focuses on the standard minimum workflow control patterns [19]. However, our definitions and algorithms can be easily extended to other control flow patterns.

Time points and duration intervals are represented by natural numbers $\mathbb{N}$. Time is measured in an atomic time unit (chronon), like minutes, hours or days. A point in time marks a point on an increasing time axis and represents the temporal distance to a given reference point, for instance the start of a process.

The maximum process duration is constrained by a deadline, that must not be exceeded. Activity instances start at a certain point in time (start event) and end at a certain point in time (end event). The distance between these two points is the actual execution duration of this activity instance. Contingent activities have a duration between their best-case (fastest) and worst-case (slowest) duration which can only be observed (but not controlled). In the following we regard all activities as contingent.

Definition 1 (Process Graph). *A* process graph $G = (N, E, \delta)$ *with a set of nodes N connected by a set of edges E with a deadline δ forms a directed acyclic graph, where n.type = activity | start | end | xor-split | xor-join | and-split | and-join, which have the usual semantics, or a temporal node with n.type = t-split | t-join | t-loop.*

$n.d_b$ is the minimum and $n.d_w$ maximum duration of a node $n \in N$ such that $0 \le n.d_b \le n.d_w$ and $n.d_b, n.d_w \in \mathbb{N}$.

Each edge $(n_1, n_2) \in E$, $n_1, n_2 \in N$, describes a precedence constraint between nodes n_1 and n_2. The predecessors and successors of a node n are denoted $n.Succ = \{m|(n,m) \in E\}$ and $n.Pred = \{m|(m,n) \in E\}$ respectively.

There is exactly one start activity and one end activity. The number of predecessors $|n.Pred|$ per node-type n.type is as follows: 0 for start, 2 for xor-joint|t-join, >1 for and-join, and 1 for all other types. And the number of successors $|n.Succ|$ per node-type n.type is restricted as follows: 0 for end, 2 for xor-split|t-split, >1 for and-split, and 1 for all other types.

A temporal split node $ts \in N$, ts.type = t-split is a special form of an xor-split with a temporal condition ts.cond = (elapsed $\le c$). The variable elapsed represents the distance between the start of the process and a point in time. A temporal loop $tl \in N$, tl.type = t-loop has a loop body $tl.B = G'$ where G' is a process graph, and a loop condition $l.cond = [P\wedge](elapsed \le c), c \in \mathbb{N}$ with the optional predicate P. The duration interval for one iteration over the loop-body is represented by $l.b_b$ and $l.b_w$. We write tsplit(n,c,u,d) for a t-split node n with threshold c, true successor u and false successor d and tloop(n,P,c,B) for a t-loop node n with predicate P, threshold c, and loop body B.

We assume that a process graph is full-blocked (proper nesting of matching pairs), and that Xor-joins and t-joins are of type simple merge [5]. Without loss of generality in this paper we only consider the temporal conditions (*elapsed* $\le c$). A temporal split $tsplit(n, c, u, d)$ compares the temporal variable *elapsed* against a constant $c \in \mathbb{N}$. If the condition is true the true successor u will be activated, otherwise the false successor d. A temporal loop $tloop(n, P, c, B)$ iterates over its body B as long as the condition is true. A temporal loop's condition specifies an upper bound in addition to a regular loop-condition. The body of a loop is again a process graph and might include temporal control structures. The variable *elapsed* is always defined relative to the start node of the (sub-)process graph.

4 Schedule and Controllability

To formalize the semantics of the proposed temporal control structures and to reason about the correctness of a given model we now introduce the concepts scenario, schedule, and controllability. In a nutshell: A scenario is a timed instance of process. It is correct, if the time stamps of the start and end events of the activities satisfy all explicit (modelled) and implicit (derived) temporal constraints. A schedule assigns start and end time intervals to each activity. A process is controllable, if it admits a schedule, such that all scenarios are valid if start and end-time are within the bounds defined in the schedule.

In a scenario time stamps for the start and the end are assigned to each node representing one out of many possible process executions.

Definition 2 (Scenario). *A scenario $\bar{S}$ for a process graph $P(N, V, \delta)$ associates each $n \in N$ and the body $l.B$ of each t-loop l with two time stamps*

$t_s, t_e \in \mathbb{N}$, *representing the start time and end time of n respectively. We call* $(n, t_s, t_e) \in \bar{S}$ *a scenario entry.*

We define a valid scenario as formalization of the conceptual semantics of control flow structures described in Sect. 3.

Definition 3 (Valid Scenario). *A scenario* $\bar{S}$ *for a process graph* $P(N, E, \delta)$ *is valid, iff:*

(1) $\forall n \in N$: $n.t_s \leq n.t_e \leq \delta$
(2) $\forall n \in N, n.type \neq t\text{-}loop : n.t_s + n.d_b \leq n.t_e \leq n.t_s + n.d_w$
(3) $\forall (m, n) \in E, m.type \neq\ t\text{-}split : m.t_e \leq n.t_s$
(4) $\forall tsplit(n, c, u, d) : n.t_s \leq c \Rightarrow n.t_e \leq u.t_s;\ c < n.t_s \Rightarrow c < n.t_e \leq d.t_s$
(5) $\forall tloop(n, True, c, B) : n.t_s \leq c \Rightarrow c < n.t_e \leq c{+}n.b_w;\ n.t_s > c \Rightarrow n.t_s = n.t_e$
(6) $\forall tloop(n, P, c, B)$: $n.t_s \leq c \Rightarrow n.t_s \leq n.t_e \leq c + n.b_w;\ n.t_s > c \Rightarrow n.t_s = n.t_e$

For the new control structures the following must hold: (4) If a t-split starts after the threshold c, the start of the false-successor must occur after the end of the t-split and therefore after c. The start time of the true-successor is not further constrained as it will not be executed. If the t-split starts before or at c, the true-successor has to start after the end of the t-split. In this case the start time of the non-executed false-successor is not further constrained. (5) If a temporal loop with the condition ($elapsed \leq c$) starts before or at c, it will run through the loop body at least until c is reached, plus one final loop-iteration (worst-case duration of the loop body). The end of the loop is always after the cut-off point c. If the loop starts after c, the loop body will not be executed (duration is 0). If the body of the loop is executed, its last iteration does not start before the beginning of the loop, and it does require at least the minimum duration of the body as distance between start and end of the loop. For the end of the loop we require that it can accommodate all durations of the loop body between best-case and worst-case duration. And finally, (6) states that t-loops with the condition $P \wedge (elapsed \leq c)$ can finish anytime before c due to the condition P, but they can last until c + duration of the loop body.

An example for one possible (valid) scenario, based on the process presented above, is visualized in Fig. 2. In this particular scenario A starts at 0 and ends at 15, and B starts at 20 and ends at 32, and so on. The t-split U ends at 80, and as $elapsed \leq 40$ the false-successor W will be chosen over V (which is given but can be neglected in this scenario, hence its start is set to 40). The loop L was not entered, as the start time of L is 80 and the condition of the temporal loop is *while* ($elapsed \leq 100$). The process ends before the deadline of 120 at 112.

A schedule defines possible execution intervals for nodes in a process graph. F (from) and T (to) represent intervals with upper bound and lower bound, of the start (s) respectively the end (e) of a node.

Definition 4 (Schedule). *A schedule S for a process graph* $P(N, E, \delta)$ *associates each* $n \in N$ *with execution intervals for the start and the end event of n: We write* $(n, [F_s, T_s], [F_e, T_e]) \in S$ *for a schedule entry.*

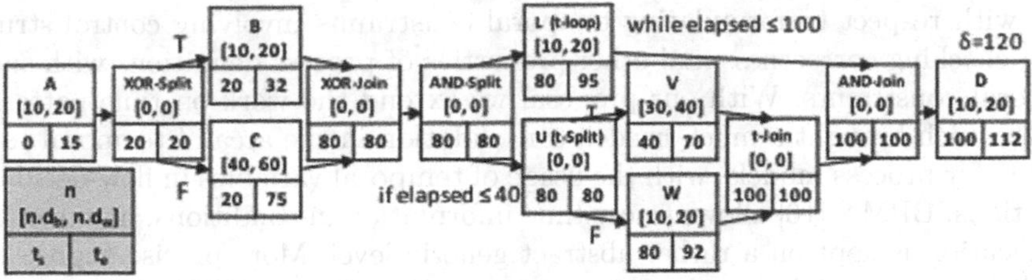

Fig. 2. Valid scenario

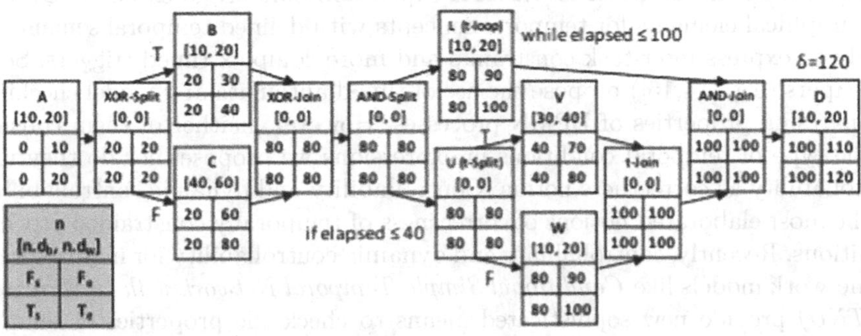

Fig. 3. Process graph with a correct schedule

An example of a (correct, controllable) schedule is shown in Fig. 3, which defines the execution intervals of activities as follows: activity A can start at 0 (between 0 and 0) and end between 10 and 20, B can start at 20 and end between 30 and 40, and so on.

The property of controllability of a process requires that there is a schedule for the process, such that all scenarios are valid for which the time-stamps of the scenarios are taken from the respective intervals of this schedule.

Definition 5 (controllability). *A process $P(N, V, \delta)$ is controllable, if it has a schedule S, such that all scenarios $\bar{S}$ are valid, iff $\forall n \in N: n.F_s \leq n.t_s \leq n.F_e$ and $n.T_s \leq n.t_e \leq n.T_e$.*

Dynamic controllability [11] allows that the start time of an activity may depend on all observed execution details (actual start and end times of activities, decisions at xor-splits) that happened before this activity. For general temporal constraints the notion of dynamic controllability is strictly more relaxed than controllability. However, for the process definitions presented here dynamic controllability is equivalent to controllability.

5 Related Work

A general overview of related work in time management for workflows and business process management are given in [3,7]. We concentrate here on related work with respect to formulating temporal constraints involving control structures, checking correctness and other properties of process definitions with such temporal constraints. With our proposal we extend the work on time patterns [2,13], which brought a much needed consolidation in the area of temporal constraints for process models, with the usage of temporal variables in flow-deciding conditions. BPMN [16] allows to use time information in conditions, however the specification is kept on a rather abstract generic level. More precise expression definition is offered by some system vendors, e.g. Oracle BPM [17]. To configure a timer event in Oracle BPM, the expressions can be written using a simple expression builder or an XPATH expression builder. [9] extended BPMN with graphical elements for temporal concepts with defined temporal semantics, mainly to express inter-task constraints and more complex timed triggers. Several papers (e.g. [14,15]) propose the use of timed automata and model checking for analysing properties of BPMN processes. However, neither of them considers the type of temporal conditions in expressions we propose, nor do they use controllability as correctness notion. Controllability and dynamic controllability are the most elaborated notions of correctness of temporally constrained process definitions. Recently, controllability and dynamic controllability for more expressive network models like *Conditional Simple Temporal Network with Uncertainty (CSTNU)* provide new sophisticated means to check the properties of temporally constrained process definitions [11]. However, they are not able to express the kind of temporal controls structures we propose here.

6 Conclusion

We proposed time dependent control structures for modeling processes as a way to better combine temporal constraints and process control modeling. We defined the semantics for temporal splits and temporal loops and defined the correctness of process models by means of the notion of controllability which is well established in temporal constraint networks. Since it is possible to calculate schedules based on the given definitions we can analyse computed schedule to indicate flaws in the process model. We conclude that this apparatus supports designers in modeling correct process respecting the temporal constraints.

Our approach offers proactive time management features in the design phase, such that temporal intervention strategies [5,6,18] aiming at the avoidance of time constraint violations can be implemented in an intuitive manner. E.g. (1) *optional execution* by skipping optional activities, (2) *parallelization of a sequence:*, (3) *alternative faster path:*, or (4) *early termination* of a late process aiming at avoiding the increase of sunk costs resulting from further process execution and exception-handling actions at the end.

This was a first expedition into the properties induced by explicit temporal control structures which opens avenues for further exploration, in particular the combination with declarative temporal constraints like upper-bound and lower-bound constraints [7].

References

1. Cardoso, J., Sheth, A., Miller, J.: Workflow quality of service. In: Kosanke, K., Jochem, R., Nell, J.G., Bas, A.O. (eds.) Enterprise Inter- and Intra-Organizational Integration. ITIFIP, vol. 108, pp. 303–311. Springer, Boston, MA (2003). doi:10.1007/978-0-387-35621-1_31
2. Cheikhrouhou, S., Kallel, S., Guermouche, N., Jmaiel, M.: Toward a time-centric modeling of business processes in BPMN 2.0. In: Proceedings of International Conference on Information Integration and Web-Based Applications & Services, p. 154. ACM (2013)
3. Cheikhrouhou, S., Kallel, S., Guermouche, N., Jmaiel, M.: The temporal perspective in business process modeling: a survey and research challenges. SOCA **9**(1), 75–85 (2015)
4. Combi, C., Posenato, R.: Controllability in temporal conceptual workflow schemata. In: Dayal, U., Eder, J., Koehler, J., Reijers, H.A. (eds.) BPM 2009. LNCS, vol. 5701, pp. 64–79. Springer, Heidelberg (2009). doi:10.1007/978-3-642-03848-8_6
5. Eder, J., Gruber, W., Pichler, H.: Transforming workflow graphs. In: Konstantas, D., Bourrières, J.P., Léonard, M., Boudjlida, N. (eds.) Interoperability of Enterprise Software and Applications, pp. 203–214. Springer, London (2006). doi:10.1007/1-84628-152-0_19
6. Eder, J., Panagos, E., Pozewaunig, H., Rabinovich, M.: Time management in workflow systems. In: Abramowicz, W., Orlowska, M.E. (eds.) BIS 1999, pp. 265–280. Springer, London (1999). doi:10.1007/978-1-4471-0875-7_22
7. Eder, J., Panagos, E., Rabinovich, M.: Workflow time management revisited. In: Bubenko, J., Krogstie, J., et al. (eds.) Seminal Contributions to Information Systems Engineering, pp. 207–213. Springer, Heidelberg (2013). doi:10.1007/978-3-642-36926-1_16
8. Eder, J., Tahamtan, A.: Temporal consistency of view based interorganizational workflows. In: Kaschek, R., Kop, C., Steinberger, C., Fliedl, G. (eds.) UNISCON 2008. LNBIP, vol. 5, pp. 96–107. Springer, Heidelberg (2008). doi:10.1007/978-3-540-78942-0_11
9. Gagne, D., Trudel, A.: Time-BPMN. In: IEEE Conference on Commerce and Enterprise Computing, CEC 2009, pp. 361–367. IEEE (2009)
10. Gillmann, M., Weikum, G., Wonner, W.: Workflow management with service quality guarantees. In: Proceedings of the 2002 ACM SIGMOD International Conference on Management of Data, pp. 228–239. ACM (2002)
11. Hunsberger, L., Posenato, R., Combi, C.: The dynamic controllability of conditional STNS with uncertainty. arXiv preprint arXiv:1212.2005 (2012)
12. Lanz, A., Posenato, R., Combi, C., Reichert, M.: Controllability of time-aware processes at run time. In: Meersman, R., Panetto, H., Dillon, T., Eder, J., Bellahsene, Z., Ritter, N., De Leenheer, P., Dou, D. (eds.) OTM 2013. LNCS, vol. 8185, pp. 39–56. Springer, Heidelberg (2013). doi:10.1007/978-3-642-41030-7_4
13. Lanz, A., Weber, B., Reichert, M.: Time patterns for process-aware information systems. Requir. Eng. **19**(2), 113–141 (2014)
14. Mallek, S., Daclin, N., Chapurlat, V., Vallespir, B.: Enabling model checking for collaborative process analysis: from BPMN to 'network of timed automata'. Enterp. Inf. Syst. **9**(3), 279–299 (2015)
15. Mendoza Morales, L.E., Monsalve, C., Villavicencio, M.: Application of formal methods to verify business processes. In: Ribeiro, L., Lecomte, T. (eds.) SBMF 2016. LNCS, vol. 10090, pp. 41–58. Springer, Cham (2016). doi:10.1007/978-3-319-49815-7_3

16. ObjectManagementGroup: Business Process Model and Notation (BPMN), Version 2.0 (2011). http://www.omg.org/spec/BPMN/2.0
17. OracleFusion: Adding delays, deadlines, and time based cycles to your process. http://docs.oracle.com/cd/E25178_01/doc.1111/e15176/timers_bpmpd.htm. Accessed 15 Apr 2017
18. Pichler, H., Wenger, M., Eder, J.: Composing time-aware web service orchestrations. In: van Eck, P., Gordijn, J., Wieringa, R. (eds.) CAiSE 2009. LNCS, vol. 5565, pp. 349–363. Springer, Heidelberg (2009). doi:10.1007/978-3-642-02144-2_29
19. van Der Aalst, W.M., Ter Hofstede, A.H., Kiepuszewski, B., Barros, A.P.: Workflow patterns. Distrib. Parallel Databases **14**(1), 5–51 (2003)

Towards Rearchitecting Meta-Models into Multi-level Models

Fernando Macías[1], Esther Guerra[2(✉)], and Juan de Lara[2]

[1] Western Norway University of Applied Sciences, Bergen, Norway
[2] Universidad Autónoma de Madrid, Madrid, Spain
esther.guerra@uam.es

Abstract. Meta-models play a pivotal role in Model-Driven Engineering, as they are used to define the structure of instance models one level below. However, in some scenarios, organizing meta-models and their instances in multi-level models spanning more than two levels yields simpler solutions. This fact has triggered the proposal of different multi-level modelling tools and approaches, although each one of them supports small variations of the multi-level concepts.

In order to benefit from multi-level technology, existing meta-models and their instances could be migrated manually, but this is error prone, costly, and requires expertise for choosing the most appropriate tool and approach. Hence, we propose an automated migration process. This way, starting from a meta-model annotated with multi-level "smells", our approach creates a neutral multi-level representation, and recommends the most appropriate tool according to the required multi-level features. We present an initial prototype, and a preliminary evaluation on the basis of meta-models developed by third parties.

1 Introduction

Modelling in Model-Driven Engineering (MDE) has traditionally adopted a two meta-level approach, where meta-models define the set of admissible models one level below. Instead, multi-level modelling (MLM) [3], also called deep modelling [5], is a modelling proposal that permits the use of an arbitrary number of meta-levels, not necessarily two. This may lead to simpler solutions – with less accidental complexity and a clear specification of classification levels – in situations where the type-object pattern or some of its variants arise [3,6].

While the dominant practice nowadays follows two-level approaches, our previous studies show that there is a considerable amount of meta-models that could benefit from multi-level technology [6]. In particular, the occurrence of the type-object pattern is common in domains like software architecture or process modelling. For example, in the latter domain, it is frequent the need to model both task types and instances, resource types and instances, agent types and instances, and so on. Using MLM would make such meta-models simpler. However, a manual rearchitecture of a large meta-model into a multi-level version is costly, tedious and error-prone.

H.C. Mayr et al. (Eds.): ER 2017, LNCS 10650, pp. 59–68, 2017.
https://doi.org/10.1007/978-3-319-69904-2_5

Several tools and approaches for MLM have emerged along the years, such as DeepTelos [11], the DPF Workbench [12], Dual Deep Modelling [15], Melanee [1], MetaDepth [5], MultEcore [13], OMLM [9], SLICER [16], XMF [4] and XModeler [7]. Each one of them has its own strengths and limitations, while many implement small variations of multi-level concepts, like attribute potency or leap potency [8]. Deciding on the tool or approach to use in order to more optimally describe the concepts in a domain can be challenging for novices, and may hamper the adoption of MLM.

To facilitate the migration of standard meta-models into a multi-level setting, we propose automated support for the rearchitecture process and the decision of the most suitable MLM approach given the problem characteristics. For this purpose, first the meta-model to be migrated needs to be annotated to indicate occurrences of multi-level modelling "smells" [6]. Then, this meta-model is automatically transformed into a multi-level neutral representation that is able to accommodate some of the most prominent MLM approaches. From this representation, a number of heuristics recommend the best suitable MLM tool for the given problem, for which a serializer synthesizes the multi-level artefact. In this short paper, we present an overview of the steps in the process, and a preliminary evaluation on some meta-models developed by third parties.

Paper organization. Section 2 introduces background on MLM and a running example. Then, Sect. 3 describes the rearchitecture process, and Sect. 4 shows a preliminary evaluation. Finally, Sect. 5 compares with related work, and Sect. 6 concludes.

2 Background and Motivation

This section illustrates the main concepts of potency-based multi-level modelling, based on an example in security policies and its encoding using either two or multiple levels.

Mouelhi et al. [14] propose a meta-model to represent access control languages (like RBAC or OrBAC) and security policies described with them. An excerpt of it is shown in Fig. 1(a). Hence, the meta-model contains elements to represent both RuleTypes and Rules, and parameter types (class ElementType) and parameter instances (class Parameter). These are two occurrences of the type-object pattern, and arise due to the need to model both types and instances at the same meta-level. In this way, the conformity relation between instances and types is reified by the three associations named type.

This solution uses classes to represent both types and instances because it assumes just one instantiation level below. Instead, should we be able to use more than two meta-levels, a simpler solution like the one in Fig. 1(b) would suffice. This model has potency 2 (indicated by the "@" symbol), which means that it can be successively instantiated at the two subsequent meta-levels. Each element inside the model receives the potency of its container element, if no specified otherwise. For example, ElementType has potency 2, and so it can be successively instantiated at the two next meta-levels. In contrast, ElementType.hierarchy has

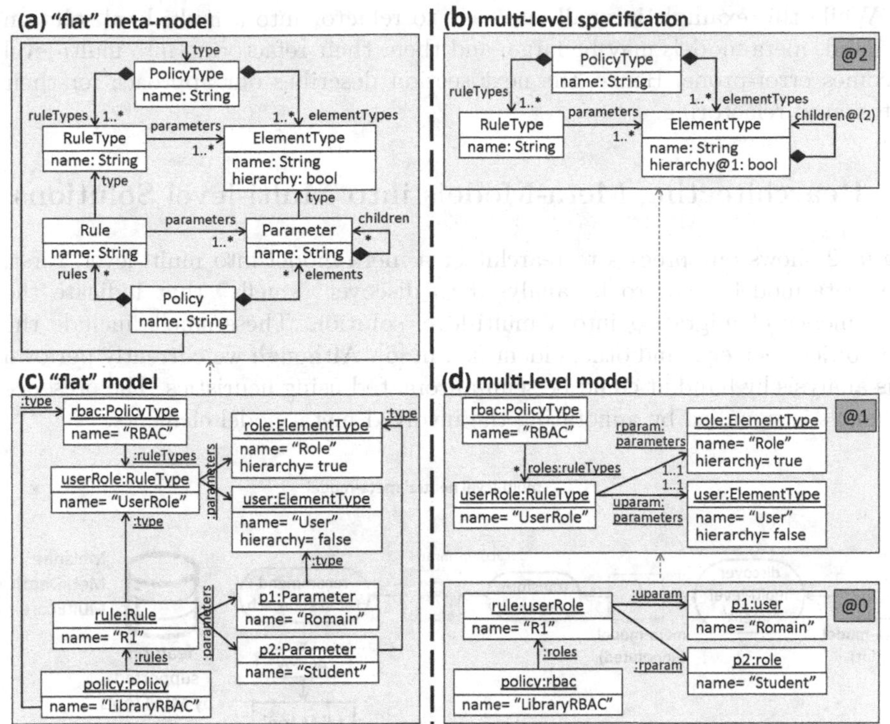

Fig. 1. Security policies: (a, c) two-level solution, (b, d) multi-level solution.

potency 1, so it can only be instantiated one level below. This multi-level model specification is roughly half the size than the flat meta-model (3 vs. 6 classes, 4 vs. 7 attributes, 4 vs. 10 associations, and 3 vs. 0 potency marks).

Figure 1(c) shows an instance of the meta-model in Fig. 1(a). It contains a small part of the definition of the RBAC language and an example of use. Hence, it defines rule type UserRole, and one instance of it named R1.

Figure 1(d) shows the equivalent multi-level version making use of two meta-levels. The upper model (with potency 1) contains the definition of the RBAC language, while the lower model (with potency 0) defines the RBAC instance. The elements in the multi-level model (e.g., rbac) are instances of a type (e.g., PolicyType), and types w.r.t. other elements (e.g., policy). This way, they have both a type and an instance facet, and so they are called clabjects (merging of the words *class* and *object*) [3]. This duality also applies to associations. This way, in the model with potency 1, associations rparam and uparam can declare cardinalities which (by default) apply to the next meta-level only. This possibility of defining cardinalities leads to a more precise model.

Altogether, in this case, the multi-level solution yields a simpler language definition (see Fig. 1(a–b)). Moreover, it permits organising models across meta-levels (see Fig. 1(c–d)), hence providing separation of concerns between language designers (e.g., the RBAC language designer within the security policies domain) and language users.

While this example is small and easy to refactor into a multi-level solution by hand, meta-models may be large, and then, their refactoring into multi-level becomes error-prone. Hence, the next section describes our approach for their automated refactoring.

3 Rearchitecting Meta-Models into Multi-level Solutions

Figure 2 shows our process to rearchitect a meta-model into multi-level. First, the meta-model needs to be analysed to discover "smells" that indicate the convenience of migrating into a multi-level solution. These smells include the type-object pattern, and others identified in [6]. Although we currently perform this analysis by hand, it could be semi-automated using heuristics. The presence of smells is signalled by annotating the involved meta-model elements.

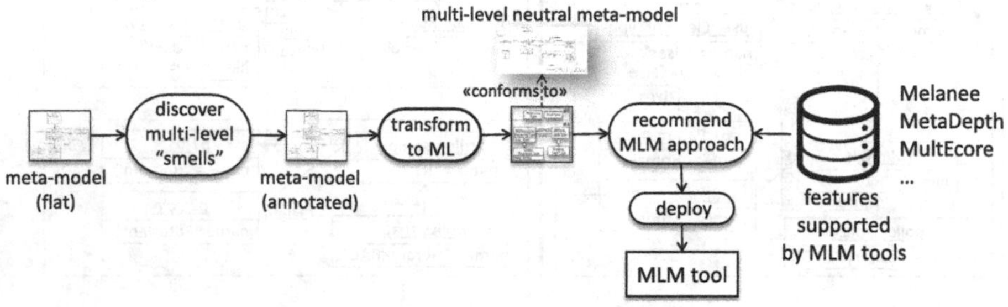

Fig. 2. Our process to rearchitect a meta-model into multi-level

In a second step, we transform the annotated meta-model into an instance of a multi-level neutral meta-model. A recommendation system analyses this model to detect the features supported, not supported, or which can be emulated by a number of MLM tools. The result is a ranked list of candidate tools. When one of such tools is selected, the neutral model is serialized into the specific format of the tool. The overall process is extensible with new smells and MLM tools.

Next, we explain the steps of the process.

(1) Discovery of multi-level smells. The first step is to annotate the occurrences of multi-level patterns in the meta-model. We take as a basis the patterns identified in [6]. These include the type-object pattern, where a class plays the role of *type*, another the role of *instance*, and a relation between them the role of *typing*. As Fig. 3 shows, the running example contains three of such occurrences. The pattern also applies to associations, in which case, their source and target classes should be in a type-object relation.

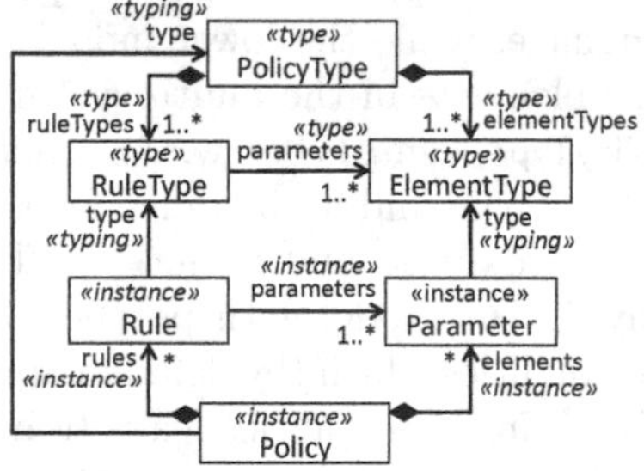

Fig. 3. Annotated meta-model

Figure 3 contains three occurrences, like association RuleType.parameters which plays the role of type for Rule.parameters.

Several heuristics are possible to automatically detect occurrences of the type-object pattern, e.g., based on naming conventions (see pairs ⟨*Name*⟩*Type* / ⟨*Name*⟩ in Fig. 3). However, at this stage, we have focussed in the translation of different variations of this pattern into a MLM setting, leaving pattern detection heuristics for future work.

One of such variations is the *static types* [6], where a superclass plays the role of type for a subclass, and the typing relation is reified as inheritance. In this case, refactoring into multi-level enables the dynamic creation of instances of the type class.

(2) Transformation into a multi-level neutral representation. We transform the annotated meta-model into an instance of the multi-level neutral meta-model shown in Fig. 4(a). It is "neutral" as it captures generalizations of multi-level concepts found in MLM tools like Melanee, MetaDepth or MultEcore.

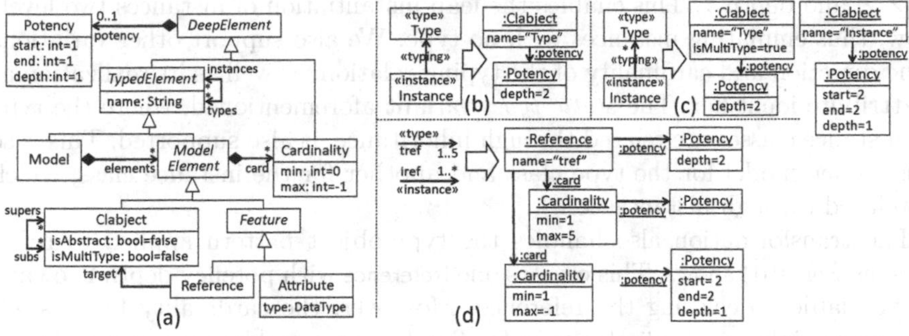

Fig. 4. (a) Multi-level neutral meta-model. Transformation of: (b) basic type-object pattern; (c) type-object with optional, multiple typing; (d) type-object of references

In this neutral meta-model, each element may have a potency governing its instantiation. In order to account for different semantics, our potency extends the classical notion [3] (explained in Sect. 2) with an interval [start..end]. This specifies a range of meta-levels where it is possible to create direct instances of the element. The number of subsequent instantiations of these instances is governed by depth, as in classical potency. The default value for the potency interval is [1..1], and the default depth is 1, which means that the element can be instantiated in the next meta-level but these instances cannot be instantiated further. This corresponds to standard two-level modelling. An interval [2..2] means that the element can be instantiated starting two levels below, and its combination with depth 1 corresponds to the notion of *leap potency* [6]. We will explain further combinations of values in the *recommending* step.

Transforming a meta-model into our multi-level neutral representation may yield a model spanning oneor several meta-levels. These are reified using the Model class. Models can hold Clabjects and Features. To account for MLM approaches supporting elements with multiple types, TypedElement declares the multi-valued reference types, and Clabject defines the flag isMultiType. Model elements can have zero or more Cardinality restrictions, constraining the number of instances that can be created at a certain level (not necessarily the next one, as in two-level modelling). The level to which the cardinality restriction applies is indicated by assigning a potency to it.

Figure 4(b), (c) and (d) show the transformation of the meta-model annotations for some representative variants of the type-object pattern. Figure 4(b) corresponds to the base case, where the instance class has a single class type. This is transformed into a clabject for the type, with default potency interval [1..1] and depth 2. This captures the possibility of creating types in the next level, and instances of them two levels below. The running example has three occurrences of this base case. Figure 4(c) tackles the situation where the instance class can have multiple, optional typing. Multiple typing is handled as the base case, but the isMultiType attribute of the produced clabject is set to true. Optional typing requires producing another clabject for the instance, with potency interval [2..2] and depth 1. This enables the leap instantiation of instances two levels below, thus emulating instances with no type. We also support other variations in the direction and cardinality of the typing relation, as well as its realization as an attribute identifier. The *static types* variant aforementioned, where the type and instance classes are related through inheritance, is also supported. This case leads to one model for the type class and another for the instance class, which are related through instantiation.

The transformation also handles the type-object pattern applied to references, as Fig. 4(d) shows. This creates one Reference with potency depth 2, owned by the clabject declaring the reference. Moreover, the cardinality bounds get transformed into two Cardinality objects. The first one captures the cardinality of the type reference and has potency 1, being enforced one level below. The second one comes from the instance reference and has leap potency 2, being applied two levels below.

As regards to the meta-model elements with no annotation, they are transformed into clabjects or features with default attribute values.

(3) Recommendation of MLM approach. After transforming the meta-model into a multi-level neutral model, we analyse it to identify the multi-level features required for the problem at hand, and which tools provide support for them. For this purpose, we have built a recommender that recognizes the required multi-level features by detecting certain patterns on the configuration of element potencies, and then counts how many of such features are either natively supported, can be emulated, or are unsupported in each tool. The recommender yields a ranking according to the number of features natively supported, and in case of tie, by the number of features that can be emulated. It also reports the unsupported required features.

Table 1 contains a summary of the patterns sought by the recommender (columns multi-level feature, start, end and depth). The last three columns show whether these features are supported, unsupported or can be emulated by three representative tools: Melanee, METADEPTH and MultEcore.

Table 1. Support of MLM concepts by tools: native support (+), emulated (∼), unsupported (−).

dimension	multi-level feature	start	end	depth	Melanee	MetaDepth	MultEcore
potency in clabjects and references	standard potency	1	1	n (n≥1)	+	+	∼ (n=∞)
	leap potency	n (n>1)	n	1	∼ (n=1)	+	∼ (n=∞)
	replicability	n (n≥1)	m (m>n)	1	− (n=1,m=n)	− (m=n)	+
	deep leap potency	n (n>1)	n	o (o>1)	− (n=1,o=1)	− (o=1)	∼ (o=∞)
	deep replicability	n (n≥1)	m (m>n)	o (o>1)	− (n=1,m=n,o=1)	− (m=n,o=1)	∼ (o=∞)
potency in attributes	attribute durability	1	n (n≥1)	1	+	+	∼ (n=∞)
	attribute mutability	n (n≥1)	m (m>n)	1	+	∼ (m=n)	− (always mutable)
instantiation	shallow ref. cardinality	1	1	1	+	+	+
	deep ref. cardinality	n (n>1)	m (m>n)	o (o>1)	−	∼ (OCL)	−
	multiple typing	-	-	-	−	+ (a-posteriori)	+ (supplementary)
	abstract types	-	-	-	∼ (potency=0)	+	+

All tools support or can emulate *standard potency*, while METADEPTH natively supports *leap potency*, which is necessary for models like the one in Fig. 4(c). Our multi-level neutral meta-model supports other variations of potency like *replicability*, where an element can be instantiated in a range of levels with depth 1, *deep replicability*, where in addition the created instances can be further instantiated, or *deep leap potency*, where instantiation starts after a level gap and can be iterated. Interestingly, none of the three tools fully support the last two options.

Regarding attributes, *durability* indicates how many levels below an attribute is instantiated, and *mutability* the range of levels where an attribute can be modified. Melanee natively supports both, while they can be emulated with the other two tools.

As for reference cardinalities, none of the tools permit their specification for levels beyond the next one, although METADEPTH can emulate this via OCL. All tools support abstract types (Melanee emulates them via clabjects with potency 0), while multiple types are possible in METADEPTH and MultEcore.

4 Experiments

We have developed a prototype tool with a recommender for Melanee, METADEPTH and MultEcore. We have used the tool to perform an initial evaluation of our process by rearchitecting the running example and four third-party meta-models which contain occurrences of the type-object pattern, as identified in [6]. Table 2 shows the size metrics before and after the rearchitecture, as well as the reduction percentage in the number of elements (clabjects, references and attributes) required to express the same information. The reduction ranges between 2% (HAL) and 50% (running example). The small reduction size for HAL and Agate is because these are the biggest meta-models and have few type-object occurrences. The reduction gain in the rest of cases is considerable.

Table 2. Results of applying our rearchitecting process to some of models analysed in [6].

meta-model	flat meta-model			multi-level version				type-object occur.		tool ranking					
	classes	refs.	attrs.	classes	refs.	attrs.	reduc.	clabject	assoc.	Melanee		MetaDepth		MultEcore	
Security Policies	7	12	7	4	5	4	50%	3	4	1	✓	2	✓	3	×
Agate	69	123	81	64	118	81	4%	6	2	2	✓	1	✓	3	✓
CloudML	21	28	26	15	17	26	23%	6	7	2	✓	1	✓	3	✓
CloudML-2.0	33	50	44	21	40	44	18%	12	5	2	✓	1	✓	3	✓
HAL	42	16	72	41	15	72	2%	1	0	2	✓	1	✓	3	✓

The table also includes the number of type-object occurrences in each meta-model, and the ranking of recommended tools based on their support of the features in Table 1. This score adds 2 points for each required multi-level feature that the tool supports natively, 1 point if the feature can be emulated, and −1 if it is unsupported. We have marked with a cross the cases in which a tool does not support some required feature.

The recommended tool for the running example is Melanee, as it supports mutability for the three attributes `name`, and it can emulate leap potency (required for reference `children`). MetaDepth appears in second place because it has native support for leap potency, but mutability needs to be emulated. MultEcore is in third place as it does not support attribute mutability as required in this case.

More details on the evaluation can be found at http://miso.es/MLeval.

5 Related Work

We are not aware of any effort for the automatic rearrangement of meta-models into multiple levels. There are just some works on manual rearchitecture [6,9], or introducing concrete multi-level elements [10]. In [6], we identified patterns where using MLM may have benefits. In [9], a standard in the oil and gas industry is recasted into multiple levels. In [10], some evolution operators allow applying the powertype pattern in models, which may imply reorganizing elements across levels. Hence, to our knowledge, ours is the first proposal towards an extensible, automated process to migrate to multi-level (though currently only the refactoring into multi-level is fully automated, but the discovery of multi-level smells is manual).

Regarding our level-neutral meta-model, the main contribution with respect to other meta-models (e.g., in MetaDepth [5] or Melanee [2]) is the generalization of potency, the possibility to specify cardinalities for levels beyond the immediate lower one, and the capability to indicate multiple typings.

6 Conclusions and Future Work

We have presented an approach for the automated rearchitecture of meta-models into multi-level specifications. The approach is based on the identification of multi-level smells, and their translation into a neutral multi-level model that can be analysed to recommend the most suitable MLM tool to transform to. We have created prototype tool support, and performed a preliminary evaluation obtaining promising results.

In the future, we plan to define annotations for other multi-level smells, and heuristics to induce them. We also plan to refine the recommendation process (e.g., to consider the cost of emulating non-native features), to migrate models together with their meta-models, and to perform a large scale evaluation.

Acknowledgements. Work supported by the Spanish MINECO (TIN2014-52129-R) and the R&D programme of the Madrid Region (S2013/ICE-3006).

References

1. Atkinson, C., Gerbig, R., Fritzsche, M.: A multi-level approach to modeling language extension in the enterprise systems domain. Inf. Syst. **54**, 289–307 (2015)
2. Atkinson, C., Kennel, B., Goß, B.: The level-agnostic modeling language. In: Malloy, B., Staab, S., Brand, M. (eds.) SLE 2010. LNCS, vol. 6563, pp. 266–275. Springer, Heidelberg (2011). doi:10.1007/978-3-642-19440-5_16
3. Atkinson, C., Kühne, T.: Reducing accidental complexity in domain models. SoSyM **7**(3), 345–359 (2008)
4. Clark, T., Sammut, P., Willans, J.S.: Super-languages: developing languages and applications with XMF, 2nd edn., CoRR, abs/1506.03363 (2015)
5. de Lara, J., Guerra, E.: Deep meta-modelling with MetaDepth. In: Vitek, J. (ed.) TOOLS 2010. LNCS, vol. 6141, pp. 1–20. Springer, Heidelberg (2010). doi:10.1007/978-3-642-13953-6_1
6. de Lara, J., Guerra, E., Sánchez Cuadrado, J.: When and how to use multi-level modelling. ACM Trans. Softw. Eng. Methodol. **24**(2), 12 (2014)
7. Frank, U.: Multilevel modeling - toward a new paradigm of conceptual modeling and information systems design. Bus. Inf. Syst. Eng. **6**(6), 319–337 (2014)
8. Gerbig, R., Atkinson, C., de Lara, J., Guerra, E.: A feature-based comparison of melanee and metadepth. In: Proceedings of MULTI@MODELS. CEUR, vol. 1722, pp. 25–34 (2016)
9. Igamberdiev, M., Grossmann, G., Selway, M., Stumptner, M.: An integrated multi-level modeling approach for industrial-scale data interoperability. SoSyM 1–26 (2016, to appear)
10. Jahn, M., Roth, B., Jablonski, S.: Remodeling to powertype pattern. In: Proceedings of PATTERNS, pp. 59–65 (2013)
11. Jeusfeld, M.A., Neumayr, B.: DeepTelos: multi-level modeling with most general instances. In: Comyn-Wattiau, I., Tanaka, K., Song, I.-Y., Yamamoto, S., Saeki, M. (eds.) ER 2016. LNCS, vol. 9974, pp. 198–211. Springer, Cham (2016). doi:10.1007/978-3-319-46397-1_15
12. Lamo, Y., Wang, X., Mantz, F., Bech, Ø., Sandven, A., Rutle, A.: DPF workbench: a multi-level language workbench for MDE. Proc. Est. Acad. Sci. **62**(1), 3–15 (2013)
13. Macías, F., Rutle, A., Stolz, V.: MultEcore: combining the best of fixed-level and multilevel metamodelling. In: MULTI@MODELS. CEUR, vol. 1722, pp. 66–75 (2016)

14. Mouelhi, T., Fleurey, F., Baudry, B.: A generic metamodel for security policies mutation. In: Proceedings of ICST, pp. 278–286. IEEE Computer Society (2008)
15. Neumayr, B., Schuetz, C.G., Jeusfeld, M.A., Schrefl, M.: Dual deep modeling: multi-level modeling with dual potencies and its formalization in F-Logic. SoSyM 1–36 (2016, to appear)
16. Selway, M., Stumptner, M., Mayer, W., Jordan, A., Grossmann, G., Schrefl, M.: A conceptual framework for large-scale ecosystem interoperability and industrial product lifecycles. Data Knowl. Eng. 1–27 (2017, in press)

Mining Goal Refinement Patterns: Distilling Know-How from Data

Metta Santiputri[1], Novarun Deb[2], Muhammad Asjad Khan[3], Aditya Ghose[3(✉)], Hoa Dam[3], and Nabendu Chaki[2]

[1] Department of Informatics, State Polytechnic of Batam, Batam 29461, Indonesia
metta@polibatam.ac.id

[2] Department of Computer Science and Engineering, University of Calcutta, Kolkata, India
novarun@acm.org, nabendu@ieee.org

[3] Decision Systems Lab, School of Computing and IT, University of Wollongong, Wollongong, NSW 2522, Australia
{aditya,hoa}@uow.edu.au

Abstract. Goal models play an important role by providing a hierarchic representation of stakeholder intent, and by providing a representation of lower-level subgoals that must be achieved to enable the achievement of higher-level goals. A goal model can be viewed as a composition of a number of *goal refinement patterns* that relate parent goals to subgoals. In this paper, we offer a means for mining these patterns from enterprise event logs and a technique to leverage vector representations of words and phrases to compose these patterns to obtain complete goal models. The resulting machinery can be quiote powerful in its ability to mine *know-how* or *constitutive norms*. We offer an empirical evaluation using both real-life and synthetic datasets.

Keywords: Goal model mining · Goal refinement · Know-how

1 Introduction

Goal models play a critical role in requirements engineering, by providing a hierarchic representation of statements of stakeholder intent, with goals higher in the hierarchy (parent goals) related to goals lower in the hierarchy (sub-goals) via AND- or OR-refinement links. Goal models encode important knowledge about feasible, available alternatives for realizing stakeholder intent represented at varying levels of abstraction. A number of prominent frameworks leverage goal models, including KAOS [8], i* [25] and Tropos [4].

There is a growing realization that data analytics (this term being liberally interpreted to denote a broad repertoire of machine learning, data mining and natural language processing techniques) have an important role to play in software engineering in general, and requirements engineering in particular. In that spirit, this paper addresses the question: *can enterprise goal models be mined*

H.C. Mayr et al. (Eds.): ER 2017, LNCS 10650, pp. 69–76, 2017.
https://doi.org/10.1007/978-3-319-69904-2_6

from readily available enterprise data? It is useful to distinguish, at this point, the exercise of mining *goal models* from the exercise of mining *goals*. That latter problem is arguably more difficult, since user goals or stakeholder intent are often never manifested in enterprise data, and are often not explicitly articulated either. Knowledge about how a goal might be refined into lower-level sub-goals is a different matter altogether. Goal refinements that have been deployed before (either explicitly or implicitly) are ultimately manifested in operational data. Our intent in this paper is to leverage data of this form.

Mining goal models adds value in a number of ways. *First*, it offers a way around the *model acquisition bottleneck* (where the high investments associated with careful modeling often prevents businesses from leveraging the full value of goal modeling). While our approach does not guarantee that all models mined will be correct and accurate, it does ensure that the goal models (or model fragments) that are mined can be quickly deployed with minimal editing (the requirement for oversight and editing by analysts remains). Overall, the approach improves the productivity of modelers/analysts; instead of starting with a "blank sheet", our machinery generates "first draft" models or model fragments that can be composed to obtain usable models. *Second*, our approach could potentially improve model quality, by mining execution histories from which "undesirable" executions have been filtered out. *Third*, model *anti-patterns* can be mined from "undesirable" execution data. *Fourth*, this machinery can be used for *goal conformance* checking.

Goal models can also be viewed as statements of *know-how*, where an AND-decomposition provides the know-how for achieving a parent goal by satisfying a set of sub-goals. Mining know-how patterns is independently useful. In particular, it permits us to use goal models as *effectors*, where a goal model is used to specify the desired state of the enterprise while decomposition via a sequence of know-how patterns enables us to identify the operational interventions which would help realize the desired state of the enterprise.

AND-refinement patterns can also be viewed as *constitutive norms* [3]. A constitutive norms specifies how the act of achieving conditions c_1, c_2, c_n *counts as* achieving condition c (we can also, without loss of generality, replace conditions with goals or actions). For instance, the acts of putting a tea bag in a cup followed by puring hot water into the cup *counts as* making tea. The account we offer in this paper can thus be also viewed as an account of constitutive norm mining.

We address two problems in this paper. First, we address the *goal refinement pattern mining problem*, where a goal refinement pattern is of the form $sg_1, sg_2, \ldots sg_n \rightarrow G$ where G is the parent goal while each sg_i is a sub-goal, and where the statement is that the act of achieving each sub-goal conjointly leads to the achievement of the parent goal. These latter are referred to as AND-refinement patterns, and are the main focus of this paper (OR-refinement patterns can be mined via small variants of the techniques discussed here, but a full discussion is omitted due to space constraints). Second, we address the problem of composing individual goal refinement patterns into *goal trees* (more generally goal graphs) which describe not only how a goal is refined into subgoals, but also how these subgoals can be further refined into sub-subgoals and so on.

We present the general approach in Sect. 2. The identification of goal refinement patterns involves mining event logs (partitioned by levels of abstraction) that leverage *temporal correlation patterns* between goals and subgoals (recall that an *event log* is a collection of time-stamped events). The composition of goal refinement patterns relies on matching subgoal in one refinement pattern with the parent goal of another such pattern - we use word2vec [20] to identify *semantic similarity* between words and phrases that appear in the goals and subgoals for this purpose. We briefly summarize the empirical evaluation contained in the full version of the paper in Sect. 3, and position this proposal in the context of related work in Sect. 4.

2 General Approach

Temporal correlation patterns relating goals and subgoals: A goal and its subgoals are typically related via *temporal correlation patterns* which impose temporal constraints on the achievement of the parent goal relative to the achievement of the subgoals. One such pattern (and the one we will leverage in the empirical evalation in this paper) requires that event denoting the achievement of the parent goal occur immediately or soon, after the events denoting the achievement of the subgoals (the event denoting the making of a cup of tea occurs immediately after the events denoting the placing of a teabag in a cup and the pouring of hot water into the cup). We shall call these *sequential correlations*. Other examples of temporal correlation patterns leverage relations from Allen's Interval Algebra [2]. In some settings, we might require the interval over which each subgoal is achieved be included entirely (using the **during** relationship from the Interval Algebra) in the interval over which the parent goal is achieved. In some settings it might make sense to relate these intervals using the **meets, finishes** or **is equal to** relations from Interval Algebra.

Mining goal refinement patterns from multi-layered event logs: Independent of which temporal correlation pattern applies in a given setting, it is critical that the input event logs are partitioned into layers based on different levels of abstraction. A key assumption underpinning this proposal is that events denoting the achievement of parent goals appear in a log of more abstract events, while events denoting the achievement of subgoals appear in logs of more refined (or lower-level) events. In other words, we assume a hierarchy of levels $L_1, L_2, \ldots$ such that L_i is always at a higher level of abstraction than L_{i+1}. The idea is that goal refinement always occurs between goals manifested by events in adjacent levels in this hierarchy. The key question to address now is: How do we obtain this partitioning/hierarchy? Possible strategies include:

- Leveraging part-whole relationships between objects: We know that a photo, a front page, an embedded chip, a visa or an expiry date are parts of a more

abstract object called a passport. Any event involving the passport photo, or a visa etc. will belong to a lower level in the hierarchy than any event involving the passport.
- Leveraging the source of the data: We know that any event from a process log is likely to be lower in an abstraction hierarchy than any event in a message log. Similarly, events that manifest in the IT infrastructure are typically lower in abstraction than events that involve applications, which in turn are lower level than events concerning business services.
- Leveraging the organizational hierarchy: We know that events associated with roles lower in the organizational hierarchy will likely be lower in the abstraction hierarchy than events associated with roles higher in the organizational hierarchy. The intuition is that employees in a business unit are usually tasked with achieving lower-level goals than the manager of that business unit. Indeed, the goals of the manager rely on the achievement of the subgoals that the employees in that unit are tasked to achieve. The employee-level goals can thus be viewed as AND-refinements of the manager-level goals.

With the abstraction hierarchy of events thus obtained, our task in now to mine (temporal) sequential correlations between events in adjacent levels of the abstraction hierarchy. Thus a passport photo check, a passport validity check, a visa check and a passport stamping event would be followed soon after by a higher-level event indicating that an immigration check has been completed. We would expect to see this pattern repeated frequently. If this frequency meets a user-specified threshold, we conclude that it is indicative of a goal refinement pattern.

Composing goal refinement patterns: The challenge in composing goal refinement patterns to obtain goal models (or goal trees) is the difficulty in relating semantically similar, but syntactically highly distinct, specifications of goals and subgoals. For instance, a subgoal might be represented in natural language as: *log labour hours for billing.* Quite separately, we might find a mined goal refinement pattern for a parent goal represented textually as: *track technician time for charging the customer.* Human intuition suggests that these two goals are semantically quite similar, and any available know-how for the latter would also be useful for the former. Our strategy is to use a state-of-the-art machinery for vector encoding of words and phrases, called *word2vec* [20] which is effective in identifying semantic similarity. Word2vec learns vector representations of words and phrases such that semantically similar ones are projected in close proximity to each other in the vector space. Given a pair of phrases, word2vec returns a real-valued measure of semantic similarity (the higher the value, the more similar the phrases are). By setting an appropriate threshold for the similarity measure (this will require domain-specific tuning), we can connect a phrase describing a subgoal in one goal refinement pattern with a phrase describing a parent goal in another goal refinement pattern.

3 Evaluation

In this section, we briefly summarize the empirical evaluation results presented in the full version of the paper.

Two distinct strategies were evaluated: (1) Sequential pattern mining for leveraging temporal correlations patterns (specifically sequential correlation patterns) between goals andsub-goals and (2) word2vec for evaluating goal-subgoal similarity.

Two distinct datasets were used for the evaluation:

- A synthetic dataset consisting of an event log of a telephone repair process[1]
- A real-life dataset consisting of data from the BPI Challenge 2015 (BPIC'15)[2] which features building permit application process in five Dutch municipalities from year 2010 until 2015.

The BIDE+ algorithm was used for sequential pattern mining.

The evaluation using Google's pre-trained word2vec model was particularly interesting [20]. Word2vec includes word vectors for a vocabulary of 3 million words and phrases that has been trained on approximately 100 billion words from a Google News dataset. Although for this evaluation, we used a pre-trained model, training a model with a smaller but more targeted and domain-specific corpora is not hard. We have done this but have not achieved results thus far that surpass the results we have obtained using the pre-trained model. We took the goal refinement patterns obtained in the evaluation using the phone repair scenario described above (8 in total), and extended these with a repertoire of 40 additional goal refinement patterns (this was necessary to be able to further refine the sub-goals initially obtained from the mining of a 2-level event log.

The Word2Vec metric tends to place two words close to each other if they are semantically similar. We found, for instance, that 'Print repair receipt for the customer' and 'Print customer service repair order' have a high similarity score even though the phrases use different vocabulary to explain the same sub-goal. The notion of similarity used here is just cosine distance (dot product of vectors). It is closer to 1 if the phrases are semantically similar. For two completely dissimilar phrases, the similarity is closer to 0. For instance, update issue status to "in repair" and "dissemble the phone components" refer to two very different goals and are very far apart semantically thus receiving a score of 0.130887. In some cases like'log labor hours for billing' and'Track technician time for charging the customer' the score is neither too high nor too low. We can use a certain threshold e.g. (0.60) to filter cases where we not fully confident of a semantic match.

Overall, the results of the empirical evaluation (contained in the full version of the paper and ommitted here due to space constraints) suggest that the combination of techniques proposed here provide a promising basis for goal model mining.

---

[1] http://www.processmining.org/_media/tutorial/repairexample.zip.

[2] https://www.win.tue.nl/bpi/doku.php?id=2015:challenge.

4 Related Work

A considerable amount of research has been reported applying data mining techniques in requirements engineering. Zawawy et al. have proposed a root-cause analysis framework [26] that mines natively generated log data to establish the relationship between a requirement and the pre- and post-conditions associated with that requirement. In [13], the authors have proposed techniques for mining dependencies from message logs and task-dependency correlations from process logs. There have been very interesting industrial and commercial applications of mining requirements from event logs. Formal verification of control systems have been performed by mining temporal requirements from simulation traces [16]. REQAnalytics [10], proposed by Garcia and Paiva, mines the usage statistics of a website and provides a roadmap for the evolution of the website's requirements specification. ACon [17] is another data mining technique that tries to address the inconsistencies that affect the contextual requirements of a system at runtime.

Sequential pattern mining has been frequently used for extracting statistically relevant patterns or sequences of values in data sets. StrProM [15], for instance, uses the Heuristics Miner algorithm to generate prefix-trees from the data stream and continuously prunes these trees to extract sequences of events. Sohrabi and Ghods use bit-wise compression techniques to represent the data sequence as a 3-dimensional array and extract frequently occurring patterns from this compressed array [23]. Hassani et al. have proposed the PIVOTMiner [14] which considers activities as interval-based events rather than the conventional single-point events. Some researchers have also tried to improve the legacy sequential mining algorithm PrefixSpan (like [5,21]). Sequential pattern mining has also been used in interesting applications that range from detecting user behavior from online surveys to mining electronic medical records and inferring the efficacy of medicines [24]. A detailed survey of sequential pattern mining algorithms is available in [1].

Previously workflow logs used to be mined for extracting the control flow within an organization and, hence, extensively used for developing process models. Schönig and his group have proposed a framework to extract the organisational structure of business processes by mining human resource allocation information from event logs [22].

Also in prior work, non-functional requirements have been extracted from text [7].

5 Conclusion

The ability to mine goal models has important implications for requirements engineering, as well as a wide variety of other settings that benefit from goal modeling. The machinery that we present can therefore provide useful directions for future research and development. This machinery can also be used to mine know-how which can support enterprise innovation strategies in significant ways. The empirical evaluation presented in the paper is preliminary in nature, but provides evidence that suggests that there is merit in pursuing this general approach. This work can be extended in a number of interesting ways. For instance, evidence of goal update in operational data could be used to reverse engineer goal models from data using intuitions from belief revision [6,11] or belief merging [18,19]. Viewing softgoals as optimization objectives (as has been done in [9]) could provide the basis for correlating goals and softgoals. Techniques for discovering process designs from legacy artefacts [12] could form the basis for an alternative approach to mining goal models.

References

1. Abbasghorbani, S., Tavoli, R.: Survey on sequential pattern mining algorithms. In: 2nd International Conference on Knowledge-Based Engineering and Innovation (KBEI), pp. 1153–1164 (2015)
2. Allen, J.F.: Maintaining knowledge about temporal intervals. Commun. ACM **26**(11), 832–843 (1983)
3. Boella, G., Broersen, J., van der Torre, L.: Reasoning about constitutive norms, counts-as conditionals, institutions, deadlines and violations. In: Bui, T.D., Ho, T.V., Ha, Q.T. (eds.) PRIMA 2008. LNCS, vol. 5357, pp. 86–97. Springer, Heidelberg (2008). doi:10.1007/978-3-540-89674-6_12
4. Bresciani, P., Perini, A., Giorgini, P., Giunchiglia, F., Mylopoulos, J.: Tropos: an agent-oriented software development methodology. Auton. Agent. Multi-Agent Syst. **8**(3), 203–236 (2004)
5. Chaudhari, M., Mehta, C.: Extension of prefix span approach with GRC constraints for sequential pattern mining. In: International Conference on Electrical, Electronics, and Optimization Techniques (ICEEOT), pp. 2496–2498 (2016)
6. Chopra, S., Ghose, A., Meyer, T.: Non-prioritized ranked belief change. J. Philos. Logic **32**(4), 417–443 (2003)
7. Cleland-Huang, J., Settimi, R., Zou, X., Solc, P.: The detection and classification of non-functional requirements with application to early aspects. In: 14th IEEE International Conference on Requirements Engineering, pp. 39–48. IEEE (2006)
8. Darimont, R., Delor, E., Massonet, P., van Lamsweerde, A.: GRAIL/KAOS: an environment for goal-driven requirements engineering. In: Proceedings of the 19th International Conference on Software Engineering, pp. 612–613. ACM (1997)
9. Dasgupta, A., Ghose, A.K.: Implementing reactive BDI agents with user-given constraints and objectives. Int. J. Agent-Oriented Softw. Eng. **4**(2), 141–154 (2010)
10. Garcia, J.E., Paiva, A.C.: Maintaining requirements using web usage data. In: International Conference on ENTERprise Information Systems/International Conference on Project MANagement/International Conference on Health and Social Care Information Systems and Technologies, CENTERIS/ProjMAN /HCist. Procedia Comput. Sci. **100**, 626–633 (2016)
11. Ghose, A., Goebel, R.: Belief states as default theories: studies in non-prioritized belief change. In: ECAI, vol. 98, pp. 8–12 (1998)
12. Ghose, A., Koliadis, G., Chueng, A.: Rapid business process discovery (R-BPD). In: Parent, C., Schewe, K.-D., Storey, V.C., Thalheim, B. (eds.) ER 2007. LNCS, vol. 4801, pp. 391–406. Springer, Heidelberg (2007). doi:10.1007/978-3-540-75563-0_27

13. Ghose, A., Santiputri, M., Saraswati, A., Dam, H.K.: Data-driven requirements modeling: Some initial results with i*. In: Tenth Asia-Pacific Conference on Conceptual Modelling (APCCM), pp. 55–64 (2014)
14. Hassani, M., Lu, Y., Wischnewsky, J., Seidl, T.: A geometric approach for mining sequential patterns in interval-based data streams. In: IEEE International Conference on Fuzzy Systems (FUZZ-IEEE), pp. 2128–2135 (2016)
15. Hassani, M., Siccha, S., Richter, F., Seidl, T.: Efficient process discovery from event streams using sequential pattern mining. In: IEEE Symposium Series on Computational Intelligence, pp. 1366–1373 (2015)
16. Jin, X., Donze, A., Deshmukh, J.V., Seshia, S.A.: Mining requirements from closed-loop control models. IEEE Trans. Comput. Aided Des. Integr. Circ. Syst. **34**(11), 1704–1717 (2015)
17. Knauss, A., Damian, D., Franch, X., Rook, A., Müller, H.A., Thomo, A.: ACon: a learning-based approach to deal with uncertainty in contextual requirements at run time. Inf. Softw. Technol. **70**, 85–99 (2016). Elsevier
18. Meyer, T., Ghose, A., Chopra, S.: Social choice, merging, and elections. In: Benferhat, S., Besnard, P. (eds.) ECSQARU 2001. LNCS, vol. 2143, pp. 466–477. Springer, Heidelberg (2001). doi:10.1007/3-540-44652-4_41
19. Meyer, T., Ghose, A., Chopra, S.: Syntactic representations of semantic merging operations. In: Ishizuka, M., Sattar, A. (eds.) PRICAI 2002. LNCS (LNAI), vol. 2417, p. 620. Springer, Heidelberg (2002). doi:10.1007/3-540-45683-X_88
20. Mikolov, T., Chen, K., Corrado, G., Dean, J.: Efficient estimation of word representations in vector space. arXiv preprint arXiv:1301.3781 (2013)
21. Patel, R., Chaudhari, T.: A review on sequential pattern mining using pattern growth approach. In: International Conference on Wireless Communications, Signal Processing and Networking (WiSPNET), pp. 1424–1427 (2016)
22. Schönig, S., Cabanillas, C., Jablonski, S., Mendling, J.: Mining the organisational perspective in agile business processes. In: Gaaloul, K., Schmidt, R., Nurcan, S., Guerreiro, S., Ma, Q. (eds.) CAISE 2015. LNBIP, vol. 214, pp. 37–52. Springer, Cham (2015). doi:10.1007/978-3-319-19237-6_3
23. Sohrabi, M.K., Ghods, V.: CUSE: a novel cube-based approach for sequential pattern mining. In: 4th International Symposium on Computational and Business Intelligence (ISCBI), pp. 186–190 (2016)
24. Uragaki, K., Hosaka, T., Arahori, Y., Kushima, M.: Sequential pattern mining on electronic medical records with handling time intervals and the efficacy of medicines. In: IEEE Symposium on Computers and Communication (ISCC), pp. 20–25 (2016)
25. Yu, E.S.: Towards modelling and reasoning support for early-phase requirements engineering. In: Proceedings of the Third IEEE International Symposium on Requirements Engineering, pp. 226–235. IEEE (1997)
26. Zawawy, H., Mankovskii, S., Kontogiannis, K., Mylopoulos, J.: Mining software logs for goal-driven root cause analysis. In: The Art and Science of Analyzing Software Data, pp. 519–554 (2015)

Goal-Oriented Regulatory Intelligence: How Can Watson Analytics Help?

Okhaide Akhigbe(✉), Susie Heap, Sakib Islam, Daniel Amyot, and John Mylopoulos

School of Electrical Engineering and Computer Science, University of Ottawa, Ottawa, Canada
{okhaide,sheap069,sisla062,damyot, jmylopou}@uottawa.ca

Abstract. Regulations are introduced by governments to ensure the well-being, safety, and other societal needs of citizens and enterprises. Governments also create programs aiming to improve awareness about and compliance with regulations. Goal models have been used in the past to conceptualize regulations and to measure compliance assessments. However, regulators often have difficulties assessing the performance of their regulations and programs. In this paper, we model both regulations and regulatory programs with the Goal-oriented Requirement Language. Using the same conceptualization framework enables asking questions about performance and about the evidence-based impact of programs on regulations. We also investigate how Watson Analytics, a cloud-based data exploration service from IBM, can be used pragmatically to explore and visualize goal satisfaction data to understand compliance issues and program effectiveness. A simplified example inspired from a Canadian mining regulation is used to illustrate the many opportunities of Watson Analytics in that context, and some of its current limitations.

Keywords: Data analytics · Data visualization · Goal models · Goal-oriented Requirement Language · GoRIM · Regulatory compliance · Regulatory intelligence · Watson Analytics

1 Introduction

Based on government policy objectives, *regulations* are introduced to ensure the well-being and safety of citizens and enterprises. Regulations aim to constrain behaviors of citizens and enterprises alike to achieve desired societal outcomes [1]. Governments also introduce and manage regulatory *programs*, which consist of events, items, activities, or processes for ensuring compliance to regulations. Regulatory programs improve awareness about and compliance with regulations by educating regulated parties about obligations and rights in relation to a regulation, and by promoting and monitoring compliance through inspections and other means [2]. While regulations routinely evolve throughout their lifetime to ensure they continue to address societal needs, it is often unclear whether they actually achieve intended societal outcomes. Do regulatory programs result in improved compliance? What do observed

H.C. Mayr et al. (Eds.): ER 2017, LNCS 10650, pp. 77–91, 2017.
https://doi.org/10.1007/978-3-319-69904-2_7

compliance levels tell us about a regulation or its supporting programs? Are they meeting their intended objectives? Over the years, governments, citizens, and interest groups have been actively involved in answering such questions, often with inconclusive results [3–5]. Current trends, including climate change and cyber threats, are driving an increased interest to quantitatively link programs and regulations with societal outcomes.

Goal models have been used successfully in the past to conceptualize and analyze regulations. Goal models capture the structure and intent of regulations, and enable compliance measurements and assessments [6, 7]. In this context, goal models put different compliance scenarios in proper perspective for stakeholders to visualize relevant regulations, laws, processes, and objectives. If we could model regulatory programs in the same manner, we could then exploit a uniform modelling framework to ask questions about performance and the evidence-based impact of programs on regulations. Such an approach will support the monitoring, analysis, and assessment of regulations and their supporting regulatory programs. Regulators collect and use much data while administering (i.e., introducing, enforcing, reviewing, and evolving) regulations. Judging from the numerous regulated parties a regulation can influence, these data exhibit the three V-properties of Big Data (velocity, variety, volume) [8]. Goal models used in regulatory contexts collect data from numerous sources that also have velocity, variety, and volume. Visualizing and deriving insight from such Big Data is very challenging today because of the dimensions required for proper analysis, including conventional ones such as time, location, and organizations, but also domain-specific ones such as the structure of regulations and programs. Towards this end, we investigate the use of *IBM Watson Analytics* [9], a cloud-based Big Data technology, to explore and visualize these different dimensions of data in order to understand compliance issues and program effectiveness at the heart of many challenges faced by regulators [10].

One contribution of this article is our proposal to use the same conceptualization framework to model both regulations and their supporting regulatory programs. This approach enables us to obtain homogeneous goal satisfaction data from the goal models of regulations and regulatory programs. The other contribution of this paper is an extended method for regulatory intelligence that exploits Watson Analytics to explore and visualize the evaluated goal satisfaction data to obtain useful insight on the regulatory process. Here, the dimensions of data analysis are the structure of the regulation and program, location, and time. We demonstrate our method using an illustrative case study inspired from the Canadian mining sector to show the potential of this tool-supported conceptualization for supporting and enhancing regulatory practices.

The rest of the paper is as follows. Section 2 provides background on the use of goal models for regulatory compliance. Section 3 discusses regulatory intelligence and how it relates to the regulatory ecosystem. Section 4 introduces the Goal-oriented Regulatory Intelligence Method, while Sect. 5 uses an illustrative case study inspired from a real regulation to describe its applicability. We present lessons learned in Sect. 6 and limitations in Sect. 7. We conclude with a summary and future work in Sect. 8.

2 Background

Goal models are often used to show compliance of information systems and business processes with one or more regulations. Here, goal models exploit various concepts (such as goals, links, and actors) to assess compliance and explore what-if scenarios to address non-compliance. The rationale is that if goal models are a useful conceptualization for eliciting, modeling, and analyzing requirements in order to capture alternatives and conflicts between stakeholder objectives [6], they can also help explore and analyze compliance [7]. The Nòmos framework [11], including its variations (Nòmos 2 [12] and Nòmos 3 [13]), is a goal-based modeling framework used to systematically generate law-compliant requirements and support requirements analysts in dealing with the problem of requirements compliance. Secure Tropos [14] is another goal-based conceptualization that has been used to support the consideration of laws and regulations during the development of secure software systems. Finally, the User Requirements Notation (URN) [15], a standard modeling language used to model and analyze requirements with two complementary views, namely the *Goal-oriented Requirement Language* (GRL) and the Use Case Map (UCM) notation, has been used to model and study the compliance of enterprises goals and business processes against regulations [16, 17]. As of 2012, the URN standard includes an indicator concept that enables enhanced compliance analysis [18, 19], and regulator-oriented reasoning about the suitability of regulations and opportunities for their evolution [20, 21].

However, these goal modelling approaches have taken into consideration neither regulatory programs nor the Big Data aspects involved in the regulatory process. Administering regulations involves more than enforcing compliance. As such, regulators, citizens, and enterprises need to get insight from the data involved in the regulatory process. Data analytics technologies such as Watson Analytics can facilitate this. Watson Analytics is a pioneering software system that uses cloud computing and multiple machine learning algorithms to analyze high volumes of data [9, 22]. Using a simple intuitive user interface, Watson Analytics enables the user to ask questions on the collected data in natural language and returns results mined from the data across different dimensions of interest. Watson Analytics understands complicated and difficult questions asked in natural language, gives evidence-based results in an appropriate visualization, and proposes related questions of potential interest about patterns, trends, and correlations. There is growing acceptance and use of Watson Analytics, and some companies have recently started using it in a regulatory compliance context [23]. However, to our knowledge, Watson Analytics has not been used from a regulator's perspective, nor has it been used with goal models, until now.

3 Regulatory Intelligence

The concept of regulatory intelligence has its origins in the heavily regulated pharmaceutical industry [24]. The motivation for regulatory intelligence is to enable pharmaceutical companies to remain locally and globally compliant to existing and new regulations. As such, definitions of *regulatory intelligence* revolve around continuously obtaining and processing data and information from multiple sources and analyzing them in the relevant context. It also includes generating and communicating meaningful outputs from these data in line with an organization's regulatory strategy [24, 25]. This implies that with regulatory intelligence, information relating to a given compliance context and its implication can be obtained, analyzed, and communicated. The regulatory ecosystem is also monitored to identify opportunities where insight obtained from the collected information can be utilized to influence future regulations. This application of regulatory intelligence is to improve decisions making and planning for pharmaceutical companies. It enables them to make and maintain their products compliance with regulations [26].

Beyond the pharmaceutical industry, in other domains, the interactions between regulators, citizens, and enterprises already involve some sort of data gathering, analysis, and communication about regulations and the regulatory process. Hence, regulatory intelligence is conducted *by regulators* using feedback from citizens and enterprises, and compliance enforcement information to administer regulations [21]. As such, from the regulator's perspective, regulatory intelligence can be used to enhance the regulatory process with data-driven support for decision-making towards introducing, enforcing, reviewing, and evolving regulations. Regulatory intelligence facilitates monitoring and assessing regulations and can be used to influence the regulatory process and ecosystem. Furthermore, analyzed data and information can be used to ascertain the relevance, effectiveness (e.g., in terms of goal satisfaction), or efficiency (e.g., in terms of costs/benefits) of regulations and their supporting regulatory programs. The regulator-oriented view of regulatory intelligence is the one adopted in this article.

4 A Method for Regulatory Intelligence

The concept of regulatory intelligence alludes to a feedback loop in the use of data from and within the regulatory ecosystem to administer regulations. In 2013, Badreddin et al. [21] proposed a regulatory intelligence method based on GRL that enables reasoning about regulations and compliance with regulation as a dimension. As discussed in Sect. 2, this method did not take regulatory programs and the amount of Big Data involved in the regulatory process, into consideration. We extend this method by incorporating a step that exploits Watson Analytics to provide a pragmatic way to explore and visualize regulations and regulatory programs as dimensions for data analysis. In addition, we explore the use of Watson Analytics to analyze the Big Data resulting from the evaluated goal models of regulations and regulatory programs to gain insights about the regulatory process. Our proposal, the *Goal-oriented Regulatory Intelligence Method* (GoRIM), shown in Fig. 1, is inspired from the method introduced by Tawhid et al. [20] for managing outcome-based regulations.

As a starting point, in the first step (Build), GRL models of the regulation and of the regulatory program are built using *jUCMNav*, a free Eclipse-based plugin for URN modeling and analysis [19, 20]. These models are built using the semi-automatic method for creating goal models of regulations from tables described by Rashidi-Tabrizi et al. [27]. The same GRL concepts are used for both types of models: goals, indicators, contribution/decomposition links, actors (optional), and dependencies

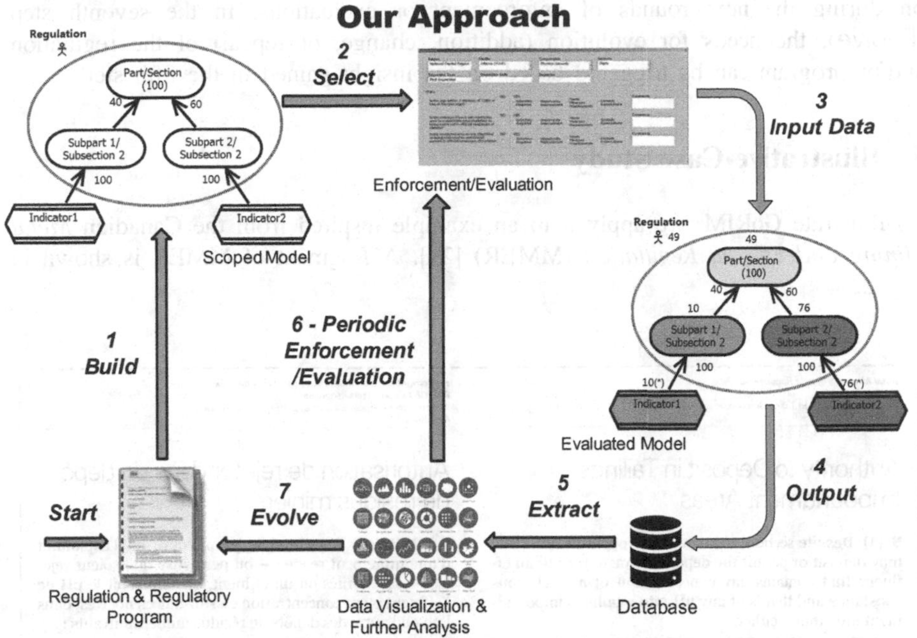

Fig. 1. The Goal-oriented Regulatory Intelligence Method (GoRIM)

to resources for conditional parts of regulations/programs (optional). Contribution levels and indicators are added manually by experts to the tabular representation of the regulations/programs as they are typically not found in the original documents. jUCMNav creates goal models by importing the tabular representation (comma-separated value file created with Excel), a format commonly used by regulators [27].

In the second step (Select), questions to be answered by inspectors/auditors (or regulated parties themselves in case of self-reporting) during periodic compliance enforcement activities for the regulation, as well as evaluations of the regulatory programs, are selected from predefined questions so that data can be fed to the indicators in the goal models. In the third step (Input Data), the data collected are input to the goal models as GRL strategies. Using GRL evaluation algorithms [28], satisfaction levels for both the regulation and program goal models, which indicate compliance and performance levels, are computed for all goals. In the fourth step (Output), snapshots of different computed compliance and performance levels can be produced for different regulated parties (companies, provinces, etc.) at different times, and stored in a database. In the fifth step (Extract), the data is extracted from the database and input into a data visualization engine (such as Watson Analytics in our case). Visualizations and further analysis can be done on large datasets to enable reporting on computed compliance and performance levels and what they mean relative to the regulation and regulatory program. Based on these computed levels, the needs for reinforcements or reevaluations can be highlighted in the sixth step (Periodic Enforcement/Evaluation). Decisions can be made on specifics to focus on during the next rounds of enforcement or evaluations. In the seventh step (Evolve), the needs for evolution (addition, change, or repeal) of the regulation and/or program can be triggered based on the insight gained in the fifth step.

5 Illustrative Case Study

To illustrate GoRIM, we apply it to an example inspired from the Canadian *Metal Mining and Effluent Regulation* (MMER) [29]. A fragment of MMER is shown in Fig. 2.

Metal Mining Effluent Regulations
PART 1 General
Authority to Deposit in Tailings Impoundment Areas
Sections 5-7

Authority to Deposit in Tailings Impoundment Areas

5 (1) Despite section 4, the owner or operator of a mine may deposit or permit the deposit of waste rock or an effluent that contains any concentration of a deleterious substance and that is of any pH into a tailings impoundment area that is either

Règlement sur les effluents des mines de métaux
PARTIE I Dispositions générales
Autorisation de rejeter dans un dépôt de résidus miniers
Articles 5-7

Autorisation de rejeter dans un dépôt de résidus miniers

5 (1) Malgré l'article 4, le propriétaire ou l'exploitant d'une mine peut rejeter — ou permettre que soient rejetés — des stériles ou un effluent, quel que soit le pH de l'effluent ou sa concentration en substances nocives, dans l'un ou l'autre des dépôts de résidus miniers suivants :

Fig. 2. A fragment of the MMER

The MMER, which aims to protect aquatic life, is the Canadian regulation that directs metal mines to conduct *Environmental Effects Monitoring* (EEM) as a condition when depositing effluents resulting from mining activities [29]. The government supports this activity through an *EMM program* (EMMP). Consider a situation where *Environment and Climate Change Canada* (ECCC), the corresponding federal regulator, wants to review and report on the performance of MMER (a regulation) and of EEMP (a program), and interesting relationships between these two artefacts. With a scenario where four provincial metal mines (in Manitoba, Nova Scotia, Ontario, and Quebec) are reviewed between 2014 and 2016, we use GoRIM and Watson Analytics to describe how this can be achieved.

Building the Goal Models: To apply GoRIM, we first build goal models for MMER and EEMP using jUCMNav. An example for MMER, based on several fragments similar to the one shown in Fig. 2, is illustrated in Fig. 3. The structure of goal models enables us to capture the regulation/program structure (part/section, subpart/subsection, rule statements, etc.), and show different relationships (contributions and decompositions). A layer of indicators at the bottom enables the measurement of various aspects of rule statements, and some indicators can contribute to many rules. The model in Fig. 3 is a simplified version of MMER; the real GRL model for this regulation is much larger, but the selected subset is sufficient to illustrate GoRIM and investigate the functionalities of Watson Analytics. A similar model exists for the supporting program (EEMP, see Fig. 4).

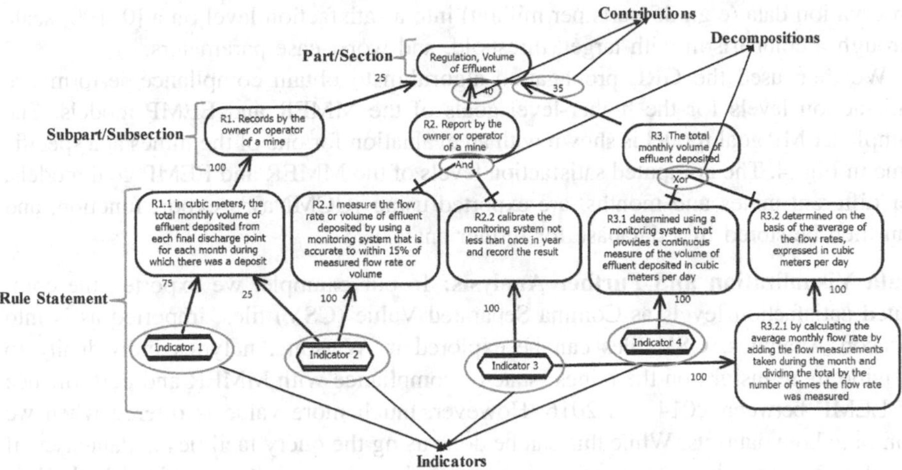

Fig. 3. Simplified MMER goal model

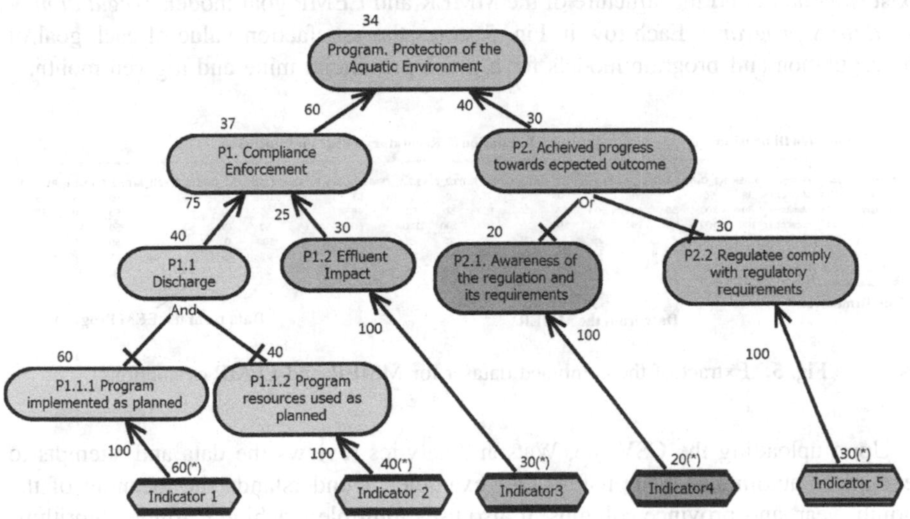

Fig. 4. Evaluated simplified EEMP goal model

Data Input, Evaluation, and Output: Next, we input data into the indicators of the regulation and program goal models via GRL strategies. We used sample compliance data for the four metal mines and evaluation data for EEMP activities from 2014 to 2016. The data we use here is synthetic as the real data and goal evaluations are confidential. GRL evaluation strategies representing each month of a year for each provincial mine were created. These GRL strategies define a set of initial values for the indicators of the MMER and EEMP goal models. Each indicator converts real observation data (e.g., 35 parts per million) into a satisfaction level on a [0–100] scale through a comparison with target, threshold, and worst-case parameters.

We then used the GRL propagation algorithm to obtain compliance/performance satisfaction levels for the higher-level goals of the MMER and EEMP models. The sample EEMP goal model is shown with an evaluation for one of the mines at a specific time in Fig. 4. The computed satisfaction levels of the MMER and EEMP goal models, for different mines and months, are exported using jUCMNav's export function, and can then be stored in a database for further analysis.

Data Visualization and Further Analysis: In our example, we exported the computed satisfaction levels as Comma Separated Value (CSV) files, imported as is into Watson Analytics. CSV files can be explored in Watson Analytics individually to provide more insight on the mines' state of compliance with MMER and performance of EEMP between 2014 and 2016. However, much more value is offered when we combine both datasets. While this can be done using the query facilities in databases (if the data is stored in a database), in our example, we manually combined both CSV files, as illustrated in Fig. 5. The combination is based on shared dimensions of interest, for example, the months between 2014 and 2016 (*time*), the provinces where the mines exist (*location*), and the structure of the MMER and EEMP goal models (*regulation & regulatory program*). Each row in Fig. 5 stores the satisfaction value of each goal of the regulation and program models for a given provincial mine and a given month.

Location Dimension **Regulation & Regulatory Program Dimension**

Month	Year	Province	MMER	R1_Ow	R2_Ow	R3_Tot	R1.1_M	R2.1_V	R2.2_C	R3.1_D	R3.2_D	R3.2.1_	EEM Program	P1_Con	P2_Ach	P1.1_D	P1.2_Ef	P2.1_R	P2.2_R	P1.1.1_	P1.1.2_
January	2014	Manitoba	38	50	0	75	50	0	0	75	0	0	61	36	100	25	75	100	50	75	25
January	2015	Manitoba	80	100	50	100	100	75	50	100	50	50	49	49	50	50	50	50	50	50	50
January	2016	Manitoba	100	100	100	100	100	100	100	100	100	100	60	68	50	75	50	50	50	75	75
February	2014	Manitoba	33	25	25	50	25	50	25	50	25	25	40	0	100	0	0	100	50	25	0
February	2015	Manitoba	58	50	50	75	50	75	50	75	50	50	47	62	25	75	25	25	25	100	75
February	2016	Manitoba	44	25	75	25	25	75	75	25	25	25	38	30	50	25	50	50	50	25	25

Time Dimension **Data from the MMER** **Data from the EEM Program**

Fig. 5. Extract of the combined dataset for MMER and EEMP evaluations

Upon uploading the CSV file, Watson Analytics reviews the data and attempts to recognizes automatically its nature. For example, it understands the meaning of the month, year, and province columns. It also uses multiple machine learning algorithms in parallel to analyze possible relationships in the data, leading to suggestions of questions and visualizations to be explored by the analyst. Figure 6 present six such *starting points*. Natural language questions in English can also be asked explicitly, as illustrated at the top of Fig. 6. When we asked the question "What is the relationship between MMER and EEM Program by year and province", Watson Analytics analyzed our question (relationships in Watson are mainly quantitative correlations), automatically selected an appropriate visualization, and suggested further related questions based on our data. The suggested questions were sorted according to their computed relevance, as outlined in Table 1. These questions reflected correctly the time and location dimensions from the dataset. However, Watson Analytics does not understand the goal-oriented structure of regulations and programs, which is a

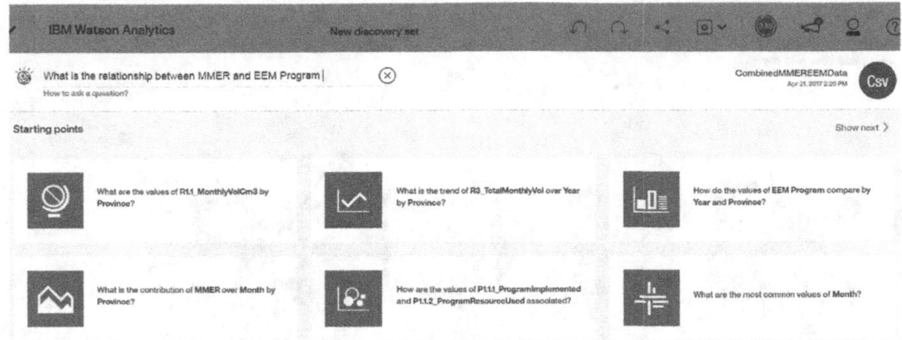

Fig. 6. Watson Analytics suggested questions, and interface to ask others based on the data

Table 1. Further questions suggested by Watson Analytics based on the initial question

Questions	Relevance Level
`What is the relationship between the` **`EEM Program`** `and` **`MMER`** `by` **`Province`** `and` **`Year`**`?`	Most Relevant
`What are the values of` **`EEM Program`** `and` **`MMER`** `by` **`Province`** `across` **`Year`**`?`	Most Relevant
`What is the breakdown of` **`EEM Program`** `by` **`Year`** `and` **`Province`**`?`	Most Relevant
`What are the values of` **`EEM Program`** `and` **`MMER`** `for` **`Year`** `and` **`Province`**`?`	Most Relevant
`How do the values of` **`EEM Program`** `and` **`MMER`** `compare by` **`Provinces`** `across` **`Year`**`?`	Most Relevant
`How are the values of` **`EEM Program`** `and` **`MMER`** `associated across` **`Year`**	Somewhat Relevant

domain-specific dimension. Although this limitation hurts the use of default navigation features at the user interface level (e.g., drilling up or down along this structure dimension), the aggregate satisfaction along such structure is still available as it was computed explicitly in the goal model by jUCMNav. For example, as shown in Fig. 4, the program satisfaction (34) combines the satisfactions of P1 (37) and P2 (30).

The Watson Analytics offering of related questions is necessary for exploring data as it provides opportunities to refine questions concerning insights desired from satisfaction data. Some proposed questions may actually have results supported by strong evidence, but still be irrelevant. Minimizing such noise still needs to be explored in future work.

Upon selecting the question "How do the values of EEM Program and MMER compare by Provinces across Year?", Watson Analytics offered the visualization shown in Fig. 7. Such a visualization offers an opportunity to analyze MMER and the EEM program together along dimensions unavailable prior to this article. For example, the regulator (ECCC) can observe that while the performance of the EEM program (the bar charts) is fairly consistent across years on average, the yearly average compliance with MMER (the trend lines) has been inconsistent. From 2014 to 2016, the metal

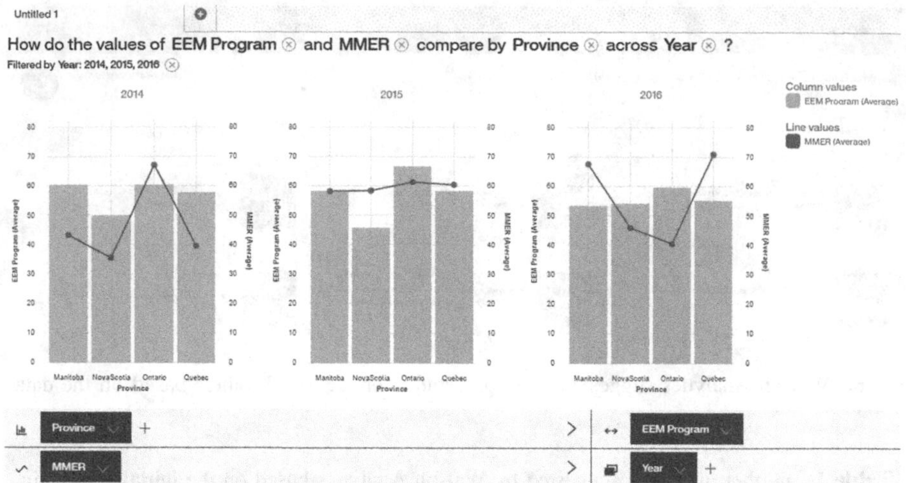

Fig. 7. Visual comparison of the EEM program and MMER by province, across years

mines in the provinces of Manitoba and Quebec have had a growing increase in their compliance levels while there has been a decrease in Ontario for the same period. The metal mine in the province of Nova Scotia had an increase in its compliance level between 2014 and 2015 and a decrease in 2016 close to its level in 2014.

With this information, the ECCC can investigate possible explanations for these observations, including what drives the MMER (Fig. 8) and the EEM program (Fig. 9).

This analysis indicates that while "R3.2.1_AvgMonthlyFlowRate" (from the goal model in Fig. 3) and "Month" is the main driver of the MMER with 46%, while "P1_ComplianceEnforcement" (from the goal model in Fig. 4) and "Province" is the main driver for the EEM program with 57%. The ECCC could explore these candidate

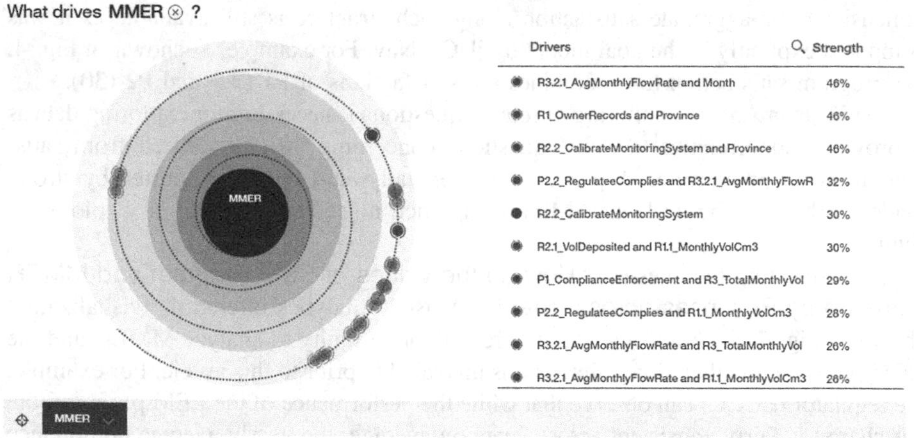

Fig. 8. Visualization showing what drives the MMER

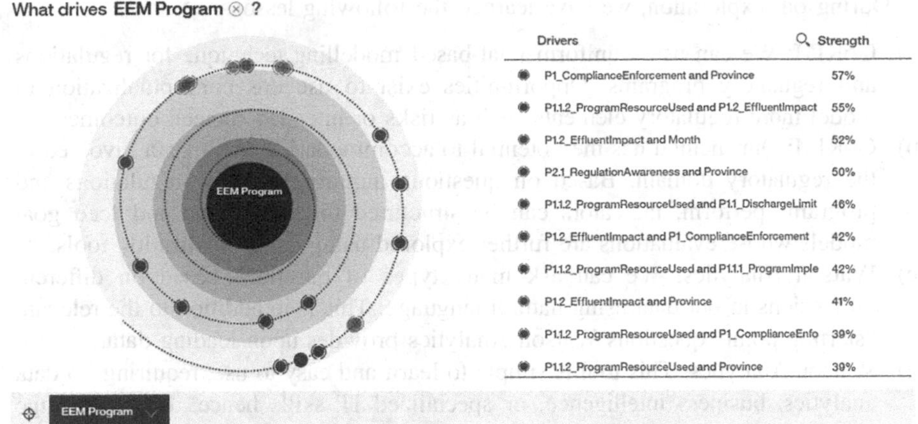

Fig. 9. Visualization showing what drives the EEM program

explanations even further or explore other visualizations or questions within Watson Analytics. Note that some proposed drivers have a low level of relevance in our context. For example, a contribution from R.3.2.1 to R3 is something known from the very structure of the goal model. How to prune out such known drivers in Watson is still under study.

6 Lessons Learned

Our exploration of GoRIM to analyze and report on compliance with a regulation (MMER) and the performance of a companion program (EEMP) were done by a Ph.D. student and two undergraduate students, under the supervision of two professors. All are co-authors of this article. The undergraduate students had no experience whatsoever with goal modelling or regulatory intelligence, whereas the PhD student and both professors had advanced knowledge. None of the participants had used Watson Analytics.

We have found Watson Analytics easy to learn and intuitive in visualizing and exploring compliance levels of regulations and performance levels of programs. While GRL offers appropriate tool-supported concepts for modeling regulations/programs and for analyzing them for one regulated party at one moment in time, Watson Analytics adds a form of analysis that was unavailable until now. Watson Analytics enables, out of the box, a combined analysis of data coming from multiple models (regulation and program), for many regulated parties and many moments in time, with opportunities for slicing, dicing, and drilling along several conventional dimensions (time and location). Suggestions for visualizations and related questions are also useful features.

During our exploration, we have learned the following lessons:

(a) GoRIM: We can use a uniform goal-based modelling technique for regulations and regulatory programs. Opportunities exist to use this conceptualization to model more regulatory elements such as risks or intended societal outcomes.
(b) GoRIM: Our method has the potential to accommodate the Big Data involved in the regulatory domain. Based on questions inquiring on how regulations and programs perform, indicators can be structured to collect data and feed goal models whose evaluations are further explored using data visualization tools.
(c) Watson Analytics: We can ask many types of questions based on different dimensions in our data using natural language. This is in addition to the relevant "starting point" questions Watson Analytics provides upon loading data.
(d) Watson Analytics: This tool is simple to learn and easy to use, requiring no data analytics, business intelligence, or specialized IT skills hence. This is a huge improvement upon the use of a conventional and heavyweight business intelligence tool (e.g., IBM Cognos) for regulatory intelligence, which was partially explored in [21]. This can lead to reductions in training costs and increased efficiency.
(e) Watson Analytics: We also like the suggestions on how to visualize and analyze data through a variety of visualization alternatives that can be tailored to suit the types of questions being asked. This is in addition to user-defined functions, which can enable regulators to explore relationships not supported by default.

7 Limitations

Although we could create and analyze goal models of regulations (MMER) and programs (EEMP) using GoRIM, we are yet to evaluate GoRIM in a real-life context. We used fake data for our analysis and have not yet obtained feedback on the usefulness of GoRIM from the regulator who provided the example used here. There are also scalability and usability concerns to be addressed due to the size of real regulations. For example, the main section of the MMER goal model, excluding the eight different schedules that further explain the regulation, already contains 273 goals. We have not yet explored the usability of Watson Analytics in the presence of hundreds of goals, as well as the impact of changes to the goal models themselves (e.g., with the addition or deletion of goals, and hence of values in the database) on the analysis features of this tool. We are also yet to explore a more complete set of functionalities from Watson Analytics for exploring regulatory intelligence data. Finally, we have observed several limitations in that technology (e.g., Watson Analytics currently understands months but not quarters, and countries/provinces/states but not cities), and there might be other such limitations affecting regulations and programs in specific domains.

8 Conclusion and Future Work

To administer regulations effectively, a feedback loop involving data from and within the regulatory process is necessary. This information exhibits the properties of Big Data, creating the need for advanced tools and technologies to enable analysis and visualization providing the insight required to make informed decisions when administering regulations and their supporting programs. This paper proposed and illustrated the Goal-oriented Regulatory Intelligence Method (GoRIM), which uses the same conceptualization (goal models) to capture and analyze regulations and regulatory programs, and supports a robust analysis of compliance data. Moreover, the method exploits Watson Analytics to analyze and report on observed compliance levels, explore what they mean relative to the regulation, and determine how supporting regulatory programs contribute to observed compliance. As such, GoRIM can offer much value to regulators who want to assess the performance of their regulations and programs. The simplicity to learn and use Watson Analytics offers an attractive, pragmatic, out-of-the-box solution to support regulatory intelligence activities.

In the near future, we plan to use GoRIM to model real regulations and programs and use real data to explore concrete relationships in the regulatory process. In addition to addressing some of the limitations from the previous section, a usability study would also help determine the parts of GoRIM and of Watson Analytics that are really usable and of value to regulators.

Acknowledgements. This work was supported financially by the National Science and Engineering Research Council of Canada (NSERC) Discovery program. We are much thankful to Colette Lacroix and IBM Canada for access to Watson Analytics. We also thank Prof. Greg Richards, Dr. Randy Giffen, and Nick Cartwright for useful discussions, as well as the reviewers for their insightful suggestions.

References

1. OECD: Recommendation of the Council on Regulatory Policy and Governance. OECD Publishing, Paris (2012)
2. OECD: The Governance of Regulators, OECD Best Practice Principles for Regulatory Policy. OECD Publishing, Paris (2014)
3. Coglianse, C.: Measuring regulatory performance: evaluating the impact of regulation and regulatory policy. OECD Expert Paper No. 1, OECD Publishing, Paris (2012)
4. Nielsen, V.L., Parker, C.: Is it possible to measure compliance? Legal Studies Research Paper No. 192, Faculty of Law, The University of Melbourne (2006). SSRN https://ssrn.com/abstract=935988
5. Parker, D., Kirkpatrick, C.: Measuring regulatory performance. The economic impact of regulatory policy: a literature review of quantitative evidence. OECD Expert Paper No. 3, OECD Publishing, Paris (2012)
6. Horkoff, J., Aydemir, F.B., Cardoso, E., Li, T., Maté, A., Paja, E., Giorgini, P.: Goal-oriented requirements engineering: a systematic literature map. In: 24th International Requirements Engineering Conference (RE), pp. 106–115. IEEE CS (2016). doi:10.1109/RE.2016.41

7. Akhigbe, O., Amyot, D., Richards, G.: Information technology artifacts in the regulatory compliance of business processes: a meta-analysis. In: Benyoucef, M., Weiss, M., Mili, H. (eds.) MCETECH 2015. LNBIP, vol. 209, pp. 89–104. Springer, Cham (2015). doi:10.1007/978-3-319-17957-5_6
8. Gandomi, A., Haider, M.: Beyond the hype: big data concepts, methods, and analytics. Int. J. Inf. Manag. **35**(2), 137–144 (2015). doi:10.1016/j.ijinfomgt.2014.10.007
9. IBM: IBM Watson Analytics: Analytics Made Easy. https://www.ibm.com/analytics/watson-analytics/us-en/index.html. Accessed 23 Apr 2017
10. Akhigbe, O., Amyot, D., Mylopoulos, J., Richards, G.: What can information systems do for regulators? A review of the state-of-practice in Canada. In: IEEE 11th International Conference on Research Challenges in Information Science (RCIS). IEEE CS (2017)
11. Siena, A., Perini, A., Susi, A., Mylopoulos, J.: A meta-model for modelling law-compliant requirements. In: Requirements Engineering and Law (RELAW), pp. 45–51. IEEE CS (2009). doi:10.1109/RELAW.2009.1
12. Ingolfo, S., Siena, A., Perini A., Susi, A., Mylopoulos, J.: Modeling laws with Nòmos 2. In: 6th International Workshop on RE and LAW (RELAW), pp. 69–71. IEEE CS (2013). doi:10.1109/RELAW.2013.6671350
13. Ingolfo, S., Jureta, I., Siena, A., Perini, A., Susi, A.: Nòmos 3: legal compliance of roles and requirements. In: Yu, E., Dobbie, G., Jarke, M., Purao, S. (eds.) ER 2014. LNCS, vol. 8824, pp. 275–288. Springer, Cham (2014). doi:10.1007/978-3-319-12206-9_22
14. Islam, S., Mouratidis, H., Jürjens, J.: A framework to support alignment of secure software engineering with legal regulations. Softw. Syst. Model. **10**(3), 369–394 (2011). doi:10.1007/s10270-010-0154-z
15. Amyot, D., Mussbacher, G.: User requirements notation: the first ten years, the next ten years. J. Softw. (JSW) **6**(5), 47–768 (2011)
16. Ghanavati, S., Amyot, D., Peyton, L.: Compliance analysis based on a goal-oriented requirement language evaluation methodology. In: 17th IEEE International Requirements Engineering Conference (RE 2009), pp. 133–142. IEEE CS (2009). doi:10.1109/RE.2009.42
17. Ghanavati, S., Amyot, D., Rifaut, A.: Legal goal-oriented requirement language (Legal GRL) for modeling regulations. In: 6th International Workshop on Modeling in Software Engineering (MiSE), pp. 1–6. ACM (2014). doi:10.1145/2593770.2593780
18. Shamsaei, A., Pourshahid, A., Amyot, D.: Business process compliance tracking using key performance indicators. In: zur Muehlen, M., Su, J. (eds.) BPM 2010. LNBIP, vol. 66, pp. 73–84. Springer, Heidelberg (2011). doi:10.1007/978-3-642-20511-8_7
19. Amyot, D., et al.: Towards advanced goal model analysis with jUCMNav. In: Castano, S., Vassiliadis, P., Lakshmanan, L.V., Lee, M.L. (eds.) ER 2012. LNCS, vol. 7518, pp. 201–210. Springer, Heidelberg (2012). doi:10.1007/978-3-642-33999-8_25
20. Tawhid, R., Braun, E., et al.: Towards outcome-based regulatory compliance in aviation security. In: 20th IEEE International Requirements Engineering Conference (RE), pp. 267–272. IEEE CS (2012). doi:10.1109/RE.2012.6345813
21. Badreddin, O., Mussbacher, G., et al.: Regulation-based dimensional modeling for regulatory intelligence. In: 6th International Workshop on Requirements Engineering and Law (RELAW), pp. 1–10. IEEE CS (2013). doi:10.1109/RELAW.2013.6671340
22. Aggarwal, M., Madhukar, M.: IBM's Watson Analytics for health care: a miracle made true. In: Cloud Computing Systems and Applications in Healthcare, pp. 117–134. IGI Global (2017). doi:10.4018/978-1-5225-1002-4.ch007
23. Anderson, F.: Watson Analytics sessions at World of Watson 2016. https://www.ibm.com/communities/analytics/watson-analytics-blog/event-watson-analytics-sessions-at-world-of-watson-2016/. Accessed 23 Apr 2017

24. Hynes, C.: Regulatory intelligence: implications for product development. In: 2014 TOPRA Module: Strategic Planning in Regulatory Affairs. http://bit.ly/2pr5UiY. Accessed 23 Apr 2017
25. Felgate, T.: What is regulatory intelligence? http://www.regulatory-intelligence.eu/2013/02/what-is-regulatory-intelligence.html. Accessed 23 Apr 2017
26. Maguire, P.: What is 'regulatory intelligence?'. Regulatory Affairs Professional Society. http://bit.ly/2oWKrNe. Accessed 23 Apr 2017
27. Rashidi-Tabrizi, R., Mussbacher, G., Amyot, D.: Transforming regulations into performance models in the context of reasoning for outcome-based compliance. In: 6th International Workshop on Requirements Engineering and Law (RELAW), pp. 34–43. IEEE CS (2013)
28. Pourshahid, A., Amyot, D., Peyton, L., Ghanavati, S., Chen, P., Weiss, M., Forster, A.J.: Business process management with the user requirements notation. Electron. Commer. Res. **9**(4), 269–316 (2009). doi:10.1007/s10660-009-9039-z
29. Justice Laws Website: Consolidated federal laws of Canada, Metal Mining Effluent Regulations. http://laws-lois.justice.gc.ca/eng/regulations/SOR-2002-222/. Accessed 23 Apr 2017

An Alternative Approach to Metainformation Conceptualisation and Use

Cesar Gonzalez-Perez(✉) and Patricia Martin-Rodilla

Institute of Heritage Sciences (Incipit), Spanish National Research Council (CSIC), Santiago de Compostela, Spain
{cesar.gonzalez-perez, patricia.martin-rodilla}@incipit.csic.es

Abstract. The growing needs to analyse and interpret large amounts of complex information has generalised the use of information about information, often called metainformation (or metadata). Metadata approaches and standards have proliferated in fields as diverse as medicine, meteorology, geography, cultural heritage or education, among others. These approaches are supposed to assist us in documenting our information by recording who has documented what, when and how, among other concerns, making the tasks of interpreting the data much easier. However, metadata approaches often suffer from a number of issues. To start with, there are too many, and users are often daunted by the task to choose among them. Secondly, metadata approaches seem to re-invent the wheel by assuming that metadata is essentially different to data (or metainformation to information) and for this reason needs a new and different set of languages and tools. Finally, many metadata approaches mix together conceptual concerns and implementation issues, thus violating well-known engineering principles of modularity and layering.

This paper presents a review of existing metadata approaches from a conceptual modelling perspective, identifies the major issues with them, and proposes a new approach based on the ConML conceptual modelling language. This new approach starts from the basis that metainformation is a particular kind of information and, as a consequence, everything that we know about information can also be applied to metainformation.

Keywords: Metadata · Metainformation · Conceptual modelling · ConML

1 Introduction

In recent decades, the increasing amount of data available for analysis and interpretation has generalised the need for rigorous approaches to express the various properties of the data being analysed. Some examples of this include registering who has created some data (i.e. its author), in which precise moment (i.e. its time of creation), for what purpose (i.e. intent), with which quality criteria (i.e. reliability), where the data comes from (i.e. provenance), etc. Data that describes other data has been called "metadata", and has been vaguely defined as "data about data" or "data that describes other data" [13, 22]. Sometimes, the term "information" is used instead of "data", and "metainformation" defined as "information about information". Although some

H.C. Mayr et al. (Eds.): ER 2017, LNCS 10650, pp. 92–105, 2017.
https://doi.org/10.1007/978-3-319-69904-2_8

distinctions may be drawn between data and information in this regard, we consider them equivalent to all effects in this paper. In addition, the term "metadata" (or "metainformation") has been used to mean very different things. At least, two separate meanings of the term are clearly visible in the literature:

- "Metadata" as the structure of other data. For example, the specification of a database table (which columns it has, which data type is used for each, etc.) is often referred to as "metadata".
- "Metadata" as a characterisation of other data. For example, the labelling of a data record (such as a row in a database table) with its author, creation date and reliability factor is usually referred to as "metadata".

In the first case, metadata is describing the structure of the data and, therefore, what scope it covers. In fact, by stating what columns a database table has, or what tables exist in the database, we are not only specifying how data is structured, but also what data we are considering to start with. In other words, metadata of the first kind determines what the domain of discourse is as much as its structure. And, in this regard, metadata of this kind is inextricably linked to the data it describes; we cannot strip a dataset of its metadata. In the second case, contrarily, metadata is an "additional layer" that we can add on top of existing data. We can enrich a dataset by capturing some properties about the data, but even if we don't, the dataset is still there. Given these major differences, we advise against using the term "metadata" to refer to the first kind of situations as described above, and prefer to use it only for the second kind. The structure and domain scope of the data is given by a data schema, information structure, type model, or an equivalent artefact; not by metadata. Metadata refers to properties of the data that are documented to aid with its analysis and interpretation. In this paper, we will only deal with "true metadata", i.e. metadata of the second kind.

In addition to this terminological problem, three additional issues exist with metadata approaches. Firstly, a very large number of metadata approaches have appeared over the last few decades. Some target a very specific domain, whereas others are general in their scope. There are metadata approaches focusing on multimedia web elements [27]; online educational environments [6]; genetic, biological and medical information [29], astronomy or meteorology [19], geography [9] or cultural heritage [8]. Approaches in these areas are extremely heterogeneous as to what they encompass, and make adoption decisions a very difficult task for tentative users. In this regard, we have reviewed 28 well-known metadata approaches as described in the literature, and selected the most common two for a detailed analysis.

Secondly, most metadata approaches start from the assumption that metadata is essentially different from plain data, and therefore whole new modelling, encoding and communication approaches are needed. In fact, as we will describe in detail in further sections, many well-known metadata approaches contain data modelling specifications that are highly redundant with already existing, "non-meta", data modelling approaches. We start from a different premise: if the "meta-" prefix in "metadata" is a qualifier of "data", then metadata must be a particular kind of data. And, applying a basic definition of subsumption (or Liskov's substitution principle [12]), we must conclude that everything we know about data, and every technology that we can employ on it, we also know, and we also can employ, on metadata. From this perspective, metadata may pose challenges that are marginally different to those of data, but we should be suspicious of apparently revolutionary deviations of metadata from plain data.

Finally, most metadata approaches contain a mixture of conceptual-level abstractions and implementation-level specifications, thus producing a "full stack" solution that ties conceptual decisions (such as whether to document the provenance of certain kinds of information) to technological and implementation ones (such as whether to store it as Unicode or ASCII, for example). Modularity, separation of concerns, and layering are well-known engineering principles that have been shown to produce more robust and maintainable products. We argue in this paper that metadata approaches should observe these principles too.

2 Existing Metadata Approaches

A large number of metadata approaches exist. Here we try to provide a glimpse of the breadth and complexity of existing approaches through the review of existing studies in which metadata approaches are compared and analysed according to different domains and uses. Firstly, we considered the semantic web as an area where metadata approaches seem to be especially popular. A relevant analysis is presented in [28] (shown as S henceforth), with a compilation of 34 standards for semantic web including also the MUSCLE compilation for multimedia elements [27], as well as *de facto* standards such as Schema.org [30]. Secondly, standardisation bodies also maintain their own aggregation works to register existing metadata approaches. The most representative is the NISO report [18] (N henceforth), which brings together 7 general standards for metadata representation, and which has worked as the seed for the ISO/IEC 11179 [10] international standard.

Thirdly, and given that metadata is, after all, about describing data, we looked at how specialists in digital humanities and information documentation (including archives and libraries, translation and language studies, communication areas and humanities and social sciences researchers) approach metadata needs. A reference work for these communities is Riley's glossary [25] (R henceforth), which indexes, visualises and briefly describes 104 metadata standards used by these professionals. This glossary also includes other previously commented catalogues such as MUSCLE [27]. Finally, many other domains possess their own metadata initiatives, such as earth sciences, biology, medicine or physics. In this regard, the Research Data Alliance (RDA) [24] is an international organisation sponsored by the European Commission as well as some American and Australian government agencies pursuing research on data-driven initiatives, and currently having over 5100 members from 122 countries. RDA maintains an active community project [23] (D henceforth) for the indexation, implementation and maintenance of metadata approaches in multiple knowledge areas, with 39 registered metadata approaches in their catalogue [2].

We have used these aggregate studies as a basis for the review of existing metadata approaches. Some overlap exists between studies, a number of metadata approaches being included and described by multiple studies. However, this overlap is not too significant: only one approach appears in all four studies, and most pairs of studies have four to six approaches in common of a grand total of 156 in total. Such a low degree of overlap indicates a considerable fragmentation as well as a notable proliferation of different metadata approaches. To make the review manageable and focused, we have considered the approaches that appear in at least two of the mentioned aggregate works, adding up to 28. Although there are many works that index or catalogue metadata approaches, works that carry out a comprehensive classification and review are less far common. One of the most complete in terms of classification criteria is [16], which proposes a classification of metadata approaches based on granularity and application domain. Application domain is indicated as domain independent (I) or domain dependent (D). In addition, granularity is quantified as the number of hierarchical levels in the metadata approach, but is further simplified as Global (G; general-purpose metadata approach), Local (L; domain-specific approach), Container (C; metadata aggregator) or Conceptual (CC; approach containing a rigorous schema definition). Table 1 shows the results of the review of metadata approaches.

Note that only one approach (ISO 15836) is present in all the aggregate works consulted, and only two of those classified as being of conceptual granularity (ISO

Table 1. Reviewed metadata approaches. Sources are indicated as R, N, S or D as per the text.

Name	Application domain	Gty.	Specific field	Source
AGLS	I: Semantic web	C	Government resources on the web	RS
Darwin Core	D: Biology	L	Biodiversity	RD
DCAT	I: Semantic web	C	Catalogue interoperability	SD
DIF	D: Earth sciences	L	Paleoclimate	RD
DIG35	D: Images	L	Images	RS
EAD	D: Humanities	C	Record description	RS
EML	D: Ecology	L	Ecology	RD
FGDC	D: Geography	L	Geospatial features	RD
FOAF	I: Semantic web	G	People	RND
FRBR	I: Humanities	CC	Bibliography	RS
ISO 15836 (Dublin core)	I	CC	Anything	RNSD
ISO 19115	D: Geography	L	Geospatial features	RSD
ISO/IEC 11179	I	CC	Organisational information	NS
ISO/IEC 13250 (topic maps)	I	CC	Topical knowledge	RS
Linked Data	I: Semantic web	G	Anything	RS
LOM	D: Education	L	Educational resources	RS
MARC	D: Humanities	C	Bibliography	RS
METS	I: Humanities	C	Data collection	RS
OAI	I: Semantic web	G	Resource exchange formats	RSD
OAIS	D	C	Preservation protocols	RS
ONIX	D: Book industry	C	Published material	RND
OWL/RDF	I: Semantic web	C	Machine-readable semantics	NSD
PMH	I: Semantic web	C	Data collection	RS
PREMIS	I: Humanities	G	Preservation of objects	RSD
RDA	I: Humanities	CC	Bibliography	RS
SKOS	I: Humanities	G	Taxonomies	RND
TEI	I: Text-based	L	Text mark-up	RS

15836 and ISO/IEC 11179) are included in most of the aggregate works. These two constitute the approaches with larger disciplinary scope and are amongst the most widely used [16]. For these reasons, both ISO 15836 and ISO/IEC 11179 represent good candidates to be analysed in depth. The following subsections present the results of this analysis.

2.1 ISO 15836 (Dublin Core)

ISO 15836, also known as Dublin Core, comprises a set of works carried out by the Dublin Core Metadata Initiative (DCMI), launched in 1995 to develop specialised metadata vocabularies that enable the construction of more advanced information search systems. Initially, Dublin Core specified 15 information descriptors that should be considered when documenting metadata for anything, such as *Creator*, *Date* or *Language*. The initial success of Dublin Core led the DCMI to promote the creation of an abstract model as well as a language specification to express Dublin Core-compliant metadata. This language is specified as a metamodel expressed in UML, as the DCMI was targeting developers, designers and software scientists as relevant stakeholders. Since 2003, the term "Dublin Core" refers to the ISO 15836 international standard [21] for the description of information resources across domains; all types of resources are describable regardless of their format, area of expertise or cultural origin. Such a wide purpose and scope explains its presence in all the revised aggregate works and its wide adoption across disciplines [20]. Some domains where Dublin Core has been used include health systems [26], Earth sciences [17], social sciences [15] or humanities [14].

The DCMI metamodel is defined in three parts: the DCMI Resource Model, the DCMI Description Set Model, and the DCMI Vocabulary Model (Fig. 1). In the DCMI metamodel, *Resources* are linguistic entities (as per their relations to terms and vocabularies) and thus correspond to information entities about things in the world that are to be described. For example, a bibliographic catalogue entry in a library is a resource under DCMI. However, resources are defined in DCMI as "anything that might be identified, i.e. an image, a service, and a collection of other resources, human beings, corporations, etc.". This definition is alluding to the entities in the world, rather than to information records about them. However, metadata is supposed to be data about data, rather than data about entities in the world. This is a significant contradiction and a potential source for confusion with the DCMI metamodel. Metadata itself corresponds to *Descriptions*, which are defined as "one or more statements about one, and only one, resource". This captures the essence of metadata satisfactorily, albeit being based on a poor definition of *Resource*. Finally, *Vocabularies* correspond to the words and terms that we use when constructing descriptions.

In addition to the confusing definition of *Resource*, there are some other conceptual weaknesses in the DCMI metamodel. Firstly, the organisation of the metamodel in three parts indicates that information about entities in the world (i.e. data) is being treated separately from the information gathered about it (i.e. metadata). In other words, the *Resources* vs. *Descriptions* dichotomy shows the differential treatment of metadata as essentially different to data, in contrast with our argument in the previous section. Consequently, under DCMI something is either data or metadata. This poses some serious problems that are discussed in the next section.

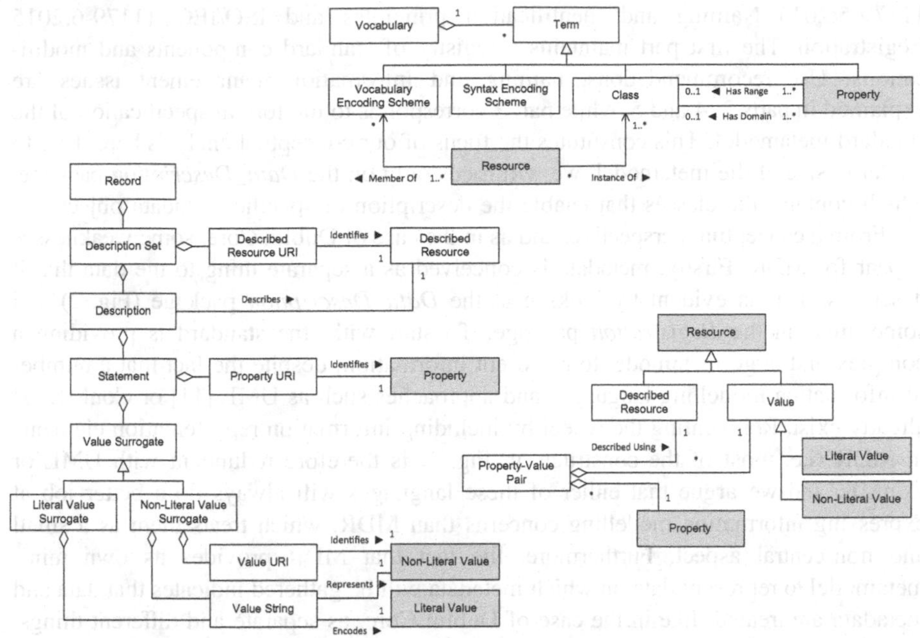

Fig. 1. Overall structure of the DCMI metamodel, including the three class families defined in the standard. Classes highlighted in grey work as connectors between the families.

Secondly, the DCMI metamodel incorporates implementation-level constructs, such as URI-related classes, together with highly abstract ones, such as *Resource* or *Description*. This is exemplified by the definition of the *Literal Value* class: "A value which uses the Unicode string as a lexical form, together with an optional language tag or datatype, to denote a resource (i.e. "literal" as defined by RDF)" [21]. Making the definition of a conceptual-level class depend on specific implementation choices such as Unicode or RDF clearly contravenes the layering and separation of concerns principles in software engineering.

2.2 ISO/IEC 11179 (Metadata Registry)

ISO/IEC 11179 Metadata Registry (MDR hereafter) is an international standard developed between 2005 and 2015 [10]. It aims at the representation of metadata structures in organisations as well as their exchange and integration in heterogeneous environments. As with Dublin Core, it is a general-purpose standard with applications in a range of disciplines. The metamodel of the standard is defined in UML as in the previous case. Good examples of ISO/IEC 11179 applications exist in e-government (including national health systems, legal or quality of service) or smart cities (including urban transport systems) [1].

The MDR metamodel is defined in six parts: ISO/IEC 11179-1:2015 Framework, ISO/IEC 11179-2:2005 Classification, ISO/IEC 11179-3:2013 Registry metamodel and basic attributes, ISO/IEC 11179-4:2004 Formulation of data definitions, ISO/IEC

11179-5:2015 Naming and identification principles and ISO/IEC 11179-6:2015 Registration. The first part maintains a registry of standard components and modifications. Use recommendations, naming and information management issues are explained in parts 2, 4 and 5, while part 3 corresponds to the formal specification of the standard metamodel. This constitutes the focus of our conceptual analysis here. Due to the large size of the metamodel, we will focus only on the *Data_Description* package, which contains the classes that enable the description of specific metadata objects.

From a conceptual perspective, and as in the case of Dublin Core, some weaknesses appear for MDR. Firstly, metadata is conceived as a separate thing to the data that it describes. This is evident by looking at the *Data_Description* package (Fig. 2) and some areas in the *Registration* package. To start with, the standard is providing a complex and large metamodel to represent information, despite the fact that a number of information modelling languages and approaches such as UML [11] or ConML [7] already exist. Reinventing the wheel by including information representation elements in MDR (i.e. most of the constructs in Fig. 2) is therefore redundant with UML or ConML, and we argue that either of these languages will always do a better job at expressing information modelling concerns than MDR, which treats them as a small and non-central aspect. Furthermore, the fact that MDR provides its own mini-metamodel to represent data on which metadata will be gathered indicates that data and metadata are treated, like in the case of Dublin Core, as separate and different things.

In summary, Dublin Core and MDR are very different metadata approaches, but they suffer from very similar problems. In the following section, we elaborate on these problems and describe the design principles for a better approach to metadata (or metainformation) management.

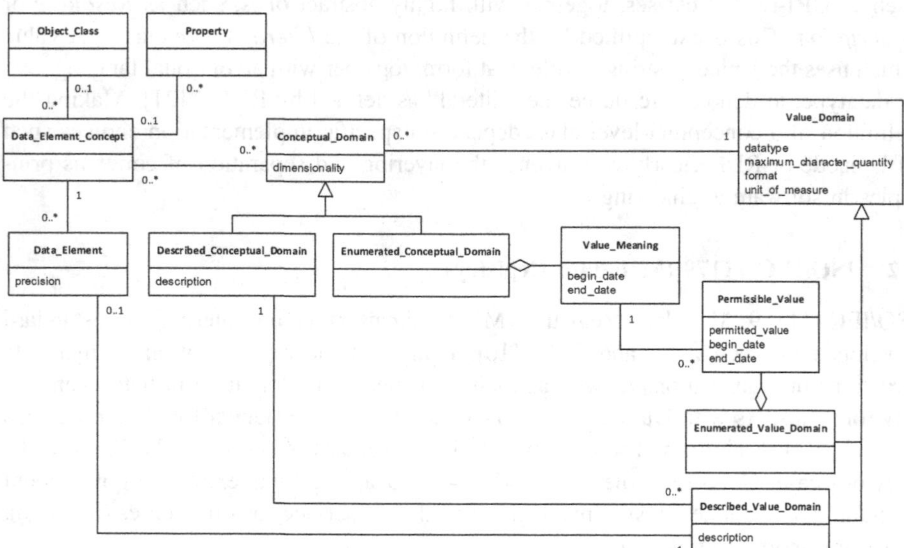

Fig. 2. Excerpt of the metamodel of the *Data_Description* package in MDR.

3 Metadata as a Conceptual Problem

The two metadata standards described in the previous section exemplify the major issues discussed in the introduction, and which are shared by the vast majority of the 28 reviewed approaches. In this section, we confront the evidence obtained from this analysis with the theoretical principles sketched in the *Introduction*, and which are elaborated here. First of all, there is a significant terminological and scope problem. For example, and as we discussed in the previous section, Dublin Core considers metadata to be the description of resources, where resources are physical entities in the world; but if this is metadata, what is plain data? In addition, the 28 reviewed approaches constitute very different kinds of artefacts, ranging from genuine metadata schemata to data modelling languages to process recommendations. To clarify this confusion, we suggest the following terminology and associated scopes (Fig. 3):

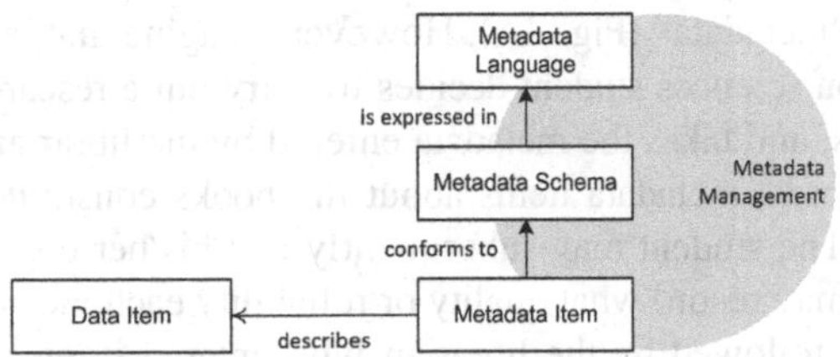

Fig. 3. Major concepts and relationships related to metadata.

- A **data item** is anything stored in a computer system, and which describes some entity in the world.
- A **metadata item** is a data item that describes a data item.
- A **metadata schema** is a specification of the structure that metadata items about a particular data item must follow. In this manner, every metadata item conforms to a metadata schema.
- A **metadata language** is a formal language that allows us to construct metadata schemata. In this manner, every metadata schema is expressed in a particular metadata language.
- **Metadata management** is the process of using metadata languages to construct metadata schemata and/or to define metadata items conforming to the latter.

According to this conceptualisation, the DCMI described in the previous section (Fig. 1) is a metadata language, although the original Dublin Core 15 information descriptors constitute a metadata schema. Similarly, the *Data_Description* package in MDR (Fig. 2) constitutes a metadata language, whereas most of its *Registration* package constitutes a specification of a metadata management approach. Of the 28 reviewed approaches in the previous section, most of them constitute metadata schemata and metadata languages.

It is worth noting that the conceptualisation proposed above is very permissible as to what may constitute a data item. In this regard, data items may correspond to M0 data (using OMG's parlance) such as objects or records in a database, but also to M1 data such as data structures, classes or other type-level specifications. Actually, data items may correspond to data at any M level. This makes sense as any kind of data maybe susceptible to being documented and described.

In addition, the relationship between the definitions of data item and metadata item has the consequence that every metadata item is also a data item. In other words, *MetaDataItem* may be seen as a subtype of *DataItem*. This fits the logic described in previous sections that metadata is not essentially different to (plain) data, but a particular kind of it. What's more, we argue that metadata is not even a subtype of data, but a role that data may take in certain situations. Consider the following scenario. A team of librarians catalogue a number of books in a computer system. The data that they enter constitutes plain data, since it describes entities in the physical world, the books. The librarians also record some metadata, such as who entered each book record, when it was done, and whether data was obtained by looking at the physical book or from a pre-existing catalogue. All these data items describe the book data, and hence we call them "metadata" (Fig. 4A). However, imagine that, at some point in the future, an information sciences student decides to carry out a research project on book cataloguing practices, and takes the metadata entered by the librarians as his/her object of study. In other words, metadata items about the books constitute the research project's primary data. The student may subsequently add his/her own metadata about it; for example, he/she may record what quality or reliability each metadata item has, what kind of process was followed by the librarian who entered it, etc. These are, in fact, meta-metadata items in relation to the original book data (Fig. 4B). In other words, the "meta-" prefix is relative, and we can easily conceive chains of meta-relationships between data items of arbitrary length.

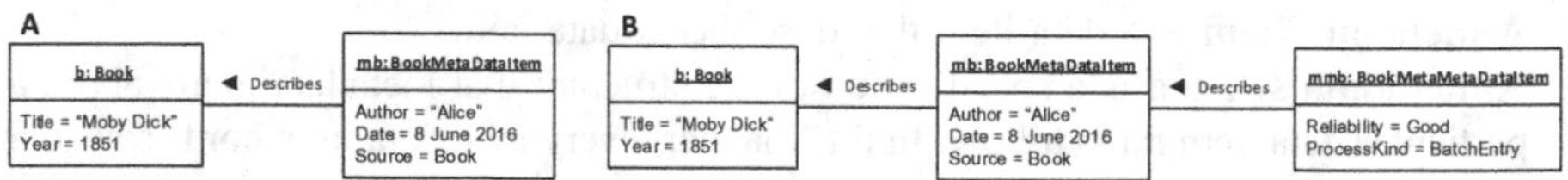

Fig. 4. Metadata and meta-metadata items. In A, *mb* constitutes metadata about *b*. In B, a third data item, *mmb*, is added, which constitutes metadata about *mb*.

In Fig. 4B, object *mb* is both plain data and metadata, depending on how we look at it. For the librarians, it is metadata about their book data; for the research student, it is data being described by further metadata. Hence our argument that metadata is not a base type (in terms of [5]), but a role. In terms of Fig. 3, this means that all the "meta" concepts in the figure can be seen as roles that their "plain data" counterparts may play. For example, we argue that a metadata schema is not essentially different from a plain data schema, but just a data schema for which the conforming data plays the role of metadata in some scenarios. Similarly, a metadata language is just a data language for which the resulting schemata happen to be used for metadata. We must conclude, then, that having a "meta" stack like in Fig. 3 does not make much sense and that, as hinted at from the beginning of this paper, *metadata is just a particular role that data may play in specific scenarios*.

According to this, we state the following design principles for a better metadata management approach:

1. Since metadata is not essentially different from data, specifically-designed complete metadata languages are not necessary. Regular data languages should suffice, perhaps complemented by some specific mechanisms to capture the "describes" relationship in Fig. 3.
2. Since data items in Fig. 3 may exist at any M level, metadata should be applicable to all of them. In particular, metadata should be applicable to any data regardless of whether it is a type (M1) or an instance (M0).
3. Since metadata is a role that data plays in some scenarios, the context of data must be taken into account. For this reason, we prefer to raise the level of abstraction and discuss "describes" relationships in terms of information rather than data.
4. Since the "describes" relationship captures a conceptual link between a piece of information and another piece of information describing the latter, we claim that implementation issues on how to encode, store, transmit or process this information should be treated as a separate concern and excluded from a metainformation management approach. In addition, and since metadata is just data, the usual encoding, storage, transmission and processing mechanisms that are used for data should be applicable to metadata as well.

Based on these design principles, we developed the metainformation features of ConML, which constitute our proposal, as described in the next section.

4 Proposed Solution

ConML [3, 7] is a conceptual modelling language especially designed to be affordable to non-specialists in information technologies, free from implementation details, and supportive of "soft" aspects such as temporality, vagueness and subjectivity, which are very relevant to the humanities [4]. Superficially, ConML resembles other well-known object-oriented modelling languages such as UML [11], having as major modelling primitives those of *Class*, *Attribute*, *Association* and *Object*. ConML is capable of capturing information in any domain at a conceptual level, very much as UML does for software and systems specifications. A comprehensive description of ConML is out of the scope of this paper.

The proposal here described builds on top of ConML by adding the minimum set of language features so that the modelling of metainformation is fully supported according to the design principles described in the previous section. Only one extra association is required in the metamodel to implement metainformation (Fig. 5).

As shown in Fig. 5, a *Describes* association has been added from *Object* to *Model Element*. This association captures the fact that, in ConML, an object may describe a number of model elements, whether they are types or instances. Adding this association has two interesting consequences. Firstly, it "reuses" a class in the metamodel (namely, *Object*) to implement metadata items. In other words, metadata items (as per Fig. 3) are objects in ConML, very much like (plain) data items. This satisfies principle number 1 in the previous section, i.e. that metadata is not essentially different from data.

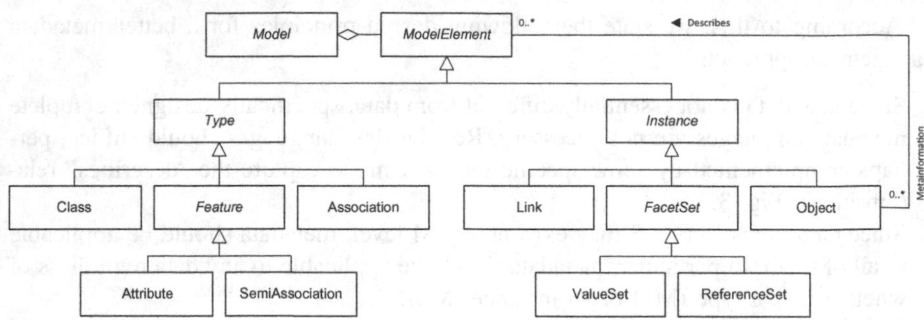

Fig. 5. ConML metamodel augmented with the *Describes* association to implement metainformation.

Secondly, it allows for chained metadata relationships (as shown in Fig. 4B), because the model element described by an object can be another object which, in turn, describes another one, and so on and so forth. Principle 2 is also satisfied, since the target of the *Describes* association, *ModelElement,* is a very abstract class from which both types and instances specialise. This means that objects acting as metainformation may be applied to anything in a model regardless of its M level, including other objects, particular values, classes, attributes, associations, etc.

In addition, design principles 3 and 4 in the previous section are also satisfied. Principle 3 is fulfilled since the *Describes* association happens between high-level, conceptual model elements (such as objects and other instances of *ModelElement*) rather than individual data atoms. This allows for a better contextualisation of the data being described as well as the metadata itself as compared to other approaches less conceptual and more implementation-oriented. Also in this regard, principle 4 is satisfied since no extra constructs are introduced in the language to describe how metainformation is encoded, stored, transmitted or processed. Since metainformation in our proposal is composed of instances of *Object*, it is open to being treated as any other collection of objects, and stored in databases, encoded as XML, or processed in any meaningful manner. Our metainformation proposal does not limit this.

It is also important to note that, in this proposal, metainformation objects may be embedded in the same model being described, or exist as part of a different model. The extension mechanisms of ConML [7, Sect. 5.9] allow for a model to refer to model elements in another model. Although metainformation objects can exist in the same metamodel being described, using a separate model results in better modularity.

So far, we have been using regular link notation to depict instances of the *Describes* association (e.g. in Fig. 4). However, we must realise that *Describes* in the ConML metamodel (Fig. 5) is not the same as a link. In fact, a link between objects captures the fact that the entities represented by the connected objects are linked, whereas *Describes* captures the fact that the connected model elements themselves, rather than the represented entities, are connected (Fig. 6).

In Fig. 6A, the *Wrote* link means that the person represented by object *p* wrote the book represented by object *b*. In Fig. 6B, however, *Describes* means that the object *mr* itself describes the object *b* itself. In other words, links happen between entities in the

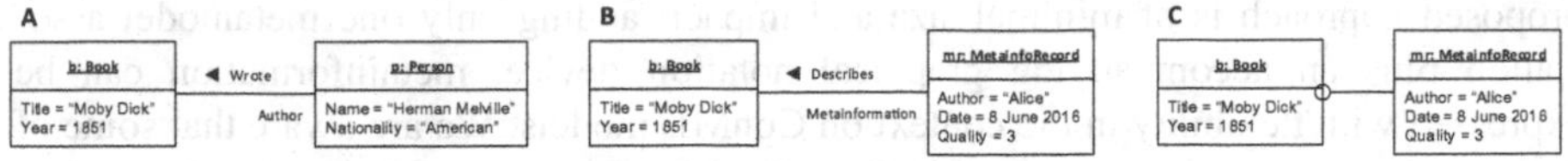

Fig. 6. Semantics of links and *Describes* relationships. In A, a link is shown. In B, a *Describes* relationship is shown using link notation. In C, the same *Describes* relationship is shown, but using special notation.

world and are represented in a model through the associated formal constructs, whereas metainformation *Describes* relationships happen between model elements themselves, without a counterpart that is external to the model. To highlight this difference, we propose that a special graphical device is used to depict *Describes* relationships. In Fig. 6C, the same *Describes* relationship is shown, but using a line connecting the involved model elements, plus a small circle overlapping the target one. This circle can be read as "applies to". Hence, Fig. 6C can be read as "the *mr* metainformation record applies to object *b*".

We said earlier in this section that *Describes* relationships connect metainformation objects to the model elements that are being described. These model elements may be objects, but also of many other types (see Fig. 5). Thus, the notation just described can be easily employed in a variety of situations involving not only objects as targets, but also classes, values or elements of other kinds. Figure 7 shows some examples. Metainformation object *mr1* in Fig. 7 applies to the *Book* class, metainformation object *mr2* applies to the *b* object, and metainformation object *mr3* applies to the *Year = 1851* value. Note how the latter is displayed with the small circle next to the attribute value, rather than intersecting the object box border.

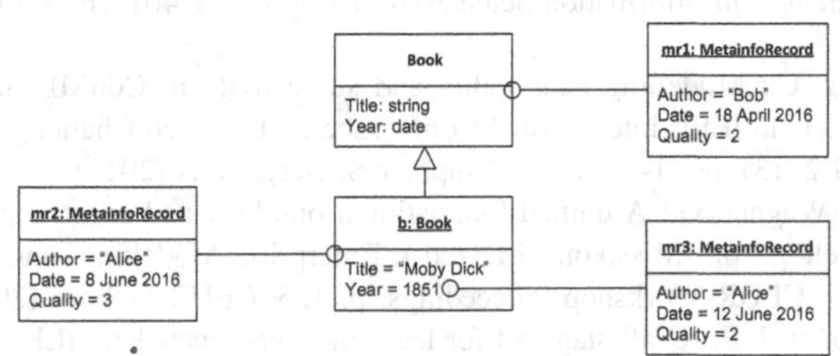

Fig. 7. Metainformation being applied to a class (*mr1*), an object (*mr2*) and a value (*mr3*).

5 Discussion and Conclusions

The proposed solution in the previous section provides several advantages to existing metadata/metainformation approaches. First of all, it satisfies the design principles described in Sect. 3 and, by doing so, avoids the abundant terminological issues in other approaches, allows for uniform treatment of information and metainformation, permits arbitrary-length chains of metainformation levels, allows the description of information elements of any kind, and avoids implementation issues. In addition, the proposed approach is of minimal size and impact: adding only one metamodel association plus an accompanying graphical notation device, metainformation can be expressed with flexibility in the context on ConML models. We are aware that some of the metadata approaches reviewed in Sect. 2 address very specific needs of metadata modelling, such as constrained domain data in DCMI. However, these needs arguably pertain to overall data/information modelling rather than to the specific case of metadata/metainformation. For example, one could argue that DCMI is superior to the approach presented here because it supports constrained domain data and ConML doesn't. However, we argue that, if metadata modelling really needs constrained domain specifications, then this feature is likely to be necessary for data modelling in general and not only for metadata modelling. Augmenting ConML with this feature (or any other) would automatically make it available for use in (plain) data as well as metadata modelling.

We conclude that a simple, unified and implementation-independent approach to metadata/metainformation management, like the one proposed here, is superior to the plethora of options currently existent which, in addition, segregate metadata from other data and pollute its conceptual modelling with implementation noise.

References

1. Bargmeyer, B.E., Gillman, D.W.: Metadata standards and metadata registries: an overview. In: International Conference on Establishment Surveys II, Buffalo, New York (2000)
2. DCC, 004-2017: Digital Curation Centre, University of Edinburgh. http://www.dcc.ac.uk/resources/metadata-standards/list
3. Gonzalez-Perez, C.: A conceptual modelling language for the humanities and social sciences. In: Rolland, C., Castro, J., Pastor, O. (eds.) 2012 6th International Conference on Research Challenges in Information Science (RCIS), pp. 396–401. IEEE Computer Society (2012)
4. Gonzalez-Perez, C.: Modelling temporality and subjectivity in ConML. In: Wieringa, R., Nurcan, S. (eds.) 7th IEEE International Conference on Research Challenges in Information Science (RCIS 2013), pp. 1–6. IEEE Computer Society, Paris (2013)
5. Guizzardi, G., Wagner, G.: A unified foundational ontology and some applications of it in business modeling. In: Missikoff, M. (ed.) Enterprise Modelling and Ontologies for Interoperability, CEUR Workshop Proceedings, p. 125. CEUR-WS.org (2004)
6. Hodgins, W., Duval, E.: Draft standard for learning object metadata. IEEE 1484.12.1-2002 (2002). https://biblio.educa.ch/sites/default/files/20130328/lom_1484_12_1_v1_final_draft_0.pdf
7. Incipit: ConML Technical Specification. Incipit, CSIC (2016). http://www.conml.org/Resources_TechSpec.aspx
8. ISO: ISO 21127:2006 Information and Documentation – A Reference Ontology for the Interchange of Cultural Heritage Information (2006). https://www.iso.org/standard/34424.html
9. ISO: ISO 19115-1:2014 Geographic information – Metadata (2014). https://www.iso.org/standard/53798.html
10. ISO: ISO/IEC 11179, Information Technology – Metadata Registries (MDR) (2015). http://metadata-standards.org/11179/

11. ISO/IEC: Information Technology – Object Management Group Unified Modeling Language (OMG UML) Part 1: Infrastructure. ISO/IEC 19505-1:2012 (2012)
12. Liskov, B., Wing, J.M.: A behavioral notion of subtyping. ACM Trans. Program. Lang. Syst. **16**(6), 1811–1841 (1994)
13. Digital Publications LLC: Glossary of Software Engineering Terms (2005). http://www.shellmethod.com/refs/seglossary.pdf
14. Macêdo, D.J., Shintaku, M., De Brito, R.F.: Dublin core usage for describing documents in Brazilian government digital libraries. In: International Conference on Dublin Core And Metadata Applications, pp. 129–135 (2015)
15. Malta, M.C., Baptista, A.A., Parente, C.: A DCAP for the social and solidarity economy. In: 2015 Proceedings of International Conference on Dublin Core and Metadata Applications, DCMI, pp. 20–29 (2015)
16. Mendez, E., Van Hooland, S.: Metadata typology and metadata uses. In: Handbook of Metadata, Semantics and Ontologies, vol. 1 (2013)
17. Mougenot, I., Desconnets, J.-C., Chahdi, H.: A DCAP to promote easy-to-use data for multiresolution and multitemporal satellite imagery analysis. In: International Conference on Dublin Core and Metadata Applications, pp. 10–19 (2015)
18. NISO: Understanding metadata. National Information Standards, p. 20 (2004)
19. Olsen, L.: Directory Interchange Format (DIF): writer's guide
20. Park, J.-R., Childress, E.: Dublin core metadata semantics: an analysis of the perspectives of information professionals. J. Inf. Sci. **35**(6), 727–739 (2009)
21. Powell, A., Nilsson, M., Naeve, A., Johnston, P.: DCMI Abstract Model (2007)
22. Radatz, J., Geraci, A., Katki, F.: IEEE standard glossary of software engineering terminology. IEEE Std. **610121990**(121990), 3 (1990)
23. RDA: RDA Metadata Directory (2017). http://rd-alliance.github.io/metadata-directory/standards/
24. RDA: Research Data Alliance (2017). https://www.rd-alliance.org/
25. Riley, J.: Glossary of Metadata Standards. Indiana University Libraries (2010)
26. Robertson, W.D., Leadem, E.M., Dube, J., Greenberg, J.: Design and implementation of the national institute of environmental health sciences Dublin core metadata schema. In: International Conference on Dublin Core and Metadata Applications, pp. 193–199 (2001)
27. Salvetti, O., Pieri, G., Di Bono, M.: WP9: a review of data and metadata standards and techniques for representation of multimedia content. MUSCLE. Network of Excellence FP6-5077-52 (2004)
28. Sicilia, M.-A.: Handbook of Metadata, Semantics and Ontologies. World Scientific, Singapore (2013)
29. Taylor, C.F., Field, D., Sansone, S.-A., Aerts, J., Apweiler, R., Ashburner, M., Ball, C.A., Binz, P.-A., Bogue, M., Booth, T.: Promoting coherent minimum reporting guidelines for biological and biomedical investigations: the MIBBI project. Nat. Biotechnol. **26**(8), 889–896 (2008)
30. Tort, A., Olivé, A.: A computer-guided approach to website Schema.org design. In: Yu, E., Dobbie, G., Jarke, M., Purao, S. (eds.) ER 2014. LNCS, vol. 8824, pp. 28–42. Springer, Cham (2014). doi:10.1007/978-3-319-12206-9_3

Schema Evolution and Foreign Keys: Birth, Eviction, Change and Absence

Panos Vassiliadis[1(✉)], Michail-Romanos Kolozoff[2], Maria Zerva[1], and Apostolos V. Zarras[1(✉)]

[1] Department of Computer Science and Engineering, University of Ioannina, Ioannina, Greece
{pvassil,mzerva,zarras}@cs.uoi.gr

[2] Upcom, Athens, Greece
libathos@hotmail.com

Abstract. In this paper, we focus on the study of the evolution of foreign keys in the broader context of schema evolution for relational databases. Specifically, we study the schema histories of a six free, open-source databases that contained foreign keys. Our findings concerning the growth of tables verify previous results that schemata grow in the long run in terms of tables. Moreover, we have come to several surprising, new findings in terms of foreign keys. Foreign keys appear to be fairly scarce in the projects that we have studied and they do not necessarily grow in sync with table growth. In fact, we have observed different cultures for the handling of foreign keys, ranging from treating foreign keys as an indispensable part of the schema, in full sync with the growth of tables, to the unexpected extreme of treating foreign keys as an optional add-on that twice resulted in their full removal from the schema of the database.

Keywords: Schema evolution · Patterns of change · Foreign keys

1 Introduction

Software evolution is an inherent part of the lifecycle of software, and schemata, carrying the architecture of a relational database are no exception to the general pattern. *Schema evolution* is necessary for schemata to align the information capacity of a database with user requirements, albeit with a cost: as the schema changes, the surrounding applications are affected both syntactically and semantically. Understanding the fundamental mechanisms and patterns behind schema evolution is of great significance as it can allow us to see problems on how databases are used, predict the change of tables in the future and adapt application development, maintenance and resource management to the forthcoming trends. Foreign keys are mechanisms that constrain data entry in relational tables, imposing that the domain of the contents of a table's attribute

M.-R. Kolozoff—Work done while in the Univ. Ioannina.

H.C. Mayr et al. (Eds.): ER 2017, LNCS 10650, pp. 106–119, 2017.
https://doi.org/10.1007/978-3-319-69904-2_9

is a subset of the contents of an attribute of another, lookup, table. Thus, foreign keys, being integrity constraints for the data of a database, are part of the schema of the database, and as such, they are unavoidably amenable to change, too. The main driver of our research is to answer the question: *how do foreign keys evolve over time?*

To the best of our knowledge, until the present paper, the question was without any answer. There are several works on the study of schema evolution [1–6, 10], which mostly focus on the macroscopic study of how the schema size grows in terms of its tables and how the surrounding code of an application relates to the underlying database (see Sect. 2). Yet, despite the importance of foreign keys as an integrity constraint that guarantees consistency among the values of different tables, the study of their evolution is a topic that –to the best of our knowledge– has never been studied in the literature before.

In this paper, we study schema evolution by placing the focus on foreign keys, rather than tables. We have collected the schema histories of a six free open-source databases that contained foreign keys, and processed them to discover the changes that occurred between subsequent releases (see Sect. 3). These data sets were *the only ones containing foreign keys*, out of a larger collection of schema histories of Free Open Source Software (FOSS) projects from different domains with adequately long stories and schema sizes. Subsequently, we studied the characteristics of foreign key evolution. Our findings, detailed in Sect. 4, include both expected and unexpected phenomena. Schemata grow over time in terms of tables. Growth is smooth and slow, with several periods of calmness. This is a well-known result from the existing literature that is also verified by our study too. Foreign keys do not necessarily grow in synch with table growth. In fact, we have observed different "cultures" for the handling of foreign keys. In two cases concerning scientific databases (Atlas, Biosql), foreign keys are an integral part of the schema, span a vast percentage of tables and co-evolve with them. In two other cases, also of scientific nature (Egee and Castor), only a subset of tables were involved in foreign key relationships and their evolution is biased: Egee (with a very small schema size) has a strong correlation of table and foreign key evolution, whereas Castor (with a small percentage of tables being involved in foreign keys) has mixed behavior throughout its history. Unexpected results came from the data sets of Content Management System (CMS) nature, SlashCode and Zabbix, where foreign keys involved only a small minority of tables. To our big surprise, foreign keys in these projects, after a period of growth, are *completely removed* from the schema with (a) a steep removal in the first case, and, (b) a slow but constant removal rate in the latter. We make a detailed discussion on the absence and extinction of foreign keys in specific environments in Sect. 5. Our data indicate that, with the exception of few environments with a strict adherence to the dictations of relational theory, foreign keys are scarce and occasionally unwanted.

All our data sets and software are openly available to the research community at our group's site at Github (https://github.com/DAINTINESS-Group).

2 Related Work

The related work on schema evolution is not abundant and, in effect, quite recent. Prior to the proliferation of Free Open Source Software (FOSS), researchers were unable to get access to the histories of schemata that they could study. To our knowledge, the only early study that exists is [5], which reports on the growth and change breakdown of the schema of a health system. Late '00s signaled the slow appearance of a set of works [1–4, 10] that continued down this road. A consistent finding in all these works is the slow expansion of the size of the schema in terms of tables, albeit with reports of a decreasing growth rate [4]. Frequently, the surrounding application is not in sync with the underlying schema (which, as a side note, signifies the importance of understanding the mechanics of schema evolution) [3, 10]. In line with these works, in [6, 7], we have assessed whether Lehman's laws of evolution apply to the case of schema evolution, and confirmed the growth of schemata over time, via the alternation of periods of concentrated modifications (mostly table insertions and occasionally including table removals) and periods of calmness with slow, or even zero growth. In [8, 9], we report on patterns of how properties of individual tables (rather than of the schema) like duration, number of attributes, or, version of birth relate to the survival or update profile of a table.

In all previous attempts, the object of study was the schema size as well as the heartbeat of change, and only lately, tables. To the best of our knowledge, the current paper is the first comprehensive effort in the literature to study the evolution of foreign keys.

3 Experimental Setup

In this section, we begin with fundamental concepts for our study. Then, we introduce the datasets that we have collected and processed using *Parmenidian Truth*[1], an open source tool we created for the purpose of this study.

3.1 Fundamentals

We treat a relational database schema as a set of relations, along with their foreign key constraints. A relation is characterized by a *name*, *a set of attributes* and *a primary key*. A *foreign key constraint*, is a pair between a set of attributes $\mathcal{S}$ in a relation, R_S, called the source of the foreign key, and a set of attributes $\mathcal{T}$ in a relation R_T, called the target of the foreign key. The foreign key constraint requires a 1:1 mapping between $\mathcal{S}$ and $\mathcal{T}$. As usual, at the extensional level, the semantics of the foreign key denote a subset relation between the instances of the source and the instances of the target attributes.

We model a database schema as a directed graph $G(V, E)$, with relations as nodes and foreign keys as directed edges, originating from their source and

[1] https://github.com/DAINTINESS-Group/ParmenidianTruth.

targeted to their target. Both nodes and edges are annotated with the respective information mentioned in the previous paragraph. If two relations have more than one foreign key with the same direction, the single edge that connects them is annotated with all the foreign key pairs involved. The *Diachronic Graph* of the history of a schema is the union of all the nodes and edges that ever appeared in the history of the schema.

The evolution history, $H = \{v^1, \ldots, v^n\}$, of a database schema can be thought of as (a) a sequence of versions, but also as (b) a sequence of revisions. Unless otherwise specified, we will treat the term history under the semantics of the former of the two representations. Each *version* of the schema v^i is a graph $G^i(V^i, E^i)$. A *transition* between two subsequent versions of the history includes a set of changes, involving (a) additions and deletions of relations and foreign keys, and, (b) relation updates in the form of changes of primary keys, modifications of attribute data types, and, attribute additions or deletions.

3.2 Datasets

The main characteristics of the six data sets that we considered in our study are given in Fig. 1. We classify the data sets in three categories as follows.

Dataset	Versions	Lifetime	Tables @Start	Tables @End	Tables @ Diach.	Table Growth	FKs@ Start	FKs@ End	FKs @ Diach.	FK Growth
Atlas	85	2 Y, 7 M	56	73	88	30%	61	63	88	0.03%
BioSQL	47	6 Y, 7 M	21	28	45	33%	17	43	79	153%
Egge	17	4Y	6	10	12	67%	3	4	6	33%
Castor	194	3Y	62	74	91	20%	6	10	13	67%
SlashCode	399	12 Y, 6 M	42	87	126	108%	0	0	47	0%
Zabbix	160	10 Y, 10 M	15	48	58	220%	10	2	38	-80%

Fig. 1. The main characteristics of the data sets.

Scientific Applications. *Atlas* is a particle physics experiment at the Large Hadron Collider at CERN, the European Organization for Nuclear Research based on Geneva, Switzerland. Atlas is notably known for its attempt to find the Higgs boson, although its scientific aims are much broader. Trigger is one of the software modules used in the Atlas project and it is responsible of filtering the very large amounts of data collected by the Collider and storing them in its database. *Biosql* is a generic relational schema that provides unified access to data from various sources, such as GenBank or Swissport that store genomic data like sequences, features, for the BioPerl, BioPython, BioJava, and BioRuby open source toolkits.

Computational Resource Toolkits. *Egee* is a data set from the homonymous EU funded project, whose goal is to provide access to computational grids. Egee is the smallest data set, frequently serving as a testbed, with a small number of releases and a small schema size. *Castor* is a hierarchical storage management (HSM) system developed at CERN, to store physics production files and user files, via command-line tools and APIs.

Content Management Systems. *SlashCode*, a software framework for web sites development; it is widely known for supporting the Slashdot website. *Zabbix* is an open source distributed monitoring solution that can be used for the monitoring of networks, servers and virtual machines. We have used the PostgreSQL version of the schema that includes foreign keys.

3.3 Data Processing

Based on our tool, *Parmenidian Truth*, we have parsed, internally represented, visualized and measured the evolution of the studied schemata. Given the history of a database, expressed as a sequence of data definition files, and consequently, a sequence of differences between subsequent versions, our tool visualizes each version of the database schema as a graph, with tables as nodes and foreign keys

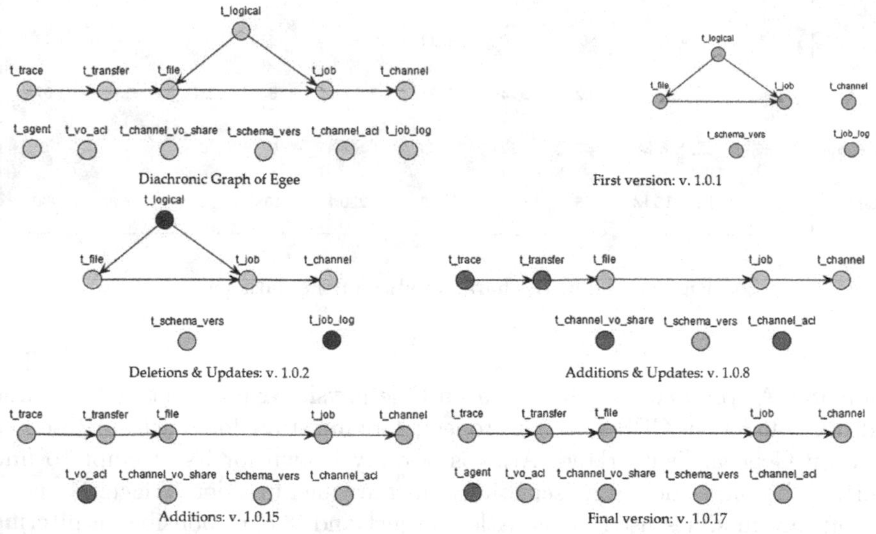

Fig. 2. The story of Egee and its diachronic graph.

as edges and produces a PowerPoint presentation, with one slide per version (appropriately annotated with color to highlight the tables affected by change). Along with the appropriate visualization provisions, the result is practically a movie on how the schema of the database has evolved. Then, the tool was also extended with measurement collection capabilities. Thus, all our measurements are also produced by the very same tool.

As an example, the evolution history of the Egee dataset is presented in Fig. 2. The first graph represents Egee's diachronic graph. The following graphs represent versions with deletions and additions that shaped the diachronic graph. In terms of coloring, our tool uses red for deleted nodes, green for added nodes, and yellow for nodes with internal updates (e.g., attribute additions, deletions or data type changes).

4 Growth and Heartbeat of Foreign Key Evolution

4.1 Total Number of Tables and Foreign Keys

In this section we quantitatively assess the evolution of the datasets that we study, with respect to the total number of tables and foreign keys throughout their entire lifetime. Figure 3 depicts the evolution of these two measures.

The different categories of schemata expose very different behaviors with respect to their growth, and especially with respect to the growth in terms of foreign keys. The first group of schemata, involving scientific databases, like Atlas and Biosql expose *growth that has expansion periods, shrinkage actions, and periods of calmness* in terms of both tables and foreign keys. The schema is of moderate size for Atlas (from 56 at start, to 73 tables at end) and of small size for Biosql (starting with 21 and ending with 28 tables), and the growth of nodes and edges is practically in sync.

Concerning the category of computational resource toolkits, Egee is very small in size and history and mostly serves as a demo example. Castor, on the other hand, has a very large percentage of nodes without edges (observe the difference of values in the y-axis). The number of tables grows from 62 to 74 tables (with the occasional removals and periods of calmness), whereas the number of foreign keys is relatively stable (from 6 to 10).

Concerning the case of the two CMS's (SlashCode and Zabbix), both CMS's go through a clear trend of expansion. Slashcode started without foreign keys at all and obtained its first set of foreign keys in version 74. *Both CMS's end up with zero foreign keys*, however! For Slashcode there is a clear phase of progressive removal, whereas for Zabbix, there is an abrupt removal of almost the entire set of foreign keys in a single transition. *The fact that developers can resort in full removal of foreign keys at some point in the lifetime of a schema is a real surprise.* We devote a dedicated discussion on this in the sequel of the paper.

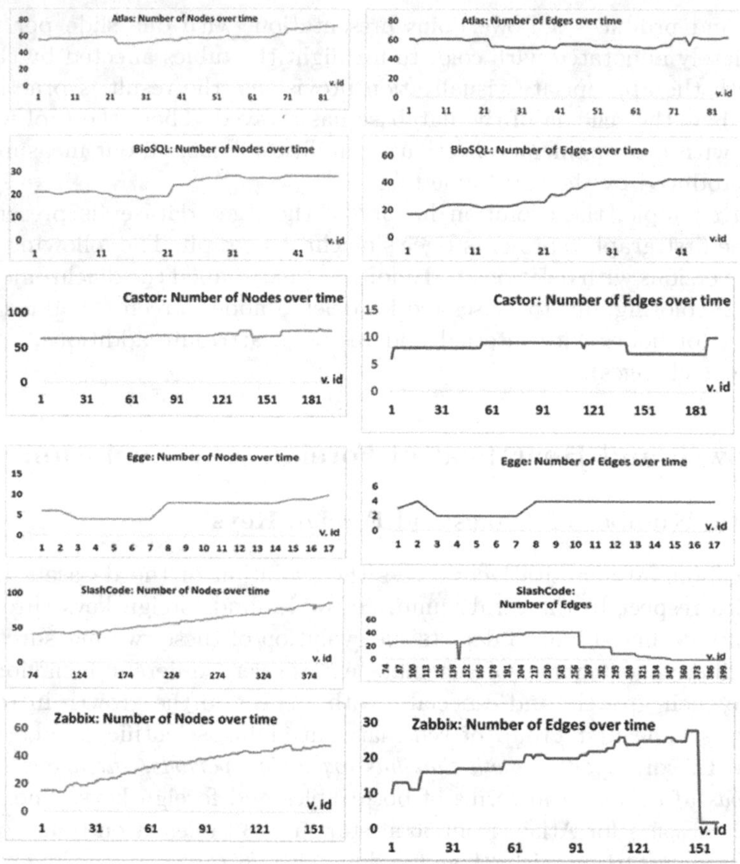

Fig. 3. Number of nodes (tables) and edges (foreign keys) over time (x-axis: version id) for the 6 studied data sets

4.2 Heartbeat of Changes

How Do Foreign Keys Germinate and Die? A first question that we wanted to explore is how does the generation and removal of foreign keys takes place. We have classified births and deaths of foreign keys in four categories. An addition of a foreign key is considered as *born with table*, when either the source or the target table is born along with the foreign key, while an *explicit addition* happens, when a foreign key is added to two existing tables. Respectively, in the case of deletions, a deletion of a foreign key is considered as *died with table*, when either the source or the target table is removed along with the foreign key, while an *explicit deletion* takes place when neither of the source or target tables gets deleted and only the foreign key is removed. In Fig. 4, we present the statistical breakdown of the creation and removal of foreign keys and we can see that different cultures for handling foreign keys exist.

			Atlas	Biosql	Egee	Castor	Slashcode	Zabbix
	Diachronic Graph	TablesDG	88	45	12	91	126	58
		FK'sDG	88	79	6	13	47	38
	Start/End	FKs@start	61	17	3	6	0	10
		FKs@end	65	52	5	10	0	2
#FKs_added ...	... in absolute numbers	Total	41	81	4	8	77	28
		Born w/ table	37	71	3	2	21	24
		Explicit addition	4	10	1	6	56	4
	... as pct	(%)Born w/ table	90%	88%	75%	25%	27%	86%
		(%)Explicit addition	10%	12%	25%	75%	73%	14%
#FKs_removed ...	... in absolute numbers	Total	37	46	2	4	77	36
		Died w/ table	25	42	2	2	16	8
		Explicit deletion	12	4	0	2	61	28
	... as pct	(%)Died w/ table	68%	91%	100%	50%	21%	22%
		(%)Explicit deletion	32%	9%	0%	50%	79%	78%

Fig. 4. Statistical breakdown on the creation and removal of foreign keys

The scientific data sets, Atlas and BioSQL, deal with *foreign keys as a regular part of the schema.* Thus, foreign keys are overwhelmingly born along with tables, and are very rarely added explicitly to existing tables (the latter percentage ranges between 10–12%), while, at the same time, they are mainly removed when one of the involved tables is removed too. Egee, coming from the category of computational resource toolkits behaves similarly.

Castor and Slashcode deal with *foreign keys as an ad-hoc add on.* In these two data sets, a very large part of the schema is without foreign keys (compare the first two data rows of Fig. 4). In Slashcode, foreign keys are introduced in v. 74. In both cases, foreign keys are added to existing tables three times more often than they are created with new tables. The death of foreign keys is also taking part without the removal of the tables: in the very few such occasions in Slashcode, the two removal methods are evenly split, but in Slashcode, explicit removals are 4:1 over removals along with table death. Remember, of course, that Slashcode is a data set were eventually all foreign keys were removed.

Zabbix is a mixture of the above behavior with a sudden *change of style.* It is clear that Zabbix started by dealing with foreign keys as a regular part of the schema: foreign keys were present at the beginning, they were mostly born with the birth of new tables and additions to existing tables were rare. Towards the end of the schema's history, however, between revision 1.150 and 1.151 *all* foreign keys are explicitly commented out and never restored back. This means that an intentional decision of treating foreign keys as a disposable add-on to the schema has been taken.

What are the Characteristics of the Heartbeat of Change of the Foreign Keys? In Fig. 5, (a) the number of foreign keys in each version of the schema history is depicted as a solid line, and, (b) the number of foreign key births and deaths is depicted via the respective bars. The bars belong to the aforementioned four categories of change.

A common theme in all the data sets is the consistent scarcity of foreign key changes (Fig. 6). Apart from the scientific data sets, where the number of foreign

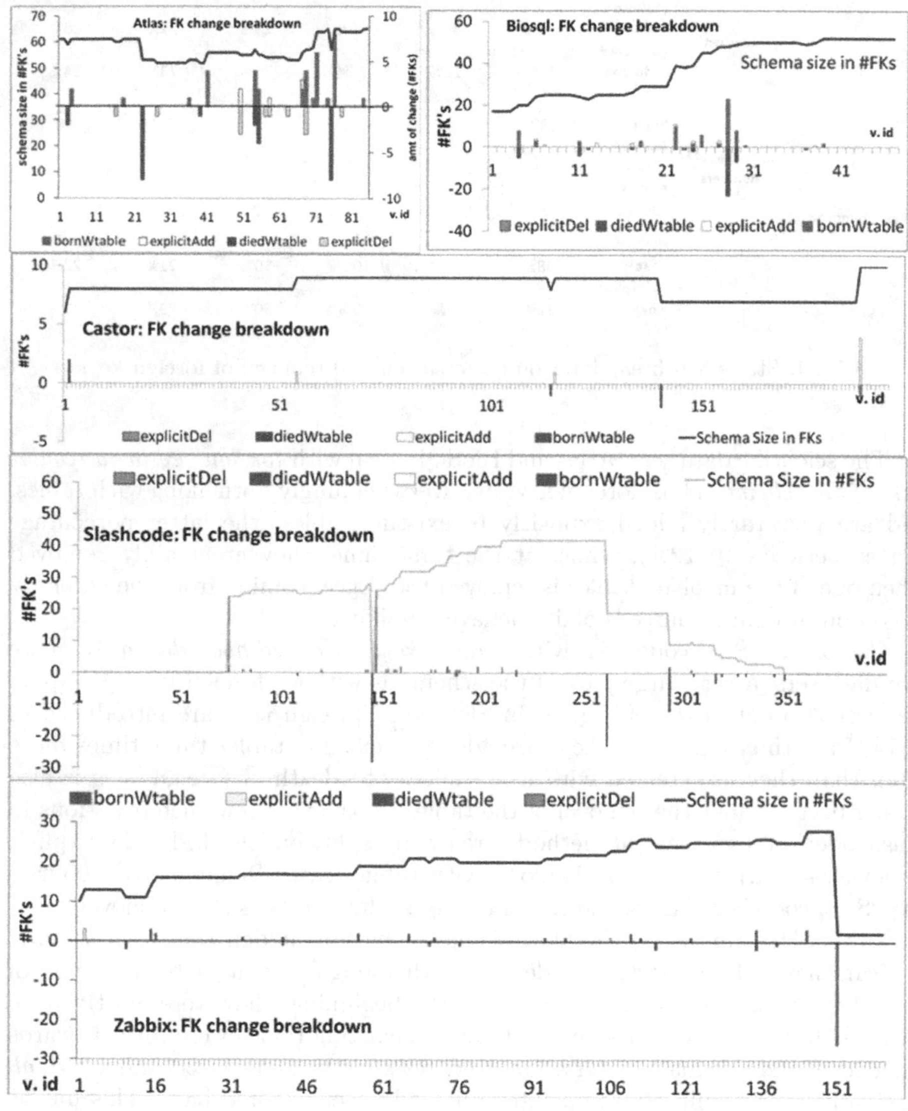

Fig. 5. Heartbeat of foreign key creation and removal

	Total # transitions	Total # transitions with FK change	Pct. of transitions with FK change
Atlas	85	25	29%
BioSQL	46	19	41%
Egee	16	3	19%
Castor	191	6	3%
Slashcode	398	34	9%
Zabbix	159	22	14%

Fig. 6. Percentage of transitions containing schema change of foreign keys

key changes is high, the rest of the datasets demonstrate a small percentage of transitions with foreign key change. As already mentioned, scientific data sets treat foreign keys as an integral part of the schema and table births and deaths come along with the respective changes. Thus the frequency of change is high. In the rest of the datasets, the additions are too few and explicit (see Fig. 4). In the case of Slashcode, if the phase of mass deletions was not part of the history, the activity would be even less.

In terms of time spread, *in most of the data sets, the events are proportionally spread in time.* Atlas is an exception to this pattern. We occasionally see (a) do-undo actions (in Atlas, Slashcode and Castor), where a revision of the schema is undone in the following commit and, (b) restructuring due to table renamings (4 times in Biosql, and twice in Zabbix).

The volume of change is also low: most changes do not exceed one foreign key, with the exceptions of explicit mass additions and deletions, as well as do-undo actions.

5 Where Did the Foreign Keys Go?

5.1 The Strange Case of the Disappearing Foreign Keys

Slashcode and Zabbix are our two CMS's that displayed the phenomenon of eventually losing all their foreign keys. Whereas for Zabbix, all our efforts for retrieving any documented reasons for the removal have been fruitless, Slashcode has an abundance of records on the removals of foreign keys. In the sequel, we report on this story.

In the first occurrence of massive foreign key removals (at version rev_1.120), 22 foreign keys were deleted. This mass removal took place due to a problem with the compatibility of the attribute types that the foreign keys referred to. The Data Definition file contains an explanatory comment for this removal:

> "Commented-out foreign keys are ones which currently cannot be used because they refer to a primary key which is NOT NULL AUTO_INCREMENT and the child's key either has a default value which would be invalid for an aut_increment field, typically NOT NULL DEFAULT '0'. Or, in some cases, the primary key is e.g. VARCHAR(20)

NOT NULL and the child's key will be VARCHAR(20). The possibility of NULLs negates the ability to add a foreign key. ⇐ That's my current theory, but it doesn't explain why discussions.topic SMALLINT UNSIGNED NOT NULL DEFAULT '0' is able to be foreign-keyed to topics.tid SMALLINT UNSIGNED NOT NULL AUTO_INCREMENT"

In the second deletion (at version rev_1.151), 10 foreign keys were removed, because some tables changed their storage engine to InnoDB from MyISAM. There was also an explanatory comment inside the corresponding sql file:

"Stories is now InnoDB and these other tables are still MyISAM, so no foreign keys between them."

The rest of the deletions happened because the foreign keys caused too many problems to the system that could not debugged, resulting in the decision to leave the schema without any foreign keys. We have retrieved several comments for these removals. At version re_1.174, where 3 foreigns keys were deleted the following comment was found:

"This doesn't work, makes createStory die. These don't work, should check why..."

At version's rev_1.189 file the comments mention:

"This doesn't work, since in the install pollquestions is populated before users, alphabetically"

Finally, at version rev_1.201 the following comment was found:

"This doesn't work, since discussion may be 0."

At the end of this process, the schema is left with zero foreign keys. Interestingly enough, the schema also contained no foreign keys at its start. Quite importantly, Slashcode's behavior holds both foreign key additions and deletions mostly happening explicitly (i.e., without the addition or removal of the involved tables). In other words, *it appears that foreign keys are treated as a disposable add-on that was removed when problems occurred.*

What do we make out of these removals? *The main problem seems to be the difficulty that developers had to face with fine details in the tuning and handling of the foreign keys. Practically, it appears that the easiest way out of this kind of problems is to comment out the respective foreign key.* We acknowledge the difficulties that occur e.g., in the case of different storage engines and the performance constraints that can drive such decisions. However, the fact that the removals of foreign keys went on as a regular practice, instead of attempting to fix the problems (some of which can be considered fairly easy fixes, like for example changing the order of table population) simply states that the essence of the contribution of foreign keys in the consistency of the schema does not seem to outweigh the need to quickly get things done.

5.2 Are Foreign Keys Unwelcome in CMS's?

One could easily suggest that the removal of foreign keys from our two CMS's is just a coincidence. Although this can certainly be the case - and we cannot verify the problem unless more studies by independent groups are performed - there is evidence to suggest that the case of CMS's suffers from an "unfriendly" attitude towards foreign keys.

In summer of 2013, we collected twenty data sets to support our work on mining evolution patterns in the history of open-source databases. The term "data set" refers to the history of the schema of a software project, represented as a sequence of files, sorted in terms of their commit timestamp, with the Data Definition Language commands that create the schema of the project's database. We have worked with the main branch of these projects. The collection includes two datasets from the biomedical domain (Ensembl and Biosql), 5 data sets from CERN (Atlas, Egee, DQ2, Castor2 and Dirac) and 13 data sets from the CMS domain (Slashcode, Zabbix, Coppermine, Dekiwiki, E107, Joomla 1.5, Mediawiki, Nucleus, phpBB, phpwiki, Tikiwiki, Typo3, Xoops).

When we turned our attention to the study of foreign keys, we came up with a surprising discovery: only two of the 13 CMSs included foreign keys (!) in contrast to all the biomedical and CERN-oriented data sets that came with foreign key usage. In the latter two families, Atlas, Castor and BioSQL are really useful for analysis. Egee is a smaller data set, in number of tables, foreign keys, and in number of revisions, as already mentioned. DQ2 comes with 55 versions in its mySQL version, out of which only the first 19 contain foreign keys. The data set starts with 2 foreign keys and ends with 1, only to be permanently dropped in the 20th version. DIRAC is quite similar case to Egee, comes with 42 versions over a very small schema, as it starts with 9 tables and 10 foreign keys at first version and ends with 15 tables and 8 foreign keys (less than in the beginning). The only data set that hides a - yet unclear - potential is Ensembl, where we have not yet managed to link the 529 files with table creation statements to the 18 files containing foreign key declarations.

In terms of the CMSs, we believe that the absence of foreign keys in the schema declaration of their database is systematic. Even the two of the 13 CMS's that adopted foreign keys at some point, eventually dropped them. We attribute the phenomenon to the combination of two factors. First, in a CMS environment, the population of the table columns where foreign keys ought to be present, mostly comes from drop-down listboxes with values. This creates the - dangerous, in our opinion - impression to the developers that the data consistency is attainable via the application. Of course, this opinion overlooks the possibility of integrity violation due to the actions of a DBA independently of the surrounding application, as well as the possibility of a bug in the population of the drop-down listboxes. Second, foreign keys impose a time lag in terms of efficiency, which developers decide not to pay, especially if they operate under the aforementioned impression of data consistency.

6 Conclusions

Summary. Our findings can be summarized as follows. For all the studied data sets, *schemata grow in the long run* in terms of tables. The usual pattern of alternation between periods of slow growth, calmness periods, spikes of extension, and occasional cleanups of the schema is present [7]. In some cases, mainly *in projects of scientific nature, foreign keys are treated as an integral part of the system*, and they are born and evicted along with table birth and eviction. At the same time, we have observed cases where *foreign keys are treated as a second-class add-on*. In these cases, there is a small subset of the tables involved in foreign keys, while birth and eviction of foreign keys is rarely performed in synch with the respective table events. In the case of CMS's we have seen *a disinclination towards having foreign keys as part of the schema*. In the data sets that we have collected, the mere existence of foreign keys is too scarce. Moreover, in the case of the two CMS's that had foreign keys in their lifetime, both *ended-up with their complete removal*. To the best of our understanding this removal was chosen due to difficulty of managing technical issues with foreign keys, that discouraged developers from trying to solve the encountered problems. The *heartbeat of foreign key change is mostly rare and small in volume*: changes of foreign keys are not really frequent and they are typically small in volume (with the exception of do-undo pairs of commits and the aforementioned massive removals).

Threats to Validity. The *scope* of our study is restricted to databases that are part of FOSS projects (and not closed ones) that have even moderate amounts of versions published on-line and also pay the price for data consistency via foreign keys. The reader should avoid over-generalizing findings to closed projects, or projects with a strict management plan. The *external validity* of our results is, of course restricted within the scope of the study. Whenever we report an observed pattern, we make clear whether it is ubiquitous in our data sets, or to what subset of the data sets it applies. We have a set of data sets from different domains (occasionally with characteristics that are domain-dependent and which we comment upon) with adequately long stories and schema sizes. Thus, we believe that patterns that appear to be either omni-present or strictly characteristic to a domain can indeed be generalized. In terms of *measurement validity*, we have tested our tools with black box testing and we have fixed any identified problems during their operation. Any processing of the input data is reported above. Although one can never exclude the possibility of occasional errors, we are confident with our results in terms of their measurement validity. We are also very sensitive to the fact that this is the first - to our knowledge - study of its kind, and consequently, it is strictly of exploratory nature. Internal validity concerns are covered by the fact that we restrain ourselves to the retrieved evidence and common knowledge. Still, more targeted experiments are needed to increase our confidence.

Importance of This Work. To the best of our knowledge, this is the first time that the study of the evolution of foreign keys is performed, and, quite importantly, at a large scale, in terms of data sets. Apart from the increase of our understanding of how schemata evolve over time with solid evidence, the study noteworthily reveals unexpected results. Although it is important not to over-generalize our findings outside the area of Free, Open Source Software that defines the scope of the study, we have now significant evidence that, unless specifically curated, foreign keys in a FOSS database can potentially be unwelcome (and thus, rare) or even completely removed by the developers. *This is a clear warning that we, as a community, need to do better (a) in terms of making systems easier at handling foreign keys and their implications, especially at the deep technical details, as well as, (b) in terms of better educating developers on the benefits and necessities behind the usage of foreign keys in their databases.*

Follow Up. Future work can continue in many directions. More studies, preferably by other groups, over other data sets, need to be performed in an attempt to be able to establish common patterns of evolution. The particularities of unusual behaviors concerning foreign keys need to be further investigated too. Mining patterns of graph evolution in the graph of foreign keys is also another path for future work.

References

1. Cleve, A., Gobert, M., Meurice, L., Maes, J., Weber, J.H.: Understanding database schema evolution: a case study. Sci. Comput. Program. **97**, 113–121 (2015)
2. Curino, C., Moon, H.J., Tanca, L., Zaniolo, C.: Schema evolution in Wikipedia: toward a web information system benchmark. In: Proceedings of ICEIS 2008. Citeseer (2008)
3. Lin, D.Y., Neamtiu, I.: Collateral evolution of applications and databases. In: Proceedings of Joint International and Annual ERCIM Workshops on Principles of Software Evolution (IWPSE) and Software Evolution (Evol) Workshops, IWPSE-Evol 2009, pp. 31–40 (2009)
4. Qiu, D., Li, B., Su, Z.: An empirical analysis of the co-evolution of schema and code in database applications. In: Proceedings of 2013 9th Joint Meeting on Foundations of Software Engineering, ESEC/FSE 2013, pp. 125–135 (2013)
5. Sjøberg, D.: Quantifying schema evolution. Inf. Softw. Technol. **35**(1), 35–44 (1993)
6. Skoulis, I., Vassiliadis, P., Zarras, A.: Open-source databases: within, outside, or beyond Lehman's laws of software evolution? In: Proceedings of 26th International Conference on Advanced Information Systems Engineering - CAiSE 2014 (2014)
7. Skoulis, I., Vassiliadis, P., Zarras, A.V.: Growing up with stability: how open-source relational databases evolve. Inf. Syst. **53**, 363–385 (2015)
8. Vassiliadis, P., Zarras, A., Skoulis, I.: Gravitating to rigidity: patterns of schema evolution - and its absence - in the lives of tables. Inf. Syst. **63**, 24–46 (2017)
9. Vassiliadis, P., Zarras, A.V., Skoulis, I.: How is life for a table in an evolving relational schema? Birth, death and everything in between. In: Proceedings of 34th International Conference on Conceptual Modeling (ER 2015), Stockholm, Sweden, 19–22 October 2015, pp. 453–466 (2015)
10. Wu, S., Neamtiu, I.: Schema evolution analysis for embedded databases. In: Proceedings of 2011 IEEE 27th International Conference on Data Engineering Workshops, ICDEW 2011, pp. 151–156 (2011)

Conceptual Modelling of Autonomous Multi-cloud Interaction with Reflective Semantics

Andreea Buga, Sorana Tania Nemeş, and Klaus-Dieter Schewe(✉)

Johannes Kepler University, Linz, Austria
{a.buga,t.nemes}@cdcc.faw.jku.at, kd.schewe@gmail.com

Abstract. Distributed systems that exploit software services from multiple clouds provide opportunities for software systems that address problems associated with systems of systems. In this paper we present an approach for the conceptual modelling of such systems, which is grounded in a distributed middleware that coordinates the client access to multiple clouds through a concept of *mediator*. Furthermore, each component of the middleware constitutes an abstract machine that is realised by three layers: a layer for normal operation, a layer for *monitoring* and detection of critical situations, and an *adaptation* layer, which in case of an identified anomaly changes the normal behaviour. The semantics of this autonomous system can be captured by *linguistic reflection*, for which reflective Abstract State Machines will be exploited.

1 Introduction

Distributed adaptive systems have recently attracted a lot of attention in research as evidenced by several surveys on adaptive systems [15,23]. Such systems consist of several components that interact concurrently and are usually distributed over a network. Components are supposed to enter or leave the collection at any time; they may also be subject to change. In order to provide guarantees for the functioning of the distributed system as a whole the emphasis is therefore on adaptivity that is realised by *monitoring* components that observe the execution of the system, and *adaptation* components that change components in case of anomalies identified by the monitoring [11]. Run-time monitoring has been addressed in various disguises focusing on the network [25], the servers [26] or the workload distribution [9,10], or using specific languages [22]. Likewise adaptation emphasises reliability [9], workload re-allocation [10], run-time optimisation [21], and runtime verification [18].

In this paper we focus on distributed adaptive systems that rely on cloud services. That is, we emphasise that the distributed systems are service-oriented exploiting software services from multiple clouds. The services themselves can

The research reported in this paper has been supported by the Christian-Doppler Society in the frame of the Christian-Doppler Laboratory for Client-Centric Cloud Computing.

H.C. Mayr et al. (Eds.): ER 2017, LNCS 10650, pp. 120–133, 2017.
https://doi.org/10.1007/978-3-319-69904-2_10

be modelled as abstract state service [19] comprising a hidden internal layer and a visible and accessible view layer on top of it. The service model has been specified using Abstract State Machines (ASMs) [4]. The services can be integrated using a mediator model [20], which can be seen as providing general skeletons for the distributed systems that can be instantiated by concrete services that are selected according to a service ontology comprising functional, categorical and SLA-based properties. The concrete interaction of a mediator instance with the service providing clouds is subject of a middleware system that handles the interaction with the clouds [5,7] and even supports the interaction between different systems through the clouds [6]. For the rigorous specification of this middleware an ambient extension of ASMs [3] has been exploited. This allows the complete model to be validated by simulation [13] and verified by model-checking [1]. Based on this work we emphasise the extension of the abstract machine model of the middleware by monitoring and adaptation layers. That is, in normal operation mode a mediator instance will be executed, for which the middleware will be exploited to realise the interaction with the clouds and the integration of the individual services. This execution is then observed by the middleware layer, for which techniques for client-side cloud monitoring will be utilised [16,17].

There are many possibilities for "critical situations" to be detected by the monitoring layer. A service may have become unavailable or may simply not react anymore. A service may still be available, but not performing well. A service may have been updated thereby changing its characteristics. A service may have become erroneous or show Byzantine behaviour. It may also be the case that a better instantiation may have become available. These are the kinds of situations we will pay mostly attention to, though there are many others, in particular in connection with security and privacy. The adaptation layer acts whenever one of these situations has been recognised. The adaptation can simply take the form of a service replacement or a replacement of a set of services, by means of which a new mediator instance will be created [8]. Our approach to adaptation is grounded in linguistic reflection, i.e. the ability of a system to change its own behaviour. For this we exploit concurrent, reflective ASMs, which provably capture all concurrent, evolving systems [24] and integrate the theories of sequential algorithms [14], unbounded parallelism [12], concurrency [2] and reflection.

The remainder of this article is organised as follows. In Sect. 2 we review the mediator model as the basis for multi-cloud interaction. In Sect. 3 we briefly look into the architecture of the middleware. Section 4 is then dedicated to the extensions concerning monitoring and adaptation. We conclude with a brief summary and outlook in Sect. 5.

2 Multi-cloud Interaction

In our conceptual specification we adopt an abstract model of software services as provided by *Abstract State Services* (AS^2) [19]. We assume that each service is provided by a cloud, but we leave open who owns the service. That is, it is possible that a service is provided by a public cloud through a third-party SaaS offer. It is also possible that the service is owned by the client running the application process, in which case it could have been uploaded to a public cloud using a IaaS or PaaS offer or it could even reside on a private server/cloud.

2.1 Abstract State Services

The key characteristic of an AS^2 is its composition of two layers: a data layer and a view layer on top of it, both combining static and dynamic aspects. The data layer consists of a set $\mathcal{S}$ of states, together with a subset $\mathcal{I} \subseteq \mathcal{S}$ of initial states, a wide-step transition relation $\tau \subseteq \mathcal{S} \times \mathcal{S}$, and a set $\mathcal{T}$ of transactions, each of which is associated with a small-step transition relation $\tau_t \subseteq \mathcal{S} \times \mathcal{S}$ $(t \in \mathcal{T})$ satisfying the postulates of a database transformation over $\mathcal{S}$.

A *run* of the data layer is an infinite sequence $S_0, S_1, \dots$ of states $S_i \in \mathcal{S}$ starting with an initial state $S_0 \in \mathcal{I}$ such that for all $i \in \mathbb{N}$ $(S_i, S_{i+1}) \in \tau$ holds, and there is a transaction $t_i \in \mathcal{T}$ with a finite run $S_i = S_i^0, \dots, S_i^k = S_{i+1}$ such that $(S_i^j, S_i^{j+1}) \in \tau_{t_i}$ holds for all $j = 0, \dots, k-1$.

As views in general are expressed by queries, i.e. read-only database transformations, we can assume that a view on a state $S_i \in \mathcal{S}$ is given by a finite run $S_i = S_0^v, \dots, S_\ell^v$ of some database transformation v with $S_i \subseteq S_\ell^v$. We can use this to define the view layer assuming that each state $S \in \mathcal{S}$ is composed as a union $S_d \cup V_1 \cup \dots \cup V_k$ such that each $S_d \cup V_j$ is a view on S_d. As a consequence, each wide-step state transition becomes a parallel composition of a transaction and an operation that "switches views on and off".

Let $\mathcal{V}$ be a finite set of (extended) views. Each view $v \in \mathcal{V}$ is associated with a finite set $\mathcal{O}_v$ of (service) operations $o_1, \dots, o_n$ such that for each $i \in \{1, \dots, n\}$ and each $S \in \mathcal{S}$ there is a unique state $S' \in \mathcal{S}$ with $(S, S') \in \tau$. Furthermore, if $S = S_d \cup V_1 \cup \dots \cup V_k$ with V_i defined by v_i and o is an operation associated with v_k, then $S' = S'_d \cup V'_1 \cup \dots \cup V'_m$ with $m \geq k-1$, and V'_i for $1 \leq i \leq k-1$ is still defined by v_i.

The AS^2 model has been formally defined in [19]. In a nutshell, in an AS^2 we have view-extended states, and each service operation associated with a view induces a transaction on the database, and may change or delete the view it is associated with, and even activate other views. These service operations are actually what is exported from the database system to be used by other systems or directly by users.

2.2 Plots and Mediators

For the model of distributed service-oriented systems suitable sequences of service operations are required. While sequencing of service operations is only implicit in the AS^2 model, algebraic expressions called *plots* will make them explicit. The service operations give rise to *elementary processes* of the form $\varphi(\boldsymbol{x})\ op[\boldsymbol{z}](\boldsymbol{y})\ \psi(\boldsymbol{x}, \boldsymbol{y}, \boldsymbol{z})$, in which *op* is the name of a service operation, $\boldsymbol{z}$ denotes input for *op* selected from the view v with $op \in Op_v$, $\boldsymbol{y}$ denotes additional input from the user, and φ and ψ are first-order formulae denoting pre- and post-conditions, respectively. The pre- and postconditions can be void, i.e. **true**, in which case they can be simply omitted. Furthermore, also simple formulae $\chi(\boldsymbol{x})$ – interpreted as tests checking their validity – constitute elementary processes. With this we obtain the following definition.

The set of *process expressions* of an AS^2 is the smallest set $\mathcal{P}$ containing all elementary processes that is closed under sequential composition $\cdot$, parallel composition $\|$, choice $+$, and iteration *. That is, whenever $p, q \in \mathcal{P}$ hold, then also pq, $p\|q$, $p+q$ and p^* are process expressions in $\mathcal{P}$. The *plot* of an AS^2 is a process expression in $\mathcal{P}$. The concept of *service mediators* [20] captures the plot of a composed AS^2. In other words, it defines a plot of an application that is yet to be constructed. The key issue is that such mediators specify service operations to be searched for, which can then be used to realise the problem at hand in a service-oriented way.

Therefore, the definition of a plot is relaxed in such a way that service operations do not belong to the same AS^2. In elementary processes we use prefixes to indicate the corresponding AS^2, so we obtain $\varphi(\boldsymbol{x})\ X : op[\boldsymbol{z}](\boldsymbol{y})\ \psi(\boldsymbol{x}, \boldsymbol{y}, \boldsymbol{z})$, in which X denotes a *service slot*, i.e. a placeholder for an actual service. Apart from this we leave the construction of the set of process expressions as above with the only difference that also $\ell\text{-}op\langle p\rangle$ is a process expression, whenever p is one. Here $\langle\cdot\rangle$ denotes a finite multiset constructor, i.e. we consider an arbitrary number of processes running in parallel, and ℓ-*op* denotes a multiset operation, which aggregates the query results of the different processes in the multiset.

A *service mediator* is a process expression with service slots. Furthermore, each service operation is associated with input- and output-types, pre- and post-conditions, and a concept in a service terminology.

2.3 Matching Services

We now need exact criteria to decide, when a service matches a service slot in a service mediator. According to [20] we can assume *service clouds* to be available, each of which providing a finite collection $\{\mathcal{A}_i \mid i \in I\}$ of AS^{2}s together with their plots and a service terminology $\mathcal{T}$, such that the defining queries of views and the associated service operations of these AS^{2}s define an instance of $\mathcal{T}$. The service terminology $\mathcal{T}$ of a service cloud (enabling to search for suitable services that match the slots of a service mediator) is given by a TBox of an appropriate service ontology. It comprises three parts:

- a *functional* description of input- and output-types as well as pre- and post-conditions telling in technical terms, what the service operation will do,
- a *categorical* description by inter-related keywords telling what the service operation does by using common terminology of the application area, and
- a *quality of service* (QoS) description of non-functional properties such as availability, response time, cost, etc.

The QoS description – usually associated with SLAs – is not needed for service discovery and merely useful to select among alternatives, but neither functional nor categorical description can be dispensed with. As for the categorical description, the terminology has to be specified. This defines an ontology in the widest sense, i.e. we have to provide definitions of "concepts" and relationships between them, such that each offered service becomes an instantiation of one or several concepts in the terminology. In this way we adopt the fundamental idea of the "semantic web". Formal details of such a service terminology are provided in [20] and shall not be repeated here.

The guideline for service matching is that the placeholder in the mediator must be replaceable by matching service operations. Functionally, this means that the input for the service operation as defined by the mediator must be accepted by the matching service operation, while the output of the matching service operation must be suitable to continue with other operations as defined by the mediator. This implies that we need supertypes and subtypes of the specified input- and output-types, respectively, in the mediator, as well as a weakening of the precondition and a strengthening of the postcondition. Categorically, the matching service operation must satisfy all the properties of the concept in the terminology that is associated with the placeholder operation, i.e. the concept associated with the matching service operation must be subsumed by that concept.

However, the matching of service operations is not yet sufficient. We also have to ensure that the projection of the mediator to a particular slot X results in a *subplot* of the plot p of the matching AS^2, i.e. a process expression q such that there exists another process expression r such that $p = q + r$ holds in the equational theory of process expressions. The *projection* of a mediator m is a process expression p_X such that $p_X = \pi_X(m)$ holds in the equational theory of process expressions, where $\pi_X(m)$ results from m by replacing all placeholders $Y : o$ with $Y \neq X$ and all conditions that are irrelevant for X by 1.

It would still be too simplistic to require that the projection of a mediator should result in a subplot of a matching service, as order may differ and certain service operations may be redundant. If for a condition $\varphi(\boldsymbol{x})$ appearing in a process expression p the equation $\varphi(\boldsymbol{x}) = \varphi(\boldsymbol{x})op[\boldsymbol{y}](\boldsymbol{z})$ holds, then $op[\boldsymbol{y}](\boldsymbol{z})$ is called a *phantom* of p.

That is, if the condition $\varphi(\boldsymbol{x})$ holds, we may execute the operation $op[\boldsymbol{y}](\boldsymbol{z})$ (or not) without changing the effect. Whenever $p = q$ holds in the equational theory of process expressions, and $op[\boldsymbol{y}](\boldsymbol{z})$ is a phantom of p with respect to condition $\varphi(\boldsymbol{x})$, we may replace $\varphi(\boldsymbol{x})$ by $\varphi(\boldsymbol{x})op[\boldsymbol{y}](\boldsymbol{z})$ in q. Each process expression resulting from such replacements is called an *enrichment of p by phantoms.*

Then an AS^2 $\mathcal{A}$ *matches* a service slot X in a service mediator m iff the following two conditions hold:

1. For each service operation $X : o$ in m there exists a service operation op provided by $\mathcal{A}$ such that
   - the input-type I_{op} of op is a supertype of the input-type I_o of o,
   - the output-type O_{op} of op is a subtype of the output-type O_o of o,
   - $pre_o \Rightarrow pre_{op}$ holds for the preconditions pre_o and pre_{op} of o and op,
   - $post_{op} \Rightarrow post_o$ holds for the postconditions $post_o$ and $post_{op}$ of o and op, and

- the concept C_o associated with o in the service terminology subsumes the concept C_{op} associated with op.

2. There exists an enrichment m_X of m by phantoms such that building the projection of m_X and replacing all service operations $X : o$ by matching service operations op from $\mathcal{A}$ results in a subplot of the plot of $\mathcal{A}$.

Once matching services for all slots in a mediator have been found, we can build an instantiation of the mediator with real services, which serves as a high-level specification of a process that exploits several services.

3 Middleware Architecture

It is clear from the definition of mediators that an instantiated mediator is a high-level specification of a distributed application that runs several services at the same time. Refining and implementing such a specification requires several add-ons. The involved services have to be started and terminated, which usually involves a log-in and authentication process. Then data have to be passed from the mediation process to the individual services, which bypass the user interaction, i.e. a control component associated with the process is needed. Furthermore, output from several services is combined, and a selection made by a user is passed back to the originating services, while non-selection leads to service termination. This must also be handled by the control component, for which we employ the *client-cloud interaction middleware* (CCIM) defined in [7].

3.1 Client-Cloud Interaction Middleware

The CCIM has been specified using ambient ASMs in order to describe formal models of distributed systems incorporating mobile components in two abstraction layers. While the algorithms of executable components are specified in terms of ASMs, their communication topology, locality and mobility are described with the terms of ambient calculus. Each ambient ASM specification can be translated into a pure ASM specification [3]. The approach provides a universal way to handle client-cloud interaction independent from particularities of certain cloud services or end-devices, while the instantiation by means of particular ambients results in specifications for particular settings. Thus, the architecture is highly flexible with respect to additional end-devices or cloud services, which would just require the definition of a particular ambient. The architecture of the CCIM integrates all novel software solutions such as Service Plot-Based Access Management, Client-to-Client Interaction (CTCI) Feature, Identity and Access Management (IdMM), Content Adaptivity, SLA Management and Security Monitoring Component into a compound single software component.

Figure 1 gives a sketch of the general architecture, in which the middleware is replicated by several components, each connected to one or more service clouds, but each cloud is connected to exactly one middleware component. Thus, there

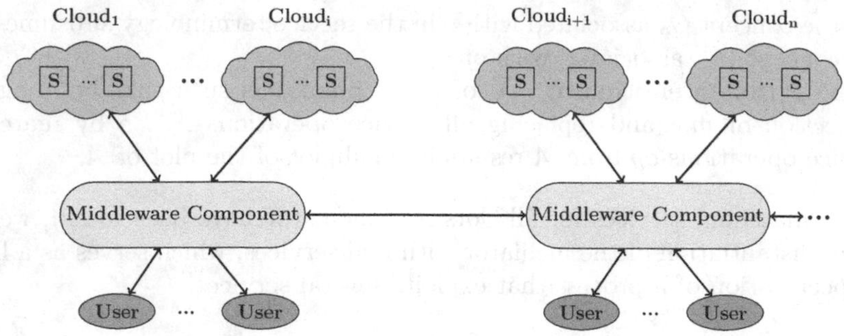

Fig. 1. General middleware architecture

are three modes of interaction: (1) interaction of users with a middleware component, (2) interaction of a middleware component with a service in one of its clouds, and (3) interaction among several middleware components.

The challenge is to keep users oblivious about the interaction among middleware components to locate individual services and to manage the transfer of results among the participating services. This challenge is addressed by the propagation of service requests among the middleware components. That is, when a middleware component receives a request for access to a particular service from a client or another middleware component, it will route the request to the middleware component owning the service, i.e. being the component that connects to the cloud, on which the service resides. Thus, a service request always comprises also routing information.

In addition to the routing of requests to access individual services each middleware component will exploit the features of the mediator model and analyse how to execute a particular mediator by extracting services that it can handle itself and those parts that have to be forwarded to other components. This is captured by an ambient ASM specification of the distributed middleware emphasizing the normal execution model. The resulting architecture for a middleware component is illustrated in Fig. 2. The normal execution mode requires the abstract machine, i.e. the ambient ASM specification, the service interfaces, the request handler that links to the users and other middleware components, and the communication handler that handles the interaction among middleware components.

3.2 CCIM Interaction Scenarios

The CCIM provides a cloud service infrastructure that permits a transparent and uniform way for clients to interact with multiple clouds. It permits to access and combine the available functions of cloud services, which may belong to various owners, and it leaves the full control over the usage of their services in the hands of the service owners. If a registered cloud user intends to subscribe to a particular service, a subscription request is sent to the cloud, which may forward

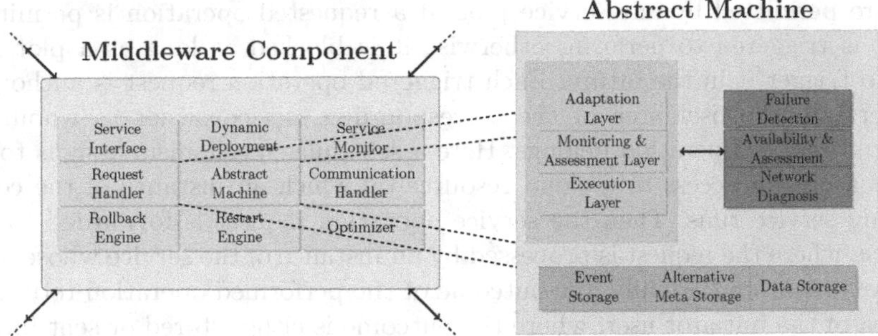

Fig. 2. Middleware components

it to such a special client corresponding to the service owner. This client responds with the *service plot*, which defines how the service can be used by the user and determines the permitted combination of service operations.

The received service plots are collected together with other available cloud functions in a personal user area by the cloud – see Fig. 3a. When the subscribed user sends a service request, it is checked whether the requested service opera-

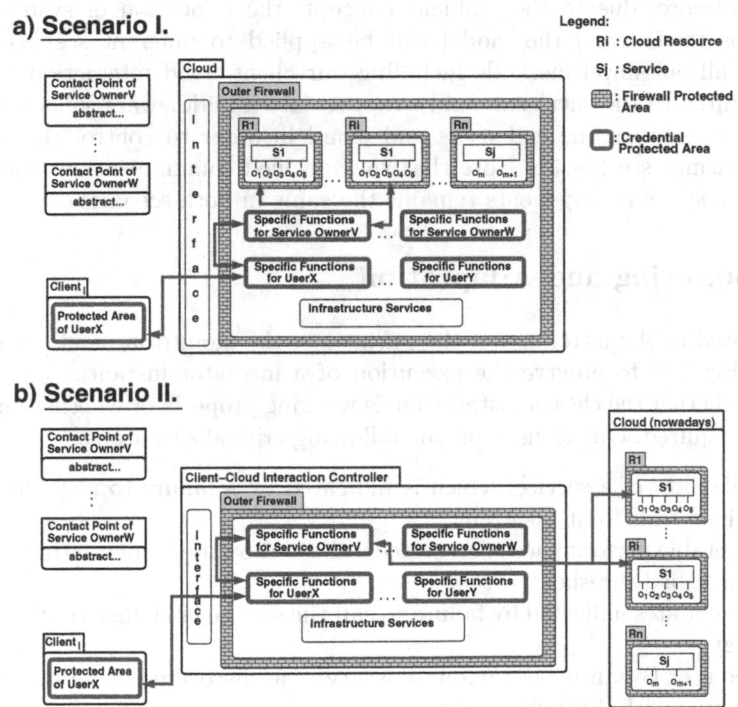

Fig. 3. Application of the CCIM according to different scenarios

tions are permitted by any service plot. If a requested operation is permitted, then it is triggered to perform, otherwise it is blocked as long as a plot may allow to trigger it in the future. Each triggered operation request is authorized to enter into the user area of the corresponding service owner to whom the requested service operation belongs. Here a scheduler mechanism assigns to the request a one-off access to a cloud resource on which an instance of the corresponding service runs. Then the service operation request is forwarded to this resource, where the request is processed by an instance of the service whose operation was requested. Finally, the outcome of the performed operation returns to the area of the initiator user, where the outcome is either stored or sent further to a given client device.

In this way, the service owners have direct influence on the service usage of particular users via the provided service plots. If a user subscribes to more than one service, he or she may have access to more than one plot. These plots are independent from each other and they can be applied concurrently. If a service owner makes available more than one service for a user, the owner has the choice either to provide independent plots for the user or to combine some functions of various services into a common service plot. This conceptual solution shows a transparent and uniform way how to provide an advanced access control mechanism for cloud services without giving up the flexibility of heterogeneous cloud access to these services.

Furthermore, due to the ambient concept, the relocation of system components is trivial, and the model can be applied to different scenarios. For instance, all our novel methods including our client-cloud interaction solution can be shifted to the client side and wrapped into a middleware software which takes place between the end users and cloud in order to control the interactions of them – see Fig. 3b. Note that the specified communication among the distributed system components remains the same in both scenarios.

4 Monitoring and Adaptation

As indicated in the introduction the purpose of the monitoring and assessment layer in Fig. 2 is to observe the execution of a mediator instantiation, and to identify, whether the chosen instatiation is working properly or whether an adaptation is required. Our focus is on the following critical situations:

- unavailability of a service, which is indicated by a failure to respond within a specified time limit (aka ping);
- unacceptable performance of a service indicated by the response time exceeding a specified threshold;
- service updates indicated by failure to call the service or changes to the service ontology;
- erroneous or Byzantine behaviour of a service as discovered by multiple equivalent usage with different results;
- identification of a better mediator instance according to the service selection criteria.

As aforementioned, in case of an identified critical situation the adaptation layer replaces one or several services, i.e. it replaces the given mediator instantiation by a new one. Its role is, therefore, essential in reconfiguring the system from a deficient execution to a normal working state. Together with the monitoring layer, it handles the internal mechanisms for problem detection and resolution.

4.1 Monitoring Ground Model

Figure 4 illustrates the interaction of the monitoring layer with the clouds. For each service there are several dedicated monitors. For the observation of the behaviour of these services, sensors are deployed across multiple clouds in order to collect environmental data that are reported to the middleware. The monitoring is part of an abstract machine as indicated in Fig. 2, which is specified using the ASM method [8]. It is important to consider that monitors are also components of the distributed system, so they can also exhibit failures. This is taken care of by assigning a trustworthiness measure to each monitor. Monitoring components with trustworthiness below a specified threshold are removed from the network of monitors.

Figure 5 shows a control-state ASM [4] for the monitors. Monitors collect data from the nodes. When starting the system, each monitor is initialized by the middleware in the `Active` state, from where it submits a heartbeat request to the node it monitors. The monitor advances afterwards to the `Wait for response` state, where it checks two guards. First, it verifies if a response to its request is received. If so, it verifies if the delay of the response is acceptable. If this condition holds, the monitor moves to the `Collect data` state. If no response is received or if the response has a big delay, the monitor moves to the `Report`

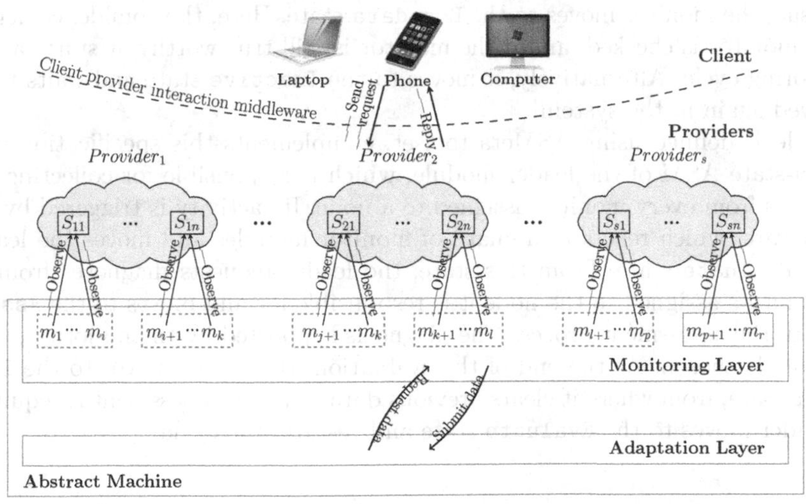

Fig. 4. Architecture of monitoring and adaptation layers

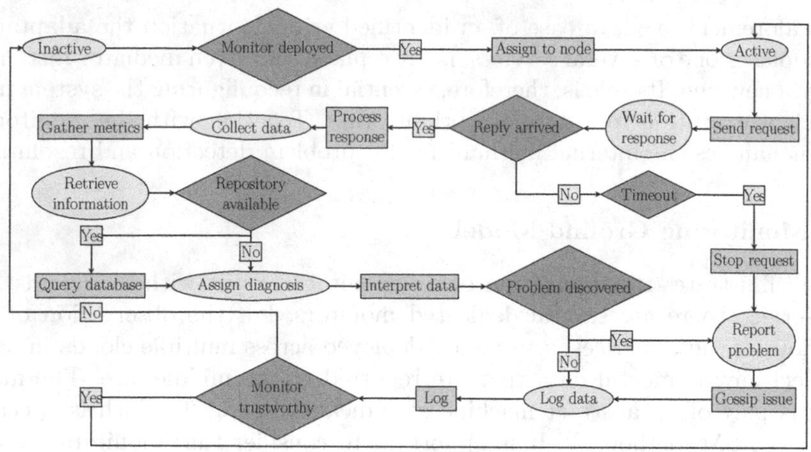

Fig. 5. Control-state ASM for the monitoring ground model

`problem` state. In the `Collect data` state the monitor gathers low level metrics (CPU, memory and storage usage, bandwidth) and then moves to the `Retrieve information` state, where it checks local storage for past monitoring data. If the repository is available, the monitor queries it. The monitor moves to the `Assign diagnosis` state, where it interprets the available data. If it discovers a problem, it moves to the `Report problem` state, otherwise it moves to the `Log data` state, where meaningful data and operation are logged. When an issue is identified, the monitor modifies a constraint that triggers a request towards the leader of the observe node, further described in Sect. 4.2, to inquire all his monitoring counterparts and carry out a collaborative diagnosis. After reporting the issue, the monitor moves to the `Log data` state. Here, the confidence degree of the monitor is checked, and if the monitor is still trustworthy, it starts a new monitoring cycle. Alternatively, it moves to the `Inactive` state and waits to be deployed again in the system.

Code 1, defined using ASMeta toolset, complements this specification by a control-state ASM of the leader module, which is responsible for collecting the diagnoses from every monitor assigned to a node. Its activity is triggered by the middleware, which reacts to a guard of monitor modules and moves the leader to the `Evaluate` state. From this state, the leader requests diagnoses from all the monitors assigned to the node it is responsible for and moves to the `Assess` state. In the assessment process, the diagnosis supported by the majority of the monitors is chosen. At the end of the evaluation, the leader moves to the `Idle leader` state, from where it clears previous data. If a new assessment is required, the leader moves to the `Evaluate` state and restarts the cycle.

```
module Leader
import Monitor
export *
signature:
    enum domain Leader_States = {IDLE_LEADER |
            EVALUATE | ASSESS}
    controlled leader_state : Leader -> Leader_States
    controlled assessment: Leader -> Diagnosis
definitions:
    rule r_AssessNode ($l in Leader) =
        if (max(failed_diagnoses($l), critical_diagnoses($l))
            = failed_diagnoses($l)) then
            if (max(failed_diagnoses($l), normal_diagnoses($l))
              = failed_diagnoses($l)) then
                assessment ($l) := FAILED
            else
                assessment ($l) := NORMAL
            endif
        else
            if(max(critical_diagnoses($l),normal_diagnoses($l))
            = critical_diagnoses($l)) then
                assessment ($l) := CRITICAL
            else
                assessment ($l) := NORMAL
            endif
        endif

rule r_RequestData ($l in Leader) = skip

rule r_ClearData ($l in Leader) = skip

rule r_LeaderProgram =
    par
        if (leader_state (self) = EVALUATE) then
            par
                r_RequestData [self]
                leader_state(self) := ASSESS
            endpar
        endif
        if (leader_state (self) = ASSESS) then
            par
                r_AssessNode [self]
                leader_state(self) := IDLE_LEADER
            endpar
        endif
        if (leader_state (self) = IDLE_LEADER) then
            seq
                r_ClearData [self]
                if (is_evaluation_needed(self)) then
                    leader_state (self) := EVALUATE
                endif
            endseq
        endif
    endpar
```

Code 1. Leader ASM module

4.2 Leader ASM

The control-state ASMs require to be specified in more details by ASM rules. The Leader module consists of three main rules shown in Fig. 6. We abstract from the protocol of requesting data from the monitors and how the data used for an evaluation is removed. The assessment process verifies the individual diagnoses and chooses the diagnosis established by the majority of the monitors.

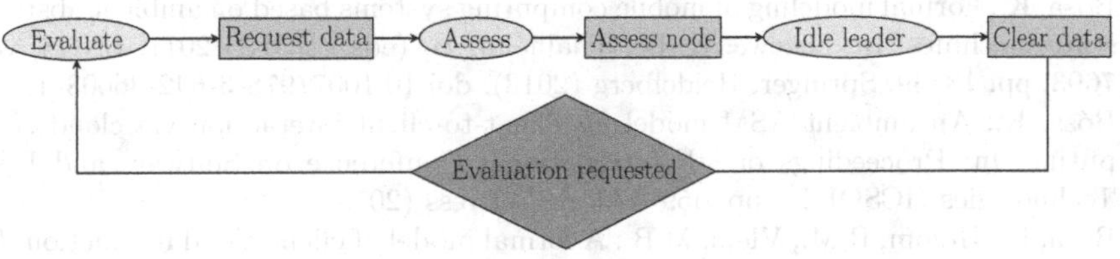

Fig. 6. Leader ASM

By analysing decisions from different counterparts we aim to improve the reliability of the process and reduce the side-effects of possible random failures of any of the monitors. In a future refinement, weights equal to the trustworthiness will be added to the contribution of each monitor. Thus, monitors that show a lower accuracy will have a smaller impact on the final evaluation.

5 Conclusion

In this paper we described an approach to the modelling of distributed, (self-) adaptive systems that are based on services supported by mutiple clouds. The general model for service-oriented systems that exploit cloud-enabled services is the mediator model from [20], which permits various instantiations of service slots by concrete services. The selection of such services is driven by a service ontology comprising functional, categorical and SLA-based characteristics. The concrete interaction with multiple clouds is realised by a middleware architecture [7]. We extend this middleware by monitoring and adaptation layers that identify the need for a change of a mediator instantiation and provide an updated one.

All parts of our approach have been specified using Abstract State Machines including the extensions covering ambient computing [3], concurrency [2] and linguistic reflection [24]. In this way the specification of any application can be subjected to rigorous simulation and model-checking using the ASMeta tools.

Our research is ongoing concerning the specification of details of the monitoring and adaptation layers, refinements towards verified implementations, and in particular concrete case studies with ASMeta.

References

1. Arcaini, P., Gargantini, A., Riccobene, E., Scandurra, P.: A model-driven process for engineering a toolset for a formal method. Softw. Pract. Exp. **41**(2), 155–166 (2011)
2. Börger, E., Schewe, K.D.: Concurrent abstract state machines. Acta Informatica **53**(5), 469–492 (2016)
3. Börger, E., Cisternino, A., Gervasi, V.: Ambient abstract state machines with applications. J. Comput. Syst. Sci. **78**(3), 939–959 (2012)
4. Börger, E., Stärk, R.: Abstract State Machines. Springer, Heidelberg (2003)
5. Bósa, K.: Formal modeling of mobile computing systems based on ambient abstract state machines. In: Schewe, K.-D., Thalheim, B. (eds.) SDKB 2011. LNCS, vol. 7693, pp. 18–49. Springer, Heidelberg (2013). doi:10.1007/978-3-642-36008-4_2
6. Bósa, K.: An ambient ASM model for client-to-client interaction via cloud computing. In: Proceedings of 8th International Conference on Software and Data Technologies (ICSOFT), pp. 459–470. SciTePress (2013)
7. Bósa, K., Holom, R.M., Vleju, M.B.: A formal model of client-cloud interaction. In: Thalheim, B., Schewe, K.D., Prinz, A., Buchberger, B. (eds.) Correct Software in Web Applications and Web Services. A Series of the Research Institute for Symbolic Computation, pp. 1–61. Springer, Cham (2014). doi:10.1007/978-3-319-17112-8_4
8. Buga, A., Nemeş, S.T.: Towards an ASM specification for monitoring and adaptation services of large-scale distributed systems. In: 41st Annual Computer Software and Applications Conference, COMPSAC Workshops 2017, Torino, Italy, 4–8 July 2017. IEEE (2017, to appear)
9. Calzarossa, M., Della Vedova, M.L., Massari, L., Petcu, D., Tabash, M.I.M., Tessera, D.: Workloads in the clouds. In: Fiondella, L., Puliafito, A. (eds.) Principles of Performance and Reliability Modeling and Evaluation. Reliability Engineering. Springer, Cham (2016). doi:10.1007/978-3-319-30599-8_20

10. Calzarossa, M., Massari, L., Tessera, D.: Workload characterization: a survey revisited. ACM Comput. Surv. **48**(3), 48:1–48:43 (2016)
11. Cheng, B.H.C., de Lemor, R., Giese, H., Inverardi, P., Magee, J. (eds.): Software Engineering for Self-Adaptive Systems. LNCS, vol. 5525. Springer, Heidelberg (2009). doi:10.1007/978-3-642-02161-9
12. Ferrarotti, F., Schewe, K.D., Tec, L., Wang, Q.: A new thesis concerning synchronised parallel computing - simplified parallel ASM thesis. Theoret. Comput. Sci. **649**, 25–53 (2016)
13. Gargantini, A., Riccobene, E., Scandurra, P.: A metamodel-based language and a simulation engine for abstract state machines. J. Univ. Comput. Sci. **14**(12), 1949–1983 (2008)
14. Gurevich, Y.: Sequential abstract state machines capture sequential algorithms. ACM Trans. Comput. Log. **1**(1), 77–111 (2000)
15. Huebscher, M., McCann, J.: A survey of autonomic computing - degrees, models, and applications. ACM Comput. Surv. **40**(3), 7 (2008). Article No. 7
16. Lampesberger, H.: Technologies for web and cloud service interaction: a survey. SOCA **10**(2), 71–110 (2016)
17. Lampesberger, H., Rady, M.: Monitoring of client-cloud interaction. In: Thalheim, B., Schewe, K.D., Prinz, A., Buchberger, B. (eds.) Correct Software in Web Applications and Web Services. A Series of the Research Institute for Symbolic Computation, pp. 177–228. Springer, Cham (2015). doi:10.1007/978-3-319-17112-8_6
18. Leucker, M., Schallhart, C.: A brief account of runtime verification. J. Log. Algebr. Program. **78**(5), 293–303 (2009)
19. Ma, H., Schewe, K.D., Thalheim, B., Wang, Q.: A theory of data-intensive software services. SOCA **3**(4), 263–283 (2009)
20. Ma, H., Schewe, K.D., Thalheim, B., Wang, Q.: A formal model for the interoperability of service clouds. SOCA **6**(3), 189–205 (2012)
21. Mirandola, R., Potena, P., Scandurra, P.: An optimization process for adaptation space exploration of service-oriented applications. In: Proceedings of 6th IEEE International Symposium on Service-Oriented System Engineering (SOSE 2011), pp. 146–151. IEEE (2011)
22. Nusayr, A., Cook, J.: Extending AOP to support broad runtime monitoring needs. In: Software Engineering and Knowledge Engineering, pp. 438–441 (2009)
23. Salchie, M., Tahvildari, L.: Self-adaptive software: landscape and research challenges. ACM Trans. Auton. Adapt. Syst. **4**(2), 14 (2009). Article No.14
24. Schewe, K.D., Ferrarotti, F., Tec, L., Wang, Q., An, W.: Evolving concurrent systems - behavioural theory and logic. In: Proceedings of Australasian Computer Science Week (ACSW 2017), pp. 77:1–77:10. ACM, Deakin University, Victoria, 31 January – 3 February 2017
25. Shin, K.S., Jung, J.H., Cheon, J.Y., Choi, S.B.: Real-time network monitoring scheme based on SNMP for dynamic information. J. Netw. Comput. Appl. **30**(1), 331–353 (2007)
26. Zeng, W., Wang, Y.: Design and implementation of server monitoring system based on SNMP. In: JCAI, pp. 680–682 (2009)

Querying Graph Databases: What Do Graph Patterns Mean?

Stephan Mennicke[1(✉)], Jan-Christoph Kalo[2], and Wolf-Tilo Balke[2]

[1] Institut für Programmierung und Reaktive Systeme, TU Braunschweig, Braunschweig, Germany
mennicke@ips.cs.tu-bs.de
[2] Institut für Informationssysteme, TU Braunschweig, Braunschweig, Germany
{kalo,balke}@ifis.cs.tu-bs.de

Abstract. Querying graph databases often amounts to some form of graph pattern matching. Finding (sub-)graphs isomorphic to a given graph pattern is common to many graph query languages, even though graph isomorphism often is too strict, since it requires a one-to-one correspondence between the nodes of the pattern and that of a match. We investigate the influence of weaker graph pattern matching relations on the respective queries they express. Thereby, these relations abstract from the concrete graph topology to different degrees. An extension of relation sequences, called failures which we borrow from studies on concurrent processes, naturally expresses simple presence conditions for relations and properties. This is very useful in application scenarios dealing with databases with a notion of *data completeness*. Furthermore, failures open up the query modeling for more intricate matching relations directly incorporating concrete data values.

Keywords: Graph databases · Query modeling · Pattern matching

1 Introduction

Over the last years, *graph databases* have aroused a vivid interest in the database community. This is partly sparked by intelligent and quite robust developments in information extraction, partly due to successful standardizations for knowledge representation in the Semantic Web. Indeed, it is enticing to open up the abundance of unstructured information on the Web through transformation into a structured form that is usable by advanced applications. A good example is the *Knowledge Graph* by Google, supporting sophisticated features in Web search. Other examples are the growing number of special interest graph databases created as part of the Linked Open Data (LOD) initiative. Most of these graphs provide *entity-centric data* from diverse domains: entities are represented as nodes connected by labeled edges (relations) to other entity nodes or attribute nodes (literals). Thereby, the nodes of a graph database are often referred to as *graph database objects*. Graph database query languages let the user query these

H.C. Mayr et al. (Eds.): ER 2017, LNCS 10650, pp. 134–148, 2017.
https://doi.org/10.1007/978-3-319-69904-2_11

graph structures in an SQL-like fashion. Examples are SPARQL as a W3C standard for querying Semantic Web data[1], Cypher as the standard query language for Neo4J[2], and Gremlin[3]. Basically, all these languages rely on the idea of graph pattern matching, complemented with suitable node substitutions. A matching mechanism common to all these query languages is graph isomorphism [12].

Unfortunately, structural identity in the sense of graph isomorphism often is too restrictive for many applications, see e. g., [4,5]. Imagine a user query for **actors being children of other actors**. One possibility to model this query as a graph pattern is depicted in Fig. 1(a). `A1` and `A2` are two nodes being connected by a `childOf` relationship, both having an `actedIn` relationship to either node `M1` or `M2`. Thereby, it is intended that nodes `A1` and `A2` represent the desired actors from the query while `M1` and `M2` are representatives for movies they acted in. Considering isomorphic matches to the graph pattern, an answer is required to have only actors acting in at least two different movies. Isomorphic matches of the pattern depicted in Fig. 1(b) are thus ruled out.

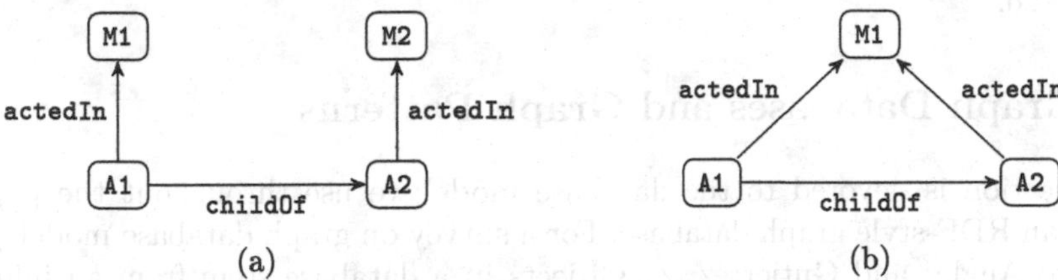

Fig. 1. Example graph patterns

Since the query in the previous paragraph is sufficiently vague, we may assume that matches to both graph patterns of Fig. 1 are intended. The reason why a single pattern is insufficient to cover the whole query is that graph isomorphism relies on a one-to-one-correspondence between the nodes of the graph pattern and that of a match. However, it would be quite sufficient to require that an object of a match incorporates in relation `actedIn` and a sequence of relations `childOf` and `actedIn`, abstracting from the concrete pattern structure. Sequences over relation symbols are henceforth called *traces*. Whether or not both actors took part in the same movies is not subject to the trace representation of the graph pattern. In fact, the patterns of Fig. 1 are indistinguishable up to traces, thus represent the same set of *trace matches*.

From Sect. 3 on, we study the influence of different graph pattern matching relations to the queries they express. All these notions are based on graph databases and graph patterns, introduced in Sect. 2. To the best of our knowledge, trace-based relations have not been investigated in the context of graph pattern matching for database querying to which we contribute so-called *failures*

[1] https://www.w3.org/TR/rdf-sparql-query/.
[2] https://neo4j.com/.
[3] http://tinkerpop.apache.org/.

originating from studies on equivalence of concurrent processes [3]. Beyond a purely topological analysis, failures express simple presence conditions for relations and properties associated with the database objects. This allows for strong correspondences in databases enjoying *data completeness*, still without the strict requirements of graph isomorphism. Therefore, we incorporate object properties in our notion of graph patterns and graph pattern matching. We include *simulation semantics* as an interesting complementation to failures, since these notions constitute incomparable matching relations, i. e., there are simulating matches to patterns that are not failure matches and vice versa. Thus, the choice in favor for failures/simulation semantics is left to the concrete application scenario. Moreover, different kinds of simulation have already been applied in several graph database tasks [1,15,17].

Since graph databases are still concerned with data in terms of attributes attached to the database objects, we propose a preliminary extension of our graph pattern model by *data predicates* and apply them to simulation-based semantics in Sect. 4. In Sect. 5, we discuss related work. We conclude our work by Sect. 6.

2 Graph Databases and Graph Patterns

This section is devoted to the database model we use throughout the paper, being an RDF-style graph database. For a survey on graph database models, we refer to Angles and Gutierrez [2]. Objects in a database stem from an infinite set of object identifiers $\mathcal{O}$. In Fig. 2, an excerpt from a graph database is given. The object identifiers used there are "Will Smith", "Jaden Smith", and "The Pursuit of Happiness". Database objects are related to other objects or concrete data values (i. e., literals) by attributes, being triples over objects, relations or properties, and objects or data values. We separate the relations between objects from properties relating an object with a concrete data value to simplify the presentation of further concepts. Object relations and properties together form the attributes of a graph database.

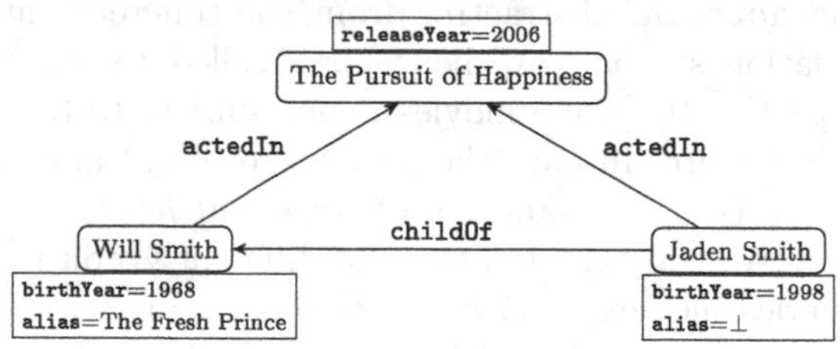

Fig. 2. A small graph database excerpt

For a fixed set of objects $O \subseteq \mathcal{O}$, relations between objects are given in terms of a directed labeled edge relation $\longrightarrow \subseteq O \times \Sigma \times O$, where Σ is a finite set of relation symbols. As an example, reconsider Fig. 2 where nodes "Will Smith" and "Jaden Smith" are connected via relation `childOf`. Properties of database objects are referenced by projection functions $\pi_p : O \to \mathcal{D}$, where p is a property from a finite set of properties P, and $\mathcal{D}$ is a usually infinite set of possible data values [2]. In Fig. 2, properties of objects are listed in an equation style within the boxes attached to each object node. Value $\bot \in \mathcal{D}$ denotes the absence of an association of property p with object o, e. g., $\pi_{\texttt{alias}}(\text{"}JadenSmith\text{"}) = \bot$ in Fig. 2. We usually leave $\bot$-valued properties implicit, e. g., $\pi_{\texttt{releaseYear}}(\text{"}WillSmith\text{"}) = \bot$, although not explicitly mentioned in Fig. 2. As a consequence, our database model is a directed edge- and node-labeled graph structure.

Definition 1. *Let Σ and P be finite alphabets such that $\Sigma \cap P = \emptyset$. A* graph database *is a 5-tuple $DB = (O, \Sigma, P, \longrightarrow, (\pi_p)_{p \in P})$ where $O \subset \mathcal{O}$ is a finite set of* objects *and $\longrightarrow \subseteq O \times \Sigma \times O$ together with $\pi_p : O \to \mathcal{D}$ $(p \in P)$ form the* attributes *of DB.*

Relation symbols range over $a, a_1, a_2, \ldots$ while we use $p, p_1, p_2, \ldots$ for properties. We abbreviate families of property functions by Π, Π', Ψ with respective projections π_p, π'_p, ψ_p. We write $o \xrightarrow{a} o'$ if $(o, a, o') \in \longrightarrow$ and $o \xrightarrow{a}$ if there is an o' with $o \xrightarrow{a} o'$. Likewise, $o \not\xrightarrow{a}$ denotes the absence of an o'.

Paths from one database object to another represent fingerprints of the topology of the database that, upon traversal, define object reachability. Capturing only the sequence of relation symbols along a path forms a *trace*.

Definition 2. *Let $DB = (O, \Sigma, P, \longrightarrow, \Pi)$ be a graph database. Relation $\longrightarrow$ extends to* relation sequences *$\sigma \in \Sigma^*$ inductively as follows: (1) $o \xrightarrow{\varepsilon} o'$ iff $o = o'$ and (2) $o \xrightarrow{\sigma \cdot a} o'$ iff there is an object $o'' \in O$ with $o \xrightarrow{\sigma} o'' \xrightarrow{a} o'$. A* trace *of $o \in O$ is a word $\sigma \in \Sigma^*$ if there is an $o' \in O$ with $o \xrightarrow{\sigma} o'$. The set of all traces of o is denoted by $\mathcal{T}_{DB}(o)$. The* traces *of DB are defined by $\mathcal{T}(DB) := \bigcup_{o \in O} \mathcal{T}_{DB}(o)$.*

For arbitrary graph databases A_1 and A_2, we denote by $A_1 \sqsubseteq_{\mathsf{T}} A_2$ that $\mathcal{T}(A_1) \subseteq \mathcal{T}(A_2)$, defining the so-called *trace preorder*. The symmetric closure of $\sqsubseteq_{\mathsf{T}}$ is called *trace equivalence* and is denoted by $\equiv_{\mathsf{T}}$.

Given a graph database $DB = (O, \Sigma, P, \longrightarrow, \Pi)$. A mechanism answering a query to DB tries finding *subgraphs* of DB, *matching* the query. A subgraph of DB is a database $A = (O', \Sigma, P, \longrightarrow', \Pi')$ where $O' \subseteq O$, $\longrightarrow' \subseteq \longrightarrow \cap (O' \times \Sigma \times O')$, and $\pi'_p = \pi_p \upharpoonright O'$ (i. e., π_p restricted to inputs from O'). We write $A \preceq DB$ if A is a subgraph of DB.

Structurally, a query to a graph database DB is given in terms of a graph pattern with nodes from some universe of nodes $\mathcal{N}$. Note that for some graph query applications, it holds that $\mathcal{N} \subseteq \mathcal{O}$ or even $\mathcal{N} \subseteq O$, as is the case for exemplar queries [17]. A *graph pattern* $\mathcal{Q}$ is itself a graph database with a finite set of nodes $N_{\mathcal{Q}} \subseteq \mathcal{N}$, relation alphabet $\Gamma \subseteq \Sigma$, a directed Γ-labeled edge relation $\longrightarrow_{\mathcal{Q}}$, and a family of property functions $\psi_p : N_{\mathcal{Q}} \to \mathcal{D}$, referred to as Ψ. We call the elements of $N_{\mathcal{Q}}$ nodes, since, without relating them to an actual database, they refer to abstract objects. An answer to a query w. r. t. graph pattern $\mathcal{Q}$ is a subgraph *matching* $\mathcal{Q}$. The most common matching mechanism in the realm of graph-based models is graph isomorphism, which we introduce here as a base-line for the matching relations to come.

Definition 3. *Let* $DB = (O, \Sigma, P, \longrightarrow, \Pi)$ *be a graph database. A* graph pattern *is a graph database* $\mathcal{Q} = (N_{\mathcal{Q}}, \Gamma, P, \longrightarrow_{\mathcal{Q}}, \Psi)$ *where* $N_{\mathcal{Q}} \subset \mathcal{N}$ *is a finite set of nodes and* $\Gamma \subseteq \Sigma$. *A subgraph* $A = (O', \Sigma, P, \longrightarrow', \Pi')$ *of DB is isomorphic to* $\mathcal{Q}$, *denoted* $A \cong \mathcal{Q}$, *iff there is a bijective function* $\nu : N_{\mathcal{Q}} \to O'$ *such that for all* $n_1, n_2 \in N_{\mathcal{Q}}$, $n_1 \xrightarrow{a}_{\mathcal{Q}} n_2$ *iff* $\nu(n_1) \xrightarrow{a}' \nu(n_2)$. *If* $\mathcal{Q} \cong A$, *A is called an* isomorphic match *of* $\mathcal{Q}$. $[\![\mathcal{Q}]\!]_{DB}^{\cong}$ *denotes the set of all isomorphic matches of* $\mathcal{Q}$.

We refer to the example patterns given in Fig. 1 by $\mathcal{Q}_a$ and $\mathcal{Q}_b$. While the graph depicted in Fig. 2 is an isomorphic match of $\mathcal{Q}_b$, it is not of $\mathcal{Q}_a$, since the bijectivity requirement cannot be fulfilled in this case. Since graph isomorphism is an equivalence relation, it holds that whenever we have two isomorphic subgraphs A_1 and A_2 of *DB*, A_1 is an isomorphic match of $\mathcal{Q}$ iff A_2 is (for every graph pattern $\mathcal{Q}$).

Besides isomorphic matches, we directly derive another query answering mechanism based on traces (cf. Definition 2). The set of all *trace equivalent matches of* $\mathcal{Q}$ is defined by $[\![\mathcal{Q}]\!]_{DB}^{\equiv_\mathsf{T}} := \{A \preceq DB \mid \mathcal{Q} \equiv_\mathsf{T} A\}$. As already mentioned, the graph patterns $\mathcal{Q}_a$ and $\mathcal{Q}_b$ are indistinguishable by traces. Hence, both include the graph depicted in Fig. 2 as a trace equivalent match. Isomorphic matches show structural identity, rather than an actual similarity. Trace-based matches may be seen as the other side of the spectrum, since they are the coarsest relations discussed in this paper. It can be shown that for every graph pattern $\mathcal{Q}$, each isomorphic match also is a trace equivalent match, but not vice versa [8].

3 Failures in Relations and Properties

We have already seen two different matching relations. In this section, we lift our considerations from a purely topological matching by step-wise incorporating properties due to the notion of failures. We then complement failures by simulation whose matches show to be incomparable with those of the failures matching relation. We introduce both notions by means of an example and by a formal definition. In the end of this section, we discuss benefits and drawbacks for each of the relations. The (counter-)examples given throughout this section are inspired by standard examples in process theory, e. g., as presented by van Glabbeek [8].

3.1 Failures

As the query graphs $\mathcal{Q}_a$ and $\mathcal{Q}_b$ of Fig. 1 have shown, graph isomorphism is sensitive to even small structural changes. In contrast, the notion of traces shows

$$\mathcal{T}(\mathcal{Q}_a) = \{\varepsilon, \texttt{actedIn}, \texttt{childOf}, \texttt{childOf} \cdot \texttt{actedIn}\} = \mathcal{T}(\mathcal{Q}_b),$$

implying that both patterns allow for the same trace matches, as e. g., the one depicted in Fig. 2. However, matching by trace equivalence does not allow for a clear differentiation of objects with different relations they participate in. Traces only require that the required relations are present in a subgraph, no matter how distributed they are over the graph. Consider the small database excerpt of Fig. 3(a) together with the graph pattern depicted in Fig. 3(b). Intuitively, the graph pattern represents the query for an actor (`A`) being resident of country (`C`), who studied in some facility (`U`). An exact, i. e., isomorphic, match is given by "Jada P. Smith". However, trace equivalence matching also allows for the combination of "Will Smith" and "Edgar F. Codd", since the former features relation `actedIn` while the latter takes part only in a `studiedIn` relation. Trace equivalence misses that "Will Smith" is *not* in a `studiedIn` relation and "Edgar F. Codd" is *not* part of an `actedIn` relationship. As long as both traces `resident`·`studiedIn` and `resident`·`actedIn` are present, a subgraph is considered a trace equivalence match. If, however, we include that after relation `resident`, neither `actedIn` nor `studiedIn` is missing, we rule out the combination of "Will Smith" and "Edgar F. Codd". This is what *failures* are for.

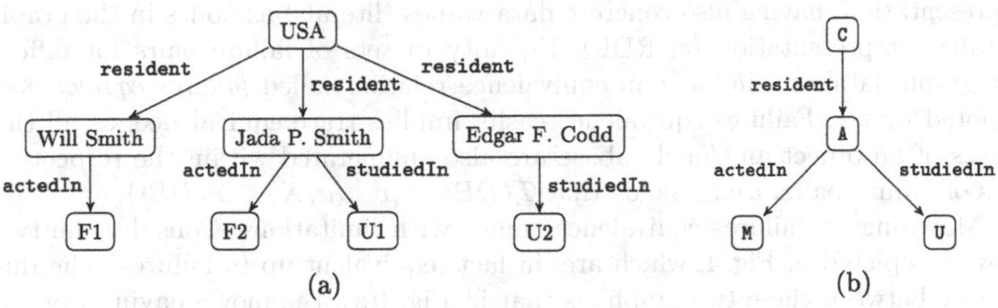

Fig. 3. (a) Another graph database excerpt with indicated `studiedIn` and `actedIn` relations such that $\pi_{\texttt{yearOfDeath}}$("Edgar F. Codd") = 2003 and $\pi_{\texttt{yearOfDeath}}$("Jada P. Smith") = $\perp$. (b) Another example graph pattern.

The central idea of *failures*, originating from studies on equivalence of concurrent processes [3], is the notion of *failure pairs*. A *failure pair of an object* o consists of a trace $\sigma \in \mathcal{T}_{DB}(o)$ and a set of relation symbols $X \subseteq \Sigma$ such that for at least one object o' with $o \xrightarrow{\sigma} o'$, o' does *not* participate in any relations $a \in X$, i. e., $o' \not\xrightarrow{a}$. Intuitively, o' *fails* in participating in relations from set X, also called *failure set*. By this representation, we naturally obtain the ability to observe that objects like "Edgar F. Codd" do not have an `actedIn` relation. In fact, the graph pattern contains no failure pair (`resident`, X) such that `actedIn` $\in X$ or `studiedIn` $\in X$, i. e., in every match, if an object is target of a relation `resident`, then it features both, an `actedIn` and a `studiedIn` relation. Thus, subgraphs containing "Edgar F. Codd" or "Will Smith" are not considered a failures equivalence match.

Often, not every characteristic of an object is expressed in terms of an interrelationship with other objects, but as associations with actual data values,

e. g., numerical properties like the year of birth or the *Erdős number*. If we omit the `actedIn` relation from the graph pattern of Fig. 3(b), we could ask for residents `A` of country `C`, who studied in facility `U`. Based on this pattern, we are now interested in all those people being still alive. We model this in the query graph $\mathcal{Q}$ by stating that $\psi_{\texttt{yearOfDeath}}(\texttt{A}) = \bot$, i. e., the property `yearOfDeath` is undefined for an object matching `A`. Therefore, "Jada P. Smith" would belong to a match of $\mathcal{Q}$, but "Edgar F. Codd" should not. In order to make failures aware of relation symbols and the (non-)existence of an association between an object and a property, we include properties in failure sets.

Definition 4. *Let* $DB = (O, \Sigma, P, \longrightarrow, \Pi)$ *be a database and* $o \in O$. *A* failure pair *of* o *is a pair* $(\sigma, X) \in (\Sigma^* \times 2^{\Sigma \cup P})$ *where* $\sigma \in \mathcal{T}_{DB}(o)$ *such that there is an object* $o' \in O$ *with* $o \xrightarrow{\sigma} o'$ *and* $\forall a \in X \cap \Sigma : o' \not\xrightarrow{a}$ *and* $\forall p \in X \cap P : \pi_p(o') = \bot$. $\mathcal{F}_{DB}(o)$ *denotes the set of all failure pairs and* $\mathcal{F}(DB) := \bigcup_{o \in O} \mathcal{F}_{DB}(o)$ *defines the failure pairs of DB. For a query graph* $\mathcal{Q}$, *define the set of* failure matches *by* $[\![\mathcal{Q}]\!]_{DB}^{\equiv_{\mathsf{F}}} := \{A \preceq DB \mid \mathcal{F}(\mathcal{Q}) = \mathcal{F}(A)\}$.

Failures still only take the topological structure of a graph pattern into account, since our family of property functions may easily be included in a graph-like representation, having also concrete data values (literals) as nodes in the graph database representation (cf. RDF). Equality of sets of failure pairs for different graph databases induces an equivalence relation called *failures equivalence*, denoted by $\equiv_{\mathsf{F}}$. Failures equivalence easily implies trace equivalence, as all the traces of an object and/or database are also enumerated within the respective sets of failure pairs, i. e., it holds that $\mathcal{T}(DB) = \{\sigma \mid (\sigma, X) \in \mathcal{F}(DB)\}$.

Matching by failures equivalence comes with limitations. Consider the two graphs depicted in Fig. 4, which are, in fact, equivalent up to failures. The difference between these two graphs is that in Fig. 4(a), the movie having won an Academy Award (Goldfinger) was directed by a writer, while in Fig. 4(b), only the movie director of the movie without any prizes attached (Quantum of Solace) also is a writer. The reason why failures equivalence does not recognize the difference is that a failure set X only accounts for exactly one step in the graph database. In order to make failures aware of the difference in Fig. 4, we would

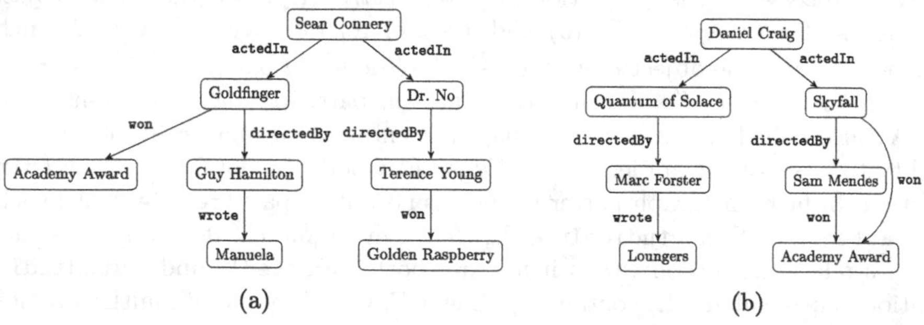

Fig. 4. Two failures equivalent graph databases, i. e., either both are failure matches of a graph pattern or none.

need that X also contains that after `actedIn` an object (here, Dr. No) does not account for the traces `won` and `directedBy` · `wrote`. For this representation, the graph database in Fig. 4(b) is not a match, since after trace `actedIn` either trace `won` or `directedBy` · `wrote` may be observed. Failures may be adapted by introducing for each $k \in \mathbb{N}$ so-called *k-failure pairs* which allow for strings of relation symbols in X of length at most k. In practice, this seems infeasible, since respecting k-failures amounts to a lot of bookkeeping. Moreover, for each k, a counterexample like the one given in Fig. 4 exists. A more elegant approach may be found in different notions of simulation, being subject of the next subsection.

3.2 Simulations

Simulations are not based on traces but rather follow the idea of relating nodes mimicking the behavior of one another. Each graph traversal step must be reflected by some step in the simulating graph. For *graph simulation equivalence*, it is necessary that one graph simulates the other and vice versa. Let us reconsider the example graphs in Fig. 3. The graph database depicted in Fig. 3(a) is a *simulation equivalence match* of the respective graph pattern if, for now, we ignore the properties attached to the objects. To establish this relationship, we need to show that the graph database (Fig. 3(b)) is capable of simulating the pattern (Fig. 3(a)) and vice versa. The respective simulations are represented in Table 1, where S_1 represents the former direction and S_2 the latter.

Table 1. Two simulations showing simulation equivalence of the graph database in Fig. 3(a) and the pattern in Fig. 3(b).

S_1: from Fig. 3(a) to Fig. 3(b)		S_2: from Fig. 3(b) to Fig. 3(a)	
USA	C	C	USA
Will Smith	A		
Jada P. Smith	A	A	Jada P. Smith
Edgar F. Codd	A		
F1	M		
F2	M	M	F2
U1	U	U	U1
U2	U		

S_1 is divided into two columns, reading a first column entry is simulated by the second column entry. Whatever relation object "USA" is in, node `C` is capable of simulating it by a respective relation, here `resident` leading to one of three persons, in turn all simulated by node `A`. Consider first "Will Smith" which is in an `actedIn` relationship with some movie object (F1, F2, U1, U2 are placeholders). Also node `A` has an outgoing edge labeled by `actedIn`, targeting node `M`. Furthermore, also the `studiedIn` relationship of the other two objects is simulated by node A, this time targeting node U. In fact, S_1 proves that the graph database is simulated by the graph pattern, since every relation in the graph is reflected by an according step in the pattern.

For the converse direction, S_2, we observe that not every node from the graph database is present in this part of the table. This is due to the simulation requirement that every node in the pattern must be simulated by some, not every possible, node in the graph database. Therefore, it is sufficient to only consider a subgraph as simulator. The edge $\texttt{C} \xrightarrow{\texttt{resident}} \texttt{A}$ is simulated by "USA" $\xrightarrow{resident}$ "Jada P. Smith". Likewise, the other relations of A are simulated by the object "Jada P. Smith". Hence, also the graph database simulates the pattern, proving that both graphs are *simulation equivalent.* When reintegrating the requirement that $\psi_{\texttt{yearOfDeath}}(\texttt{A}) \neq \bot$, object "Edgar F. Codd" needs to be excluded from a match.

Formally, a simulation between two graph databases, e. g., a graph pattern and a subgraph, is a relation over the nodes of the first graph database and that of the second. For each pair of nodes (n_1, n_2) in that relation, two conditions must hold. First, if n_1 has a defined value for property p, i. e., $\pi_p(n_1) \neq \bot$, n_2 also has a defined value for p. Second, if $n_1 \xrightarrow{a} n_1'$, then there must be a node n_2' such that $n_2 \xrightarrow{a} n_2'$ and n_2' simulates n_1'.

Definition 5. *Let DB be a graph database, $A = (O, \Sigma, P, \longrightarrow, \Pi)$ a subgraph of DB, and $\mathcal{Q} = (N_\mathcal{Q}, \Gamma, P, \longrightarrow_\mathcal{Q}, \Psi)$ a graph pattern. A simulates $\mathcal{Q}$, denoted $\mathcal{Q} \sqsubseteq_S A$, iff there is a relation $S \subseteq N_\mathcal{Q} \times O$ such that (a) for every $n \in N_\mathcal{Q}$ there is an $o \in O$ with $(n, o) \in S$ and (b) for every $(n, o) \in S$, it holds that (1) for all $p \in \mathcal{P}$, $\psi_p(n) \neq \bot$ implies $\pi_p(o) \neq \bot$ and (2) $n \xrightarrow{a}_\mathcal{Q} n'$ implies that there is an $o' \in O$ such that $o \xrightarrow{a} o'$ and $(n', o') \in S$. If $A \sqsubseteq_S \mathcal{Q}$ and $\mathcal{Q} \sqsubseteq_S A$, A and $\mathcal{Q}$ are* simulation equivalent, *denoted $A \simeq \mathcal{Q}$. The set of* simulation equivalence matches *of $\mathcal{Q}$ is defined by $[\![\mathcal{Q}]\!]^{\simeq}_{DB} := \{A \preceq DB \mid A \simeq \mathcal{Q}\}$.*

Compared to the original definitions (cf. [3,8]), we require that each node n of the graph pattern is simulated by at least one object o of the match. Omitting condition (a) entails simulation equivalence trivially holds between every two graphs, e. g., by means of the empty simulation. Others [15,17] avoid this issue by requiring maximality of simulation S, which means every other simulation is a subset of S. This requirement is unnecessarily restrictive for our purposes.

Please note, for establishing simulation equivalence, the respective simulations S_1, S_2 do not need to coincide in that $S_1 = S_2^{-1}$. Our example simulations in Table 1 already feature two very different simulations. If, however, there is a simulation S such that S^{-1} is also a simulation, then S is called a *bisimulation.* If between two graph databases there exists a bisimulation, we call them bisimilar ($\leftrightarroweq$). So far, all the relations introduced throughout this paper are interrelated as depicted in Fig. 5. A matching relation with a left-to-right path to another matching relation implies that other matching relation. It also means that the sets of matches of graph pattern $\mathcal{Q}$ are ordered by set inclusion. Graph isomorphism is primed ($\cong'$), since the hierarchy is only properly reflected if also graph

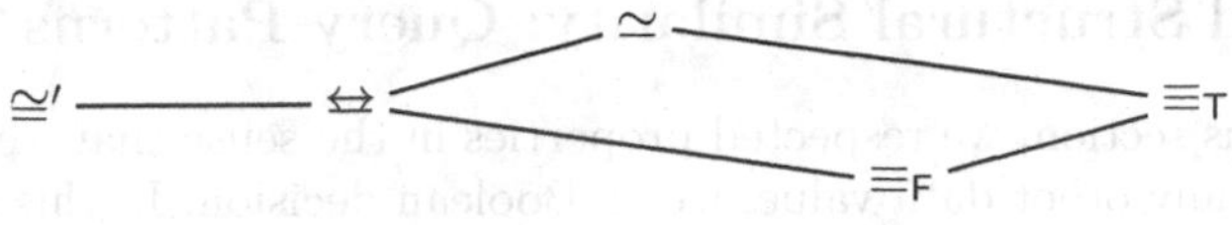

Fig. 5. The hierarchical order of the presented matching relations from [8]

isomorphism handles undefined properties. Therefore, we simply require for an isomorphism ν that for each $p \in P$, $\psi_p(n) \neq \bot$ iff $\pi_p(\nu(n)) \neq \bot$.

As already mentioned, simulation equivalence and failures equivalence are incomparable matching relations. We have shown the graphs depicted in Fig. 3 to be simulation equivalent by simulations S_1 and S_2 (cf. Table 1). As discussed in the previous subsection, these two graphs differ in their sets of failures, since the graph database contains the failure pair (`resident`, {`actedIn`}) while the graph pattern does not demonstrate this failure pair. Furthermore, the graph databases depicted in Fig. 4 are equivalent up to failures, but simulation tells them apart, as none of the graphs simulates the other. Suppose there is a simulation S showing that the graph in Fig. 4(b) simulates the graph in Fig. 4(a). Since none of the graphs is empty, there must be an object o simulating "Goldfinger", i. e., ("Goldfinger", o) $\in S$. There is only one candidate for o, namely "Skyfall", since only then relations `directedBy` and `won` may be reflected properly. But then also "Sam Mendes" ought to simulate "Guy Hamilton", which cannot be fulfilled. Thus, the graphs are not equivalent up to simulation, showing the incomparability of simulation equivalence and failures equivalence.

In practice, the choice of the matching relation depends strongly on the underlying data model. For traditional relational databases, usually a *closed-world* is assumed, thus information not being in the database can be seen as *false* [10]. As an example, the absence of the `studiedIn` relation for "Will Smith" in Fig. 3(a) means that "Will Smith" did not attend university. Therefore, a failure query using this information can only return matches with actors that did not attend any university. In the Semantic Web, on the other hand, data is usually interpreted as incomplete [16]. The absence of information does not imply that it cannot be true, but just that the information is not known, at least to the current state of the database. As a consequence, querying an open-world assumption-based database by failures would not be meaningful. In such a scenario, a simulation-based matching relation is preferable. It is even advisable to lose the equivalence matching, resulting in the requirement that a match should only simulate the query, but not vice versa. Without care, the set of matches becomes quite large and, again, less meaningful. Applications and adjustments to the simulation requirement yields reasonable matching sizes [15,17].

4 Beyond Structural Similarity: Query Patterns

In the previous section, we respected properties in the sense that we distinguish value $\perp$ from any other data value, i. e., a Boolean decision. In this section, our goal is to handle concrete data values alongside the graph pattern matching relations, letting the presented framework appear in a relational interpretation of graph database knowledge. We exemplify two ways to achieve this goal by means of simulation, which can easily be adapted to bisimulations and graph isomorphism. First, predicates over properties expressing attribute comparisons are directly attached to the nodes of the query graph. Second, global query predicates are introduced in order to express attribute comparisons between different nodes. Finally, we give a brief discussion on data integration into trace-based matchings.

Consider the example from the introduction with the graph pattern $\mathcal{Q}_a$ in Fig. 1(a). We extend the query, now asking for **actors being children of other actors, who acted in movies released after the year 2000**. Therefore, the graph pattern needs to be associated with the requirement that a match for `M1` has a release year greater than or equal to 2000, which may be expressed by the first-order formula $\varphi = \texttt{releaseYear} \geq 2000$ attached to node `M1`. Intuitively, the graph database depicted in Fig. 2 constitutes a match for simulation equivalence and the aforementioned property. Formally, however, we need to establish some assumptions before being able to integrate data values into the query matching, yielding two notions of *query pattern*.

The key assumption is that each property $p \in P$ has a *type* t, denoted $p \vdash t$, e. g., $\texttt{releaseYear} \vdash \mathbb{Z}$. For concrete data values $c \in \mathcal{D}$, $c \vdash t$ also denotes that c is a constant of type t. Furthermore, each type t is equipped with a set of binary predicates Θ_t, e. g., for type $\mathbb{Z}$ we have $\Theta_{\mathbb{Z}} = \{=, \neq, <, \leq, >, \geq\}$ with the expected meaning. As a base, we allow for comparisons of properties $p \in P$ with constants $c \in \mathcal{D}$ by predicates $\theta \in \Theta_t$ as $p\,\theta\,c$ whenever p and c have type t. Also properties $p_1, p_2 \in P$ may be compared by θ, i. e., $p_1\,\theta\,p_2$ whenever $p_1, p_2 \vdash t$. We allow the usual propositional connectives of conjunction ($\wedge$) and disjunction ($\vee$) as well as the constant **True** with the usual meaning. The following grammar summarizes the set of formulas we allow for *query predicates* (**QP**):

$$\varphi ::= \textbf{True} \;\big|\; p\,\theta\,c \;\big|\; p_1\,\theta\,p_2 \;\big|\; \varphi \wedge \varphi \;\big|\; \varphi \vee \varphi$$

where $c \in \mathcal{D}$ and $p, p_1, p_2 \in P$ with $c, p, p_1, p_2 \vdash t$ and $\theta \in \Theta_t$. Please note that the language **QP** contains features of first-order logics established in the context of graph pattern matching (e. g., [6]) or graph query languages (e. g., SPARQL).

Let $\mathcal{Q}$ be a graph pattern with set of nodes $N_{\mathcal{Q}}$. Then function $\Phi : N_{\mathcal{Q}} \rightarrow$ **QP** associates a formula φ with every node $n \in N_{\mathcal{Q}}$. We denote by φ_n that $\Phi(n) = \varphi$. A *local query pattern* is a pair $(\mathcal{Q}, \Phi)$. A simulation equivalence match $A = (O, \Sigma, P, \longrightarrow, \Psi)$ of $\mathcal{Q}$ features one simulation $S \subseteq N_{\mathcal{Q}} \times O$ showing that A simulates $\mathcal{Q}$. We evaluate the formulas φ_n alongside this simulation S. A is a simulation equivalence match of $(\mathcal{Q}, \Phi)$ iff (1) A is a simulation equivalence match of $\mathcal{Q}$ and (2) for all $(n, o) \in S$, $o \models \varphi_n$. Thereby, the satisfaction relation is defined inductively over φ_n as follows:

- $o \models$ **True**
- $o \models p\,\theta\,c$ if $\psi_p(o) \neq \bot$ and $\psi_p(o)\,\theta\,c$,
- $o \models p_1\theta\,p_2$ if $\psi_{p_1}(p) \neq \bot$, $\psi_{p_2} \neq \bot$, and $\psi_{p_1}\,\theta\,\psi_{p_2}$,
- $o \models \varphi_1 \wedge \varphi_2$ if $o \models \varphi_1$ and $o \models \varphi_2$, and
- $o \models \varphi_1 \vee \varphi_2$ if $o \models \varphi_1$ or $o \models \varphi_2$.

In our example, we would associate every node except for `M1` with predicate **True** and $\varphi_{\texttt{M1}} = \texttt{releaseYear} \geq 2000$. Indeed, the graph database depicted in Fig. 2 is a simulation equivalence match for the query pattern $(\mathcal{Q}_a, \Phi)$, because the match of `M1` satisfies the required property of the release year.

Sometimes it is necessary to compare properties of different nodes in a match, e. g., when we ask for **actors that were born in the same year**. Works on data path querying, see Libkin et al. [14] for an overview, included comparisons of data values alongside regular path queries by so-called *binding operators*. Such a binding operator stores a data value at some point of the path, which may later be compared with another data value in another part of the path. Since our setting features a whole graph pattern $\mathcal{Q}$, we may directly access the properties of pattern nodes and compare them. The syntax of such a *global query predicate* is the same except for the access of properties. Instead of referencing p, p_1, p_2 directly, we now access them via the node identifiers. Suppose we have nodes `A1` and `A2`. Then predicate $\texttt{A1.birthYear} = \texttt{A2.birthYear}$ states the aforementioned global requirement. As a consequence, a *query pattern* is a triple $(\mathcal{Q}, \Phi, \varphi_g)$ where $\mathcal{Q}$ is a graph pattern, Φ a function assigning local predicates to nodes in $\mathcal{Q}$, and φ_g is a global query predicate. The local predicates as well as the global predicates need to be satisfied. Please note that by global predicates the local ones get obsolete, formally. However, we believe that from a query modeling perspective, local predicates deserve their existence in our framework.

For bisimilarity and graph isomorphism, the adaptations for simulation equivalence directly carry over to the respective mechanisms in these matching relations, i. e., bisimulations S and isomorphisms ν. In contrast, for trace-based semantics as matchings by failures, integration is not as easy as for simulation-based matchings. One way is surely the already mentioned extensions of regular path queries [13,14]. For failure pairs (σ, X), integrating not only relations and properties in X, but also local predicates that must (not) be satisfied by an object with $o \xrightarrow{\sigma} o'$ seems feasible. Alternatively, the local predicates approach could also be integrated. We strongly believe that path queries can be adapted to work like failures equivalence matching, whose proof of effectiveness shall be subject to future work.

5 Related Work

Graph Pattern Matching is an extensively studied topic in various domains of computer science [7]. Its applications range from social network analysis, over structural analysis of chemical entities to various applications in the database domain, particularly in graph databases. In these domains, graph pattern matching is usually based on the idea of (sub-)graph isomorphism. Recently, emerging applications showed a trend of studying and using other graph pattern matching relations with the goal of reducing structural requirements of the answer graphs. For example, recent works have implemented the idea of simulation for graph pattern matching [4,5]. Indeed, experiments have shown advantages of simulation-based matching relations when analyzing social network patterns, as they offer the possibility to collapse several nodes into one node and vice versa.

With regard to *graph databases*, graph isomorphism has become the most common principle for query answering [12]. Almost every graph query language is built on graph pattern matching, using homomorphisms such as graph isomorphism, for retrieving results from the database. Recently, also in this field, different forms of *simulation* with lower runtime complexity compared to subgraph isomorphism have been analyzed to improve performance. On the downside, this performance improvement comes with a loss of topology for graph queries as criticized by Ma et al. [15]. Therefore, topologically more restrictive matching relations, also based on simulation, have been introduced [6,15]. On the one hand there is dual simulation, a form of simulation that also considers ingoing edges of nodes. Thereby, source and target of a relation are rigorously handled equally important. However, as in the case of simulation, if a graph database contains one dual simulating match, the whole database may be seen as a match. Strong simulation overcomes this issue by extending dual simulation in such a way that (1) the size of a match is bounded by the diameter of the pattern and (2) all occurring nodes and edges to match nodes and edges in the pattern [15]. Trace-based relations and, thereupon, comparative studies w. r. t. the expressed queries have not been performed.

Similar to the graph queries considered in our work, *approximate graph queries* are not restricted to returning structurally and semantically identical results. Many approximate graph query models rely on measures of pattern similarity by graph edit distances [18,19]. In comparison to our work, approximate queries might return results with a totally different structure than the query, leading to answers fulfilling only a fraction of the requirements of the original graph pattern. Also, node label similarity is studied for approximate queries [11].

6 Conclusion

We compared the meaning of failures and simulation, both originating from the studies of concurrent processes, compared to the standard matching relations, for graph database querying. Based on an overview of the restrictions arising from isomorphic matching, we showed the advantages and semantic differences of failures and simulation. Furthermore, we extended our query model by the possibility of also comparing data values, originally motivated by the findings on failures. From a modeling perspective, we provided an interplay of global and local query predicates.

Although not the focus of a conceptual model, we briefly discuss the combined complexity (database and pattern as input) of the presented relations. Compared to graph isomorphism, boiling down to the well-known NP-complete problem of subgraph isomorphism, simulations may be computed in PTIME [9]. For the trace preorder as well as the failures preorder we are facing the problem of language inclusion for nondeterminstic automata, thus rendering the respective matching problems PSPACE-complete.

Many more matching relations exist, summarized in the *linear-time branching-time spectrum* by van Glabbeek [8]. We believe that the existing knowledge on these relations may be used to get new insights on graph database querying, even if only to locate new relations in the spectrum. Since relations in the spectrum are mainly concerned with process equivalence, the domain of graph database queries may also produce insights, giving birth to not yet studied matching relations. Strong simulation [15] is such a new relation. We strongly believe, the key to include more relations is the value a matching relation holds beyond complexity considerations.

Graph patterns as we use them include a design-decision influencing every theory about graph pattern matching, namely the pattern relation symbols (Γ) are graph database symbols. Foremost in the Semantic Web, queries are stated without knowledge of the database internals, especially the names of the relations and properties. An extension of our work may assume a similarity relation of relation symbols such that traces do not have to be identical but character-wise *similar*. Furthermore, the notions discussed in this paper may be a starting point for a typing method, helping to align relation and property names.

References

1. Abriola, S., Barceió, P., Figueira, D., Figueira, S.: Bisimulations on data graphs. In: KR 2016, pp. 309–318. AAAI Press (2016)
2. Angles, R., Gutierrez, C.: Querying RDF data from a graph database perspective. In: Gómez-Pérez, A., Euzenat, J. (eds.) ESWC 2005. LNCS, vol. 3532, pp. 346–360. Springer, Heidelberg (2005). doi:10.1007/11431053_24
3. Brookes, S.D., Hoare, C.A.R., Roscoe, A.W.: A theory of communicating sequential processes. J. ACM **31**(3), 560–599 (1984)
4. Brynielsson, J., Högberg, J., Kaati, L., Mårtenson, C., Svenson, P.: Detecting social positions using simulation. In: ASONAM 2010, pp. 48–55 (2010)
5. Fan, W.: Graph pattern matching revised for social network analysis. In: ICDT 2012, pp. 8–21. ACM, New York (2012)
6. Fan, W., Li, J., Ma, S., Tang, N., Wu, Y., Wu, Y.: Graph pattern matching: from intractable to polynomial time. PVLDB Endow. **3**(1–2), 264–275 (2010)
7. Gallagher, B.: Matching structure and semantics: a survey on graph-based pattern matching. In: Papers from the AAAI FS 2006, pp. 45–53 (2006)
8. van Glabbeek, R.J.: The linear time - branching time spectrum. In: Baeten, J.C.M., Klop, J.W. (eds.) CONCUR 1990. LNCS, vol. 458, pp. 278–297. Springer, Heidelberg (1990). doi:10.1007/BFb0039066
9. Henzinger, M., Henzinger, T., Kopke, P.: Computing simulations on finite and infinite graphs. In: FOCS 1995, pp. 453–462. IEEE Computer Society (1995)
10. Imielinski, T., Lipski Jr., W.: Incomplete information in relational databases. J. ACM **31**(4), 761–791 (1984)
11. Khan, A., Wu, Y., Aggarwal, C.C., Yan, X.: NeMa: fast graph search with label similarity. PVLDB Endow. **6**(3), 181–192 (2013)

12. Lee, J., Han, W.S., Kasperovics, R., Lee, J.H.: An in-depth comparison of subgraph isomorphism algorithms in graph databases. PVLDB Endow. **6**(2), 133–144 (2012)
13. Libkin, L., Martens, W., Vrgoč, D.: Querying graph databases with XPath. In: ICDT 2013, pp. 129–140. ACM, New York (2013)
14. Libkin, L., Martens, W., Vrgoč, D.: Querying graphs with data. J. ACM **63**(2), 14:1–14:53 (2016)
15. Ma, S., Cao, Y., Fan, W., Huai, J., Wo, T.: Strong simulation: capturing topology in graph pattern matching. ACM Trans. Database Syst. **39**(1), 4:1–4:46 (2014)
16. Motik, B., Horrocks, I., Sattler, U.: Bridging the gap between OWL and relational databases. In: WWW 2007, pp. 807–816. ACM, New York (2007)
17. Mottin, D., Lissandrini, M., Velegrakis, Y., Palpanas, T.: Exemplar queries: a new way of searching. VLDB J. **25**(6), 741–765 (2016)
18. Zheng, W., Zou, L., Lian, X., Wang, D., Zhao, D.: Efficient graph similarity search over large graph databases. IEEE Trans. Knowl. Data Eng. **27**(4), 964–978 (2015)
19. Zheng, W., Zou, L., Peng, W., Yan, X., Song, S., Zhao, D.: Semantic SPARQL similarity search over RDF knowledge graphs. PVLDB Endow. **9**(11), 840–851 (2016)

Scaffolding Relational Schemas and APIs from Content in Web Mockups

Alfonso Murolo(✉), Sybil Ehrensberger, Zera Asani, and Moira C. Norrie

Department of Computer Science, ETH Zurich, 8092 Zurich, Switzerland
{alfonso.murolo,norrie}@inf.ethz.ch

Abstract. Web developers often use an interface-driven design process where mockups are gradually refined before being implemented using a platform or framework. We propose a tool, DataMockups, that supports the creation of digital mockups and then generates a relational schema automatically based on sample content and some assumptions on its structure. This aims at reducing development effort, and the database knowledge required by developers. Sample content may be entered manually or automatically using data extracted from similar existing websites. A relational schema is inferred from the data content, and then translated to an SQL database definition before generating a server-side API. To support schema evolution, the generated API provides schema abstractions that offer robustness to future schema modifications. We report on a case study for the schema inference and a performance evaluation of the data detection algorithm.

Keywords: Schema generation · Digital mockups · Interface-driven development · Scaffolding · Relational schema

1 Introduction

The research community has proposed model-driven approaches to web development that support automatic code generation and improved maintenance. However, as confirmed by a recent survey [1], many practitioners have no formal education in computer science or software engineering and are unfamiliar with data modelling techniques and database technologies. They instead tend to use an interface-driven approach, starting from a mockup that depicts the visual look of the website, its layout and navigation as well as how the content will be presented. Mockups come in many forms and have many uses including requirements analysis, graphical design and obtaining customer feedback, especially when real content is used to create the mockups [2]. For example, Protostrap[1] offers interface prototyping to simulate the real application, with real data.

Hence, methods such as AppForge [3], RAINBOW [4] and Mavo [5] have been proposed to allow application designers to generate database models or code from interface prototypes. However, many existing methods either restrict their

[1] http://protostrap.ch/.

H.C. Mayr et al. (Eds.): ER 2017, LNCS 10650, pp. 149–163, 2017.
https://doi.org/10.1007/978-3-319-69904-2_12

analysis to specific types of prototypes, or require extensive annotations following a specific set of rules which could impose cognitive load on the developers.

We therefore decided to investigate techniques to automatically generate code from high-fidelity web mockups. This paper presents DataMockups, a design tool for creating digital mockups and then generating database code from real sample content. Based on some assumptions and minimal annotations by the user, DataMockups uses a combination of structural and visual cues to generate a relational database schema together with an API for managing data. It is also possible to populate the generated database with data items extracted from the sample content. Further, by integrating the general web data extraction tool DeepDesign [6], developers can reuse data published on similar existing websites as an alternative to manually providing their own content samples. This work represents a significant advance over earlier work where we generated custom post types for WordPress based on the detection, extraction and management of individual entities [7]. In contrast, DataMockups generates full relational database schemas together with an API to manage entities and relationships. This is done using a bottom-up clustering algorithm and analysing the occurrences of elements in the clusters as well the containment relationships between clusters.

2 Background

The web engineering research community has tended to focus on model-driven web engineering (MDWE) using automatic code generation to reduce the development effort, while ensuring quality and consistency in websites [8–10]. While MDWE has had its successes, interface-driven approaches based on mockups are commonly used in practice. DENIM [11] was an early research project that generated HTML from mockups of web pages at different levels of detail. Since then, commercial tools such as Balsamiq[2] and Mockingbird[3], which offer UI prototyping and wireframing, have become widely used.

Other recent research has considered how automated website composition and code generation can be brought to the mockup design stage. MockAPI [12] introduces a metamodel for user-defined annotations that drive the derivation of an API prototype, with the goal of supporting agile methods in the creation of RESTful APIs for web services. ELECTRA [13] is a follow-on project which still targets the generation of APIs for web services but proposes an alternative hybrid approach combining agile methods, mock-up driven development and coding. MockupDD [14] took this further by translating annotations to MDWE models, or to code generated automatically. They have shown that development using MockupDD is faster and less error-prone than traditional MDWE processes. We note that all of these approaches rely on extensive use of annotations according to a metamodel to generate the necessary models and/or code. Mavo [5] introduces additional properties and expressions to HTML5 for schema-specific annotations in the markup, with the goal of defining data schemas and data-driven behaviour.

[2] https://balsamiq.com/.
[3] https://gomockingbird.com/.

In contrast to these approaches, our aim was to investigate the extent to which database code could be generated automatically based on real content used in high-fidelity mockups and with a minimum of user input. Based on an analysis of the structure and styling of the sample content, a database schema is derived and then used to generate a database together with an API to manage it. Optionally, the database may be populated with data items extracted from the sample content, and the sample content may come from existing websites as well as high-fidelity mockups. The user provides minimal annotations by labelling groups of fields with a name.

The database community has also proposed methods to generate schemas from UIs or their prototypes. GUAVA [15] generates schemas from forms of standalone applications. AppForge [3] allows developers to define schemas through the creation of web-based forms and views in a WYSIWYG editor. While this approach allows the inference of complex schemas, its views can only be designed in the form of nested tables, lists or charts. RAINBOW [4] also uses forms to support a two-way inference between interfaces and relational schemas.

Our methods build on extensive previous research addressing web data extraction, including the specific problem of *wrapper induction*. However, the main difference to much of this research is that we perform the analysis in the browser at runtime, taking into account modern web design and development practices, and relying on a single sample page. Most of the methods used for web data extraction use either structural cues based on the Document Object Model (DOM) or a series of visual cues such as the position of bounding boxes or typographic information, or some combination of both. One of the most effective measures used to detect similarities based on structural cues is the tree edit distance [16] and its variants, such as the pq-gram distance [17].

RoadRunner [18] and IEPAD [19] are systems that use structural analysis to extract data from a set of pages and a single page, respectively, while ViDE [20] is an example of a system that focuses on the use of visual cues. The latter works purely on the rendered web page and extracts first records and then fields using similarity clustering based exclusively on visual cues. While the authors acknowledge that this approach is too expensive for real-time use, we were able to build on some of their ideas while keeping our approach more tied to HTML and CSS to avoid complex visual processing. Similar to ViDE, our approach makes use of a content-rich area, which is indicated by the user in our case.

DataMockups is integrated with a Chrome extension called DeepDesign [7], which we created to extract data from arbitrary web pages in order to create custom post types within a theme editor for WordPress [6]. DeepDesign also uses a mixed analysis of structural, visual and content-related cues but, in contrast to the DataMockups extraction algorithm, works in a top-down rather than bottom-up manner. We compare the approaches in detail later in the paper.

3 The DataMockups Tool

The DataMockups design tool allows users to create mockups for different projects (see Fig. 1). Being a web application, it runs in a general-purpose browser and

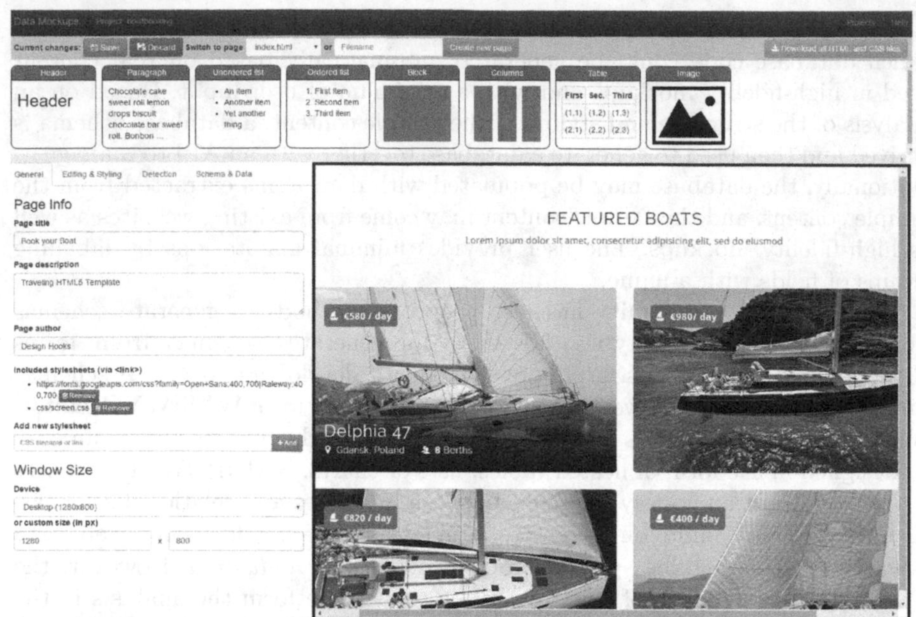

Fig. 1. DataMockups tool showing a high-fidelity mockup of a boat rental website from the case study, with a control panel (left) and elements that can be inserted (top).

exploits CSS positioning, customisations and capabilities of automatic arrangement using flexible box layout (Flexbox). We will now introduce the various features of the design tool and the development support provided by the system.

Mockup Design. There is a page switcher at the top, together with the option to create new mockups in the current project. Via the tabs on the left, the user can customise the mockup pages, the design viewport and the CSS rules for the page and individual elements. Elements can be inserted using drag-and-drop from the palette of elements located above the mockup. Although any HTML element could be supported, we currently offer only headings, paragraphs, lists, blocks, tables and pictures which are the most common elements in web pages and, in our opinion, best suited for hosting content in a mockup scenario.

It is important to note that mockups are responsive and hence an element dropped into a mockup is not assigned an absolute or relative position using pixel-based offsets from reference points, but instead is inserted into the document flow using a novel approach based on Flexbox. When an element is dragged onto the page, a purple overlay on a hovered target element is used to indicate where the inserted element will be placed if released. In the case of Fig. 2, the new element would be introduced on the left side of the existing one.

Content Editing. The content of dropped elements can be modified as in any WYSIWYG editor. On a double-click, elements can be given style customisations or transformed into links to other pages.

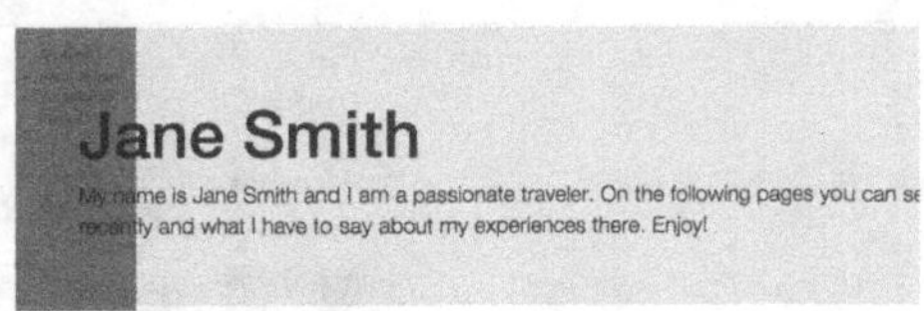

Fig. 2. A screenshot of the mouse overlay for positioning.

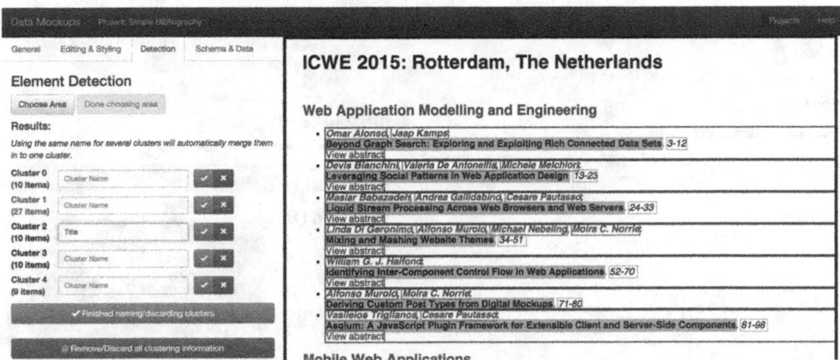

Fig. 3. Clusters detected by DataMockups in a mockup containing publications. In the screenshot, the user is hovering on the yellow cluster (Cluster 2), and corresponding elements in the mockup are highlighted. (Color figure online)

Since it can be tedious to enter sample data content, we offer the possibility for users to reuse data from existing similar websites using the integrated DeepDesign tool [7]. For example, if a website for a research group is being created, the developer will want to include a list of publications in the mockup. Instead of entering the list manually, they could for example go to their DBLP page and extract publication data from there. This would be done by running the DeepDesign browser plugin in a separate browser tab containing the DBLP page. The user would be required to label the fields of an example publication within that page, execute a matching process and then click on a button to send the data to the DataMockups tool. A new element would then appear in the palette at the top of the DataMockups window, which could be dragged into the design causing the entire set of matched publication records to be inserted in the mockup, reusing the style information of the source website.

Schema Formation. Once content has been placed into the mockups, the process of generating a database schema can begin. The first step involves detecting groups of similar data items within a page and is accessed via the *Detection* tab. Although technically not required, the user is asked to first select the area within the page where the content to be analysed is located as this reduces the processing costs significantly. Elements in the selected area are clustered together by visual and structural similarity, with the goal of having elements with similar meaning in the same cluster. Figure 3 shows an example with publications where titles, authors, pages and the publications themselves form different clusters.

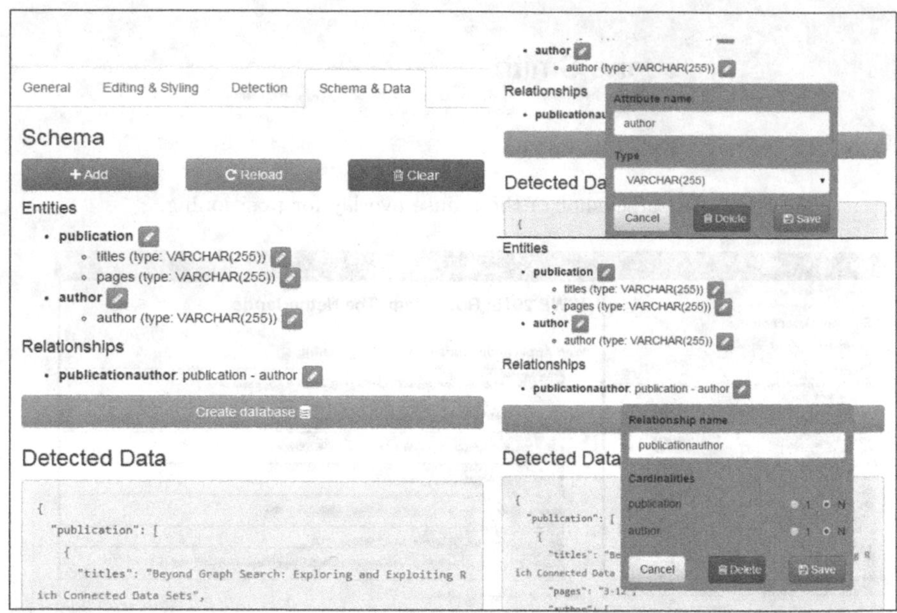

Fig. 4. A schema detected (left) which can be modified by the user (right).

The different clusters are listed on the left of Fig. 3 and hovering on the cluster name highlights all the elements in the mockup belonging to that cluster which, along with the visual cue of colour-coding, allows users to easily see how data has been matched. Users are required to give the clusters names, for example *author*, *title* and *publication*. The system then stores the clusters for use in the schema formation step. If data comes from an external website via DeepDesign, it is already clustered and labelled so this first detection step is skipped.

Schema formation is performed via the *Schema & Data* tab. An entity-relationship (ER) schema is inferred iteratively and automatically through analysis of the saved clusters and content from one mockup at a time. Some tuning of the generated schema may be required, for example to refine the type of an attribute or the cardinality of a relationship. This can be done through customisation options as shown in Fig. 4. To generate the database code, DataMockups prepares an XML representation of the schema in terms of the entities, relationships and attributes, together with their associated data types.

Database and API Generation. Once the ER schema has been finalised, a user can start the final step of generating the database. They first have to specify a few parameters such as the database name, the address of the database server and access credentials. Then the ER schema is mapped into a relational schema and the corresponding SQL generated.

Everything until this point is done on the client. The DataMockups server is responsible for generating the database and API, as well as managing projects and exporting the HTML and CSS files of the mockups. An overview of the architecture is given in Fig. 5. If the database server is reachable from the DataMockups server machine, the database can be created directly. Otherwise, the user exports SQL scripts and executes them manually. The user also receives an object-oriented PHP-based API that is able to manage the entities and relationships in the schema as well as the HTML and CSS of the mockups for further development. Since it is likely that a website under development and its schema will be modified in the future, our aim was to provide an object-oriented API which would be as change-proof as possible. We achieved this by making all calls to the API go through a so-called *Naming Service* that keeps track internally of the structure of the schema. When the database and naming service go out of sync, e.g. the developer tries to access a field which was added to the database after the code was generated, our API performs a query on the *INFORMATION_SCHEMA* table of the database to resynchronise the naming service and allow the API to access the new fields. In the case that more entities are added (i.e. tables), the API offers a class that provides similar interface abstractions to access any table in the database. While this means that newer entities will not have their own database management class, developers will still be able to use the generated API to interact with the database.

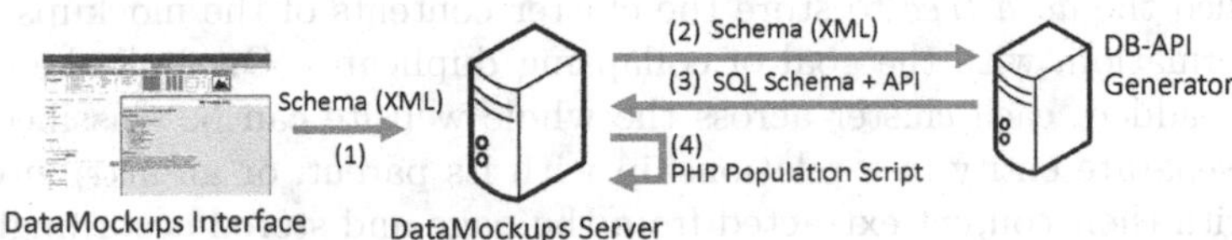

Fig. 5. The generation flow across the architecture of DataMockups. The XML defines the generated schema and API, and is used to create the database.

4 Data Detection and Schema Formation

The detection process performs a clustering of all the elements contained in the selected area of the web page, based on the assumption that the granularity of the DOM elements is enough to distinguish different tuples, entities and fields in the design. Each clustered page can contribute to the detected schema. The first parent element containing the selected area is also included in the clustering. Visually hidden elements are excluded from the clustering, i.e. elements with CSS properties such as *visibility:hidden* or *display:none*. Clearly, the overall assumption is that designed elements to be analysed are representative of the complexity of the schema being modeled.

All of these elements are used as input to a hierarchical clustering algorithm implemented with an external library[4]. The distance metric is the pq-gram edit

[4] http://harthur.github.io/clusterfck/.

distance [17] implemented in a library called JQGram[5] since it has performance advantages over the tree-edit distance. The labels of the nodes in the tree are the node names, e.g. DIV, P, and SPAN. Children of the nodes in the pq-gram input tree are the children of the nodes in the DOM tree, joined with the set of associated CSS classes. This allows visual rules to be taken into account without having to compare the entire set of CSS rules, thereby reducing runtime costs. The parameters for the pq-gram algorithm are left at the default ($P = 2$, $Q = 3$).

The pq-gram edit distance returns a distance value in the interval [0,1]. The stopping criterion for the hierarchical clustering is set to 0.8, meaning that the clustering will stop if all clusters are at least at a distance of 0.8 or more from each other. Clusters are assigned an ID and labelled by the user. The elements in a cluster are assigned a *data-cluster* property with the name as the value. This enables multiple clusters with the same naming scheme to be easily merged. Elements extracted from external websites using the DeepDesign tool are imported with these properties already assigned.

The schema formation makes two assumptions. The first is that links between clusters (such as membership or connection through relationships) are reflected in the mockup through a containment relationship in the DOM. The second assumption is that if elements of the same cluster contain identical content (e.g. the same author name) then they are matched as the same value.

The schema formation is done in two steps. First, for each mockup page, we add all the elements with a data-cluster attribute (called *cluster elements*) to a tree called the *data tree* to store the cluster contents of the mockups for the schema formation, with the goal of collapsing duplicates. Once all the clusters have been added, each cluster across the whole website can be classified as an entity, a separate entity in a relationship with its parent, or an attribute of its parent, with their content extracted from the page and stored accordingly.

The first step in adding a mockup examines all cluster elements in the mockup. For each cluster element c, we add it to the tree, creating node c_n. Cluster elements added to the tree follow the hierarchical structure that comes from the mockups: for example, if a cluster element *publication* contains many cluster elements of *authors*, the tree will contain a node for the *publication* with many children belonging to cluster *authors* (see Fig. 6). Each node c_n will also hold the reference to the corresponding cluster element c in the mockup page.

If an element e similar to c_n already exists in the tree (in terms of content and of the cluster they belong to), we mark them as mergeable. Once all the cluster elements for a mockup have been added to the tree, we iterate over the mergeable elements and mark the tree node for c_n as merged with e through a reference as long as their children do not conflict content-wise (*naive merge*). The same is attempted for the parents of e and c_n. Furthermore, in a merge operation from m to t, the children of m are merged with those of t and removed from m. Nodes which have been previously merged cannot then be targeted for a merge. Therefore, the *data tree* realises a graph, where all nodes can be bidirectionally

[5] https://github.com/hoonto/jqgram.

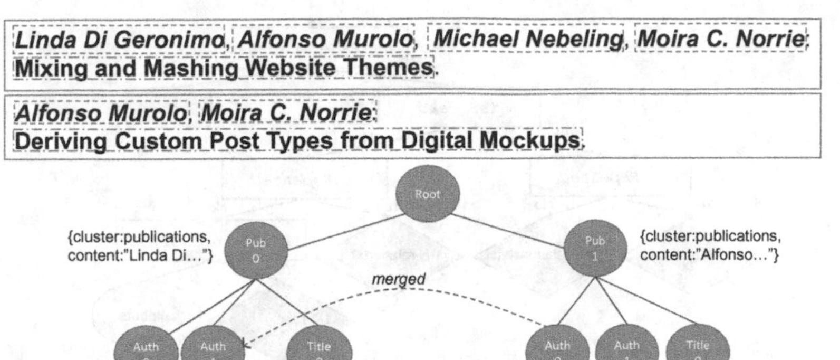

Fig. 6. A simplified example of a single mockup housing publications and the corresponding data tree. Borders show the publications (solid), authors (dashed), and titles (mixed). For simplicity, we hide the second merge that would occur. The two publications cannot be merged, since the title nodes are conflicting.

navigated in the parent-children relationship (as in a classic tree), but augmented with the merging references, which can only be navigated unidirectionally.

Once the *data tree* is constructed, the second step starts: the graph is analysed to distinguish which clusters should become entities, entities in relationships, or attributes. Iterating over the list of clusters, for each cluster *cl*, we identify all the parent clusters *p* which have *cl* as a child. For each *cl* and respective parent *p* (if any) in the *data tree*, we define cl_p as the elements of *cl* which have *p* as a parent cluster in the *data tree*. We then consider:

- whether *cl* is a child of other clusters in the *data tree* (*hasParentCluster*)
- whether, following merge links, the ratio of unique contents in cl_p to the total count of contents of cl_p is below a certain threshold (*isSpread*)
- whether any element in cl_p has any siblings of the same cluster (*isRepeated*)
- whether any of the nodes of *cl* has children clusters (*hasChildClusters*)

The decision tree leading the classification of each cluster is shown in Fig. 7. Our implementation uses a threshold of 0.95 in the *isSpread* function, since our goal was to flexibly allow some content to appear a few times and still be considered as an attribute. If a cluster is spread, we consider it an entity in a relationship with its parent. Every time the user adds a new mockup to the data tree, the schema is re-inferred using the new information, and the resulting schema can be viewed directly. The evolution of the schema depends on the order in which the mockups are added, even though the final result will be the same.

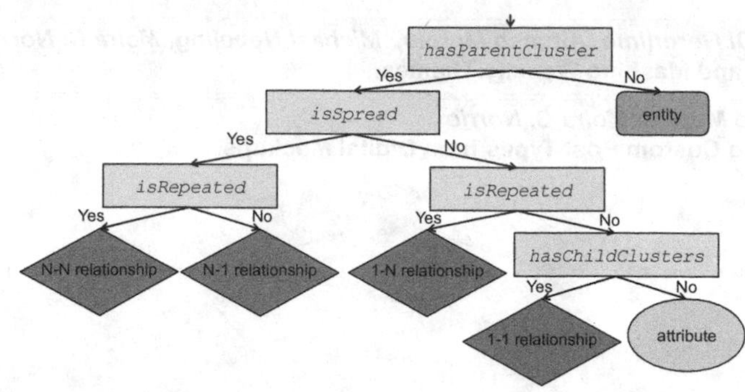

Fig. 7. The decision tree that leads to the classification of clusters.

5 Evaluation

We report on two evaluations of DataMockups. The first was a case study to evaluate the quality of the generated schemas. The second was a performance evaluation of the element detection component executed on different websites.

5.1 Case Study for Schema Formation

We aimed at assessing the quality of the schema formation algorithm by creating projects with data from 10 different data-intensive application domains related to online databases, shops and rental platforms, which are typical targets of data extraction systems. For each project, we designed multiple list pages showing results of different queries together with mockup pages showing the detailed information for some single items in these lists. An exception was the application known as FoodCASE which presents all details in the list pages.

To test the schema inference in isolation, an MSc student created and annotated these 49 mockups manually and directly fed them to the schema formation, with the default threshold for *isSpread* of 0.95. We list the projects in Table 1, and have made them available online[6] together with the resulting schemas in the form of SQL statements. As a metric, we considered the number of major mismatches (e.g. cardinality mismatches, mis-identified entities), and of minor mismatches (e.g. fields of the wrong data type) when comparing the generated schema with ones produced by a PhD student (with several years of experience in database design) while considering the same mockups.

The projects were generally correctly analysed and produced meaningful schemas. No minor mismatches occurred, with DataMockups being able to analyse the content and detect dates, integers, and floating point numbers in the content. Two projects, **Movies** and **Blog**, were inferred correctly with no mismatches detected. These two projects were quite interesting in terms of the schemas involved.

[6] http://dev.globis.ethz.ch/datamockups/DataMockups_casestudy.zip.

Table 1. All the projects used for the case study. We also report the total number of mockups compared to the number of mockups after which the schema inference reached a stable condition and did not alter the inferred schema (order dependent). The last column reports the number of major (M) and minor (m) mismatches.

Project	Domain description	Mockups	Mism.
Recipe website	Recipes with instructions, categories, times of preparation and ingredients	4/3	1M
Movie DB	Movies (with title, rating, date, description), genres, actors	7/4	0
Blog	Posts with categories, comments, authors	5/1	0
Clothes shop	Products (with title, a picture, prices, categories, description, etc.), different sizes of dresses	5/2	3M
Job search	Jobs (with title, salary, description), job types, qualification requirements, company offices in different locations	5/2	2M
Book Store	Books (with title, picture, description, genre, date, publisher) and authors	4/2	3M
Boat rental	Boat with picture, price, name, cabins, year of construction and sleeping berths	5/2	1M
Laptop shop	Products with a name, picture, price, description, RAM, color, model code, hard drive size, operating system and manufacturer	5/3	1M
Flat rental	Apartments with picture, price, name, address, size, additional information, amount of rooms and the district where they are located	6/2	1M
Food CASE	Food composition database (subset). Foods can have categories and sub-categories, and various composition measurements which vary by measurement unit	3/1	3M

In the **Movies** project, Movies have M-N relationships with both Genres and Actors. Other clusters such as the picture, the title, the movie rating, the release date, and the description were identified as attributes of the Movie entity.

In the **Blog** project, which was of similar complexity, the entities recognised were Posts (with attributes of title, content and date), Authors (with the name), Comments (with the comment date and the comment text), and Categories (with the category name). The pair *(Posts, Authors)* was recognised as a 1-N relationship, similarly to *(Posts, Comments)* and *(Comments, Authors)*. *(Posts, Categories)* was correctly identified as an M-N relationship.

In the other projects, two main types of major mismatches occurred:

- Type 1: *(a)* an attribute wrongly modeled into a different entity or *(b)* vice versa
- Type 2: the wrong multiplicity being determined for a relationship between two entities

Type 1a occurred in various cases: the preparation times of **Recipes**, the sleeping berths in the boats of the **Boat rental**, hard drive sizes for the **Notebook shop**, the number of rooms for the **Flat rental**. All of these projects were otherwise inferred correctly. Type 1b occurred for the publisher and the genre fields in the **Book Store**, the city in the **Job Search**, and the category field in the **Clothes** shop due to a lack of sample data. Type 1 mismatches occurred a total of 8 times.

The second type of mismatch, the wrong multiplicity, occurred 5 times: once in the **Clothes** project, once in the **Job Search**, once in the **Book Store** and twice in the **FoodCASE** project. Almost all of these (the exception being the Clothes and FoodCASE projects which will be discussed later) were connected to a lack of representative sample data, which was connected to a total of 7 major mismatches across the whole experiment. This highlights how critical the sample data is to the process of schema formation. We now discuss some mismatches in specific projects which are especially interesting for our schema inference.

Clothes: As previously mentioned, in this shop project, a Type 2 mismatch occurred: the Size of the clothes was generated as a separate entity involved in a 1-N relationship with Products. This case is particularly interesting since it highlights two critical aspects of the approach: the dependency on the labelling (and therefore on the mockup design), and the complexity of the schemas supported. In these mockups, the *size* and the *availability* were designed with a text label (i.e. *"Size: S,M"* and *"In stock")*. In reality, an expert database designer may separate the sizes and have the dresses in an M-N relationship (a dress can have many sizes, and a size can apply to many dresses). However, since the finest granularity in the DOM for DataMockups was the single text element "S,M" being annotated as "size", this became a 1-N relationship. This suggests that the system should, in some cases, also have a finer granularity than DOM elements to support the recognition of such lists and interpret these as multiple elements. Also, the availability could apply to the relationship *(dress,size)*, but DataMockups does not yet support the detection of relationships with attributes, accounting for an additional major mismatch.

FoodCASE: To test schema formation on a more complex example, we used it with a subset of data from the application FoodCASE[7] which was developed within a European project on food sciences. Since members of our research group were responsible for developing the database behind it, this enabled us to compare the inferred schema with the real one. The generated schema has foods in an M-N relationship with the composition measurements (Type 2 error), which in turn are in a 1-N relationship with a measurement unit, e.g. kcal, or kJ, and with the component which is a string describing the type of measurement, such as "Energy, kiloJoule". Foods are also in a 1-N relationship with a subcategory which in turn is in a 1-N relationship with a parent category. While such a schema can be complicated in terms of querying, it is almost semantically correct. In reality, the database designers show a major difference in having an N-ary

[7] http://www.foodcase.ethz.ch/index_EN.

relationship to easily relate different foods to different measurement types and measurement units, adding relationship attributes. In addition, the real schema allows foods to belong to more categories, which is the second mentioned Type 2 mismatch, possibly related to the limitation of our sample data.

Summarising, the experiments show promising results and also two main types of errors which need to be addressed. To tackle errors of Type 1*a*, it is possible to lower the *isSpread* threshold, with a level of success that depends on the sample data provided. Providing more data for a mis-classified cluster will also affect the calculations for *isSpread*. While this shows room for improvement, we plan to experiment with some questions the user could be asked to refine the defined schema if the confidence in the decision for *isSpread* is insufficient. In our experiments, most errors of Type 1*b* and Type 2 were connected to a limitation of the sample data, so providing representative data is important to avoid these; however, tuning the *isSpread* threshold may also have an effect, depending on the data. Alternatively, we also allow users to fine tune the detected multiplicities to address Type 2 mismatches. Finally, some unsupported cases still need to be addressed, namely the detection of N-ary relationships, of relationship attributes, and the handling of content which is more fine grained than the DOM.

5.2 Performance Evaluation

We evaluated the performance of the element detection component on live websites using four pages: a publications page similar to the one in Fig. 3, a DBLP page, a Google search results page and a results page from Twitter. The goal was to assess the feasibility of the element detection approach on external web pages, without selecting any area, then introducing a selection of a content-rich area and finally introducing some code optimisations (e.g. filtering hidden elements). Results on these four pages showed that the technique without selecting a content-rich area on external web pages is practically infeasible (93 s on the Google page, while it did not terminate in Twitter and DBLP within two minutes and the browser became unresponsive). Introducing area selection and optimisations could make it feasible (3.7 s of total runtime on Google). In this case, the mockup publication page only took 141 ms while the DBLP page took almost 2 s. The only page which was still very expensive was Twitter, which took 71 s. This technique may therefore only be suitable for the smaller pages occurring in mockups where it performs well, while DeepDesign performs much better when extracting data from live web pages.

6 Conclusion

We have shown how DataMockups can be used to create digital mockups and automatically generate database code from sample content. The system clusters content based on structural and style-related cues, and then generates a schema by analysing it to detect relationships between the clusters. The inferred schema is sent to a generation service that creates an SQL database definition and a PHP-based server-side API, which can be used to optionally populate the database with the content from the mockup. As an alternative to manually providing sample content, data can be extracted from existing websites.

Our inspection of a number of cases in our case study showed that the quality of the generated schemas was generally good, but identified a number of cases where the methods require refinement. The comparison of the DataMockups approach to data detection with that of DeepDesign [7], suggests that our hybrid approach of using the former for content created manually and the latter for the importation of content from external sites with larger volumes of data is justified. Finally, we cannot claim that our approach is completely general: we plan to improve the freedom in the design by introducing a *recursive merging* strategy, and to experiment with more complex datasets and designs to improve the performance as well as the quality of the schemas.

Acknowledgments. We would like to thank Loris Diana for his work on the realisation of the DB-API-Generator.

References

1. Norrie, M.C., Geronimo, L., Murolo, A., Nebeling, M.: The forgotten many? A survey of modern web development practices. In: Casteleyn, S., Rossi, G., Winckler, M. (eds.) ICWE 2014. LNCS, vol. 8541, pp. 290–307. Springer, Cham (2014). doi:10.1007/978-3-319-08245-5_17
2. Blakeley-Silver, T.: WordPress 2.8 Theme Design: Create Flexible, Powerful, and Professional Themes for Your WordPress Blogs and Websites. Packt Publishing Ltd. (2009)
3. Yang, F., Gupta, N., Botev, C., Churchill, E.F., Levchenko, G., Shanmugasundaram, J.: WYSIWYG development of data driven web applications. Proc. VLDB Endow. **1**(1), 163–175 (2008)
4. Ramdoyal, R., Cleve, A.: From pattern-based user interfaces to conceptual schemas and back. In: Jeusfeld, M., Delcambre, L., Ling, T.-W. (eds.) ER 2011. LNCS, vol. 6998, pp. 247–260. Springer, Heidelberg (2011). doi:10.1007/978-3-642-24606-7_19
5. Verou, L., Zhang, A.X., Karger, D.R.: Mavo: creating interactive data-driven web applications by authoring HTML. In: Proceedings of 29th Annual Symposium on User Interface Software and Technology, pp. 483–496. ACM (2016)
6. Murolo, A., Norrie, M.C.: Deriving custom post types from digital mockups. In: Cimiano, P., Frasincar, F., Houben, G.-J., Schwabe, D. (eds.) ICWE 2015. LNCS, vol. 9114, pp. 71–80. Springer, Cham (2015). doi:10.1007/978-3-319-19890-3_6
7. Murolo, A., Norrie, M.C.: Revisiting web data extraction using in-browser structural analysis and visual cues in modern web designs. In: Bozzon, A., Cudre-Maroux, P., Pautasso, C. (eds.) ICWE 2016. LNCS, vol. 9671, pp. 114–131. Springer, Cham (2016). doi:10.1007/978-3-319-38791-8_7
8. Hennicker, R., Koch, N.: A UML-based methodology for hypermedia design. In: Evans, A., Kent, S., Selic, B. (eds.) UML 2000. LNCS, vol. 1939, pp. 410–424. Springer, Heidelberg (2000). doi:10.1007/3-540-40011-7_30
9. Ceri, S., Fraternali, P., Bongio, A.: Web modeling language (WebML): a modeling language for designing web sites. Comput. Netw. **33**(1–6), 137–157 (2000)

10. Houben, G.-J., Barna, P., Frasincar, F., Vdovjak, R.: Hera: development of semantic web information systems. In: Lovelle, J.M.C., Rodríguez, B.M.G., Gayo, J.E.L., Puerto Paule Ruiz, M., Aguilar, L.J. (eds.) ICWE 2003. LNCS, vol. 2722, pp. 529–538. Springer, Heidelberg (2003). doi:10.1007/3-540-45068-8_99
11. Newman, M.W., Lin, J., Hong, J.I., Landay, J.A.: DENIM: an informal web site design tool inspired by observations of practice. Hum.-Comput. Interact. **18**(3), 259–324 (2003)
12. Rivero, J.M., Heil, S., Grigera, J., Gaedke, M., Rossi, G.: MockAPI: an agile approach supporting API-first web application development. In: Daniel, F., Dolog, P., Li, Q. (eds.) ICWE 2013. LNCS, vol. 7977, pp. 7–21. Springer, Heidelberg (2013). doi:10.1007/978-3-642-39200-9_4
13. Rivero, J.M., Heil, S., Grigera, J., Robles Luna, E., Gaedke, M.: An extensible, model-driven and end-user centric approach for API building. In: Casteleyn, S., Rossi, G., Winckler, M. (eds.) ICWE 2014. LNCS, vol. 8541, pp. 494–497. Springer, Cham (2014). doi:10.1007/978-3-319-08245-5_35
14. Rivero, J.M., Grigera, J., Rossi, G., Luna, E.R., Montero, F., Gaedke, M.: Mockup-driven development: providing agile support for model-driven web engineering. Inf. Softw. Technol. **56**(6), 670–687 (2014)
15. Terwilliger, J.F., Delcambre, L.M.L., Logan, J.: The user interface is the conceptual model. In: Embley, D.W., Olivé, A., Ram, S. (eds.) ER 2006. LNCS, vol. 4215, pp. 424–436. Springer, Heidelberg (2006). doi:10.1007/11901181_32
16. Tai, K.: The tree-to-tree correction problem. J. ACM **26**(3), 422–433 (1979)
17. Augsten, N., Böhlen, M., Gamper, J.: Approximate matching of hierarchical data using Pq-grams. In: Proceedings of 31st International Conference on Very Large Data Bases, VLDB Endowment (2005)
18. Crescenzi, V., Mecca, G., Merialdo, P.: Roadrunner: towards automatic data extraction from large web sites. In: Proceedings of 27th International Conference on Very Large Data Bases. Morgan Kaufmann (2001)
19. Chang, C., Lui, S.: IEPAD: information extraction based on pattern discovery. In: Proceedings of 10th International Conference on World Wide Web. ACM (2001)
20. Liu, W., Meng, X., Meng, W.: Vide: a vision-based approach for deep web data extraction. IEEE Trans. Knowl. Data Eng. **22**(3), 447–460 (2010)

SourceVote: Fusing Multi-valued Data via Inter-source Agreements

Xiu Susie Fang[1(✉)], Quan Z. Sheng[1], Xianzhi Wang[2], Mahmoud Barhamgi[3], Lina Yao[4], and Anne H.H. Ngu[5]

[1] Department of Computing, Macquarie University, Sydney, Australia
xiu.fang@students.mq.edu.au, michael.sheng@mq.edu.au
[2] School of Information Systems, Singapore Management University, Singapore, Singapore
sandyawang@gmail.com
[3] LIRIS Laboratory, Claude Bernard Lyon1 University, Villeurbanne, France
mahmoud.barhamgi@liris.cnrs.fr
[4] School of Computer Science and Engineering, UNSW, Sydney, Australia
lina.yao@unsw.edu.au
[5] Department of Computer Science, Texas State University, San Marcos, USA
angu@txstate.edu

Abstract. *Data fusion* is a fundamental research problem of identifying true values of data items of interest from conflicting multi-sourced data. Although considerable research efforts have been conducted on this topic, existing approaches generally assume every data item has exactly one true value, which fails to reflect the real world where data items with multiple true values widely exist. In this paper, we propose a novel approach, *SourceVote*, to estimate value veracity for multi-valued data items. SourceVote models the endorsement relations among sources by quantifying their two-sided inter-source agreements. In particular, two graphs are constructed to model inter-source relations. Then two aspects of source reliability are derived from these graphs and are used for estimating value veracity and initializing existing data fusion methods. Empirical studies on two large real-world datasets demonstrate the effectiveness of our approach.

Keywords: Data integration · Data fusion · Multi-valued data items · Inter-source agreements

1 Introduction

Last few years have witnessed a sheer amount of data produced and communicated among numerous sources over the Web. Unfortunately, these sources possess varying qualities and in many cases provide conflicting information on the same data items. This poses great challenges to data integration research on discovering true values from multi-sourced data, or the *data fusion* problem [7]. Considerable research efforts have been conducted to resolve this issue [8]. However, most of them assume that every data item has exactly one true value, i.e.,

H.C. Mayr et al. (Eds.): ER 2017, LNCS 10650, pp. 164–172, 2017.
https://doi.org/10.1007/978-3-319-69904-2_13

single-valued assumption. This assumption fails to reflect the reality where many data items have multiple true values [15], e.g., the authors of a book. Given a data item, although we can simply concatenate and regard the values provided by the same source as a single joint value, like what previous methods do, the sets of values provided by different sources may overlap and implicitly support one another, making the concatenation unreasonable. For example, a source may claim "Charlie Booty, Lily James, Tim Roth" while another source may claim "Charlie Booty, Lily James" as the cast of the film "Broken". Apparently, the latter set is covered by the former set and therefore partially supports the former set. Since neglecting this hint may greatly impair the data fusion accuracy on multi-valued data items, we define and conduct focused study on a new topic called the *multi-valued data fusion* problem.

To the best of our knowledge, few research efforts have been devoted to the multi-valued issue in the field of truth discovery. We identify the challenges of multi-valued data fusion and the disadvantages of existing approaches as follows. Firstly, all existing methods require initializing source reliability, and for many of them, source reliability initialization impacts their performance in terms of convergence rate and accuracy. Secondly, there are implicit endorsement relations among sources when they provide some values in common. Intuitively, a source endorsed by more sources is regarded more authoritative and its provided values can be more trusted. Unlike other widely studied source relations such as copying relations, endorsement relations among sources are neglected by the previous work. Thirdly, sources may exhibit different behavioral features on multi-valued data items: some sources may provide erroneous values, leading to false positives, while some other sources may provide partial true values without making mistakes, leading to false negatives. While these two types of errors are equivalent for single-valued data items, for multi-valued data items, differentiating these errors is crucial for identifying the complete true value set. In a nutshell, our work makes three main contributions: (i) we propose a graph-based model, called *SourceVote*, as a solution to the multi-valued data fusion problem. It uses two graphs, i.e., $\pm$*Agreement Graph*, to model the two-sided endorsement relations among sources. Random walk computations are applied on both graphs to derive two-sided vote counts of sources and to finally estimate value veracity; (ii) we further derive two-sided source reliability from the two graphs to better estimate sources' quality and initialize existing data fusion methods; (iii) we conduct extensive experiments on two large real-world datasets. The results show that SourceVote consistently outperforms the baselines.

2 Related Work

Except uniformly initializing source reliability as 0.8 [10], most previous work helps data fusion methods to initialize source reliability based on prior knowledge, which is obtained by either semi-supervised methods [2] or leveraging an external trustful information source [3]. In comparison, our approach automatically derives source reliability by capturing source endorsement relations without using any prior knowledge. The Web-link based data fusion methods [6,9] are the closest to our method. They compute the trustworthiness of sources and the truthfulness of values by using PageRank, where each link between a source and a value represents the source provides that value. However, they make single-valued assumption. To the best of our knowledge, *multi-valued data fusion* is rarely studied by the previous work. LTM (Latent Truth Model) [15] and the method proposed by Wang et al. [13] are two probabilistic models that take multi-valued objects into consideration. Waguih and Berti-Equille [10] conclude with extensive experiments that this type of models make strong assumptions on the prior distributions of latent variables, which render the modeled problem intractable and inhibitive to incorporating various considerations, and cannot scale well. Wang et al. [11] analyze the unique features of MTD and propose an MBM (Multi-truth Bayesian Model). However, they make strong assumptions on the copying of false information among sources and the independent provisioning of correct information by sources. It also requires initialization of several parameters including source reliability and copy probabilities of copiers. Recently, Wang et al. [12] design three models for enhancing existing truth discovery methods. Their experiments show that those models are effective in improving the accuracy of multi-truth discovery using existing truth discovery methods. However, LTM and MBM still performed better than those enhanced methods. None of the above methods takes the endorsement relations among sources into consideration. Different from them, our approach assumes no prior distribution or source dependency and requires no initialization of source reliability. Therefore, it is robust to various problem scenarios and insensitive to initial parameters.

3 The SourceVote Approach

The multi-valued data fusion problem involves three explicit inputs: (i) a set of *multi-valued data items*, denoted as O. Each $o \in O$ may have multiple true values; (ii) a set of *data sources*, denoted as S. Each $s \in S$ provides potential values on a subset of O; (iii) *claimed values*, denoted as V. Each $v \in V$ represents a value claimed by a source on a data item. Given a data item o, we denote the set of sources that provide values on it as S_o, and the set of all claimed values on it as V_o. In addition, we can derive several implicit inputs from the explicit inputs. Suppose the source s provides some specific values on item o (i.e., *positive claims*), denoted as ${V_{s_o}}^+$. By incorporating the *mutual exclusion assumption*, we believe s at the same time disclaims all the other values of o (i.e., *negative claims*), denoted as ${V_{s_o}}^-$, satisfying $V_o - {V_{s_o}}^+$.

To differentiate false positives and false negatives made by sources and to model source quality more precisely in multi-valued scenarios, our model focuses on two aspects of source reliability: *positive (resp., negative) precision*, the probability of the positive (resp., negative) claims of a source being true (resp., false). Note that the truth and source reliability are closely related. We formally define the multi-valued data fusion problem as follows:

Definition 1. ***Multi-Valued Data Fusion Problem.*** *Given a set of data items (O) and the conflicting values (V) claimed by a set of sources (S), the goal is to identify a set of true values (V_o^*) from V for each data item o, satisfying that V_o^* is as close to the ground truth as possible.* □

For multi-valued data items, sources may provide the same, overlapping, or totally different sets of values from one another. Generally, values agreed by the majority of sources are more trustworthy. Therefore, if the positive claims of a source are agreed by the majority of other sources, this source is likely to have high positive precision; likewise, if the negative claims of a source are disclaimed by the majority of sources, this source would be of high negative precision. That means the agreements among sources indicate endorsement, which further motivates us to model the quality of a source by quantifying the agreements and endorsement relations among data sources.

Given a data item o, we formally define the common values claimed by two sources as *inter-source agreement*. We consider two-sided inter-source agreements based on mutual exclusion. In particular, *+agreement*, the agreement between two sources (e.g., s_1 and s_2) on their positive claims of o, (denoted by $A_o{}^+(s_1, s_2)$) is calculated as:

$$A_o{}^+(s_1, s_2) = V_{s_{1_o}}{}^+ \cap V_{s_{2_o}}{}^+ \tag{1}$$

Similarly, *−agreement*, the agreement between two sources on their negative claims of o (denoted by $A_o{}^-(s_1, s_2)$) is calculated as:

$$A_o{}^-(s_1, s_2) = V_{s_{1_o}}{}^- \cap V_{s_{2_o}}{}^- = V_o - (V_{s_{1_o}}{}^+ \cup V_{s_{2_o}}{}^+) \tag{2}$$

The positive (resp., negative) precision of a source is endorsed by the +agreement (resp., −agreement) between this source and the other sources.

In this section, we present a graph-based approach, called *SourceVote*, as a solution to multi-valued data fusion, which is a two-step process: (i) creating two graphs based on agreements among sources (Sect. 3.1), and (ii) assessing two-sided source quality based on the graphs and further use the assessment results to estimate value veracity or initialize data fusion methods (Sect. 3.2).

3.1 Creating Agreement Graphs

By quantifying the two-sided inter-source agreements, we can construct two fully connected weighted graphs, namely *±agreement graphs*. In each graph, vertices represent sources, each directed edge depicts that one source agrees with/endorses another source, and the weight on each edge denotes the endorsement degree between the two sources. In particular, +agreement (resp., −agreement) graph models the +agreement (resp., −agreement) among the sources.

To construct the +agreement graph, we first formalize the endorsement from one source to another (e.g., $s_1 \rightarrow s_2$) on their positive claims. Specifically, for each data item that they both cover, we calculate the endorsement based on the

+agreement between the two sources. Then, we sum up the endorsement on all their overlapping data items as follows,

$$E^+(s_1, s_2) = \sum_{o \in O_{s_1} \cap O_{s_2}} \frac{|A_o{}^+(s_1, s_2)|}{|V_{s_{2o}}{}^+|} \tag{3}$$

where O_s denotes the set of data items covered by s. Then, we calculate the weight on the edge from s_1 to s_2 as:

$$W^+(s_1 \to s_2) = \beta + (1-\beta) \cdot \frac{E^+(s_1, s_2)}{|O_{s_1} \cap O_{s_2}|} \tag{4}$$

In Eq. (4), we add a "*smoothing link*" with a small weight between every pair of vertices, where β is the smoothing factor to guarantee the graph's full connectivity and the convergence of random walk computations. For our experiments, we simply set $\beta = 0.1$ (empirical studies [5] show this setting generally yields more accurate estimation). Finally, we normalize the weights of all out-going links of each vertex by dividing each weight by the sum of weights on all out-going links from this vertex. This normalization allows us to interpret the edge weights as the transition probabilities in random walk computations. We construct the –agreement graph in a similar way.

3.2 Estimating Value Veracity and Source Reliability

To derive two-sided source reliability (positive and negative precision) from the two graphs, the measurements should capture two features: (i) vertices with more input edges are assigned higher precision because those sources are endorsed by a large number of sources and should be more trustworthy[1]; (ii) endorsement from a source with more input edges should be more trusted because both the authoritative sources and the sources endorsed by authoritative sources are more likely to be trustworthy. We adopt *Fixed Point Computation Model* (FPC) to capture the transitive propagation of source trustworthiness through agreement links based on the ±agreement graphs [1].

By applying FPC, we obtain the ranking scores of the two-sided precision of each source among all the sources. Specifically, we refer to each agreement graph as a Markov chain, where vertices serve as the states and the weights on edges as transition probabilities between the states. We calculate the asymptotic stationary visiting probabilities of the Markov random walk, where for each graph, all visiting probabilities sum up to 1. Although, in this way, the visiting probabilities may not reflect the sources' real positive and negative precision, such feature renders the visiting probabilities of each source in the two graphs comparable. For this reason, we can count the visiting probability of each source in the +agreement (resp., –agreement) graph as the vote for its positive (resp., negative) claims being true (resp., false). We denote the corresponding vote count

[1] Here we neglect the smoothing links, i.e., no link would be there between two sources in the graphs if no common value exists between the two sources.

of each source as $\mathcal{V}^+(s)$ (resp., $\mathcal{V}^-(s)$) and further estimate the veracity of each claimed value as follows:

$$Veracity(v) = \begin{cases} True; & \text{if } \sum_{s \in S_v^+} \mathcal{V}^+(s) > \alpha \cdot \sum_{s \in S_v^-} \mathcal{V}^-(s) \\ False; & otherwise \end{cases} \quad (5)$$

where α is the source confidence factor, ${S_v}^+$ (resp., ${S_v}^-$) represents the set of sources that claim (resp., disclaim) v regarding o. Given a single-valued data item, if a source claims a value, the source certainly disclaims all the other potential values. However, sources may not know the number of true values on the data items and thus do not necessarily reject negative claims on multi-valued data items. Therefore, we adopt a new mutual exclusion definition [11] and further add a source confidence factor, $\alpha \in (0, 1)$, to differentiate the confidence of each source on its positive claims and negative claims.

To further quantify the two-sided source reliability based on the calculated visiting probabilities, we apply a two-step normalization process: (i) given the source which has the highest visiting probability in the +agreement graph (resp., –agreement graph), we first manually evaluate the positive precision (resp., negative precision) of the source, and then divide the evaluated positive precision (resp., negative precision) by the visiting probability to derive the *normalization rate*; (ii) normalizing the visiting probabilities of all sources as positive precision or negative precision, by multiplying the corresponding normalization rates.

Note that most existing methods start with initializing source reliability as a default value, e.g., set source reliability as 0.8 [10]. Such initialization may fundamentally impact the convergence rate and precision of methods. According to Li et al. [7], "*knowing the precise trustworthiness of sources can fix nearly half of the mistakes in the best fusion results*". As constructing and computing our agreement graphs can be easily realized and require no initialization of source reliability, our approach can be applied to existing methods for more precise source reliability initialization.

4 Experiments

We used two real-world datasets, including the *Parent-Children Dataset* [9] and the *Book-Author Dataset* [14]. To compare our method with traditional data fusion algorithms, we investigated the existing approaches that can be modified to tackle the multi-valued data fusion problem. As a result, we identified six methods as baselines: Voting, Sums (Hubs and Authorities) [6], Average-Log [9], TruthFinder [14], 2-Estimates [4], LTM [15], and MBM [11].

4.1 Comparison of Data Fusion Methods

Table 1 shows the performance of different approaches on the two datasets. The results show that our approach consistently achieved the best recall and F_1 score among the methods. Compared with the two existing multi-valued data fusion

Table 1. Comparison of different methods: the best and second best performance values are in bold.

Method	Book-Author dataset				Parent-Children dataset			
	Precision	Recall	F_1 score	Time(s)	Precision	Recall	F_1 score	Time(s)
Voting	**0.84**	0.63	0.72	**0.07**	**0.90**	0.74	0.81	**0.56**
Sums	**0.84**	0.64	0.73	0.85	**0.90**	0.88	0.89	1.13
Avg-Log	**0.83**	0.60	0.70	0.61	**0.90**	0.88	0.89	**0.75**
TruthFinder	**0.84**	0.60	0.70	0.74	**0.90**	0.88	0.89	1.24
2-Estimates	0.81	0.70	0.75	**0.38**	**0.91**	0.88	0.89	1.34
LTM	0.82	0.65	0.73	0.98	0.88	**0.90**	0.89	0.99
MBM	**0.83**	**0.74**	**0.78**	0.67	**0.91**	0.89	**0.90**	2.17
SourceVote	0.81	**0.77**	**0.79**	0.63	**0.90**	**0.92**	**0.91**	0.91

methods (LTM and MBM), SourceVote had the lowest execution time. This is because LTM conducted complicated Bayesian inference over a probabilistic graphical model, and MBM includes time-consuming copy detection. Moreover, Both LTM and MBM are iterative approaches; in contrast, our approach is based on a simpler graph-based model. Although our approach achieved no significantly superior precision, the recall was improved drastically. For F_1 score, SourceVote consistently achieved the highest values for both datasets. The results reveal that our approach performs the best overall among all these baseline methods, which is consistent with our expectation because it makes no prior assumption and considers the endorsement relations among sources by combining with the graph-based method.

4.2 Empirical Studies of Different Concerns

We conducted experiments on the aforementioned baselines[2], to validate the feasibility of modeling source reliability by quantifying two-sided inter-source agreements and the feasibility of using SourceVote to initialize the existing data fusion methods. Figure 1(a) describes the performance comparison of the SourceVote initialized methods with their original versions on the Book-Author dataset. The results show that initializing source reliability by applying *SourceVote* almost led to better performance of all methods, indicated by higher precision and recall, and lower execution time. This reflects that the source reliability evaluated by *SourceVote* is more accurate than the widely applied default value of 0.8. With precise initialization, all methods achieved faster convergence speed. We also investigated the performance of SourceVote by tuning the values of the source confidence factor α from 0 to 1 on both datasets. Figure 1(b) shows the impact of α on the performance of SourceVote on the Book-Author dataset. The overall

[2] Note that we did not apply *SourceVote* to *Voting*, because *Voting* assumes all sources are equally reliable.

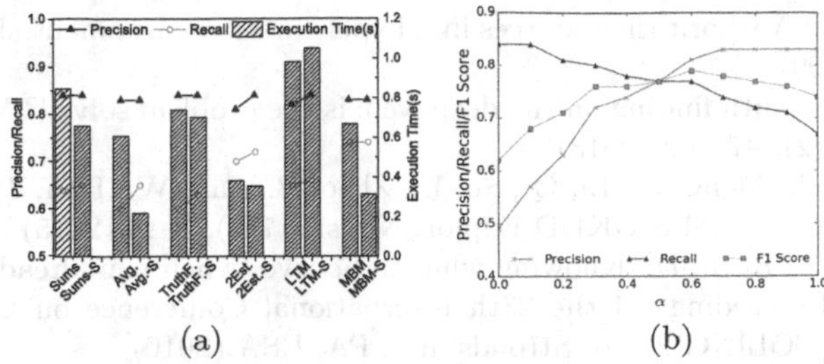

Fig. 1. (a) Comparison between the original versions of representative existing data fusion methods and the versions that apply SourceVote for precise source reliability initialization. The latter versions are marked by suffix "-s". (b) Performance of SourceVote under varying source confidence factor, i.e., α.

performance of SourceVote peaked at the point of $\alpha = 0.6$ with an F_1 score of 0.79, which is consistent with our intuition that source confidence on positive claims should be more respected. For $\alpha \in [0.3, 0.9]$, the lowest F_1 score of SourceVote is 0.76, which is still higher than the other baseline methods. The experimental results on Parent-Children dataset showed the similar results.

5 Conclusion

In this paper, we have proposed a novel approach, *SourceVote*, to address the multi-valued data fusion problem. Our approach models the endorsement relations among sources by quantifying the agreements among sources on their positive and negative claims. Two aspects of sources reliability are derived from the modelled relations. Due to the compact feature of SourceVote, it can be leveraged to initialize and improve the existing data fusion methods. Experimental results on two large real-world datasets show that our approach outperforms the state-of-the-art data fusion methods.

References

1. Brin, S., Page, L.: The anatomy of a large-scale hypertextual web search engine. Comput. Netw. ISDN Syst. **30**(1–7), 107–117 (1998)
2. Dong, X.L., et al.: Less is more: selecting sources wisely for integration. VLDB Endow. (PVLDB) **6**(2), 37–48 (2013)
3. Dong, X.L., et al.: Knowledge vault: a web-scale approach to probabilistic knowledge fusion. In: Proceedings of the 20th ACM SIGKDD International Conference on Knowledge Discovery and Data Mining (KDD 2014), New York, USA (2014)
4. Galland, A., et al.: Corroborating information from disagreeing views. In: Proceedings of the Third ACM International Conference on Web Search and Data Mining (WSDM 2010), New York, USA (2010)
5. Gleich, D.F., et al.: Tracking the random surfer: empirically measured teleportation parameters in pagerank. In: Proceedings of the 19th International World Wide Web Conference (WWW 2010), Raleigh, NC, USA (2010)

6. Kleinberg, J.: Authoritative sources in a hyper-linked environment. J. ACM **46**(5), 604–632 (1999)
7. Li, X., et al.: Truth finding on the deep web: is the problem solved? VLDB Endow. (PVLDB) **6**(2), 97–108 (2013)
8. Li, Y., Gao, J., Meng, C., Li, Q., Su, L., Zhao, B., Fan, W., Han, J.: A survey on truth discovery. ACM SIGKDD Explor. Newsl. **17**(2), 1–16 (2015)
9. Pasternack, J., Roth, D.: Knowing what to believe (when you already know something). In: Proceedings of the 23th International Conference on Computational Linguistics (COLING 2010), Stroudsburg, PA, USA (2010)
10. Waguih, D.A., Berti-Equille, L.: Truth discovery algorithms: an experimental evaluation. arXiv preprint (2014). arXiv:1409.6428
11. Wang, X., et al.: An integrated Bayesian approach for effective multi-truth discovery. In: Proceedings of the 24th ACM International Conference on Information and Knowledge Management (CIKM 2015), Melbourne, Australia (2015)
12. Wang, X., et al.: Empowering truth discovery with multi-truth prediction. In: Proceedings of the 25th ACM International Conference on Information and Knowledge Management (CIKM 2016), pp. 881–890 (2016)
13. Wang, X., et al.: Truth discovery via exploiting implications from multi-source data. In: Proceedings of the 25th ACM International Conference on Information and Knowledge Management (CIKM 2016), pp. 861–870 (2016)
14. Yin, X., et al.: Truth discovery with multiple conflicting information providers on the web. In: Proceedings of the 13th ACM SIGKDD International Conference on Knowledge Discovery and Data Mining (KDD 2007), San Jose, California, USA (2007)
15. Zhao, B., et al.: A Bayesian approach to discovering truth from conflicting sources for data integration. The VLDB Endow. (PVLDB) **5**(6), 550–561 (2012)

Level-Aware Ecosystem Transformations for Industrial Lifecycle Interoperability

Matt Selway(✉), Markus Stumptner, Michael Schrefl, and Andreas Jordan

Advanced Computing Research Centre, University of South Australia, Adelaide, Australia
{matt.selway,andreas.jordan}@unisa.edu.au, mst@cs.unisa.edu.au, schrefl@dke.uni-linz.ac.at

Abstract. Interoperability between heterogeneous software ecosystems at increasing scale remains a major challenge. The automated translation of data between the data models and languages built around official or de facto standards is best addressed using model-driven engineering techniques, but requires handling both data and multiple levels of metadata within a single model. In this paper we demonstrate the use of the SLICER multi-level modelling framework as the basis for creating conceptual and executable mappings between diverse data and metadata across multiple levels. We show how an interoperability designer can abstract from the details of specific models, enrich them with SLICER semantics, and develop mappings between them. We present a case study in the industrial plant engineering domain to map plant information for lifecycle information management, demonstrating how the methodology produces alignment across highly heterogeneous standards.

Keywords: Metamodelling · Conceptual models · Multilevel modelling · Ecosystem interoperability

1 Introduction

Lack of interoperability between computer systems remains one of the largest challenges of computer science and costs industry tens of billions of dollars each year [4,15]. Continued efforts to solve interoperability through standards for data exchange have failed as *heterogeneous ecosystems* form around different standards. These ecosystems comprise large groups of software systems built around different standards that must interact to support the entire system lifecycle and where, even within a given industry, the standards are not universally applied. Therefore, the issue of interoperability remains for both intra- and inter-ecosystem interactions.

To enable sensor-to-boardroom reporting, the effort to establish and maintain interoperability solutions must be drastically reduced. This can be achieved using model transformations based on high-level conceptual models. However, the traditional approach using two-level models as the starting point for integration is inadequate as they can lead to omission or distortion of domain level

H.C. Mayr et al. (Eds.): ER 2017, LNCS 10650, pp. 173–181, 2017.
https://doi.org/10.1007/978-3-319-69904-2_14

relationships, even for deceptively simple problems such as the classic Lassie-Dog-Breed example [1]. This significantly increases the burden on the mapping designer, possibly leading to more complex mappings with hidden weaknesses, and makes maintenance and updates more laborious. This is particularly relevant since an interoperability solution is affected by changes in *any* of the systems involved.

Instead, the development of high-level conceptual models and model transformations is best suited to multi-level modelling (MLM) approaches, which can express the multi-level nature of the domain without imposing a traditional two-level structure. For example, in the creation of an engineering part or plant in the Oil & Gas industry, different concepts are considered primitive objects during different lifecycle stages: during design, the specification for a (type of) pump has its own lifecycle (e.g. creation, revisions, obsolescence), while in operations the same object is considered a type with respect to physical pumps that have their own lifecycle (e.g. manufacturing, operation, end-of-life). Moreover, the same objects are viewed differently at the organisational level: e.g., through concepts providing cross-classifications of objects at other levels. Hence, there appear to be three levels of data: business, specification, and physical entity. These domain properties should be reflected in a flexible conceptual framework that simplifies the creation of mappings by the interoperability designer.

One such approach is SLICER [12], a flexible MLM-based conceptual framework for building joint (meta)models that encompass the heterogeneities of different information ecosystems and serve as the common representation of information transferred across an ecosystem (cf. Fig. 1). SLICER allows interoperability designers to factor out the meaning of the models being studied, assisted by automated inference and consistency checking, allowing their successful integration and interoperability. In this paper we leverage SLICER to create executable mappings between models consisting of multiple levels of (meta)data. The interoperability designer first abstracts from the details of a specific source or target model. The system then assists in identifying the SLICER distinctions to *enrich* the models and reformulate them into consistent multi-level models. The designer then develops the mappings between the models. We present a case study in the industrial plant engineering domain to map plant information for lifecycle information management and demonstrate how the methodology produces alignment across highly heterogeneous standards.

The remainder of this paper is structured as follows: Sect. 2 briefly introduces the SLICER framework on which we build our model mappings; we then use a simplified industrial case study to describe the methodology for creating mappings using SLICER, in which the model undergoes multi-level enrichment Sect. 3 followed by the definition of mappings Sect. 4; finally, we conclude and discuss future directions in Sect. 5.

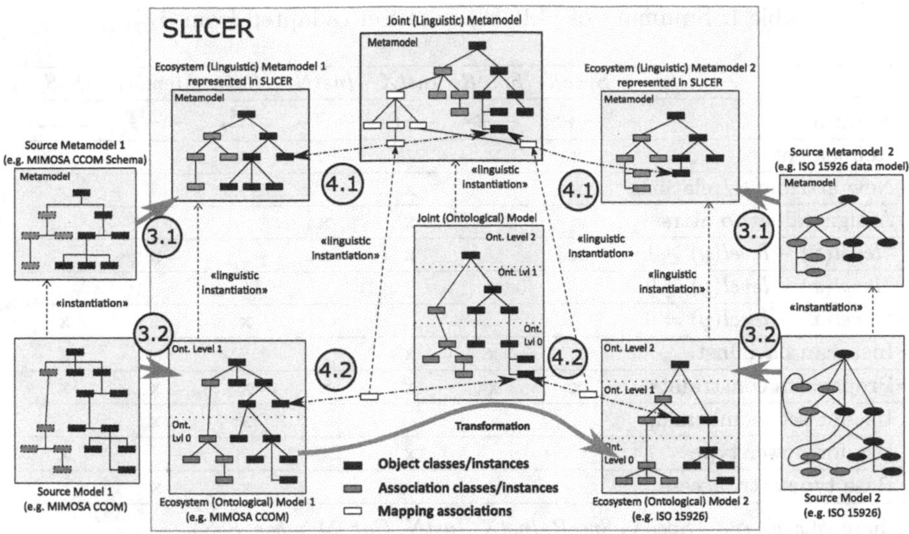

Fig. 1: Ecosystem interoperability through a joint metamodel (numbers refer to sections of this paper).

2 Brief Introduction to SLICER

SLICER is based around five core relations (two with two sub-relations each) and the use of explicit descriptions (i.e. sets of constraints) for an object: the full definition of SLICER can be found in [13]. The relations include: Standard Instantiation (*InstN*) and Instantiation with Extension (*InstX*), Specialisation by Refinement (*SpecR*) and Specialisation by Extension (*SpecX*), Subset by Specification (*SbS*), Categorisation (*Cat*), and Membership (*Member*) A summary of the SLICER relationships, their features, and notation is shown in Table 1. In contrast to other MLM approaches—such as Melanee [2] and FMML^X[5]—SLICER has unique characteristics, including:

- Existence and subordination of levels is dynamic, determined by the relations: i.e. no a priori specified levels or *potency* values for the depth of instantiation.
- Instantiation determined by value assignment to attributes defined at the higher-level: *InstN* assigns *all* attributes of an object, otherwise *InstX*.
- Specialisation determined by the addition of new attributes to the sub-concept: a specialisation that introduces new attributes is *SpecX*, otherwise *SpecR*.
- Model levels are *not* levels of instantiation: non-instantiation relations, such as *SpecX*, introduce new model levels.
- Incorporates the power type pattern [10] through *SbS*: a specification concept is linked to a partitioned concept (its base type) such that the instances of the former are subclasses of the latter (but not necessarily the inverse). Allows constraints to be defined across instantiation levels. Multiple *SbS* relations may refer to the same base type, supporting restricted multiple-inheritance.

Table 1: Summary of SLICER notation (adapted from [13])

	SpecX	*SpecR*	*InstX*	*InstN*	*Cat*	*Member*	*SbS*
Notation	—+▷	—▷	- - -|>	- - ->	$\xrightarrow{Cat}$	-·-·->	$\xrightarrow{SbS}$
Refinement	x	x					
New attributes/relations	x		x				
Assign values to attrs.			x	x			
[a] $level(x) - level(y) \geq 1$	x		x	x		x	
[a] $level(x) - level(y) \geq 0$		x					
[a] $level(x) - level(y) = 0$					x		x
Inst. can have inst.	x	x	x			x	x
Propagates constraints	x	x	x	x	x	x	x
Use for set membership					x	x	
Use for power type			x				x
Base type attr. access					x	x	x

[a] Where $\phi(x, y), \phi \in \{SpecX, SpecR, InstX, InstN, Cat, Member, SbS\}$.

- Differentiates categorisation from instantiation: categorisation is basic set membership, where an object can have multiple categories (if it conforms to the membership criteria), while instantiation is generally limited to a single type and imposes value assignment to attributes defined by the type. *Cat* links a category to its base type, *Member* links an object to a category.
- Includes explicit descriptions of constraints with intuitive propagation across multiple levels of instantiation: e.g., a constraint between a specification concept and its base type is propagated firstly to the instances of the specification type (which are subclasses of the base type) and again to their instances.

3 Multi-level Enrichment

Complex standards typically comprise a data model and reference data containing instances of multi-level patterns (see [8]) as a workaround for being defined in a two-level language. Therefore, the source/target models must undergo semantic and multi-level enrichment at both the linguistic (i.e. data model/schema) and ontological dimensions (i.e. reference data instances) [6]. In Fig. 1, the thick grey arrows labelled with numbers identify the steps and their corresponding sections below. After the initial conversion into SLICER, instances of specific SLICER relations are identified to help identify hidden semantics, improve model comparisons, and assist the definition and structuring of the joint metamodel [13]. We demonstrate this process in the context of the OGI Pilot—an instance of the Open Industry Interoperability Ecosystem (OIIE) initiative[1] that aims for the automated, model-driven transformation of data during the asset lifecycle

[1] http://www.mimosa.org/open-industrial-interoperability-ecosystem-oiie.

between two of the major data standards in the Oil & Gas industry ecosystem. MIMOSA CCOM [9], one of the major standards, is a two-level domain model defined in UML using XML for information exchange, exhibiting many of the multi-level patterns. For brevity, we focus on the concept Asset (representing individual assets such as a physical pump) and their types (i.e. AssetType), of which a simplified extract is illustrated in Fig. 2a. The upper box illustrates the MIMOSA CCOM data model, while the lower box contains its instances.

3.1 Mapping the Linguistic Dimension to SLICER

Mapping the linguistic dimension requires transformation of both the implementation language and linguistic metamodel. This requires mapping them to SLICER primitives—e.g. objects, attributes, instantiation, and specialisation—using knowledge of the model and analysis of its constructs. For MIMOSA CCOM, its definition in UML is converted: its classes, attributes, associations, etc. are mapped to SLICER primitives. We then identify aspects of the CCOM metamodel (i.e. specific attributes, etc.) that also map to SLICER primitives: e.g., the *type* association (see Fig. 2a) maps to SLICER instantiation, *superType* maps to specialisation, and the Attribute and AttributeType concepts become SLICER attributes. Moreover, the CCOM concept Model represents both specific (revisions of) models of assets, through the *model* association, and the definition of attribute specifications for AssetTypes, through *modelTemplate*. The attributes of an Asset merge those of the *modelTemplate*s and the *model*. Therefore, we infer specialisation between the Model of an Asset and its AssetTypes and the *model* association is another instantiation relation. The result is a unified view of objects that enables the enrichment of non-SLICER models with SLICER distinctions.

3.2 Enriching the Ontological Dimension

Next, instances of general relations in the ontological model, i.e. the reference data, are classified according to their subrelations (*InstN*, *InstX*, *SpecR*, and *SpecX*) in an automated fashion. Only the ontological attributes are analysed to prevent unexpected extension relations between objects that implement different linguistic types, e.g., when comparing an instance of Model to an AssetType. The bottom of Fig. 2a illustrates the enriched version of the CCOM example: bracketed attributes are from linguistic instantiation, attributes prefixed by '/' are derived from a mapping rule. After identifying the semantic distinctions, level assignment is performed automatically. Level stratification aids the interoperability designer by showing the alignments of separate model hierarchies as objects are mapped. Such alignments can be a simple indicator of correct mappings, while level (and other constraint) violations indicate possibly missing concepts and/or incorrect mappings as levels are determined dynamically from the content of the models.

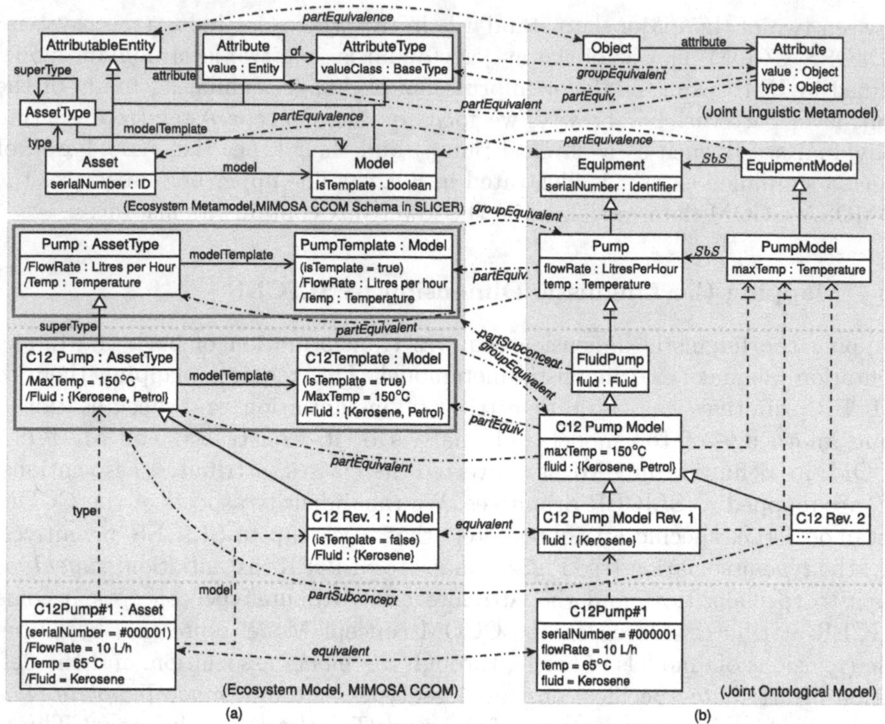

Fig. 2: CCOM → joint metamodel mapping example. (For clarity, instantiation relations between mappings are omitted.)

4 Multi-level Mappings

SLICER is extended with conceptual relations allowing the interoperability designer to define mappings between elements of different models. Unlike typical model transformation languages, such as those surveyed in [7], we define transformations at the conceptual level by leveraging SLICER's object descriptions to specify declarative mappings that enable cross-model consistency checking while providing execution semantics along the lines of transformation operators [3,14].

4.1 Semantic Mapping Relations

Conceptual and semantic relations for interoperability, such as those described by [11] in a two-level modelling context, have been known for a long time. Rather than being defined at a single meta-level and used by a single instance level, mappings in a multi-level context can occur at any level and can instantiate higher-level mappings. Using SLICER we define a taxonomy of mapping relations along the lines of [3,11,14]. To flexibly handle model variations, individual mapping relations are not necessarily bidirectional nor are inverse relations implied. Moreover, mappings can be composed to form a pattern that can be reused in the identification of mappings from the joint model to other targets.

This taxonomy includes, but is not limited to, the following relations (for brevity we do not discuss attribute, association, or functional mappings):

Equivalent(x, y) x and y represent the *same* thing (concept or object). For concepts, this implies they have the same extension (i.e. instances) across the integrated model; different models may have different sets of instances at any one time, but they can be transformed from one to the other. The description of the relation specifies the attribute level equivalences.

Subconcept(x, y) x is an (unknown) *subconcept* of y; the extension of x may completely overlap that of a known subconcept of y without implying equivalence as the extensions *may* differ. Moreover, x may overlap multiple known subconcepts: during transformations, the generated instances are classified using the descriptions. The inverse, *superconcept*(y, x), is not implied (nor vice versa).

Partial mappings (*partEquivalent*(x, y), *partSubconcept*(x, y), etc.) some part (defined by the description of the relation instance) of x is equivalent/subconcept/etc. to (possibly part-of) of y. Applies when an element of one model conceptually covers only some part of another, either because the model excludes some aspect or because it maps to multiple objects/concepts.

Group mappings (inverse of the partial relations) map a group of elements to an element, or multiple elements, of another model.

4.2 Defining Joint Model Mappings

Figure 2 illustrates the mapping between the CCOM example (left) and a simple joint (ontological) model (JM) that was created, in part, by also examining ISO15926-based models. At the top, CCOM Asset has a (bidirectional) partial equivalence to JM Equipment, with a similar mapping between Model and EquipmentModel. This reveals the *SbS* nature of the relationship between Asset and Model since the instances of Model are subtypes of Asset through instances of AssetType. This is shown by C12 Rev. 1 of the enriched CCOM model and its equivalent in JM. Grouping Pump with its *modelTemplate* provides an equivalence to JM Pump. The inverse relations identify how Pump would be split between the asset type and model template during a reverse transformation.

FluidPump, which has no equivalent in the CCOM model, is mapped using the *partSubconcept* relation indicating that it (and its subtypes) are a subtype of CCOM Pump. This mapping could be automatically determined by the equivalence of its supertype in the JM with CCOM Pump; however, additional constraints can be added for consistency when transforming unmapped subtypes.

Using the AssetType/*modelTemplate* pattern, C12 Pump is *groupEquivalent* to C12 Pump Model. Although seemingly inconsistent (C12 Pump Model only *refines* its super type), the extension in the hierarchy to their common parent (i.e. Pump) maintains consistency. Importantly, this mapping clarifies the instantiation of */MaxTemp* from Pump Model, otherwise undefined in the CCOM model.

The mappings and their descriptions allow C12Pump#1 of the CCOM model, for example, to be transformed into its equivalent in the JM. Similarly, C12 Rev. 2 could be instantiated in the CCOM model, replacing the *partSubconcept* to C12 Pump with equivalence relations to the newly instantiated elements. Such generated relations denote instances of mappings of a higher level.

5 Conclusion

We have presented a SLICER-based conceptual modelling approach to designing model transformations between complex, multi-level models and demonstrated its use for defining conceptual and executable mappings between diverse data and metadata across multiple levels. Using the approach an interoperability designer can abstract from the details of a specific source or target model and develop mappings between them using enriched semantics provided by SLICER. We give a case study in the industrial plant engineering domain in which we transform the linguistic and ontological models of MIMOSA CCOM into SLICER and then use the mapping relations to link them to a joint (meta)model, demonstrating how to produce alignment across highly heterogeneous standards. Future work will address mappings related to categories and specification types, which are basic concepts in SLICER that would facilitate identification of mappings.

Acknowledgements. This research was funded in part by the South Australian Premier's Research and Industry Fund grant no. IRGP 37.

References

1. Atkinson, C., Kühne, T.: The essence of multilevel metamodeling. In: Gogolla, M., Kobryn, C. (eds.) UML 2001. LNCS, vol. 2185, pp. 19–33. Springer, Heidelberg (2001). doi:10.1007/3-540-45441-1_3
2. Atkinson, C., Gerbig, R.: Flexible deep modeling with melanee. In: Modellierung (Workshops). LNI, vol. 255, pp. 117–122. GI (2016)
3. Berger, S., Grossmann, G., Stumptner, M., Schrefl, M.: Metamodel-based information integration at industrial scale. In: Petriu, D.C., Rouquette, N., Haugen, Ø. (eds.) MODELS 2010. LNCS, vol. 6395, pp. 153–167. Springer, Heidelberg (2010). doi:10.1007/978-3-642-16129-2_12
4. Fiatech: Advancing interoperability for the capital projects industry: a vision paper. Technical report, Fiatech, Feburary 2012
5. Frank, U.: Multilevel modeling. Bus. Inf. Syst. Eng. **6**(6), 319–337 (2014)
6. Igamberdiev, M., Grossmann, G., Selway, M., Stumptner, M.: An integrated multi-level modeling approach for industrial-scale data interoperability. Softw. Syst. Model. **16**, 1–26 (2016)
7. Kusel, A., Schönböck, J., Wimmer, M., Kappel, G., Retschitzegger, W., Schwinger, W.: Reuse in model-to-model transformation languages: are we there yet? Softw. Syst. Model. **14**(2), 537–572 (2015)
8. de Lara, J., Guerra, E., Cuadrado, J.S.: When and how to use multilevel modelling. ACM Trans. Softw. Eng. Methodol. **24**(2), 12:1–12:46 (2014)

9. MIMOSA: Open Systems Architecture for Enterprise Application Integration (2014)
10. Odell, J.J.: Power types. JOOP **7**, 8–12 (1994)
11. Schrefl, M., Neuhold, E.J.: Object class definition by generalization using upward inheritance. In: Proceedings of ICDE, pp. 4–13. IEEE Computer Society (1988)
12. Selway, M., Stumptner, M., Mayer, W., Jordan, A., Grossmann, G., Schrefl, M.: A conceptual framework for large-scale ecosystem interoperability. In: Johannesson, P., Lee, M.L., Liddle, S.W., Opdahl, A.L., López, Ó.P. (eds.) ER 2015. LNCS, vol. 9381, pp. 287–301. Springer, Cham (2015). doi:10.1007/978-3-319-25264-3_21
13. Selway, M., Stumptner, M., Mayer, W., Jordan, A., Grossmann, G., Schrefl, M.: A conceptual framework for large-scale ecosystem interoperability and industrial product lifecycles. Data Knowl. Eng. **109**, 85–111 (2017). Online first
14. Wimmer, M., Kappel, G., Kusel, A., Retschitzegger, W., Schoenboeck, J., Schwinger, W.: Surviving the heterogeneity jungle with composite mapping operators. In: Tratt, L., Gogolla, M. (eds.) ICMT 2010. LNCS, vol. 6142, pp. 260–275. Springer, Heidelberg (2010). doi:10.1007/978-3-642-13688-7_18
15. Young, N., Jones, S.: SmartMarket report: interoperability in construction industry, Technical report. McGraw Hill (2007)

Conceptual Modeling: Enhancement Through Semiotics

Veda C. Storey[1] and Bernhard Thalheim[2](✉)

[1] Computer Information Systems, J. Mack Robinson College of Business, Georgia State University, Atlanta, GA, USA
vstorey@gsu.edu

[2] Department of Computer Science, Christian-Albrechts-University, Kiel, Germany
thalheim@is.informatik.uni-kiel.de

Abstract. Conceptual modeling uses languages to represent the real world. Semiotics, as a general theory of signs and symbols, deals with the study of languages and is comprised of syntax, semantics, and pragmatics. Pragmatics includes the explicit representation of the intentions of users. A common assumption is that all levels of database design (user, conceptual, logical, and physical) can be modeled using the same language. However, languages at the conceptual level are often enhanced by concepts that attempt to capture inherent pragmatics. This research proposes that concepts from semiotics can provide the background needed to understand an application. Specifically, pragmatics and semantics are considered at both the user and conceptual level, based on proposed constraints.

Keywords: Conceptual modeling · Languages · Semiotics · Semantics · Constraints

1 Introduction

Conceptual models act as mediators between the application and an implementation [11]. Conceptual modelers often attempt to model situations that occur in the real world using one language as a construction mechanism, and a model for a schema. Representing how the world operates must be described at the right level of specification. This tends to be done, for example, using an entity-relationship diagram as a modeling tool. However, it is difficult to expect one language to be able to handle all phases of modeling. Semantic issues need to be captured and modeled during both the design phases. The objective of this research, therefore, is to understand how to create better conceptual models by considering these different levels of abstraction and how they might be addressed. Although language is usually the main vehicle for modeling, additional understanding is needed for collaboration among stakeholders. Semiotics, as a general theory of signs and symbols, deals with the study of languages, and could serve as the needed background. The contributions are to: propose that models should be defined from the perspective of semiotics, and propose an additional set of constraints.

H.C. Mayr et al. (Eds.): ER 2017, LNCS 10650, pp. 182–190, 2017.
https://doi.org/10.1007/978-3-319-69904-2_15

2 Modeling Challenges in Conceptual Modeling

Levels of Abstraction. Many modeling languages are applied at different levels of abstraction. Business issues might be applied at the application level. Prescription issues for implementation are at a detailed level of specification. Although different, they are often all represented by an entity-relationship diagram.

Semantics. Semantics (meaning of terms) is challenging [5]. Constraints are often used as a surrogate for business rules [6]. Attempting to capture and represent semantics in terms of first-order predicate logic seems restrictive. Implicit or lexical semantics contribute to complete semantics.

Inclusion Constraints. These could be class-based; for example, a student is a person. The person identification is reused for student as a co-existence constraint, expressible via identification (becoming a foreign key constraint in the relational model). Then an enforcement mechanism can be: (1) canonically declared based on reference existence and reference enforcement; or (2) expressed by the on-*event*-if-*condition*-then-*action* (ECA) paradigm. The enforcement can be refined for control, application, optimization, and exception handling. If the inclusion constraint is not class-based, but value-based, then support and enforcement become more challenging. For example, the *Student* type may use an attribute *Name,* which corresponds to a person's *Name* in a type *Person.*

Cardinality Constraints. These have two main approaches to define their semantics: look-up and participation. Look-up works well for binary associations without relationship attributes. Participation constraints mix two different kinds of semantics with rigidity for extreme cases, despite the need to represent normal cases. 'Min/Max' captures the absolute extreme for all potential cases. The 'min' captures a (generalized) inclusion constraint; 'max' is intended to capture a (generalized) multiplicity constraint. For a relationship where the minimum participation could be '0' (someone is a student but not taking courses yet), a null value would be allowed in an implementation. However, a "*normal*" interpretation of the relationship is that a student must be registered for at least one course (null not allowed). Cardinality constraints impact other constraints in the schema [3].

Implicit Constraints. Constraints can be implicit or hidden due to syntax construction. The eER modeling language uses relationship types with inherent (construction) inclusion and existence constraints as *based-on constraints*. Relationship objects reference their component objects; for example, entity objects. Therefore, the relationship objects can only exist if the corresponding entity object exists, making the semantics implicit, based upon the way in which relationships are constructed and used. They become explicit in the corresponding SQL specification.

Type Semantics. eER modeling uses a Salami-slice strategy, oriented on the homogeneity of types and thus on decomposition into small, meaningful semantic units. Things in the application domain are multifaceted. A human is represented via a *Person* type that is separated from the *Student* type, which is associated via an IsA relationship (or subclass), to the *Person* type. At the same time, *Student* can be associated with other types, such as: *student_engagement*, *student_facilities, dormitory*, etc. Depending upon the view, a student might best be considered using the notion of a student or the notion of the more general object, person. Research has analyzed classification challenges [4].

Implicit Representation of Viewpoints. At the application level, it might be beneficial to consider user viewpoints that are represented as views [11]. For instance, a student might best be considered, including more general objects, e.g. person.

Separation of Syntax and Semantics. The separation of syntax and semantics is generally problematic. Most modelers learn a language using simple problems. However, real world problems are complex, so one language, or modeling technique, is not appropriate for all. It is impossible to represent a business problem at an application level of abstraction and implementation issues based on a singleton diagram. The problem is understanding and representing semantics.

Restricted and Mixed Semantics. Instead of general constraint frames, specific cases are often considered; e.g., mapping ratios (1:N, N:M, 1:1) to capture some binary relationship semantics. Sometimes, N:M ratios declare the maximum to be higher than 1. Look-up and participation cardinalities may be used with the same syntactic notion.

3 Models, Expressions, and Stakeholder Levels

Models and Conceptual Models. The notion of a *model* is complex and not necessarily well understood; similarly, for the process of modeling. Consider four perspectives: (1) the origins to be considered by the model; (2) the profile of the model (e.g. its function, purpose, or goal); (3) the stakeholders or the community of practice that the model must satisfy; and (4) the context within which the model and the origins are considered. The first two perspectives are internal; the second two, external.

A model is guided on its background [10]: the *grounding* of the model (paradigms, postulates, theories, culture, and conventions); and the *basis* for the model (e.g. languages used, concepts and conceptions, community, and commonly accepted practices). The *basis* of a model may change on demand. The perceptions of users might need to be represented in a model. Multiple coherent perceptions, a description of a system, or an augmented system might also be useful. A model can have many different purposes: to describe or explain a situation; specify and represent a concept someone has in mind; to aid in communication among stakeholders; or to decompose complex situations. A *model* is a well-formed, adequate and dependable artifact, commonly accepted by its community of practice within a given context [10, 11].

Semiotics of Signs: Icons, Symbols and Indexes. Semiotics, the study of the theory of signs, emphasizes the properties of things in their capacity. It is reasonable to apply semiotics to aid in this understanding since, before using a modeling language, it is first necessary to understand the language and its inherent bias.

Syntax refers to the arrangement of words in sentences and phrases. Syntax should be simple, parsimonious, and harmonic.

Semantics is concerned with the meaning of sentences and defines the interpretation of a sentence in the real world, depending on its context. It refers to the meaning of signs and what they represent in the real world.

Pragmatics considers the relationship between parts of sentences or signs and their users within a situation and context. It is user-dependent.

Although language is the main vehicle for modeling, semiotics is the background needed for understanding so that collaboration among stakeholders can result. Syntax, semantics, and pragmatics may follow different paradigms, leading to some effective use. The strictness of first-order predicate logic might be inappropriate during modeling. It is, however, needed in the final result. For example, natural utterances use the connective "and/or" with the meaning of logical OR. Similar observations can be made for all connectives, especially, for quantifiers.

Syntax has been well investigated for formal languages. Semantics can be defined in a variety of ways; e.g. for evaluation of variables, incorporation of context, scope of states, exceptions, and matching between syntactic language and semantic structure [8]. Problems arise when pragmatics is taken into consideration because the pragmatic interpretation depends on the community of practice, its culture, scope and attention.

Syntax, semantics and pragmatics of models are all important issues, and depend upon the needs of a model and its context.

Abstraction Levels of Stakeholders. At the application level, the perceptions of the users must be considered and combined with the context. At the conceptual modeling level, the resulting conceptual model must be based on what was developed at the application level. The logical level is typically based on an understanding of the platform, with the best practice being to use models that are mappings or compilations of the conceptual model.

4 Illustrative Example

A *conceptual database model* consists of a conceptual schema and a number of view schemata [11]. The view schemata are the result of transformations [1, 9] that map the viewpoints of the application level to sub-schemata of the conceptual schemata.

Consider a student-dormitory-course schema in Fig. 1. Suppose a student is enrolled in several programs at a university. The dormitory association is dependent upon the program that a student takes. Specifically, a student lives in a dormitory that corresponds to the program (business, music, etc.) in which the student is enrolled. A student might obtain some financial support from a program, depending upon the level of completion of the program. A student makes courses that are required for a given program. The credit hours assigned to a course, may vary across courses, depending upon whether the course is intended for one program, or whether it is a mandatory or elective course. Any course can only be counted one time towards one program. A student is required to take a minimum number of classes per term. If a student fails a course, then the student may retake the course, up to a maximum of three times. A course has an associated tuition fee that must be within the limits of a given term, which may vary from term to term.

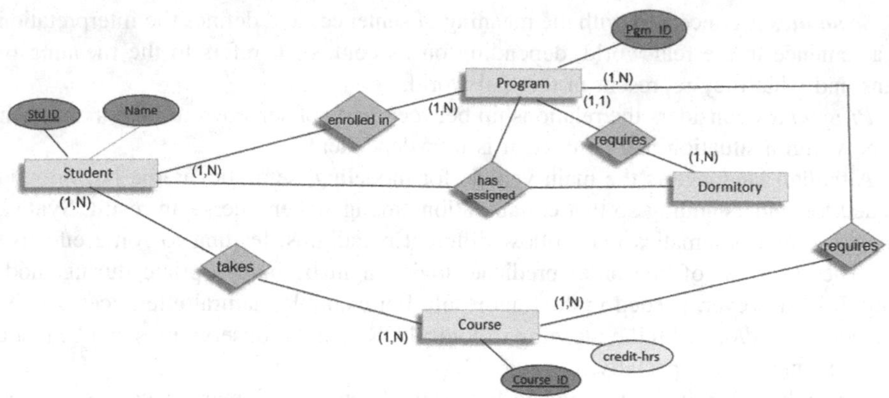

Fig. 1. Entity-relationship model of student-dormitory application

There are, however, some aspects of this situation that are difficult to model.

- A student can only take a course a maximum of three times. This might be overcome by adding a separate entity, called class or section, and a relationship; Course has Classes, with min/max cardinalities of (0, 3) from student to class.
- A course can have different credit hours depending upon the program.
- A student can have multiple majors, which requires a decision about the dormitory to which a student should be assigned.
- The normal case for *enrolled in* does not capture freshmen who are not enrolled.
- The student must take courses that are required by the program.

These problems are at the application level. Someone must represent the university situation correctly and implement the corresponding results into a database. Also, involved is the end-user, a student. The database designer must attempt to models these in one conceptual model.

5 Semiotics Reconsidered

Semantics and Pragmatics at the Application Level. Models at the application level have their own origins that they represent, profile, context, and community. The origins are consolidated perception models, enhanced by situation models that are commonly accepted in the application domain. Each community has a community-specific model; that is, a “local-as-design” approach. Objects under consideration are not homogeneous, for example, a department is considered together with its department head. Or, a student view incorporates all of the classes a student takes and refers to a university program class view from the university administration. A student is typically enrolled in one and only one program. There might be other students. Generalization and specialization follow natural semantics.

Models at this level of abstraction can be used at the conceptual level for communication and negotiation within and between communities of practice. Semantics and pragmatics differ based on the perception and understanding within the communities. Models may not be complete. Semantics may not be rigid. Objects are often considered to be holistic; for example, students together with their courses based on their programs. Therefore, we are not bound to normal data type construction. Constraints typically consider normal cases instead of extreme ones. Class planning might not require that students take classes, but student planning is based on the minimum and maximum credit hours a student must acquire in a given term.

Models at the application level have their own coherence. The underlying model allows us to integrate the different models. Models at the user level are typically not denotative but connotative, and follow cultural or community interpretations. For this reason, ontologies are appropriate for specifying domain-specific content [2].

Model Semantics at the Conceptual Level. A conceptual data model reflects, integrates and harmonizes the user views. Types specify homogeneous classes and are decomposed accordingly. The functionality definition is based on an entity-relationship algebra and given only after the structure model is complete. Constraints refine the structure; that is, semantics are defined only after the syntax is complete. The entity-relationship schema uses a diagram that is assumed to be complete, and represents its component at the same level of granularity and precision. Pragmatics tend to be hidden in a conceptual model, even though it is, in essence, an underlying model. It is assumed to be defined though external views.

Constraints at the Application Level and Conceptual Level. Constraints are generally considered valid for all of an application. However, a user's community might consider the 'normal' case or abstract (generalize) from exceptions, or omit them. Users use different scope, context, origins, and purposes. E.g., cardinality constraints represent some aspect, within specific semantics and pragmatics.

The Nature of Constraints. At the conceptual level, pragmatics must be handled by syntax and semantics. Cardinality constraints can do so, but are rigid and based on participation or lookup definition [7]. In the participation approach, extreme cases are included, in an attempt to represent exceptional cases. For example, an (1, N) constraint states that a corresponding relationship must exist for all entity classes. One solution is to use a harmonization of all user models and integrate them into the conceptual model. In this "global-as-design" approach, user views represent the external views of users, resulting in the challenge of properly representing finer semantics and pragmatics of these views. Due to the "local-as-view" design, constraints are introduced from the user's point of view. A conceptual model should harmonize all of these views to provide a holistic view of all constraints. A similar harmonization can occur at the logical level.

In Fig. 1, a freshman could be enrolled in a program or not. If the freshman is enrolled, then a dormitory can be assigned based on the program enrolled. Later the freshman might also take courses. Then, a student is either a normal student, a student who does not take courses, or a student who does not have yet a dormitory. At the logical level, we can use tables for each of these specific cases and define a view that combines them. At the logical level, horizontal decomposition can be applied [10]. A relation type can be decomposed by selection expressions E1, …, En into separate types, provided this decomposition forms a partition on the class for this type. Therefore, we might also use a conceptual type, made up of conceptual base types. The base type has semantics without any context, but all subclasses are identified.

Objectives for Developing Better Constraints. Semantics can vary, depending on the user. This results in problems when mapping to a conceptual model, so the conceptual model should be more flexible. In most practices, normalization deals with the exceptional case where semantics causes a change of structure and the schema. That is, semantics drives syntax, in contrast to "semantics follows syntax." DBMS provide a much finer means for integrity maintenance. Maintenance can be deferred (eager or lazy integrity enforcement). Consistency can be supported at the row level. Integrity constraints can be maintained at the application level. Integrity can be made through views. Finally, flexible strategies may be used, besides the no-action and rollback approach; for example, on the basis of triggers or stored procedures.

These observations show that conceptual integrity constraints can be more elaborated if we can map the constraints to DBMS features. Here, we simply aim to show how semantics and syntax can be developed in a holistic approach. We further assume that pragmatics is defined at the application level, based on views, leading to the following observations and requirements.

(1) DBMS technology must provide a better way of treating syntax and semantics at the conceptual level, which captures pragmatics at the user level.
(2) A holistic view is needed for integrated usage of syntax together with semantics.
(3) Flexibility is required for changes needed to accommodate new technology.
(4) A mapping procedure for advanced integrity constraints should be supported.

Proposed Extensions of Integrity Constraints by Context as Part of Semantics.

1. *Actions* on a database are insert, delete and update for: a single object, one class, or objects tightly bundled via class inclusion constraints. Actions might be defined as an *action pattern*. This extends single-object actions to a complex object action while disabling the basic actions whenever a complex pattern exists.
2. The *scope pattern* is a view-defining query. This query defines either a single type view or, in general, the view schema on the conceptual schema.
3. *Enforcement style pattern* is for constraints that are timed as eager (default) or lazy (with(out) delay) enforcement, after an action (default), or as control before an action, with a level statement (e.g. DBMS, transaction, and interface levels).
4. *Reaction pattern* is for immediate enforcement or exception handling with a timed exit sub-pattern or timed enforcement, based on an enforcement obligation.

The above illustrates the need to deal with structure versus semantics. They can be formally defined and implemented. Then, in contrast to traditional approaches in which "semantics follows syntax," syntax and semantics may be treated as a whole.

Holistic View. A *conditional integrity constraint* is a pair of a context and a constraint. Constraints can be combined to partition a problem based on a scope pattern. For example, cardinality constraints Card(R, R') = (1, 1) are for R = *enrolled_in*, and

R' = *Student* with a selection predicate for: freshmen, a student who does not yet have an assigned dormitory, and students who did not yet take courses. The cardinality constraint is only valid for "normal" students. Adding an attribute *term* to the type *takes* could ensure that a student has not taken a course more than three times.

For example, for freshman with a dormitory, we may use a relaxed enforcement style. For freshman without a dormitory, we might use an interface style. That is, an insertion of such a student is only possible by an encapsulated insertion of the student, the programs, and the dormitory with a temporary insertion into the corresponding basic types; and a transfer of the object to another basic class whenever additional data are inserted. However, problems that exist or can be deduced for these constraints are not usually considered. All user needs cannot be represented by semiotics. View integration is difficult with global constraints, and usually completed based on user views. From a semiotics perspective, the user view should be considered as much as possible.

6 Conclusion

Many problems arise from the need to carry out modeling at multiple levels, depending upon the stakeholders. Since semiotics deals with language, it is proposed as an underlying basis from which to understand and capture semantics at different levels of abstraction. Additional conditional constraints are needed to model context, namely, action, scope, enforcement style and reaction.

Acknowledgements. This research was supported by the J. Mack Robinson College of Business, Georgia State University. Thanks to Melinda McDaniel for her assistance.

References

1. Embley, D.W., Mok, W.Y.: Mapping conceptual models to database schemas. In: Embley, D., Thalheim, B. (eds.) Handbook of Conceptual Modeling, pp. 123–163. Springer, Heidelberg (2011). doi:10.1007/978-3-642-15865-0_5
2. Gruber, T.R.: A translation approach to portable ontology specifications. Knowl. Acquis. **5** (2), 199–220 (1993)
3. Hartmann, S.: On the characterization and construction of entity-relationship database populations obeying cardinality constraints. Ph.D. thesis, University Rostock (1996)
4. Parsons, J., Wand, Y.: Using cognitive principles to guide classification in information systems modeling. MIS Q. **32**(4), 839–868 (2008)
5. Storey, V.C.: Relational database design based on the entity-relationship model. Data Knowl. Eng. **7**(1), 47–83 (1991)
6. Storey, V.C.: Understanding semantic relationships. VLDB J. **2**(4), 455–488 (1993)
7. Storey, V.C.: Comparing relationships in conceptual modeling: mapping to semantic classifications. IEEE Trans. Knowl. Data Eng. **17**(11), 1478–1489 (2005)
8. Schewe, K.-D., Thalheim, B.: About semantics. In: Schewe, K.-D., Thalheim, B. (eds.) SDKB 2010. LNCS, vol. 6834, pp. 1–22. Springer, Heidelberg (2011). doi:10.1007/978-3-642-23441-5_1

9. Thalheim, B.: Entity-Relationship Modeling-Foundations of Database Technology. Springer, Berlin (2000)
10. Thalheim, B.: Syntax, semantics and pragmatics of conceptual modelling. In: Bouma, G., Ittoo, A., Métais, E., Wortmann, H. (eds.) NLDB 2012. LNCS, vol. 7337, pp. 1–10. Springer, Heidelberg (2012). doi:10.1007/978-3-642-31178-9_1
11. Thalheim, B., Tropmann-Frick, M.: Enhancing entity-relationship schemata for conceptual database structure models. In: Johannesson, P., Lee, M.L., Liddle, S.W., Opdahl, A.L., López, Ó.P. (eds.) ER 2015. LNCS, vol. 9381, pp. 603–611. Springer, Cham (2015). doi:10.1007/978-3-319-25264-3_47

Conceptual Modeling and Requirements

Towards an Ontology for Privacy Requirements via a Systematic Literature Review

Mohamad Gharib[1(✉)], Paolo Giorgini[2], and John Mylopoulos[2]

[1] DiMaI, University of Florence, Viale Morgagni 65, Florence, Italy
mohamad.gharib@unifi.it
[2] DISI, University of Trento, 38123 Povo, Trento, Italy
{paolo.giorgini,john.mylopoulos}@unitn.it

Abstract. Privacy has been frequently identified as a main concern for systems that deal with personal information. However, much of existing work on privacy requirements deals with them as a special case of security requirements, thereby overlooking key aspects of privacy. In this paper, we address this problem by proposing an ontology for privacy requirements. The ontology is mined from the literature through a systematic literature review whose main purpose is to identify key concepts/relationships for capturing privacy requirements. In addition, identified concepts/relations are further analyzed to identify redundancies and semantic overlaps.

Keywords: Privacy ontology · Privacy requirements · Privacy by Design (PbD) · Requirements engineering

1 Introduction

Increasing numbers of today's systems deal with personal information (e.g., information about citizens, customers, etc.), where such information is protected by privacy laws [1]. Accordingly, privacy has become a main concern for system designers. In other words, dealing with privacy related concerns is a must these days because privacy breaches may result in huge costs as well as long-term consequences [2]. Privacy breaches might be due to lack of appropriate security policies, bad security practices, attacks, data thefts, etc. [1,3]. However, most of these breaches can be avoided if privacy requirements of the system-to-be were captured properly during system design (e.g., Privacy by Design (PbD)) [3,4]. Nevertheless, most existing work on privacy requirements often deal with them either as non-functional requirements (NFRs) with no specific techniques on how such requirements can be met [5], or as security requirements (e.g., [4,6], etc.), i.e., focusing mainly on confidentiality and overlooking important privacy aspects such as anonymity, pseudonymity, unlinkability, unobservability, etc.

On the other hand, privacy is an elusive and vague concept [4,7]. Although several efforts have been made to clarify the concept by linking it to more refined concepts such as secrecy, personhood, control of personal information, etc., there

H.C. Mayr et al. (Eds.): ER 2017, LNCS 10650, pp. 193–208, 2017.
https://doi.org/10.1007/978-3-319-69904-2_16

is no consensus on the definition of these concepts or which of them should be used to analyze privacy [7]. This has resulted in much confusion among designers and stakeholders, and has led in turn to wrong design decisions. In this context, a well-defined privacy ontology that captures privacy related concepts along with their interrelations would constitute a great step forward in improving the quality of privacy-aware systems.

Ontologies have proven to be a key success factor for eliciting high-quality requirements, as they facilitate and improve the job of requirements engineers [8]. Privacy is a social concept. Accordingly, a privacy ontology should conceptualize privacy requirements in their social and organizational context. Since most systems these days are socio-technical systems, consisting not only of technical components but also of humans along with their interrelations, where different kinds of vulnerabilities might manifest themselves [1,9].

This paper applies systematic review techniques to survey available literature to identify key concepts/relationships for capturing privacy requirements[1]. Then, we further analyze these concepts/relations to identify the key ones in order to propose a novel ontology that can be used to capture privacy requirements. This paper is therefore intended to be a starting point to address the problem of identifying a core privacy ontology.

The rest of the paper is organized as follows; Sect. 2 describes the review process and the protocol underlining this systematic review. We present and discuss the review results and findings in Sect. 3. In Sect. 4 we propose a novel ontology for privacy requirements engineering. We discuss threats to validity in Sect. 5. Related work is presented in Sect. 6, and we conclude and discuss future work in Sect. 7.

2 Review Process

Following [10,11], the review process (depicted in Fig. 1) consists of three main phases: 1- planning the review, 2- conducting the review, and 3- reporting the results of the review.

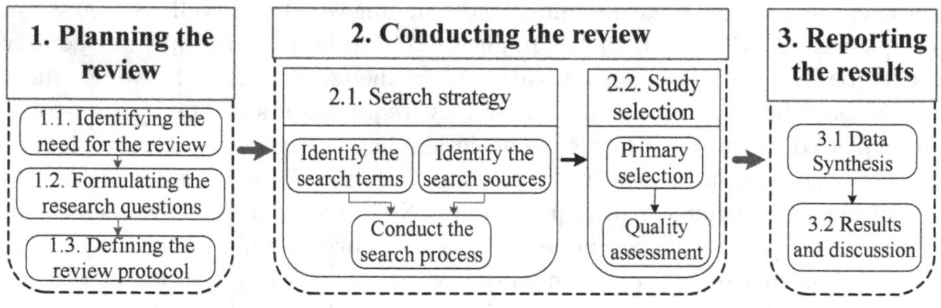

Fig. 1. The systematic review process

[1] A detailed version of the systematic literature review can be found at [12].

2.1 Planning the Review

This phase is very important for the success of the review, for it is here that we define the research objectives and the way in which the review will be carried out. This includes three main activities:

1.1 Identifying the need for the review, which can be done by identifying and reviewing any existing systematic reviews related to privacy ontologies[2].

1.2 Formulating the research questions, which is a very critical activity since these questions are used to derive the entire systematic review methodology [10]. Therefore, we formulate the following four Research Questions (RQ) to identify the main privacy concepts that have been presented in the literature:

RQ1: What are the privacy concepts/relations that have been used to capture privacy requirements?

RQ2: What are the key concepts/relations that have been used for capturing privacy requirements?

RQ3: Do existing privacy studies cover the key privacy concepts/relations, i.e., what is the degree of coverage of each study with respect to a gold standard defined by the union of all concepts proposed in the literature.

RQ4: What are the coverage limitations of existing privacy studies?

1.3 Defining the review protocol that specifies the methods to be followed while conducting the systematic review. Based on [10,11], a review protocol should specify the following: the strategy that will be used to search for primary studies selection; study selection criteria; study quality assessment criteria; data extraction and dissemination strategies. In the rest of this section, we discuss how we specify and perform each of these activities.

2.2 Conducting the Review

This phase is composed of two main activities: 1- search strategy; and 2- study selection, where each of them is composed of several sub-activities.

Search Strategy. The search strategy aims to find as many studies relating to the research questions as possible using an objective and repeatable search strategy [10]. The search activity consists of three main sub-activities: 1- identify the search terms, 2- identify the literature resources, and 3- conduct the search process.

Identify the Search Terms. Following [10,11], we derived the main search terms from the research questions. In particular, we used the Boolean AND to link the major terms, and we use the Boolean OR to incorporate alternative synonyms of such terms. The resulting search terms are: (Privacy AND (ontology OR ontologies OR taxonomy OR taxonomies) OR (Privacy requirements).

---

[2] Secondary studies can be found in the related work section.

Identify the Literature Resources. Five electronic database sources were used to primarily extract data for this research. These include: IEEE Xplore, Springer, ACM library, Google Scholar, and CiteSeerX. The selection criteria for the studies sources are based on the opinion of the authors of this work as experts in both ontological and requirements engineering. In particular, IEEE Xplore and Springer are the publishers of the main journals and conferences concerning requirements engineering such as RE journal, SoSym, ICSE RE, ER, CAiSE, etc. While ACM library, Google Scholar and CiteSeerX index the main scientific publications in the field of computer science and information science.

Conduct the Search Process. The search process (shown in Fig. 2) consists of two main stages:

Search stage 1. We have used the search terms to search the six electronic database sources, and only papers with relevant titles have been selected;

Search stage 2. The reference lists of all primary selected papers were carefully checked, and several relevant papers (25 papers) were identified and added to the list of the primary selected papers.

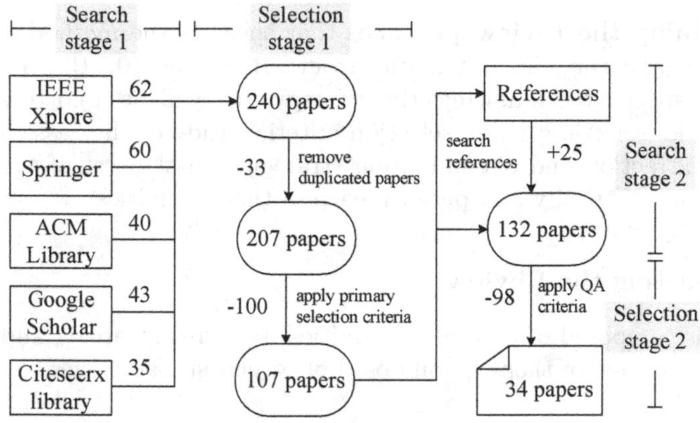

Fig. 2. Paper search and selection process

Study Selection. The selection process (shown in Fig. 2) consists of two main stages.

Selection stage 1 (primary selection). Searching the electronic database source returned 240 relevant papers, among which we have identified and removed 33 duplicated papers. Next, we have applied the primary selection criteria on the remaining 207 papers. In particular, we have read the abstract, introduction, and then we skimmed through the rest of paper. We removed all the papers that are not published in the English language, and we excluded all papers that are not related to any of our research questions. Moreover, when we were able to identify multiple version of the same paper, only the most complete one was included. Finally, we excluded any paper that has been published before 1996, since we were not able to find any concrete work related to our research before 1996. The primary selection inclusion and exclusion criteria are shown in Table 1. The outcome of this selection stage was 107 papers, i.e., we have excluded 100 papers.

Table 1. Primary selection inclusion and exclusion criteria

Inclusion criteria	Exclusion criteria
a. Papers related to at least one of the research questions	a. Papers that are not published in the English language
b. Relevant papers that are published from 1996 to 2016	b. If a paper has several versions only the most complete one is included

Selection stage 2 (Quality Assessment (QA)). At this stage, the QA criteria have been applied to the papers that have resulted from the first selection stage (107 papers) along with the papers that have resulted from the second search stage (25 papers), for a total of 132 papers. In order to identify the most relevant studies that can be used to answer our research questions, we formulated five QA questions (shown in Table 2) to evaluate the relevance, completeness, and quality of the studies, where each question has only two answers: Yes = 1 or No = 0. The quality score for each study is computed by summing the scores of its QA questions, and the paper is selected only if it scored at least 4. As a result, 98 papers were excluded and 34 were selected.

Table 2. Quality assessment questions

Quality assessment questions	
Q1	Are the objectives of the proposed work clearly justified?
Q2	Are the proposed concepts/relations clearly defined?
Q3	Does the work propose sufficient concepts/relations to deal with privacy aspects?
Q4	Have the concepts/relations been applied to project/case study, or have they been justified by appropriate examples?
Q5	Does the work add value to the state-of-the-art?[a]

[a]Evaluated based on the number of citations taking into consideration the year of publication.

2.3 Reporting the Results

The final phase of the systematic review involves summarizing the results, and it consists of two main activities: 1- data synthesis; and 2- results and discussion.

Data Synthesis is described as follows: Data related to *RQ1* were extracted directly from the list of selected papers (shown in Table 3). To answer *RQ2*, the

Table 3. Summary of the privacy related concepts and relations identified in the studies

			[13]	[3]	[14]	[15]	[16]	[17]	[9]	[18]	[19]	[20]	[21]	[22]	[23]	[24]	[4]	[5]	[7]	[25]	[26]	[27]	[28]	[29]	[30]	[31]	[32]	[33]	[6]	[34]	[35]	[36]	[37]	[2]	[38]	[39]
Organizational	Agentive	**actor**	X	X	X	X	X	X	✓	✓	X	✓	X	✓	✓	✓	X	✓	✓	X	X	X	✓	X	X	✓	X	X	✓	X	X	✓	X	X	✓	✓
		role	X	X	X	X	X	X	✓	✓	X	✓	X	X	X	X	X	✓	X	✓	X	X	✓	X	✓	X	X	X	✓	X	X	X	X	X	✓	✓
		agent	✓	X	X	X	X	X	✓	✓	X	✓	X	X	X	X	X	✓	X	X	✓	X	✓	X	✓	X	✓	X	✓	X	X	X	X	X	✓	✓
		user		-	-																									-				-		-
		stakeholder									-			-			-											-						-		
		person																		-																
		is_a	X	X	X	X	X	X	✓	X	X	✓	X	X	X	X	X	✓	X	X	X	X	✓	X	✓	X	X	X	✓	X	X	X	X	X	✓	X
		plays	X	X	X	X	X	X	✓	X	X	✓	X	X	X	X	X	✓	X	X	X	X	✓	X	✓	X	X	X	✓	X	X	X	X	X	✓	X
	Intentional	**goal**	✓	X	X	✓	X	X	✓	✓	X	✓	X	✓	✓	X	X	✓	X	X	✓	X	✓	X	✓	X	X	X	✓	X	X	✓	✓	X	✓	X
		objective												-		-										-		-								
		task							-	-		-			-			-			-		-		-				-			-	-		-	
		action		-	-				-	-	-			-					-																	
		refinement	✓	X	X	X	X	X	✓	✓	X	✓	X	X	X	X	X	✓	X	X	✓	X	✓	X	✓	X	X	X	✓	X	X	✓	X	X	✓	X
	Informational	asset	-			-		-		-	-		-	-					-	-		-			-		-	-		-						
		information	X	✓	✓	X	X	✓	✓	X	X	✓	X	X	X	X	X	X	✓	X	X	X	X	✓	X	X	X	✓	X	X	X	X	✓	✓	✓	✓
		data		-	-														-	-														-		-
		resource				-			-	-		-		-	-			-					-													
		personal info	X	✓	✓	X	X	X	X	X	X	X	X	X	X	X	X	X	✓	X	X	X	X	X	X	X	X	X	X	X	X	X	X	✓	X	✓
		sensitive info																	-									-								-
		part_of	X	X	X	X	X	X	X	X	X	X	X	X	X	X	X	X	✓	X	X	X	X	X	X	X	X	X	X	X	X	X	X	X	✓	X
		own	✓	X	✓	X	X	X	X	✓	X	✓	X	X	X	X	X	X	✓	✓	X	X	X	X	✓	X	X	X	✓	X	X	X	X	X	✓	X
	Interaction	**obj deleg.**	X	X	X	X	X	X	✓	X	X	✓	X	X	X	X	X	✓	X	X	X	X	✓	X	✓	X	X	X	✓	X	X	✓	X	X	X	X
		perm. deleg.	X	X	X	X	X	X	✓	X	X	✓	X	X	X	X	X	X	X	X	X	X	✓	X	✓	X	X	X	✓	X	X	X	X	X	✓	X
		info provision	X	X	X	X	X	X	✓	X	X	✓	X	✓	X	X	X	X	X	X	X	X	✓	X	✓	X	X	X	✓	X	X	X	X	X	✓	X
		monitor	✓	X	X	X	X	X	X	X	X	✓	X	X	X	X	X	X	X	X	X	X	X	X	X	X	X	✓	X	X	X	X	X	X	✓	X
		obj trust	X	X	X	X	X	X	X	X	X	✓	X	✓	X	X	X	X	X	X	X	X	X	X	X	X	X	✓	X	X	X	✓	X	X	✓	X
		perm trust	X	X	X	X	X	X	X	X	X	✓	X	X	X	X	X	X	X	X	X	X	X	X	X	X	X	✓	X	X	X	X	X	X	✓	X
Risk		risk				-					-		-								-	-			-							-	-	-	-	-
		threat	X	X	X	X	X	X	X	✓	✓	X	✓	✓	X	X	✓	X	X	✓	X	✓	✓	✓	✓	✓	✓	✓	X	✓	✓	X	X	✓	X	X
		inten. threat	✓	X	X	X	X	✓	✓	X	X	X	X	X	✓	X	X	X	X	✓	X	X	X	X	✓	X	✓	X	X	X	X	X	X	X	X	X
		casual threat	✓	X	X	X	X	X	X	X	✓	X	X	X	✓	X	X	X	X	✓	X	X	X	X	X	X	X	X	X	X	X	X	X	X	X	X
		vulnerability	✓	X	X	✓	✓	X	✓	✓	✓	X	X	✓	✓	X	X	✓	X	✓	X	✓	✓	X	X	✓	✓	X	X	✓	X	X	X	X	X	X
		attack				-	-		-		-		-	-	-			-					-	-				-								
		attacker	✓	X	X	X	✓	X	✓	✓	✓	X	X	✓	✓	✓	X	X	X	X	X	X	✓	✓	✓	✓	✓	✓	X	✓	X	X	X	✓	X	X
		attack method	X	X	X	X	✓	X	✓	✓	X	X	X	X	X	X	X	X	X	X	X	X	✓	X	X	X	✓	X	X	X	X	X	X	X	X	X
		impact	X	X	X	X	✓	X	✓	X	X	X	X	✓	✓	X	X	X	X	✓	X	✓	✓	X	✓	X	✓	X	X	X	X	X	X	✓	X	X
		threaten	✓	X	X	X	X	X	✓	✓	X	X	X	X	✓	X	X	X	X	✓	X	X	X	X	X	✓	X	X	✓	X	X	X	X	X	✓	X
		exploit	X	X	X	X	✓	X	✓	✓	✓	X	X	✓	X	X	X	X	X	✓	X	✓	✓	X	X	✓	✓	X	X	X	X	X	X	X	X	X
Treatment		countermeasure	-				-	-	-	-	-		-								-	-		-	-	-		-			-		-			
		mitigate	✓	X	X	X	✓	X	X	✓	✓	X	X	X	X	X	X	X	X	✓	✓	X	X	X	X	✓	✓	X	X	X	X	✓	✓	X	X	X
		control								-	-									-					-		-									-
		treatment																								-										
		s/p goal	✓	X	X	✓	X	X	✓	✓	X	✓	✓	✓	✓	X	✓	✓	X	✓	X	✓	✓	X	✓	✓	✓	✓	✓	X	X	X	X	X	✓	X
		s/p constraint	X	X	X	X	X	X	✓	X	X	X	X	X	X	X	X	✓	X	X	X	X	X	✓	✓	X	X	X	X	X	X	X	X	X	X	X
		s/p policy	X	X	✓	X	X	X	✓	X	✓	X	X	X	X	X	X	✓	X	X	X	X	X	X	X	X	X	X	X	X	X	X	X	X	X	X
		s/p mechanism	X	X	✓	✓	X	X	✓	X	✓	X	X	X	X	X	X	✓	X	X	X	X	X	X	X	X	X	X	X	X	X	X	X	X	X	X
Privacy		**sec/priv req.**	✓	✓	X	X	X	X	✓	X	✓	✓	✓	✓	✓	X	X	✓	X	X	X	✓	X	X	✓	✓	✓	X	✓	✓	✓	X	X	X	✓	✓
		confidentiality	✓	X	X	X	X	X	✓	✓	✓	✓	✓	X	X	X	X	X	✓	X	X	X	✓	✓	X	X	X	✓	✓	X	X	X	X	✓	✓	✓
		integrity	-						-	-	-	-	-					-					-	-				-	-		-				-	
		availability	-						-	-	-	-	-					-					-	-				-	-		-				-	
		non-repudiation	✓	X	X	X	X	X	X	X	X	X	✓	X	X	X	X	X	X	X	X	X	X	X	X	X	X	X	X	X	X	X	X	X	✓	X
		notice	X	✓	X	X	X	X	X	X	X	X	X	X	X	X	X	✓	✓	X	X	X	X	X	X	X	X	X	X	X	X	X	X	X	X	✓
		anonymity	X	X	X	X	X	X	X	X	X	X	X	X	X	X	X	✓	✓	X	X	X	X	X	X	X	X	X	X	X	X	X	X	✓	X	✓
		transparency	X	X	X	X	X	X	X	X	X	X	X	X	X	X	X	X	X	X	X	X	X	X	X	X	X	X	X	X	X	X	X	✓	✓	✓
		accountability	X	X	X	X	X	X	X	X	X	X	✓	X	X	X	X	X	X	X	X	X	X	X	X	X	X	✓	X	X	X	X	X	X	✓	X

contents of the 34 selected studies were further analyzed to identify privacy related concepts/relations, and list them in a comprehensive table (Table 3), which has been used to identify the key concepts/relations for capturing privacy requirements. To answer *RQ3*, data were derived from the percentage of the key concepts/relations categories that each selected study cover. *RQ4* can be answered by categorizing the studies into four groups based on the concepts categories that they do not cover.

3 Review Results and Discussion

This section presents and discusses the findings of this review.

RQ1: *What are the privacy concepts/relations that have been used to capture privacy requirements?* The review has identified 34 studies that can be used for capturing privacy requirements. The list of the selected studies that answers our first research question is presented in the upper part of Table 3.

RQ2: *What are the key concepts/relations that have been used for capturing privacy requirements? RQ2* is intended to capture the key concepts for a privacy ontology, taking into account overlap in meaning among concepts found in the 34 studies, which ensures that the ontology is not too fine-grained, in the sense that it includes many similar concepts that might confuse modelers. Each of the 34 selected studies has been carefully investigated to identify concepts/relations that can be used for capturing privacy requirements. The result is shown in Table 3, where 55 concepts and relations have been identified[3], which have been grouped into four main groups based on their type: 27 Organizational concepts (8 agentive entities, 5 intentional entities, 8 informational entities, 6 entities' interaction), 10 risk, 8 treatment, and 9 privacy concepts. Among the 55 identified concepts and relations, we have selected 38 key concepts and relations (17 organizational, 9 risk, 5 treatment, and 7 privacy) that can be used for capturing privacy requirements in their social and organizational context, and they are shown in **Bold** typeset in Table 3. Each of the selected concepts and relations has been chosen based on the authors' experience taking into consideration two main criteria: (1) its importance for capturing privacy requirements; and (2) the frequency of its appearance in the selected studies[4].

RQ3: *Do existing privacy studies cover the key privacy concepts/relations?* We answer *RQ3* by comparing the privacy related concepts/relations presented in each selected study with the key privacy concepts/relations identified while answering *RQ2*. In Table 3, we use (✓) when the study presents a key privacy concept/relation, and (-) when the study presents a normal privacy concept/relation. In addition, we use (X) to mark when a study misses a key concept/relation. Considering Table 3, it is easy to note that most studies miss key privacy concepts/relations[5].

RQ4: *What are the coverage limitations of existing privacy studies?* We answer this question by categorizing the studies into four non-mutually exclusive groups (**G1-4**) based on the concepts categories (e.g., organizational, risk, treatment, and privacy) that studies do not appropriately cover. Based on the

[3] In the case of multiple synonyms, some were omitted.

[4] The frequency of appearance for each concept/relation can be found in [12].

[5] The percentage of the concepts/relations covered by each study can be found in [12].

previous categories, we have 15 studies that do not appropriately cover all the four concepts categories, and 13 studies that do not appropriately cover three categories. 5 studies do not appropriately cover two categories, and one study does not appropriately cover only one category.

4 A Novel Privacy Ontology

Several recent studies stress the need for addressing privacy concerns during the system design (e.g., Privacy by Design (PbD) [3,4]). Nevertheless, based on the results of this review, it is easy to note that no existing study covers all the key privacy concepts and relations that have been identified in the review, and without such ontology it is almost impossible to address main privacy concerns during the system design. Therefore, proposing such ontology would be a viable solution for this problem. To this end, we propose a novel privacy ontology based on the key privacy concepts and relations identified in Table 3. Figure 3 presents the meta-model of the ontology as a UML class diagram. For reasons of readability, multiplicity and other constraints have been left out. The concepts of the ontology are organized into four main dimensions:

(1) Organizational dimension. This dimension includes the organizational concepts of the system in terms of its agentive entities, their objectives and informational entities, their social dependencies and expectations concerning such dependencies.

Agentive entities: represent the active entities of the system, we have selected three concepts along with two relations: *Actor* represents an autonomous entity that has intentionality and strategic goals, and it cover two entities, a *role* that is an abstract characterization of an actor in terms of a set of behaviors and functionalities, and *roles* can be a specialization (*is_a*) of one another. An *agent* that is an autonomous entity, which has a specific manifestation in the system, and it can *plays* a role or more.

Intentional entities: the behavior of actors is determined by the objectives they aim to achieve. Therefore, we adopt the goal concept to represent such objectives. A *goal* is a state of affairs that an actor intends to achieve, and it can be refined through *and/or-decompositions* of a root goal into finer sub-goals. *And-decomposition* implies that the achievement of a root-goal requires the achievement of all its sub-goals. While in *Or-decomposition* the achievement of any of its sub-goals is enough.

Informational entities: *information* represents any informational entity without intentionality. Information can be composed of several parts, and we adopt the *part_of* concept to capture the relation between an information entity and its sub-parts. In the context of this work, we differentiate between two main types of information: *personal information*, any information that can be *related* (directly or indirectly) to an identified or identifiable legal entity (e.g., names, addresses) [14,39]; and *public information*, any information that cannot be *related* (directly

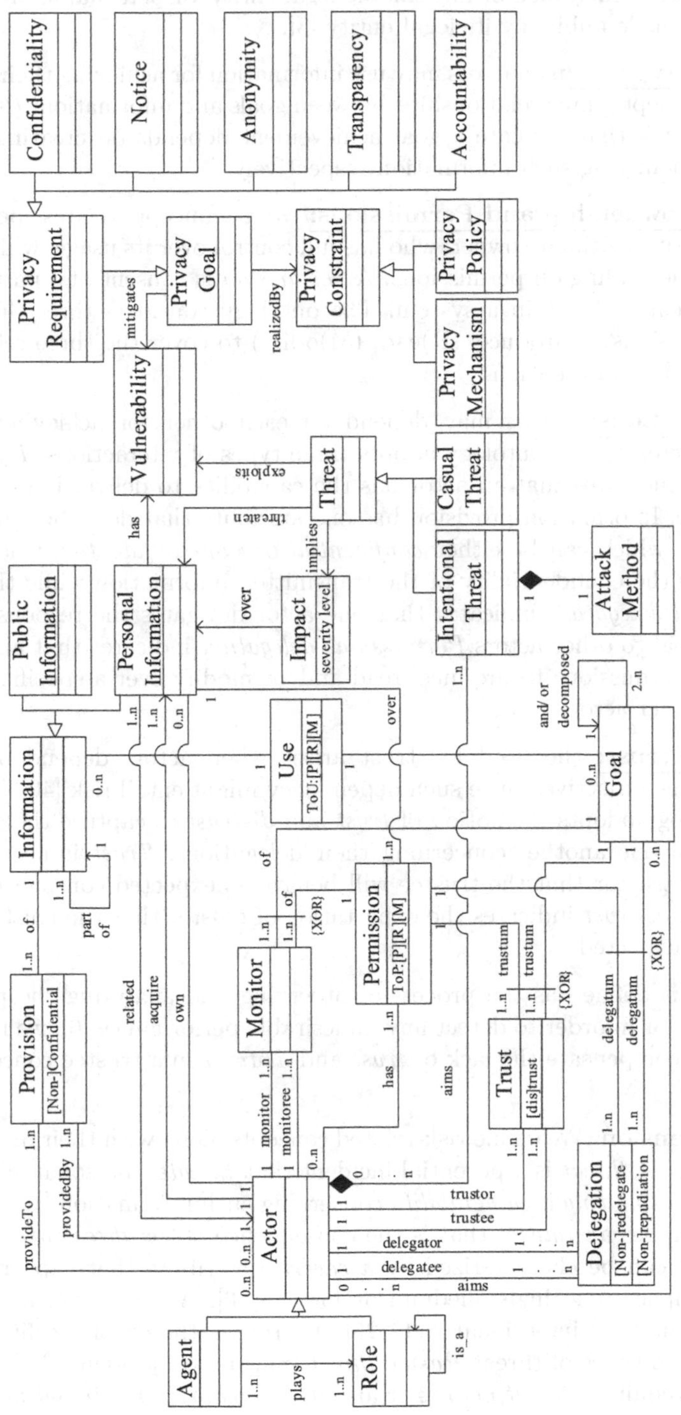

Fig. 3. The meta-model of the proposed privacy ontology

or indirectly) to an identified or identifiable legal entity, or personal information that has been made public by its legal entity [3].

Information type of use: actors may use information for achieving their goals. The ontology adopts three relationships between goals and information: *Produce*, *Read*, and *Modify* that indicate a goal achievement depends on creating, consuming, and modifying such information respectively.

Information ownership and Permissions: *own* concept relates personal information to its legitimate owner, who has full control over its usage, which can be controlled depending on permissions. A *permission* is consent of a particular use of a particular object in a system. The ontology considers three different types of permissions ((P)roduce, (R)ead, (M)odify) to cover the three relations between goals and information.

Entity interactions: actors may depend on each other for achieving their objectives. Therefore, the ontology adopts three types of interactions. *Information provision* indicates that an actor has the capability to deliver information to another one. Information provision has one attribute that describes the provisioning type, which can be either *confidential* or *non-confidential*, where the first guarantee the confidentiality of the transmitted information while the last does not. *Goal delegation* indicates that one actor delegates the responsibility to achieve a goal to other actors.*Permissions delegation* indicates that an actor delegates the permissions to produce, read and/or modify over a specific information to another actor.

Entity social trust: the need for trust arises when actors depend on one another for some objectives since such dependency might entail risk [40]. Therefore, our ontology adopts the notion of *trust* and *distrust* to capture the actors' expectations of one another concerning their delegations. *Trust* indicates the expectation of trustor that the trustee will behave as expected considering the trustum; while *distrust* indicates the expectation of trustor that the trustee will not behave as expected.

Monitoring: is defined as the process of observing and analyzing the performance of an actor in order to detect any undesirable performance [6], we rely on monitoring to compensate the lack of *trust* and *distrust* in a trustee concerning the trustum.

(2) Risk dimension. We define risk-related concepts along with their interrelations as follows: *A threat* is a potential incident that *threaten* personal information (asset) by *exploiting* a *vulnerability* concerning such information [15,21,32]. Each threat implies an *impact* that is the consequence of the *threat over* information, and it can be characterized by a *severity* attribute that captures the level of the impact (e.g. high, medium or low) [8,16]. A *threat* can be either natural, accidental, or intentional [8,17,25]. Therefore, the ontology differentiates between two types of threat, *casual threat* (natural or accidental): a threat that does not require a *threat actor* nor an *attack method. Intentional threat*: a threat that require a *threat actor* and a presumed *attack method* [22,34]. *Threat* *actor* is an actor that aims for achieving the *intentional threat* [23,31,32], and *attack method* is a standard means by which a *threat actor* carries out an *intentional threat* [8,28,32]. Finally, *a vulnerability* is a weakness related to personal information that can be exploited by a *threat* [15,31,32].

(3) Treatment dimension. This dimension introduces countermeasure concepts to mitigate risks, we adopted a high abstraction level countermeasure concepts to capture the required protection/treatment (e.g., privacy goal), which can be refined into concrete protection/treatment constraints (e.g., mechanisms or policies) to be implemented. The concepts of the treatment dimension are: *a privacy goal* defines an aim to counter threats and prevents harm to personal information by satisfying privacy criteria concerning such information. *A privacy constraint* is defined as a design restriction that is used to realize/satisfy a privacy goal, constraints can be either a privacy policy or privacy mechanism. *A privacy policy* is a privacy statement that defines the permitted and/or forbidden actions to be carried out by actors of the system toward information. *A privacy mechanism* is a concrete technique to be implemented for helping towards the satisfaction of privacy goal (attribute).

(4) Privacy dimension. The concepts of this dimension are: *Privacy requirement* that is used to capture owner/data subject privacy needs at a high abstraction level, and it is specialized from the *privacy goal* concept. Moreover, *privacy requirement* is further specialized into five more refined concepts:

1- Confidentiality, means personal information should be kept secure from any potential leaks and improper access [3,7,33]. We rely on the following principles to analyze confidentiality: *(i) Non-disclosure*, personal information can only be disclosed if the owner's consent is provided [3,14,33]. Moreover, *non-disclosure* covers information transmission that is why we differentiate between two types of information provision (confidential and non-confidential). *(ii) Need to know*, an actor should only use information if it is strictly necessary for completing a certain task [3,38]. *(iii) Purpose of use*, personal information should only be used for specific, explicit, legitimate purposes and not further used in a way that is incompatible with those purposes [7,33,39].

2- Notice, data subject should be notified when its information is being collected [7,33,39]. *Notice* is considered mainly to address situations where personal information related to a legitimate entity is being collected without her knowledge.

3- Anonymity, the identity of owner should not be disclosed unless it is required [7,33], i.e., the identifiers of owner (e.g., name, social security number, address, etc.) should be removed if they are not required and information still can be used for the same purpose after their removal. In other words, if the identifiers are not required for the task, they can be easily removed, and information can be used without linking it back to its owner/data subject (unlinkability).

4- Transparency, owner should be able to know who is using her information and for what purposes [21,33,39]. We rely on two principles to analyze transparency: *(i) Authentication*, a mechanism aims at verifying whether actors are who they claim they are [38]; and *(ii) Authorization*, a mechanism aims at verifying whether actors can use information in accordance with their credentials [33].

5- Accountability, owners should have a mechanism available to them to hold information users accountable for their actions concerning information [21,33]. We rely on two principles to analyze accountability: *(a) Non-repudiation*, the delegator cannot repudiate she delegated; and the delegatee cannot repudiate she accepted the delegation [21,38]; *(b) Non-re-delegation*, the delegatee is requested by the delegator not to re-delegate the delegatum [38].

5 Threats to Validity

Following Runeson and Höst [41], we classify threats to validity under four types:

1- Construct threats: is concerned with the extent to which a study measures what it claims to be measuring [41]. We have identified the following threats: **(i) Poor conceptualization:** occurs when few factors are considered to analyze the subject of the study. To avoid this threat, we followed the best practices in the area to define the criteria while searching for and selecting the related studies (e.g., inclusion and exclusion criteria, QA criteria, etc.). **(ii) Systematic error:** may occur while designing and conducting the review. To avoid such threat, the review protocol has been carefully designed based on well-adopted methods, and it has been strictly followed during the different phases of the review.

2- Internal threats: is concerned with factors that have not been considered in the study, and they could have influenced the investigated factors [41]. One internal threat has been identified, **Publication bias:** refers to a situation where positive research results are more likely to be reported than negatives ones [11]. Our review focused on identifying privacy related concepts/relations, and there are no positive nor negative research results in such case. Despite this, we have specified clear inclusion and exclusion criteria, and QA criteria while searching for/selecting the studies.

3- External threats: is concerned with to what extent the results of the study can be generalized [41]. One internal threat has been identified, **Completeness:** it is almost impossible to capture all related studies, yet our review protocol and search strategy were very carefully designed to cover as much as possible of the related studies. To mitigate this limitation, we performed a manual scan of the references of all the primary selected studies in order to identify those studies that were missed during the first search stage. However, we cannot guarantee that we have identified all the main available studies, which can be used to answer our research questions.

4- Reliability threats: is concerned with to what extent the study is dependent on the researcher(s). The search terms, search sources, QA questions, etc. are all available, and any researcher can repeat the review and she should get similar results. However, the researcher should consider the time when the search was performed (March 2016).

6 Related Work

There are few systematic reviews concerning privacy ontologies. For instance, Souag et al. [42] performed a systematic review that proposes an analysis and a typology of existing security ontologies. While Blanco et al. [43] conducted a systematic review with a main aim for identifying, extracting and analyzing the main proposals for security ontologies. Fabian et al. [44] present a conceptual framework for security requirements engineering by mapping the diverse terminologies of different security requirements engineering methods to that framework. Finally, a security ontology for capturing security requirements have been presented in [8]. However, the focus these studies was security, rather than privacy.

7 Conclusions and Future Work

We have conducted a systematic review with a main purpose of identifying the key concepts/relations for capturing privacy requirements. The objectives of the research were considered to have been achieved since the research questions posed have been answered. Moreover, we used the identified concepts/relations for proposing a privacy ontology to be used by software engineers while dealing with privacy requirements. This ontology can be used to search among alternative ways of fulfilling privacy requirements and choose ones that do best with respect to stakeholder-defined objective functions, such as cost or risk. For future work, we aim to develop core privacy ontology to be used by software/security engineers while dealing with privacy requirements. To achieve that, we are planning to contact the authors of the selected studies to get their feedback concerning the proposed privacy ontology. Finally, we plan to evaluate the completeness and validity of the ontology by deploying it to capture privacy requirements for two real case studies that belong to different domains.

References

1. Gharib, M., Salnitri, M., Paja, E., Giorgini, P., Mouratidis, H., Pavlidis, M., Ruiz, J.F., Fernandez, S., Della Siria, A.: Privacy requirements: findings and lessons learned in developing a privacy platform. In: The 24th International Requirements Engineering Conference (RE), pp. 256–265. IEEE (2016)
2. Hong, J.I., Ng, J.D., Lederer, S., Landay, J.A.: Privacy risk models for designing privacy-sensitive ubiquitous computing systems. In: Proceedings of the 5th Conference on Designing Interactive Systems: Processes, Practices, Methods, and Techniques, pp. 91–100. ACM (2004)
3. Labda, W., Mehandjiev, N., Sampaio, P.: Modeling of privacy-aware business processes in BPMN to protect personal data. In: Proceedings of the 29th Annual ACM Symposium on Applied Computing, pp. 1399–1405. ACM (2014)
4. Kalloniatis, C., Kavakli, E., Gritzalis, S.: Addressing privacy requirements in system design: the PriS method. Requirements Eng. **13**(3), 241–255 (2008)

5. Mouratidis, H., Giorgini, P.: Secure tropos: a security-oriented extension of the tropos methodology. J. Softw. Eng. Knowl. Eng. **17**(2), 285–309 (2007)
6. Zannone, N.: A requirements engineering methodology for trust, security, and privacy. Ph.D. thesis, University of Trento (2006)
7. Solove, D.J.: A taxonomy of privacy. Univ. Pa. Law Rev. **154**, 477–564 (2006)
8. Souag, A., Salinesi, C., Mazo, R., Comyn-Wattiau, I.: A security ontology for security requirements elicitation. In: Piessens, F., Caballero, J., Bielova, N. (eds.) ESSoS 2015. LNCS, vol. 8978, pp. 157–177. Springer, Cham (2015). doi:10.1007/978-3-319-15618-7_13
9. Liu, L., Yu, E., Mylopoulos, J.: Security and privacy requirements analysis within a social setting. In: 11th International RE Conference, pp. 151–161. IEEE (2003)
10. Kitchenham, B.: Procedures for performing systematic reviews. UK Keele Univ. **33**, 1–26 (2004)
11. Kitchenham, B., Charters, S.: Guidelines for performing systematic literature reviews in software engineering. Technical report, Keele University (2007)
12. Gharib, M., Giorgini, P., Mylopoulos, J.: Ontologies for privacy requirements engineering: a systematic literature review. arXiv preprint arXiv:1611.10097 (2016)
13. Van Lamsweerde, A.: Elaborating security requirements by construction of intentional anti-models. In: Proceedings of the 26th International Conference on Software Engineering, pp. 148–157. IEEE Computer Society (2004)
14. Braghin, S., Coen-Porisini, A., Colombo, P., Sicari, S., Trombetta, A.: Introducing privacy in a hospital information system. In: Proceedings of the Fourth International Workshop on Software Engineering for Secure Systems, pp. 9–16. ACM (2008)
15. Singhal, A., Wijesekera, D.: Ontologies for modeling enterprise level security metrics. In: Proceedings of the Sixth Annual Workshop on Cyber Security and Information Intelligence Research, p. 58. ACM (2010)
16. Wang, J.A., Guo, M.: OVM: an ontology for vulnerability management. In: Proceedings of the 5th Annual Workshop on Cyber Security and Information Intelligence Research, p. 34. ACM (2009)
17. Velasco, J.L., Valencia-García, R., Fernández-Breis, J.T., Toval, A., et al.: Modelling reusable security requirements based on an ontology framework. J. Res. Pract. Inf. Technol. **41**(2), 119 (2009)
18. Souag, A., Salinesi, C., Wattiau, I., Mouratidis, H.: Using security and domain ontologies for security requirements analysis. In: Computer Software and Applications Conference Workshops (COMPSACW), pp. 101–107. IEEE (2013)
19. Tsoumas, B., Gritzalis, D.: Towards an ontology-based security management. In: 20th International Conference on Advanced Information Networking and Applications (AINA), vol. 1, pp. 985–992. IEEE (2006)
20. Giorgini, P., Massacci, F., Mylopoulos, J., Zannone, N.: Modeling security requirements through ownership, permission and delegation. In: 13th International Conference on Requirements Engineering, pp. 167–176. IEEE (2005)
21. Kang, W., Liang, Y.: A security ontology with MDA for software development. In: 2013 International Conference on Cyber-Enabled Distributed Computing and Knowledge Discovery (CyberC), pp. 67–74. IEEE (2013)
22. Massacci, F., Mylopoulos, J., Paci, F., Tun, T.T., Yu, Y.: An extended ontology for security requirements. In: Salinesi, C., Pastor, O. (eds.) CAiSE 2011. LNBIP, vol. 83, pp. 622–636. Springer, Heidelberg (2011). doi:10.1007/978-3-642-22056-2_64
23. Elahi, G., Yu, E., Zannone, N.: A modeling ontology for integrating vulnerabilities into security requirements conceptual foundations. In: Laender, A.H.F., Castano,

S., Dayal, U., Casati, F., de Oliveira, J.P.M. (eds.) ER 2009. LNCS, vol. 5829, pp. 99–114. Springer, Heidelberg (2009). doi:10.1007/978-3-642-04840-1_10
24. Sindre, G., Opdahl, A.L.: Eliciting security requirements with misuse cases. Requirements Eng. **10**(1), 34–44 (2005)
25. Fenz, S., Ekelhart, A.: Formalizing information security knowledge. In: Proceedings of the 4th International Symposium on Information, Computer, and Communications Security, pp. 183–194. ACM (2009)
26. Asnar, Y., Moretti, R., Sebastianis, M., Zannone, N.: Risk as dependability metrics for the evaluation of business solutions: a model-driven approach. In: Third Conference on Availability, Reliability and Security, ARES 2008, pp. 1240–1247. IEEE (2008)
27. den Braber, F., Dimitrakos, T., Gran, B.A., Lund, M.S., Stølen, K., Aagedal, J.: The CORAS methodology: model-based risk assessment using UML and up. UML Unified Process 332–357 (2003)
28. Elahi, G., Yu, E., Zannone, N.: A vulnerability-centric requirements engineering framework: analyzing security attacks, countermeasures, and requirements based on vulnerabilities. Requirements Eng. **15**(1), 41–62 (2010)
29. Jürjens, J.: UMLsec: extending UML for secure systems development. In: Jézéquel, J.-M., Hussmann, H., Cook, S. (eds.) UML 2002. LNCS, vol. 2460, pp. 412–425. Springer, Heidelberg (2002). doi:10.1007/3-540-45800-X_32
30. Matulevičius, R., Mayer, N., Mouratidis, H., Dubois, E., Heymans, P., Genon, N.: Adapting secure tropos for security risk management in the early phases of information systems development. In: Bellahsène, Z., Léonard, M. (eds.) CAiSE 2008. LNCS, vol. 5074, pp. 541–555. Springer, Heidelberg (2008). doi:10.1007/978-3-540-69534-9_40
31. Røstad, L.: An extended misuse case notation: including vulnerabilities and the insider threat. In: International Working Conference on Requirements Engineering: Foundation for Software Quality, pp. 33–34. Springer (2006). doi:10.1.1.106.8353
32. Mayer, N.: Model-based management of information system security risk. Ph.D. thesis, University of Namur (2009)
33. Dritsas, S., Gymnopoulos, L., Karyda, M., Balopoulos, T., Kokolakis, S., Lambrinoudakis, C., Katsikas, S.: A knowledge-based approach to security requirements for e-health applications. J. E-Commer. Tools Appl. **2**, 1–24 (2006)
34. Lin, L., Nuseibeh, B., Ince, D., Jackson, M., Moffett, J.: Introducing abuse frames for analysing security requirements. In: 11th Requirements Engineering International Conference, pp. 371–372. IEEE (2003)
35. Avizienis, A., Laprie, J.C., Randell, B., Landwehr, C.: Basic concepts and taxonomy of dependable and secure computing. IEEE Trans. Dependable Secure Comput. **1**(1), 11–33 (2004)
36. Asnar, Y., Giorgini, P., Massacci, F., Zannone, N.: From trust to dependability through risk analysis. In: The Second International Conference on Availability, Reliability and Security, ARES 2007, pp. 19–26. IEEE (2007)
37. Asnar, Y., Giorgini, P., Mylopoulos, J.: Risk modelling and reasoning in goal models, DIT-06-008. Technical report, Universitá degli studi di Trento (2006)
38. Paja, E., Dalpiaz, F., Giorgini, P.: STS-tool: security requirements engineering for socio-technical systems. In: Heisel, M., Joosen, W., Lopez, J., Martinelli, F. (eds.) Engineering Secure Future Internet Services and Systems. LNCS, vol. 8431, pp. 65–96. Springer, Cham (2014). doi:10.1007/978-3-319-07452-8_3
39. Van Blarkom, G., Borking, J., Olk, J.: Handbook of privacy and privacy-enhancing technologies. Privacy Incorporated Software Agent Consortium, The Hague (2003)

40. Gharib, M., Giorgini, P.: Analyzing trust requirements in socio-technical systems: a belief-based approach. In: Ralyté, J., España, S., Pastor, Ó. (eds.) PoEM 2015. LNBIP, vol. 235, pp. 254–270. Springer, Cham (2015). doi:10.1007/978-3-319-25897-3_17
41. Runeson, P., Höst, M.: Guidelines for conducting and reporting case study research in software engineering. Empir. Softw. Eng. **14**(2), 131–164 (2009)
42. Souag, A., Salinesi, C., Comyn-Wattiau, I.: Ontologies for security requirements: a literature survey and classification. In: Bajec, M., Eder, J. (eds.) CAiSE 2012. LNBIP, vol. 112, pp. 61–69. Springer, Heidelberg (2012). doi:10.1007/978-3-642-31069-0_5
43. Blanco, C., Lasheras, J., Valencia-García, R., Fernández-Medina, E., Toval, A., Piattini, M.: A systematic review and comparison of security ontologies. In: 3rd Conference on Availability, Reliability and Security, pp. 813–820. IEEE (2008)
44. Fabian, B., Gürses, S., Heisel, M., Santen, T., Schmidt, H.: A comparison of security requirements engineering methods. Requirements Eng. **15**(1), 7–40 (2010)

What Happens to Intentional Concepts in Requirements Engineering if Intentional States Cannot Be Known?

Ivan J. Jureta(✉)

Fonds de la Recherche Scientifique – FNRS and Namur Digital Institute, Université de Namur, Namur, Belgium
ivan.jureta@unamur.be

Abstract. I assume in this paper that the proposition "I cannot know your intentional states" is true. I consider its consequences on the use of so-called "intentional concepts" for Requirements Engineering. I argue that if you take this proposition to be true, then intentional concepts (e.g., goal, belief, desire, intention, etc.) start to look less relevant (though not irrelevant), despite being the focus of significant research attention over the past three decades. I identify substantial problems that arise if you use instances of intentional concepts to reflect intentional states. I sketch an approach to address these problems. In it, intentional concepts have a less prominent role, while notions of time, uncertainty, prediction, observability, evidence, and learning are at the forefront.

Keywords: Requirements engineering · Goals · Intentionality · Foundations

1 Introduction

In this paper, I assume that the proposition "I cannot know your intentional states" is true. I call this the *Non-Verifiable Intentionality Proposition* (NVIP hereafter). I analyze its consequences on conceptualizations proposed and used for representation and reasoning about system requirements.

What does it mean exactly that I cannot know your intentional states? Here, it means that I cannot know accurately what you want, need, desire, or more broadly, your exact emotions, moods, beliefs, etc. I can talk and make assumptions about your intentional states. Based on communication and other cues, I may believe to have evidence that some of my assumptions are true. But ultimately, I have no reproducible means to ascertain in a clear-cut way if any of those assumptions I have, about your intentional states, are right or wrong. All I have is my own internal cognitive apparatus. While I may be making these assumptions, and doing the usual things we do when thinking about what others might think, I cannot ascertain that I am right or wrong.

The reason NVIP matters is that so-called "intentional concepts" have a central role in Requirements Engineering (RE) research for several decades now. The basic and persistent idea in RE is that requirements need to reflect the purpose of the system-to-be, and that purpose originates in the intentional states of system stakeholders. Roughly, if stakeholders desire that system does something, then we will carry

H.C. Mayr et al. (Eds.): ER 2017, LNCS 10650, pp. 209–222, 2017.
https://doi.org/10.1007/978-3-319-69904-2_17

this over to a requirements model as an instance of an intentional concept, namely "goal", and that goal will one of the goals that the system-to-be should be engineered to achieve.

In this paper, I am concerned with what happens to intentional concepts if we assume that intentional states cannot be known. My argument is structured as follows:

1. I start from the observation that intentional concepts, such as "goal", "desire", "intention", "belief", have played, and continue to play a central role in many research contributions in Requirements Engineering for almost three decades so far. Section 2 identifies some of these concepts, recalls their role and common definitions in RE research, and what they have been proposed for in RE practice.
2. I argue that if you use intentional concepts in RE, then you must make additional assumptions. I call these Requirements Intentionality Assumptions (RIA). I identify them in Sect. 3 and relate them to long-standing topics in philosophy, on folk psychology and social cognition, and on metarepresentations in psychology and linguistics.
3. In Sect. 4, I identify six problems which arise if you take NVIP to be true and you want to use intentional concepts for RE. I argue that these problems exist when instances of intentional concepts are used to convey assumed intentional states. I further argue that the presence of these problems leads to the conclusion that instances of intentional concepts give low quality requirements.
4. Assuming you agreed with me that the problems identified in Sect. 4 should be taken seriously, or that you at least remain open to further debate, I use Sect. 5 to sketch an alternative requirements concept to address the problems.
5. In Sect. 6, I discuss limitations, summarize conclusions, and identify some of many open questions.

Motivation for this paper comes from the tension I experience between the research I do in RE and my practice of it as participant in software product design and development teams over the last ten years. I have helped design and launch about a dozen software products and businesses. Despite my own arguments in RE research in favor of intentional concepts, some of these ventures have suffered from taking requirements to convey predominantly intentional states. It looked consequently worth exploring the consequences of NVIP being true.

2 Intentional Concepts in Requirements Engineering

This Section uses well-cited prior research to recall common ideas on intentional concepts in RE, and the "goal" concept specifically. The goal concept and the ideas around it are so influential, that there exists Goal-Oriented RE, a field on its own within RE. In a survey of Goal-Oriented RE [1], we have the following.

> "A goal is an objective the system under consideration should achieve. Goal formulations thus refer to intended properties to be ensured; they are optative statements as opposed to indicative ones, and bounded by the subject matter.
>
> Goals may be formulated at different levels of abstraction, ranging from high-level, strategic concerns (such as 'serve more passengers' for a train transportation system or 'provide

ubiquitous cash service' for an ATM network system) to low-level technical concerns (such as 'acceleration command delivered on time' for a train transportation system or 'card kept after 3 wrong password entries' for an ATM system).

[…] The system which a goal refers to may be the current one or the system-to-be; both are involved in the RE process. High-level goals often refer to both systems. The system-to-be is in essence composite; it comprises both the software and its environment and is made of active components such as humans, devices, and software. As opposed to passive ones, active components have choice of behavior; henceforth we will call them agents. Unlike requirements, a goal may in general require the cooperation of a hybrid combination of multiple agents to achieve it.

[…] Goal identification is not necessarily an easy task. Sometimes they are explicitly stated by stakeholders or in preliminary material available to requirements engineers. […] In our experience, goals can also be identified systematically by searching for intentional keywords in the preliminary documents provided, interview transcripts, etc."

In everyday language, a goal is the object of a person's ambition, something that they act to achieve. In Goal-Oriented RE, there are goals of (or held by) people or systems. A system can have a goal in the sense that the system, with all the machines, software and people involved, should achieve that goal. Goals come from people related to the system. They are generically called "stakeholders" in this paper.

But are these goals used to reflect intentional states of system stakeholders? If yes, then these goals are what is called "intentional concepts"; if not, they are something else. Consider that question more carefully and four cases turn up.

In **Case A**, I say that the system should do something because I want it, and I want the system to do it with me, or on its own for me. I want the automated thermostat to regulate temperature in my home based on my past settings, inside and outside temperature, air quality, etc. In this case, it is me who wants that, and the system will have that goal because I had that desire, and I want the system to be designed to satisfy that desire. Case A is me who defines system's goals to reflect, and because of my own understanding of my intentional states. In this case, I am the requirements engineer and I am the system stakeholder. This makes for a short route - relative to other cases below - from intentional states to requirements. Clearly, "goal" is in this case an intentional concept.

In **Case B**, I may prefer to deal with my thermostat without the system, but I happen to be the one who should design requirements for a system which regulates home temperature automatically on behalf of its users. In this case, I conclude through requirements elicitation that there are people who want to have temperature automatically regulated. It is not me who is in or has the intentional states which are reflected in the goal. It is someone else. I believe they have these intentional states, and since I should design a system to act accordingly, I give that system the goal which reflects these intentional states. Case B is a longer route (than Case A) from intentional states to requirements. I form beliefs about stakeholders' desires, and I give the system goals to reflect desires.

In Case A and Case B, goals are intentional concepts, owing their content and existence to the need to capture something about intentional states.

Now, you may argue that goals are nothing but a different and more practical name for (some types of) requirements, and that there is no need to worry so much about their relationship to intentional states. That is a possible reading of Goal-Oriented RE. We could say that it is more useful to get requirements from talking about goals, and that this is because system stakeholders may find goals to be a more convenient conceptualization, a better abstract tool, or easier to talk about, when trying to identify what a system should do with and for them.

Let us call that reading *Light Intentionality*. It consists of using nouns such as "goal" to talk about requirements, while at the same time not explicitly relating them to intentional states. There are problems with that view. Take some goal instance and ask why it exists in a requirements model or specification. The likely answer is that someone wants the system to do something and the goal represents that. If the goal reflects stakeholders' goals, then you are talking about intentional states.

There is a way to distance oneself from intentional states and hold on to Light Intentionality. It consists of focusing not on intentional states as the origin of goals, but on what stakeholders communicate. This Case C is the view from Zave and Jackson [2], who argued that requirements come from "optative statements":

> "Statements in the 'optative' mood describe the environment as we would like it to be and as we hope it will be when the machine is connected to the environment. Optative statements are commonly called 'requirements.'"

In this third case, we find goals or requirements in optative statements.[1] That is, she is the recipient of communication, and treats optative statements as a cue to document goals which reflect what the optative statements are conveying.

So far, in Case A and Case B, an instance of a goal concept is a representation of something about intentional states. In Case C, a goal instance is a representation of something communicated in a specific way.

Observe that you could hold the view that there are no substantial differences between Case B and Case C, if you assume that communication reflects intentional states. This is an argument Mylopoulos, Faulkner, and I presented in the so-called Core Ontology for Requirements [3]: there, we said that there are intentional states, they are conveyed by system stakeholders to requirements engineers via communication, that the requirements engineer look for speech acts to identify instances of different types of information used when doing RE. For goals specifically, we said that they are a record of desires expressed through specific kinds of speech acts.

The strongest relationship of intentional states to requirements seems to be in Yu's iStar modeling language [4]. This is the foundation for Tropos [5], and was an important influence on Techne [6]. In iStar models, goals always belong to agents. Some agents are people, others are (parts of) machines (software and hardware). The language has more than goals, with its notion of intentional dependency, tasks, and the modeling of the rationale of agent's actions using intentional concepts: i.e., agents do things because they hold goals, know means to achieve goals, and these means are tasks they can perform and resources they have access to. An important notion in iStar is that we are modeling the rationale that agents have for collaborating with others, using intentional concepts.

---

[1] As a side note, Zave and Jackson's requirements are van Lamsweerde's goals (even if van Lamsweerde's uses "requirement" as something else, namely a goal which a single agent is responsible for; that makes no difference in this paper).

If Case C is Light Intentionality, then Case A and Case B fall under something we can call *Hard Intentionality*, where requirements are closely tied to intentional states.

If unhappy with these cases, you could argue that whatever intentional states may be, we should focus on understanding how the system-to-be will be used and we can leave the debate of the why as somehow separate. Which business processes, use cases, scenarios, standard operating procedures should the system do or support? This is Case D, in which - for the purposes of this paper - I put all scenario and process-based conceptualizations of requirements. There, requirements reflect ways of doing things.

But isn't Case D Light Intentionality too? If the system should be made to do as is done now, those current processes are still done for some purpose, and that purpose must have been desired, wanted, needed, etc. by someone at some point in the past. If the system needs to do something in ways not done now, these new ways reflect, again, what someone must be wanting, needing, etc. Case D looks like Light Intentionality.

The role of the notion of system purpose is in fact critical in RE. A major change, as far as I can tell, between system design and engineering before RE set itself up as a discipline of research and industry, and after, is that with RE, we should first identify and specify the system's purpose before anything gets made.

The discussion in this section circles back to the observation that requirements need to ensure a system is made to fit its purpose, and that purpose originates in what is wanted, needed, desired, etc. by those who have a say when that system is being designed. Seems non-controversial.

To be clear, not all requirements originate in a system's purpose, some originate in the properties of the environment where the system should run. These properties can be neutral to intentional states: gravity on Mars is weaker than on Earth, whatever we may desire about that. But these neutral environment properties still should, so to speak, go through intentional states of stakeholders: what if I need to design a shuttle to land on Mars for stakeholders who do not believe that gravity there is different from here? So not only goals matter, there are other intentional states to consider. The point here is that, again, intentional states matter for RE.

3 Requirements Intentionality Assumptions

Goal-oriented RE, especially in Yu's work and our own Core Ontology for Requirements and Techne, uses the language of folk psychology. That language appears clearly elsewhere in computer science, in some strands of artificial intelligence. Bratman [7] suggested an explanation of rational behavior through notions of belief, desire, and intention. The so-called BDI model [8] was one of the foundational ideas in research on Multi-Agent Systems for instance. Intentional notions play an important role in research from Levesque [9], Halpern [10], and others on knowledge, belief, awareness, etc., in a computational context. What is folk psychology?

> "Folk psychology is a network of principles which constitutes a sort of common-sense theory about how to explain human behavior. These principles provide a central role to certain propositional attitudes, particularly beliefs and desires. The theory asserts, for example, that if someone desires that p, and this desire is not overridden by other desires, and he believes an action of kind K will bring it about that p, and he believes that such an action is within his

power, and he does not believe that some other kind of action is within his power and is a preferable way to bring it about that p, then ceteris paribus, the desire and the beliefs will cause him to perform an action of kind K. The theory is largely functional, in that the states it postulates are characterized primarily in terms of their causal relations to each other, to perception and other environmental stimuli, and to behavior." [11, 12]

Using intentional concepts for RE means subscribing to the ideas outlined above. It means seeing human behavior in a certain way, as propositional attitudes and causal links between them. It means, for example, that actions are explained in terms of an interplay of beliefs, desires, choices, and commitments.

For illustration, consider how Cohen and Levesque [9] use the language of folk psychology when defining the notion of "intention" of a computational agent.

"Intention will be modeled as a composite concept specifying what the agent has chosen and how the agent is committed to that choice. First, consider the desire that the agent has chosen to pursue as put into a new category. Call this chosen desire, loosely, a goal. By construction [in their formal framework], chosen desires are consistent. We will give them possible world semantics, and hence the agent will have chosen a set of worlds in which the goal/desire holds. Next, consider an agent to have a persistent goal if he has a goal (i.e., a chosen set of possible worlds) that will be kept as long as certain conditions hold. […] Persistence involves an agent's internal commitment to a course of events over time. Although a persistence goal is a composite concept, it models a distinctive state of mind in which agents have both chosen and committed to a state of affairs. We will model intention as a kind of persistent goal."

The first quote in this Section illustrates the language that folk psychology uses for describing, explaining, and making predictions of human behavior. The second quote is an illustration of how that language becomes a tool for motivating, describing, and explaining design choices when we make formal models of computational agents.

Folk psychology is used in the same way in RE. We need concepts and relationships, and we need to construct specialized (formal or not) languages for the representation and reasoning about requirements. We can use the language of folk psychology to motivate and justify our designs of these abstract toolsets. For instance, we can say that goal instances capture conditions which are desired by stakeholders, which amounts to defining goals by appealing to intentional states. We can then say that goals can be inconsistent if there are beliefs that they cannot be achieved together; we can define a concept, such as "domain assumption" in the Core Ontology for Requirements, to capture conditions that are the object of such beliefs. By drawing on folk psychology, we can construct conceptualizations of requirements which are inspired by and grounded in various folk psychology ideas. As discussed in Sect. 2, this has already been done in RE, specifically in Goal-Oriented RE.

If we do that in RE, we should assume that there is something to folk psychology. That at the very least it is a useful language for describing internal dynamics of individual human behavior as well as of social or collective behavior, even if that language may prove to be deficient in constructing valid explanations of human behavior, as Churchland [13] and others have argued (see debates in, e.g., [11, 12]).

If requirements capture intentional states, then intentional states justify the presence of requirements.

The first part of Requirements Intentionality Assumptions (RIA hereafter, both in singular and plural) are, then, assumptions that folk psychology makes about mechanisms producing human behavior. It is, for example, that actions are a function of beliefs and desires.

The second part of RIA is that the language used in folk psychology is useful for describing, explaining, predicting, generalizing patterns of human behavior and its causes. This means that it is useful to talk of desires, beliefs, intentions, and such, when communicating with others about human behavior.

The third part of RIA is the proposition that we can explain why there is such and such requirement on grounds of there being, and being communicated, intentional states of those who have a stake in the system-to-be. That is, some requirements exist because some intentional states exist and have been conveyed by stakeholders to requirements engineers.

The fourth part of RIA is that we should talk about requirements of systems using folk psychology concepts, that there are important relationships between folk psychology concepts and requirements concepts. They are connected in that it is unclear what the latter are, if we untie them from the former.

What I have argued so far, is that if you use intentional concepts in RE, then you should take either the Weak Intentionality or the Hard Intentionality stance. More importantly, whichever of those two you take, you should take RIA seriously. You can see RIA as that batch of ideas that tie conceptualizations of requirements to the broad and malleable folk psychology conceptualizations of human behavior.

Accepting RIA seems indeed to make sense when doing RE, if we see RE as a collective activity where the ability of a requirements engineer to identify (the right) requirements depends strongly on their ability to "read other people's minds", that is, to make assumptions about others' intentional states. The following passage is a neat description of what seems to be going on when RE is done too, even if it is taken from a contribution to cognitive science on how intentional states may be shared.

> "[H]uman beings, and only human beings, are biologically adapted for participating in collaborative activities involving shared goals and socially coordinated action plans (joint intentions). Interactions of this type require not only an understanding of the goals, intentions, and perceptions of other persons, but also, in addition, a motivation to share these things in interaction with others - and perhaps special forms of dialogic cognitive representation for doing so. The motivations and skills for participating in this kind of 'we' intentionality are woven into the earliest stages of human ontogeny and underlie young children's developing ability to participate in the collectivity that is human cognition." [14]

All that I said so far in this section may seem like common sense or common knowledge. Folk psychology, despite vocal critics (Churchland, Stich and others), remains an important conceptualization of individual human behavior (i.e., an important body of theories of mind), as well as an important part of models of how people collaborate. It is also taken seriously in pragmatics.

> "Pragmatic studies of verbal communication start from the assumption [...] that an essential feature of most human communication, both verbal and non-verbal, is the expression and recognition of intentions. On this approach, pragmatic interpretation is ultimately an exercise in metapsychology, in which the hearer infers the speaker's intended meaning from evidence she has provided for this purpose. An utterance is, of course, a linguistically-coded piece of evidence, so that verbal comprehension involves an element of decoding. However, the decoded

linguistic meaning is merely the starting point for an inferential process that results in the attribution of a speaker's meaning." [15]

The case for making the assumptions in RIA seems strong, if we take it that RE involves communication in the above sense, that it involves collaboration, and that requirements reflect intentional states.

Taking intentional concepts in RE seriously means, I have argued, taking RIA seriously. And that means subscribing to many other things, namely specific theories of mind, collective action, and communication. As I illustrated above, intentional concepts are a gateway to theories which seem to be widely shared in their respective research communities. Subscribing to them does not look controversial. You could even argue that it is not clear how we would talk about requirements, if we could not speak in terms of what stakeholders may think, want, need, believe, or know.

4 Problems

According to NVIP, I cannot know your intentional states. In more precise terms, I have no reproducible way to verify if my assumptions about your intentional states are true. "True" here means correspondence of what I assume your intentional states to be to the actual intentional states you are in. The best I can do is have assumptions about your intentional states, and search for cues in communication if I am right or wrong [15].

If I see you ordering a cup of coffee with a friend, I may believe that you want to drink coffee. But you may in fact be ordering coffee as a courtesy to your friend who wanted to have a chat over coffee. Did you desire coffee, or was it the chat with the friend, or both, or something else? How can I find evidence that supports my assumptions about why you want to have that coffee? I can ask you, I can observe, I might ask others their beliefs about your intentional states, infer from answers and observations, update my current beliefs, and then do it all over again. Looking for evidence this way is consistent with assumptions in RIA.

But if you take NVIP to be true, then there is no procedure which can move you from assumptions about others' intentional states to knowledge of their intentional states. No evidence will ever get you to know my true intentional states. While that may seem a strong statement, it is consistent with criticisms of the existence of intentional states for example. It is not a new idea.

Why does that matter for RE? It matters because if you use intentional concepts and you take NVIP to be true, then you should conclude that you can never know that you got the right requirements from stakeholders. The right ones being those which accurately reflect their true intentional states. Indeed, you cannot know stakeholder's intentional states. Therefore, instances of your intentional concepts are at best your bets that you got their intentional states right (and that you got metarepresentations [16] of those intentional states right). If they are not the right requirements, then solving these requirements, i.e., designing a system which is expected to satisfy them, will give a system that is solving the wrong problem.

If, instead, you use intentional concepts and take NVIP to be false, then you seem to be capable of actual mind-reading. I will not take line of argument seriously in the rest of the paper.

One reason why NVIP should be taken seriously, and intentional concepts less than they are, is that this makes us recognize that instances of intentional concepts do not correspond and do not reflect something we know. At best, they reflect what we believe to have understood that stakeholders were communicating. We fall back to the Zave and Jackson's idea that requirements are due to optative statements.

Unfortunately, it gets worse. Remember that above, the "right" requirements are those that fit stakeholders' true intentional states. It turns out that these are probably not the right requirements.

When we ask stakeholders what they want, or if we introspect what we may want from a system (or what they may want), we make assumptions not about our (their) current intentional states, but about our (their) future intentional states. Looks like a lot of mental work, especially when there is innovation in the system-to-be.

If you ask me what I expect from a driverless car (which I have not experienced at the time of writing), I must tell you what I will desire in that future, in which I will have that driverless car that you are designing for me. I must imagine some pieces or aspects of that future. I must imagine myself in it. I must imagine that which you have yet to design and build for me, and I must imagine how I would feel about it, what I would believe about it, and so on. Notice that as I do so, while operating with only bounded rationality [17], I am focusing on imagining an isolated experience (being driven in a driverless car), and am disregarding any other experience which I could have also imagined, and which may be related to my imagined intentional states about that system. What if I also imagined that driverless cars were in fact moving not on roads, but in the air, yet I am afraid of flying?

Now that's a mess. If I cannot know your current intentional states, can I know better your future intentional states? Do you know better your future intentional states? From personal experience, I cannot claim to know what I will like or dislike in a few months or years. Can you?

It is worse than that if there is innovation in the system's design. Not only am I asking you about your future intentional states, I am asking you about your future intentional states about phenomena which you have never experienced. Would you have known in 1995 if you would desire an iPhone made in 2017? Would you have known in 1995 if you would prefer one button or two buttons on the front face of a smartphone? Could you have experienced a smartphone in 1995? No. Unless you just came back from the future. As Marty McFly says in a "Back to the Future" movie: This is heavy.

Taking NVIP seriously leads to the conclusion that if we want to get requirements from intentional states, we are trying to get them from current intentional states which are about hypothesized future intentional states, which themselves can be about phenomena we may never have experienced. What are, then, the right requirements?

The unavoidable conclusion is that there are several substantial problems which arise if we are looking for the right requirements in intentional states.

- **Non-Verifiable Intentionality Problem:** Instances of intentional concepts are about intentional states, yet NVIP tells us we cannot know these intentional states.
- **Uncertain Intentionality Problem:** Because the system-to-be does not exist yet at the time its requirements are being specified, instances of intentional concepts are about future intentional states. These seem even less amenable to being known than present intentional states. These are not intentional states experienced when requirements are elicited.
- **Speculative Intentionality Problem:** Because the system-to-be may generate new experiences, and these experiences are not known by system stakeholders at the time stakeholders communicate their intentional states, instances of intentional concepts are about intentional states that would arise in the future if stakeholders in that future have lived these presently unknown experiences.

There is more bad news. Time passes from when requirements are elicited and specified, to when the system-to-be is made and runs and can be experienced (used) by its stakeholders. Intentional states conveyed at requirements elicitation time may have expired, or at least changed enough that they are in fact no longer satisfied (to the same extent) by the system-to-be. I call this the **Expiring Intentionality Problem**.

There are even more problems. What if what is said is not entirely true? Or more broadly, what if there is no reason to trust that what is communicated genuinely reflects true intentional states? What if both the mode and content of communication of intentional states are distorted, for example, to provide partial information? What if what is said is, so to speak, cheap talk (i.e., it is said but has no bearing on what is done)? I call all such cases the **Distorted Intentionality Problem**; there are interesting nuances between these cases, but are not important for this paper.

Even if there are only the best intentions, people forget to mention information which may turn out to be critical for making sense of intentional states that they may be in. They may omit important conditions, observations, remarks. They may fail to mention what is obvious to them, even if it may not be apparent at all to aliens coming from other domains. This is called the **Incomplete Intentionality Problem** in this paper.

In short, requirements which originate in intentional states come together with six problems: non-verifiability, uncertainty, speculation, expiry, distortion, and incompleteness.

Do these problems matter? The success of RE has two dimensions. One is that the system runs according to its requirements specification. The other is that it meets expectations of its stakeholders. These are called, respectively, engineering quality and service quality (as in quality of services that the system provides to its stakeholders).

Engineering quality can be high, yet the delivered system may fail to deliver service quality. This is because engineering quality is fitness to a specification, while service quality critically depends on how well the specification satisfies the right requirements. If the six problems are present, we cannot know if we have the right requirements. The specification, even if precise, comprehensive, and clear, will involve the risk that the system satisfies the wrong, or perhaps only a subset of the right requirements.

As an aside, note that this risk is solved partly through RE methods, and partly by freezing and requiring formal approval of the frozen the specification. But freezing the specification does not imply that intentional states will also be frozen.

5 Sketching a Solution

By demoting intentional states among lesser sources of requirements, we should answer two questions. Where do we preferably get requirements from, if not from intentional states? How do these other sources deal with problems identified in Sect. 4?

The first step is to avoid the language of folk psychology and use the word "requirement" instead of "goal" for top-level, most abstract requirements. The next step is to identify necessary properties for the requirement concept.

Non-Verifiable Intentionality Problem exists because the content of a requirement is a statement about something that cannot be observed, and thus, whose relationship to that statement cannot be reproducibly verified. We therefore need requirements to be statements which are verifiably reproducible. This also means that the statement that makes the requirement should be treated as a hypothesis which needs to be verified. It follows that, for each requirement we need to answer the following questions.

- **Hypothesis:** Which hypothesis is/are stated in the requirement?
- **History:** How was the hypothesis formulated? Where did the hypothesis originate?
- **Verification:** How can the hypothesis be reproducibly verified?
- **Instrument:** What is used to establish the hypothesis-experience relationship?

In a venture where I took part, a high-level requirement was that the system will remove the bias that brokers introduce in the price of road freight transportation. The hypothesis is that prices paid by shippers to carriers, via the system, will be systematically lower than historical broker-set prices for comparable shipments (similar freight, routes, etc.). The entire system was in fact designed to verify that hypothesis. The history of the hypothesis was the observation by the founders, that freight brokers charge inconsistent prices for similar freight and routes, that is, that prices do not reflect market conditions, but broker's ability to exploit information asymmetries. Verification amounts to the entire lifecycle of the system, while the system itself is the instrument. Another requirement, which has a more modest scope, was that market participants will perform the onboarding of their resources (freight, equipment, drivers, etc.) by themselves. The history was that it requires less resources to have the customers provide, by themselves, the required information about resources. Verification process involves building a prototype of the onboarding process, then having a small sample of select prospects use that prototype. The prototype was only part of the instrument, the other part being a questionnaire filled out by observing how customers did it, and by interviewing customers about the experience of using the prototype.

For verification to be reproducible, its steps and instruments need to be accessible to others. It follows, for example, that neither one's own mind can be the instrument, nor one's own thinking the verification process. This makes prototypes more interesting instrument than, say, a textual specification.

Uncertain Intentionality Problem exists because requirements are about the future. The problem with the future is that we must wait to experience it. Waiting costs. If what we say about the future matters today, then our current actions depend on that which we expect in the future. A requirement thus involves the risk of being a wrong prediction. That risk is proportional to the cost of waiting to verify the prediction. It follows that we should minimize the time to verify the prediction. A requirement's age is thus an input to the estimation of the risk it carries of being wrong. **Age** and **Risk** become necessary properties of any requirement. Risk is in two parts, as it is necessary to describe the outcomes expected in case the hypothesis does not fit experience, and a description (probability?) that this happens. If waiting costs, then risk will be a function of a requirement's age.

Speculative Intentionality Problem can be addressed by approximating to stakeholders sooner the unknown future experience that they speculate about. Stakeholders should learn requirements, rather than get them from speculation, through use of instruments which approximate the new experience. Moreover, this needs to happen in a proxy environment which provides conditions resembling as much as possible the conditions in which the stakeholders expect to use the system-to-be. Requirements should originate in observable phenomena which requirements engineers can experience in similar ways in which stakeholders already do. It is practices and conditions in an environment that clash with the elusive internal ambitions and motives of stakeholders, leading them to have requirements in the first place.

When trying to learn requirements for a system which should match shippers in need of freight transportation, with carriers, go to shippers to do the work they do now, and go to carriers to do what they do, and finally, go to brokers who mediate most transactions in the freight transportation market. When trying to design a system which uses AI to provide instructions for improving one's running, take time to become even a novice running coach and work under an expert. This is hard to do, it takes significant time, it requires interested parties in proxy environments, who are willing to open their practices to newcomers. It also places a greater burden on requirements engineers, who can no longer take interviews and distant observation too seriously, but have to apply themselves to doing that which in fact generates requirements in the first place.

To reduce speculation, requirements engineers learn by doing stakeholders' actions in the proxy environment, while stakeholders learn through changing their past actions using instruments designed to validate hypotheses. Each requirement comes with its own set of **Practices** that requirements engineers need to be interested in, in that the system will rely on and change these practices, and **Proxy Environments** in which these practices can be realized in approximate conditions.

Expiring Intentionality Problem is due to the unknown lifetime of a requirement. This is addressed in several ways. One is by minimizing the Age of the requirement by which we do a first verification of the hypothesis. Another is by repeating verification, if we observe cues that the requirement may be expiring. In the earlier example, of the hypothesis that market participants will on-board by themselves their resources, an **Expiry Cue** was that some of the stakeholders asked for features that would enable the operations department of the firm to on-board customers' resources on their behalf (suggesting that stakeholders are predicting that not all customers are willing to perform on-boarding on their own).

To address the *Distorted Intentionality Problem*, there are distortion cues to monitor for. For example, inconsistencies in the information that stakeholders provide are such a cue. But the main direct means to identify distortion is, as above, early verification, since it confronts stakeholders with an approximation of their future experience. Same applies to the *Incomplete Intentionality Problem*, in that there are cues to look out for, while early verification should help stakeholders identify incompleteness.

6 Discussion and Conclusions

At best, this paper is an exploratory identification and analysis of six problems which arise if intentional concepts are used to represent stakeholders' intentional states, under the assumption that intentional states are an important source of requirements. The arguments laid out are theoretical claims, supported only by personal experience, but not by rigorous reproducible research. Despite these important drawbacks, the argument is worth considering, given that it reaches novel conclusions, yet starts from non-controversial and well known premises.

I started from the assumption that I cannot know your intentional states. This led me to identify a set of properties of a "requirement" concept which distances itself from intentional concepts. To the best of my knowledge, the properties have not been tied to the requirement concept in the past, and have not been used to describe intentional concepts in RE.

The paper raises many new and interesting questions. What does it mean exactly to learn requirements? How can that be facilitated? How do we elicit information useful for the formulation of the hypotheses? How can we verify these hypotheses, and what are the merits and limitations of alternative verifications? What are the consequences of the need for early verification on how we refine requirements? Which instruments to use for verification, and how do they compare? And so on.

References

1. Van Lamsweerde, A.: Goal-oriented requirements engineering: a guided tour. In: Proceedings of Fifth IEEE International Symposium on Requirements Engineering, pp. 249–262 (2001)
2. Zave, P., Jackson, M.: Four dark corners of requirements engineering. ACM Trans. Softw. Eng. Methodol. **6**(1), 1–30 (1997)
3. Jureta, I.J., Mylopoulos, J., Faulkner, S.: Revisiting the core ontology and problem in requirements engineering. In: Proceedings of 16th IEEE International Requirements Engineering Conference RE 2008, vol. 2008, pp. 71–80 (2008)
4. Yu, E.S.K.: Towards modelling and reasoning support for early-phase requirements engineering. In: Proceedings of ISRE 1997 3rd IEEE International Symposium on Requirements Engineering, pp. 226–235 (1997)
5. Castro, J., Kolp, M., Mylopoulos, J.: Towards requirements-driven information systems engineering: the Tropos project. Inf. Syst. **27**(6), 365–389 (2002)
6. Jureta, I.J., Borgida, A., Ernst, N.A., Mylopoulos, J.: Techne: towards a new generation of requirements modeling languages with goals, preferences, and inconsistency handling. In: Proceedings of 2010 18th IEEE International Requirements Engineering Conference RE 2010, no. May 2016, pp. 115–124 (2010)
7. Bratman, M.: Intentions, Plans, and Practical Reason (1987)

8. Rao, A.S., Georgeff, M.P.: BDI agents: from theory to practice. In: ICMAS, vol. 95, pp. 312–319 (1995)
9. Cohen, P.R., Levesque, H.J.: Intention is choice with commitment. Artif. Intell. **42**(2–3), 213–261 (1990)
10. Fagin, R., Halpern, J.Y.: Belief, awareness, and limited reasoning. Artif. Intell. **34**(1), 39–76 (1987)
11. Horgan, T., Woodward, J.: Folk psychology is here to stay. Philos. Rev. **44**(2), 399–419 (1985)
12. Stich, S., Ravenscroft, I.: What is folk psychology? Cognition **50**(1–3), 447–468 (1994)
13. Churchland, P.: Eliminative materialism and the propositional attitudes. J. Philos. **78**(2), 67–90 (1981)
14. Tomasello, M., Carpenter, M., Call, J., Behne, T., Moll, H.: Understanding and sharing intentions: the origins of cultural cognition. Behav. Brain Sci. **28**(5), 675–91–735 (2005)
15. Sperber, D., Wilson, D.: Pragmatics, modularity and mind-reading. Mind Lang. **17**(1–2), 3–23 (2002)
16. Wilson, D., Sperber, D.: Meaning and Relevance. Cambridge University Press, Cambridge (2012)
17. Simon, H.A.: A behavioral model of rational choice. Q. J. Econ. **69**(1), 99–118 (1955)

Goal Models for Acceptance Requirements Analysis and Gamification Design

Luca Piras(✉), Elda Paja, Paolo Giorgini, and John Mylopoulos

University of Trento, Trento, Italy
{luca.piras,elda.paja,paolo.giorgini,john.mylopoulos}@unitn.it

Abstract. The success of software systems highly depends on user engagement. Thus, to deliver engaging systems, software has to be designed carefully taking into account *Acceptance Requirements*, such as "70% of users will use the system", and the psychological factors that could influence users to use the system. Analysis can then consider mechanisms that affect these factors, such as *Gamification* (making a game out of system use), advertising, incentives and more.

We propose a *Systematic Acceptance Requirements Analysis Framework* based on *Gamification* for supporting the requirements engineer in analyzing and designing engaging software systems. Our framework, named *Agon*, encompasses both a methodology and a meta-model capturing acceptance and gamification knowledge. In this paper, we describe the *Agon Meta-Model* and provide examples from the gamification of a decision-making platform in the context of a European Project.

Keywords: Acceptance requirements · Gamification · Goal modeling · Requirements engineering · Human behavior

1 Introduction

Usage is becoming the main factor that determines the success of a software system [10,11,15], especially so for social software such as Twitter and Facebook. In fact, the human aspect has to be deeply taken into account and addressed by building into a system strategies for stimulating the user to carry out activities that the system supports. For instance, if we consider Facebook, its success resides mainly on people's participation in platform activities. In fact, if people stop posting videos, comments, etc., the entire system would be deemed a failure. Thus, to guarantee the success of such a system, it is essential that users use the functionality of the system [10,11]. According to this, in order to maximize the usage and participation, favoring the success of a system, it is important to analyze and design a system considering also elements for engaging the user [15]. Such elements have been called *Acceptance Requirements* [10,11].

Acceptance Requirements and how to fulfill them have been receiving much attention in the literature [3,5,10–12,15]. Fulfilling such requirements calls for expertise such as psychologists, sociologists or marketing experts [11,15], and this

H.C. Mayr et al. (Eds.): ER 2017, LNCS 10650, pp. 223–230, 2017.
https://doi.org/10.1007/978-3-319-69904-2_18

makes the design process even more complex, error-prone and time-consuming than for vanilla software. Unfortunately, few requirements engineering studies and practices consider adequately such strategical concerns [11].

In order to tackle this acceptance requirements problem, we need systematic, tool supported methodologies able to: (i) guide the analyst in properly and accurately analyzing and eliciting *Acceptance Requirements* [10,11]; (ii) support in finding and designing operationalization solutions (e.g., through *Gamification*) [10,11]; (iii) provide suggestions concerning which psychological (acceptance) strategies and (gamification) best practices to employ in relation to the typologies of users the analyst has to engage (e.g., on the basis of acceptance and gamification knowledge conceptualized and modeled as meta-models) [10,11]; (iv) reason with the knowledge of conceptual models, mentioned in the previous point, to supply the analyst with proper suggestions [10,11].

In a previous short paper [10] we propose a preliminary version of *Agon*, an *Acceptance Requirements Framework based on Gamification.* Agon supports all the elements discussed above with a methodology: a *Systematic Acceptance Requirements Analysis* based on *Gamification.* This methodology is founded on and uses a *Multi-Layer Meta-Model* that represents acceptance and gamification knowledge. This paper is an extension of [10], focusing on the *Agon Multi-Layer Meta-Model.* The paper presents a detailed description of the models and examples from a real case study, in the context of a European project, where we employed Agon and its meta-model for gamifying a decision-making platform.

The next sections of this work are organized as follows. Section 2 introduces: (i) the *Acceptance Requirements*; (ii) the European project of the decision-making platform we gamified by using the *Agon Meta-Model*; (iii) how acceptance requirements are important in the context of the previous point. Section 3 provides an overview of the *Agon Multi-Layer Meta-Model* and illustrates in detail the meta-models that compose it. Finally, Sect. 4 concludes.

2 Acceptance Requirements and the PACAS Project

Acceptance Requirements are defined over a set of `Functions`, that are supposed to be accepted, and a target set of users, `Participants`, that must use the functions. Thus, they constitute a special class of quality requirements [6] represented as: `Acceptance[{Functions}, Participants]` $\geq$ `N%`. Each acceptance requirement imposes a constraint, `N%`, on the percentage of intended users actually agree to use the functions. The task for the designers is to deploy psychological, cognitive and behavioral mechanisms to spur users to use the functions.

In the following, we introduce the *Participatory Architectural Change MAnagement in ATM Systems* (PACAS[1]) European project (ATM stands for Air Traffic Management) and explain why acceptance requirements are important in its context (EATMA). The European Air Traffic Management Architecture (EATMA) is composed of many procedures that are continuously discussed,

[1] http://www.pacasproject.eu/.

innovated and improved concerning safety, security, organizational and economical aspects. This requires complex architectural change management activities involving many heterogeneous stakeholders from various institutions, agencies, and companies. The stakeholders, decision makers having different expertise, to find a solution, deal with many concurrent multidisciplinary variables, needs and constraints coming from different realities. They should collaborate and participate actively to the decision making process for finding an agreement fulfilling safety, security, organizational and economical aspects. Thus, the critical part is to guarantee that all the stakeholders participate actively and continuously to the process for designing high-quality solutions.

This process is enacted by using a platform for managing EATMA architectural changes. Therefore, our aim has been to make the platform able to motivate the stakeholders to participate and collaborate actively. We used the Agon methodology and the Agon meta-model, described in this paper, for analyzing acceptance requirements and operationalizing them for gamifying the platform. The full case study is available at [9]. An extract of acceptance requirements we defined for PACAS is: `Acceptance[{Propose Change Management, Report AsIs Details, Propose Alternative, ...}, Decision Makers]` $\geq$ `80%`. Thus, we identified the set of crucial functions of the platform that need full users' participation to satisfy platform objectives. For instance, from the previous definition, we decided to motivate decision makers, above all, concerning the usage of the platform for proposing a new change management, reporting collaboratively details of the procedures to be improved, finding problems and parts to be enhanced and proposing alternative solutions. By using the Agon meta-model, described in the next section, we refined these acceptance requirements and operationalized them by gamifying functions highlighted above [9].

3 The Agon Multi-Layer Meta-Model

Here, we start giving an overview of the Agon multi-layer meta-model and, in the next sub-sections, we describe each model composing the entire meta-model.

The Multi-Layer Meta-Model. The *Agon Multi-Layer Meta-Model* is shown in Fig. 1 with an example from the PACAS case study. The example is described step by step in the next sub-sections. The meta-model is composed of 4 abstraction layers and at each level there is a goal model [2]. In order to design the Agon meta-model, we extended the *NFR Framework* [2], and in the following sub-sections we describe all the elements at each layer. At the moment of writing, the meta-model counts 281 goals and 393 relations. It represents the acceptance and gamification knowledge and, we are continuously improving it by adding new elements. This is necessary because new acceptance and gamification concepts have been continuously appearing in the literature, thus, it is important to apply updates for keeping the meta-model as much as possible close to the reality and, therefore, precise and effective.

From the acceptance level to the gamification level (Fig. 1) we have the *Acceptance Meta-Model* (AMM), the *Tactical Meta-Model* (TMM) and the *Gamifica-*

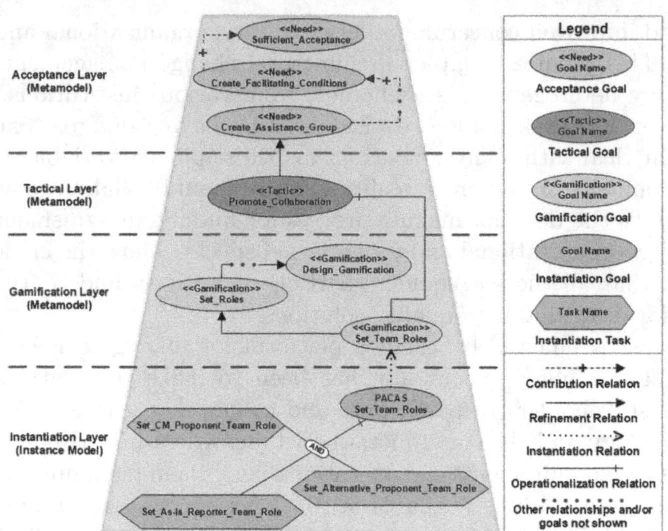

Fig. 1. The Agon multi-layer meta-model

tion Meta-Model (GMM)). Them are meta-models including generic concepts not referring to a particular domain (e.g., the one of PACAS). In fact, them are composed of: (i) psychological strategies (AMM); (ii) tactics (TMM) as high-level goals AMM and GMM have in common; (iii) gamification solutions (GMM). In the bottom layer, there is the *Instance Model* (IM). IM is not a meta-model, it instantiates generic goals of the upper level (GMM) by specifying them in relation to the distinct domain of the system to gamify (e.g., PACAS).

The requirements analyst, following the Agon methodology, a *Systematic Acceptance Requirements Analysis based on Gamification*, uses the Agon meta-model starting from the top, the most abstract layer (AMM), and going towards the bottom layers (GMM and IM). This activity is semi-automatic because, at each layer, the analyst uses reasoning techniques applied to goal models [7] and automatically receives suggestions related respectively to acceptance, tactical and gamification solutions to employ in the gamification of the system. This activity is also interactive, because the analyst at each layer, on the basis of suggestions received and her knowledge regarding the domain of the system to gamify, takes further decisions (e.g., discarding parts of the solutions proposed).

Morever, Agon is composed also of another fundamental model, the *User Context Model* (UCM) (designed with *Context Dimension Trees* [8]), that characterizes the intended users to engage through context variables such as gender, age, expertise, kind of player [1], etc. These variables are crucial elements used during the reasoning activity described above. Indeed, relations of the Agon models are annotated by *Context Dependent Rules* (CDRs) defined on UCM variables. CDRs are evaluated to decide if to keep or discard some relations and connected elements. The idea behind this, is to reason over acceptance and gamification knowledge, the meta-model, selecting the solutions (goals) that are the most suitable ones for the users to motivate.

In the following sub-sections, we describe all the Agon models by providing some examples from the PACAS case study. The complete case study, the Agon meta-model (with full models) and the Agon glossary can be found online at [9].

The User Context Model. Different people are stimulated by different psychological factors and gamification solutions [1,5,14,15]. This is captured by UCM that includes users' characteristics to consider for the selection of acceptance and gamification strategies that can affect positively a specific kind of user. Thus, the analyst instantiates UCM on the basis of the user's characteristics and, when Agon executes reasoning over AMM, TMM and GMM, considers the UCM instantiation for evaluating CDRs (annotated in the relations of the models) to select the most suitable solutions for the intended users. CDRs are rules (we extracted them from the literature [1,5,14,15]) composed of expression based on the UCM variables. For example, in Fig. 2 there is an extract from the meta-model specifying that: (i) if you are dealing with socializers (or other user's kinds expressed by the CDR starting with `(C2[Socializer] OR ...`) challenges tackled in team (`Team Challenges`) are preferred [15]; (ii) if you are dealing with males or achiever, etc., (`(C7[Male] OR C1[Achiever] ...`) personal challenges (`Personal Challenges`) are suggested [15].

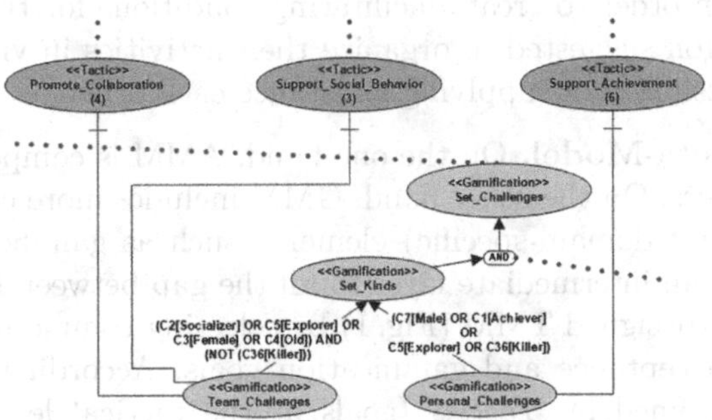

Fig. 2. Context dependent rules, gamification goals and tactics

The Acceptance Meta-Model. AMM is composed of *Needs* (legend in Fig. 1) to be satisfied for maximizing the possibility that intended users accept to use the system. We designed AMM by carrying out a wide literature review of technology acceptance models (e.g., the Unified Theory of Acceptance and Use of Technology (UTAUT) [14], the Technology Acceptance Model (TAM2), etc.; full list in [10]) and merging the most relevant concepts in a model, the Agon AMM.

The main structure of AMM (Fig. 3) and related CDRs are based on the UTAUT model [14]. The root goal is the `Sufficient Acceptance` need. It is the most abstract goal and it means to make that most of the intended users accept to use a software. This receives positive contributions (all the

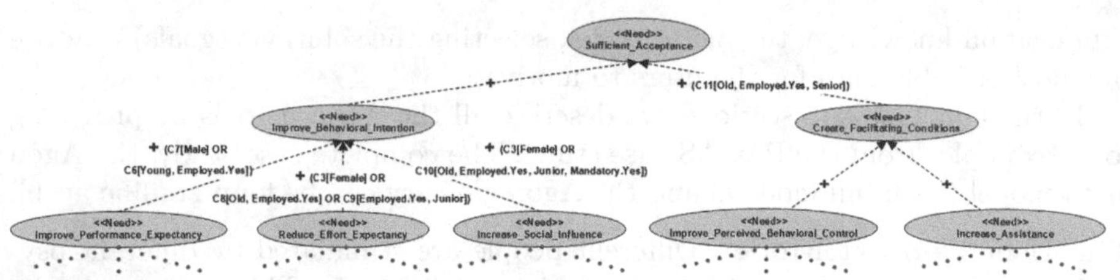

Fig. 3. An extract of the Agon acceptance meta-model based on UTAUT [14]

relations in AMM are contributions) by two high-level needs (Fig. 3): (i) `Improve Behavioral Intention` that in turn receives positive contributions from `Improve Performance Expectancy`, `Reduce Effort Expectancy` and `Increase Social Influence`; (ii) `Create Facilitating Conditions` that in turn receives positive contributions from `Improve Perceived Behavioral Control` and `Increase Assistance`.

Around the main high-level needs we inserted relevant concepts of other technology acceptance models. For instance, needs that provide positive contributions to `Increase Assistance` come from [13]. Those needs are not shown in Fig. 3 for the sake of space, but we can refer on the example from PACAS in Fig. 1, where it is shown one of them: `Create Assistance Group`. In fact, the idea is that, in order to create facilitating conditions for the decision makers of PACAS, Agon suggested to organize their activities in virtual groups for increasing the possibility of supplying assistance each other.

The Tactical Meta-Model. On the one hand, AMM is composed of abstract psychological factors. On the other hand, GMM includes more concrete (though still generic, i.e. not domain-specific) elements such as gamification solutions. Thus, it is needed an intermediate layer to fill the gap between the two (Fig. 1). With this aim, we designed TMM (Fig. 1) by selecting common high-level qualities able to tie acceptance and gamification goals. According to this, acceptance needs are refined by *Tactics* (goals at the tactical level) that in turn are operationalized by gamification goals (Fig. 1). Continuing the example in Fig. 1, at the AMM level Agon proposes to enable users to assist each other in groups and, at the tactical level it is refined by promoting collaboration (`Promote Collaboration`) among the PACAS decision makers. This leads Agon to select gamification goals able to operationalize the collaboration promotion (we discuss this in the next sub-section). Other tactics are shown in Fig. 2.

The Gamification Meta-Model. GMM is built on gamification concepts and best practices we extracted by carrying out a wide review of the literature and of success cases from the industry (some resources [3,4,12,15]). GMM supports mainly: badges, levels, paths, leader-boards of various kinds, redeemable points, reputation points, experience points, karma points, skill points, gamified trainings, gamified tutorials, game roles, unlockable powers, gamified tours, avatars, suggestions and tricks, gamified forums, team and personal challenges, gamified communities and gamified markets with redeemable rewards and making gift policies.

The main relationship used at the GMM level (Figs. 1 and 2) is that of refinement. Furthermore, gamification goals operationalize or give positive/negative contributions to tactics (Fig. 2). For instance, the challenges concept is represented in Fig. 2 (`Set Challenges`) with: `Team Challenges` and `Personal Challenges`. According to the CDRs indicated, team challenges are suggested for socializers, explorers, etc., and them operationalize the `Promote Collaboration` and `Support Social Behavior` tactics. Continuing the PACAS example in Fig. 1, at the tactical level Agon suggests to promote collaboration and, at the gamification level, it is operationalized by arranging teams and team roles (`Set Team Roles`) for PACAS decision makers.

The Instantiation Model. Solutions obtained at the gamification level are the result of acceptance and tactic reasoning and are the most suitable for the intended users, but are generic, independent from a specific domain. Therefore, GMM goals need to be instantiated in relation to the specific domain of the system to gamify. So far, the process is semi-automatic and interactive, while at the instantiation level the analyst has to create the IM. Agon helps the analyst by providing her with a notation based on the *NFR Framework* [2] supporting goals, tasks, and relations such as instantiations, refinements and operationalizations. Concluding the example from the PACAS case study (Fig. 1), at the gamification level, Agon suggests to operationalize the collaboration through the definition of teams and team roles for the users. This suggestion is valuable and suitable for the intended users, but it is still abstract, thus, the analyst creates the IM (Fig. 1) by instantianting the `Set Team Roles` gamification goal and defining the purposes of each team roles. Those purposes are specific of the PACAS domain. For instance, `Set As-Is Reporter Team Role` defines a team responsible for reporting the current as-is situation of an ATM procedure. While, `Set Alternative Proponent Team Role` describes a team in charge of proposing alternative solutions for improving an ATM procedure.

4 Conclusion

In this paper, we focus on a fundamental component of our Agon framework, the *Agon Meta-Model*. It captures acceptance and gamification knowledge and facilitates a systematic acceptance requirements analysis based on gamification. Moreover, we have provided examples from a real case study that we conducted in the context of the PACAS European project[2]. This case study concerns the gamification of the PACAS platform by using Agon. Moreover, preliminary evaluations conducted with non-experts (master students) and experts (experts on gamification and requirements engineering from the PACAS project) confirmed the usefulness of Agon. In order to collect more evidences regarding the Agon

[2] http://www.pacasproject.eu/.

usefulness, we are employing Agon also in the context of other European projects, for instance in the Vision project[3] for gamifying a privacy platform.

Acknowledgments. This project has received funding from the SESAR Joint Undertaking under grant agreement No. 699306 under European Union's Horizon 2020 research and innovation programme.

This work was partially supported by ERC Advanced Grant 267856, titled "Lucretius: Foundations for Software Evolution."

References

1. Bartle, R.: Hearts, clubs, diamonds, spades: players who suit MUDs. J. MUD Res. **1**, 19 (1996)
2. Chung, L., Nixon, B., Yu, E., Mylopoulos, J.: Non-Functional Requirements in Software Engineering, vol. 5. Springer, Heidelberg (2012)
3. Hamari, J.: Do badges increase user activity? a field experiment on the effects of gamification. Comput. Hum. Behav. **71**, 469–478 (2015)
4. Kazhamiakin, R., Marconi, A., Perillo, M., Pistore, M., Valetto, G., Piras, L., Avesani, F., Perri, N.: Using gamification to incentivize sustainable urban mobility. In: 1st International Smart Cities Conference (ISC2). IEEE (2015)
5. Koivisto, J., Hamari, J.: Demographic differences in perceived benefits from gamification. Comput. Hum. Behav. **35**, 179–188 (2014)
6. Li, F.L., Horkoff, J., Mylopoulos, J., Guizzardi, R., Guizzardi, G., Borgida, A., Liu, L.: Non-functional requirements as qualities, with a spice of ontology. In: 22nd International Requirements Engineering Conference (RE), pp. 293–302. IEEE (2014)
7. Nguyen, C.M., Sebastiani, R., Giorgini, P., Mylopoulos, J.: Multi-objective reasoning with constrained goal models. Requir. Eng. J. p. 1–37 (2016)
8. Orsi, G., Tanca, L.: Context modelling and context-aware querying. In: Moor, O., Gottlob, G., Furche, T., Sellers, A. (eds.) Datalog 2.0 2010. LNCS, vol. 6702, pp. 225–244. Springer, Heidelberg (2011). doi:10.1007/978-3-642-24206-9_13
9. Piras, L., Giorgini, P., Mylopoulos, J.: Models, case studies and the glossary of Agon (an Acceptance Requirements Framework). https://pirasluca.wordpress.com/home/acceptance/
10. Piras, L., Giorgini, P., Mylopoulos, J.: Acceptance requirements and their gamification solutions. In: 24th IEEE International Requirements Engineering Conference (RE). IEEE (2016)
11. Piras, L., Paja, E., Cuel, R., Ponte, D., Giorgini, P., Mylopoulos, J.: Gamification solutions for software acceptance: a comparative study of requirements engineering and organizational behavior techniques. In: 11th IEEE International Conference on Research Challenges in Information Science (RCIS). IEEE (2017)
12. Schell, J.: The Art of Game Design: A Book of Lenses. CRC Press, Boca Raton (2014)
13. Thompson, R., Higgins, C., Howell, J.: Personal computing: toward a conceptual model of utilization. MIS Q. **15**, 125–143 (1991)
14. Venkatesh, V., Morris, M., Davis, G., Davis, F.: User acceptance of information technology: toward a unified view. MIS Q. **27**, 425–478 (2003)
15. Zichermann, G., Cunningham, C.: Gamification by Design: Implementing Game Mechanics in Web and Mobile Apps. O'Reilly Media Inc, Sebastopol (2011)

[3] http://www.visioneuproject.eu/.

Modeling Regulatory Ambiguities for Requirements Analysis

Aaron K. Massey[1(✉)], Eric Holtgrefe[1], and Sepideh Ghanavati[2]

[1] Department of Information Systems, University of Maryland, Baltimore County, Baltimore, USA
{akmassey,eholtgr1}@umbc.edu

[2] Department of Computer Science, Texas Tech University, Lubbock, USA
sepideh.ghanavati@ttu.edu

Abstract. Lawyers and policy makers regularly and intentionally use ambiguous language in laws, regulations, and other legal texts. Although ambiguity has important policy benefits, such as interpretive resilience in an ever-changing world, it frustrates engineers and businesses seeking to build software systems that are demonstratively compliant with legal obligations. In this vision paper, we propose a method for modeling legal texts alongside models of software requirements or design artifacts. Our approach allows engineers to reason about regulatory ambiguity separately from their system under development and then trace interpretive decisions made about the legal text to affected requirements models. When a regulation is updated or case law demands a new interpretation of a regulation, engineers can evaluate the effect of the changes on the current design and respond appropriately. Inspired by User Requirements Notation, our proposed method can be implemented as an extension to Legal-GRL.

Keywords: Requirements engineering · Ambiguity modeling · Regulatory compliance

1 Introduction

Regulatory Compliance Software Engineering (RCSE) is an emerging field of interdisciplinary research focused on the development of systematic approaches to building, maintaining, and verifying software systems that must comply with laws and regulations. Laws, regulations, and policy documents, and other legal texts are simultaneously useful and challenging as a source of requirements for software engineers [16]. One of the reasons for this challenge is the use of intentional ambiguity as a means of interpretive resilience in rapidly changing technical environments. For example, specifying a particular encryption algorithm is less resilient than using an ambiguous phrase like "reasonable encryption" because if a specified algorithm were broken, then the law would need to be updated. Unfortunately, any ambiguity in a legal text, whether intentional or

H.C. Mayr et al. (Eds.): ER 2017, LNCS 10650, pp. 231–238, 2017.
https://doi.org/10.1007/978-3-319-69904-2_19

not, must be identified, classified, and disambiguated during requirements engineering [13]. That is, at some point "reasonable encryption" will have to be interpreted to identify a particular algorithm prior to implementation.

Current approaches to RCSE focus on performing an interpretation of legal texts, including the resolution of ambiguity, and linking each interpretation back to the subsection of the policy document from which it came. On the surface, this seems to be all that is needed, but interpreting legal texts is more nuanced than this procedure supports. For example, lawyers cannot give a "definitive" interpretation of a law; they can only give an opinion based on how they believe a court or regulator would interpret the text for a particular situation. As a result, many requirements engineering approaches to regulatory requirements fundamentally require legal domain expertise that is not currently supported by goal modeling, requirements modeling, or other standard software engineering modeling activities. New approaches must be developed to support increased participation of non-legal domain experts, provide flexibility in the face of a changing regulatory environment, and incorporate modeling of regulatory requirements in the software development lifecycle.

In this paper, we propose a method for modeling legal texts alongside models of software requirements or design artifacts. Our approach allows engineers to reason about regulatory ambiguity separately from their system under development and then trace interpretive decisions made about the legal text to the affected requirements models. The goal of this approach is to support reanalysis of ambiguities in the event of regulatory change or updated engineering requirements. By identifying, categorizing, and modeling ambiguities, we can document how those ambiguities are resolved by requirements models or other design artifacts. When a regulation is updated or case law demands a new interpretation of a regulation, engineers can evaluate the effect of the changes on the current design and respond appropriately.

The remainder of this paper is structured as follows. Section 2 details related work in regulatory requirements and goal modeling. Section 3 describes our proposed methodology for constructing an ambiguity model and present an example of its use. Section 4 discusses the implications of our method and details possible future work.

2 Related Work

Policy makers write abstract, intentionally ambiguous language to ensure the laws and policies they construct outlast the current generation of technologies. On the other hand, engineers developing software systems must interpret these laws and regulations to address their specific cases and to ensure compliance. Recent research [5,13] demonstrates that ambiguity and vagueness in privacy policies increase privacy risks and decrease the user trust and willingness to share the personal data.

Analyzing and resolving ambiguities has been a research topic in requirements engineering and analysis for decades. Most engineering approaches to analyzing and resolving ambiguities involve developing tools [8] and techniques based on natural language processing [14,15,18] or machine learning approaches [17,19]. The goal of these approaches is to resolve—once and for all—ambiguities in requirements with a single, definitive interpretation (e.g., identify the correct antecedent to an ambiguous pronoun). Herein, we avoid definitive resolution in favor of modeling options and supporting reuse and re-examination of interpretive decisions.

In our prior work [13], we developed a taxonomy and a classification methodology for legal ambiguities, consisting of seven types of ambiguity: Lexical, Syntactic, Semantic, Vagueness, Incompleteness, Referential, and Other. Understanding an ambiguity's classification supports disambiguation of that ambiguity. This taxonomy was designed to be broadly applicable, but it is not guaranteed to be comprehensive. Our ambiguity taxonomy describes the process of classifying ambiguities according to their types [13]. Our methodology presented herein can be adapted to other methods for classifying ambiguities.

We use User Requirements Notation (URN) [9] for modeling ambiguities derived from our taxonomy. URN combines Goal-oriented Requirements Language (GRL) [2–4] with Use Case Maps (UCM) [6] in one single notation and provides traceability between the two. GRL includes 'lightweight' mechanisms to help extending the language with the help of metadata, rules, concerns, and links. The Use Case Map notation is used to model scenarios and use cases in terms of a set of responsibilities assigned to *components* (▭) , which represent actors, agents, roles, software modules, systems or sub-systems. Paths start with *start points* (●) and traverse through elements along the way until they reach the *end points* (▮) . Paths contain *responsibilities* (✕) which indicate where actions, activities, or transformations are needed. They can be performed in sequence, concurrently (⊣⊏) , or as alternatives (⤙) . UCM also includes static or dynamic stubs (◇) to model parts of a scenario or a process as a plug-in map. URN has an open source tool-support, called jUCMNav [1], which is a plugin for the Eclipse development environment.[1]

Legal-URN [7] is an extension to the URN framework that helps requirements engineers analyze the compliance of business and software requirements with privacy-related regulations. jUCMNav has been extended to capture concepts from Legal-URN. In our approach, we first model ambiguities with Use Case Maps and then provide links from the ambiguity models to Legal-URN models to perform this analysis. The ultimate goal of our approach is to develop a new form of contribution link that connects regulatory ambiguities with traditional modeling elements. Although we do not develop the syntax herein, we discuss how it would support our ambiguity models in Sect. 4.

3 Constructing Ambiguity Models

In this section, we discuss how to develop ambiguity models. We adopt and extend UCM to model ambiguities in legal statements. First, we identify and

[1] http://eclipse.org/.

classify ambiguities in the legal text we wish to model. Herein, we employ the approach introduced in our prior work [13], but we believe similar approaches to ambiguity identification may also suffice. Regardless of the technique chosen, we recommend examining the complete text prior to modeling because this prevents modeling of ambiguities that are resolved or clarified elsewhere in the regulation.

After classification, we follow the process outlined in Algorithm 1. In general, we use static or dynamic stubs (◇) to model legal text. When the legal text includes an ambiguity, we tag the stub with ambiguity marker as («amb»). Specifically, the steps of our approach are as follows. First, model each subsection of a legal statement with a stub. These represent legal statements to be detailed in a plug-in map. Next, model the plug-in map of each related stub. If modeling an ambiguity, use a stub with an ambiguity marker. If modeling another sub-path, use a regular stub. If modeling a non-ambiguous task, use a responsibility (✕) or other appropriate UCM element. Finally, we model the ambiguities tagged with ambiguity markers using new plug-in maps. The plug-in map includes a path, AND- or OR- Fork(s), and Join elements depending on the semantics of the legal text and ambiguity elements (⊡).

Algorithm 1: Algorithm for Modeling Ambiguities

```
FnRecursive(an element of a legal text) begin
    if the element under examination is atomic and not ambiguous then
        model any requirements using traditional techniques;
    else if the element under examination is atomic and ambiguous then
        create a stub on the path;
        document the ambiguity inside the stub;
    else
        create a stub on the path;
        recursively apply this algorithm to each sub-element;
```

We illustrate how our approach for modeling ambiguities works using a section from the Health Insurance Portability and Accountability Act (HIPAA)[2]. We selected §164.312, which contains the technical safeguards regulations for HIPAA, because this article has been used extensively in our prior work [10–12] examining those systems. To start the modeling process, we construct an outline of §164.312 with each subsection modeled using a stub because none of them are ambiguous. After completing this step, we follow the recursive step of the algorithm to model the first stub in §164.312 which is (a) Access Control.

(a) Access Control contains two subparts, labeled as (1) Standard and (2) Implementation Specifications. Subpart (a)(1) contains an ambiguity,[3] thus

[2] Pub. L. No. 104–191, 110 Stat. 1936 (1996).

[3] All ambiguity identification is relative to the interpreter. There is no "ground truth" in ambiguity identification. However, for the sake of simplicity, we refer to Subpart (a)(1) as "containing" an ambiguity. In reality, without an interpreter, these same words are neither ambiguous nor unambiguous.

we model it as a stub with ambiguity marker, («amb»). Subpart `(a)(2)` is modeled as a stub and it includes four separate statements as: `(i)` Unique User Identification; `(ii)` Emergency Access Procedure; `(iii)` Automatic Logoff, and `(iv)` Encryption and Decryption. We further expand the stub for `(a)(2)` in another plug-in map. The first three statements of this subpart are ambiguous.[4] Thus, these three are modeled with stubs with ambiguity markers. The fourth statements does not include any ambiguity so it is modeled with a UCM responsibility element.

During this portion of the modeling, we are only interested in three things: (1) reflecting the structure of the actual legal text we are modeling, (2) accurately identifying ambiguity stubs, and (3) accurately modeling unambiguous statements with traditional methods. We are neither resolving nor prioritizing ambiguities because we want resolution, prioritization, and other analyses to be independent of identification. If identification and classification are not separated from other analysis, then the model is not easily reused.

Next, we expand stubs with ambiguity markers into detailed paths with ambiguity elements. As mentioned above, statement `(a)(2)(ii)` was found to be ambiguous. This statement reads as follows:

> `(a)(2)(ii)` Emergency access procedure: Establish (and implement as needed) procedures for obtaining necessary electronic protected health information during an emergency.

Our analysis found two ambiguities, one syntactic and one vagueness. The phrase *and implement as needed* allows the whole statement to have multiple valid meanings. (e.g., A procedure may be 'established' or 'established and implemented'.) In addition, the phrase *during an emergency* is vague in that no definition for an emergency is provided.

At this point, requirements engineers may begin the task of resolving these ambiguities. Resolution may take many forms, but whatever form it takes for a given project, the data necessary to perform an ambiguity resolution should be recorded here as attributes of the ambiguity stubs. In our prior work, we examined intentionality [13]. That is, did the author of the legal text intend for this ambiguity to be written as ambiguous in the way that we identified it. For `(a)(2)(ii)`, we believe the syntactic ambiguity is not intentional (When would you establish and not implement a procedure?) and the vagueness is intentional (Emergencies are difficult to define with clarity). Regardless the resolution approach taken, all data necessary for resolution should be recorded as attributes of the ambiguity stubs. The goal of this step is to support reuse and facilitate changing legal or engineering requirements.

We model these two ambiguities with ambiguity elements (⬡) which is added to UCM models as an extension. To complete the ambiguity model, we must lay each ambiguity out on the path. Our approach has two options, the ambiguities are independent or one must be resolved before the other. For `(a)(2)(ii)`, we

[4] Again, based on our interpretation.

decided that both of ambiguities determine the actor and their responsibilities. As a result, we model them in parallel and with AND-fork paths.

Figure 1 illustrates modeling the second of these, including the type of ambiguity, which details our analysis of §`164.312(b)` which reads as follows:

> Implement hardware, software, and/or procedural mechanisms that record and examine activity in information systems that contain or use electronic protected health information.

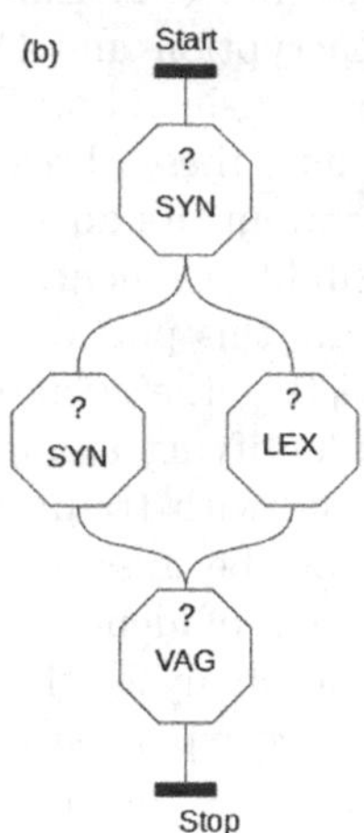

Fig. 1. Ambiguity identified in §164.312(b)

This legal statement includes four ambiguities: two syntactic ambiguities, a lexical ambiguity and a vagueness, summarized in Table 1. We believe all four ambiguities are relatively easy to disambiguate and this text can be implemented by software engineers. They do, however, have a strict ordering, as shown in Fig. 1.

Due to space constraints, we now focus our analysis on the lexical ambiguity resulting from the phrase "…that contain or use electronic protected health information." The "contain and use" part of this phrase is confusing. Does "contain" refer to "having access to some data" or "keeping some data apart from"? No separation of data is explicitly mentioned, so it would be easy to assume the former meaning is correct. However, in this case the word "contain" is superfluous. Any "use" of the data would require access to it. So perhaps the latter meaning of "contain" is correct? This ambiguity is

Table 1. Ambiguities found in `164.312(b)`

Type	Phrase	Rationale
Syntactic	"Implement hardware, software, and/or procedural mechanisms that…"	Does the "that" clause apply to the hardware, the software, the procedural mechanisms or some combination of them?
Syntactic	"…that record and examine activity…"	Do the mechanisms need to be implemented for a system that only records activity?
Lexical	"…that contain or use electronic protected health information."	Does contain mean "have access to" or "keep separate from the rest of the system"?
Vagueness	"Implement hardware, software, and/or procedural mechanisms that record and examine activity in information systems that contain or use electronic protected health information."	The statement is quite broad. What is actually needed?

also localized and does not affect the meaning of the entire statement. Because both this lexical ambiguity and the second syntactical ambiguity (see Table 1) can be resolved independently and without affecting the resolution of the first syntactical ambiguity, we modeled them in parallel.

4 Discussion and Summary

Although ambiguity has important policy benefits, such as interpretive resilience in an ever-changing world, it frustrates engineers seeking to interpret their meaning and demonstrate due diligence in complying with legal obligations. In this vision paper, we proposed a method for modeling ambiguities in legal texts alongside models of software requirements or design artifacts. We presented an example model that demonstrate how our approach supports engineers as they reason about regulatory ambiguity and come to a disambiguation or resolution strategy. When a regulation is updated or case law demands a new interpretation of a regulation, engineers can evaluate the effect of the changes on the current design and respond appropriately.

Because regulations can change over time, interpretations may also change. A structural model of regulatory ambiguity supports easier change impact analysis because updates to legal texts are denoted with structural changes. For example, consider §`170.314` and §`170.315`. These two sections of HIPAA represent the meaningful use certification criteria for EHR systems for 2014 and 2015, respectively. They are remarkably similar in structure, so if an EHR vendor seeking to transition from 2014 compliance to 2015 compliance used an ambiguity model, many of the implications of the changes could easily be identified.

By modeling legal documents as they are structured to support reuse and reanalysis, we support discussion between the analysts and legal experts as they seek to resolve ambiguities in system design. If ambiguity identification and classification were interleaved with ambiguity resolution, then any change in the regulations may require analysts to either re-identify and re-classify the ambiguities or to undo the resolution process, whatever it may have been (disambiguation, prioritization, etc...).

By choosing to model the text in a way that supports multiple interpretations and without a definitive interpretation or resolution in mind, we can meaningfully support analysts seeking to incorporate ambiguity resolution with traditional modeling approaches. Many ambiguity types can only be resolved with domain experts, and for these analysts cannot reach a valid conclusion without a consultation. Unfortunately, by resolving these directly and documenting only the resolution, requirements engineers risk non-compliance resulting from future changes, including changes to regulations, changes to customer requirements, or even simple staff turnover. In essence, the resolved ambiguity has become tacitly hidden, with no indication that the ambiguity existed at all.

References

1. Amyot, D.: JUCMNav. http://jucmnav.softwareengineering.ca/ucm/bin/view/ProjetSEG/WebHome, October (2016)
2. Amyot, D., Ghanavati, S., Horkoff, J., Mussbacher, G., Peyton, L., Yu, E.: Evaluating goal models within the goal-oriented requirement language. Int. J. Intell. Syst. **25**(8), 841–877 (2010)
3. Amyot, D., Horkoff, J., Gross, D., Mussbacher, G.: A lightweight GRL profile for i* modeling. In: Heuser, C.A., Pernul, G. (eds.) ER 2009. LNCS, vol. 5833, pp. 254–264. Springer, Heidelberg (2009). doi:10.1007/978-3-642-04947-7_31
4. Amyot, D., et al.: Towards advanced goal model analysis with jUCMNav. In: Castano, S., Vassiliadis, P., Lakshmanan, L.V., Lee, M.L. (eds.) ER 2012. LNCS, vol. 7518, pp. 201–210. Springer, Heidelberg (2012). doi:10.1007/978-3-642-33999-8_25
5. Bhatia, J., Breaux, T.D., Reidenberg, J.R., Norton, T.B.: A theory of vagueness and privacy risk perception. In: 24th International RE Conference, Beijing, China, September 2016
6. Buhr, R., Casselman, R.: Use Case Maps for Object-Oriented Systems. Prentice-Hall, Upper Saddle River (1995)
7. Ghanavati, S.: Legal-URN Framework for Legal Compliance of Business Processes. PhD thesis, University of Ottawa, Ottawa, Canada (2013)
8. Gordon, D.G., Breaux, T.D.: Reconciling multi-jurisdictional legal requirements: a case study in requirements water marking. In: 20th IEEE International RE Conference, pp. 91–100, September 2012
9. ITU-T. User Requirements Notation (URN) - Language definition. Technical Report ITU-T Z.151, ITU-T, October 2012
10. Massey, A.K., Otto, P.N., Antón, A.I.: Evaluating legal implementation readiness decision-making. IEEE Trans. Softw. Eng. **41**(6), 545–564 (2015)
11. Massey, A.K., Otto, P.N., Hayward, L.J., Antón, A.I.: Evaluating existing security and privacy requirements for legal compliance. Requir. Eng. **15**, 119–137 (2010)
12. Massey, A.K., Rutledge, R.L., Antón, A.I., Hemmings, J.D., Swire, P.P.: A strategy for addressing ambiguity in regulatory requirements. https://smartech.gatech.edu/handle/1853/54573 (2015)
13. Massey, A.K., Rutledge, R.L., Antón, A.I., Swire, P.P.: Identifying and classifying ambiguity for regulatory requirements. In: 22nd International Conference on RE, pp. 83–92, August 2014
14. Nigam, A., Arya, N., Nigam, B., Jain, D.: Tool for automatic discovery of ambiguity in requirements. Int. J. Comput. Sci. Issues **9**(5) (2012)
15. Osborne, M., MacNish, C.K.: Processing natural language software requirement specifications. In: 2nd International Conference on RE, pp. 229–236, April 1996
16. Otto, P.N., Antón, A.I.: Addressing legal requirements in RE. In: 2007 15th IEEE International RE Conference, RE 2007, pp. 5–14 (2007)
17. Popescu, D., Rugaber, S., Medvidovic, N., Berry, D.M.: Reducing ambiguities in requirements specifications via automatically created object-oriented models. In: Paech, B., Martell, C. (eds.) Monterey Workshop 2007. LNCS, vol. 5320, pp. 103–124. Springer, Heidelberg (2008). doi:10.1007/978-3-540-89778-1_10
18. Umber, A., Bajwa, I.S.: Minimizing ambiguity in natural language software requirements specification. In: 2011 Sixth International Conference on Digital Information Management, pp. 102–107, September 2011
19. van Bussel, D.: Detecting ambiguity in requirements specifications. PhD thesis, Tilburg University (2009)

An Experimental Evaluation of the Understanding of Safety Compliance Needs with Models

Jose Luis de la Vara[1(✉)], Beatriz Marín[2], Clara Ayora[3], and Giovanni Giachetti[4]

[1] Departamento de Informática, Universidad Carlos III de Madrid, Leganés, Spain
jvara@inf.uc3m.es

[2] Facultad de Ingeniería, Universidad Diego Portales, Santiago, Chile
beatriz.marin@mail.udp.cl

[3] R&D Department, Treelogic, Madrid, Spain
claraayora@gmail.com

[4] Universidad Tecnológica de Chile INACAP, Santiago, Chile
ggiachetti@inacap.cl

Abstract. *Context:* Most safety-critical systems have to fulfil compliance needs specified in safety standards. These needs can be difficult to understand from the text of the standards, and the use of conceptual models has been proposed as a solution. *Goal:* We aim to evaluate the understanding of safety compliance needs with models. *Method:* We have conducted an experiment to study the effectiveness, efficiency, and perceived benefits in understanding these needs, with text of safety standards and with UML object diagrams. *Results:* Sixteen Bachelor students participated in the experiment. Their average effectiveness in understanding compliance needs and their average efficiency were higher with models (17% and 15%, respectively). However, the difference is not statistically significant. The students found benefits in using models, but on average they are undecided about their ease of understanding. *Conclusions:* Although the results are not conclusive enough, they suggest that the use of models could improve the understanding of safety compliance needs.

Keywords: Safety-critical system · Safety standard · Safety compliance needs · Model · Understanding · Comprehension · Experiment

1 Introduction

Safety-critical systems are those whose failure cam harm people, property, or the environment [12]. These systems must comply with safety standards, e.g., IEC 61508 for a wide range of industries, DO-178C in avionics, EN 50128 in railway, and ISO 26262 in automotive, as a way of assuring that they do not pose undue risks [13]. Safety standards specify safety compliance needs that must be satisfied [7], such as requirements to fulfil, data to manage, and activities to execute. System suppliers must

H.C. Mayr et al. (Eds.): ER 2017, LNCS 10650, pp. 239–247, 2017.
https://doi.org/10.1007/978-3-319-69904-2_20

understand and follow these needs, but this can be difficult. The standards are typically large textual documents that consist of hundreds of pages and define thousands of criteria for compliance. Ambiguity and inconsistencies are also usual in their text [12]. Practitioners have indeed acknowledged issues in understanding the standards [5, 13].

As a solution, several authors have argued that conceptual models of safety compliance needs can help practitioners understand these needs, e.g. [14]. However, there exists little evidence of the extent to which the use of models improves this understanding. Prior analyses are either based on experts' perceptions [7, 14], not on actual model usage, or have only provided preliminary insights from pilot studies [6]. There is also a general lack of experiments related to safety certification [12].

We aim to fill the gaps regarding the analysis of the understanding of safety compliance needs with models. To this end, we have conducted an experiment to study the effectiveness, efficiency, and perceived benefits of understanding the needs with models. Sixteen Bachelor students answered questions about safety compliance needs in DO-178C and in EN 50128, using their text and models (UML object diagrams). The students also indicated their opinion about the use of models.

The paper is organised as follows. Section 2 presents the background, and Sect. 3 the experiment process. Section 4 reports the results and Sect. 5 our conclusions.

2 Background

Model-based approaches for the specification of safety compliance needs have been proposed for specific standards or parts of them (e.g. IEC 61508 [14]), and for specific compliance needs (e.g. related to processes [3]). Modelling standards for system assurance and certification have also been published [8]. Some studies have reported that models are used in industry for safety certification purposes [5, 13].

For the experiment, we have used a holistic generic metamodel for the specification of safety compliance needs [7]. This metamodel supports the specification of different types of these needs: information about requirements, artefacts, and processes, and about their applicability. The metamodel can be used for different standards from several domains and has been validated with practitioners and data from real projects.

Regarding **related work**, we run a pilot experiment [6] to validate the experiment design, adjust it for the experiment reported in this paper, and derive hypotheses. We found both evidence and counterevidence of the improvement in the understanding of safety compliance needs with the use of models.

In other studies, experts have agreed that models of safety standards are easy to understand [7, 14]. There are also some experiments related to safety certification (e.g. [1, 4]), including on model-based approaches. Experiments that have evaluated the comprehension of model-based artefacts (e.g. [2, 9]) have shown benefits in their use. Others have compared textual and graphical representations (e.g. [15, 17]). The results of understanding tasks with models were better in some cases, and with text in others.

3 Experiment Process

We used the guidelines by Wohlin et al. [19] to design the experiment. The goal is to analyse the use of models to specify safety compliance needs for the purpose of evaluation with respect to effectiveness, efficiency, and perceived benefits of understanding safety compliance needs from the point of view of the researcher in the context of Bachelor students in Computer Science and Engineering.

We formulated three research questions (RQs):

- RQ1. Does the use of models increase the effectiveness of understanding safety compliance needs?
- RQ2. Does the use of models increase the efficiency of understanding safety compliance needs?
- RQ3. Do users find benefits in the use of models to understand safety compliance needs?

The subjects of the experiment are 16 students of a 3rd-year course on "Software development projects management" of a Bachelor's Degree in Computer Science and Engineering at Carlos III University of Madrid, Spain. In this course the students have to plan the development and validation of an application and to design it according to the ESA PSS-05-0 software engineering standard [10]. In the experiment the subjects have to identify safety compliance needs from excerpts of the text of safety standards and from models of these excerpts, and indicate their opinion about the models.

Based on the results of the pilot experiment [6], we formulate two null hypotheses that we aim to reject:

- $H_{1,0}$: There is no significant difference in the effectiveness of understanding safety compliance needs with the text of safety standards and with models.
- $H_{2,0}$: There is no significant difference in the efficiency of understanding safety compliance needs with the text of safety standards and with models.

The independent variables are: (1) the means used to represent safety compliance needs (model or text), and; (2) the standard considered (DO-178C requirements process or EN 50128 integration process, which are different to the standard used in the course). To represent the instances of the holistic metamodel, we use UML object diagrams.

Two dependent variables are the effectiveness and efficiency. In line with related work, e.g. [2, 4], we use the F-measure (F_s) to quantify the effectiveness. It is based on the precision and recall in identifying safety compliance needs. We use the formulas for cases in which it is possible that a subject does not answer a question [9]. We use the effectiveness and the time (in minutes) to quantify efficiency ($Effy_s$) [1, 15].

$$precision_s = \frac{\sum_i |answer_{s,i} \cap correct_i|}{\sum_i |answer_{s,i}|} \qquad recall_s = \frac{\sum_i |answer_{s,i} \cap correct_i|}{\sum_i |correct_i|}$$

$$F_s = 2 \times \frac{precision_s \times recall_s}{precision_s + recall_s} \qquad Effy_s = 100 \times \frac{F_s}{minutes}$$

The third dependent variable is the perceived benefits in understanding safety compliance needs. It is evaluated with a questionnaire and a 5-point Likert scale (see Sect. 4.3) about the use of models to specify and to understand the needs [7].

The subjects are randomly divided into four groups in a within-subject 2 × 2 factorial design [18]: (1) DO-178C model (for the first task) and EN 50128 text (for the second task); (2) EN 50128 model and DO-178C text; (3) DO-178C text and EN 50128 model, and; (4) EN 50128 text and DO-178C model. The execution of the experiment is planned for a maximum of two hours, one for training and one for performing the tasks. The first author, as main expert in safety certification, was the main responsible for material preparation and the rest of authors validated it.

The subjects work offline and with the material[1] of each task printed: an introductory page, a two-page excerpt of a standard or models of the excerpts, and seven free-text questions. The subjects have to identify 11 safety compliance needs to correctly complete the questionnaire, the same in the text and in the model. The subjects need to record the time when they start and finish each task, and complete an opinion questionnaire.

Despite our effort to ensure experiment **validity**, some threats could impact it. For internal validity, we mitigated fatigue effects by running the experiment in the morning and having a break between the training and the tasks. Learning effects were mitigated by using different experimental objects, with similar size and complexity, in the two tasks. Regarding external validity, the use of students as subjects might concern the generalization of results. Nonetheless, recent studies argue that there are minor differences when students or practitioners are used [16]. Students can be regarded as novice practitioners [2], and it cannot be claimed that experience greatly helps practitioners better understand safety compliance needs [5]. We are also aware that the sample size is limited, but the number of students of the course was a constraint. The creation of the experimental material might be threatened by the interpretation of the standards (construct validity). To mitigate this threat, we used parts of standards for which we had access to models validated by practitioners. For conclusion validity, we use dependent variables that are widely used in experiments with a similar purpose, e.g. [2, 4]. To analyse the statistical significance of the results, we use parametric tests when normality of data was confirmed and non-parametric tests otherwise, and a 0.05 level for the p-value. Finally, the selection of a given graphical notation (UML object diagram) affects conclusion validity.

4 Results and Interpretation

This section presents the results of the experiment and how we interpret them. No subject had knowledge about the standards used in the experiment or the parts of them. Their experience with UML class or object diagrams was homogeneous and similar to our expectations for 3rd-year Bachelor students in Computer Science and Engineering.

[1] https://sites.google.com/site/jldelavara/material/msac2016.

4.1 Effectiveness of Understanding (RQ1)

Table 1 shows the effectiveness of understanding safety compliance needs with models and with the text of standards. In addition to the value of the F-measure for each subject (F), the table shows the precision (P) and recall (R). Their mean values are similar to or higher than those in other experiments related to safety certification, e.g. [1, 4], thus we regard subjects' overall effectiveness as acceptable and valid.

Table 1. Effectiveness and efficiency of understanding safety compliance needs

Group	Subj.	Effectiveness						Efficiency			
		Models			Text			Models		Text	
		P	R	F	P	R	F	T	Effy	T	Effy
1	**1**	0.67	0.91	**0.77**	0.55	0.55	**0.55**	18.88	**4.07**	13.75	**3.97**
	2	0.18	0.27	**0.21**	0.82	0.82	**0.82**	19.5	**1.1**	16	**5.11**
	3	0.83	0.91	**0.87**	0.5	0.45	**0.48**	18.65	**4.66**	25.73	**1.86**
	4	0.5	0.73	**0.59**	0.64	0.64	**0.64**	26.03	**2.28**	16.57	**3.84**
2	**5**	0.67	0.73	**0.7**	0.38	0.45	**0.42**	14	**4.97**	11.63	**3.58**
	6	0.75	0.82	**0.78**	0.47	0.73	**0.57**	18.08	**4.33**	17.58	**3.25**
	7	0.69	0.82	**0.75**	0.2	0.36	**0.26**	19.23	**3.9**	18.42	**1.40**
	8	0.62	0.73	**0.67**	0.36	0.36	**0.36**	26.12	**2.55**	14.38	**2.53**
3	**9**	0.62	0.73	**0.67**	0.4	0.56	**0.46**	22.92	**2.91**	17.5	**2.64**
	10	0.33	0.36	**0.35**	0.24	0.56	**0.33**	16.12	**2.16**	21.33	**1.56**
	11	0.87	0.64	**0.74**	0.62	0.73	**0.67**	15.77	**4.67**	21.93	**3.04**
	12	0.58	0.64	**0.61**	0.41	0.64	**0.5**	21.05	**2.89**	26.42	**1.89**
4	**13**	0.31	0.36	**0.33**	0.67	0.73	**0.7**	15.28	**2.18**	22.98	**3.03**
	14	0.29	0.45	**0.36**	0.8	0.73	**0.76**	21.32	**1.68**	25.32	**3.01**
	15	0.64	0.64	**0.64**	0.5	0.55	**0.52**	19.5	**3.26**	29.93	**1.74**
	16	0.56	0.82	**0.67**	0.33	0.18	**0.24**	29.83	**2.23**	32.58	**0.72**
Mean		0.57	0.66	0.61	0.49	0.56	0.52	20.14	3.12	20.75	2.7
Median		0.62	0.73	0.67	0.49	0.55	0.51	19.37	2.9	19.87	2.8
Std. deviation		0.2	0.2	0.19	0.18	0.17	0.17	4.33	1.19	6.042	1.14

The mean effectiveness with models is 17% higher than with the text of standards, and the median is 30% higher. This initial overall result suggests that the use of models improves the effectiveness of understanding safety compliance needs. According to the Shapiro-Wilk test, the sample for effectiveness with models is non-normal (p-value = 0.049 < 0.05), thus we selected the Wilcoxon test for $H_{1,0}$. The test result determines that the difference in the effectiveness when using models is not statistically significant (p-value = 0.096 > 0.05). Therefore, $H_{1,0}$ cannot be rejected and the results are not conclusive enough to confirm that the use of models improves the effectiveness of understanding safety compliance needs.

Despite the lack of statistical significance, we argue that most of the evidence from the results suggests that the use of models could improve the effectiveness of understanding compliance needs. In addition to the differences of the means and the medians, the effectiveness with models is higher for 12 out of the 16 subjects (75%). The highest effectiveness (0.87) is with models, as a result of the highest precision (0.83) and recall (0.91). The effectiveness is above 0.7 for six subjects with models and for only two with text. We conjecture that the lack of statistical significance is due to sample size. This could be addressed in follow-up experiments. We have not observed any potentially relevant correlation between subject's experience and effectiveness.

When comparing the results with those from the pilot experiment [6], we consider that the results are coherent. The initial average gain in effectiveness from using models in the pilot was a 2%, but it raised up to 15% when an issue with a question about applicability information was taken into account. This is close to the 17% average gain in the experiment.

4.2 Efficiency of Understanding (RQ2)

Table 1 shows the results regarding efficiency of understanding safety compliance needs with models and with text. The table includes the data of the time spent in the tasks (T; in minutes) and the efficiency outcome (Effy). The mean effectiveness with models is 15% higher and the median 3%. The results from the Shapiro-Wilk test for normality shows that both the sample for efficiency with models and the sample for efficiency with text of safety standards are normal (p-value > 0.05). Therefore, we selected the paired t-test for $H_{2,0}$. The test result determines that the difference in efficiency is not statistically significant (p-value = 0.173 > 0.05). Thus, $H_{2,0}$ cannot be rejected and the results are not conclusive enough to confirm that the use of models improves the efficiency of understanding safety compliance needs.

Although there is no statistical significance, some aspects of the results make us believe that the use of models could improve the efficiency of understanding of safety compliance needs. We have argued above that the results suggest that effectiveness could increase with models, and efficiency is directly based on effectiveness. The efficiency is above 4.0 for four subjects when using models, and only for one when using text. The lack of statistical significance might be an effect of sample size.

As counter evidence of the increase in efficiency when using models, the average time to execute the tasks is only a 3% higher with the text of safety standards. With such a little decrease in time when using models, it is not likely that efficiency improvement is significant unless effectiveness improvement also is. The mean gain in efficiency with models is also lower (15%) than the mean gain in effectiveness (17%). Finally, the efficiency is above 3.0 for seven subjects when using models and for eight when using the text.

In the pilot experiment [6] the efficiency of understanding compliance needs with models was quite lower than with the text (24%). This might have been a result of issues in the experimental design that the adjustments for this experiment have mitigated.

4.3 Perceived Benefits in the Use of Models (RQ3)

Figure 1 shows the results about the subject's perceived benefits in the use of models to understand safety compliance needs. The numbers in the bars indicate the data points of each possible answer for the corresponding statement.

The median of four statements is *Agree*, and at least three subjects strongly agreed on them. No subject disagreed that "*The models help in understanding the relationships between the concepts*", and the statements with the highest number of subjects that disagreed or strongly disagreed are "*The models help in understanding the concepts*" and "*The models are easy to understand*" (7 subjects; 44%). In addition to the latter statement, some subject strongly disagreed that "*The models are easier to understand than the text of the safety standards I have dealt with*". "*The models are easy to understand*" is also the only statement for which no subject strongly agreed.

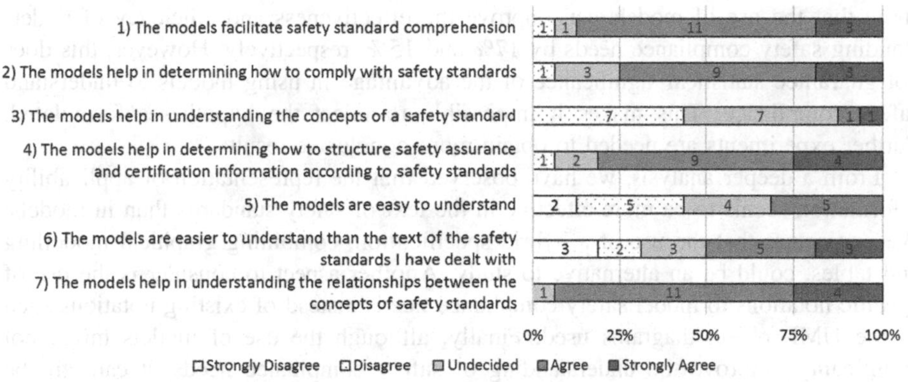

Fig. 1. Perceived benefits in the use of models to understand safety compliance needs

Despite the overall benefits found, the models do not seem to be regarded as easy to understand or easier to understand than the text. This could be due to the graphical notation used in the experiment. The experience with UML might also influence the perceived benefits. We plan to gain deeper insights into this aspect by running the experiment with students of courses on model-driven engineering.

In the pilot experiment [6], the widest agreement was on "*The models help in understanding the relationships between the concepts*" too, and the ratio of subjects that disagreed or strongly disagreed that "*The models are easy to understand*" was higher. The latter is also the only statement for which some practitioner disagreed in [7], and all the practitioners agreed or strongly agreed upon the former. Interestingly, the median in the study with practitioners, the pilot experiment, and the experiment for "*The models are easier to understand than the text of the safety standards I have dealt with*" is *Undecided* or *Undecided-Agree*. This supports the proposal of investigating notations that could be more suitable to represent compliance needs. Different graphical notations might help to increase the perception of the benefits.

Most of the practitioners that provided feedback on a model of IEC 61508 [14] regarded it as easy to understand. The model was presented as a class diagram, and these practitioners might have more experience with UML than our subjects. In experiments on security assessment (e.g. [11]), the number of positive aspects regarding perceived ease of use and perceived usefulness was higher for models than for text.

5 Conclusion

The textual descriptions of compliance needs in safety standards can be difficult to understand. The use of conceptual models has been proposed as a solution, but there is a lack of empirical evidence that confirms the benefits of this usage. This paper has presented an experiment with 16 subjects, separated into four different groups, that interpreted models and textual specifications of safety compliance needs. The results show that the use of models can improve the effectiveness and efficiency of understanding safety compliance needs by 17% and 15%, respectively. However, this does not guarantee statistical significance of the advantage in using models to understand safety compliance. This makes it impossible to reject the hypotheses formulated. Further experiments are needed to obtain more conclusive results.

From a deeper analysis, we have observed that the representation of applicability information seems to be more effective in the text of safety standards than in models. We conjecture that the use of a hybrid specification, combining graphical modelling and tables, could be an alternative to study. Another aspect to consider is the use of specific notations to model safety compliance needs instead of existing notations such as the UML object diagrams used. Finally, although the use of models might not significantly improve the understanding of safety compliance needs, it can still be beneficial for safety certification, e.g. for automated compliance management [14].

As main future work, we plan to conduct new experiments to evaluate different modelling approaches to specify safety compliance needs (e.g. BPMN and goal models). We expect that, as a consequence, we will be able to draw stronger conclusions and to guide the selection of adequate specification style alternatives according to the safety compliance needs to be represented.

Acknowledgments. The research leading to this paper has received funding from the AMASS project (H2020-ECSEL grant agreement no 692474; Spain's MINECO ref. PCIN-2015-262) and the AMoDDI project (Ref. 11130583). We also thank the subjects that participated in the experiment.

References

1. Abdulkhaleq, A, Wagner, S.: A controlled experiment for the empirical evaluation of safety analysis techniques for safety-critical software. In: EASE 2015, pp. 16:1–16:10 (2015)
2. Abrahão, S., et al.: Assessing the effectiveness of sequence diagrams in the comprehension of functional requirements. IEEE Trans. Softw. Eng. **39**(3), 327–342 (2013)

3. Ayora, C., et al.: Variability management in process families through change patterns. Inform. Softw. Tech. **74**, 86–104 (2016)
4. Briand, L., et al.: Traceability and SysML design slices to support safety inspections: a controlled experiment. ACM Trans. Softw. Eng. Meth. **23**(1), 9:1–9:43 (2014)
5. de la Vara, J.L., et al.: An industrial survey on safety evidence change impact analysis practice. IEEE Trans. Softw. Eng. **42**(12), 1095–1117 (2016)
6. de la Vara, J.L., et al.: Do models improve the understanding of safety compliance needs? Insights from a pilot experiment. In: ESEM, pp. 32:1–32:6 (2016)
7. de la Vara, J.L., et al.: Model-based specification of safety compliance needs for critical systems: a holistic generic metamodel. Inform. Softw. Tech. **72**, 16–30 (2016)
8. de la Vara, J.L., et al.: An analysis of safety evidence management with the structured assurance case metamodel. Comput. Stand. Interfaces **50**, 179–198 (2017)
9. De Lucia, A., et al.: An experimental comparison of ER and UML class diagrams for data modelling. Empir. Softw. Eng. **15**(5), 455–492 (2010)
10. ESA. Software engineering and standardisation (2006). http://www.esa.int/TEC/Software_engineering_and_standardisation/TECBUCUXBQE_0.html
11. Labunets, K., et al.: An experimental comparison of two risk-based security methods. In: ESEM, pp 163–172 (2013)
12. Nair, S., et al.: An extended systematic literature review on provision of evidence for safety certification. Inform. Softw. Tech. **56**(7), 689–717 (2014)
13. Nair, S., et al.: Evidence management for compliance of critical systems with safety standards: a survey on the state of practice. Inform. Softw. Tech. **60**, 1–15 (2015)
14. Panesar-Walawege, R.K., et al.: Supporting the verification of compliance to safety standards via model-driven engineering. Inform. Softw. Tech. **55**(5), 836–864 (2013)
15. Razali, R., et al.: Experimental comparison of the comprehensibility of a UML-based formal specification versus a textual one. In: EASE (2007)
16. Salman, I., et al.: Are students representatives of professionals in software engineering experiments? In: ICSE (2015)
17. Sharafi, Z., et al.: An empirical study on the efficiency of graphical vs. textual representations in requirements comprehension. In: ICPC (2013)
18. Vegas, S., et al.: Crossover designs in software engineering experiments: benefits and perils. IEEE Trans. Softw. Eng. **42**(2), 120–135 (2016)
19. Wohlin, C., et al.: Experimentation in Software Engineering, 2nd edn. Springer, Heidelberg (2012)

Foundations

Cardinality Constraints with Probabilistic Intervals

Tania Katell Roblot and Sebastian Link(✉)

Department of Computer Science, University of Auckland, Auckland, New Zealand
{t.roblot,s.link}@auckland.ac.nz

Abstract. Probabilistic databases accommodate well the requirements of modern applications that produce large volumes of uncertain data from a variety of sources. We propose an expressive class of probabilistic cardinality constraints which empowers users to specify lower and upper bounds on the marginal probabilities by which cardinality constraints should hold in a data set of acceptable quality. The bounds help organizations balance the consistency and completeness targets for their data quality, and provide probabilities on the number of query answers without querying the data. Algorithms are established for an agile schema-driven acquisition of the right lower and upper bounds in a given application domain, and for reasoning about the constraints.

Keywords: Cardinality constraint · Data and knowledge intelligence · Decision support · Probability · Requirements engineering · Summaries

1 Introduction

Background. Cardinality constraints help us understand the semantics of data. They enforce bounds on the number of data patterns that occur in application domains. Cardinality constraints were introduced in Chen's seminal ER paper [3], and have attracted interest and tool support ever since. A cardinality constraint $card(X) \leq b$ stipulates for an attribute set X and a positive integer b that a relation must not contain more than b different tuples with matching values on all the attributes in X. For example, a social worker may not handle more than five cases at a time. This expressiveness makes cardinality constraints invaluable in applications such as data integration, modeling, and processing.

Motivation. Relational databases target applications with certain data, such as accounting and payroll. Modern applications, such as data integration and information extraction, produce large volumes of uncertain data. For example, RFID (radio frequency identification) can track endangered species of animals, such as the Alpine Shrew in Slovenia. Here it is sensible to apply probabilistic databases. Figure 1 shows two probabilistic relations (p-relation), which are probability distributions over a finite set of possible worlds, each being a relation.

A goal in requirements acquisition is (i) to specify all constraints that apply to the application domain, and (ii) not to specify any others. This enables us

H.C. Mayr et al. (Eds.): ER 2017, LNCS 10650, pp. 251–265, 2017.
https://doi.org/10.1007/978-3-319-69904-2_21

r1:

w1 (p1=0.75)

rfid	time	zone
as2	6	z1
as2	7	z1
as3	15	z7
as3	16	z8
as3	17	z9
as10	10	z11
as11	10	z12
as12	10	z13
as4	11	z3
as5	12	z3
as6	13	z3
as7	14	z3

w2 (p2=0.15)

rfid	time	zone
as1	8	z4
as1	8	z5
as1	8	z6
as2	5	z1
as2	6	z1
as2	7	z1
as4	11	z3
as5	12	z3
as6	13	z3
as7	14	z3
as8	9	z2
as9	9	z2

w3 (p3=0.1)

rfid	time	zone
as1	8	z4
as1	8	z5
as1	8	z6
as2	5	z1
as2	6	z1
as2	7	z1
as4	11	z3
as5	12	z3
as6	13	z3
as7	14	z3
as8	9	z2
as9	9	z2
as0	9	z2

r2:

w1 (p1=0.8)

rfid	time	zone
as10	10	z11

w2 (p2=0.15)

rfid	time	zone
as2	5	z1
as2	6	z1
as2	7	z1
as8	9	z2
as9	9	z2

w3 (p3=0.05)

rfid	time	zone
as2	5	z1
as2	6	z1
as2	7	z1
as8	9	z2
as9	9	z2
as0	9	z2
as1	8	z4
as1	8	z5

Fig. 1. Probabilistic relations r_1 and r_2 over TRACKING={rfid, time, zone}

to (i) restrict instances to those which are meaningful for the domain, and (ii) permit all meaningful instances. Cardinality constraints therefore address the consistency and completeness dimensions of data quality. Here, consistency in relations requires us to specify all meaningful constraints, while we can only access the complete set of meaningful relations if we do not specify any meaningless constraints. As depicted in Fig. 2, we aim at consistency and completeness.

In probabilistic databases, one may speak of a cardinality constraint when it holds in all possible worlds. Hence, a cardinality constraint holds with marginal probability one, which means that the probabilities of the worlds in which the constraint holds add up to one. However, due to the veracity inherent to probabilistic databases, and the variety of sources the data originates from, one must not expect to satisfy the completeness criteria with this definition. Such definition does also not make sensible use of probabilities, contrary to what would be expected of probabilistic databases. In our running example, the cardinality constraint *card(time)* ≤ 3 has marginal probability 1 in both r_1 and r_2, *card(time, zone)* ≤ 2 has marginal probability 0.9 in r_1 and 0.95 in r_2, and *card(time, zone)* ≤ 1 has marginal probability 0.75 in r_1 and 0.8 in r_2.

We propose the new class of *cardinality constraints with probabilistic intervals*, or p-CCs for short, which stipulate lower and upper bounds on the marginal probability by which a cardinality constraint holds in a probabilistic database.

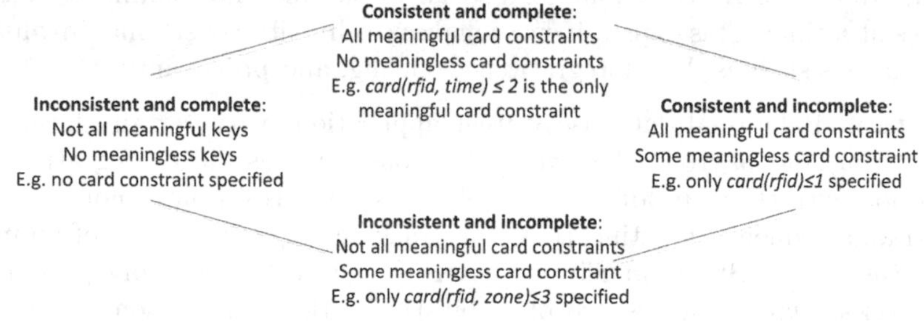

Fig. 2. Consistency and completeness dimensions as controlled by cardinality constraints

For example, we may specify the p-CCs *card(time, zone)* $\leq 2 \in [0.9, 0.95]$ and *card(time, zone)* $\leq 1 \in [0.75, 0.8]$. *Data quality:* Our main use-case for p-CCs is their ability to balance the consistency and completeness targets for the quality of probabilistic data. In fact, consistency means that for each CC the specified lower (upper) bound is not too high (low), and completeness means that for each CC the specified lower (upper) bound is not too low (high). Once consolidated, p-CCs can control these data quality dimensions during updates. When new data arrives, p-CCs can help detect anomalous patterns of data in the form of p-CC violations. *Query estimation:* In a different showcase, p-CCs can be used to infer probabilities on the maximum number of query answers without querying any portion of the potentially big data source. The query `SELECT` *rfid* `FROM` TRACKING `WHERE` *zone*='z2' `AND` *time*='9'; asks for the *rfid* of Alpine Shrews recorded in zone 'z2' at '9'am. Reasoning about our p-CCs tells us that at most 3 answers will be returned with probability 1, at most 2 answers with a probability in [0.9,0.95], and at most 1 answer with a probability in [0.75,0.8]. A service provider may return approximate costs to a customer, who can decide whether to pay for the service. The provider does not utilize unpaid resources for querying the potentially big data source to return the feedback.

Contributions. Our contributions are as follows. *Modeling:* We propose p-CCs *card*$(X) \leq b \in [l, u]$ as a natural class of integrity constraints over uncertain data. Their main use is to help organizations balance consistency and completeness targets for the quality of their data. P-CCs can distinguish meaningful from meaningless patterns in large volumes of uncertain data from a variety of sources, and estimate the probability bandwidths for numbers of query answers. *Reasoning:* While sets of p-CCs can be unsatisfiable, we establish an efficient algorithm to decide satisfiability. We characterize the implication problem of satisfiable sets of p-CCs by a simple finite set of Horn rules, and a linear time algorithm. This enables organizations to reduce the overhead of data quality management by p-CCs to a minimal level necessary. *Acquisition:* For the schema-driven acquisition of the right probabilistic intervals, we show how to summarize concisely any given satisfiable set of p-CCs as an Armstrong PC-base sketch. Such a sketch is a perfect semantic summary of all p-CCs currently perceived meaningful by analysts. The base consists of two PC-sketches: one that satisfies every cardinality constraint with the exact marginal probability that is the perceived best lower bound for the domain, and one that is the perceived best upper bound. Any flaws with these perceptions are explicitly pointed out in the sketches, either as unreasonably high lower bounds or unreasonably low upper bounds. For example, Table 1 shows an Armstrong PC-base sketch for the set of p-CCs that are satisfied by both p-relations r_1 and r_2 in Fig. 1. For each sketch, Γ shows which patterns of data must occur in how many rows (represented in column *card*) in which possible worlds (represented by the world identifiers in column ι). The symbol $*$ represents some value that is unique in each world derived from the sketch. Π defines the probability distribution over the possible worlds. The first (second) PC-sketch represents the p-relation r_1 (r_2, respectively) from Fig. 1. While all implied p-CCs are satisfied

Table 1. Two PC-sketches that form an Armstrong PC-base for the set of p-CCs that hold on both p-relations r_1 and r_2 in Fig. 1

Γ					Π	
card	*rfid*	*time*	*zone*	ι	ι	$\Pi(\iota)$
3	as1	8	*	2,3	1	.75
2	as2	*	z1	1,2,3	2	.15
1	as2	*	z1	2,3	3	.1
2	*	9	z2	2,3		
1	*	9	z2	3		
3	as3	*	*	1		
3	*	10	*	1		
4	*	*	z3	1,2,3		

Γ					Π	
card	*rfid*	*time*	*zone*	ι	ι	$\Pi(\iota)$
1	*	*	*	1	1	0.80
3	as2	*	z1	2, 3	2	0.15
2	*	9	z2	2, 3	3	0.05
1	*	9	z2	3		
2	as1	8	*	3		

by both p-relations, every non-implied p-CC is violated in at least one p-relation. For example, the implied p-CC $card(time,zone) \leq 2 \in [0.92, 0.93]$ is satisfied by both p-relations, while the non-implied p-CC $card(time,zone) \leq 1 \in [0.75, 0.79]$ is violated by r_2. It is important to point out the challenges we have overcome. While sets of p-CCs do not enjoy single Armstrong databases, our new concept of an Armstrong base makes it possible to apply this toolkit to the requirements acquisition of p-CCs. Moreover, most sets of p-CCs require Armstrong sketches to represent infinite p-relations, as these are necessary whenever there is some attribute A for which no p-CC $card(A) \leq b \in [1, 1]$ is implied by the given p-CC set. The frequent challenge of finitely representing infinite p-relations is overcome by using the symbol ∞ to represent an infinite number of rows of a data pattern. This points out the potential incompleteness of the acquired requirements.

Organization. We discuss related work in Sect. 2. P-CCs are introduced in Sect. 3. Computational problems are characterized in Sect. 4. The acquisition framework is established in Sect. 5. We conclude and mention future work in Sect. 6. All proofs are available in Roblot's PhD thesis [13].

2 Related Work

Cardinality constraints are an influential contribution of data modeling. They were already present in Chen's seminal paper [3], and are now part of all major languages for data modeling, including UML, EER, ORM, XSD, and OWL. Cardinality constraints have been extensively studied [5,7,8,10–12,18]. Our work subsumes relations as p-relations that consist of one possible world only.

Poor data quality is arguably the biggest inhibitor to deriving value from big data [16]. P-CCs provide a well-founded, yet manageable approach to balance consistency and completeness targets. The concept of p-CCs is new but naturally derived from previous research.

In work on possibilistic CCs [6] tuples are attributed some degree of possibility and CCs some degree of certainty saying to which tuples they apply.

Possibility theory can be a qualitative approach, while probability theory is a quantitative approach to uncertainty. Our research therefore complements the qualitative approach to CCs in [6].

P-CCs extend previous work on keys and CCs, in which only lower bounds were considered in [2,14]. Our extension causes significant differences. First, p-CCs are more expressive as upper bounds smaller than 1 can be specified by them. Consequently, consistency and completeness targets can be addressed better. Second, sets of p-CCs with intervals may not be satisfiable by any p-relation. In contrast, every set of CCs with only lower bounds is satisfiable. Third, while implication and inference problems become more complex for intervals, we succeed in establishing linear time algorithms. Fourth, while keys and CCs with only lower bounds enjoy representations by a single Armstrong PC-sketch, p-CCs require two PC-sketches. This is also an interesting novelty for Armstrong databases: So far, research on constraint elicitation [4,9] has only considered representations by a single Armstrong instance, but constraint sets for which two or fewer instances form an Armstrong base have not been considered. Our work also extends previous work on keys with probabilistic intervals [1]. CCs are more expressive than keys, the sources of inconsistencies become larger, the implication and inference problems become more challenging, and the construction of Armstrong instances become more sophisticated.

3 Cardinality Constraints with Probabilistic Intervals

We fix concepts from probabilistic databases and introduce the central notion of p-CCs. We use the symbol $\mathbb{N}_1^\infty$ to denote the positive integers together with the symbol ∞ for infinity, to which the order $<$ extends.

A *relation schema* is a finite set R of attributes A. Each attribute A is associated with a domain *dom*(A) of values. A tuple t over R is a function that assigns to each attribute A of R an element $t(A)$ from the domain *dom*(A). A *relation* over R is a finite set of tuples over R. Relations over R are also called *possible worlds* of R here. An expression *card*$(X) \leq b$ with some non-empty subset $X \subseteq R$ and $b \in \mathbb{N}_1^\infty$ is called a *cardinality constraint over* R. In what follows, we will always assume that a subset of R is non-empty without mentioning it explicitly. A cardinality constraint *card*$(X) \leq b$ over R is said to *hold* in a possible world w of R, denoted by $w \models$ *card*$(X) \leq b$, if and only if there are not $b+1$ different tuples $t_1, \cdots, t_{b+1} \in W$ such that for all $1 \leq i < j \leq b+1$, $t_i \neq t_j$ and $t_i(X) = t_j(X)$. A *probabilistic relation* (p-relation) over R is a pair $r = (\mathcal{W}, P)$ of a finite non-empty set $\mathcal{W}$ of possible worlds over R and a probability distribution $P : \mathcal{W} \rightarrow (0, 1]$ such that $\sum_{W \in \mathcal{W}} P(W) = 1$ holds. Figure 1 shows two p-relations over relation schema TRACKING={*rfid,time,zone*}. World W_2 of r_1, for example, satisfies the cardinality constraints *card*(*rfid*) ≤ 3, *card*(*time*) ≤ 3, *card*(*zone*) ≤ 4, *card*(*rfid, time*) ≤ 3, *card*(*rfid, zone*) ≤ 3, and *card*(*time, zone*) ≤ 2 but violates the CC *card*(*time, zone*) ≤ 1. The *marginal probability* $m_{X,b,r}$ of a cardinality constraint *card*$(X) \leq b$ in the p-relation r is the sum of the probabilities of those possible worlds in r which satisfy *card*$(X) \leq b$. We will now introduce the central notion of a key with probabilistic intervals.

Definition 1. *A* cardinality constraint with probabilistic intervals, *or* p-CC, *over relation schema R is an expression card(X) $\leq b \in [l, u]$ where $\emptyset \neq X \subseteq R$, $b \in \mathbb{N}_1^\infty$, $l, u \in [0, 1]$, and $l \leq u$. The p-CC card(X) $\leq b \in [l, u]$ over R is* satisfied by, *or said to* hold in, *the p-relation r over R if and only if $l \leq m_{X,b,r} \leq u$.*

In our running example, the p-relations r_1 and r_2 from Fig. 1 both satisfy the p-CCs *card(rfid, time)* $\leq 1 \in [0.75, 0.95]$, *card(rfid, zone)* $\leq 2 \in [0.75, 0.8]$, *card(time, zone)* $\leq 2 \in [0.9, 0.95]$ and *card(time, zone)* $\leq 1 \in [0.75, 0.8]$, but r_1 violates the p-CC *card(time, zone)* $\leq 2 \in [0.95, 0.95]$ and r_2 violates the p-CC *card(time, zone)* $\leq 2 \in [0.9, 1]$. The reasons for the violations are that $m_{\{rfid,time\},2,r_1} = 0.9$ and $m_{\{rfid,time\},2,r_2} = 0.95$, respectively.

It is useful to look at lower and upper bounds separately. A CC with lower bound, or *l-CC*, is of the form *card(X)* $\leq b \in [l, 1]$ and we write (*card(X)* $\leq b, \geq l$). Similarly, a CC with upper bound, or *u-CC*, is of the form *card(X)* $\leq b \in [0, u]$ and we write (*card(X)* $\leq b, \leq u$). For example, the p-CC *card(time, zone)* $\leq 2 \in [0.9, 0.95]$ can be rewritten as the l-CC (*card(time, zone)* $\leq 2, \geq 0.9$) and the u-CC (*card(time, zone)* $\leq 2, \leq 0.95$). Hence, a p-relation satisfies a p-CC iff it satisfies the corresponding l-CC and u-CC. L-CCs have been studied in [14]. In the following, we will first study u-CCs, and then combine u-CCs with l-CCs.

4 Reasoning Tools

When using p-CCs to manage consistency and completeness targets for data quality, their overhead should be minimized. This requires us to reason about p-CCs efficiently. We will establish fundamental tools to identify efficiently (i) if a given set of p-CCs is satisfiable, and (ii) the largest lower and smallest upper bounds on the probability by which a given CC is implied by a given set of p-CCs. This helps optimize the efficiency of updates and query answers. The results are required for our acquisition framework later.

Computational Problems. Let $\Sigma \cup \{\varphi\}$ denote a set of constraints over relation schema R. We say that Σ is *satisfiable*, if there is some p-relation over R that satisfies all elements of Σ. We say Σ *implies* φ, denoted by $\Sigma \models \varphi$, if every p-relation r over R that satisfies Σ, also satisfies φ. We use $\Sigma^* = \{\varphi : \Sigma \models \varphi\}$ to denote the *semantic closure* of Σ. Let $\mathcal{C}$ denote a class of constraints. The *$\mathcal{C}$-satisfiability problem* is to decide for a given relation schema R and a given set Σ of constraints in $\mathcal{C}$ over R, whether Σ is satisfiable. The *$\mathcal{C}$-implication problem* is to decide for a given relation schema R and a given satisfiable set $\Sigma \cup \{\varphi\}$ of constraints in $\mathcal{C}$ over R, whether Σ implies φ. If $\mathcal{C}$ denotes the class of p-CCs, then the *$\mathcal{C}$-inference problem* is to compute for a given relation schema R, a given satisfiable set Σ of constraints in $\mathcal{C}$, and a given cardinality constraint *card(X)* $\leq b$ over R the largest probability l and the smallest probability u such that Σ implies *card(X)* $\leq b \in [l, u]$. We will characterize the computational problems for the class of u-CCs first. Subsequently, we then combine these results with those from [14] for the class of l-CCs to characterize the class of p-CCs.

4.1 Cardinality Constraints with Upper Bounds

Satisfiability Problem. While every set of l-CCs is satisfiable, this is not the case for every set of u-CCs. However, satisfiable sets are easy to characterize.

Theorem 1. *A set Σ of u-CCs over relation schema R is satisfiable iff Σ does not contain a u-CC of the form $(card(R) \leq b, \leq u)$ where $u < 1$ and Σ does not contain a u-CC of the form $(card(X) \leq \infty, \leq u)$ where $u < 1$. The satisfiability problem for u-CCs can thus be decided with one scan over the input.* □

Axioms. We determine the semantic closure by applying *inference rules*. For a set $\mathfrak{R}$ of inference rules let $\Sigma \vdash_{\mathfrak{R}} \varphi$ denote the *inference* of φ from Σ by $\mathfrak{R}$. That is, there is some sequence $\sigma_1, \ldots, \sigma_n$ such that $\sigma_n = \varphi$ and every σ_i is an element of Σ or is the conclusion that results from an application of an inference rule in $\mathfrak{R}$ to some premises in $\{\sigma_1, \ldots, \sigma_{i-1}\}$. Let $\Sigma^+_{\mathfrak{R}} = \{\varphi : \Sigma \vdash_{\mathfrak{R}} \varphi\}$ be the *syntactic closure* of Σ under inferences by $\mathfrak{R}$. $\mathfrak{R}$ is *sound* (*complete*) if for every satisfiable set Σ over every R we have $\Sigma^+_{\mathfrak{R}} \subseteq \Sigma^*$ ($\Sigma^* \subseteq \Sigma^+_{\mathfrak{R}}$). The (finite) set $\mathfrak{R}$ is a (finite) *axiomatization* if $\mathfrak{R}$ is both sound and complete. The following set $\mathfrak{U}$ of inference rules

$$\frac{}{(card(R) \leq \infty, \leq 1)} \quad \text{(Maximum, } \mathcal{M}\text{)} \qquad \frac{(card(XY) \leq b + b', \leq u)}{(card(X) \leq b, \leq u + u')} \quad \text{(Relax, } \mathcal{R}\text{)}$$

forms a finite axiomatization for the implication of u-CCs. Here, R denotes the underlying relation schema, $X \neq \emptyset$ and Y form attribute subsets of R, $b + b' \in \mathbb{N}_1^\infty$, $b \in \mathbb{N}_1$, and u, u' as well as $u + u'$ are probabilities.

Theorem 2. *$\mathfrak{U}$ forms a finite axiomatization for u-CCs.* □

For example, $\Sigma = \{(card(rfid, time) \leq 2, \leq 0.95)\}$ implies the u-CC $\varphi = (card(rfid) \leq 1, \leq 0.97)$, but not the u-CC $\varphi' = (card(rfid) \leq 3, \leq 0.97)$. Indeed, φ can be inferred from Σ by applying $\mathcal{R}$ to $(card(rfid, time) \leq 2, \leq 0.95)$. By definition, it is redundant to verify that a given p-relation satisfies an implied p-CC. In particular, the larger the given p-relation, the more time we save by avoiding redundant validation checks.

Algorithms. Computing Σ^* and checking whether $\varphi \in \Sigma^*$ is not feasible. We will now establish a linear-time algorithm for computing the smallest probability u, such that $(card(X) \leq b, \leq u)$ is implied by Σ. The following theorem allows us to decide the implication problem for u-CCs to a single scan of the input.

Theorem 3. *Let $\Sigma \cup \{(card(X) \leq b, \leq u)\}$ denote a satisfiable set of u-CCs over R. Then Σ implies $(card(X) \leq b, \leq u)$ iff (i) $u = 1$ or (ii) there is some $(card(X') \leq b', \leq u') \in \Sigma$ such that $X \subseteq X'$, $b \leq b'$ and $u' \leq u$ hold.* □

Algorithm 1. Inference

Require: $R, \Sigma, card(X) \leq b$ with satisfiable set Σ of u-CCs
Ensure: $\min\{u : \Sigma \models (card(X) \leq b, \leq u)\}$
$u \leftarrow 1$;
for all $(card(X') \leq b', \leq u') \in \Sigma$ **do**
  if $X \subseteq X'$ **and** $b \leq b'$ **and** $u' < u$ **then**
    $u \leftarrow u'$;
return u;

Theorem 3 enables us to design Algorithm 1, which returns for a given satisfiable set Σ of u-CCs, and a given cardinality constraint $card(X) \leq b$ over R the smallest probability u such that $(card(X) \leq b, \leq u)$ is implied by Σ. Starting with $u = 1$, the algorithm scans all input keys $(card(X') \leq b', \leq u')$ and resets u to u' whenever u' is smaller than the current u, X is contained in X' and b is at most b'. We use $|\Sigma|$ and $|R|$ to denote the total number of attributes that occur in Σ and R, respectively.

Theorem 4. *On input $(R, \Sigma, card(X) \leq b)$, Algorithm 1 returns in $\mathcal{O}(|\Sigma|+|R|)$ time the minimum u with which $(card(X) \leq b, \leq u)$ is implied by Σ.* □

Given $R, \Sigma, (card(X) \leq b, \leq u)$ as an input to the implication problem for u-CCs we can use Algorithm 1 to compute $u_{X,b} := \min\{u' : \Sigma \models (card(X) \leq b, \leq u')\}$ and return an affirmative answer if and only if $u_{X,b} \leq u$.

Theorem 5. *The implication problem of u-CCs is decidable in linear time.* □

Given $\Sigma = \{(card(rfid, time) \leq 2, \leq 0.95)\}$ and $card(rfid) \leq 3$, Algorithm 1 returns $u_{rfid,3} = 1$. In particular, if $\varphi' = (card(rfid) \leq 3, \leq 0.97)$ as before, we conclude that Σ does not imply φ' as $1 \not\leq 0.97$.

4.2 Cardinality Constraints with Probabilistic Intervals

Every p-CC set Σ is the union of the l-CC set $\Sigma_l := \{(card(X) \leq b, \geq l) \mid (card(X) \leq b \in [l, u]) \in \Sigma\}$ and the u-CC set $\Sigma_u := \{(card(X) \leq b, \leq u) \mid (card(X) \leq b \in [l, u]) \in \Sigma\}$. While every l-CC set is satisfiable [14], and satisfiability for u-CCs requires one scan over the input, the satisfiability problem for p-CCs requires two scans. For example, the p-CC set $\Sigma = \{(card(rfid, zone) \leq 2 \in [0.75, 0.8], card(rfid) \leq 1 \in [0.85, 0.9]\}$ is not satisfiable.

Theorem 6. *A set Σ of p-CCs over relation schema R is satisfiable iff $\Sigma_l \cup \Sigma_u \cup \{(card(R) \leq 1, \geq 1)\} \cup \{(card(X) \leq \infty, \geq 1) \mid (card(X) \leq \infty, \leq q) \in \Sigma_u\}$ does not contain $(card(X) \leq b, \geq p)$, $(card(X') \leq b, \leq q)$ such that $X \subseteq X'$, $b \leq b'$ and $q < p$.* □

No Interaction. We can show that every satisfiable set of p-CCs does not exhibit any interaction between its l-CCs and u-CCs. We say that *there is no interaction between* u-CCs and l-CCs if for every relation schema R, every satisfiable set Σ of p-CCs, every l-CC $(card(X) \leq b, \geq p)$ and every u-CC $(card(X) \leq b, \leq q)$ over R, the following hold:

- $\Sigma_u \cup \Sigma_l \models (card(X) \leq b, \geq p)$ if and only if $\Sigma_l \models (card(X) \leq b, \geq p)$,
- $\Sigma_u \cup \Sigma_l \models (card(X) \leq b, \leq q)$ if and only if $\Sigma_u \models (card(X) \leq b, \leq q)$.

Hence, there is no interaction between u-CCs and l-CCs iff it is true that the p-CC $card(X) \leq b \in [p, q]$ is implied by a satisfiable set Σ of p-CCs iff (i) $(card(X) \leq b, \geq p)$ is implied by Σ_l, and (ii) $(card(X) \leq b, \leq q)$ is implied by Σ_u.

Theorem 7. *There is no interaction between u-CCs and l-CCs.* □

Firstly, we can simply combine our axiomatizations for u-CCs and l-CCs into one for p-CCs.

Theorem 8. *The union of $\mathfrak{U}$ from Theorem 2 and $\mathfrak{P}$ from [14] forms a finite axiomatization for p-CCs.* □

Secondly, we can combine our inference algorithms for u-CCs and l-CCs to obtain an efficient inference algorithm for p-CCs.

Theorem 9. *Given a satisfiable set Σ of p-CCs, and some $card(X) \leq b$ over R, we can return in $\mathcal{O}(|\Sigma| + |R|)$ time the maximum l and the minimum u such that $card(X) \leq b \in [l, u]$ is implied by Σ.* □

Thirdly, the implication problem of p-CCs can be decided efficiently.

Theorem 10. *The implication problem of p-CCs is decidable in linear time.* □

Example 1. Consider the set of p-CCs that hold on both p-relations in Fig. 1. A cover Σ for this set is: $card(rfid) \leq 3 \in [1, 1]$, $card(time) \leq 3 \in [1, 1]$, $card(zone) \leq 4 \in [1, 1]$, $card(rfid, time) \leq 1 \in [0.75, 0.95]$, $card(rfid, zone) \leq 2 \in [0.75, 0.8]$, $card(time, zone) \leq 2 \in [0.9, 0.95]$, and $card(time, zone) \leq 1 \in [0.75, 0.8]$. To decide if $card(time, zone) \leq 2 \in (0.91, 0.94)$ is implied by Σ we check if $(card(time, zone) \leq 2, \geq 0.91)$ is implied by Σ_l and if $(card(time, zone) \leq 2, \leq 0.94)$ is implied by Σ_u. While the first condition is true, the second condition fails. Consequently, the p-CC is not implied by Σ.

5 Acquiring Probabilistic Intervals

A main inhibitor to the uptake of probabilistic cardinality constraints is the difficulty to determine the probabilistic interval that applies to the underlying application domain. For that task, analysts should communicate with domain experts. However, the challenge is to overcome the following disconnect: Analysts know database concepts but not the domain, while domain experts know the domain but not database concepts. To connect analysts and domain experts, we establish a computational tool that helps them to jointly consolidate requirements. Analysts will use our algorithm to compute for any given satisfiable set of p-CCs that they perceive meaningful, two user-friendly summaries that perfectly represent the set. The summaries represent simultaneously for all cardinality constraints their lowest and highest marginal probabilities, respectively, that quality data sets in the target domain should exhibit. The two data summaries are then inspected jointly with the domain experts to identify and rectify any flaws with the perception of the meaningful constraints. The constraints are revised until analysts and domain experts are satisfied.

5.1 Summarizing Abstract Sets of P-CCs as Armstrong PC-bases

Our results will show that every satisfiable set Σ of p-CCs can be summarized as a pair of PC-sketches such that all given p-CCs are satisfied by the two p-relations the PC-sketches represent, and all those p-CCs not implied by Σ are violated by at least one of the p-relations. The notion of a PC-sketch generalizes the concept of an *Armstrong database*, which is a *single* database instance that satisfies a constraint if and only if it is implied by the given constraint set [4]. The reason why p-CCs require two instances is simple: Each instance can only represent one marginal probability, but p-CCs generally require a lower and an upper bound on the marginal probability. So, unless every given p-CC has the same lower and upper bounds, we require two p-relations.

Definition 2. *Let Σ be a satisfiable set of p-CCs over R. A pair of p-relations r_1, r_2 forms an Armstrong p-base for Σ if for all p-CCs φ over R it holds that r_1 and r_2 satisfy φ if and only if Σ implies φ.*

For example, the p-relations r_1, r_2 from Fig. 1 form an Armstrong p-base for the set Σ of p-CCs from Example 1. It is worth emphasizing the effectiveness of the definition: Knowing that r_1, r_2 form an Armstrong p-base for a given Σ enables us to reduce *every* instance $\Sigma \cup \{\varphi\}$ of the implication problem to simply checking if both r_1 and r_2 satisfy φ. Knowing that u-CCs and l-CCs do not interact, we can compute r_1, r_2 such that *every* instance $\Sigma \cup \{card(X) \leq b\}$ of the inference problem is reduced to simply computing the lower (upper) bound l (u) in $card(X) \leq b \in [l, u]$ as the marginal probability m_{X,b,r_1} (m_{X,b,r_2}) of $card(X) \leq b$ in r_1 (r_2). For example, $card(time, zone) \leq 2 \in [0.91, 0.94]$ is not implied by Σ from Example 1 as the given upper bound 0.94 is smaller than the marginal probability 0.95 of $card(time, zone) \leq 2$ in r_2.

Computational Strategy. For a given satisfiable set Σ of p-CCs over R we want to compute two p-relations r_1, r_2 that form an Armstrong p-base for Σ. Our strategy is to compute r_1 (r_2) such that for all $card(X) \leq b$ over R, the marginal probability m_{X,b,r_1} (m_{X,b,r_2}) equals the largest (smallest) probability $p_{X,b}$ such $(card(X) \leq b, \geq p_{X,b})$ $(card(X) \leq b, \leq p_{X,b})$ is implied by Σ_l (Σ_u). Let us recall the computation of $r_1 = (\mathcal{W}_1, P_1)$ first [14].

Lower Bounds. Let $p_1 < \cdots < p_n$ denote the different probabilities that occur in Σ_l. Furthermore, let $p_0 \leftarrow 0$, and if $p_n < 1$, then we set $n \mapsto n+1$ and define $p_n \leftarrow 1$. Then $\mathcal{W}_1 = \{w_1, \ldots, w_n\}$ where the possible world w_i is an Armstrong relation for the set $\Sigma^l_{p_i} = \{card(X) \leq b \mid (card(X) \leq b, \geq p) \in \Sigma_l \cup \{(card(R) \leq 1, \geq 1)\}$ such that $p \geq p_i\}$ and $P_1(w_i) = p_i - p_{i-1}$ for $i = 1, \ldots, n$. This construction yields a p-relation r_1 that is Armstrong for Σ_l [14]. That is, for an arbitrary l-CC φ it holds that Σ_l implies φ if and only if r_1 satisfies φ. The marginal probability of an arbitrary $card(X) \leq b$ in r_1 is therefore the largest probability $p_{X,b}$ such that $(card(X) \leq b, \geq p_{X,b})$ is implied by Σ_l. For example, the p-relation r_1 from Fig. 1 is Armstrong for the set Σ_l induced by the set Σ of p-CCs from Example 1. To make the presentation self-contained, we briefly recall how to compute the possible worlds as Armstrong relations for the sets of cardinality constraints (CCs). An Armstrong relation w for a given set Σ of CCs over relation schema R violates all CCs $card(X) \leq b$ over R which are not implied by Σ. However, $\Sigma \models card(X) \leq b$ if and only if $X = R$ or $b = \infty$ or there is some $card(Z) \leq b' \in \Sigma$ where $Z \subseteq X$ and $b' \leq b$. Hence, if $\Sigma \not\models card(X) \leq b$, then $X \neq R$, $b < \infty$ and for all $card(Z) \leq b' \in \Sigma$ where $Z \subseteq X$ we have $b' > b$. Our strategy is thus to find for all subsets X, the smallest upper bound b_X that applies to the set X. In other words, $b_X = \inf\{b \mid \Sigma \models card(X) \leq b\}$. Moreover, if $b_{XY} = b_X$ for some attribute sets X, Y, then it suffices to violate $card(XY) \leq b_{XY} - 1$. For this reason, the set $dup_\Sigma(R)$ of *duplicate sets* is defined as $dup_\Sigma(R) = \{\emptyset \subset X \subset R \mid b_X > 1 \wedge (\forall A \in R - X(b_{XA} < b_X))\}$. For each duplicate set $X \in dup_\Sigma(R)$, we introduce b_X new tuples $t^X_1, \ldots, t^X_{b_X}$ that all have matching values on X and all have unique values on all the attributes in $R - X$. An Armstrong relation for Σ is obtained by taking the disjoint union of $\{t^X_1, \ldots, t^X_{b_X}\}$ for all duplicate sets X. For example, each possible world of the p-relation r_1 is an Armstrong relation for the corresponding set $\Sigma^l_{p_i}$ induced by the given p-CC set Σ from Example 1. For instance, consider the sets $\Sigma^l_{0.75}$, $\Sigma^l_{0.9}$ and Σ^l_1, together with their duplicate sets and associated cardinalities. Following the construction above, we obtain the worlds $w1$, $w2$ and $w3$ of the p-relation r_1 in Fig. 1. Each of these is an Armstrong relation for its corresponding CC-set. For instance, the world $w2$ of r_1 is Armstrong for the set $\Sigma^l_{0.9} = \{card(rfid) \leq 3, card(time) \leq 3, card(zone) \leq 4, card(time, zone) \leq 2\}$.

Upper Bounds. Let $p_1 < \cdots < p_n$ denote the different probabilities in Σ_u. If $p_n < 1$, then $n \mapsto n+1$ and define $p_n \leftarrow 1$. The construction of the p-relation r_1 for the lower bounds relies on traditional Armstrong relations as its possible worlds. In contrast, we construct the worlds of the p-relation r_2 for the upper bounds without reference to traditional Armstrong relations. For probability p, we define $\Sigma^u_p = \{card(X) \leq b \mid \exists (card(X) \leq b, \leq p') \in \Sigma_u \wedge (p' < p)\}$. The sets $\Sigma^u_{p_i}$ tell us to violate all those input cardinality constraints in world w_i whose upper bound probability is smaller than p_i. In particular, $\Sigma^u_{p_1} = \emptyset$, so the world w_1 with probability p_1 must satisfy every cardinality constraint, which is achieved by populating w_1 with a single tuple only. The world w_1 is not used, if $p_1 = 0$. If $n > 1$, we violate input constraints with upper bound probability smaller than p_i in world w_i, for $i = 2, \ldots, n$. For that purpose, let $cand_i$ consist of those attribute sets Y such that there is some $card(X) \leq b \in \Sigma^u_{p_i}$ with $Y \subseteq X$. For each $X \in cand_i$, let $b_{X,i} := \sup\{b \mid \exists card(Y) \leq b \in \Sigma^u_{p_i} \wedge X \subseteq Y\}$. That is, $b_{X,i}$ denotes the maximum upper bound b such that $card(X) \leq b$ holds with probability at most p_{i-1}. To show that $card(X) \leq b_{X,i}$ does not hold with any probability larger than p_{i-1}, it suffices to introduce $b_{X,i} + 1$ different tuples in w_i with matching values on all attributes in X. Furthermore, it suffices to apply this construction to every attribute set which is maximal, with respect to set containment, among those attribute sets with the same upper integer bound. Hence, we define the duplicate sets as $dup^u_i := \{X \in cand_i \mid \forall Y \in cand_i(X \subset Y) \Rightarrow b_{X,i} \neq b_{Y,i}\}$, and then set $b_{X,i} \leftarrow b_{X,i}+1$ for all $X \in dup^u_i$. For $i = 2, \ldots, n$, the world w_i of r_2 then has probability $p_i - p_{i-1}$ and is the disjoint union of the tuple sets $\{t^X_1, \ldots, t^X_{b_{X,i}}\}$ for each $X \in dup^u_i$. The given construction yields an Armstrong p-relation $r_2 = (\mathcal{W}_2 = \{w_1, \ldots, w_n\}, P_2 : w_i \mapsto p_i - p_{i-1})$ for Σ_u. That is, the marginal probability of an arbitrary $card(X) \leq b$ in r_2 is the smallest probability $p_{X,b}$ such that $(card(X) \leq b, \leq p_{X,b})$ is implied by Σ_u. Consequently, r_1 and r_2 form an Armstrong p-base for Σ.

Example 2. We illustrate our construction on the running example with Σ from Example 1. We obtain $\Sigma^u_{0.8} = \emptyset$, $\Sigma^u_{0.95} = \{card(rfid, zone) \leq 2, card(time, zone) \leq 1\}$, and $\Sigma^u_{1.0} = \{card(rfid, time) \leq 1, card(rfid, zone) \leq 2, card(time, zone) \leq 1, card(time, zone) \leq 2\}$. The duplicate sets and their cardinalities are: dup_2 contains $\{rfid, zone\}$ and $\{time, zone\}$ with $b_{\{rfid,zone\},2} = 3$ and $b_{\{time,zone\},2} = 2$, and dup_3 contains $\{rfid, zone\}$, $\{time, zone\}$, and $\{rfid, time\}$ with $b_{\{rfid,zone\},3} = 3$, $b_{\{time,zone\},3} = 3$, and $b_{\{rfid,time\},3} = 3$. The worlds $w1$, $w2$ and $w3$ of the p-relation r_2 in Fig. 1 are the result of our construction.

Armstrong Sketches. While the construction of Armstrong p-relations works well in theory, a problem occurs with their actual use in practice. In many cases, the Armstrong relation will be infinite and therefore of no use. These cases occur exactly if there is some attribute $A \in R$ for which $b_A = \infty$, in other words, if there is some attribute for which no finite upper bound has been specified. For a practical solution we use sketches as introduced in [14], which are finite representations of possibly infinite relations. In a relation we introduced for each duplicate set X with associated cardinality b_X, b_X-many tuples $t^X_1, \ldots, t^X_{b_X}$ that all have matching values on X and all have unique values on all the attributes in $R-X$. The idea of a sketch is to represent these b_X-many tuples by a single tuple which has matching values with the t^X_i tuples on X, and carries the placeholder $*$ on all remaining attributes in $R-X$. Indeed, $*$ is a placeholder for values that are unique across all tuples in a relation. In addition, we record the cardinality b_X in a new column *card* together with this tuple. This provides a convenient finite summarization of a possibly infinite number of tuples. The notion of Armstrong sketches can be suitably extended to Armstrong p-sketches and Armstrong p-base sketches, the latter just being pairs of Armstrong p-sketches.

Example 3. An Armstrong p-sketch for the set Σ_u of p-CCs in Example 1 is given as follows. It is easy to see how the tuples in this sketch can be unfolded to obtain the Armstrong p-relation r_2 in Fig. 1.

$\varsigma_1(p_1 = 0.8)$

$card_1$	*rfid*	*time*	*zone*
1	*	*	*

$\varsigma_2(p_2 = 0.15)$

$card_2$	*rfid*	*time*	*zone*
3	as2	*	z1
2	*	9	z2

$\varsigma_3(p_3 = 0.05)$

$card_3$	*rfid*	*time*	*zone*
3	as2	*	z1
3	*	9	z2
3	as1	8	*

Naturally the question arises whether Armstrong p-base sketches always exist. We say that p-CCs *enjoy* Armstrong p-base sketches, if for every relation schema R and for every finite satisfiable set Σ of p-CCs over R there is some p-base sketch over R that is Armstrong for Σ.

Theorem 11. *Prob. cardinality constraints enjoy Armstrong p-base sketches.*

Armstrong PC-base Sketches. Probabilistic conditional databases, or short PC-tables [17] are a popular system that can represent any given probabilistic database concisely. Considering our aim of finding concise data samples of p-CCs, we use PC-sketches to summarize each Armstrong p-sketch even further. A PC-sketch of a p-sketch consists of two tables Γ and Π in which Π summarizes the probability distribution, and Γ stores all tuples of a p-sketch together with the identifiers of worlds in which the tuple occurs. Since we have sketches, the same tuple is recorded multiple times and with cardinalities that represent the difference $b^j_X - b^i_X$ between its multiplicity b^j_X in w_j and its multiplicity b^i_X already recorded for the last possible world w_i in which it occurs.

Example 4. The PC-sketch on the right of Table 1 summarizes the p-sketch from Example 3. The third and fourth row of Γ show that $(*, 9, z2)$ occurs twice in ς_2 and three times in ς_3. This is because $X = \{time, zone\}$ is a duplicate set in dup_2 and dup_3 with cardinalities $b^2_X = 2$ and $b^3_X = 3$, respectively.

Our main result can be summarized as follows.

Theorem 12. *For every satisfiable set Σ of p-CCs over relation schema R, our construction above results in an Armstrong PC-base sketch for Σ in which the total number of possible worlds is at most two larger than the sum of the distinct lower bounds in Σ_l and the distinct upper bounds in Σ_u.*

The time complexity of finding Armstrong PC-base sketches is inherently exponential. Precisely exponential means that there is an algorithm which requires exponential time and that there are cases in which the number of tuples in the output is exponential in the input size. Note that there are also cases where the number of tuples in some Armstrong PC-base sketch for Σ is logarithmic in $|\Sigma|$.

Theorem 13. *The time complexity to find an Armstrong PC-base sketch for a given satisfiable set Σ of p-CCs is precisely exponential in $|\Sigma|$.*

6 Conclusion and Future Work

We empower users to stipulate lower and upper bounds on the marginal probability by which cardinality constraints shall hold on large volumes of uncertain data. The constraints provide a principled, yet manageable mechanism to control the consistency and completeness targets for the quality of uncertain data. Our axiomatic and algorithmic reasoning tools minimize the overhead in using the constraints for applications. Our findings for the semantic summarization of these constraints have been implemented as a tool that provides effective support for the efficient acquisition of the right bounds that hold in a given application domain [15]. In future research we will investigate the usefulness of our framework for constraint acquisition. This will require us to extend empirical measures from certain [9] to probabilistic data. Intriguing is the question whether PC-sketches, p-sketches, or their finite p-relations (if available) are more useful.

References

1. Brown, P., Ganesan, J., Köhler, H., Link, S.: Keys with probabilistic intervals. In: Comyn-Wattiau, I., Tanaka, K., Song, I.-Y., Yamamoto, S., Saeki, M. (eds.) ER 2016. LNCS, vol. 9974, pp. 164–179. Springer, Cham (2016). doi:10.1007/978-3-319-46397-1_13
2. Brown, P., Link, S.: Probabilistic keys. IEEE Trans. Knowl. Data Eng. **29**(3), 670–682 (2017)
3. Chen, P.P.: The entity-relationship model - toward a unified view of data. ACM Trans. Database Syst. **1**(1), 9–36 (1976)
4. Fagin, R.: Horn clauses and database dependencies. J. ACM **29**(4), 952–985 (1982)
5. Ferrarotti, F., Hartmann, S., Link, S.: Efficiency frontiers of XML cardinality constraints. Data Knowl. Eng. **87**, 297–319 (2013)
6. Hall, N., Köhler, H., Link, S., Prade, H., Zhou, X.: Cardinality constraints on qualitatively uncertain data. Data Knowl. Eng. **99**, 126–150 (2015)
7. Hartmann, S., Köhler, H., Leck, U., Link, S., Thalheim, B., Wang, J.: Constructing Armstrong tables for general cardinality constraints and not-null constraints. Ann. Math. Artif. Intell. **73**(1–2), 139–165 (2015)
8. Jones, T.H., Song, I.Y.: Analysis of binary/ternary cardinality combinations in entity-relationship modeling. Data Knowl. Eng. **19**(1), 39–64 (1996)
9. Langeveldt, W., Link, S.: Empirical evidence for the usefulness of Armstrong relations in the acquisition of meaningful functional dependencies. Inf. Syst. **35**(3), 352–374 (2010)
10. Liddle, S.W., Embley, D.W., Woodfield, S.N.: Cardinality constraints in semantic data models. Data Knowl. Eng. **11**(3), 235–270 (1993)
11. McAllister, A.J.: Complete rules for n-ary relationship cardinality constraints. Data Knowl. Eng. **27**(3), 255–288 (1998)
12. Queralt, A., Artale, A., Calvanese, D., Teniente, E.: OCL-Lite: finite reasoning on UML/OCL conceptual schemas. Data Knowl. Eng. **73**, 1–22 (2012)
13. Roblot, T.: Cardinality constraints for probabilistic and possibilistic databases. Ph.D. thesis, Department of Computer Science, The University of Auckland (2016)
14. Roblot, T., Link, S.: Probabilistic cardinality constraints. In: Johannesson, P., Lee, M.L., Liddle, S.W., Opdahl, A.L., López, Ó.P. (eds.) ER 2015. LNCS, vol. 9381, pp. 214–228. Springer, Cham (2015). doi:10.1007/978-3-319-25264-3_16

15. Roblot, T.K., Link, S.: URD: a data summarization tool for the acquisition of meaningful cardinality constraints with probabilistic intervals. In: 33rd IEEE International Conference on Data Engineering, ICDE 2017, San Diego, CA, USA, 19–22 April 2017, pp. 1379–1380. IEEE Computer Society (2017)
16. Saha, B., Srivastava, D.: Data quality: the other face of big data. In: Cruz, I.F., Ferrari, E., Tao, Y., Bertino, E., Trajcevski, G. (eds.) IEEE 30th International Conference on Data Engineering, ICDE 2014, Chicago, IL, USA, March 31–April 4 2014, pp. 1294–1297. IEEE Computer Society (2014)
17. Suciu, D., Olteanu, D., Ré, C., Koch, C.: Probabilistic Databases. Synthesis Lectures on Data Management. Morgan & Claypool Publishers, San Rafael (2011)
18. Thalheim, B.: Fundamentals of cardinality constraints. In: Pernul, G., Tjoa, A.M. (eds.) ER 1992. LNCS, vol. 645, pp. 7–23. Springer, Heidelberg (1992). doi:10.1007/3-540-56023-8_3

Contextual Keys

Ziheng Wei, Sebastian Link[(✉)], and Jiamou Liu

Department of Computer Science, University of Auckland, Auckland, New Zealand
{z.wei,s.link,j.liu}@aucklanduni.ac.nz

Abstract. Much work has been done on extending the relational model of data to encompass incomplete information. In particular, a plethora of research has examined the semantics of integrity constraints in the presence of null markers. We propose a new approach whose semantics relies exclusively on fragments of complete data within an incomplete relation. For this purpose, we introduce the class of contextual keys. Users can specify the context of a key as a set of attributes that selects the subrelation of tuples with no null marker occurrences on the attributes of the context. Then the key uniquely identifies the tuples within the subrelation. The standard notion of a key over complete relations is the special case of a contextual key whose context consists of all attributes. SQL unique constraints form the special case of a contextual key whose context coincides with the set of key attributes. We establish structural and computational characterizations of the associated implication problem, and of their Armstrong databases. The computation of Armstrong databases has been implemented in a tool, and experiments provide insight into the actual run-time behavior of the algorithms that complement our detailed computational complexity analysis.

Keywords: Armstrong relation · Data and knowledge intelligence · Decision support · Incomplete data · Key · Reasoning · Requirements analysis

1 Introduction

Keys are core enablers for data management. They are fundamental for understanding the structure and semantics of data. Given a collection of entities, a key is a set of attributes whose values uniquely identify an entity in the collection. For example, a key for a relational table is a set of columns such that no two different rows have matching values in each of the key columns. Keys are essential for many other data models, including semantic models, object models, probabilistic models, XML, RDF, and graphs. They help in many classical areas of data management, including data modeling, database design, indexing, and query optimization. Knowledge about keys enables us to (i) uniquely reference entities across data repositories, (ii) minimize data redundancy at schema design time to process updates efficiently at run time, (iii) provide better selectivity estimates in cost-based query optimization, (iv) provide a query optimizer with new

H.C. Mayr et al. (Eds.): ER 2017, LNCS 10650, pp. 266–279, 2017.
https://doi.org/10.1007/978-3-319-69904-2_22

access paths that can lead to substantial speedups in query processing, (v) allow the database administrator to improve the efficiency of data access via physical design techniques such as data partitioning or the creation of indexes and materialized views, and (vi) provide new insights into application data. Modern applications raise the importance of keys further. They facilitate the data integration process, help with the detection of duplicates and anomalies, provide guidance in repairing data, and return consistent answers to queries over dirty data. The discovery of keys is one of the core activities in data profiling.

An important and rich area of research is to extend the relational model of data to encompass incomplete information. This is due to the importance of incomplete information for applications. A plethora of different extensions exist, but many are based on the use of a special symbol as placeholder for incomplete information, also known as the *null marker*. The semantics of the null marker can vary greatly, for example "unknown at present" [8], "non-existence" [25], "inapplicable" [4,8], "no information" [31] and "open" [7]. Similarly, several extensions of the notion of a key from complete to incomplete relations have been investigated in the research literature. Examples constitute SQL's primary and candidate keys as well as `UNIQUE` constraints [15], weak and strong keys [21], Codd keys [9], possible and certain keys [15,17,18], and key sets [22,27]. Candidate keys are minimal sets of attributes that enable us to uniquely identify tuples in an incomplete relation and where no null markers are permitted to occur in the columns of the key. They are a result of Codd's principle of entity integrity. The principle has been challenged by several researchers, including Thalheim [27], Levene and Loizou [22], and Köhler et al. [17]. For example, certain keys can uniquely identify rows in a table even though null markers may occur in the key columns. Similarly, for all pairs of distinct tuples there is some key in a key set on which the two tuples have no null marker occurrences and are unique.

Table 1 shows an incomplete relation, where $\perp$ denotes a null marker occurrence. Interestingly, this relation does not satisfy any candidate key, any certain key, nor any key set. It does not satisfy any candidate key as null markers occur in *Department* and *Manager*, and there are different tuples with the same value on *Employee*. The relation violates every certain key since the two null marker occurrences may be replaced by the values *Toys* and *Burns*, respectively, resulting in two different tuples that have matching values on all attributes. The relation violates every key set because the first and second tuple are incomplete on *Department* and on *Manager*, and have matching values on *Employee*.

Table 1. A relation with no candidate key, no certain key, and no key set

Employee	Department	Manager
Homer	Toys	Burns
Homer	$\perp$	$\perp$
Marge	Toys	Burns

Common to all extended notions of keys is the target of uniquely identifying all tuples in incomplete relations, even tuples with null marker occurrences. The example in Table 1 shows that this target cannot always be achieved. In fact, any semantics of a key that depends on the interpretation of null markers can easily become problematic. This holds especially when data is integrated from different sources, which may rely on different interpretations of null markers. Interestingly, SQL's `UNIQUE` constraint enforces uniqueness only for those tuples of an incomplete relation that are complete on the attributes of the `UNIQUE` constraint. For example, the incomplete relation in Table 1 satisfies the unique constraints `UNIQUE`(*Employee, Department*) and `UNIQUE`(*Employee, Manager*), but violates the unique constraints `UNIQUE`(*Employee*) and `UNIQUE`(*Department, Manager*). This approach sparked our idea of giving up any false hope that tuples can be uniquely identified in the presence of null marker occurrences. In SQL's `UNIQUE` constraint this given set of attributes forms the unique constraint itself. That, however, is a requirement that should be relaxed, as the incomplete relation in Table 1 illustrates. In fact, `UNIQUE`(*Employee, Department*) can distinguish between the first and third tuple by the values on *Employee* already, and does not require values on *Department*. Note that uniqueness only holds for the tuples which are complete on *Employee* and *Department*, and uniqueness does not hold for the tuples that are complete on *Employee* only.

Motivated by these examples, we propose the new notion of *contextual keys* for incomplete relations. Contextual keys target the unique identification of those tuples in an incomplete relation that are complete on a user-specified set of attributes. Contextual keys consist of a pair of attributes (C, K) such that $K \subseteq C$. The user-specified set of attributes C is called the *context* of the contextual key, and selects the *scope* of the key, which is defined as the subset of tuples in a given incomplete relation that are complete on all the attributes of the context. The set K of a contextual key (C, K) is called the key and uniquely identifies tuples in the scope of the key. For example, ({*Employee, Department*},{*Employee*}) and ({*Employee, Manager*},{*Employee*}) are both contextual keys that are satisfied by the incomplete relation in Table 1. Here, both contexts {*Employee, Department*} and {*Employee, Manager*} have the same scope in the incomplete relation, which consists of the first and third tuple, and the key {*Employee*} uniquely identifies tuples in this scope. The incomplete relation in Table 1 does not satisfy any of the following contextual keys: ({*Employee*},{*Employee*)}, ({*Employee, Department*},{*Department*}) and ({*Employee, Manager*},{*Manager*}). In particular, SQL's constraint `UNIQUE`(X) is satisfied by an incomplete relation if and only if the relation satisfies the contextual key (X, X).

This paper introduces contextual keys, and provides first evidence that they exhibit good computational properties. Due to its importance in automating data management, we are interested in the axiomatic and algorithmic characterizations of the implication problem associated with contextual keys. We also want to provide computational support for the acquisition of contextual keys that are meaningful for an application domain. We will now detail our contributions.

Contributions. Our contributions are at least threefold. Firstly, we propose a novel class of keys for incomplete databases, named contextual keys. Secondly, we characterize the implication problem of contextual keys by a finite axiomatization and by a linear-time algorithm. An immediate application of the algorithm is to compute a non-redundant set of contextual keys, thereby minimizing the overhead of enforcing contextual keys on relations. Thirdly, we investigate structural and computational properties of Armstrong relations for contextual keys, providing a computational tool that aids with the acquisition of contextual keys. While the problem of finding an Armstrong relation is precisely exponential, our algorithm is conservative in its use of time and space, as the output Armstrong relation is guaranteed to have a number of tuples that is at most quadratic in the minimum number of tuples required. For transfer into practice, we have implemented our algorithm in a prototype system. Experiments with the prototype system complement our theoretical complexity analysis, and illustrate - on average - how quickly Armstrong relations for contextual keys can be computed, how many tuples our output contains, and how many null markers occur in the output. For example, for a fixed schema with 15 attributes, and a set of contextual keys with 100 attributes, our algorithm computes an Armstrong relation with 86 tuples and 200 null marker occurrences in about 10 s.

Organization. We discuss related work in Sect. 2. Our central notion of contextual keys is introduced in Sect. 3, where we also characterize the associated implication problem axiomatically and algorithmically. In Sect. 4 we investigate structural and computational properties of Armstrong relations. Finally, we conclude and sketch future work in Sect. 5. We refer the interested reader to [30] for the proofs of our results.

2 Related Work

While about 100 different classes of data dependencies are known [28], keys arguably constitute the most import class among all of them. Keys have been studied in-depth on complete data [23,28], and have been extended to most other data models, including nested [29], object-relational [13], XML [10–12], and models of uncertainty [2,3,5,14].

The first section has already examined various proposals for notions of keys over incomplete relations. These include candidate keys that respect Codd's principle of entity integrity [9], possible and certain keys [15], weak and strong keys [21], as well as key sets [22,27]. Contextual keys are different from all of these proposals in the sense that they do not target the unique identification of all tuples in an incomplete relation. The idea of contextual keys is to target the unique identification of only those tuples that are complete on a user-specified set of attributes. This idea generalizes SQL's `UNIQUE` constraint where the user-defined set coincides with the set of attributes on which the values are unique. We believe contextual keys are particularly useful in modern applications, such as data integration, where different occurrences of missing information may require different semantics. The semantics of contextual keys is clearly defined as it does not depend on the semantics of null marker occurrences. Furthermore, contextual keys empower users to link their completeness requirements on the quality of their data with their uniqueness requirements.

In our research we investigate the same computational problems that have been studied for previous notions of keys. More specifically, we tackle the associated implication problem as well as the structural and computational properties of Armstrong relations. The importance of these problems is well-established in the literature and practice. Efficient solutions to the implication problem help address many data management problems, as listed in the introduction. Furthermore, Armstrong relations are useful for the acquisition of meaningful contextual keys, similar to the case of Armstrong relations for other classes of data dependencies [1,19,20,26].

3 Fundamentals of Contextual Keys

Let $\mathfrak{A} = \{A_1, A_2, \cdots\}$ be a countable and infinite set of distinct symbols, called *attributes*. A *relation schema* is a finite, non-empty set of attributes, normally denoted as R. Each attribute $A \in \mathfrak{A}$ is associated with a domain $dom(A)$. We assume that the domain of every attribute contains a distinguished null marker, which we denote by $\perp$. This is for simplicity, and we emphasize that $\perp$ is not a domain value but a marker. In what follows we will use the relation schema STAFF = {*Employee*, *Department*, *Manager*} from Table 1 as a running example for illustrating our concepts and results. We refer to the attributes *Employee*, *Department*, *Manager* as E, D, and M, respectively.

A *tuple* t over R is a function which maps each $A \in R$ to a value in $dom(A)$, namely $t(A) \in dom(A)$. A *relation* r over R is a finite set of tuples over R. The size of the relation, denoted as $|r|$ is the number of tuples the relation contains. Let $X = \{A_1, A_2, \cdots, A_m\}$ be a set of attributes. For simplicity, we sometimes write X as $A_1A_2\cdots A_m$, and the union of X and another attribute set Y as XY. Let $X \subseteq R$. For a tuple t over R, we use the notation $t(X)$ to denote the projection of t onto X. To stipulate completeness, we say a tuple t over R is X-*total* if and only if $t(A) \neq \perp$ for all $A \in X$. Furthermore, We use r^X to denote $\{t \in r \mid t\ is\ X\text{-total}\}$.

A *constraint* of a class $\mathcal{C}$ is a statement which enforces semantic properties on a given collection of data. For instance, *keys* are a class of integrity constraints which stipulate that the identity of tuples is determined by the values on a given set of attributes. Let Σ be a set of constraints over class $\mathcal{C}$. We use $|\Sigma|$ to denote the number of constraints in Σ, and $||\Sigma||$ to denote the total number of attributes in Σ. For a class $\mathcal{C}$ of integrity constraints, we are interested in the implication problem associated with $\mathcal{C}$. The $\mathcal{C}$-implication problem is to decide whether for an arbitrary given relation schema R, and an arbitrarily given set $\Sigma \cup \{\varphi\}$ of integrity constraints from class $\mathcal{C}$ on R, Σ implies φ (written as $\Sigma \models \varphi$), that is, whether every relation over R that satisfies all the elements in Σ also satisfies φ. Solutions to the implication problem provide users with a better understanding of the interaction of the integrity constraints, and algorithms can be developed that compute better representations of a set of integrity constraints. For example, a set Σ' is said to be a *cover* of Σ if and only if Σ and Σ' are satisfied by the same relations. A cover Σ' is said to be *non-redundant* if and only if for all $\sigma \in \Sigma'$ it is the case that $\Sigma' - \{\sigma\}$ does not imply σ. Being able to decide the implication problem, we can easily compute a non-redundant cover for Σ by successively checking for all $\sigma \in \Sigma$ whether $\Sigma - \{\sigma\}$ implies σ and removing σ from Σ whenever that is the case. In practice, checking whether all the constraints in a non-redundant cover are satisfied by a relation ensures that the overhead of constraint validation is minimized. Clearly, the more tuples in a relation, the more time we save when validating constraints with a non-redundant cover.

Next we formally introduce a new class of keys for incomplete relations which we call *contextual keys*.

Definition 1. A contextual key (CK) *over a relation schema* R *is a statement of the form* (C, K) *where* $K \subseteq C \subseteq R$. *The attribute set* C *is called the* context *of the contextual key. A relation* r *over* R satisfies *the* CK (C, K), *denoted as* $r \models (C, K)$, *if and only if for all* $t, t' \in r^C$, $t(K) = t'(K)$ *implies* $t = t'$. *We call* r^C *the scope of* r *with respect to the context* C.

Next we illustrate the notion of a contextual key on our running example.

Example 1. The incomplete relation r in Table 1 satisfies the contextual keys (ED, E) and (EM, E), but it violates the contextual keys (E, E), (ED, D), and (EM, M). For example, r satisfies (ED, E), since the scope of r with respect to the context ED consists of the first and third tuple of r, and the values of these tuples on E are different. Similarly, r does not satisfy (E, E), since the scope of r with respect to the context E is the relation r itself, but the values of the first and second tuples on E are the same.

For what follows, we require the following concepts. Let R be a relation schema. We define a partial order $\sqsubseteq_R$ over R as $\{((C_1, K_1), (C_2, K_2)) \mid C_1 \subseteq C_2 \subseteq R, K_1 \subseteq K_2 \subseteq R\}$. For any $((C_1, K_1), (C_2, K_2)) \in \sqsubseteq_R$, we write $(C_1, K_1) \sqsubseteq_R (C_2, K_2)$, or $(C_1, K_1) \sqsubset_R (C_2, K_2)$ if $C_1 \subset C_2$ or $K_1 \subset K_2$. We may omit the subscript R, if R is clear from the context. Let Σ be a set of CKs over R. We define the set $\mathsf{CL}(\Sigma) = \{(C, K) \mid \Sigma \not\models (C, K), K \subseteq C \subseteq R\}$. The set of *contextual anti-keys* of Σ is $\Sigma^{-1} = \{(C, K) \in \mathsf{CL}(\Sigma) \mid \neg\exists(C', K') \in \mathsf{CL}(\Sigma) : (C, K) \sqsubset (C', K')\}$. Let r be a relation over R. We say t_1 and t_2 *exactly agree* on (C, K) if and only if $t_1(K) = t_2(K)$ and $t_1(A) = \perp \vee t_2(A) = \perp$ for all $A \in R \setminus C$. The *agree set* of r is $ag(r) = \{(C, K) \mid t_1, t_2$ exactly agree on (C, K) for all distinct $t_1, t_2 \in r\}$.

A sensible first step in solving the implication problem is to discover a set of *inference rules* that allows us to mechanically derive exactly those constraints from a given set Σ that are implied. We apply inference rules of the form $\frac{\text{premises}}{\text{conclusion}}$. Let $\mathfrak{R}$ be a set of inference rules over class $\mathcal{C}$ and φ a constraint of $\mathcal{C}$. We say that φ is *derivable* from Σ with respect to $\mathfrak{R}$, denoted by $\Sigma \vdash_{\mathfrak{R}} \varphi$, whenever there is some finite sequence $\sigma_1, \sigma_2, \ldots, \sigma_n$ such that $\sigma_n = \varphi$ and for every $i < n$, $\sigma_i \in \Sigma$ or σ_i results from the conclusion of some inference rule in $\mathfrak{R}$ with $\sigma_1, \ldots, \sigma_{i-1}$ as premises.

To reason about CKs, we introduce the set $\mathfrak{B}$ of inference rules as shown in Table 2. Our goal is to show that $\mathfrak{B}$ is a sound and complete set of inference rules for contextual keys. This goal can be realized by using the following syntactic characterization of $\mathfrak{B}$.

Table 2. Axiomatization $\mathfrak{B}$

$\dfrac{}{(R,R)}$	$\dfrac{(C,K)}{(CC',KK')}$
(R-axiom)	*(Superkey)*

Theorem 1. *Let $\Sigma \cup \{(C,K)\}$ be a set of* CKs *over a relation schema R. $\Sigma \vdash_{\mathfrak{B}} (C,K)$ if only if there is $(C',K') \sqsubseteq (C,K)$ where $(C',K') \in \Sigma \cup \{(R,R)\}$.*

We will now illustrate the usefulness of Theorem 1 on our running example.

Example 2. Given the set $\Sigma = \{(ED,E),(EM,E)\}$ we can use Theorem 1 to conclude that there is a derivation of the contextual keys (ED,ED) and (EM,EM) from Σ by $\mathfrak{B}$ since $(ED,E) \sqsubseteq (ED,ED)$ and $(EM,E) \sqsubseteq (EM,EM)$ hold. Similarly, we can use Theorem 1 to conclude that there is no derivation of the contextual key (E,E) from Σ by $\mathfrak{B}$ since neither $(ED,E) \sqsubseteq (E,E)$ nor $(EM,E) \sqsubseteq (E,E)$ hold.

Using Theorem 1, we can establish the following axiomatic characterization.

Theorem 2. *$\mathfrak{B}$ forms a finite axiomatization for the implication of* CK*s.*

We apply Theorem 2 to our running example.

Example 3. Recall that we inferred in Example 2 that we can use $\mathfrak{B}$ to derive the contextual keys (ED,ED) and (EM,EM) from $\Sigma = \{(ED,E),(EM,E)\}$, but we cannot use $\mathfrak{B}$ to derive the contextual key (E,E) from Σ. Based on the soundness of $\mathfrak{B}$ we can further conclude that the contextual keys (ED,ED) and (EM,EM) are implied by Σ. Furthermore, based on the completeness of $\mathfrak{B}$ we can conclude that the contextual key (E,E) is not implied by Σ.

The axiomatization can be used to explicitly enumerate all contextual keys that are implied by a given set Σ. In practice, however, one may not be interested in all contextual keys that are implied, but only be interested whether a given contextual key φ is implied by Σ. In such situation, an explicit enumeration of all implied constraints is inefficient and does not make good use of the additional input φ. For this purpose, our final contribution of this section is a linear-time algorithmic characterization of the implication problem associated with contextual keys. In fact, we use Theorem 1 to obtain this algorithm.

The correctness of Algorithm 1 follows from Theorems 1 and 2, and the linear-time complexity is easy to observe from the algorithm.

Algorithm 1. Implication of contextual keys

INPUT: A set $\Sigma \cup \{(C, K)\}$ of contextual keys over relation schema R
OUTPUT: TRUE, if $\Sigma \models (C, K)$; FALSE, otherwise
`CK` := FALSE
for each $(C', K') \in \Sigma \cup \{(R, R)\}$ **do**
  if $C' \subseteq C$ and $K' \subseteq K$ **then**
    `CK` := TRUE
return `CK`

Theorem 3. *Algorithm 1 decides the implication problem of contextual keys* $\Sigma \models (C, K)$ *in time* $\mathcal{O}(||\Sigma \cup \{(R, R)\}||)$.

We conclude this section by a final example.

Example 4. Using $R = EDM$, $\Sigma = \{(ED, E), (EM, E)\}$ and $\varphi = (E, E)$ as input, Algorithm 1 returns FALSE, since there is no $(C', K') \in \Sigma \cup \{(R, R)\}$ such that $C' \subseteq \{E\}$ and $K' \subseteq \{E\}$.

4 Armstrong Relations for Contextual Keys

Contextual keys can enforce important application semantics within a database system. However, a fundamental problem is to acquire those contextual keys that are meaningful in a given application domain. Database designers usually do not know the domain well and domain experts do not know database constraints. We will now establish computational support for overcoming the communication barrier between designers and experts. As illustrated in Fig. 1, designers think in terms of an abstract set Σ of contextual keys they perceive meaningful. For them to communicate their current perceived understanding to domain experts, we will establish an algorithm that computes from a given set Σ a relation r_Σ that perfectly represents Σ. That is, r_Σ satisfies all contextual keys in Σ and violates all contextual keys that are not implied by Σ. Relations with this property are known as *Armstrong relations* [6]. If designers currently perceive an actually meaningful contextual key as meaningless, then this contextual key will be violated in r_Σ. The point is that domain experts will easily notice this violation because the contextual key is meaningful. The experts can then alert the designers to this inconsistency with the application semantics, and the designer can include the meaningful contextual key in their set Σ. Such process can be repeated until both designers and experts are happy. The other direction,

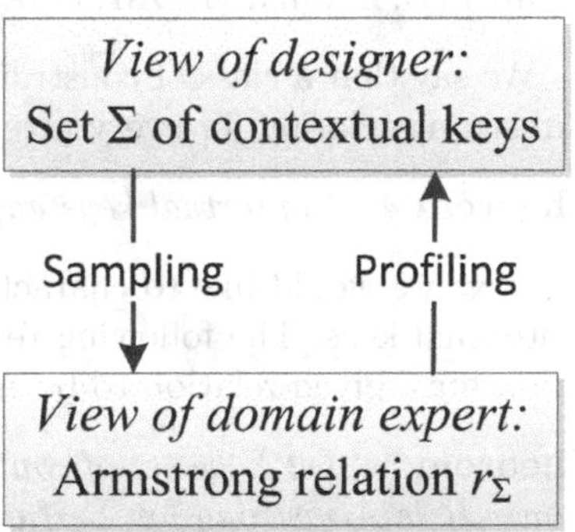

Fig. 1. Acquisition framework

in which one provides computational support for identifying the set Σ of contextual keys that hold in a given relation, is beyond the focus of this article. However, research into this direction is useful as the domain expert may want to change values in an Armstrong relation, or legacy data becomes available to the designers. For the remainder of this section, we will investigate computational and structural properties of Armstrong relations for contextual keys. We begin with the definition of Armstrong relations for contextual keys.

Definition 2. *Let Σ be a set of contextual keys over relation schema R. A relation r over R is* Armstrong *for Σ if and only if the following property holds for all contextual keys (C, K) over R: $r \models (C, K)$ if and only if $\Sigma \models (C, K)$.*

Note the beauty of this definition: Given an Armstrong relation r for Σ, one can reduce *every* instance $\Sigma \models \varphi$ of the implication problem for contextual keys to checking whether φ holds on r. In fact, if r satisfies φ, then Σ implies φ; and if r does not satisfy φ, then r is not implied by Σ.

Example 5. The relation r in Table 1 is Armstrong for the set

$$\Sigma = \{(ED, E), (EM, E)\}$$

over the relation schema $R = EDM$. It is indeed easy to observe that r satisfies (ED, ED) and (EM, EM), which are therefore implied by Σ. Similarly, r violates (E, E), and (EDM, DM) which are therefore not implied by Σ.

We say that a class of constraints $\mathcal{C}$ *enjoys* Armstrong relations if there is an Armstrong relation for every given set of constraints of $\mathcal{C}$.

Theorem 4. *Contextual keys enjoy Armstrong relations.*

Next we would like to characterize the structure of Armstrong relations for contextual keys. The following result establishes a necessary and sufficient condition for a given relation to be Armstrong for a given set of contextual keys.

Theorem 5. *Let Σ be set of contextual keys over relation schema R. A relation r over R is Armstrong for Σ if and only if $\Sigma^{-1} \subseteq ag(r) \subseteq \mathsf{CL}(\Sigma)$.*

We apply Theorem 5 to our running example.

Example 6. The relation r in Table 1 is indeed Armstrong for

$$\Sigma = \{(ED, E), (EM, E)\}$$

because every contextual anti-key is an exact agree set of r, and every exact agree set is a contextual key not implied by Σ. In fact, the contextual anti-keys of Σ are (E, E) and (EDM, DM), which are the exact agree sets of the first and second tuple, and the first and third tuple, respectively. Moreover, the exact agree set of the second and third tuple is $(EDM, \emptyset)$, which is not implied by Σ.

Given Theorem 5, it is not difficult to see that Algorithm 2 computes a relation that is Armstrong for a given set Σ of contextual keys.

In fact, Algorithm 2 always computes an Armstrong relation with conservative use of space.

Theorem 6. *For every set Σ of contextual keys, Algorithm 2 computes an Armstrong relation for Σ with $|\Sigma^{-1}|+1$ tuples. This number is at most the square of the minimum number of tuples required by any Armstrong relation for Σ.*

Algorithm 2. Computing Armstrong relations

INPUT: A set Σ of contextual keys over a relation schema R
OUTPUT: An Armstrong relation r for Σ
Let t_0 be a tuple over R where $t(A) = 0$ for all $A \in R$;
$r_{\text{Armstrong}} \leftarrow \{t_0\}$;
$i \leftarrow 1$;
for each $(C, K) \in \Sigma^{-1}$ **do**
  Let t_i be a tuple over R
  $t_i(A) \leftarrow \begin{cases} 0 & \text{, if } A \in K \\ i & \text{, if } A \in C \setminus K \\ \bot & \text{, if } A \in R \setminus C \end{cases}$
  $i++$;
  $r_{\text{Armstrong}} \leftarrow r_{\text{Armstrong}} \cup \{t_i\}$;
return $r_{\text{Armstrong}}$;

In practice, it may be important to focus the attention of the designers and domain experts to certain fragments of an Armstrong relation. For rows, it makes perfect sense to loop through the anti-keys and look at each row pair whose agree set is the anti-key. For columns, one may give the users of the algorithm full control over which columns should be highlighted. One sensible choice would be to inspect the columns in the context of an anti-key.

The following example demonstrates a worst case scenario in which the size of every Armstrong relation is exponential in the input size.

Example 7. Let $R = \{A_1, A_2, \ldots, A_{2n}\}$ where n is a positive integer. Let $\Sigma = \{(A_{2i-1}A_{2i}, A_{2i-1}A_{2i}) \mid i = 1, \ldots, n\}$ be a set of CKs over R. If $n = 2$, then

$$\Sigma^{-1} = \{(A_1A_3, A_1A_3), (A_1A_4, A_1A_4), (A_2A_3, A_2A_3), (A_2A_4, A_2A_4)\}$$

In general, $|\Sigma^{-1}| = 2^n$ where Σ has size $4n$. □

As evidenced by Example 7, there is no algorithm that can compute Armstrong relations in polynomial time in the input. Extending the currently best known strategy of computing the set Σ^{-1} of anti-keys from traditional to contextual keys [26], we establish a characterization of anti-keys that will provide us with an iterative algorithm to compute them.

Lemma 1. *Let $\Gamma = \Sigma \cup \{(C, K)\}$ be a set of contextual keys over a relation schema R. If $(U, X) \in \Gamma^{-1}$, then the following must hold:*

1. *$(U, X) \in \Sigma^{-1}$, or*
2. *there exists $A \in K$ such that $(U, XA) \in \Sigma^{-1}$, or*
3. *there exists $A \in C \setminus K$ such that $(UA, X) \in \Sigma^{-1}$.*

Lemma 1 will give us an iterative algorithm for computing the anti-keys for a given set of contextual keys. However, in each iteration we still need to validate for each candidate anti-key that it is indeed an anti-key. This can be done efficiently as formally documented now.

Algorithm 3. Computing contextual anti-keys

INPUT: A set Σ of contextual keys over a relation schema R
OUTPUT: Σ^{-1}
$\Sigma \leftarrow \Sigma \cup \{(R, R)\}$;
$\Sigma' \leftarrow \emptyset$;
$\Sigma^{-1} \leftarrow \{(R, R)\}$;
for each $(C, K) \in \Sigma$ **do**
  $\Sigma' \leftarrow \Sigma' \cup \{(C, K)\}$
  for each $(U, X) \in \Sigma^{-1}$ **do**
    if $(C, K) \sqsubseteq (U, X)$ **then**
      $\Sigma^{-1} \leftarrow \Sigma^{-1} \setminus \{(U, X)\}$
      for each $A \in C \setminus K$ **do**
        $\Sigma^{-1} \leftarrow \Sigma^{-1} \cup \{(U \setminus \{A\}, X \setminus \{A\})\}$
      for each $A \in K$ **do**
        $\Sigma^{-1} \leftarrow \Sigma^{-1} \cup \{(U, X \setminus \{A\})\}$
  for each $(U, X) \in \Sigma^{-1}$ **do**
    if $\exists A \in U \setminus X\ \forall (C', K') \in \Sigma' : (C', K') \not\sqsubseteq (U, XA)$ or $\exists A \in R \setminus U\ \forall (C', K') \in \Sigma' : (C', K') \not\sqsubseteq (UA, X)$ **then**
      $\Sigma^{-1} \leftarrow \Sigma^{-1} \setminus \{(U, X)\}$;
return Σ^{-1};

Lemma 2. *Validating whether a given contextual key is an anti-key for a given set Σ of contextual keys over relation schema R can be done in time $\mathcal{O}(|R| \cdot ||\Sigma||)$.*

Algorithm 3 iteratively examines the input keys in Σ. For each input key (C, K) it checks if any anti-key in Σ^{-1} contains (C, K). The algorithm constructs $\Gamma^{-1} = (\Sigma \cup \{(C, K)\})^{-1}$ from those contextual anti-keys which belong to Σ^{-1} by eliminating attributes in K or $C \setminus K$.

To evaluate the efficiency of our approach, we conducted experiments with Algorithms 2 and 3. We randomly generated sets of CKs over a relation schema R. For each set Σ of randomly generated CKs, we set a series of parameters: $n \in \{10, 20, \ldots, 100\}$, $k \in \{5, 6, \ldots, 15\}$ where $n = ||\Sigma||$ and $k = |R|$. In the experiments, we run each possible setting of the parameters 500 times and measure the average running time of the algorithm in milliseconds, the average number of tuples and null markers in the output Armstrong relation.

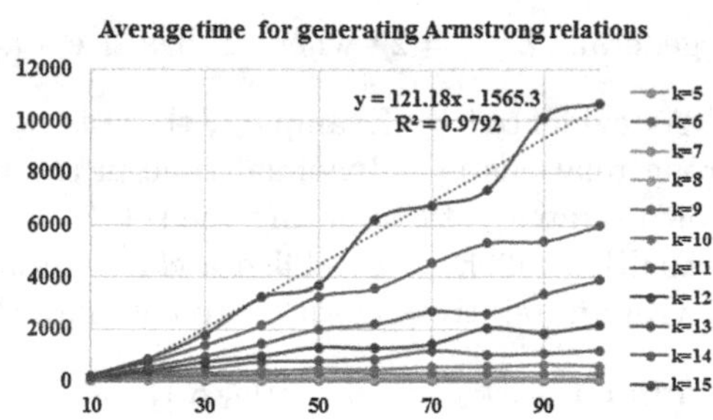

Fig. 2. Average computing time

Figure 2 illustrates that the average running time shows a linear growth with respect to the input size and a fixed schema. Similarly, Fig. 3 illustrates that the size of Armstrong relations and the number of null marker occurrences grow slowly with increasing input size.

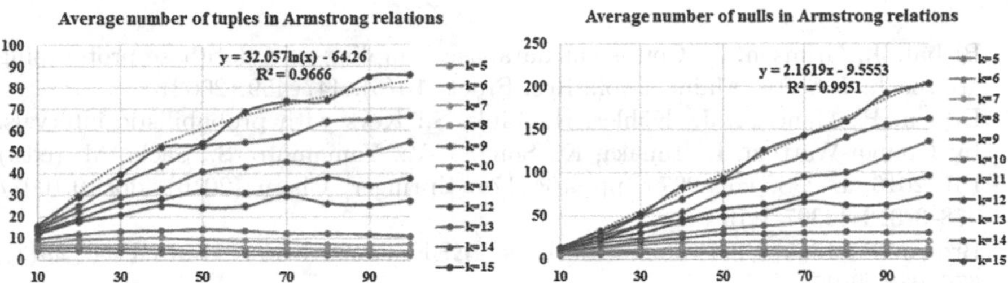

Fig. 3. Average sizes and average number of null markers in Armstrong relations

Indeed, with smaller sizes and fewer occurrences of null markers, Armstrong relations become more comprehensible to domain experts. With faster run times, communication between designers and domain experts improves in terms of frequency and efficiency.

5 Conclusion and Future Work

We have investigated a new class of keys over incomplete relations, named contextual keys. Contextual keys target the unique identification of those tuples in a relation that are complete on a user-specified set of attributes. This approach ensures that the unique identification is independent of any interpretation of null marker occurrences. In order to unlock the vast usefulness of contextual keys for processing data, we have studied two fundamental problems associated with contextual keys. We have established axiomatic and algorithmic characterizations of the implication problem, enabling us to reason efficiently about contextual keys and to minimize the overhead of enforcing them within a database system. We have further established structural and computational properties of Armstrong relations for contextual keys, enabling us to represent any set of contextual keys in the form of a user-friendly data sample. Our theoretical and experimental analysis shows that Armstrong relations can be computed efficiently and that their size is reasonably small in order to be effective for the acquisition of contextual keys that are meaningful in a given application domain.

In the future, it will be interesting to investigate the discovery problem for contextual keys. The problem is to compute a cover of the set of contextual keys that hold in a given relation. Solutions to this problem will complete our acquisition framework, in which the cover of a set of constraints can be translated back and forth between an abstract set of constraints and an Armstrong relation for this set. Another important avenue of future research will lead to the investigation of other classes of contextual constraints, such as functional dependencies, join dependencies, or inclusion dependencies. This may have important applications in schema design [16,24].

References

1. Bisbal, J., Grimson, J.: Consistent database sampling as a database prototyping approach. J. Softw. Maint. Evol.: Res. Pract. **14**(6), 447–459 (2002)
2. Brown, P., Ganesan, J., Köhler, H., Link, S.: Keys with probabilistic intervals. In: Comyn-Wattiau, I., Tanaka, K., Song, I.-Y., Yamamoto, S., Saeki, M. (eds.) ER 2016. LNCS, vol. 9974, pp. 164–179. Springer, Cham (2016). doi:10.1007/978-3-319-46397-1_13
3. Brown, P., Link, S.: Probabilistic keys. IEEE Trans. Knowl. Data Eng. **29**(3), 670–682 (2017)
4. Codd, E.F.: Missing information (applicable and inapplicable) in relational databases. ACM SIGMOD Rec. **15**(4), 53–53 (1986)
5. Demetrovics, J., Katona, G.O.H., Miklós, D., Seleznjev, O., Thalheim, B.: Asymptotic properties of keys and functional dependencies in random databases. Theor. Comput. Sci. **190**(2), 151–166 (1998)
6. Fagin, R.: Horn clauses and database dependencies. J. ACM (JACM) **29**(4), 952–985 (1982)
7. Gottlob, G., Zicari, R.: Closed world databases opened through null values. VLDB **88**, 50–61 (1988)
8. Grant, J.: Null values in a relational data base. Inf. Process. Lett. **6**(5), 156–157 (1977)
9. Hartmann, S., Leck, U., Link, S.: On Codd families of keys over incomplete relations. Comput. J. **54**(7), 1166–1180 (2011)
10. Hartmann, S., Link, S.: Unlocking keys for XML trees. In: Schwentick, T., Suciu, D. (eds.) ICDT 2007. LNCS, vol. 4353, pp. 104–118. Springer, Heidelberg (2006). doi:10.1007/11965893_8
11. Hartmann, S., Link, S.: Efficient reasoning about a robust XML key fragment. ACM Trans. Database Syst. **34**(2), 10:1–10:33 (2009)
12. Hartmann, S., Link, S.: Expressive, yet tractable XML keys. In: Kersten, M.L., Novikov, B., Teubner, J., Polutin, V., Manegold, S. (eds.) EDBT 2009, pp. 357–367. ACM, New York (2009)
13. Khizder, V.L., Weddell, G.E.: Reasoning about uniqueness constraints in object relational databases. IEEE Trans. Knowl. Data Eng. **15**(5), 1295–1306 (2003)
14. Koehler, H., Leck, U., Link, S., Prade, H.: Logical foundations of possibilistic keys. In: Fermé, E., Leite, J. (eds.) JELIA 2014. LNCS (LNAI), vol. 8761, pp. 181–195. Springer, Cham (2014). doi:10.1007/978-3-319-11558-0_13
15. Köhler, H., Leck, U., Link, S., Zhou, X.: Possible and certain keys for SQL. VLDB J. **25**(4), 571–596 (2016)
16. Köhler, H., Link, S.: SQL schema design: foundations, normal forms, and normalization. In: Özcan, F., Koutrika, G., Madden, S. (eds.) Proceedings of the 2016 International Conference on Management of Data, SIGMOD Conference 2016, San Francisco, CA, USA, 26 June–01 July 2016, pp. 267–279. ACM (2016)
17. Köhler, H., Link, S., Zhou, X.: Possible and certain SQL keys. PVLDB **8**(11), 1118–1129 (2015)

18. Köhler, H., Link, S., Zhou, X.: Discovering meaningful certain keys from incomplete and inconsistent relations. IEEE Data Eng. Bull. **39**(2), 21–37 (2016)
19. Langeveldt, W.D., Link, S.: Empirical evidence for the usefulness of Armstrong relations in the acquisition of meaningful functional dependencies. Inf. Syst. **35**(3), 352–374 (2010)
20. Le, V.B.T., Link, S., Ferrarotti, F.: Empirical evidence for the usefulness of Armstrong tables in the acquisition of semantically meaningful SQL constraints. Data Knowl. Eng. **98**, 74–103 (2015)
21. Levene, M., Loizou, G.: Axiomatisation of functional dependencies in incomplete relations. Theor. Comput. Sci. **206**(1), 283–300 (1998)
22. Levene, M., Loizou, G.: A generalisation of entity and referential integrity in relational databases. RAIRO-Theor. Inf. Appl. **35**(2), 113–127 (2001)
23. Levene, M., Loizou, G.: A Guided Tour of Relational Databases and Beyond. Springer Science & Business Media, Berlin (2012)
24. Link, S., Prade, H.: Relational database schema design for uncertain data. In: Mukhopadhyay, S., Zhai, C., Bertino, E., Crestani, F., Mostafa, J., Tang, J., Si, L., Zhou, X., Chang, Y., Li, Y., Sondhi, P. (eds.) Proceedings of the 25th ACM International on Conference on Information and Knowledge Management, CIKM 2016, Indianapolis, IN, USA, 24–28 October 2016, pp. 1211–1220. ACM (2016)
25. Makinouchi, A.: A consideration on normal form of not-necessarily-normalized relation in the relational data model. In: Proceedings of the Third International Conference on Very Large Data Bases, 6–8 October 1977, Tokyo, Japan, pp. 447–453 (1977)
26. Mannila, H., Raihä, K.: Design by example: an application of Armstrong relations. J. Comput. Syst. Sci. **33**(2), 126–141 (1986)
27. Thalheim, B.: On semantic issues connected with keys in relational databases permitting null values. Elektron. Informationsverarbeitung und Kybern. **25**(1/2), 11–20 (1989)
28. Thalheim, B.: Dependencies in Relational Databases. Teubner, Leipzig (1991)
29. Thalheim, B.: The number of keys in relational and nested relational databases. Discrete Appl. Math. **40**(2), 265–282 (1992)
30. Wei, Z., Link, S., Liu, J.: Contextual keys. Technical report 508, (2017). www.cs.auckland.ac.nz/research/groups/CDMTCS/researchreports/
31. Zaniolo, C.: Database relations with null values. J. Comput. Syst. Sci. **28**(1), 142–166 (1984)

A Comprehensive Formal Theory for Multi-level Conceptual Modeling

João Paulo A. Almeida[1(✉)], Claudenir M. Fonseca[1], and Victorio A. Carvalho[2]

[1] Ontology and Conceptual Modeling Research Group (NEMO), Federal University of Espírito Santo (UFES), Vitória, ES, Brazil
jpalmeida@ieee.org, claudenirmf@gmail.com

[2] Research Group in Applied Informatics, Informatics Department, Federal Institute of Espírito Santo (IFES), Colatina, ES, Brazil
victorio@ifes.edu.br

Abstract. Multi-level modeling extends the conventional two-level classification scheme to deal with subject domains in which classes are also considered instances of other classes. In the past, we have explored theoretical foundations for multi-level conceptual modeling and proposed an axiomatic theory for multi-level modeling dubbed MLT. MLT provides concepts for multi-level modeling along with a number of rules to guide the construction of sound multi-level conceptual models. Despite the benefits of MLT, it is still unable to deal with a number of general notions underlying conceptual models (including the notions used in its own definition). In this paper, we present an extension of MLT to deal with these limitations. The resulting theory (called MLT*) is novel in that it combines a strictly stratified theory of levels with the flexibility required to model abstract notions that defy stratification into levels such as a universal "Type" or, even more abstract notions such as "Entity" and "Thing".

Keywords: Conceptual modeling · Multi-level modeling · Metamodeling

1 Introduction

The vast majority of conceptual modeling techniques are based on notions such as "class" and "type", capturing what subject matter experts refer to as "kinds", "categories" and "sorts" in their accounts of a subject domain. In several subject domains, the categorization scheme itself is part of the subject matter, and thus experts make use of categories of categories in their accounts. For instance, considering the software development domain [15], project managers often need to plan according to the *types of tasks* to be executed during the software development project (e.g. "requirements specification", "coding"). They may also need to classify those *types of tasks* giving rise to *types of types of tasks*. In this case, "requirements specification" and "coding" could be considered as examples of "technical task types", as opposed to "management task types". Finally, during project development, they need to track the execution of individual tasks (e.g. specifying the requirements of the system X). Thus, to describe the conceptualization underlying the software development domain, one needs to

H.C. Mayr et al. (Eds.): ER 2017, LNCS 10650, pp. 280–294, 2017.
https://doi.org/10.1007/978-3-319-69904-2_23

represent entities of different (but nonetheless related) classification levels, such as *tasks (specific individual occurrences), types of tasks,* and *types of types of tasks.* Other examples of multiple classification levels come from domains such as that of organizational roles (or professional positions) [8], biological taxonomy [26] and artifact types (e.g., product types) [29].

These subject domains require us to break the two-level divide between classes and instances, admitting classes that are also instances of other classes, and suggesting that there could be a multitude of classification 'levels' or meta-levels. The need to support the representation of subject domains dealing with multiple classification levels has given rise to what has been referred to as multi-level modeling [21]. Techniques for multi-level conceptual modeling must provide modeling concepts to deal with types in various levels and the relations that may occur among them. In the last decades, several approaches for the representation of multi-level models have been worked out, including those mostly focused on multi-level modeling from a model-driven engineering perspective (e.g. [14, 23]) and those that propose modeling languages for models with multiple levels of classification (e.g. [3, 22]). These approaches embody conceptual notions that are key to the representation of multi-level models, such as the existence of entities that are simultaneously types and instances, the iterated application of instantiation across an arbitrary number of (meta) levels, the possibility of defining attributes and values at the various type levels, etc.

Despite the recent advances in multi-level modeling approaches and tools, the literature on multi-level modeling still lacks a language-independent formal theory that captures the foundational concepts underlying multi-level modeling. We believe that such a theory could facilitate the identification of the characterizing features a multi-level approach should possess, being useful to support the proposal of well-founded multi-level modeling approaches. Further, it could be used as a foundation to clarify the semantics of existing approaches as well as to relate and harmonize different approaches to multi-level modeling.

In the past, the search for such a theory has led us to propose the MLT multi-level modeling theory [10]. MLT is founded on a basic instantiation relation and characterizes the concepts of individuals and types, with types organized in 'orders' and related by instantiation. MLT has been used successfully to analyze and improve the UML support for modeling the powertype pattern [11], to uncover problems in multi-level taxonomies on the Web [6], to found an OWL vocabulary that supports the representation of multi-level vocabularies in the Semantic Web [5], and to provide conceptual foundations for dealing with types at different levels of classification both in core [8] and in foundational ontologies [9].

While the theory has been fruitful for these applications, it is unable to account for types that defy a strict stratification scheme. This rules out abstract and general types such as "Entity" and "Type" (which are instances of themselves). We have observed that these types correspond to general notions that are ubiquitous in comprehensive conceptualizations (see e.g., the core of the Semantic Web with the notion of "Resource" or "Thing" [31, 32], (Foundation) Ontologies such as UFO [16], Cyc [13], DOLCE and BFO [25] with their notions of "Entity" or "Thing", Telos [28] with the notions of "Property"). Failure to account for such types restricts the generality of the theory, which motivates us to extend it.

This paper presents MLT*, which extends MLT with a focus on improving its generality. The theory is formally defined through axiomatization in first-order logic, building up on a primitive instantiation relation. In order to account for types that defy a strict classification scheme, we introduce the notions of orderless and ordered types. We precisely define the relations that may occur between orderless and ordered types, and define rules that apply to these relations. We show that the two-level scheme and the strictly stratified schemes are special cases allowed by the theory. We further show how MLT* is general enough to account for the types that are used in its own definition. We aim to provide a theory that is *comprehensive* enough as a semantic foundation for various multi-level modeling techniques.

All definitions of MLT* have been specified and tested with the support of Alloy [19]. Alloy allows the specification of first-order logic based models and supports model simulation (model finding) and verification (model checking) through exhaustive search in finite models. The rules that arise from the definitions and axioms in MLT* have been defined as assertions and verified in Alloy[1].

This paper is further structured as follows: Sect. 2 presents requirements for a comprehensive theory for multi-level modeling; Sect. 3 presents MLT*, addressing the set of requirements defined in Sect. 2; Sect. 4 discusses the implications of the theory to the practice of multi-level conceptual modeling and finally Sect. 5 presents concluding remarks and topics for further investigation.

2 Requirements for a Comprehensive Multi-level Theory

We establish here key requirements for a theory on multi-level modeling, substantiating these requirements with sources from the literature on multi-level modeling and justifying them based on the nature of multi-level phenomena.

First of all, an essential requirement for a multi-level modeling theory is to account for *entities of multiple classification levels*, which are related through chains of instantiation between the involved entities (requirement **R1**). This means that the theory must admit entities that represent both types (class) and instances (object) simultaneously [1], diverging thereby from the traditional two-level scheme, in which classification (instantiation) relations are only admitted between classes and individuals.

The size of chains of instantiation may vary according to the nature of the phenomena being captured and according to the model purposes. Because of this, a general-purpose theory should *admit an arbitrary number of classification levels* (**R2**) (including the two-level scheme as a special case). The ability to deal with an arbitrary number of levels is identified as a key a requirement by many authors (e.g., see [13, 14]). Several examples of three and four level models are available in the literature as well as in structured data repositories such as Wikidata (in which there are more than 17,000 classes involved in multi-level taxonomies [6]).

[1] See https://github.com/nemo-ufes/mlt-ontology.

Further, in previous work, some of us have found empirical evidence to support the claim that representations capturing chains of instantiation can benefit greatly from rules for organizing entities into levels [6]. We have found that over 87% of the classes in multi-level taxonomies in Wikidata were involved in errors that could have been prevented with some support to detect the inadequate use of instantiation (and its combination with subtyping) [6]. Based on this evidence, we consider that a multi-level modeling theory *should define principles (rules) for the organization of entities into levels* (**R3**). An example of this sort of principle, which is adopted in some prominent multi-level modeling approaches, is the so-called strict metamodeling principle [1], which prescribes the arrangement of elements into levels mandating that elements of a level only instantiate elements of the level immediately above.

While these principles are intended to guide the modeler in producing sound models, they should not obstruct the representation of genuine multi-level phenomena. The strict metamodeling principle, for example, excludes from the domain of enquiry abstract notions such as a universal "Type" or, an even more abstract notion such as "Thing". This is because their instances may be related in chains of instantiation, conflicting with the stratification imposed by the principle. Given that these general notions are ubiquitous in comprehensive conceptualizations (see e.g., the core of the Semantic Web with the notion of "Resource" or "Thing" [31, 32], (Foundation) Ontologies such as UFO [16], Cyc [13], DOLCE and BFO [25] with their notions of "Entity" or "Thing", Telos [28] with the notions of "Property"), we conclude that a comprehensive multi-level modeling theory should *admit types that defy a strictly stratified classification scheme* (**R4**) (with the general notion of "type" or "class" and the universal notion of "entity" or "thing" as paradigmatic special cases).

Finally, an important characteristic of domains spanning multiple levels of classification is that there are domain rules that apply to the instantiation of types of different levels. For example, in a conceptual model encompassing the notions of "Dog Breed" and "Dog", all instances of "Dog Breed" (e.g. "Collie" and "Beagle") are types whose instances are instances of "Dog". Hence, in this setting, instances of "Dog Breed" specialize "Dog". Given the recurrence of this kind of scenario [24], which in the past motivated the powertype pattern [30], a comprehensive multi-level modeling theory should be able *to account for the rules that govern the instantiation of related types at different levels* (**R5**).

3 MLT*: A Theory for Multi-level Modeling

This section presents MLT* showing how it satisfies the requirements defined in Sect. 2. Section 3.1 describes basic notions of the theory (in order to satisfy requirements R1 and R2); Sect. 3.2 discusses how types can be organized into strictly stratified levels (addressing R3); Sect. 3.3 accounts for types that defy the rigid stratification scheme (addressing R4); finally, Sect. 3.4 discusses the various structural relations that can be established between types (addressing R5). Throughout the sections we discuss the rules that arise from the formalization of the theory.

3.1 Basic Notions

The notions of *type* and *individual* are central for our multi-level modeling theory. *Types* are predicative entities that can possibly be applied to a multitude of entities (including types themselves). Particular entities, which are not types, are considered *individuals*. Each type is characterized by an *intension, which* is used to judge whether the type applies to an entity (e.g., whether something is a Person, a Dog, a Chair) (it is also called *principle of application* in [16]). If the intension of a type *t* applies to an entity *e* then it is said that *e is an instance of t.* Thus, the *instance of* relation (or *instantiation* relation) maps a type to the entities that fall under the type. The set of instances of a type is called the *extension* of the type [17]. We assume that the theory is only concerned with types with non-trivially false intensions, i.e., with types that have possible instances in the scope of the conceptualization being considered.

MLT* is formalized in first-order logic, quantifying over all possible individuals and types in a subject domain. The theory is built up from the instantiation relation, which is formally represented by a binary predicate iof(e, t) that holds if an entity e is instance of an entity t (denoting a type). For instance, the proposition iof (John, Person) denotes the fact that "John" is an instance of the type "Person". Note that here we do not account for modal or temporal aspects of instantiation; see [10] for a treatment of modal aspects where instantiation is 'world-indexed' and represented with a ternary predicate.

Using the iof predicate, we can define the ground notion of *individual* (D1). An entity is an individual iff it does not possibly play the role of type in instantiation relations. Conversely, an entity is a type iff it plays the role of type in instantiation relations, i.e., if there is some (possible) entity which instantiates it (D2). Definitions D1 and D2 create a dichotomy with all elements in the domain of quantification being considered either types or individuals.

$$\forall x(\text{individual}(x) \leftrightarrow \neg\exists y(\text{iof}(y,x))) \tag{D1}$$

$$\forall x(\text{type}(x) \leftrightarrow \exists y(\text{iof}(y,x))) \tag{D2}$$

We assume that all types are ultimately grounded on individuals (A1). Thus the transitive closure of the instantiation relation (iof'), always leads us from a type to one or more individuals:

$$\forall t(\text{type}(t) \rightarrow \exists x(\text{individual}(x) \wedge \text{iof}'(x,t))) \tag{A1}$$

Note that the definitions so far allow us to satisfy R1, as we place no restrictions on the kinds of entities that may instantiate a type. Thus, the theory would admit a model such as the one illustrated in Fig. 1. The figure depicts a chain of instantiation, with "Man" and "Woman" instantiating "PersonTypeByGender", and "John" and "Bob" instantiating "Man", while "Ana" instantiates "Woman". We use a notation inspired in the class and object notations of UML, and we use dashed arrows to represent relations that hold between the elements, with labels to denote the relation that applies (in this case *instance of*). This notation is used in all further diagrams in this paper. It is important to highlight here that our focus is not on the syntax of a multi-level modeling language and we use these diagrams to illustrate the concepts intuitively. Further, no constraint is placed on the size of instantiation chains, and thus, the theory would admit a model such as the one illustrated in Fig. 2 (satisfying R2).

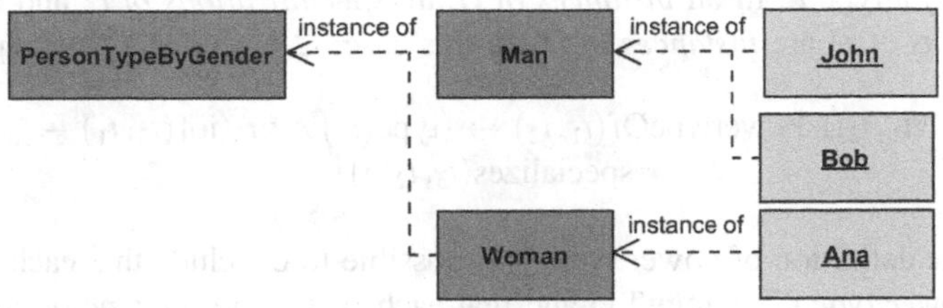

Fig. 1. An instantiation chain, where "Man" and "Woman" are both instances and classes.

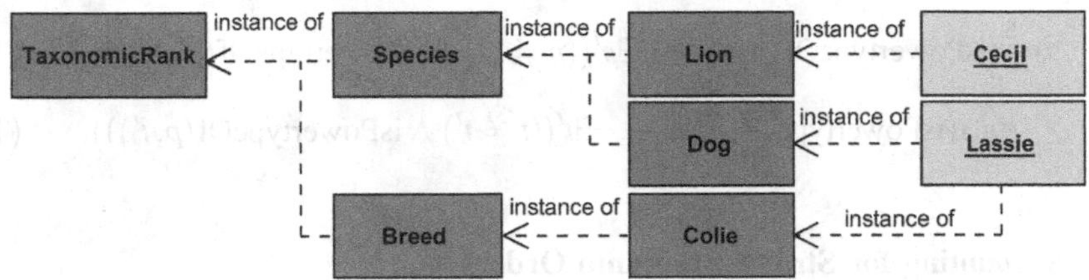

Fig. 2. A four-level instantiation chain with representing a biological domain.

We define some basic structural relations, starting with the ordinary specialization between types. A type *t specializes* another type *t'* iff in all possible instances of *t* are also instances of *t'*. According to this definition every type *specializes* itself. Since this may be undesired in some contexts, we define the *proper specialization* relation in which *t proper specializes t'* iff *t specializes t'* and *t* is different from *t'*.

$$\forall t_1, t_2(\text{specializes}(t_1, t_2) \leftrightarrow (\text{type}(t_1) \wedge \forall e(\text{iof}(e, t_1) \rightarrow \text{iof}(e, t_2)))) \quad \text{(D3)}$$

$$\forall t_1, t_2(\text{properSpecializes}(t_1, t_2) \leftrightarrow (\text{specializes}(t_1, t_2) \wedge \neg(t_1 = t_2))) \quad \text{(D4)}$$

We consider two types equal iff the sets of all their possible instances are the same [10][2]. This definition of equality only applies to elements which are not *individuals*, hence the 'guard' conditions on the left-hand side of the implication:

$$\forall t_1, t_2((\text{type}(t_1) \wedge \text{type}(t_2)) \rightarrow (t_1 = t_2) \leftrightarrow \forall x(\text{iof}(x, t_1) \leftrightarrow \text{iof}(x, t_2))) \quad \text{(D5)}$$

Building up on the specialization definition, we can now address the notion of powertype. Here we employ the seminal notion proposed by Cardelli [7]. According to

[2] See [10] for a refinement of identity and specialization concerning modal distinctions.

[7], the same way specializations are intuitively analogous to subsets, *power types* can be intuitively understood as powersets. The powerset of a set A, is the set whose elements are **all** possible subsets of A including the empty set and A itself. Thus, "if A is a type, then Power(A) is the type whose elements are **all** the subtypes of A" (including A itself) [7]. Following Cardelli's definition, we define that a type *t1 is power type of* a type *t2* iff all *instances of t1* are *specializations of t2* and all possible *specializations of t2* are *instances of t1*. In this case, *t2* is said the base type of *t1*:

$$\forall t_1, t_2(\text{isPowertypeOf}(t_1, t_2) \leftrightarrow (\text{type}(t_1) \land \forall t_3(\text{iof}(t_3, t_1) \leftrightarrow \text{specializes}(t_3, t_2)))) \tag{D6}$$

Given the definition of power type, it is possible to conclude that each type has at most one *power type* (Theorem T1) and that each *type* is *power type of*, at most, one other type (Theorem T2). (These theorems are proved in [10], which suggests a concrete syntactic constraint for a multi-level model: only one higher-order type can be linked to a base type through the *is power type of* relation.).

$$\forall p, t(\text{isPowertypeOf}(p, t) \rightarrow \neg\exists p'((p \neq p') \land \text{isPowertypeOf}(p', t))) \tag{T1}$$

$$\forall p, t(\text{isPowertypeOf}(p, t) \rightarrow \neg\exists t'((t \neq t') \land \text{isPowertypeOf}(p, t'))) \tag{T2}$$

3.2 Accounting for Stratification into Orders

Note that, thus far, the theory does not impose a principle of organization for the entities into (strictly stratified) 'levels'. In order to account for such kinds of principles, we use the notion of type order. Types whose instances are individuals are called *first-order types*. Types whose instances are *first-order types* are called *second-order types*. Those types whose extensions are composed of *second-order types* are called *third-order types*, and so on.

Types that follow this strictly ordered scheme are called *ordered* types. To define such a scheme formally, we define a notion of 'basic type'. A basic type is the most abstract type in its type order. For example, "Individual" is a basic type since it is the most abstract of all first-order types, classifying all instances of first-order types, i.e., all possible individuals. We define the constant "Individual" as follows:

$$\forall t((t = \text{Individual}) \leftrightarrow \forall x(\text{individual}(x) \leftrightarrow \text{iof}(x, t))) \tag{A2}$$

Like "Individual", there are basic types for each subsequently higher order, i.e., every instance of the basic type of an order i ($i > 1$) specialize the basic type of the order immediately below ($i - 1$). This is formalized by D7. (Note that i is only used to improve the intuition in the definition, and is not formally a variable).

$$\forall b_i(\text{basictype}(b_i) \leftrightarrow (\text{type}(b_i) \land ((\forall x(\text{individual}(x) \leftrightarrow \text{iof}(x, b_i)) \lor \exists b_{i-1}(\text{basictype}(b_{i-1}) \land \forall t_{i-1}(\text{specialize}(t_{i-1}, b_{i-1}) \leftrightarrow \text{iof}(t_{i-1}, b_i)))))) \tag{D7}$$

A consequence of this definition of basic type is that the basic type of an order i ($i > 1$) is the *powertype* of the basic type at the order immediately below ($i - 1$), showing that the basic types are formed by the cascaded application of the powertype pattern. This is reflected in the following theorem (T3), which is the result of applying D6 to D7:

$$\forall b_i(\text{basictype}(b_i) \leftrightarrow (\forall x(\text{individual}(x) \leftrightarrow \text{iof}(x, b_i)) \vee \exists b_{i-1}(\text{basictype}(b_{i-1}) \wedge \text{isPowertypeOf}(b_i, b_{i-1})))) \quad \text{(T3)}$$

Every ordered type that is not a basic type (e.g., a domain type) is an instance of one of the basic higher-order types (e.g., "1stOT", "2ndOT"), and, at the same time proper specializes the basic type at the immediately lower level (respectively, "Individual" and "1stOT"). Figure 3 illustrates this pattern. Since "Person" applies to individuals, it is instance of "1stOT" and proper specializes "Individual". The instances of "PersonTypeByGender" are specializations of "Person" (e.g. "Man" and "Woman"). Thus, "PersonTypeByGender" is instance of "2ndOT" and proper specializes "1stOT".

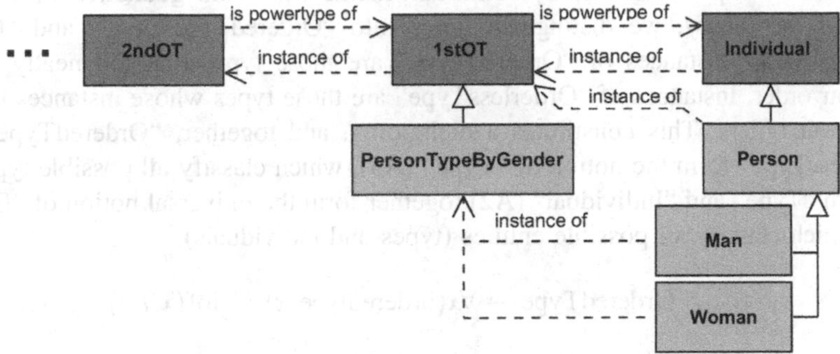

Fig. 3. Illustrating an important basic pattern of MLT and its intra-level structural relations.

Note that, the ellipsis in the left-hand side of the figure indicates that the theory admits an unbound number of higher-order basic types. Nevertheless, we have been careful not to necessitate the existence of such types in the theory. This means that the theory has finite models, and thus can be subject to analysis using a finite model checker/finder such as Alloy, which we have employed for verification of all theorems discussed here.

Having defined the structure of basic types we can define ordered type as a type that specializes one of the basic types (D8). Conversely, we can define *orderless types* as in D9.

$$\forall x(\text{orderedtype}(x) \leftrightarrow \exists b(\text{basictype}(b) \wedge \text{specializes}(x, b))) \quad \text{(D8)}$$

$$\forall x(\text{orderlesstype}(x) \leftrightarrow \text{type}(x) \wedge \neg\text{orderedtype}(x)) \quad \text{(D9)}$$

We can account now for a strictly stratified scheme. In this case, it would suffice to add an axiom stating that all types are ordered types, which would rule out types whose instances belong to different orders. The stratified scheme is thus a restriction of the more general theory we have, which admits *orderless types*.

Moreover, we can see that the theory can be further constrained to account for the two-level scheme as a particular case. For a two-level theory it would suffice to add to the strictly stratified scheme an axiom stating that there is a unique basic type (which would be "Individual").

3.3 Beyond Strictly Stratified Types

While a strictly stratified approach imposes a useful principle of organization for entities in multi-level models, it rules out types whose instances transcend this strict structure, i.e., types that have instances belonging to different levels or strata. For example, consider the type whose instances are all types admitted ("Type"). This type itself defies stratification into orders, since its instances are types at various different orders (e.g., "Lion", "Species", "Taxonomic Rank", etc.).

In order to capture the strictly stratified scheme while still guaranteeing the generality of the theory, we distinguish types into "OrderedType" (A3) and "OrderlessType" (A4). Instances of "OrderedType" are those types that fall neatly into a particular order. Instances of "OrderlessType" are those types whose instances belong to different orders. This constitutes a dichotomy, and together, "OrderedType" and "OrderlessType" form the notion of "Type" (A5), which classify all possible types. In their turn "Type" and "Individual" (A2) together form the universal notion of "Entity" (A6), which classify all possible entities (types and individuals).

$$\forall t(t = \text{OrderedType} \leftrightarrow \forall x(\text{orderedtype}(x) \leftrightarrow \text{iof}(x,t))) \quad \text{(A3)}$$

$$\forall t(t = \text{OrderlessType} \leftrightarrow \forall x(\text{orderlesstype}(x) \leftrightarrow \text{iof}(x,t))) \quad \text{(A4)}$$

$$\forall t((t = \text{Type}) \leftrightarrow \forall x(\text{type}(x) \leftrightarrow \text{iof}(x,t))) \quad \text{(A5)}$$

$$\forall t(t = \text{Entity} \leftrightarrow \forall x(\text{iof}(x,t))) \quad \text{(A6)}$$

The classification scheme formed by MLT* is presented in Fig. 4. A number of interesting observations can be made about the top-layer of MLT*. First of all, MLT*, differently from MLT, is able to account for the types used in its definition. All entities admitted are instances of "Entity", including all possible types and all possible individuals. All possible types are instances of "Type" and ultimately specializations of "Entity" (since their instances are entities). "Type" is thus the *powertype of* "Entity". All elements added in MLT* are instances of "OrderlessType", including (curiously) "OrderedType" (since its instances are types at different orders).

The instantiation relation has the following logical properties as a consequence of the definitions and axioms of the theory: whenever instantiation involves solely ordered types, it is *irreflexive*, *antissymetric* and *antitransitive*, leading to a strict stratification of types. When instantiation involves any orderless types, none of these properties can

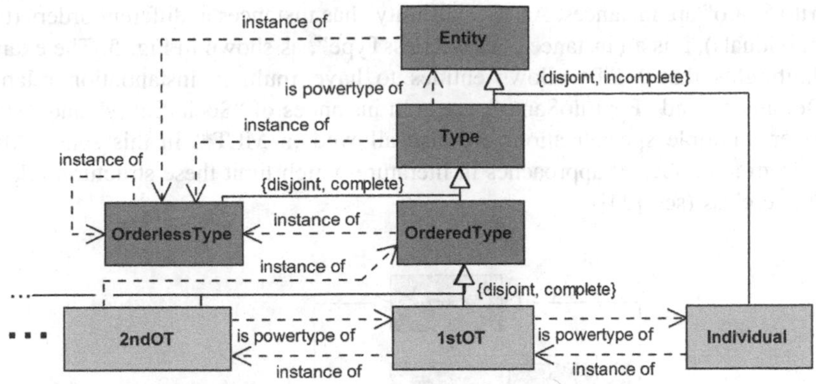

Fig. 4. MLT* classification scheme.

be asserted, as there are situations in which it is *reflexive* (e.g., "Type" is instance of itself), *symmetric* (e.g., "Entity" is instance of "Type" and vice-versa) as well as *transitive* (e.g., "OrderedType" is instance of "Type" which is instance of "Entity" and "OrderedType" is also instance of "Entity"). Further, an orderless type is never an instance of an ordered type. These characteristics of instantiation can be used to rule out models that violate the theory.

Table 1 summarizes the rules that concern which types of entities may be related through structural relations along with the logical properties of these relations.

Table 1. Summary of constraints on MLT* relations.

Relation (t → t')	Domain	Range	Constraint	Properties
specializes(t, t')	Orderless	Orderless	if *t* and *t'* are ordered types, they must be at the same type order	Reflexive, antissymetric, transitive
	Ordered	Orderless		
	Ordered	Ordered		
properSpecializes(t, t')	Orderless	Orderless		Irreflexive, antissymetric, transitive
	Ordered	Orderless		
	Ordered	Ordered		
isPowertypeOf(t, t')	Orderless	Orderless	*t* cannot be a first-order type if *t* and *t'* are ordered types, *t* must be at a type order immediately above the order of *t'*	Irreflexive, antissymetric, antitransitive
	Ordered	Ordered		

The notion of "Orderless Type" is useful not only for the domain-independent entities forming MLT*, but also for general notions in specific subject domains. Consider, for example, the domain of social entities in which a "Social Entity" is defined as an entity that is created by a social normative act. Instances of "Social Entity" include specific states of Brazil (individuals) such as "Rio de Janeiro" and "Espírito Santo", but also the first-order type "State" of which "Rio de Janeiro" and

"Espírito Santo" are instances. As "SocialEntity" has instances at different orders (types and individuals), it is an instance of "OrderlessType", as shown in Fig. 5. The example also highlights that MLT* allows entities to have multiple instantiation relations. "RioDeJaneiro" and "EspíritoSanto", are both instances of "SocialEntity" and "State". Moreover, multiple specializations are also allowed in MLT*. In this sense, MLT* differs from a number of approaches in literature which limit these structural relations to a single class (see [24]).

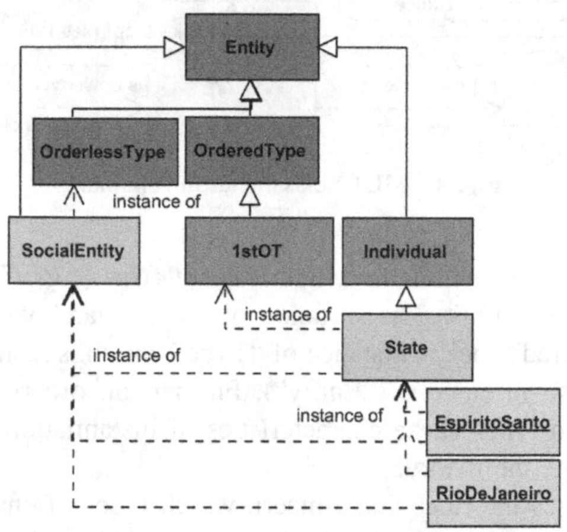

Fig. 5. Example of orderless type in domain model.

The same mechanism that allows us to model *bona fide* self-instantiating types such as "Entity" and "Type" would permit a modeler to introduce paradoxical types, such as the type of all types that are not self-instantiated (the so-called Russellian property, due to Russell [18]). This type is paradoxical since it is both an instance and not an instance of itself. Note that this possibility does not threaten the overall consistency of the theory. This is because we do not assume in MLT* that there are types corresponding to any expressible unifying condition (i.e., we do not assume that given an arbitrary logical condition F, we can define the type with extension $[x \mid F(x)]$). Types here, instead, are explicitly recognized entities describing intentionally identified properties shared by their instances. Lacking the ability to prove or introduce the existence of types in this sense, we are under no threat of such paradoxes [27].

3.4 Cross-Level Structural Relations

So far, the only *cross-level structural relations* we have considered is Cardelli's power type relation. Another definition of *power type* that has had great influence in the literature was proposed by Odell [30]. In order to satisfy R5, and account for the variations of the power type pattern in the literature, MLT* defines the categorization cross-level relation based on Odell's notion power type.

A type *t categorizes* a type *t'* iff all instances of *t* are proper specializations of *t'*. Note that, differently from the *is powertype of* relation (due to Cardelli), *t'* is not an instance of *t*, and further not all possible specializations of *t'* are instances of *t*. For instance, “EmployeeType” (with instances “Manager” and “Researcher”) *categorizes* “Person”, but is not the *powertype* of “Person”, since there are specializations of “Person” that are not instances of “EmployeeType” (“Child” and “Adult” for example).

MLT* also defines some variations of the categorization relation. A type *t completely categorizes* a type *t'* iff every instance of *t'* is instance of at least one instance of *t*. Moreover, a type *t disjointly categorizes* a type *t'* iff every instance of *t'* is instance of at most one instance of *t*. Further, *t partitions t'* iff every instance of *t'* is instance of exactly one instance of *t*. For example, “PersonTypeByGender” *partitions* “Person” into “Man” and “Woman”, and thus each instance of “Person” is either a “Man” or a “Woman” and not both. “EmployeeType” incompletely *categorizes* “Person”, and thus there are persons that are not instances of “Manager”, “Researcher” (or any other possible instance of “EmployeeType”). This kind of constraint is usually represented in UML through a generalization set, see [10] for a detailed comparison.

Rules concerning the types of entities that may be related through the variations of categorization and the logical properties of these relations are summarized in Table 2.

Table 2. Summary of constraints on MLT* categorization relations.

Relation (t → t')	Domain	Range	Constraint	Properties
categorizes(t, t') *disjointlyCategorizes(t, t')*	Orderless	Orderless	*t* cannot be a first-order type if *t* and *t'* are ordered types, *t* must be at a type order immediately above the order of *t'*	Irreflexive, antissymetric, nontransitive
	Ordered	Orderless		
	Ordered	Ordered		
completelyCategorizes(t, t') *partitions(t, t')*	Orderless	Orderless		Irreflexive, antissymetric, antitransitive
	Ordered	Ordered		

4 Implications for Multi-level Modeling Approaches

We have observed in the literature that multi-level approaches often opt for one of two extremes: (i) to define relations that support the representation of instantiation chains, without necessarily binding a type to some level (what is referred to as a level-blind approach in [4], e.g., Kernel [12]), or (ii) to consider all classes to be strictly stratified. Some approaches that opt for (i) are able to account for all types which can be admitted by MLT*, however, they fail on providing rules to guide the use of the various structural relations (including instantiation). As shown in [6], this lack of guidance has serious consequences for the quality of the resulting representation. Approaches that opt for the other end of the spectrum (ii), lack support to a number of important abstract notions, including those very general notions that are used to articulate multi-level domains (such as “types”, “clabjects”, “entities”). This is the case of Melanee [3] and MetaDepth [22]. The combination of both approaches in our theory places it in a unique position in multi-level modeling approaches.

A few other knowledge representation approaches (such as Telos [20] and Cyc [13]) have, like MLT*, drawn distinctions between orderless and ordered types. Differently from MLT*, however, Telos does not provide rules for the various structural relations, including instantiation and specialization. (Mechanisms to address R5 in Telos were added with the notion of MGI in Deeptelos [21]). In its turn, Cyc, which employs a conceptual architecture for types that is most similar to MLT*'s top layer, includes rules for instantiation and specialization [13]. However, it does not address the cross-level relations (and associated rules) we discuss here.

MLT* shows that there is no dilemma between requirements R3 (to define principles for the organization of entities into levels) and R4 (to admit types that defy a strictly stratified scheme). It suggests the possibility of extending existing multi-level approaches that currently meet R3 but fail to meet R4 in order to meet both. For example, extensions of Melanee and MetaDepth could be worked out to allow some kind of selective stratification, beyond what is currently supported with the so-called star potency, in order to fully enable the representation of orderless types.

Further, since MLT* reveals that there is no inconsistency between powertype and clabject-based approaches, we consider it possible to extend clabject-based approaches such as Melanee and MetaDepth to support the representation of MLT* cross-level relations (in order to satisfy R5). Finally, we consider it possible to extend Deeptelos by including variations of the so-called MGI mechanism to capture the MLT* cross-level relations (and thereby fully address R5 in Deeptelos).

5 Conclusions and Future Work

In this paper, we have proposed a multi-level modeling theory that can account for the classification scheme underlying current multi-level modeling approaches. We have aimed for a simple but comprehensive approach in that it encompasses stratified and non-stratified schemes, and is able to accommodate the variations for the powertype pattern in the literature. We should stress that it is not our intention in this paper to propose a multi-level language, and that our use of a notation inspired in UML has been solely illustrative. As discussed in [16], a reference theory can be used to inform the revision and redesign of a modeling language, not only through the identification of semantic overload, construct deficit, construct excess and construct redundancy, but also through the definition of modeling patterns and semantically-motivated syntactic constraints. Thus, a natural application for MLT* is to inform the design of a well-founded multi-level conceptual modeling language or to promote the redesign of a language such as UML into a multi-level modeling language. This is the subject of ongoing research which will be reported soon.

Due to space limitations, we have not been able to address here the use of features (attributes and associations). In a multi-level context, since types are also instances, feature assignment in types becomes relevant, along with relations between features across different levels. Some of us have already addressed this issue previously [10] using the notion of 'regularity feature' in MLT, however, revisiting the notion in light of MLT* is still the subject of further investigation. This is particularly important to account for the deep characterization mechanisms in potency-based approaches [2].

Acknowledgements. This research is funded by CNPq (grants numbers 311313/2014-0, 461777/2014-2 and 407235/2017-5), CAPES (23038.028816/2016-41) and FAPES (69382549). Claudenir M. Fonseca is funded by CAPES. We thank Giancarlo Guizzardi for fruitful discussions in topics related to this paper.

References

1. Atkinson, C., Kühne, T.: Meta-level independent modelling. In: International Workshop on Model Engineering at 14th European Conference on Object-Oriented Programming, pp. 1–4 (2000)
2. Atkinson, C., Kühne, T.: Reducing accidental complexity in domain models. Softw. Syst. Model. **7**, 345–359 (2008)
3. Atkinson, C., Gerbig, R.: Melanie: multi-level modeling and ontology engineering environment. In: Proceedings of the 2nd International Master Class on MDE Modeling Wizards. ACM (2012)
4. Atkinson, C., Gerbig, R., Kühne, T.: Comparing multi-level modeling approaches. In: Proceedings of the 1st International Workshop on Multi-Level Modelling (2014)
5. Brasileiro, F., Almeida, J.P.A., Carvalho, V.A., Guizzardi, G.: Expressive multi-level modeling for the semantic web. In: Groth, P., Simperl, E., Gray, A., Sabou, M., Krötzsch, M., Lecue, F., Flöck, F., Gil, Y. (eds.) ISWC 2016 Part I. LNCS, vol. 9981, pp. 53–69. Springer, Cham (2016). doi:10.1007/978-3-319-46523-4_4
6. Brasileiro, F., Almeida, J.P.A., Carvalho, V.A., Guizzardi, G.: Applying a multi-level modeling theory to assess taxonomic hierarchies in Wikidata. In: Proceedings of the Wiki Workshop 2016 at 25th International Conference on Companion on World Wide Web, pp. 975–980 (2016)
7. Cardelli, L.: Structural subtyping and the notion of power type. In: Proceedings of the 15th ACM Symposium of Principles of Programming Languages, pp. 70–79 (1988)
8. Carvalho, V.A., Almeida, J.P.A.: A semantic foundation for organizational structures: a multi-level approach. IEEE EDOC **2015**, 50–59 (2015)
9. Carvalho, V.A., Almeida, J.P.A., Fonseca, C.M., Guizzardi, G.: Extending the foundations of ontology-based conceptual modeling with a multi-level theory. In: Johannesson, P., Lee, M.L., Liddle, S.W., Opdahl, A.L., López, Ó.P. (eds.) ER 2015. LNCS, vol. 9381, pp. 119–133. Springer, Cham (2015). doi:10.1007/978-3-319-25264-3_9
10. Carvalho, V.A., Almeida, J.P.A.: Towards a well-founded theory for multi-level conceptual modeling. Softw. Syst. Model. **10**, 1–27 (2016). Springer
11. Carvalho, V.A., Almeida, J.P.A., Guizzardi, G.: Using a well-founded multi-level theory to support the analysis and representation of the powertype pattern in conceptual modeling. In: Nurcan, S., Soffer, P., Bajec, M., Eder, J. (eds.) CAiSE 2016. LNCS, vol. 9694, pp. 309–324. Springer, Cham (2016). doi:10.1007/978-3-319-39696-5_19
12. Clark, T., Gonzalez-Perez, C., Henderson-Sellers, B.: A foundation for multi-level modelling. In: Proceedings of Workshop on Multi-Level Modelling, MODELS, pp. 43–52 (2014)
13. Foxvog, D.: Instances of instances modeled via higher-order classes. In: 28th German Conference on AI Foundational Aspects of Ontologies (FOnt 2005), pp. 46–54 (2005)
14. Frank, U.: Multilevel modeling. Bus. Inf. Syst. Eng. **6**, 319–337 (2014)
15. Gonzalez-Perez, C., Henderson-Sellers, B.: A powertype-based metamodelling framework. Softw. Syst. Model. **5**, 72–90 (2006)

16. Guizzardi, G.: Ontological Foundations for Structural Conceptual Models. University of Twente, Enschede (2005)
17. Henderson-Sellers, B.: On the Mathematics of Modeling, Metamodelling, Ontologies and Modelling Languages. Springer, Heidelberg (2012)
18. Irvine, A.D., Deutsch, H.: Russell's paradox. In: The Stanford Encyclopedia of Philosophy (2016). https://plato.stanford.edu/archives/win2016/entries/russell-paradox/
19. Jackson, D.: Software Abstractions: Logic, Language and Analysis. The MIT Press, Cambridge (2006)
20. Jarke, M., et al.: ConceptBase – a deductive object base for meta data management. J. Intell. Inf. Syst. **4**, 167–192 (1995)
21. Jeusfeld, M.A., Neumayr, B.: DeepTelos: multi-level modeling with most general instances. In: Comyn-Wattiau, I., Tanaka, K., Song, I.-Y., Yamamoto, S., Saeki, M. (eds.) ER 2016. LNCS, vol. 9974, pp. 198–211. Springer, Cham (2016). doi:10.1007/978-3-319-46397-1_15
22. de Lara, J., Guerra, E.: Deep meta-modelling with MetaDepth. In: Proceedings of the 48th International Conference, TOOLS 2010, Málaga, Spain (2010)
23. de Lara, J., et al.: Extending deep meta-modelling for practical model-driven engineering. Comput. J. **57**(1), 36–58 (2014)
24. de Lara, J., Guerra, E., Cuadrado, J.S.: When and how to use multilevel modelling. ACM Trans. Softw. Eng. Methodol. **24**, 1–46 (2014)
25. Masolo, C., Borgo, S., Gangemi, A., Guarino, N., Oltramari, A.: Ontology library. In: WonderWeb Deliverable D18 (2003)
26. Mayr, E.: The Growth of Biological Thought: Diversity, Evolution, and Inheritance. The Belknap Press, Cambridge (1982)
27. Menzel, C.: Knowledge representation, the world wide web, and the evolution of logic. Synthese **182**, 269–295 (2011)
28. Mylopoulos, J., et al.: Telos: representing knowledge about information systems. ACM Trans. Inf. Syst. (TOIS) **8**, 325–362 (1990)
29. Neumayr, B., Grün, K., Schrefl, M.: Multi-level domain modeling with M-objects and M-relationships. In: Proceedings of 6th Asia-Pacific Conf. Conceptual Modeling, New Zealand (2009)
30. Odell, J.: Power types. J. Object-Oriented Program. **7**(2), 8–12 (1994)
31. W3C: RDF Schema 1.1 (2014). https://www.w3.org/TR/2014/REC-rdf-schema-20140225/
32. W3C: OWL 2 Web Ontology Language-Document Overview (Second Edition) (2012). https://www.w3.org/TR/2012/REC-owl2-syntax-20121211

Alignment-Based Trace Clustering

Thomas Chatain[1(✉)], Josep Carmona[2], and Boudewijn van Dongen[3]

[1] LSV, ENS Paris-Saclay, CNRS, Inria, Cachan, France
chatain@lsv.ens-cachan.fr
[2] Universitat Politècnica de Catalunya, Barcelona, Spain
jcarmona@cs.upc.edu
[3] Eindhoven University of Technology, Eindhoven, The Netherlands
b.f.v.dongen@tue.nl

Abstract. A novel method to cluster event log traces is presented in this paper. In contrast to the approaches in the literature, the clustering approach of this paper assumes an additional input: a process model that describes the current process. The core idea of the algorithm is to use model traces as centroids of the clusters detected, computed from a generalization of the notion of *alignment*. This way, model explanations of observed behavior are the driving force to compute the clusters, instead of current model agnostic approaches, e.g., which group log traces merely on their vector-space similarity. We believe alignment-based trace clustering provides results more useful for stakeholders. Moreover, in case of *log incompleteness*, *noisy logs* or *concept drift*, they can be more robust for dealing with highly deviating traces. The technique of this paper can be combined with any clustering technique to provide model explanations to the clusters computed. The proposed technique relies on encoding the individual alignment problems into the (pseudo-)Boolean domain, and has been implemented in our tool DARKSIDER that uses an open-source solver.

1 Introduction

The ubiquity of digital data has made organizations to become more than ever data-oriented. This has a clear implication on the way decisions are taken in an organization, where nowadays an unprecedent focus is put to the evidences hidden in the data. *Process mining* is an emerging field which focuses on analyzing *event logs* which contain the data corresponding to process executions. Process mining techniques focus on discovering, analyzing and enhancing evidence-based process models [1].

Trace clustering has been used as a method to partition event logs in a way that more homogeneous sublogs are obtained, with the hope that process discovery techniques will perform better on the sublogs than if applied to the original log [1]. Several techniques have been proposed in the last decade for trace clustering [2–8]. They can be partitioned into *vector space approaches* [2,4], *context aware approaches* [5,6] and *model-based approaches* [3,7,8].

H.C. Mayr et al. (Eds.): ER 2017, LNCS 10650, pp. 295–308, 2017.
https://doi.org/10.1007/978-3-319-69904-2_24

All the aforementioned clustering algorithms consider only the event log as input, and use different internal representations for producing the clusters.

We present a different view on clustering event log traces, by assuming that a process model exists. This assumption is realistic in many contexts, e.g., in *Process-Aware Information Systems* (PAIS), process models are often available [9]. Notice that due to the evolving nature of processes, this assumption by no means invalidates the motivation of this work: processes in a organization evolve and/or change frequently, and therefore process mining (and consequently, clustering) techniques may be very useful to be aligned with the reality, even if a process model exists.

Most of the aforementioned algorithms for trace clustering are centroid-based, i.e., for each cluster a representative (often a vector of features) is the reference of the cluster when computing distances. Furthermore, in some algorithms this representative may not be one of the log traces (e.g., if applying *k-means*). By using these model agnostic approaches, the grouping of event log traces may have no relation at all with the executions of the underlying process.

The approach we propose in this paper puts the available process model as a first citizen in trace clustering: clusters computed have as centroid a process model execution. This way, even in case of deviations, incomplete or noisy traces, or even drifts in the process model (e.g., dealing with the process of winter sales, while the traces correspond to summer sales), a process explanation of the traces in each cluster is available, so that stakeholders can relate them more reliably to the underlying process.

The clustering approach of this paper has as core operation the novel concept of *multi-alignments*, which is also a contribution of the paper. Multi-alignments are a generalization of the notion of *alignments* [10]. Intuitively, given a trace representing a real process execution, an optimal alignment provides the best trace the process model can provide to reproduce the observed behavior. Then observed and model traces are rendered in a two-row matrix denoting the synchronous/asynchronous moves between individual activities of model and log, respectively. Multi-alignments generalize alignments in that not one but a collection of observed traces is considered, while still the model produces a single trace that globally aligns well (i.e., its at minimal global distance) with the observed traces. Multi-alignments are shown graphically as an $(n+1)$-row matrix, where the first n rows correspond to the observed traces, and the $n+1$ row denotes the model trace. An example of multi-alignment for four observed traces and a model with behavior according to the regular expression[1] $A; ((B1; C1)||(B2; C2)||(B3; C3)); D$ is shown in Fig. 1.

The clustering approach of this paper is guided by the computation of multi-alignments. More specifically, clusters in our algorithm are multi-alignments. Informally, given a threshold distance, the approach produces a set of multi-alignments that covers (if possible) the set of traces in the event log. Several variations of the initial algorithm proposed in this paper can be envisioned as

[1] Operators ; and || denote sequential and parallel composition, respectively.

A	$B1$				$C1$	$B2$	$C2$	$B3$	$C3$					D	trace 1
A		$B2$	$C2$	$B1$	$C1$			$B3$	$C3$					D	trace 2
A								$B3$	$C3$	$B1$	$C1$	$B2$	$C2$	D	trace 3
A	$B1$	$B2$	$C2$		$C1$			$B3$	$C3$					D	trace 4
A	$B1$	$B2$	$C2$		$C1$			$B3$	$C3$					D	model trace

Fig. 1. A model trace which is an optimal multi-alignment for four log traces.

future work, e.g., hierarchical or density based, or which allow rising the given distance to guarantee a full covering of the traces in the event log.

The paper is organized as follows: Sect. 2 provides the necessary background for the understanding of the paper. Then in Sect. 3 the formal description and algorithmic computation of multi-alignments is provided. The overall method for alignment-based clustering is presented in Sect. 4. The evaluation of the techniques is reported in Sect. 5. Finally, Sect. 6 concludes the paper and provides lines for future research.

2 Preliminaries

2.1 Petri Nets

Definition 1 ((Labeled) Petri Net System). *A* labeled Petri net system *(or simply* Petri net*) [11] is a tuple $N = \langle P, T, \mathcal{F}, m_\bot, m_\top, \Sigma, \lambda\rangle$, where P is the set of places, T is the set of transitions (with $P \cap T = \emptyset$), $\mathcal{F} \subseteq (P \times T) \cup (T \times P)$ is the flow relation, $m_\bot$ is the initial marking, $m_\top$ is the final marking, Σ is an alphabet of actions and $\lambda : T \to \Sigma$ labels every transition by an action.*

A marking is an assignment of a non-negative integer to each place. If k is assigned to place p by marking m (denoted $m(p) = k$), we say that p is marked with k tokens. Given a node $x \in P \cup T$, we define its pre-set ${}^\bullet x \stackrel{\text{def}}{=} \{y \in P \cup T \mid (x, y) \in F\}$ and its post-set $x^\bullet \stackrel{\text{def}}{=} \{y \in P \cup T \mid (y, x) \in F\}$.

A transition t is *enabled* in a marking m when all places in ${}^\bullet t$ are marked. When a transition t is enabled, it can *fire* by removing a token from each place in ${}^\bullet t$ and putting a token to each place in $t^\bullet$. A marking m' is *reachable* from m if there is a sequence of firings $\langle t_1 \dots t_n\rangle$ that transforms m into m', denoted by $m[t_1 \dots t_n\rangle m'$. A firing sequence $u = \langle t_1 \dots t_n\rangle$ is called a *run* if it can fire from the initial marking: $m_\bot[u\rangle$; it is called a *full run* if it additionally reaches the final marking: $m_\bot[u\rangle m_\top$. We write $Runs(N)$ for the set of full runs of Petri net N. Given $u = \langle t_1 \dots t_n\rangle \in Runs(N)$, the sequence of actions $\lambda(u) \stackrel{\text{def}}{=} \langle\lambda(t_1) \dots \lambda(t_n)\rangle$. is called a *trace* of N.

The set of reachable markings from $m_\bot$ is denoted by $[m_\bot\rangle$, and form a graph called *reachability graph.* A Petri net is *k-bounded* if no marking in $[m_\bot\rangle$ assigns more than k tokens to any place. A Petri net is *safe* if it is 1-bounded. In this paper we assume safe Petri nets.

2.2 Foundations of Alignments

We survey definitions for alignments and some variations. The interested reader can refer to [10] for the seminal work on alignments where a complete formalization can be found.

An event log is a collection of traces, where a trace may appear more than once. Formally:

Definition 2 (Event Log). *An* event log L *(over an alphabet of actions Σ) is a multiset of traces $\sigma \in \Sigma^*$.*

Given a Petri net N (typically obtained using process mining techniques, and supposed to model the behavior of an observed system), and an observed trace σ in a log, the aim of alignments is to find the full run u of the model N that mostly resembles σ, i.e. such that $\lambda(u)$ is close to σ, for some notion of distance $dist(\sigma, \lambda(u))$.

Example 1. An example of alignment is shown in Fig. 2: given the model in Fig. 2(a) and the trace $\langle C, D \rangle$, the model produces the trace $\langle A, C, B, D \rangle$, as shown in the upper row of Fig. 2(b).

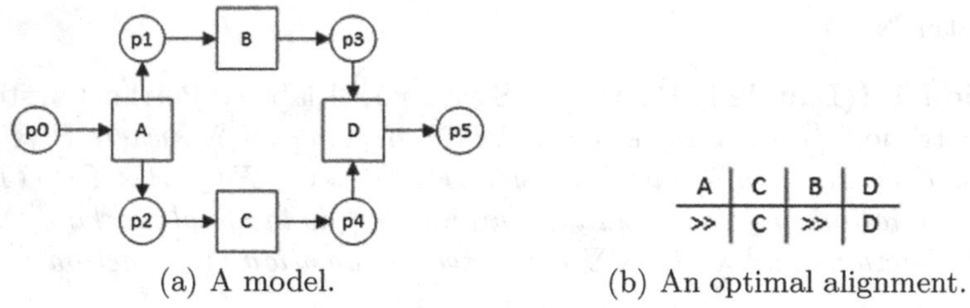

(a) A model.

A	C	B	D
>>	C	>>	D

(b) An optimal alignment.

Fig. 2. Example of alignment between observed and modeled behavior.

A traditional choice for the distance $dist(\sigma, \gamma)$ is Levenshtein's edit distance (which counts how many deletions and insertions are needed to transform σ to γ). Another possible choice is Hamming distance, which simply counts the number of positions in which σ and γ differ: for two traces $\sigma = \langle \sigma_1 \ldots \sigma_n \rangle$ and $\gamma = \langle \gamma_1 \ldots \gamma_n \rangle$ of equal length n, Hamming distance is defined as $\left| \{ i \in \{1 \ldots n\} \mid \gamma_i \neq \sigma_i \} \right|$; when one trace is shorter than the other, we pad it and count every occurrence of the padding symbol as a mismatch with the longer trace.

Most of the definitions in this article are valid for any choice of distance (in particular Levenshtein and Hamming). For readability, some of the most technical developments are done only for Hamming distance, and we give insights on how to adapt them to Levenshtein's distance. In the example of Fig. 2, the trace produced by the model is at distance 2, independently of the distance considered. Our tool DARKSIDER mostly uses Levenshtein's distance.

Definition 3 (δ-Alignment, (Optimal) Alignment). *Given a (log) trace σ, and a Petri net model N, a δ-*alignment *of σ to N is a full run u of N such that $dist(\sigma, \lambda(u)) \leq \delta$.*

Clearly there exist δ-alignments for all values of δ larger or equal to a minimal value which we denote $\delta_{\min}(\sigma, N)$ (or simply $\delta_{\min}$ when σ and N are clear from the context). An optimal alignment *(or simply* alignment*) is a $\delta_{\min}(\sigma, N)$-alignment of σ to N.*

In Example 1, the 2-alignment represented by the run $\langle A, C, B, D\rangle$ is provided for the observed trace $\langle A, C\rangle$, which is an optimal alignment.

3 Multi-alignments

We now present multi-alignment as a generalization of the notion of alignments. This new notion will be used in the rest of the paper as basis for the clustering approach proposed. We refer the reader to the example in the introduction (Fig. 1) for an example of multi-alignment.

3.1 Formalization of Multi-alignments

The following definition relies on a notion of distance *dist*, which can be chosen depending on the context. For instance, Hamming distance and Levenshtein's edit distance are valid choices (see discussion in Sect. 2.2).

Definition 4 (Multi-alignments, Optimal Multi-alignments). *Given a finite collection $\mathcal{C}$ of (log) traces, a model N and some $\delta \in \mathbb{N}$, a δ-*multi-alignment *of $\mathcal{C}$ to N is a full run $u \in Runs(N)$ such that*[2] *$\sum_{\sigma\in\mathcal{C}} dist(\sigma, \lambda(u)) \leq \delta$. Clearly, there is a minimal δ for which a δ-multi-alignment exists. We denote it by $\delta_{\min}(\mathcal{C}, N)$ (or simply by $\delta_{\min}$ when $\mathcal{C}$ and N are clear from the context). A $\delta_{\min}$-multi-alignment is simply called an optimal multi-alignment of $\mathcal{C}$ to N.*

Given a log L, interesting instantiations deserve a comment. First, it is clear that if $|\mathcal{C}| = 1$, then the notion of multi-alignment collapses into the traditional notion of alignment from [10]. If $\mathcal{C} = L$, then the corresponding optimal multi-alignment represents the model trace that aligns optimally with all the traces in the log. However, for models containing alternative executions, to consider $\mathcal{C} = L$ may incur into high multi-alignment distances.

3.2 Encoding Multi-alignments Using Pseudo-Boolean Constraints

Computing multi-alignments is an NP-complete problem.[3]

[2] We understand the $\sum$ as a sum over a multiset, taking multiplicities into account. For instance, with the multiset $A = \{1, 1\}$, we get $\sum_{i\in A} i = 2$.

[3] More precisely, the problem of existence of a δ-multi-alignment for given $\mathcal{C}$, N and δ (represented in unary), is NP-complete. For NP-hardness, we use a reduction from the problem of reachability of a marking m in a 1-safe acyclic Petri net N, known to be NP-complete [12,13], to the existence of a 0-multi-alignment with the empty collection $\mathcal{C} = \emptyset$.

In order to compute a multi-alignment of $\mathcal{C}$ to N, our tool DARKSIDER constructs a pseudo-Boolean[4] formula $\Phi(N, \mathcal{C})$ and calls a solver (currently MINISAT+ [14]) to find an optimal solution. Every optimal solution to the formula is interpreted as a multi-alignment.

The formula $\Phi(N, \mathcal{C})$ characterizes a δ-multi-alignment $u = \langle t_1 \dots t_n \rangle \in Runs(N)$, with $\delta = \sum_{\sigma \in \mathcal{C}} dist(\sigma, \lambda(u))$. For simplicity, we present the encoding for Hamming distance as *dist*. Later we discuss how to adapt the encoding to Levenshtein's edit distance.

For the encoding, we need to fix a bound on the length $n = |u|$ of the δ-multi-alignment. In principle n could be exponential in $|T|$, simply because multi-alignments are full runs and there are models for which the final marking is reachable only after firing sequences of exponential length in $|T|$. Nevertheless, the distance $dist(\sigma, \lambda(u))$ between a full run u of length n is at least $n - |\sigma|$.[5] Hence u cannot be a δ-multi-alignment for δ smaller than $n - \min_{\sigma \in \mathcal{C}} |\sigma|$. Since in practice we are interested with δ of the order of the length of the log traces, we can bound n to, for instance, twice the length of the longest trace in $\mathcal{C}$: $n = 2 \times \max_{\sigma \in \mathcal{C}} |\sigma|$.

The formula $\Phi(N, \mathcal{C})$ is coded using the following Boolean variables:

- $\tau_{i,t}$ for $i = 1 \dots n$, $t \in T$ means that transition $t_i = t$.
- $m_{i,p}$ for $i = 0 \dots n$, $p \in P$ means that place p is marked in marking m_i reached after firing $\langle t_1 \dots t_i \rangle$ (remind that we consider only safe nets, therefore the $m_{i,p}$ are Boolean variables).
- $\delta_{i,\sigma}$ for $i = 1 \dots n$, $\sigma \in \mathcal{C}$, means that σ and $\lambda(u)$ mismatch at position i, i.e. $\lambda(t_i) \neq \sigma_i$.

The total number of variables is smaller than $n \times (|T| + |P| + |\mathcal{C}|)$.

Let us decompose the formula $\Phi(N, \mathcal{C})$.

- The fact that $u = \langle t_1 \dots t_n \rangle \in Runs(N)$ is coded by the conjunction of the following formulas:
  - Initial marking:

$$\left(\bigwedge_{p \in m_\bot} m_{0,p} \right) \wedge \left(\bigwedge_{p \in P \setminus m_\bot} \neg m_{0,p} \right)$$

  - Final marking:

$$\left(\bigwedge_{p \in m_\top} m_{n,p} \right) \wedge \left(\bigwedge_{p \in P \setminus m_\top} \neg m_{n,p} \right)$$

[4] Pseudo-Boolean constraints are generalizations of Boolean constraints. They allow one to specify constant bounds on the number of variables which can/must be assigned to true among a set V of variables. We write them as $a \leq \sum_{v \in V} v \leq b$. Pseudo-Boolean constraints are not more expressive but can be upto exponentially more concise than Boolean constraints. Some pseudo-Boolean solvers also offer to search for a solution minimizing a pseudo-Boolean objective of the same form $\sum_{v \in V} v$: number of variables assigned to true among V.

[5] This holds as well for Hamming or edit distance.

• The transitions are enabled when they fire:

$$\bigwedge_{i=1}^{n} \bigwedge_{t \in T} (\tau_{i,t} \implies \bigwedge_{p \in {}^{\bullet}t} m_{i-1,p})$$

• Token game (for safe Petri nets):

$$\bigwedge_{i=1}^{n} \bigwedge_{t \in T} \bigwedge_{p \in t^{\bullet}} (\tau_{i,t} \implies m_{i,p})$$

$$\bigwedge_{i=1}^{n} \bigwedge_{t \in T} \bigwedge_{p \in {}^{\bullet}t \setminus t^{\bullet}} (\tau_{i,t} \implies \neg m_{i,p})$$

$$\bigwedge_{i=1}^{n} \bigwedge_{t \in T} \bigwedge_{p \in P, p \notin {}^{\bullet}t, p \notin t^{\bullet}} (\tau_{i,t} \implies (m_{i,p} \iff m_{i-1,p}))$$

– One and only one t_i for each i, can be expressed concisely as a pseudo-Boolean constraint:

$$\sum_{i=1}^{n} \sum_{t \in T} \tau_{i,t} = 1$$

– Now, we look for a solution minimizing the quantity $\delta = \sum_{\sigma \in \mathcal{C}} dist(\sigma, \lambda(u))$ (total number of mismatches), which is coded as:

$$\sum_{\sigma \in \mathcal{C}} \sum_{i=1}^{n} \delta_{i,\sigma}$$

with the $\delta_{i,\sigma}$ correctly affected w.r.t. $\lambda(t_i)$ and σ_i:

$$\bigwedge_{\sigma \in \mathcal{C}} \bigwedge_{i=1}^{n} \left(\delta_{i,\sigma} \iff \bigvee_{t \in T,\ \lambda(t) = \sigma_i} \tau_{i,t} \right)$$

Notice that, as such, the formula $\Phi(N, \mathcal{C})$ characterizes multi-alignments u of a fixed length n. But in fact, what we need is to accept any u of length less or equal to n. There is a simple trick for this: we simply add to the Petri net N a new transition with the final marking $m_\top$ as pre- and post-set, and labeled with a special padding symbol. This transition allows N to 'wait' once in the final marking.

Size of the Formula. In the end, the first part of the formula ($u = \langle t_1 \dots t_n \rangle \in Runs(N)$) is coded by a pseudo-Boolean formula of size $O(n \times |T| \times |P|)$.

The second part of the formula (minimization of the mismatches) is coded by a pseudo-Boolean minimization objective of size $O(n \times |\mathcal{C}| \times |T|)$.

The total size for the coding of the formula $\Phi(N, \mathcal{C})$ is

$$O\left(n \times |T| \times \left(|P| + |\mathcal{C}|\right)\right).$$

Encoding of Levenshtein's Edit Distance. The encoding that we have presented above is for multi-alignments w.r.t. Hamming distance (see discussion in Sect. 2.2). For Levenshtein's edit distance, the basic idea is to let the multi-alignment model trace "wait" for the log traces. This corresponds to the blanks in the matrix shown in Fig. 1. For this it suffices to add to the Petri net N a new transition with empty pre- and post-set, and labeled with a special padding symbol. When counting the mismatches between the multi-alignment trace $\lambda(u)$ and a model trace σ, a blank compared to another action costs 1 (it corresponds to a deletion if one transforms σ to $\lambda(u)$). Symmetrically, the log trace is also allowed to "wait" for the multi-alignment.

There is now a subtlety: since the multi-alignment is compared with several log traces together, at some point it may have to wait for only some of the traces. This should count for the computation of the distance between $\lambda(u)$ and these traces, but not between $\lambda(u)$ and the other traces which do not need to wait. The solution is to let the latter wait without counting any mismatch at this point between them and $\lambda(u)$. This situation happens at the end of the multi-alignment shown in Fig. 1 when the multi-alignment has to wait for trace 3, while trace 1, 2 and 4, which "are ready", wait like the multi-alignment.

In the end, this may lengthen the representation of the multi-alignment: in the worst case, for log traces of length l, one may have to insert $l - 1$ blanks before each symbol of the multi-alignment.

3.3 Partial Covering of the Log Traces

We have defined a multi-alignment as a full run u of the model N which minimizes its distance to a collection $\mathcal{C}$ of (log) traces. Now, if the collection $\mathcal{C}$ contains very different traces, it makes sense to focus on a subset of $\mathcal{C}$ containing sufficiently similar traces. For this we adapt a little bit the notion of multi-alignment in order to leave the choice of a subset of $\mathcal{C}$ to be considered: instead of minimizing the sum of distances to the log traces $\sigma \in \mathcal{C}$, we fix a distance threshold d and look for a $u \in Runs(N)$ which maximizes the number of log traces which are at distance $\leq d$ to u.

Definition 5 (Optimal Partial Covering). *Given a collection $\mathcal{C}$ of (log) traces, a model N and a distance threshold $d \in \mathbb{N}$, we say that a full run $u \in Runs(N)$ of N* covers *a log trace $\sigma \in \mathcal{C}$ if $dist(\sigma, \lambda(u)) < d$. We say that u is an* optimal partial covering *of $\mathcal{C}$ for the distance threshold d if no full run of N covers strictly more log traces of $\mathcal{C}$ than u.*

As an example, consider the following collection of log traces, the model shown in Fig. 3, and set the distance threshold to $d = 4$.

```
t1: A C E B D G H F
t2: A C E G H F D B
t3: A C AC AA AF AI AJ AD AH X2 AG AB D B
t4: A E C G H F D B
t5: A C AA AC AF AJ AI AD AH X2 AG AB D B
```

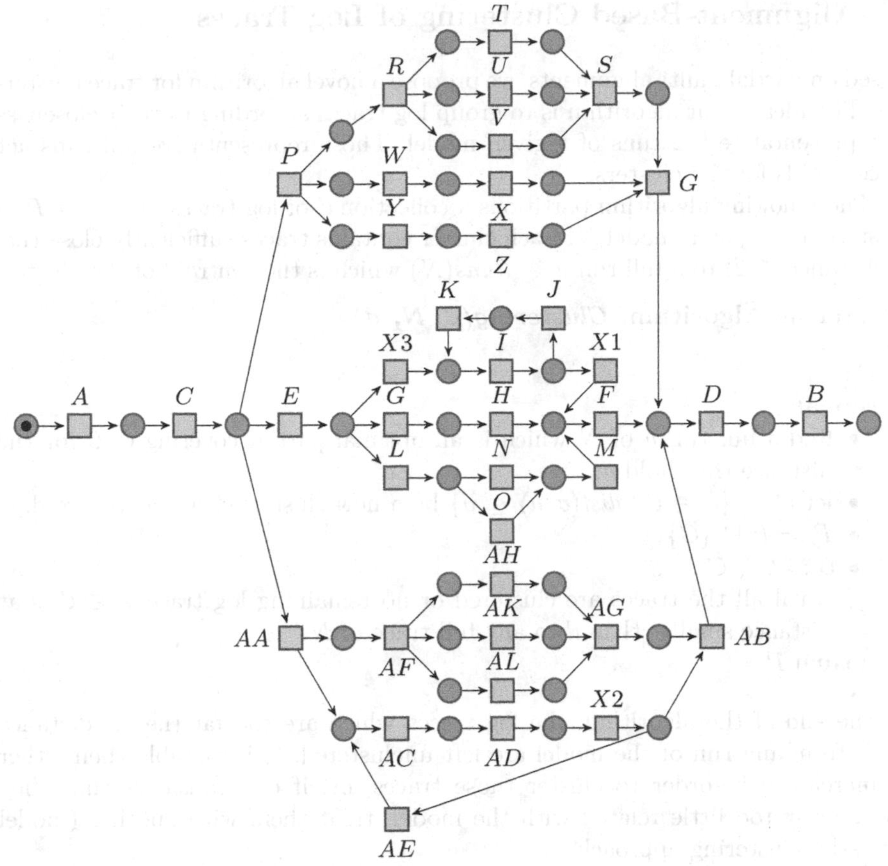

Fig. 3. M1 example (taken from [15]).

The full run $u_1 = \langle A, C, E, G, H, F, D, B\rangle$ covers traces t1, t2 and t4. The full run $u_2 = \langle A, C, AA, AC, AF, AI, AJ, AD, AH, X2, AG, AB, D, B\rangle$ covers the others. No other full run covers more traces, so u_1 is an optimal partial covering.

The problem of finding an optimal partial covering u of the log traces can be encoded as a pseudo-Boolean optimization problem following the same lines as the encoding presented for multi-alignments in Sect. 3.2. We use additional variables b_σ for $\sigma \in \mathcal{C}$ with the constraint that b_σ can be assigned to true only if σ is covered by the full run u:

$$b_\sigma \implies \sum_{i=1}^{n} \delta_{i,\sigma} \leq d .$$

Now we express our objective of covering as many log traces as possible, as the pseudo-Boolean maximization objective $\sum_{\sigma \in \mathcal{C}} b_\sigma$.

4 Alignment-Based Clustering of Log Traces

Based on partial multi-alignments, we propose a novel algorithm for trace clustering. The idea of our algorithm is to group log traces according to their closeness to representative full runs of a given model. Those representative full runs act as centroids for the clusters.

The following algorithm partitions a collection $\mathcal{C}$ of log traces into a set P of clusters relying on a model N. Each cluster contains traces sufficiently close (i.e. at distance $\leq d$) to a full run $u \in \mathit{Runs}(N)$ which is the centroid of the cluster.

Clustering Algorithm. ***Clustering($\mathcal{C}$, N, d)***

- $P := \emptyset$
- **repeat**
  - find a full run u of N which is an optimal partial covering of $\mathcal{C}$ for the distance threshold d;
  - let $C = \{\sigma \in \mathcal{C} \mid \mathit{dist}(\sigma, u) \leq d\}$ be a new cluster with u as centroid.
  - $P := P \cup \{C\}$
  - $\mathcal{C} := \mathcal{C} \setminus C$

  until all the traces are clustered or no remaining log trace $\sigma \in \mathcal{C}$ is at distance smaller than d to any full trace of N.
- **return** P

At the end of the algorithm, the log traces which are too far (i.e. at distance $> d$) from any run of the model are left unclustered. It is possible then either to increase d in order to cluster those traces, or, if one considers that they are anyway too little related with the model, treat them with another (model agnostic) clustering approach.

5 Implementation and Experiments

We have implemented the theory of this paper in our tool DARKSIDER, which was initially focused on computing *anti-alignments* [16]. DARKSIDER is available at http://www.lsv.ens-cachan.fr/~chatain/darksider. DARKSIDER is written in OCaml. For each cluster computed, it constructs the pseudo-Boolean formulas described in Sect. 3.2 and calls the pseudo-Boolean solver MINISAT+ [14]. When an (optimal) solution is found, DARKSIDER analyses it and displays the corresponding multi-alignment according to the truth values of the variables $\tau_{i,t}$.

To show the capabilities of the tool, we have focused on a synthetic medium-size example (model M1, 40 places and 39 transitions). Figure 3 shows the example. The model contains the typical constructs for a process: sequence, choice, concurrency and loops. It was originally presented in [15], together with a log containing 500 cases of varying sizes. We want to illustrate four different aspects of the contributions of this paper: tool usability, comparison with another clustering approach, combination with other approaches, and resilience to noise.

Tool Usability. By assigning values to the few parameters the tool has (that control the length and the distance of the multi-alignments computed), one can obtain a clustering in few minutes. We have run the clustering algorithm with distance[6] 4 and setting 15 as maximal length for a run. As a result, we have obtained 8 clusters, covering 499 traces. The 8 centroids are:

```
c1: A C E G H F D B
c2: A C P W R Y X U Z V T S Q D B
c3: A C AA AF AC AD AE AC AH AJ AI AD AG AE AC
c4: A C AA AC AF AH AJ AI AD AG X2 AB D B
c5: A C E X3 I J K I J K I J K I J
c6: A C AA AF AI AH AJ AC AD AG X2 AB D B
c7: A C P R W Y U Z V T S X Q D B
c8: A C AA AF AJ AI AC AH AD AG AE AC AD AE AC
```

corresponding to the following partitioning of the log in number of traces: (206, 135, 115, 31, 8, 2, 2, 1), respectively. Notice that most of the centroids are full runs of the model (c1, c2, c4, c6, c7), the others are only prefixes of full runs, truncated to the maximal size (15) that we imposed to centroids. One can see that the aforementioned centroids cover most of the case variants of the model in Fig. 3. For instance, centroid c5 corresponds to the following cluster:

```
t1: J J E I C K I A K I B J F D
t2: A C J I J K I J K F I E D B
t3: A J C K E I J K I J I F D B
t4: C J A E F I J K I D J K I B
t5: A C E J J K I J K I I F D B
t6: A C E I J K I J K B I K I J F D J
t7: A C I K J K E J I I J K I J F D B
t8: A C E I J K I K D I F J K I K I J J J B
```

Overall, the approach can be tuned to provide a coarse-view of the traces (like the one examplified here), or by decreasing the distance, to get a more fine-grained view with more clusters of smaller size. For instance, if we set maximal distance 3 instead of 4, we get 18 clusters.

Comparison with Other Clustering Approach. We compare the results produced by our tool with the technique from [8]. This technique maps every case to a profile vector, and builds a similarity matrix. This matrix is used as input for a *Markov* cluster algorithm, which returns the clustering. In essence, this clustering approach is meant to group together traces with similar labels and behavior. For the same example, this technique provides 18 clusters of sizes ranging from 1 upto 137 traces. A key difference with our approach is the restriction on the traces to be included in a cluster: this approach only obtains clusters with traces having the same length. For instance, the following is an example of one of the clusters obtained by the aforementioned technique:

---

6 For efficiency reasons, DARKSIDERuses currently an ad-hoc distance intermediate between Hamming and Levenshtein.

```
t1: A C E J J K I J K I I F D B
t2: C J A E F I J K I D J K I B
t3: A J C K E I J K I J I F D B
t4: A C J I J K I J K F I E D B
t5: J J E I C K I A K I B J F D
```

To force having the same length within a cluster may be the reason why more clusters are obtained in [8]. In case of loops, this can be misleading, as it can be seen in the cluster computed by our tool corresponding to centroid c5, where different iterations of the loop (I,J,K) are combined into the same cluster. We believe this is a good feature of our approach, since the core information is the same even if two traces have different number of loop iterations.

Combination with Other Clustering Approach. The theory of this paper can be applied to enrich the information provided by other (model agnostic) trace clustering approaches. Once clusters are produced by any trace clustering technique, obtaining multi-alignments for each one would then provide the model-based centroids as our approach provides. For instance, for the cluster provided above from the approach in [8], our tool produced a multi-alignment having the following model sequence $\langle A, C, E, X3, I, J, K, I, J, X1, F, D, B\rangle$. Also, traces that are left uncovered by our approach (since they are beyond the distance considered) can then be clustered with other approaches that do not consider the model.

Resilience to Noise. We have inserted noise into the initial log using the available plugins in the open source tool ProM. The noise insertion was removing and swapping activities in every trace, with a 10% of probability for each one of the noise operations. Accordingly, the clustering approach was computed (with the same parameters) on the same model and the noisy log. Due to the significant insertion of noise, 19 clusters were detected now, and 63 traces out of the 500 became unclustered (compared to the one trace unclustered for the initial log)[7]. In spite of this, some of the centroids were preserved, which give rise to detecting some of the clusters similar to the initial log. For instance the centroid c1 was again detected, and centroids equivalent (variations of the available concurrency in the model) to c2, c4, c6, c7 were computed. We performed the same experiment but now with a 20% of probability for each one of the noise operations. The results obtained in terms of centroids and clusters were very similar. Hence, by focusing at the model-based centroid and not at the cluster level, a certain invariance in the results, even in the presence of significant noise, can be obtained. Also, notice that unclustered traces represent model-based outliers that can be then analyzed apart, to drill down the analysis in those cases.

[7] If more flexible distance parameters are applied, a clustering with only 10 traces unclustered can be computed.

6 Conclusion and Perspectives

An important dimension in process mining is to extract from a large log with many traces, high-level information about families of similar traces which may correspond to different executions of the same parts of the model. The techniques in the literature do not consider the process model for solving this task. For the first time, this paper puts the process model as a main actor in trace clustering.

The notion of multi-alignments defined in this paper is a crucial one to facilitate alignment-based clustering. Multi-alignments incorporate the idea of grouping similar traces within the problem of aligning observed behavior with the model. They provide a typical trace which represents as well as possible the behavior of a cluster of similar log traces. These high-level alignments can be viewed as a way to enrich, and at the same time compress, the alignment information. We envision future applications of multi-alignments that will go beyond trace clustering.

Although currently the tool can provide clustering results in few minutes for medium-sized instances, future work will be devoted to improve the efficiency of computing multi-alignments, which is the core part of the clustering algorithm. Our tool computes exact solutions to the optimal multi-alignment problem, which has a cost in terms of efficiency. Finding efficient heuristics for computing reasonable approximations is an interesting perspective, as has been done recently [17]. By considering several traces at the same time, this work opens the door to significant reduction in the overall complexity of aligning an event log and a model, since the number of alignment problems to solve may be considerably lower.

We plan to do an extensive comparison of our technique with respect to other clustering techniques in the literature, over a comprehensive set of benchmarks. We will also show possible combinations of these approaches with ours, with the aim of improving the interpretation of the clustering information obtained.

Acknowledgements. We thank Bart Hompes for facilitating the clustering results of his tool for the example used in the experiments. This work has been partially supported by funds from the Spanish Ministry for Economy and Competitiveness (MINECO), the European Union (FEDER funds) under grant COMMAS (ref. TIN2013-46181-C2-1-R).

References

1. van der Aalst, W.M.P.: Process Mining — Discovery, Conformance and Enhancement of Business Processes. Springer, Berlin (2011)
2. Greco, G., Guzzo, A., Pontieri, L., Saccà, D.: Discovering expressive process models by clustering log traces. IEEE Trans. Knowl. Data Eng. **18**(8), 1010–1027 (2006)
3. Ferreira, D., Zacarias, M., Malheiros, M., Ferreira, P.: Approaching process mining with sequence clustering: experiments and findings. In: Alonso, G., Dadam, P., Rosemann, M. (eds.) BPM 2007. LNCS, vol. 4714, pp. 360–374. Springer, Heidelberg (2007). doi:10.1007/978-3-540-75183-0_26

4. Song, M., Günther, C.W., van der Aalst, W.M.P.: Trace clustering in process mining. In: Ardagna, D., Mecella, M., Yang, J. (eds.) BPM 2008. LNBIP, vol. 17, pp. 109–120. Springer, Heidelberg (2009). doi:10.1007/978-3-642-00328-8_11
5. Bose, R., van der Aalst, W.M.P.: Context aware trace clustering: towards improving process mining results. In: Proceedings of the SIAM International Conference on Data Mining, SDM 2009, 30 April – 2 May 2009, Sparks, Nevada, USA, pp. 401–412 (2009)
6. Bose, R.P.J.C., van der Aalst, W.M.P.: Trace clustering based on conserved patterns: towards achieving better process models. In: Rinderle-Ma, S., Sadiq, S., Leymann, F. (eds.) BPM 2009. LNBIP, vol. 43, pp. 170–181. Springer, Heidelberg (2010). doi:10.1007/978-3-642-12186-9_16
7. Weerdt, J.D., vanden Broucke, S.K.L.M., Vanthienen, J., Baesens, B.: Active trace clustering for improved process discovery. IEEE Trans. Knowl. Data Eng. **25**(12), 2708–2720 (2013)
8. Hompes, B., Buijs, J., van der Aalst, W., Dixit, P., Buurman, H.: Discovering deviating cases and process variants using trace clustering. In: Proceedings of the 27th Benelux Conference on Artificial Intelligence (BNAIC 2015), Hasselt, Belgium, 5–6 November 2015
9. Dumas, M., van der Aalst, W.M.P., ter Hofstede, A.H.M.: Process-Aware Information Systems: Bridging People and Software Through Process Technology. Wiley, Hoboken (2005)
10. Adriansyah, A.: Aligning observed and modeled behavior. Ph.D. thesis, Technische Universiteit Eindhoven (2014)
11. Murata, T.: Petri nets: properties, analysis and applications. Proc. IEEE **77**(4), 541–574 (1989)
12. Stewart, I.A.: Reachability in some classes of acyclic Petri nets. Fundam. Inform. **23**(1), 91–100 (1995)
13. Cheng, A., Esparza, J., Palsberg, J.: Complexity results for 1-safe nets. In: Shyamasundar, R.K. (ed.) FSTTCS 1993. LNCS, vol. 761, pp. 326–337. Springer, Heidelberg (1993). doi:10.1007/3-540-57529-4_66
14. Eén, N., Sörensson, N.: Translating pseudo-boolean constraints into SAT. JSAT **2**(1–4), 1–26 (2006)
15. Taymouri, F., Carmona, J.: Model and event log reductions to boost the computation of alignments. In: Proceedings of the 6th International Symposium on Data-driven Process Discovery and Analysis (SIMPDA 2016), Graz, Austria, 15–16 December 2016, pp. 50–62 (2016)
16. Chatain, T., Carmona, J.: Anti-alignments in conformance checking — the dark side of process models. In: Kordon, F., Moldt, D. (eds.) PETRI NETS 2016. LNCS, vol. 9698, pp. 240–258. Springer, Cham (2016). doi:10.1007/978-3-319-39086-4_15
17. Taymouri, F., Carmona, J.: A recursive paradigm for aligning observed behavior of large structured process models. In: La Rosa, M., Loos, P., Pastor, O. (eds.) BPM 2016. LNCS, vol. 9850, pp. 197–214. Springer, Cham (2016). doi:10.1007/978-3-319-45348-4_12

Conceptual Modeling in Specific Context

The Conceptual Modelling of Dynamic Teams for Autonomous Systems

Rick Evertsz[1(✉)], John Thangarajah[1], and Michael Papasimeon[2]

[1] RMIT University, Melbourne, Australia
{rick.evertsz,john.thangarajah}@rmit.edu.au
[2] Defence Science and Technology Group, Melbourne, Australia
michael.papasimeon@dsto.defence.gov.au

Abstract. The concept of a 'team' is key in multi-agent decision-making applications such as for combat operations and disaster management. Although there are a number of team-oriented agent programming approaches, conceptual modelling of teams is not fully addressed. In this paper we present TDF-T, an extension of the TDF agent design methodology that addresses the requirements of team oriented modelling; in particular, team hierarchies, dynamic team formation, and team coordination. These concepts encapsulate team tactical behaviour which is essential to our user community who need to build and deploy complex team-based simulation applications. We show positive results in a user study that evaluates comprehension and maintainability of TDF-T models.

Keywords: Autonomous systems · Multi-agent systems · Organisational modelling · Team modelling

1 Introduction

There is a growing community involved in computationally modelling team-based decision-making behaviour; for example, to build multi-agent tactical simulations or teams of autonomous aircraft in domains such as air combat (e.g. [3,6,11]). In such applications, teams of agents are created to drive autonomous systems, or to support *what-if* simulation scenarios that help answer questions such as how best to build an air defence capability.

With the advent of increasingly sophisticated hardware, including autonomous platforms such as Unmanned Aerial Systems, many scenarios have become very complex and difficult to model; for example, where teams need to achieve joint goals in uncertain and highly dynamic environments. As such, the type of operational analysis that is being conducted has evolved from modelling, simulating and analysing *single agent systems* to *multi-agent systems in organisational contexts*. This has meant that concepts such as *teams*, *joint goals*, *shared beliefs* and *team roles* have become increasingly important, and it is critical that these concepts now be represented as *first order* constructs in any modelling methodology.

H.C. Mayr et al. (Eds.): ER 2017, LNCS 10650, pp. 311–324, 2017.
https://doi.org/10.1007/978-3-319-69904-2_25

Another problem for those developing computational models is the lack of a common language for the specification of team behaviour. The development of team models usually requires collaboration between several communities with different skill sets and perspectives, for example, domain experts, operations analysts and software engineers. Within a given project, each community tends to use a different approach. For example, domain experts typically rely on natural language and informal diagrams, whereas software engineers might use UML [13] or go straight to program code. This makes communication difficult, and the links between the products of each community is tenuous and easily lost as the modelling process moves from domain experts through to software engineers.

The final significant problem in team modelling has been the fact that computational models are usually tied to a specific implementation platform, and transferring the models to another platform entails reimplementation.

The aforementioned three drivers are the primary motivation for the team modelling concepts and methodology presented in this paper, namely, the need for (i) first order team constructs, (ii) a shared modelling representation for all users, and (iii) platform independence.

In this work, our research objective has been to develop a methodology and representation for modelling teams that is (i) easy for domain experts to understand, (ii) straightforward for operations analysts to apply, and (iii) for software engineers to use, debug and maintain. We want the representation to be easy to understand because this will help with knowledge elicitation and model validation. If domain experts can understand the representation, then it gives them a sense of ownership over the unfolding models, allowing them to relate the subsequent team behaviour back to the models so that they can directly critique any shortcomings.

We have found over the last 20 years, working with groups who are modelling team behaviour, that domain experts will talk about a team as an *abstract entity*. They conceptualise the team as having an overall goal (*desire*) to achieve through the cooperative actions of its team members, and as having specific situational awareness (*beliefs*) guiding its choices, as well as committing to particular solutions (*intentions*). This perspective is a close match to the BDI (Beliefs, Desires, Intentions) paradigm [19], and so we selected an existing BDI-based modelling methodology for extension with team modelling concepts; namely TDF (Tactics Development Framework) [10].

This paper contributes a practical approach to the conceptual modelling of autonomous teams by (i) extending the TDF methodology with additional steps, and with explicit team modelling concepts such as team hierarchies, dynamic team formation, and team coordination (Sect. 4), (ii) mapping it to an established teams implementation platform, JACK Teams [8] (Sect. 5.1), and providing a preliminary evaluation (Sect. 5) indicating that, for team-based scenarios, the TDF-T (TDF-Teams) extension is intuitive, and it is straightforward for new users to see how team-oriented designs can be changed to encompass greater variation in behaviour.

2 Background

This section briefly introduces important background to TDF-T, namely theoretical and practical research into teams, team modelling in AOSE (Agent Oriented Software Engineering) methodologies, the BDI paradigm, and TDF.

2.1 Team Oriented Programming and AOSE

From a philosophical perspective, there has been considerable debate about whether a team should be modelled as a separate entity or merely an aggregation of the different (mental) attributes of the agents that constitute it. According to Bratman [5], a shared intention is nothing more than the aggregation of the intentions of individuals. Searle [21], on the other hand, argues that there has to be such a thing as *collective intention* if a team is to perform adequately.

Theoretical work on teaming tends to focus on formal aspects such as Cohen and Levesque's *Joint Intentions Theory* [7], and Grosz's work on *SharedPlans* [12], whereas practical work on team oriented programming is concerned with the challenges of building real systems (e.g. Machinetta [20], JACK Teams [8] and JaCaMo [4]).

In team oriented programming, coordinated behaviour is expressed at a high-level of abstraction, relying on the team-based platform to reify the team structures and behaviour in terms of individual agents and sub-teams. Team oriented programming typically organises a team in terms of the roles and responsibilities of the team members; these specify the goals they can achieve as well as their other capabilities. Depending on the platform, other aspects can be specified in the team definition, for example, the procedures a team member can use to achieve its goals, and coordination constraints that are applied when agents are engaged in joint activities.

Teams are essentially collections of *agents* that work towards a common goal [14]. Consequently, much of the early work on the computational modelling of teams was carried out within the field of multi-agent systems [22]. AOSE is concerned with how to specify, design, implement, validate and maintain multi-agent systems, and was identified early on as an important prerequisite for their successful development, e.g. [16]. Akbar [1] lists 75 AOSE methodologies, and another survey [15] identifies only seven that incorporate some form of organisational modelling; namely, ASPECS, Extended Gaia, INGENIAS, MaSE, the AGR model, Moise+, and OperA. According to [15], of these, only the first four specifically address teaming in the sense of explicitly supporting the representation of a *joint goal* that all team members work towards. However, they only partially address our modelling requirements (Sect. 3). For example, none fully support dynamic team formation or the expression of team coordination strategies of arbitrary complexity; only INGENIAS offers diagrammatic team views.

2.2 TDF and the BDI Paradigm

Effective team behaviour requires some degree of individual autonomy coupled with an ability to coordinate with peers, while balancing reactivity with proactivity. These attributes, namely *autonomy*, *social ability*, *reactivity* and *proactivity*, are characteristic of BDI agent-based systems.

The BDI model is a particularly parsimonious conception of rational agency, characterising agents as reasoning in terms of their *beliefs* about the world, *desires* (often modelled as *goals*) that they would like to achieve and the *intentions* that they are committed to. Apart from its intuitive appeal as a model of decision making [17], it is a powerful computational abstraction for building sophisticated, goal-directed and reactive reasoning systems.

Operationally, a BDI agent performs a continuous loop in which it updates its beliefs to reflect the current state of the world, deliberates about what to achieve next (reacting to changes in the environment or pursuing its own goals), finds an applicable plan from a predefined plan library, and executes the next step in that plan. Each time around this cycle, it effectively reconsiders its options, yielding goal-oriented behaviour that is also responsive to environmental change.

TDF [10] is an extension of the BDI-based Prometheus [18] AOSE methodology; the latter has been in use for over 15 years. Whereas Prometheus targeted fairly static problems, TDF was developed to tackle highly dynamic tactical scenarios, and so it extended Prometheus with richer goal structures and ways of expressing the conditions under which a goal should be adopted or dropped. Relevant aspects of TDF are covered in more detail during the presentation of TDF-T in Sect. 4.

3 Team Modelling Requirements

In developing TDF-T, we adopted the following requirements, based on previous work on team modelling (including the research mentioned in Sect. 2.1), our air combat stakeholder's objectives, as well as our previous experience working with other groups engaged in modelling a wide range of team-oriented tactical domains.

- R1 **First class team entities** – In a team modelling methodology, teams should be primary entities. A major shortcoming of earlier approaches has been that the designer had to find *implicit* ways to model teams [15], for example, modelling them as organisations.
- R2 **Team structures** – Modelling a *team structure* entails defining *what* constitutes a team, and how situational factors can affect its structure.
- R3 **Joint goals** – A team is formed to achieve a (relatively short term) *goal* and so is, to some extent, ephemeral. This focus on an immediate *joint goal* is fundamental, and is what differentiates teams from longer term organisational structures.
- R4 **Dynamic team structures** – Scenarios such as those found in air combat are highly dynamic, and so team structures need to be adaptable to any significant changes in the tactical situation.

R5 **Team roles** – The dynamic formation of teams, as well as their reorganisation in response to tactical changes, is facilitated by the notion of *role*, that is, what roles a team needs to have filled, and who can fill those roles.

R6 **Sub-teams** – Domains, such as air combat, require teams to be composed of sub-teams, and for those sub-teams to be composed of further sub-teams, and so on.

R7 **Flexible team coordination strategies** – Methodologies, such as Moise+, support coordination by mapping goal schemes into a sub-team structure. This approach is too rigid to handle some of the very dynamic scenarios we have encountered in tactical domains.

R8 **Intuitive representation for domain experts** – In practice, the development and validation of team models relies critically on the input of domain experts. Therefore, it is vital that they can understand and take ownership of the evolving models. They typically lack a background in computer science, and so comprehension is facilitated by *diagrammatic* views rather than formal, text based ones.

4 TDF-T Methodology, Conceptual Model, and Tool

TDF-T is a team oriented extension of the TDF methodology, that addresses the teaming requirements, R1 through R8, outlined in Sect. 3. As a practical methodology, it addresses four overarching modelling concerns:

- **Process.** Guidelines on the sequence of steps to be followed in modelling a team oriented scenario.
- **Artefacts and Relationships.** The conceptual artefacts defined in the diagrams, and how those artefacts should relate to one another. For example, how team artefacts are structured in a team hierarchy in terms of team/subteam relationships.
- **Diagrams and Iconography.** The diagrams created at each step of the process, and the set of icons used. Provides guidance on the diagrams needed to represent a team oriented model, and what aspects those diagrams highlight.
- **Route to Implementation.** Software support for creating and editing design diagrams, and a method for mapping those designs to implementation.

4.1 TDF-T Process

TDF-T follows the original TDF methodology [10] by dividing the modelling process into three main stages, and augments them with the team-oriented extensions highlighted in *italics* below.

- **System Specification.** Identification and diagramming of system-level artefacts and relationships, namely scenarios, missions, goals, roles, incoming percepts, outgoing actions, and external actors interacted with. Scenarios outline specific use cases, whereas missions are more general descriptions of the situations the system needs to handle, and typically encompass a number of individual scenarios. Missions have top-level goals to pursue, and these map to lower level sub-goals. These goals and sub-goals are aggregated into the roles that will be responsible for their performance. The interaction with the environment is diagrammed by showing, for each scenario, the percepts that are received from external actors, and the actions that the system can perform. At this stage, although some of the roles are specified, their enactment by either teams or agents isn't specified until the Architectural Design stage.

- **Architectural Design.** Specification of the internal structural aspects of the system, namely agent types and role enactments, *team types*, *team role enactments*, and *team structures*. Here, the abstract roles are mapped to the entity types that will enact them computationally. In the case where a role needs to be enacted by a group of entities *collectively* working towards any of the role's goals, a *team type* must be specified. In a running system, the team *enacts* the role in question, that is, it performs the computational activities required to achieve the role's currently active goal(s). In practice, some team members may need to delegate their activities, and this leads to a hierarchical team/sub-team structure of arbitrary depth, specified in a *team structure* diagram.
- **Detailed Design.** Definition of the internal details of agents and *teams*, i.e. tactics, plan diagrams, *team coordination plans*, messages sent/received, and internal beliefs (data) held by each agent or *team*. Team coordination plans are critical to effective team performance; without a coordination mechanism, a team will not be able to synchronise its activities so as to achieve the overall joint goal.

4.2 TDF-T Artefacts and Relationships

In addition to the artefacts/relationships already in TDF, TDF-T tackles the team modelling requirements (Sect. 3) by providing (i) teams/sub-team relationships (requirements R1, R2 and R6; Fig. 2), (ii) team coordination plans (requirement R7; Fig. 4), (iii) role/team relationships (requirement R5; Fig. 1), (iv) dynamic conditions (requirement R4; Fig. 2) that define how a team structure should be modified in response to changes in the tactical situation and the goals (requirement R3) being pursued by the team. These artefacts and relationships are described further in the context of the various diagrams that they appear in.

4.3 TDF-T Diagrams and Iconography

The TDF-T methodology involves the development of a number of diagrams that provide an overview of different aspects of the team-based system being modelled. To address requirement R8, the diagrams and iconography were developed with input from domain experts from undersea warfare, air combat, and firefighting domains; nevertheless, they are not specific to those domains. In addition

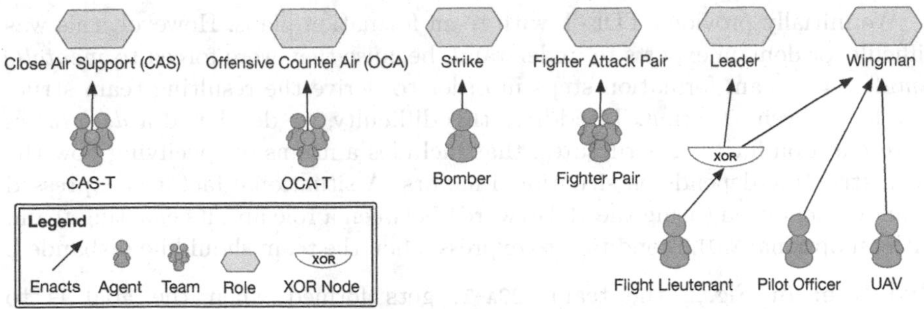

Fig. 1. Agent and team role enactments

to the diagrams offered by TDF [10] (p. 227), TDF-T adds (i) *team* role enactments (Fig. 1), (ii) *team structure* diagrams (Fig. 2), (iii) *team overview* diagrams (Fig. 3), (iv) *team tactics* diagrams (Fig. 3), and (v) *team coordination plan* diagrams (Fig. 4).

Role Enactment Diagram (Architectural Design) Overview: Since teams and agents *enact* roles, i.e. implement the functionality denoted by the goals that a given role can achieve, TDF-T shows the mapping between roles and teams/agents. For a given application, these role enactment definitions delimit the space of possible team hierarchies, because a team can only take on the roles it is defined as being able to enact.

Example: Figure 1 shows some role enactments from an air combat scenario. Note that, in principle, a given role can be enacted by more than one entity, in this case, the `Wingman` role can be enacted by a `Flight Lieutenant`, `Pilot Officer` or `UAV` agent. Also, an entity can potentially enact more than one role; in this example, an agent of type `Flight Lieutenant` can enact either the `Leader` or `Wingman` roles, but never both, as shown by the *exclusive OR node* (`XOR`). If it were possible for a `Flight Lieutenant` to take both roles simultaneously in a team, then the `XOR` node would be omitted, and the choice would be made when the specific team instance is created, as defined by the constraints within its *team structure* definition (see Sect. 4.3).

Team Structure Diagrams (Architectural Design) Overview: As indicated by requirement R4, TDF-T needs to support dynamic team structures. Typical tactical scenarios are highly dynamic, i.e. the situation can change significantly and unexpectedly within a short timeframe. Consequently, a static team structure will not suffice; a team modelling representation needs to support the representation of the structure of a team, how that structure depends on the tactical situation, and the conditions under which the team should be dismantled. Team oriented programming languages typically address this need by providing primitives for *procedurally* specifying the required steps (cf. JACK Teams' team formation plans [8]).

We initially provided TDF-T with team formation plans. However, this was difficult for domain experts to understand, because they were forced to *mentally simulate* the team formation steps in order to derive the resulting team structure for a given situation. To address this difficulty, we developed a *declarative* representation for team structures, that includes a means of specifying how the team structure depends on situational factors. A situational factor is expressed as an arc condition (using the `IF` keyword) between a role and its enacting team, with an optional `WHILE` condition to express when the team should be disbanded.

Example: In Fig. 2, the team, `OCA-T`, gets formed when the goal is to `Provide close air support` (due to space constraints, we have not shown the Role Overview diagram that maps this goal to the `Close Air Support (CAS)` role that this team enacts). Team formation is triggered by the system's adoption of the goal in question, and the team exists for as long as the goal remains active. If the goal is achieved, or is dropped for some reason, the team is dismantled. As shown in the diagram, a `CAS-T` team needs a `Strike` role filled, as well as an `Offensive Counter Air (OCA)` role (cardinality is shown inside the role icon, i.e. `[1]`). These are enacted by the `Bomber` and `OCA-T` teams.

The `OCA-T` team will comprise two `Fighter Attack Pair` role fillers if there are between 5 and 8 enemy fighters; otherwise, if there are between 1 and 4 enemy fighters, then only one role filler is required. The `WHILE` denotes that the subteam exists as long as the `WHILE` condition remains true. So, in this example, if there were 5 enemy fighters, two `Fighter Pair` teams would be formed. If at any time, the number of enemy fighters dropped to 4, then only one `Fighter Pair` would be needed, and so the team would be dismantled and a new team formed. This could happen due to enemy losses during air combat, or because the initial estimate of the number of incoming fighters was wrong, and the true value only became apparent once they were within visual range.

Team Overview Diagrams (Detailed Design) Overview: The Team Overview diagram provides a high level summary of a team and its properties, and shows the *goals* the team can achieve, the *tactics* it can use to achieve those goals, individual *plans* that are separate from its tactics, and *beliefs* that it maintains.

Example: The lefthand side of Fig. 3 presents a small part of the Team Overview diagram for the `Fighter Pair` team. It shows that the team handles two goals. The `Single side offset` goal is handled by two plans, with the context in which each plan applies shown as an arc label between goal and plan. Two tactics are available to handle the `Pincer attack` goal, and each applies in a different context (see arc labels). Both plans and both tactics read from, and write to, the belief set `Enemy situation`, as denoted by the bidirectional arcs.

Tactics Overview Diagrams (Detailed Design) Overview: The concept of a *tactic* is somewhat similar to the concept of a *capability* in AOSE. Tactics

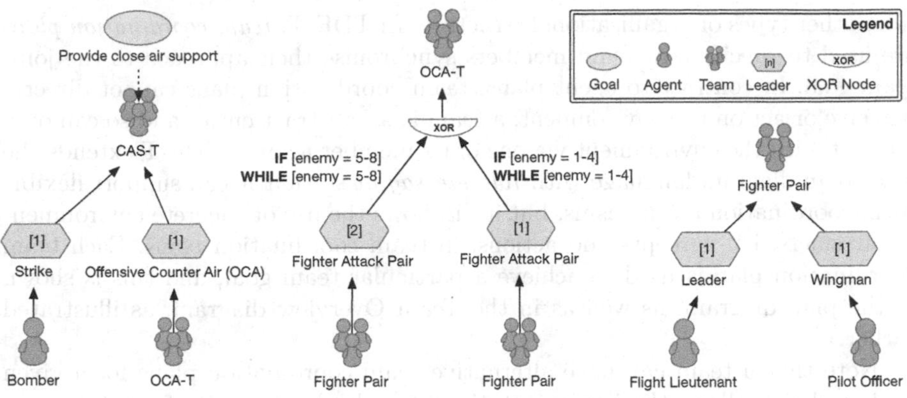

Fig. 2. CAS-T, OCA-T and Fighter Pair team structures

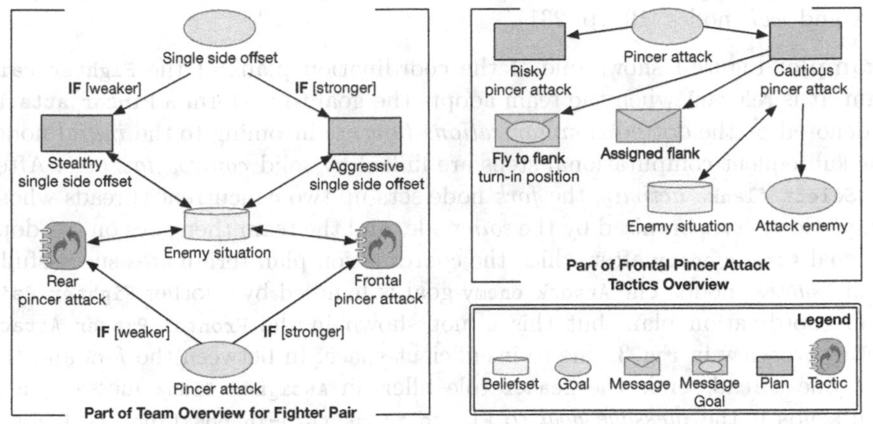

Fig. 3. Team overview and tactics overview diagrams

decompose agent and team functionality into a collection of reusable components, and incorporate aspects of design patterns, such as a *problem description* and an accompanying *solution description* (see [10] (p. 232)).

Example: The righthand side of Fig. 3 presents a small part of the `Frontal pincer attack` tactic. It applies to the goal `Pincer attack`. This diagram shows two of the plans the tactic has for tackling the goal, and shows the `Assigned flank` message and `Fly to flank turn-in position` message goal, that is sent to the `Leader` and `Wingman` role fillers, as shown in the team coordination plan (Fig. 4). One of the tactic's belief sets, `Enemy situation`, is shown in the diagram.

Team Coordination Plans (Detailed Design) Overview: As mentioned earlier, the notion of *joint goal* is the key differentiator that distinguishes teams from other types of organisational structure. In TDF-T, *team coordination plans* are used to specify how team members synchronise their approach to the joint team goal. In contrast to agent plans, team coordination plans cannot directly perceive or act on the environment; a team is an abstract entity and so can only interact with the environment via one of its member agents. TDF-T extends the TDF plan diagram language with *role messaging* so that it can support flexible team coordination mechanisms, but it disallows the use of concrete environmental artefacts, i.e. percepts and actions, in team coordination plans. Each team coordination plan is used to achieve a particular team goal, and this is shown in the plan diagram, as well as in the Team Overview diagram, as illustrated earlier.

Note that a team can have alternative team coordination plans for a given goal, and this allows the implementation of multiple strategies for achieving a particular team goal. In addition to the icons shown in Fig. 4, TDF-T coordination plans support *activity*, *data*, *decision/merge*, *failure*, *asynchronous goal*, *note* and *wait* nodes [10] (p. 231).

Example: Figure 4 shows one of the coordination plans of the `Fighter Pair` team. It is relevant when the team adopts the goal to perform a `Pincer attack`, as denoted by the dotted *communications flow* arc incoming to the *initial* node. The subsequent computational steps are linked by solid *control flow* arcs. After the `Select flanks` *activity*, the *fork* node sets up two concurrent threads whose completion is synchronised by the *join* node, and the team then goes on to adopt the goal `Attack enemy` after which the coordination plan terminates successfully at the *success* node. The `Attack enemy` goal is handled by another `Fighter Pair` team coordination plan, but this is not shown in the `Frontal Pincer Attack` tactics overview in Fig. 3, due to insufficient space. In between the *fork* and the *join*, one thread sends the `Leader` role filler an `Assigned flank` message, and then sends it the *message goal* to `Fly to flank turn-in position`, as denoted by the *communications flow* arcs. The thread proceeds to the *join* once the `Fly to flank turn-in position` is achieved. The other thread is analogous but messages the `Wingman` instead.

The scope of role references is important in team coordination plans. Messages or goals can target role fillers within the team, but cannot reference roles outside of the team or, if the team is a sub-team, roles in its parent team or any of its parent's ancestors. Thus, in this example, the `Fighter Pair` team can reference its `Leader` and `Wingman` roles, but cannot refer to the `Strike` role of the `CAS-T` *ancestor* team (Fig. 2). If the `Fighter Pair` team needs to coordinate with the `Strike` role filler, then this must be encoded in a team coordination plan at the level of the `CAS-T` team. This constraint is imposed because the `Fighter Pair` team cannot assume that it is a sub-team of a team that has a `Strike` role filler.

4.4 TDF-T Tool

The TDF-T Tool extends the TDF Tool [10] (p. 232) to represent the team-oriented diagrams and concepts presented in this paper. It is currently a working

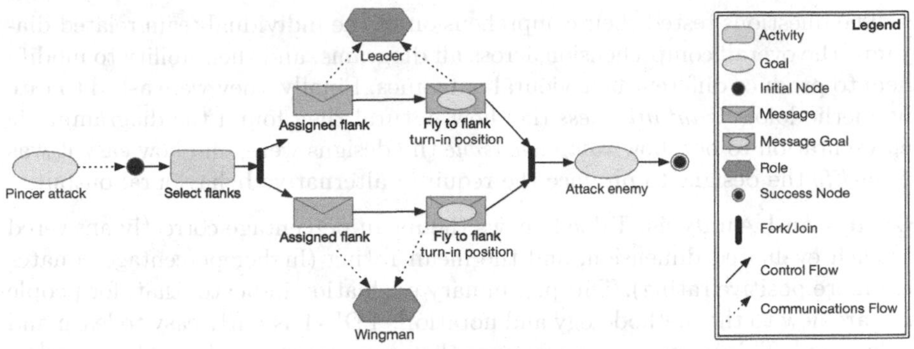

Fig. 4. Cautious pincer attack - team coordination plan (Fighter Pair team)

prototype that offers type safety by constraining what can go in a diagram and what relationships can be defined therein. It also supports propagation of relationships across diagrams. Work is ongoing to extend the tool to mirror the functionality of the TDF Tool by providing consistency checking of team-oriented designs, and code generation capabilities.

5 Evaluation

We conducted a preliminary evaluation of the *understandability* and *maintainability* of TDF-T designs. Previously, evaluations of TDF (without teams) indicated that domain experts found its representation to be easy to understand [9], and that participants with a sound UML background found TDF designs to be significantly easier to understand and modify than equivalent UML ones [10]. The objective of the current study was to obtain an indication of how easily TDF-T can be understood by those who are new to the notation, and whether they can see how to modify a design to produce different behaviour. One of our stakeholder's key objectives for TDF-T is for it to be easy to understand and critique, so that domain experts and model builders can have a common diagrammatic representation for expressing and discussing team behaviour. The following evaluation, though preliminary, is a first step in assessing whether this is the case.

Participants. 13 participants took part in the evaluation; chosen because they either had a software engineering background or were experienced in modelling tactics.

Method. All participants were given a 15 minute presentation of the TDF-T notation, and were then given 7 design diagrams to study that targeted the teaming aspects of TDF-T. The design diagrams were based on a submarine defence case study [2]. The participants were given unlimited time to answer the 11 questions, and took between 20 to 30 min to complete the questionnaire.

The questions tested their comprehension of the individual team related diagrams, the overall comprehension across all diagrams, and their ability to modify them to produce different behavioural outcomes. Finally, they were asked to rate the methodology's *intuitiveness* (i.e. how natural they found the diagrammatic representation to be), how *comprehensible* the designs were, and how easy it was to *modify* the designs to produce the required alternative behavioural output.

Results and Analysis. Table 1 shows the mean percentage correctly answered for each evaluated dimension, and the mean rating (higher percentage equates to a more positive rating). This preliminary evaluation indicates that, for people who are new to the methodology and notation, TDF-T is fairly easy to learn and understand. This is encouraging because they were given a real-world case study. As expected, the overall intuitiveness rating was lower, as the notation was new to the participants and most of them had many years of UML modelling experience, requiring a shift in perspective. However, the participants were able answer most of the questions correctly and rated TDF-T highly on the dimensions of ease of understanding and modification.

Table 1. Test scores and ratings for TDF-T evaluation

Dimension	Mean (%)	σ	Rating	Mean (%)	σ
Goal structures	100	0.00	Intuitiveness	61	0.80
Roles, Goals, Teams	97	0.16	Ease of understanding	74	0.70
Team coordination	93	0.30	Ease of modification	83	0.88
Comprehension	82	0.37			
Modification	100	0.00			

Though promising, this evaluation needs to be followed up with a more extensive study that looks at how TDF-T facilitates the interaction between domain experts and modellers working on a real-world project together. Our stakeholder is planning to run such a study in the air combat domain, looking at scenarios that have been modelled using other approaches, that are not necessarily agent based.

5.1 Implementation

A software design methodology is most useful when it can be mapped to supporting programming platforms. With respect to TDF-T, we investigated BDI agent programming languages that could support the methodology and found two contenders in JaCaMo [4] and JACK Teams [8]. We found JACK Teams to be more suitable for our implementation than JaCaMo, as there was a more direct mapping from TDF-T to JACK Teams for most concepts. JACK Teams also supports the rich goal decomposition constructs that TDF-T provides, whilst the goal decomposition in JaCaMo is less suited to our needs, because it is expressed via `parallel` and `sequential` goals and it is not straightforward to express more flexible team coordination in terms of messaging.

6 Discussion

This paper presented TDF-T, a team-oriented extension of TDF, which supports the diagrammatic specification of dynamic team structures, and team coordination plans.

In developing TDF-T, we surveyed related work in team oriented programming, organisation-based methodologies, and also the philosophical work that underpins team concepts (as outlined in Sect. 2.1). We developed and evaluated various approaches to modelling teams and eventually settled on what is presented in this paper, as it met the requirements outlined in Sect. 3. For example, to make the case studies easier to model and understand, we abandoned team formation plans, and instead developed a declarative representation for dynamic team structures. Furthermore, we initially used the widely adopted Business Process Model and Notation (BPMN[1]) to represent team coordination plans. However, as we developed our case studies, the diagrams became overly complex and difficult to understand, due to the large set of possible BPMN design elements. Although we tried using a subset, this required modification of the standard definitions of some BPMN elements. To simplify team coordination plans, we dispensed with BPMN and chose to use the TDF plan diagram notation, augmented to include team coordination constructs as detailed in Sect. 4.3.

Although our preliminary evaluation of TDF-T was positive, there are shortcomings. TDF-T does not include a formal model of the environment (also true of TDF) and does not incorporate the notion of norms (social or organisational). Both of these aspects are well formulated in JaCaMo [4], though JaCaMo lacks some of the team specific modelling constructs of TDF-T, due to design choices in Moise+. As such we see the current version of TDF-T as complementary to JaCaMo and we will look into incorporating into TDF-T some of the organisational features of JaCaMo, including the normative aspects.

References

1. Akbari, O.Z.: A survey of agent-oriented software engineering paradigm: towards its industrial acceptance. J. Comput. Eng. Res. **1**(2), 14–28 (2010)
2. Akbori, F.: Autonomous-agent based simulation of anti-submarine warfare operations with the goal of protecting a high value unit. Master's thesis (2004)
3. Bisht, S., Malhotra, A., Taneja, S.B.: Modelling and simulation of tactical team behaviour. Def. Sci. J. **57**(6), 853 (2007)
4. Boissier, O., Bordini, R.H., Hübner, J.F., Ricci, A., Santi, A.: Multi-agent oriented programming with JaCaMo. Sci. Comput. Program. **78**(6), 747–761 (2013)
5. Bratman, M.: Faces of Intention: Selected Essays on Intention and Agency. Cambridge University Press, Cambridge (1999)

[1] http://www.bpmn.org.

6. Case, D.M., DeLoach, S.A.: Obaa++: an agent architecture for participating in multiple groups. In: Proceedings of the 2014 International Conference on Autonomous Agents and Multi-agent Systems, pp. 1367–1368. International Foundation for Autonomous Agents and Multiagent Systems (2014)
7. Cohen, P.R., Levesque, H.J.: Teamwork. Nous **25**(4), 487–512 (1991)
8. Evertsz, R., Fletcher, M., Jones, R., Jarvis, J., Brusey, J., Dance, S.: Implementing industrial multi-agent systems using JACK^{TM}. In: Dastani, M.M., Dix, J., El Fallah-Seghrouchni, A. (eds.) ProMAS 2003. LNCS, vol. 3067, pp. 18–48. Springer, Heidelberg (2004). doi:10.1007/978-3-540-25936-7_2
9. Evertsz, R., Thangarajah, J., Ly, T.: A BDI-based methodology for eliciting tactical decision-making expertise. In: Sarker, R., Abbass, H.A., Dunstall, S., Kilby, P., Davis, R., Young, L. (eds.) Data and Decision Sciences in Action. LNMIE, pp. 13–26. Springer, Cham (2018). doi:10.1007/978-3-319-55914-8_2
10. Evertsz, R., Thangarajah, J., Yadav, N., Ly, T.: A framework for modelling tactical decision-making in autonomous systems. J. Syst. Softw. **110**(C), 222–238 (2015). doi:10.1016/j.jss.2015.08.046
11. Giachetti, R.E., Marcelli, V., Cifuentes, J., Rojas, J.A.: An agent-based simulation model of human-robot team performance in military environments. Syst. Eng. **16**(1), 15–28 (2013)
12. Grosz, B.J., Kraus, S.: Collaborative plans for complex group action. Artif. Intell. **86**(2), 269–357 (1996)
13. Heaton, L.: Unified modeling language (UML): superstructure specification, v2.0. Object Management Group, Technical report (2005)
14. Horling, B., Lesser, V.: A survey of multi-agent organizational paradigms. Knowl. Eng. Rev. **19**(04), 281–316 (2004)
15. Isern, D., Sánchez, D., Moreno, A.: Organizational structures supported by agent-oriented methodologies. J. Syst. Softw. **84**(2), 169–184 (2011)
16. Kinny, D., Georgeff, M., Rao, A.: A methodology and modelling technique for systems of BDI agents. In: Van de Velde, W., Perram, J.W. (eds.) MAAMAW 1996. LNCS, vol. 1038, pp. 56–71. Springer, Heidelberg (1996). doi:10.1007/BFb0031846
17. Norling, E.: Folk psychology for human modelling: extending the BDI paradigm. In: Proceedings of AAMAS 2004, pp. 202–209. IEEE Computer Society (2004)
18. Padgham, L., Winikoff, M.: Developing Intelligent Agent Systems: A Practical Guide, vol. 1. Wiley, Hoboken (2004)
19. Rao, A., Georgeff, M., et al.: BDI agents: from theory to practice. In: Proceedings of the First ICMAS (1995), pp. 312–319, San Francisco (1995)
20. Schurr, N., Maheswaran, R., Scerri, P., Tambe, M.: From STEAM to Machinetta: the evolution of a BDI teamwork model. Cognition and Multiagent Interaction: From Cognitive Modeling to Social Simulation 2004 (2006)
21. Searle, J.R.: Responses to critics of the construction of social reality. Philos. Phenomenol. Res. **57**(2), 449–458 (1997)
22. Wooldridge, M.: An Introduction to Multiagent Systems. Wiley, Hoboken (2008)

Conceptual Modeling for Genomics: Building an Integrated Repository of Open Data

Anna Bernasconi(✉), Stefano Ceri, Alessandro Campi, and Marco Masseroli

Dipartimento di Elettronica, Informazione e Bioingegneria,
Politecnico di Milano, Milan, Italy
{anna.bernasconi,stefano.ceri,alessandro.campi,marco.masseroli}@polimi.it

Abstract. Many repositories of open data for genomics, collected by world-wide consortia, are important enablers of biological research; moreover, all experimental datasets leading to publications in genomics must be deposited to public repositories and made available to the research community. These datasets are typically used by biologists for validating or enriching their experiments; their content is documented by metadata. However, emphasis on data sharing is not matched by accuracy in data documentation; metadata are not standardized across the sources and often unstructured and incomplete.

In this paper, we propose a conceptual model of genomic metadata, whose purpose is to query the underlying data sources for locating relevant experimental datasets. First, we analyze the most typical metadata attributes of genomic sources and define their semantic properties. Then, we use a top-down method for building a global-as-view integrated schema, by abstracting the most important conceptual properties of genomic sources. Finally, we describe the validation of the conceptual model by mapping it to three well-known data sources: TCGA, ENCODE, and Gene Expression Omnibus.

Keywords: Conceptual model · Data integration · Genomics · Next Generation Sequencing · Open data

1 Introduction

Thanks to Next Generation Sequencing, a recent technological revolution for reading the DNA, a huge number of genomic datasets have become available. Sequencing machines perform the *primary data analysis* and produce raw datasets (a single human genome requires about 200 GB). Computationally expensive pipelines, collectively regarded as *secondary data analysis* [30], are then applied to raw data for extracting signals from the genome (such as: mutations, expression levels, peaks of binding enrichment, chromatin states, etc.), thereby producing **processed genomic data**, which are much smaller in size.

Processed datasets are collected by worldwide consortia, such as TCGA (The Cancer Genome Atlas) [36], ENCODE (the Encyclopedia of DNA Elements) [28],

H.C. Mayr et al. (Eds.): ER 2017, LNCS 10650, pp. 325–339, 2017.
https://doi.org/10.1007/978-3-319-69904-2_26

Roadmap Epigenomics [19], and 1000 Genomes [27]; moreover, it is customary for authors of biological articles to publish their processed datasets on repositories such as GEO (the Gene Expression Omnibus) [4]. These datasets constitute a wealth of information, as they are open and can be used for secondary research. Processed datasets are used in *tertiary data analysis* for giving a global sense to heterogeneous genomic and epigenomic signals, thereby answering complex biological queries. Several systems are dedicated to tertiary data analysis, including FireCloud[1], SciDB-Paradigm4 [26], and BLUEPRINT [1]. In the context of the GeCo Project[2], we developed GMQL [17,23], a high-level query language for genomics; we also proposed GDM [24], a unifying model for processed data formats.

While a lot of efforts are made for the production of genomic datasets, much less emphasis is given to the structured description of their content. Such descriptions, collectively regarded as *metadata*, are fundamental for understanding how each biological sample was processed, to which biological or clinical condition it is associated, which technological process has been used for its production, and so on. There is no standard for metadata, thus each source/consortium enforces some rules autonomously; a conceptual design for metadata is either missing or, when present, overly complex and useless[3]. In summary, in spite of a growing interest on tertiary data analysis and of the availability of many valuable data sources, genomic metadata are lacking a conceptual model for understanding which sources and datasets are most suitable for answering a genomic question.

One of the far-reaching goals of the GeCo project is the development of an integrated repository of open processed data, supporting both structured and search queries; the GMQL prototype[4] already integrates data from three repositories (TCGA, ENCODE, and Roadmap Epigenomics) and structured methods for periodically loading and keeping updated their contents. To overcome the lack of standards, metadata are stored in GMQL as generic attribute-value pairs; with such format, metadata are used for the initial selection of relevant datasets. However, we are aware of the fact that attribute-value pairs are just providing a viable solution, but do not carry enough semantics.

In this paper, we present the **Genomic Conceptual Model (GCM)**, a conceptual model for describing metadata of genomic data sources. GCM is centered on the notion of the *experiment item*, typically a file containing genomic regions and their properties, which is analyzed from three points of view:

- The *technology* used in the experiment, including information about item containers and their formats.
- The *biological* process observed in the experiment, in particular the sample being sequenced (derived from a tissue or a cell culture) and its preparation, including its donor.

[1] https://software.broadinstitute.org/firecloud/.

[2] Data-Driven Genomic Computing, http://www.bioinformatics.deib.polimi.it/geco/, ERC Advanced Grant, 2016–2021.

[3] At https://www.encodeproject.org/profiles/graph.svg see the conceptual model of ENCODE, an ER schema with tens of entities and hundreds of relationships, which is neither readable nor supported by metadata for most concepts.

[4] http://www.bioinformatics.deib.polimi.it/GMQL/interfaces/.

- The *management* of the experiment, describing the organizations/projects which are behind the production of each experiment.

The conceptual schema is constructed top-down, based on a systematic analysis of metadata attributes and of their properties in many genomic sources, and then verified bottom-up, on TCGA, ENCODE, and GEO; we show that ER schemas describing these sources can be constructed as subsets of GCM. Arbitrary queries on GCM can be propagated to sources, using the *global-as-view* approach [20]. We also show that GCM provides the skeleton to a simple query interface, similar to the one provided by DeepBlue [2]. Driven by GCM, we will add many more data sources to our integrated repository of open data for genomics.

2 Design of GCM

2.1 Analysis of Metadata Attributes

Most data sources provide interfaces for metadata extraction; these are based on simple query templates or application programming interfaces (APIs), and enable the selection of experimental data. Some sources also provide tabular descriptions of the metadata that can be more systematically queried, or enable the extraction of matching metadata in semistructured format (XML or JSON files).

Taxonomy of Metadata Attributes. As a first step in developing GCM, we defined a taxonomy of the main properties of metadata attributes; we then systematically applied the taxonomy to each considered source, so as to better characterize its content. According to our taxonomy, attributes are:

- **contextual (C)** when they are present (or absent) only within specific contexts, typically because another attribute takes a specific value. In such cases, there is an *existence dependency* between the two attributes.
- **dependent (D)** when the domain of their possible values is restricted, typically because another attribute takes a specific value. In such cases, there is a *value dependency* between the two attributes.
- **restricted (R)** when their value must be chosen from a controlled vocabulary.
- **single-valued (S)** when they assume at most one value for each specific experiment.
- **mandatory (M)** when they must have a value, either for all experiments or within a specific context.

The resulting taxonomy is shown in Table 1; it includes orthogonal features, and we targeted both completeness and minimality. By default (and in most cases), attributes do not have any of the above properties. Very few attributes are mandatory and unfortunately sources do not always agree on them; in many cases they are named and typed somehow differently.

Table 1. Taxonomy of features for metadata attributes

Level	Symbol	Feature	Default
Source	C	Contextual	Non-contextual
	D	Dependent	Independent
	R	Restricted	Free
	S	Single-valued	Multi-valued
	M	Mandatory	Optional
Integrated Repository	H	Human Curated	Extracted
	O	Ontological	Ordinary

We use these five categories to describe the attributes that are included in the conceptual model, as explained in the next section; we label the attributes with a feature vector, e.g. $Type^{[RSM]}$ denotes *Type* as an attribute which is mandatory, restricted and single-valued, while $Pipeline^{[D(Technique)S]}$ denotes *Pipeline* as a single-valued attribute with a value dependency from the attribute *Technique*.

Source Analysis. We examined several sources; among them TCGA and ENCODE provide the most comprehensive collection of metadata attributes.

- **TCGA** reports many experiment pipeline-specific metadata attributes; out of them we selected 22 attributes, common to all pipelines, which are the most interesting from a biological point of view (Table 2).
- **ENCODE** includes both a succinct and an expanded list of metadata attributes; while the expanded list has over 2000 attributes, the succinct list has 49 attributes for experiments, 44 attributes for biosamples, and 28 attributes for file descriptions.

Other Properties. We next define properties that we could not observe in the sources, but will be used for characterizing the metadata attributes of our integrated repository (they are also included in Table 1). Accordingly, attributes are:

- **human curated (H)** when their value is provided by a curator of the repository (and not extracted from the underlying data source).
- **ontological (O)** when an interface supports similarity-based matches based upon semantic properties, e.g. through the connection to external ontologies.

Rules. Rules may be used for expressing existence and value dependencies.

- The **existence dependency** *Technique* = "Chip-seq" $\rightarrow$ M(*Target*) indicates that *Target* is a mandatory attribute if *Technique* takes the value "Chip-seq", while *Technique* $\neq$ "Chip-seq" $\rightarrow$ NULL(*Target*) indicates that *Technique* is not specified otherwise.

Table 2. TCGA metadata attributes analysis

C	D	R	S	M	Dependency	Attribute
			×	×		clinical.demographic.id
			×			clinical.demographic.year_of_birth
		×	×	×		clinical.demographic.gender
		×	×	×		clinical.demographic.ethnicity
		×	×	×		clinical.demographic.race
			×	×		biospecimen.sample.id
		×	×	×		biospecimen.sample.sample_type
	×	×	×		sample_type	biospecimen.sample.tissue_type
			×	×		generated_data_files.data_file.⟨type⟩.id
		×	×	×		generated_data_files.data_file.⟨type⟩.data_type
	×	×	×	×	data_type	generated_data_files.data_file.⟨type⟩.data_format
			×	×		generated_data_files.data_file.⟨type⟩.file_size
	×	×	×	×	data_type	generated_data_files.data_file.⟨type⟩.experimental_strategy
×		×	×		data_type	generated_data_files.data_file.⟨type⟩.platform
	×	×	×	×	data_type	analysis.⟨workflow⟩.workflow_type
			×	×		analysis.⟨workflow⟩.workflow_link
			×	×		case.case.id
			×			case.case.primary_site
	×		×		primary_site	case.case.disease_type
			×	×		administrative.program.name
			×	×		administrative.project.name
			×			administrative.tissue_source_site.name

- The following **value dependency** connects the *DataType* and *Format* attributes: *DataType* = "raw data" → *Format* = "fastq".

In the next section we show examples of both existence and value dependencies, that complement the conceptual model specification; when the dependencies are specified for attributes belonging to different entities, they hold for all the instance pairs connected with an arbitrary join path connecting the two entities (this is not ambiguous because the conceptual model is acyclic).

2.2 Genomic Conceptual Model

We next designed the Genomic Conceptual Model top-down, inclusive of the most relevant metadata attributes as scouted from the various sources, building the entity-relationship schema represented in Fig. 1. The schema includes the principal concepts; other source-specific concepts can be made available in

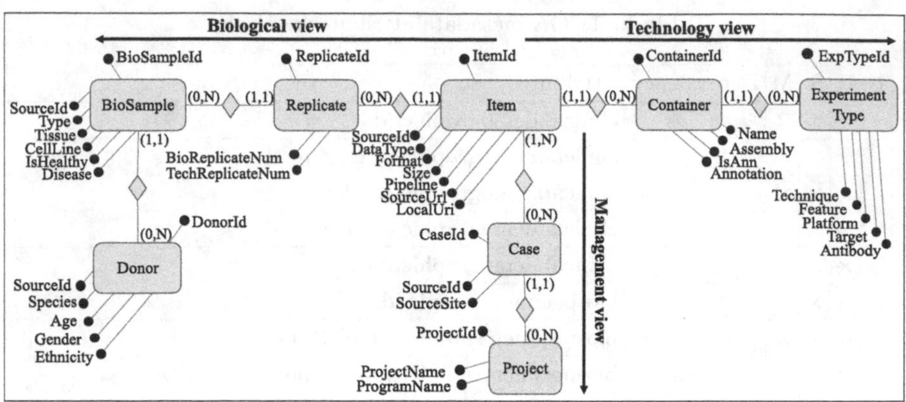

Fig. 1. Genomic conceptual model

semi-structured form aside from this schema (e.g. all clinical diagnosis conditions available for the donor in TCGA). The model is centered on the ITEM entity, which represents an elementary experimental unit. Three sub-schemata (or views) depart from the central entity, recalling a classic star-schema organization that is typical of data warehouses; they respectively describe biological, technological, and management aspects.

Central Entity. We next describe the attributes of the ITEM entity and associate each of them with their feature vector. The $SourceId^{[SM]}$ and $DataType^{[RSM]}$ respectively denote the item identifier within the source and the item's data type, and must always be included; *DataType* denotes the specific content of the ITEM, e.g. "peak". $Format^{[D(DataType)RSM]}$ denotes the ITEM data file format (e.g. ["fastq", "bam", "wiggle", "bed", "tsv", "vcf", "maf", "xml"]) and depends on *DataType* (e.g. "bed" format is compatible with "peak" and not compatible with "read"). Other attributes are: $Size^{[SM]}$, $SourceUrl^{[M]}$, $LocalUri^{[C(Format)SM]}$, and $Pipeline^{[D(Technique)S]}$.

The use of the last three attributes requires some discussion. Recall that we intend to build an integrated repository that contains only processed data, while in many cases the sources include also the raw data. In our metadata repository we include items relative to both raw and processed data with a reference to the related file in the original source within the *SourceUrl* attribute, that can be multi-valued in case the same data file is derived from different sources. In addition, items relative to processed files also exhibit an attribute *LocalUri* (see rule 1 in Listing 1, at the end of this section) indicating their physical location in our data repository. *Pipeline* is a descriptor of the specific parameters adopted in the pipeline used for producing the processed data. The descriptor is interpreted in the general context of the *Technique* used for producing several items of the same type and format; hence, the feature vector notation for *Pipeline*. Providing parameters and references to the raw data is relevant in the case of processed data, as sometimes biologists resort to original raw data for reprocessing; however, in the data sources such attributes may be missing or hidden within textual attributes.

Biological View. This view consists of a chain of entities: ITEM-REPLICATE-BIOSAMPLE-DONOR describing the biological process leading to the production of the ITEM. All relationships are many-to-one, hence an ITEM is associated with a given REPLICATE, each associated with a given BIOSAMPLE, each associated with a DONOR.

DONOR represents the individual of a specific organism from which the biological material is derived. It has attributes $SourceId^{[S]}$ (donor identifier relative to a source) and $Species^{[RSM]}$; $Age^{[S]}$, $Gender^{[RS]}$, and $Ethnicity^{[RS]}$ are other optional attributes of interest.

BIOSAMPLE describes the material sample taken from a biological entity and used for the experiment. Its $SourceId^{[M]}$ is an identifier of the bio-sample within a source, mandatory but also multi-valued (when the same sample is linked to different sources). $Type^{[RSM]}$ is restricted to the values ["cell line", "tissue"]. Based on the value of this attribute, either $Tissue^{[CSMO]}$ or $CellLine^{[CSMO]}$ becomes mandatory, but not both of them; this dependency is expressed by rules 2 and 3. $IsHealthy^{[RS]}$ is Boolean and $Disease^{[C(IsHealthy)D(Tissue)O]}$ contextually depends on *IsHeathy*, as expressed by rule 4, and can be multi-valued; moreover, its values depend on *Tissue* because given diseases can only be related to given tissues. We marked *Tissue*, *CellLine* and *Disease* as ontological[5], as we intend to extend the values of these attributes with their synonyms and generalizations/specializations, so as to ease their search; for example, the *Tissue* "blood vessel" will match the terms "vessel", "arteries" and "veins". Preliminary work for giving an extended ontological interpretation to ENCODE metadata is reported in [11].

REPLICATE is used when multiple material samples are generated from the same BIOSAMPLE, giving rise to items that are replica for the same experiment. This entity is relevant in some epigenomic data sources (such as ENCODE), that differentiate between technical and biological replication; such distinction is not present in most of the other sources.

Technology View. This view consists of a chain of entities: ITEM-CONTAINER-EXPERIMENTTYPE describing the used technology leading to the production of the ITEM. Through this chain, an ITEM is associated by means of (1:N) relationships to a given CONTAINER of a given EXPERIMENTTYPE.

[5] We will use the BRENDA Tissue and Enzyme Source Ontology [32] for tissues, the Cell Line Ontology [31] for cell lines, and the Human Disease Ontology [33] for human diseases.

Container is used to describe common properties of homogeneous items - sharing the same data structure and produced by the same experiment type. Its attributes include $Name^{[SM]}$ and $Assembly^{[C(DataType)D(Species)RSM]}$; *Assembly* is only present for items of particular types (see rule 5) and is restricted to a smaller vocabulary according to the *Species* (e.g., see rules 16 and 17). The Boolean attribute $IsAnn^{[RSM]}$ is used for distinguishing experimental items from known annotations (i.e., regarding known genomic regions): when true, $Annotation^{[C(IsAnn)RSM]}$ exists (see rules 6 and 7); annotations have a restricted vocabulary, including: ["Gene", "Exon", "TSS", "Promoter", "Enhancer", "Cpg-Island"].

ExperimentType refers to the specific methods used for producing each item. It includes the mandatory attribute $Technique^{[RSM]}$ (e.g., ["Chip-seq", "Dnase-seq", "RRBS", ...]). $Feature^{[D(Technique)RSMH]}$ is a mandatory manually curated attribute that we add to denote the specific feature described by the experiment (e.g., "Copy Number Variation", "Histone Modification", "Transcription Factor"). The value of $Platform^{[C(DataType)RSM]}$ illustrates the NGS platform used for sequencing and depends on the *DataType* of the item (see rule 8). When the *Technique* is "Chip-seq", the two attributes $Target^{[C(Technique)RSM]}$ and $Antibody^{[C(Technique)D(Target)RSM]}$ are present (see rules 9–12). The *Target* value is usually aligned to the vocabulary of UniProtKB[6]. The *Antibody* value depends on the *Target* since it is specific against that antigen.

Management View. This view consists of a chain of entities: Item-Case-Project describing the organizational process for the production of each item and the way in which items are grouped together to form a case.

Case represents a set of items that are gathered together, because they participate to a same research objective.

Project represents the project or program, occurred at a given institution (e.g., individual laboratory or consortium) that was responsible of the production of the item. $ProjectName^{[S]}$ and $ProgramName^{[S]}$ may be present, but none of them is mandatory.

Dependencies. Rules 1–12 of Listing 1 exhaustively describe the existence dependencies of the global schema. Rules 13–17 show some examples of value dependencies. Note that an attribute can be contextual but not mandatory (such as *Disease*, rule 4), contextual and mandatory (such as *Target*, rules 9 and 10), and also mandatory but not contextual (such as *Technique*). Note also that, when an attribute is marked as mandatory and the related information is missing from the source, then either human curation or rule-based management are needed.

[6] http://www.uniprot.org/uniprot/.

```
Item.Format="bed" → M(Item.LocalUri)
BioSample.Type="tissue" → M(BioSample.Tissue)
BioSample.Type="cell_line" → M(BioSample.CellLine)
BioSample.IsHealthy → NULL(BioSample.Disease)
Item.DataType in ["aligned read","peak","signal"] → M(Container.Assembly)
Container.IsAnn → M(Container.Annotation)
NOT(Container.IsAnn) → NULL(Container.Annotation)
Item.DataType="raw data" → M(ExperimentType.Platform)
ExperimentType.Technique="Chip-seq" → M(ExperimentType.Target)
ExperimentType.Technique≠"Chip-seq" → NULL(ExperimentType.Target)
ExperimentType.Technique="Chip-seq" → M(ExperimentType.Antibody)
ExperimentType.Technique≠"Chip-seq" → NULL(ExperimentType.Antibody)
--------------------------------------------------------------------
Item.DataType="raw data" → Item.Format="fastq"
BioSample.Tissue="liver" → BioSample.Disease ∈ ["viral hepatitis","liver lymphoma",...]
BioSample.Tissue="liver" → BioSample.Disease ∉ ["acute leukemia","pilorus cancer",...]
Donor.Species="Homo sapiens" → Container.Assembly ∈ ["GRCh38", "hg19", "hs37d5"]
Donor.Species="Mus musculus" → Container.Assembly ∈ ["mm9", "mm10", "GRCm38"]
```

Listing 1. Examples of existence and value dependencies

2.3 Source-Specific Views of GCM

We verify that the global-as-view approach really captures the three data sources considered, by showing them as *views of GCM* in Fig. 2; we use the following notation:

- We place the attributes of each source in the same position as in GCM, but we use for them the name that we found in the documentation of each source; missing attributes correspond to white circles.
- We cluster the conceptual entities corresponding to a single concept in the original source by encircling them within grey shapes. The entity names corresponding to the original source are reported with a bold bigger font on the clustered shape (e.g. Series in GEO) or directly on the new entity (e.g., Case in TCGA) when this corresponds to the name given in our GCM.
- We indicate specific relationship cardinalities where GCM differs from the source, using a bold font (e.g., see (1,1) from Item to Case in ENCODE).
- We enclose fixed human curated values in inverted commas and use the functions notation *tr*, *comb*, and *curated* to describe a transformation of a source field, a combination of multiple source fields, and curated fields, respectively.

Note that the Gene Expression Omnibus (GEO) source is at the same time a very rich public repository of genomic data (as most research publications include links to experimental data uploaded to GEO), but is also a very poor source of metadata, which are not well structured and often lack information; hence our mapping effort is harder and less precise for GEO than for the more organized TCGA and ENCODE sources[7]. The mapping to GEO captures as well the mapping to Roadmap Epigenomics, another relevant source of public data.

[7] Textual analysis to extract semantic information from the GEO repository is reported in [12]; we plan to reuse their library.

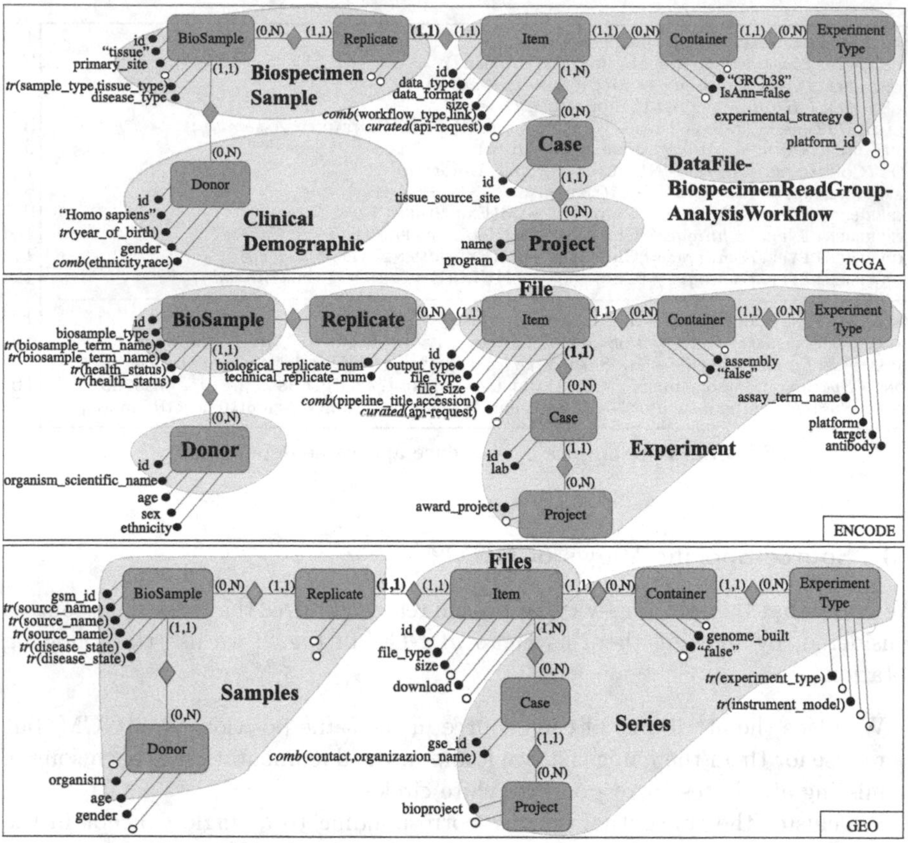

Fig. 2. Source-specific views of GCM for TCGA, ENCODE, and GEO

2.4 User-Friendly Interface

An important side effect of providing a global and integrated view of data sources is the ability to build user-friendly query interfaces for selecting items from multiple data sources. We show a mock-up of an interface that supports conjunctive

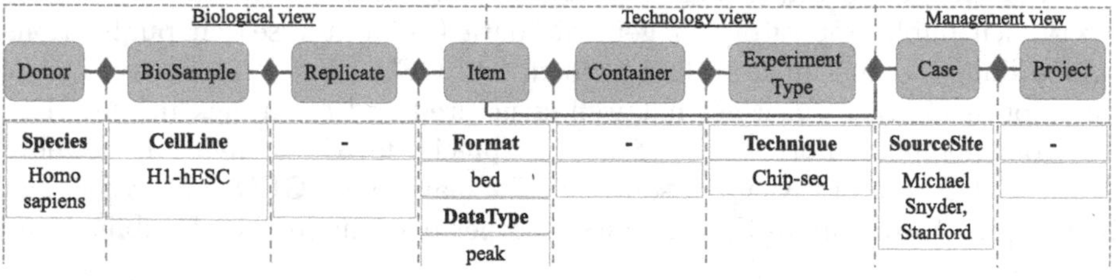

Fig. 3. Retrieval interface mock-up

queries over our entities, very similar to the user interface currently provided by DeepBlue [2] (Fig. 3); attributes are rendered by pop-up lists and values are then entered by users, with autocomplete support.

3 Building the Integrated Repository

In this section, we describe high level rules for loading the content of the integrated repository from the original data sources, with a global-as-view approach. These transformations drive our approach.

3.1 Available Repositories at the Sources

Most genomic repositories offer Web interfaces for accessing their metadata. In addition, some of them offer Web APIs for querying the metadata, used for accessing storage structures for metadata (typically relational tables). Table 3 describes the schemas of the tables available at TCGA[8], ENCODE, and GEO[9]. TCGA and ENCODE tables result from the translation of a hierarchical json format representation (the only one provided by the sources) into a relational representation that has required several normalization steps and simplifications for illustration purposes. GEO tables result from a selection of a small subset of attributes used for mapping GEO to GCM.

Table 3. Relational schema of TCGA(T), ENCODE(E), and GEO(G) repositories

T.Case(**id**,project_id,disease_type,primary_site,tissue_source_site)
T.Project(**id**,name,program)
T.ClinicalDemographic(**id**,case_id,year_of_birth,gender,ethnicity,race)
T.BiospecimenSample(**id**,case_id,sample_type,tissue_type)
T.BiospecimenReadGroup(**id**,sample_id,platform_id)
T.DataFile(**id**,readgroup_id,workflow_id,data_type,data_format,size,experimental_strategy)
T.AnalysisWorkflow(**id**,workflow_type,workflow_link)
E.Donor(**id**,organism_scientific_name,age,sex,ethnicity)
E.Biosample(**id**,donor_id,biosample_type,biosample_term_name,health_status)
E.Replicate(**id**,biosample_id,experiment_id,biological_replicate_num,technical_replicate_num)
E.Experiment(**id**,assembly,assay_term_name,target,antibody,lab,award_project,platform)
E.File(**id**,experiment_id,output_type,file_type,file_size,pipeline_title,pipeline_accession)
G.File(**id**,gsm_id,file_type,size,download)
G.Gse(**id**,organization_name,contact,bioproject,experiment_type)
G.Gsm(**id**,gse_id,organism,age,gender,source_name,disease_state,genome_built,instrument_model)

[8] The metadata is provided in the NCI Genomic Data Commons portal, https://docs.gdc.cancer.gov/Data_Dictionary/viewer/.

[9] GEO information can be retrieved through the R package *GEOmetadb* [37].

3.2 Mapping Rules

Mapping rules are used to describe how data are loaded from the sources into the integrated repository; for illustration purposes, in Table 4 we provide some of the mappings, related to the Donor, BioSample, Case, and ExperimentType entities. Each mapping rule is a logic formula with variables in its left end side (LHS) which are computed from the variables in its right end side (RHS). The order of the LHS variables is the same reported in our global schema in Fig. 1 and the order of the RHS variables is the same reported in Table 3 for each source. As an example, the entity ExperimentType of the global schema is filled with data from ENCODE's entity Experiment, together with data from TCGA's BiospecimenReadGroup and DataFile (joined on the *readgroup_id* attribute), and data from GEO's Gse and Gsm (joined on the *gse_id* attribute).

Table 4. Examples of mapping rules for building the integrated repository from the sources

LHS		RHS
Donor(*SID*,*SP*,*AGE*,*G*,*E*)	⊇	E.Donor(*SID*,*SP*,*AGE*,*G*,*E*)
Donor(*SID*,"Homo S.",*tr*(*Y*),*G*,*comb*(*ET*,*R*))	⊇	T.ClinicalDemographic(*SID*,_,*Y*,*G*,*EY*,*R*)
Donor(_,*SP*,*AGE*,*G*,_)	⊇	G.Gsm(_,_,*SP*,*AGE*,*G*,_,_,_,_)
BioSample(*SID*,*T*,*tr*(*BT*),*tr*(*BT*),*tr*(*HS*),*tr*(*HS*))	⊇	E.Biosample(*SID*,_,*T*,*BT*,*HS*)
BioSample(*SID*,"tissue",*PS*,_,*tr*(*ST*,*TT*),*DIS*)	⊇	T.BiospecimenSample(*SID*,*CID*,*ST*,*TT*), T.Case(*CID*,_,*DIS*,*PS*,_)
BioSample(*SID*,*tr*(*SN*),*tr*(*SN*),*tr*(*SN*),*tr*(*D*),*tr*(*D*))	⊇	G.Gsm(*SID*,_,_,_,_,*SN*,*D*,_,_)
Case(*SID*,*SS*)	⊇	E.Experiment(*SID*,_,_,_,_,_,*SS*,_)
Case(*SID*,*SS*)	⊇	T.Case(*SID*,_,_,_,*SS*)
Case(*SID*,*tr*(*O*,*C*))	⊇	G.Gse(*SID*,*O*,*C*,_,_,_)
ExperimentType(*TE*,*comb*(*TE*,*T*),*P*,*T*,*A*)	⊇	E.Experiment(_,_,*TE*,*T*,*A*,_,_,*P*)
ExperimentType(*TE*,*tr*(*TE*),*P*,_,_)	⊇	T.BiospecimenReadGroup(*RGID*,_,*P*), T.DataFile(_,*RGID*,_,_,_,_,*TE*)
ExperimentType(*tr*(*TE*),*tr*(*TE*),*tr*(*P*),_,_)	⊇	G.Gse(*EID*,_,_,_,*TE*), G.Gsm(_,*EID*,_,_,_,_,_,_,*P*)

As we already discussed in Sect. 2.3, the values of some of the attributes are acquired exactly as they are in the original source, others need the application of simple manually provided functions for textual transformation (denoted as *tr*), others are computed as textual combination of multiple source fields (denoted as *comb*, and finally others need manual curation (values are enclosed in inverted commas). As an example, Donor.*Ethnicity* corresponds to a combination of the attributes *race* and *ethnicity* of the ClinicalDemographic table, taken from TCGA source. *Tissue* and *CellLine* attributes of the BioSample are both produced by *biosample_term_name* of ENCODE which uses this attribute for both of them - the content of this attribute depends on the value of *biosample_type* (either "cell_line" or "tissue"). Relevant integration efforts are addressed towards defining a shared set of homogenized values for each attribute. The values of the global attributes, given to the LHS variables, are to be intended as already homogenized to the reference ontologies (as indicated in Sect. 2.2), or to the chosen finite restricted dictionaries. Notice that all the mappings preliminarily perform a value homogenization step, implicit in the integration process.

4 Related Works

A long stream of research tackled the problem of providing integrated access to multiple, heterogeneous sources. A survey of very preliminary works is [14]. Buneman et al. [6] described the problem of querying and transforming scientific data residing in structured files of different formats. Along that work, BioKleisli [8] and K2 [9] describe early systems supporting queries across multiple sources. BioKleisli was a federated database offering an object-oriented model; its main limitation was the lack of a global schema, imposing users to know the structure of underlying sources. To improve this aspect, K2 included GUS (Genomics Unified Schema), an extensive relational database schema supporting a wide range of functional genomics data types. The BioProject [3] database was recently established to facilitate the organization and classification of project metadata submitted to NCBI, EBI and DDBJ databases.

A common approach in integrated data management is data warehousing, consisting of a-priori integration and reconciliation of data extracted from multiple sources, such as in EnsMart/BioMart [13,34]. Along this direction, [22] describes a warehouse for integrating genomic and proteomic information using generalization hierarchies and a modular, multilevel global schema to overcome differences among data sources. ER modeling (and UML class diagrams) were used in [5]; models describe protein structures and genomic sequences, with rather complex concepts aiming at completely representing the underlying biology. [35] is a biomedical data warehouse supporting a data model (called BioStar) capturing the semantics of biomedical data and providing some extensibility to cope with the evolution of biological research methodologies.

Many other works [10,15,16,18,21,25,29] present conceptual models for explaining biological entities and their interactions in terms of conceptual data structures. With our approach, similar to DeepBlue [2], we instead use conceptual modeling for driving the continuous process of metadata integration and for offering high-level query interfaces on metadata for locating relevant datasets, under the assumption that users will then manage these datasets for solving biological or clinical questions. Similarly to DeepBlue, we hide the data source differences so as to provide easy-to-use interfaces, but differently from them we disclose the semantic properties of the underlying sources and the metadata integration process; moreover, we cover a broader spectrum of sources and provide a richer set of concepts, including the management view.

5 Conclusions

The interest on an integrated repository for genomics stems from the huge amount of resources that are becoming available. In this paper we provide GCM, a genomic conceptual model capable of capturing the metadata of heterogeneous sources with a global-as-view approach. The model is supported by a method for conceptually designing global metadata through source attribute analysis and is validated by using three data sources: TCGA, ENCODE, and GEO.

Our GMQL system already provides access to datasets from TCGA, ENCODE, and Roadmap Epigenomics, that were identified as the most relevant in the course of collaborative projects with many biologists; we already developed some tools for automatically importing such datasets and for converting them to an integrated format, e.g., TCGA2BED [7]. Thanks to GCM, we can also provide a coherent semantics to the metadata of integrated sources; throughout the GeCo project we plan to add more sources, according to needs of biologists, and to continuously integrate their metadata within GCM.

Acknowledgement. This research is funded by the ERC Advanced Grant project GeCo (Data-Driven Genomic Computing), 2016–2021.

References

1. Adams, D., et al.: BLUEPRINT to decode the epigenetic signature written in blood. Nat. Biotechnol. **30**(3), 224–226 (2012)
2. Albrecht, F., et al.: DeepBlue epigenomic data server: programmatic data retrieval and analysis of epigenome. Nucleic Acids Res. **44**(W1), W581–W586 (2016)
3. Barrett, T., et al.: BioProject and BioSample databases at NCBI: facilitating capture and organization of metadata. Nucleic Acids Res. **40**(D1), 57–63 (2012)
4. Barrett, T., et al.: NCBI GEO: archive for functional genomics data sets – update. Nucleic Acids Res. **41**(Database issue), D991–D995 (2013)
5. Bornberg-Bauer, E., Paton, N.W.: Conceptual data modelling for bioinformatics. Brief. Bioinform. **3**(2), 166–180 (2002)
6. Buneman, P., et al.: A data transformation system for biological data sources. In: International Conference on Very Large Data Bases, pp. 158–169 (1995)
7. Cumbo, F., et al.: TCGA2BED: extracting, extending, integrating, and querying The Cancer Genome Atlas. BMC Bioinform. **18**(6), 1–9 (2017)
8. Davidson, S.B., et al.: Biokleisli: a digital library for biomedical researchers. Int. J. Digit. Libr. **1**(1), 36–53 (1997)
9. Davidson, S.B., et al.: K2/Kleisli and GUS: experiments in integrated access to genomic data sources. IBM Syst. J. **40**(2), 512–531 (2001)
10. El-Ghalayini, H., et al.: Deriving conceptual data models from domain ontologies for bioinformatics. In: 2006 2nd Information and Communication Technologies, ICTTA 2006, vol. 2, pp. 3562–3567 (2006)
11. Fernández, J.D., et al.: Ontology-based search of genomic metadata. IEEE/ACM Trans. Comput. Biol. Bioinform. **13**(2), 233–247 (2016)
12. Galeota, E., Pelizzola, M.: Ontology-based annotations and semantic relations in large-scale (epi)genomics data. Brief. Bioinform. **18**(3), 403–412 (2017)
13. Haider, S., et al.: BioMart Central Portal - unified access to biological data. Nucleic Acids Res. **37**(Web Server issue), 23–27 (2009)
14. Hernandez, T., Kambhampati, S.: Integration of biological sources: current systems and challenges ahead. SIGMOD Rec. **33**(3), 51–60 (2004)
15. Idrees, M., et al.: A review: conceptual data models for biological domain. JAPS, J. Anim. Plant Sci. **25**(2), 337–345 (2015)

16. Ji, F., Elmasri, R., et al.: Incorporating concepts for bioinformatics data modeling into EER models. In: ACS/IEEE International Conference on Computer Systems and Applications, pp. 189–192. IEEE Computer Society, Washington, DC, USA (2005)
17. Kaitoua, A., Pinoli, P., Bertoni, M., Ceri, S.: Framework for supporting genomic operations. IEEE Trans. Comput. **66**(3), 443–457 (2017)
18. Keet, M.C.: Biological data and conceptual modelling method. J. Concept. Model. **29**(1), 1–14 (2003)
19. Kundaje, A., et al.: Integrative analysis of 111 reference human epigenomes. Nature **518**(7539), 317–330 (2015)
20. Lenzerini, M.: Data integration: a theoretical perspective. In: Symposium on Principles of Database Systems, PODS, pp. 233–246. ACM, New York, NY, USA (2002)
21. Louie, B., et al.: Data integration and genomic medicine. J. Biomed. Inform. **40**(1), 5–16 (2007)
22. Masseroli, M., Canakoglu, A., Ceri, S.: Integration and querying of genomic and proteomic semantic annotations for biomedical knowledge extraction. IEEE/ACM Trans. Comput. Biol. Bioinform. **13**(2), 209–219 (2016)
23. Masseroli, M., et al.: GenoMetric Query Language: a novel approach to large-scale genomic data management. Bioinformatics **31**(12), 1881–1888 (2015)
24. Masseroli, M., et al.: Modeling and interoperability of heterogeneous genomic big data for integrative processing and querying. Methods **111**, 3–11 (2016)
25. Rechenmann, F.: Data modeling: the key to biological data integration. EMBnet. J. **18**(B), 59–60 (2012)
26. Anonymous paper. Accelerating bioinformatics research with new software for big data to knowledge (BD2K), Paradigm4, April 2015. www.paradigm4.com
27. Consortium 1000Genomes: A map of human genome variation from population-scale sequencing. Nature **467**(7319), 1061–1073 (2010)
28. Consortium ENCODE: An integrated encyclopedia of DNA elements in the human genome. Nature **489**(7414), 57–74 (2012)
29. Reyes Román, J.F., Pastor, Ó., Casamayor, J.C., Valverde, F.: Applying conceptual modeling to better understand the human genome. In: Comyn-Wattiau, I., Tanaka, K., Song, I.-Y., Yamamoto, S., Saeki, M. (eds.) ER 2016. LNCS, vol. 9974, pp. 404–412. Springer, Cham (2016). doi:10.1007/978-3-319-46397-1_31
30. Roy, A., et al.: Massively parallel processing of whole genome sequence data: an in-depth performance study. In: Proceedings of the 2017 ACM International Conference on Management of Data, SIGMOD 2017, Chicago, Illinois, USA, 14–19 May 2017, pp. 187–202. ACM, New York (2017)
31. Sarntivijai, S., et al.: CLO: the cell line ontology. J. Biomed. Semant. **5**(1), 37 (2014)
32. Schomburg, I., et al.: BRENDA in 2013: new options and contents in BRENDA. Nucleic Acids Res. **41**(Database issue), D764–D772 (2013)
33. Schriml, L.M., et al.: Disease Ontology: a backbone for disease semantic integration. Nucleic Acids Res. **40**(Database issue), 940–946 (2012)
34. Smedley, D., et al.: The BioMart community portal: an innovative alternative to large, centralized data repositories. Nucleic Acids Res. **43**(W1), 589–598 (2015)
35. Wang, L., et al.: BioStar models of clinical and genomic data for biomedical data warehouse design. Int. J. Bioinform. Res. Appl. **1**(1), 63–80 (2005)
36. Weinstein, J.N., et al.: The cancer genome atlas pan-cancer analysis project. Nat. Genet. **45**(10), 1113–1120 (2013)
37. Zhu, Y., et al.: Geometadb: powerful alternative search engine for the gene expression omnibus. Bioinformatics **24**(23), 2798–2800 (2008)

Towards Thinking Manufacturing and Design Together: An Aeronautical Case Study

Thomas Polacsek[1], Stéphanie Roussel[1(✉)], François Bouissiere[2], Claude Cuiller[2], Pierre-Eric Dereux[2], and Stéphane Kersuzan[2]

[1] ONERA, Toulouse, France
{thomas.polacsek,stephanie.roussel}@onera.fr
[2] AIRBUS, Blagnac, France
{francois.boussiere,claude.cuiller,pierre-eric.dereux, stephane.kersuzan}@airbus.fr

Abstract. The construction of complex objects, such as an aircraft, requires the creation of a dedicated industrial system. By industrial system, we mean all the material and immaterial means used to manufacture the object (labour, machines, factories, etc.). Classically, the industrial system is specified when the aircraft design is already engaged. In other words, the specifications of the product are the requirements of the industrial system. This approach presents two major drawbacks: firstly, the industrial system can inherit blocking constraints that could be easily removed by changing the aircraft design, and secondly, both continue to evolve during the lifetime of the aircraft programme. In this paper, we address the problem of having a global view of design and manufacturing. Starting from an industrial case study, the Airbus A320 aircraft manufacturing, we proposed a model-based approach, firsts steps towards tools for specifying together and consistently the design of an aircraft and its manufacturing system.

Keywords: Model-based systems engineering · Simultaneous engineering · Manufacturing · Aeronautics · Factory of the future

1 Introduction

Nowadays, the aeronautical market moves very quickly, especially due to the emergence of new airline companies. Indeed, these companies have requirements on their aircraft fleet either regarding the performances of the aircraft, the associated costs, or more specific features. Aircraft manufacturers need to align their current aircraft models with these requirements quickly if they want to remain competitive. But the development cycle of an aircraft is, today, very long compared to the evolution of the market. In fact, the aircraft architectural design is carried out sequentially by first considering the requirements related to the performance of the product (number of passengers, consumption, etc.), defining the major components of the aircraft, and then defining the associated industrial

H.C. Mayr et al. (Eds.): ER 2017, LNCS 10650, pp. 340–353, 2017.
https://doi.org/10.1007/978-3-319-69904-2_27

system.[1] This results in a low reactivity to adapt the product to these potential new clients.

On another aspect, the demand for aircraft has been growing for decades, especially for some short-haul aircraft families. In this context, there is a need for increasing the production rate on the manufacturing lines. But the production schedule is already so tight that it has become very difficult and costly to reach higher rates. As the aircraft manufacturers do not wish to deeply modify the current industrial system, they are introducing modifications in the architecture design that *"simplify"* manufacturing. For instance, a heavy and large aircraft element, thus difficult to handle by operators, may have to be installed in non-ergonomic conditions, like arms raised upward for a long duration. If this element is moved to a more accessible location, or replaced by smaller elements, gains in installation time can be expected. In order to evaluate the impact of a modification of the architectural design on the industrial system, one has classically to go through the whole development cycle and specially define in detail the industrial operations associated to the new design. This process is very time-consuming and results again in a low reactivity in regards with the market demand.

One way to shorten the development cycle and hence increase the reactivity of aircraft manufacturers is to think the design of aircraft architecture and manufacturing system together instead of sequentially, which is also called *simultaneous engineering*. The concept of simultaneous engineering between the design office and production is relatively old [12]. Used in the automotive industry, especially in the supply chain [7], its implementation in our context raises some issues due to aeronautics particularities. Indeed, an aircraft is a very complex and bulky object, composed of many components, and requiring manufacturing operations that are often manual and relying on a very specific know-how. In addition, aeronautical regulations impose very strong certification constraints on the design and the manufacturing of the aircraft. All of this constrains and limits the evolution of the design and production methods, mainly due to the efforts necessary to provide justifying elements for the compliance with the regulations. Lastly, until today, production volumes, limited to a few hundred aircraft per year, had not yet prompted an evolution of production methods.

In this paper, we present a recent initiative from Airbus to incrementally develop the A320 aircraft family and increase the production rate on a specific manufacturing line. The concepts we describe here are still preliminary but are based on a real industrial use-case for which significant efforts have been provided to collect very heterogeneous data (documents, interviews, plans, etc.). We show how this industrial problem has been addressed so as to think aircraft architectural design and manufacturing system together. Therefore, the contribution is a first step towards an aeronautical simultaneous engineering.

This paper is organized as follows. We first present the specificities of simultaneous engineering dedicated to aeronautics in Sect. 2.1. In Sect. 3, we describe

[1] By industrial system we mean all the material and non-material means used to construct an aircraft (labour, machines, factories, methods, tools, etc.).

the industrial use-case and we define a first model of the manufacturing line. In Sect. 4, we define a generic pattern for a model of design and manufacturing that can be instantiated at different levels of abstraction. Finally, Sect. 5 concludes this paper by bringing up the short-term and long-term perspectives.

2 Simultaneous Engineering for Aeronautics

In this section, we describe the specificities of simultaneous engineering for the aeronautics domain. We first detail the current aircraft development cycle. Then, we highlight the main objectives to reach.

2.1 A Sequential Development Cycle

In the aeronautics industry, the *aircraft architect* manages the interactions between many different entities and the contribution of many different disciplines. These interactions include negotiations amongst engineering disciplines (e.g. aerodynamics, loads, safety, thermal), business functions (e.g. finance, procurement) and production. In fact, because they have a global picture, the main goal of the aircraft architect is to ensure that the aircraft fulfils its operational performance requirements just as well as its production requirements.

The design and development of an aircraft, such as the A320, follows today a very traditional cascading cycle, starting from very high level requirements refined to lower level requirements that are then transformed into specifications. More precisely, in this sequential cascade approach, the preliminary project steps are devoted exclusively to the overall aircraft specification and sizing. These steps are in fact a consultation between the aircraft architects, the design offices and the European national companies that make up the *European Economic Interest Grouping* (EEIG). After dispatching the main activities between the members of the EEIG, each major component of the aircraft (fuselage, cockpit, wings, tails, systems, landing gear, ...) is defined in detail. The result is the detailed aircraft design and constitutes the starting point used for the definition of the industrial system.

Because of this sequential definition, the design of the industrial system is completely out of synchronisation with the engineering activities. Therefore, the difficulties of defining an industrial system that implements the detailed design are only grasped late in the development process. Moreover, this division between design and production is a constraint for the new challenges of the aeronautics industry. First of them is the capability to quickly modify the product to meet the market demand and second the need to increase the production rate.

The spectrum of market demand can be quite large. For instance, one customer might want to improve the performances of the aircraft or make it compliant with a specific regulation. Generally, this implies some modifications of the aircraft design. However, because the demand is expressed when the aircraft is already designed and industrial system build deep modifications of the industrial system are not an option. That is why the architects have to ensure that the current industrial system will be able to handle the design modifications. For that, they need to evaluate the impact of a modification of the design on the production system.

Today, such an evaluation cannot be done directly because the architects use high level abstract elements such as a wing or landing gear while the manufacturing engineers handle screws, cables, etc. In fact, to perform this evaluation, it is necessary to perform all the steps of the development cycle: preliminary design, detailed design and industrial definition. The industrial definition includes the creation of assembly operations dedicated to the new design, the identification of the physical equipment necessary to manufacture along with the associated tooling, and the scheduling of the manufacturing steps. Then, the evaluation is performed mostly manually following different criteria: impact on the production rate, additional costs, etc. This process is time-consuming and has a significant cost.

Regarding the production rate, the increase in air traffic and the arrival of new airlines lead to the need to produce more aircrafts. For cost reasons, the production rate must be increased without deeply modifying the industrial system. Indeed, increase the size of the assembly line or build a new factory requires a very unfavorable financial investment. Therefore, a possible option, with a limited effect of the industrial system, is to introduce design modifications to make manufacturing operations *simpler*.

An example is illustrated on Fig. 1: after a study of the assembly line, it appears that a bottleneck for the increase of the production rate is related to the installation of an air conditioning circuit (pipe). A part of this circuit passes through a very narrow area, which makes the installation particularly difficult. The architects propose to modify the path of this circuit in the aircraft, and to make it pass through an area more accessible to the operators.

In this case, the process to increase the production rate consists in the following steps:

1. identify the manufacturing bottlenecks and their causes;
2. analyse the installation instructions in order to establish the links between the design elements and the installation operations (duration, aircraft zones, number of operators needed for the operations);
3. create a new architecture design that removes the bottleneck;
4. define the corresponding manufacturing elements as described previously and evaluate the resulting benefits on the industrial system performance.

Again, this process is too time-consuming compared to the required reactivity. Moreover, it can sometimes reveal to be a waste of time if a new design does not have the expected positive effects on the production.

2.2 Objectives of the Simultaneous Engineering

As we have seen, the architectural work begins at high-level of abstraction and finishes at complete detailed description design level. However, due to the successive design refinements, it is excessively difficult to evaluate the impact of new

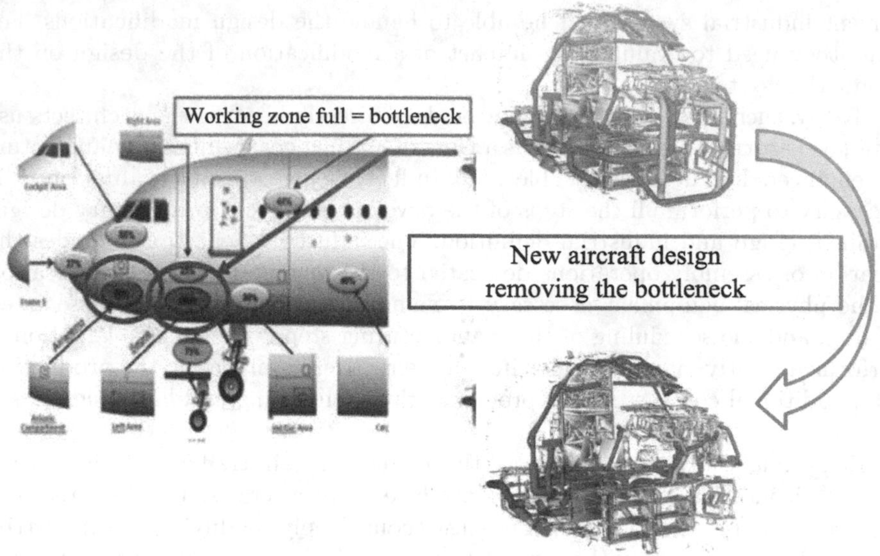

Fig. 1. New aircraft concept design to remove a bottleneck

architecture proposals on the production. To reduce the time and cost, there is a real need for tools allowing to assess the impacts on the manufacturing without the detailed definition of the final product, i.e. tools that can be used at the same level of abstraction as the one used by the architect. To address this, Airbus has decided to carry out a simultaneous engineering activity between the design office and the production department.

The purpose of this activity is to switch from the sequential development cycle as described in the previous subsection and illustrated on Fig. 2a to a progressive development cycle as illustrated on Fig. 2b. More precisely, on Fig. 2a, the pyramid represents the evolution from high-level design (top of the pyramid) to a final design (bottom of the pyramid) from which a manufacturing can be implemented. The manufacturing impact can only be assessed when a final design is achieved. The aim of the simultaneous engineering is to allow the architect to quickly study aircraft design proposals regarding the expected benefits on the production. It can be split up into two objectives:

(a) *consider consistently about design and manufacturing at any level of abstraction.* As illustrated on Fig. 2a, it is currently possible to reason about design at several levels of abstraction. Hence, the objective is to have high-level abstractions of the manufacturing model, one for each level of the design. On Fig. 2b, this corresponds to the right pyramid;
(b) *assess the manufacturing performances thanks to its abstract models.* If such an evaluation is possible at any abstract level, then it allows to have a feedback on the impact of the design at any time. On Fig. 2b, this feedback is represented by the left arrow that goes from the right pyramid to the left one.

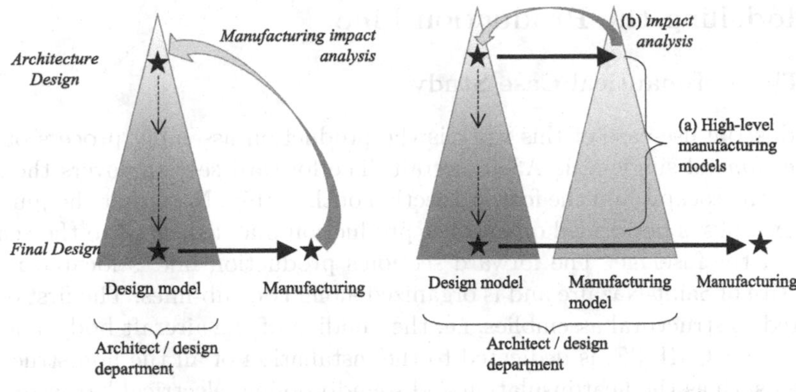

(a) Current development process. (b) Enhanced development process.

Fig. 2. Towards an enhanced model for the aircraft architect

With such a structure, the first advantage is the capacity for the architects to evaluate at any time the foreseen impact on the manufacturing process, which avoids the current time-consuming process. The second advantage is the possibility to specify much earlier the industrial system associated to a design. In fact, such a specification based on conceptual models allows all stakeholders to anticipate the difficulties in the industrial implementation of an architecture design, even for high-level ones.

In a long-term perspective, the evaluation could consist in a complete chain of methods and tools. For instance, at each abstract level of design, one could consider several high-level industrial systems and choose the one that gives the best performances, or even optimize the overall industrial system. Tools could also support the architects in design tasks by automatically checking properties directly on the model and finding the best possible configuration according to a set of constraints as it is done in [4,5] with logic-based solvers.

In a short-term perspective, we focus on an essential part of the evaluation: the estimation of the impact on the production rate. More precisely, we want to plug our model to automatic tools that would generate the optimal sequence of high-level installation operations and therefore give a clue of an expected production rate. This means that conceptual manufacturing models must be compliant with operational research tools dedicated to scheduling [8,10]. In order to reach this short-term objective, we first need to achieve the first sub-goal and model the manufacturing at different abstract levels. Hence, for the time being, starting from raw data, we focus on the definition of high-level manufacturing models. More precisely, we first model the current assembly line and we abstract this model while taking into account architecture design elements. Contrary to approaches developed in [2,6,13], we do not aim at defining a generic framework for simultaneous engineering but a framework dedicated to aeronautics. Nevertheless, we hope that this preliminary work will support a larger reflection in the future.

3 Modelling the Production Line

3.1 The Aeronautical Case Study

The industrial use-case of this work is the production assembly process of *forward sections* of single-aisle A320 aircraft. The forward section covers the nose fuselage, the cockpit and the forward section of the cabin. Note that the junction with the wings is performed on another production line dedicated to the central section of the fuselage. The forward section's production line is located in the French site of Saint-Nazaire and is organized along two sub-lines. The first one is dedicated to structural assemblies, i.e. the building of the aircraft body, and the second one, COMETE, is dedicated to the installation of all the non-structural elements such as the heat insulation and soundproofing, electrical harnesses and equipping, air conditioning circuits, etc.

In this use-case, we focus on the COMETE production line. It is composed of 14 stations on which manufacturing activities, i.e. equipments installation, are distributed. The installation process is organized as a *pulse line*, meaning that the section to equip and the associated tooling are transferred every X hours from one station to another. The equipments installation always starts in station 1 with a completely unequipped section, and always finishes on station 14 with a completely equipped one.

As the A320 aircraft family is quite old, its production was not foreseen for high production rates. At this time, a production rate of one plane per month was a remarkable performance. Nowadays, the rate reaches 50 planes per month in order to meet the market demand. Nevertheless, due to the weight of this program's history, most of manufacturing activities are still manual ones. Technologies used on the line are highly reliable and low cost but have almost not evolved since the beginning. Moreover, work zones are still cramped and make operators' tasks quite tedious, especially with high production rates.

The objective is to develop solutions that allow to reach a rate of 63 planes per month. In order to minimize industrial risks, these solutions cannot deeply modify the production line. Moreover, the solution that would consist in building a second identical production line is out of scope.

3.2 Data Retrieval and Analysis

Modelling the manufacturing process requires an in-depth understanding of its building blocks and the interactions between them. In fact, many competences and trades are involved and they can sometimes be quite far from the architect's world. Thus, the first part of the study, which is still on-going work, consists in retrieving and analysing data about the manufacturing line.

Due to the A320 program's age, significant part of the documentation is still not digitalized, the human knowledge is quite tremendous but is mostly shared orally and some rules can even be implicit. Consequently, we had to go to the Saint-Nazaire site regularly in order to interview the different actors, understand and question their practises.

From those interviews and from the engineering and manufacturing database, we have built and/or retrieved several relevant pieces of information:

- the PERT (Program Evaluation and Review Technique) diagram - this diagram contains the manufacturing scheduling, i.e. the order in which the equipment are currently installed on the section. For the A320 program, this scheduling is manually built by a *Time Evaluation Agent*;
- equipment installation descriptions - documents detailing the sequences of activities performed during the installation, the impacted geographic zones of the forward section, the list of physical parts concerned and the number of operators required;
- a list of all the physical parts to be installed on each station of the line.

Note that most of these pieces of information are paper documents with heterogeneous structures and formats and therefore have been analysed manually, which represents a significant work. From this analysis, we have identified seven major concepts in the COMETE manufacturing line. They are connected together as presented in the UML model of Fig. 3.

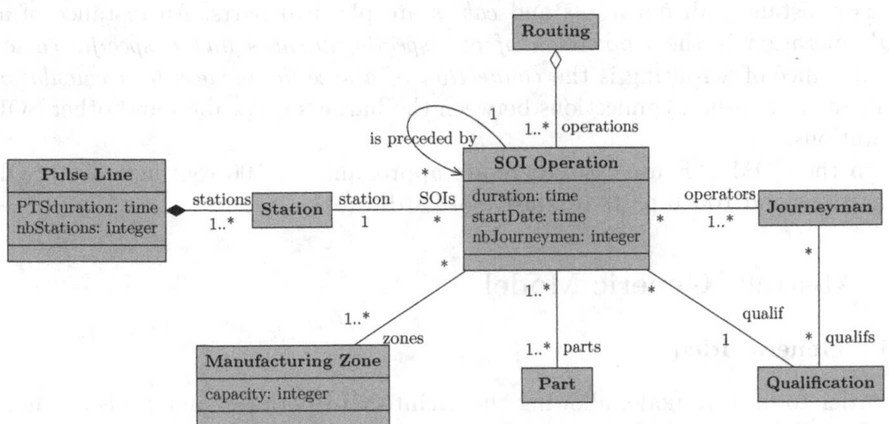

Fig. 3. UML model of the manufacturing line

The concepts and their features are:

- **Part**: physical elements of the aircraft.
- **Station**: the physical space in which the section is equipped along with the associated tools and parts. Because the physical space and the time during which the forward section stays at the station are often merged, station represents also a temporal interval called the *Product Time Slot* (PTS).
- **Pulse Line**: set containing *nbStations* stations that altogether deliver completely equipped forward sections every X hours, where X denotes the duration of the *Product Time Slot*.

- **Manufacturing Zone**: physical space in the forward section. In fact, forward section is divided into manufacturing zones that are characterized by their geographic perimeter and the maximum number of operators that can simultaneously work in them (i.e. its *capacity*).
- **SOI Operation** (Standard Operating Instruction): sequence of atomic manufacturing activities on the forward section.

  The set of parts that are assembled in the nose section during these activities is associated to the SOI operation. One SOI operation cannot fall on more than one station. The realization of one SOI operation requires *nbJourneymen* operators that have a specific qualification.

  It starts at *startDate* and lasts *duration*. The SOI operation covers at least one manufacturing zone. Finally, there are precedences constraints between SOI operations, meaning that some SOI operations cannot start before some other are finished.
- **Routing**: set containing SOI operations that correspond to interconnected parts. A routing groups operations into high level tasks.
- **Journeyman**: operator that performs the SOI operations. Each journeyman has at least one qualification.

For instance, all *harnesses* and *cables* are physical parts. An instance of a SOI operation is the *connection of one specific harness and a specific cable.* An instance of a routing is the *connection of a specific harness to a calculator* that involves several connections between the harness and cables and other SOI operations.

In the COMETE use-case, there are approximately 500 routings, 3500 SOI operations and 10000 parts (exclusive of hardware).

4 Abstract Generic Model

4.1 General Idea

In order to have a model allowing the architect to perform simultaneous engineering of the aircraft design and the industrial system, we must create a correspondence between dynamic elements, in our case manufacturing operations, and static elements. Let us take the simple example of an air conditioning circuit. In the design world, such a circuit, pipe, is defined by static attributes such as geometry, materials, etc. In the manufacturing world, it is linked to the operations necessary for its installation. The concept of pipe object makes sense in both worlds and can therefore be seen as a bridge between them. More generally, we consider that the physical elements constituting the aircraft, are the contact points of these two worlds.

The junction between design and manufacturing could be achieved by coupling two distinct models along with transformation rules for instance [9]. We did not choose this solution for three reasons. First, there is a significant risk of drift between the two models. Indeed, in the future, it is possible that the models change without their coupling being updated, or even worse that they become completely incompatible with one another. The second reason is more practical. Whether in the design or the manufacturing worlds, there is only one aircraft. Therefore, it is better to have a unique model of the aircraft that can be shared by all stakeholders, rather than heterogeneous models that would suggest that the real object may be different depending on the context. Finally, the third reason is related to our goal, which is to enable the architect to understand the interactions between architecture and production. Hence, it is not a matter of having two distinct models, but rather an integrated model of the aircraft, with a design part and a production part.

On the other side, we do not intend to merge inextricably the production and the design models. We must foresee that models of each world may evolve in the future, without each evolution of the one necessarily impacting the other. Hence, our idea is to define a global model with two parts and a very limited number of objects shared between the parts. In this model, shared objects define a "*contact area*", i.e. the bridge, between the manufacturing and the design. This allows each trade to update its model without impacting the other as long as it does not touch the objects of the contact area.

As discussed previously, we need to define high-level of abstraction for the manufacturing model. Like [14] with architectural frameworks, we have chosen an approach in views, where each view corresponds to a layer of abstraction. However, unlike the macro-models defined in [11] that are composed of layers of abstraction with rules explaining how to pass from one level to the other, we have privileged simplicity. For the moment, we choose to define a high-level abstract model with *abstract* classes that can be specialized in *concrete* ones for each level of abstraction.

4.2 Pattern

An outline of this abstract model is illustrated on Fig. 4. This model must be specialized in each view, i.e. in each abstraction level. For reasons of legibility, we chose to include only the most important attributes and classes. On the generic pattern of this figure, concepts relating to design are on the left and those relating to production on the right. The bridge between the two worlds is represented here by the abstract classes *Physical Element* and *Zone*.

Physical Element is specialized as follows:

- at high-level of abstraction, in the class *Sub-element*. A Sub-element is a set of parts that has a business meaning in a stage of the production process. A set of sub-elements defines a component of the aircraft which corresponds to a part of the aircraft (wing, front section, etc.), manufactured by different production sites and delivered for assembly to the factories which realize the final assembly;
- at low-level of abstraction, in the class *Part* presented in Sect. 3.

For instance, the air conditioning pipe as mentioned in the example of Sect. 2.1 is a *Sub-element* and belongs to a high-level view. All the pipes sections are instances of *Part* and belong to the low-level view.

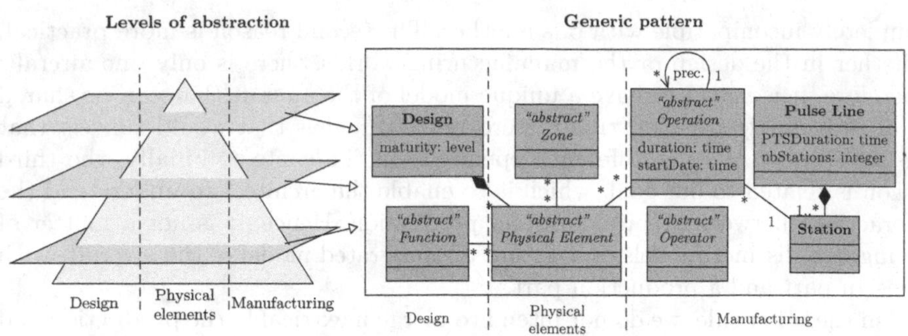

Fig. 4. Prototype of a generic class diagram for aeronautics simultaneous engineering

The abstract class *Zone* corresponds to the location of physical elements in the aircraft. At low-level, it specializes in *Manufacturing Zone* as defined in Sect. 3.

On the design side, an aircraft architecture proposal is represented by a *Design*, which is associated with a maturity level and composed of physical elements. Here, a Design is the realization of an architecture, i.e. the definition of all physical elements (parts, sections, etc.) composing the aircraft, the technical way they are assembled together and associated to the *Function* which are fullfilled. So, each *Physical Element* is connected with an aircraft *Function*. These functions are related to the aircraft operational life: power generation, fuel storing, providing means of communication etc. The class *Function* is abstract and it generalizes as follows:

- at high-level of abstraction, in service functions to users (pilots, passengers, cabin crew, etc.), without presupposing how these functions are performed;
- at low-level of abstraction, in *Elementary Functions* which are all the technical functions necessary to perform the hight-level users services.

On the manufacturing side, the pattern contains two concrete classes for the manufacturing: the *Pulse Line* and the *Station* as described in the Sect. 3. In fact, these elements constitute the structure of any industrial system and must consequently be present at any level of abstraction. Operations, represented by the abstract class *Operation*, are carried out on each station and correspond to actions performed on a station. An operation has *duration* and a *startDate*. At a high-level of abstraction, operations are specialized in the class *Action* which consists in equipping the aircraft with a *Sub-element* like fixing a pipe. At low-level of abstraction, operations are specialized in SOI operations (see Sect. 3). Finally, the abstract class *Operator* corresponds to the actor performing the *Operation*. An operator could be a human or a robot. We choose not to represent the relation between *Operator* and *Operation* in this generic pattern. Indeed, for higher abstract levels, architect might not be able to express such a relation. However, it could be useful to characterize the different kind of operators.

The Fig. 5 represents two specialisations of the generic pattern for the manufacturing side. The lower part of the figure shows how the UML model of manufacturing defined in the Sect. 3 and illustrated on Fig. 3 is transformed to be compliant with the generic pattern. We can remark that there are no robots on the current production line, so *Journeyman* is the only class specializing *Operator*.

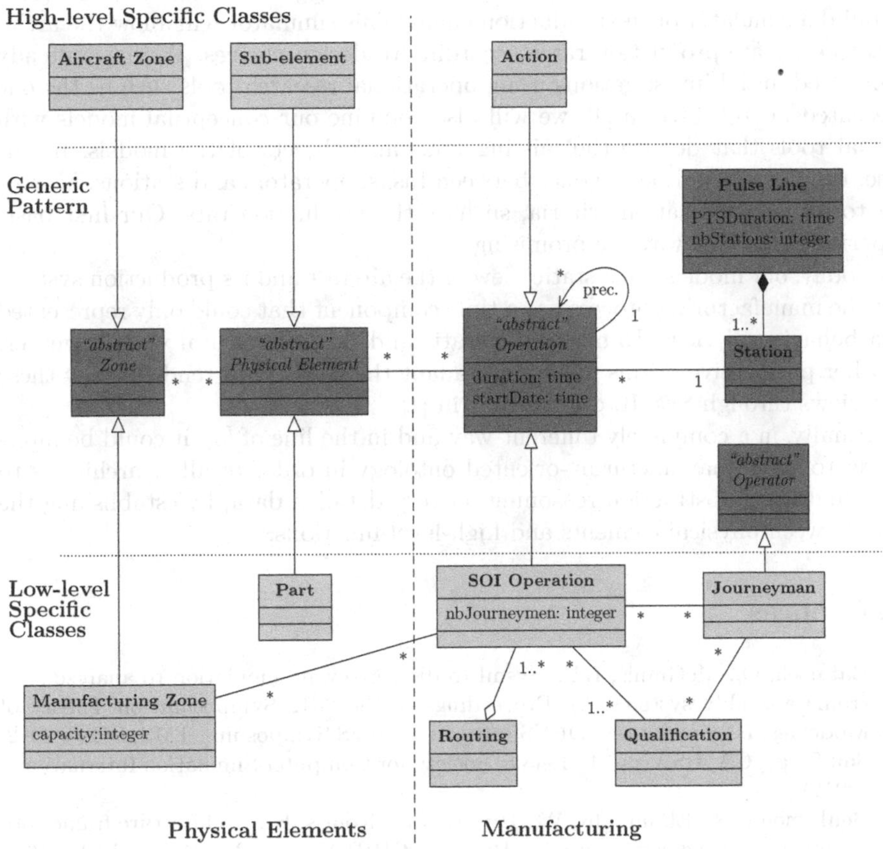

Fig. 5. UML class diagram, manufacturing part, low-level.

5 Conclusion and Perspectives

In this article, we present an industrial case study and demonstrate the need for having a model-based framework to embrace design and industrial system of complex products such as aircraft. After studying the manufacturing reality, especially the data retrieval and the precise understanding of the domain which have mobilized most of our efforts so far, we have given a first draft of a model for a simultaneous engineering of the aircraft design and its production. This model-based approach allows the definition of the different concepts, the analysis of the problem and the communication between the design and manufacturing teams by providing a common system of reference. Moreover, it is a first step towards a simultaneous engineering digital framework to carry out studies of impact of architecture on the production.

In future work, we will refine the manufacturing part of the model in order to build a simulator of the production chain. This simulator will allow the architect to estimate production rates according to design choices. We have already conducted initial investigations using operational research tools such as the one presented in [10]. Like in [4], we will also combine our conceptual models with formal tools that deduce the missing links and objects of the models. In our case, the links would be the ones between tasks, operators and stations, according to some optimization criteria, such as the production rate. Our first basic experiments in this way are promising.

Today, our models are a static view of the aircraft and its production system, but the manufacturing process has a time component that could only represented in a behavioural view. To model the static and the behavioural views together, another perspective of this paper is to adapt the works that tend to unify these two views through SysML diagrams as in [1].

Finally, in a completely different way and in the line of [3], it could be interesting to use a manufacturing-oriented ontology in order to allow architects to have high-level abstraction reasoning on very detailed data, by establishing the link between physical elements and high-level functions.

References

1. Batarseh, O., McGinnis, L.F.: Sysml to discrete-event simulation to analyze electronic assembly systems. In: Proceedings of the 2012 Symposium on Theory of Modeling and Simulation - DEVS Integrative M&S Symposium, TMS/DEVS 2012, San Diego, CA, USA, pp. 48:1–48:8. Society for Computer Simulation International (2012)
2. Benkamoun, N., ElMaraghy, W., Huyet, A.L., Kouiss, K.: Architecture framework for manufacturing system design. Procedia CIRP **17**, 88–93 (2014). doi:10.1016/j.procir.2014.01.101
3. Bruno, G., Antonelli, D., Villa, A.: A reference ontology to support product lifecycle management. Procedia CIRP **33**, 41–46 (2015)
4. Delmas, R., Doose, D., Pires, A.F., Polacsek, T.: Supporting model based design. In: Bellatreche, L., Mota Pinto, F. (eds.) MEDI 2011. LNCS, vol. 6918, pp. 237–248. Springer, Heidelberg (2011). doi:10.1007/978-3-642-24443-8_25
5. Delmas, R., Polacsek, T.: Formal methods for exchange policy specification. In: Salinesi, C., Norrie, M.C., Pastor, Ó. (eds.) CAiSE 2013. LNCS, vol. 7908, pp. 288–303. Springer, Heidelberg (2013). doi:10.1007/978-3-642-38709-8_19
6. Demoly, F., Yan, X., Eynard, B., Rivest, L., Gomes, S.: An assembly oriented design framework for product structure engineering and assembly sequence planning. Robot. Comput. Integr. Manuf. **27**(1), 33–46 (2011)

7. Göpfert, I., Schulz, M.: Logistics integrated product development in the German automotive industry: current state, trends and challenges. In: Kreowski, H.J., Scholz-Reiter, B., Thoben, K.D. (eds.) Dynamics in Logistics, pp. 509–519. Springer, Heidelberg (2013). doi:10.1007/978-3-642-35966-8_43
8. Graham, R.L.: Bounds for certain multiprocessing anomalies. Bell Syst. Tech. J. **45**(9), 1563–1581 (1966)
9. Herrmann, C., Krahn, H., Rumpe, B., Schindler, M., Völkel, S.: An algebraic view on the semantics of model composition. In: Akehurst, D.H., Vogel, R., Paige, R.F. (eds.) ECMDA-FA 2007. LNCS, vol. 4530, pp. 99–113. Springer, Heidelberg (2007). doi:10.1007/978-3-540-72901-3_8
10. Pralet, C., Verfaillie, G.: Dynamic online planning and scheduling using a static invariant-based evaluation model. In: Borrajo, D., Kambhampati, S., Oddi, A., Fratini, S. (eds.) Proceedings of the Twenty-Third International Conference on Automated Planning and Scheduling, ICAPS 2013, Rome, Italy, 10–14 June 2013. AAAI (2013)
11. Salay, R., Mylopoulos, J., Easterbrook, S.: Using macromodels to manage collections of related models. In: van Eck, P., Gordijn, J., Wieringa, R. (eds.) CAiSE 2009. LNCS, vol. 5565, pp. 141–155. Springer, Heidelberg (2009). doi:10.1007/978-3-642-02144-2_15
12. Shenas, D.G., Derakhshan, S.: Organizational approaches to the implementation of simultaneous engineering. Int. J. Oper. Prod. Manag. **14**(10), 30–43 (1994)
13. Sprock, T., McGinnis, L.F.: Analysis of functional architectures for discrete event logistics systems (DELS). Procedia Comput. Sci. **44**, 517–526 (2015)
14. Wisnosky, D.E., Vogel, J.: DoDAF Wizdom: A practical guide to planning. Managing and Executing Projects to Build Enterprise Architectures Using the Department of Defense Architecture Framework (DoDAF) (2004)

OCL$_{\mathsf{UNIV}}$: Expressive UML/OCL Conceptual Schemas for Finite Reasoning

Xavier Oriol(✉) and Ernest Teniente

Universitat Politècnica de Catalunya, Barcelona, Spain
{xoriol,teniente}@essi.upc.edu

Abstract. Full UML/OCL is so expressive that most reasoning tasks are known to be undecidable in schemas defined with these languages. To tackle this situation, literature has proposed mainly three decidable fragments of UML/OCL: UML with no OCL, UML with limited OCL and no maximum cardinality constraints (OCL-Lite), and UML with limited OCL with no minimum cardinality constraints (OCL$_{\mathsf{UNIV}}$). Since most conceptual schemas make use of OCL together with min and max cardinalities, this poses a strong limitation to current proposals. In this paper, we go beyond these limits by showing that OCL$_{\mathsf{UNIV}}$ with *acyclic* min cardinality constraints and path acyclicity constraints also preserves decidability. In this way, we establish a language that can deal with most of UML/OCL identified constraint patterns. We also empirically test the expressiveness of this language through different UML/OCL case studies.

Keywords: UML · OCL · Decidability · Reasoning

1 Introduction

Reasoning on UML/OCL conceptual schemas is aimed at answering questions regarding what kind of instances does a UML/OCL conceptual schema admit. This is known to be crucial in the specification stage of software development. Indeed, reasoning about what kind of instances does a UML/OCL schema admit allows to assess whether the UML/OCL schema is correct or not. In this way, we can avoid the propagation of conceptual errors to the other stages of software development [1].

For instance, consider the UML/OCL schema in Fig. 1 specifying a soccer league competition. This domain includes *Leagues*, identified by year, and *Teams* enrolled in these leagues. Teams play *Matches* during a league, for which we store the goals made and the *Stadium* in which they took place. The UML schema is complemented with some OCL constraints that describe the *primary key attributes* of each class, ensure that no team has a match with itself, ensure that a league is *finished* when all teams have played against all other teams, and ensure that the unique unfinished league is the last one, whose finishing date is later than any date of its matches.

By taking a closer look at this UML/OCL schema, we may realize that it accepts an instance of a match among two teams of different leagues. This clearly

H.C. Mayr et al. (Eds.): ER 2017, LNCS 10650, pp. 354–369, 2017.
https://doi.org/10.1007/978-3-319-69904-2_28

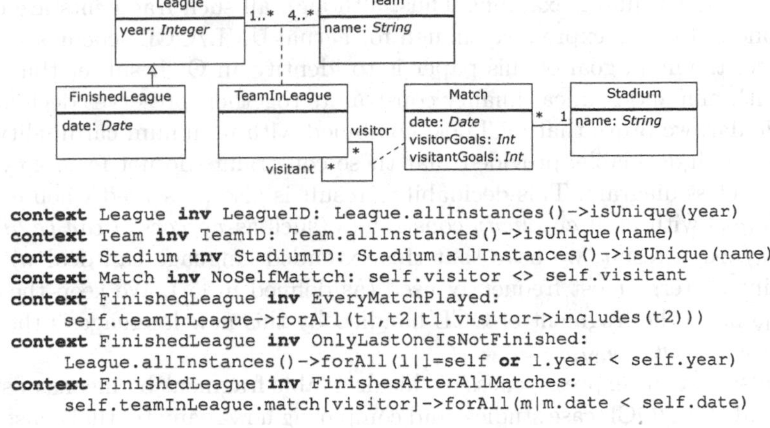
League
year: Integer
1..*
4..*
Team
name: String
FinishedLeague
date: Date
TeamInLeague
visitor
*
visitant
*
Match
date: Date
visitorGoals: Int
visitantGoals: Int
*
1
Stadium
name: String
context League inv LeagueID: League.allInstances()->isUnique(year)
context Team inv TeamID: Team.allInstances()->isUnique(name)
context Stadium inv StadiumID: Stadium.allInstances()->isUnique(name)
context Match inv NoSelfMattch: self.visitor <> self.visitant
context FinishedLeague inv EveryMatchPlayed:
self.teamInLeague->forAll(t1,t2|t1.visitor->includes(t2)))
context FinishedLeague inv OnlyLastOneIsNotFinished:
League.allInstances()->forAll(l|l=self or l.year < self.year)
context FinishedLeague inv FinishesAfterAllMatches:
self.teamInLeague.match[visitor]->forAll(m|m.date < self.date)

Fig. 1. UML schema and OCL constraints

indicates that there is an error in the UML/OCL schema and, thus, an OCL constraint preventing such situation should be incorporated to it. It is worth noting that, incorporating new constraints in the conceptual schema means propagating such changes into the other software artifacts (in particular, operation design-contracts and code), thus, it is crucial to reason that no constraint is missing/lacking in the conceptual schema in order to avoid the propagation of this mistake to the rest of artifacts.

Unfortunately, it is well-known that reasoning on UML/OCL schemas is undecidable [2]. That is, there is no algorithm that can reason over a UML/OCL schema ensuring termination and a correct output. The cause of the undecidability relies on the high expressiveness of UML/OCL schemas. Indeed, UML schemas with general OCL constraints have an expressive power beyond first-order logics. Thus, since reasoning about the satisfiability of first-order logic theories is undecidable and a UML schema with general OCL constraints can encode a first-order theory, the undecidability result of first-order logic reasoning is inherited by reasoning on UML/OCL schemas.

To mitigate this issue, one option is to reduce the expressiveness of UML/OCL into some fragment whose reasoning problems are decidable. To the best of our knowledge, three such fragments have been identified in the literature:

- UML schemas alone: that is full UML features with no OCL constraints [2].
- OCL-Lite: a fragment of UML/OCL which, in essence, forbids the usage of maximum cardinalities in the UML schema [3].
- OCLUNIV: a fragment of UML/OCL which, in essence, forbids the usage of minimum cardinalities in the UML schema [4].

Clearly, all three proposed languages lack critical features making them strongly limited. Indeed, UML/OCL schemas tend to make use of OCL constraints and minimum and maximum cardinality constraints together, as required by our running example. Thus, although all such fragments are decidable, none of them is expressive enough for actual UML/OCL schemas.

Hence, the main goal of this paper is to identify an OCL subset that, combined with min and max cardinality constraints together, preserves decidability. In particular, we prove that OCL_{UNIV} combined with minimum cardinality constraints is still decidable, provided that these constraints do not form a cycle in the UML class diagram. This decidability result is also preserved when extending OCL_{UNIV} with path *acyclicity* constraints (such as *no person can be his own ancestor*). As a result, we have that this extended language can deal with the constraint patterns most frequently used (as defined in [5]). We keep the name OCL_{UNIV} since the fragment of OCL handled by this new language is the same as the original OCL_{UNIV}.

We also test the expressiveness of this decidable fragment by means of studying several UML/OCL case studies, and comparing how many textual constraints could we encode in the language proposed in this paper and how many in OCL-Lite. With this experiment, we show that, while OCL-Lite could cover 56% of the constraints of the case studies, our OCLuniv could handle the 82%. In addition, our OCL_{UNIV} required only deleting 1 minimum cardinality constraint to ensure decidability (i.e., acyclicity in the class diagrams associations) while OCL-Lite required removing all the maximum cardinality constraints in the schemas (a total of 69).

In conclusion, we can state that the language identified in this paper is currently the most expressive one for specifying UML/OCL schemas while ensuring finite reasoning on them. Thus, any complete UML/OCL schema reasoner (such as [6]) receiving as input a schema written in our language never hangs while checking its correctness.

2 Preliminaries

We start from a logic encoding of a UML class diagram into a logic schema based on [6], and the weak acyclicity result stating that any logic schema with no cycles involving existential variables can be reasoned in finite time [7,8]. We summarize all these notions in the following:

UML Class Diagram and Compatible Classes. A UML class diagram is a diagram which contains a hierarchy of classes, n-ary associations among these classes (where some of them might be reified, i.e., association classes), and attributes inside the classes. In addition, a UML class diagram might be annotated with minimum/maximum cardinality constraints over its association-ends/attributes, and hierarchy constraints (that is, disjoint/complete constraints). In this paper, we say that two classes C_1 and C_2 are *compatible* if they have a common superclass SC in the hierarchy.

Terms, Atoms, Literals, and Positions. A *term* t is either a variable or a constant. An *atom* is formed by a n-ary *predicate* p together with n terms, i.e., $p(t_1, \ldots, t_n)$. We may write $p(\overline{t})$ for short, and say that the position $p[i]$ is occupied by the term t_i. If all the terms of an atom are constants, we say that the atom is *ground.* A literal l is either an atom $p(\overline{t})$, or a built-in literal $t_i \; \omega \; t_j$, where ω is an arithmetic comparison (i.e., $<, \leq, =, \neq$).

Logic Encoding of the UML Class Diagram. We formalize each class C in a class diagram with attributes $\{A_1, \ldots, A_n\}$ by means of a base atom $c(Oid)$ together with n atoms of the form $cA_i(Oid, A_i)$, each association R between classes $\{C_1, \ldots, C_k\}$ by means of a base atom $r(C_1, \ldots, C_k)$, and each association class R between classes $\{C_1, \ldots, C_k\}$ with attributes $\{A_1, \ldots, A_n\}$ by means of a base atom $r(C_1, \ldots, C_k)$ together with n atoms $rA_i(C_1, \ldots, C_k, A_i)$.

Dependencies. A *Tuple-Generating Dependency (TGD)* is a formula of the form $\forall \overline{x}, \overline{z}. \; \varphi(\overline{x}, \overline{z}) \rightarrow \exists \overline{y}. \; \psi(\overline{x}, \overline{y})$ where $\varphi(\overline{x}, \overline{z})$ is a conjunction of literals, and $\psi(\overline{x}, \overline{y})$ a conjunction of atoms. A *Disjunctive Embedded Dependency (DED)* is a variation of TGDs where disjunctions are admitted in the conclusion of the rule. In particular, they follow the form: $\forall \overline{x}, \overline{z}. \; \phi(\overline{x}, \overline{z}) \rightarrow \bigvee \exists \overline{y}. \; \psi(\overline{x}, \overline{y})$. A *ded* is a *denial* if its right hand side is an empty disjunction: $\forall \overline{x}. \; \phi(\overline{x}) \rightarrow \perp$. From now on, we omit the logic quantifiers since they can be understood by context.

Dependency Graph and Weak Acyclicity. Given a set of *deds*, its *dependency graph* is a directed graph obtained as follows. There is a vertex for each position of all *ded* predicates, and for each *ded* of the form $\phi(\overline{x}, \overline{y}) \rightarrow \bigvee \psi(\overline{x}, \overline{z})$, there is a *universal edge* from a position $p[i]$ of ϕ to a position $r[j]$ of ψ iff: there is a variable $x \in \overline{x}$ occupying both $p[i]$ and $r[i]$. Moreover, there is an *existential edge* from a position $p[i]$ of ϕ to a position $r[j]$ of ψ iff there is a variable $x \in \overline{x}$ occupying $p[i]$, and there is a variable $z \in \overline{z}$ occupying $r[i]$. A set of *deds* is said to be *weakly acyclic* iff its *dependency graph* does not contain any cycle involving an existential edge.

3 The OCL$_{\mathsf{UNIV}}$ Language

OCL$_{\mathsf{UNIV}}$ is a fragment of OCL which does not make use of existential variables (i.e., it does not have the *exists* OCL construct and it limits all the other constructs to avoid emulating it). Under the point of view of first-order logics, it is the fragment of OCL that can be described by means of the first-order constructs $\vee$, $\wedge$ and $\forall$; avoiding $\exists$ and limiting the usage of $\neg$ accordingly. The OCL$_{\mathsf{UNIV}}$ language was firstly described as a fragment of OCL which can be efficiently checked by means of SQL queries with no need of subqueries [9], and as a fragment whose constraints can be mantained (i.e. repaired) in finite time [4].

We reproduce its grammar here for the sake of self-containment of the paper:

```
ExpBool ::= ExpBool and ExpBool        | ExpBool or ExpBool
          | ExpOp
ExpOp   ::= Path->excludesAll(Path)    | Var.Member->includesAll(Path)
          | Path->excludes(Path)       | Var.Member->includes(Var)
          | Path->isEmpty()            | Path->forAll(Var| ExpBool)
          | Path OpComp Constant       | not Path.oclIsKindOf(Class)
          | Path OpComp Path           | Path.oclIsKindOf(Class)
Path    ::= Var.Nav                    | Class.allInstances().Nav
          | Var                        Class.allInstances()
Nav     ::= Role.Nav                   | oclAsType(Class).Nav
          | Role                       | Attribute
          | oclAsType(Class)
```

With regard to semantics, the basic property of OCL$_{\mathsf{UNIV}}$ is that its logic encoding provides as a result *deds* of the form: $\phi(\overline{x}, \overline{y}) \rightarrow \bigvee \psi(\overline{x})$ or denials $\phi(\overline{x}) \rightarrow \bot$ [4]. In any case, note the absence of existentials variables $\overline{z}$ of typical deds.

For instance, the OCL$_{\mathsf{UNIV}}$ constraints in Fig. 1 would be encoded as follows:

```
1) LeagueYear(l, y), LeagueYear(l2, y), l≠l2 → ⊥
2) TeamName(t, n), TeamName(t2, n), t≠t2 → ⊥
3) StadiumName(s, n), StadiumName(s2, n), s≠s2 → ⊥
4) Match(tl, tl) → ⊥
5) TeamInLeage(t, l), TeamInLeage(t2, l) → Match(t, l, t2, l)
6) FinishedLeage(f),LeagueName(l,n),l≠f,LeagueYear(f,y),LeagueYear(l,z),z<y → ⊥
7) FinishedLeage(f), LeagueDate(f, d), MatchDate(tl, l, tl2, l2, d2), d < d2 → ⊥
```

Moreover, since the OCL$_{\mathsf{UNIV}}$ language is strongly-typed, all its valid expressions satisfy the type conformance specified in the OCL standard. This fact implies that, for each variable x in some *ded* codifying some OCL$_{\mathsf{UNIV}}$ constraint, the UML class of two different positions occupied by x are compatible. Intuitively, this is because each variable x stands for some UML instance of class C obtained when evaluating an OCL$_{\mathsf{UNIV}}$ expressions, and UML instances of C can only be obtained in OCL$_{\mathsf{UNIV}}$ expressions of a type compatible with C.

For instance, in the ded 4 above, we see that the variable *t1* holds two different positions in the *Match* predicate. This implies that both positions codify two compatible types. Indeed, if we take a look at the diagram, we see that *Match* is a recursive association and thus, both positions have the same type.

4 Decidability of OCL$_{\mathsf{UNIV}}$ with Min Cards and Path Acyclicity

Reasoning whether a UML/OCL schema satisfies a given property is aimed at checking whether the schema admits a consistent sample instantiation witnessing the property. For instance, checking whether the schema in our example satisfies that *Match* is *lively*, requires identifying whether this schema admits an instantiation containing, at least, one instance of *Match* without violating any integrity constraint.

The cause for undecidability is always the new objects that must be created to repair the constraints violated by the sample instantiation being built. Indeed, such new objects might violate other constraints that require creating new objects, thus, potentially stacking into an endless process of creating new objects.

For instance, assume that we have a UML class diagram with classes *Employee*, *Department*, and *Project* such that *each employee should be assigned to at least one department, each department should be assigned to at least one project*, and that *each project should have at least two employees.* Clearly, if we want to check whether *Employee* is *lively*, we need to instantiate one employee in the schema. Then, to satisfy the constraints, we will have to instantiate one department for this employee. Similarly, we will need to instantiate one project for the department and, then, we need a new employee for the project, thus potentially entering into an infinite loop.

Intuitively, a UML class diagram with acyclic minimum cardinality constraints avoids this kind of loops. Moreover, OCL$_{\text{UNIV}}$ constraints (and path acyclicity constraints) guarantee that no new object needs to be created to satisfy the constraints. Thus, the combination of OCL$_{\text{UNIV}}$ constraints with path acyclicity constraints into UML class diagrams with no minimum cardinality constraints cycles is decidable.

In the following we formalize the proof of this statement. We start by proving that reasoning on UML class diagrams with no min cardinality cycles and no OCL constraints is decidable. To facilitate the proofs, we begin with the assumption that min cardinalities are 1 or 1..*, and that all hierarchies are *complete*. Then, we show that incorporating OCL$_{\text{UNIV}}$ constraints preserves decidability. Finally, we incorporate path acyclicity constraints and generalize our results to min cardinality constraints with boundaries different than 1, and incomplete hierarchies.

4.1 Reasoning on UML Class Diagrams with No Min Card Cycles Is Decidable

We say that there is a *min cardinality cycle* in a UML class diagram if there is a directed cycle in the UML class diagram formed by association roles whose min cardinality is one and/or hierarchy constraints (taken upwards or downwards, i.e., in both directions of the hierarchy). Then, we say that a UML class diagram is weakly acyclic if it does not contain any min cardinality cycle. Formally:

Definition 1. *A* min cardinality cycle *on class C is a sequence of association-role names $r_0, \ldots, r_n$ s.t.:*

1. *Forms a cycle, i.e., the UML class of r_n is compatible with C.*
2. *Each association-role r_i has a min cardinality 1 (or is a navigation from an association class to one of its members).*
3. *It is a valid path, i.e., C can navigate to r_0, and the UML class of r_{i-1} can navigate to a role/association-class r_i for every $i > 1$. We consider that a*

UML class can navigate through a role r_i if it has a role property called r_i, or some of its compatible classes have it.

Equivalently, there is a *min cardinality cycle* if we can build an OCL path that starts from class C, navigates uniquely through roles whose min cardinality is 1 (or from association classes to its members since an instance of an association class always one member for each association-end), possibly using *oclAsType* to cast some (intermediate) path result to some other compatible classes into which continue navigating, and whose final result is (a collection) of a type compatible with C.

Definition 2. *A UML class diagram is* weakly acyclic *iff it does not contain any min cardinality cycle for any of its classes.*

In the following, we prove that reasoning on a *weakly acyclic* UML class diagram is decidable. We do so by showing that the logic encoding of a *weakly acyclic* UML schema results into a *weakly acyclic* set of *deds*, which are well-known to be decidable [7,8].

Theorem 1. *Reasoning on a weakly acyclic UML class diagram is decidable.*

Proof. The proof starts from the logic encoding of the UML constraints present in the class diagram. In particular, we see that there are only 6 kinds of rules generated by the encoding of constraints in this language [1]:

- Integrity Reference Rules: Assoc(x, y,...) → Class(x)
- Minimum cardinality rules: Class(x) → Assoc(x, y,...)
- Maximum cardinality rules: Assoc(x, y,...) ∧ Assoc(x, y2,...) → ⊥
- Hierarchy constraints: Subclass(x) → Class(x)
- Disjoint constraints: Subclass1(x) ∧ Subclass2(x) → ⊥
- Complete constraints: Class(x) → Subclass1(x) ∨... ∨ SubclassN(x)

Now we see that, if the UML class diagram is weakly acyclic, these kinds of rules form a weakly acyclic set of deds. We do this by contraposition. That is, we show that if there is a cycle in the deds, we can find a min cardinality cycle in the class diagram.

If there is a cycle in the deds, there is, for sure, an existential edge. The unique rules that generate an existential edge are the min cardinality rules, so, there must be a min cardinality constraint in the UML class diagram. We use this class to generate a min cardinality cycle. Indeed, each edge that appears in the cycle in the deds can be seen either as a navigation through a min cardinality 1 role, or the navigation to the class of the association, a superclass or a subclass. We can generate the min cardinality cycle by simply picking the role names of the min cardinality constraint deds appearing in the deds cycle. Since the deds form a cycle, for sure, the navigations ends with the original class C. □

Up to here, we know that reasoning on weakly acyclic UML schemas is decidable. Now, we generalize this condition in order to ensure good expressiveness.

In particular, it is quite frequent to find a binary association in a UML class diagram with a min cardinality 1 in both association-ends. This forms a trivial cycle in the UML class diagram, and thus, a cycle in its logic encoding.

Assume, for instance, that the (reified) association *TeamInLeague* in our example has a min cardinality 1 in both association-ends: *Team* and *League*. In such case, the logic encoding contains the following cycle:

```
8) Team(t), → TeamInLeague(t, l)
9) TeamInLeague(t, l), → League(l)
10) League(l) → TeamInLeague(t, l)
11) TeamInLeague(t, l) → Team(t)
```

This kind of cycles do not affect the decidability of the schema. Intuitively, this is because everytime we *repair* the ded 9 creating a new league l for some team t we are actually repairing the ded 10 that says that each league (such as l) should have at least one team. Thus, ded 10 is not triggered, and the repairing process does not loop forever.

Formally, this kind of cycles satisfy the third decidability theorem identified in [1], which states that when creating new instances to repair such kind of constraints, those instances do not get stacked into an infinite loop.

Therefore, cycles involving only one (non-recursive) association with min cardinalities in both association ends do not break decidability.

4.2 Incorporating OCL$_{\mathsf{UNIV}}$

We assume now that the UML class diagram is complemented with OCL$_{\mathsf{UNIV}}$ constraints and show that decidability is still preserved. The basic idea is that these constraints do not create new objects to be repaired, but reclassify them among compatible classes or add new associations to them. Thus, no new cycles with new existential edges are added.

It might seem that an OCL$_{\mathsf{UNIV}}$ constraint can create a new *universal edge* that is involved within a cycle with some existential edge (given by some min card constraint). However, we show that, if this is the case, then, there is a min cardinality cycle in the UML class diagram alone (and thus, the UML class diagram would not be weakly acyclic). The intuition behind this fact is that, given a ded cycle involving an OCL$_{\mathsf{UNIV}}$ constraint, we can build a UML min card cycle by simply bypassing OCL$_{\mathsf{UNIV}}$ constraints. This is because OCL$_{\mathsf{UNIV}}$ cannot make an existing object become an instance of an arbitrary class, but can only reclassify objects into compatible classes (whose propagations are already taken in account when searching for min cardinality cycles through hierarchies).

We start stating two intermediate Propositions that make the overall proof easier:

Proposition 1. *Given a set of* deds *encoding a UML class diagram, if a position* $r[i]$ *encodes objects compatible with class* C*, then, there is a universal-path (i.e., a path formed by* universal edges *in the dependency graph) from* $r[i]$ *to* $C[0]$.

Proof. There are two different cases: r might encode either a class or an association (the case of association classes is treated similarly).

Assume r is a predicate encoding a class R. If R is compatible with C we have that, in the UML class diagram, R is connected to C through hierarchies. This connection is represented in the dependency graph through *deds* encoding hierarchy constraints (intuitively, to go upwards a hierarchy), and *complete* constraints (intuitively, to go downwards a hierarchy). Both kinds of *deds* only generate universal edges and, so, there is a universal-path between them.

Assume r is a predicate encoding an association R and $r[i]$ encodes the i-th member of the association R, whose UML class is RC. If RC is compatible with C, we have a universal path between the positions $rc[0]$ and $c[0]$ (as we have seen previously). Now, because of the ded encoding the integrity reference constraint, there is also a universal edge from $r[i]$ to $rc[0]$. So, there is a universal path between $r[i]$ and $c[0]$. □

With this result at hand, we can prove that, if there is a cycle in the *deds* encoding a UML schema with OCL$_{\mathsf{UNIV}}$ constraints, then, there is a min cardinality cycle in the UML schema. The proof is based on showing that, if there is a cycle in the *deds*, and such cycle uses some universal edge generated from a *ded* encoding an OCL$_{\mathsf{UNIV}}$ constraint, we can build a new cycle without using such *ded* by means of replacing such edge for the universal path stated in Proposition 1.

Proposition 2. *If there is a cycle in the* deds *encoding a UML schema with OCL$_{\mathsf{UNIV}}$ constraints, then, there is a min cardinality cycle in the UML schema.*

Proof. Take a cycle in the *deds*. If such cycle does not use any edge resulting from a ded encoding an OCL$_{\mathsf{UNIV}}$ constraint, then, there is a min cardinality cycle in the UML class diagram (see proof of Theorem 1).

If such cycle uses an edge coming from the *ded* of a OCL$_{\mathsf{UNIV}}$ constraint, we are going to see that we can create a new cycle avoiding such *ded*. Assume that the edge is from positions $r[i]$ to position $s[j]$. First, because OCL$_{\mathsf{UNIV}}$ does not create existential variables, such edge is going to be a universal edge. Then, because OCL$_{\mathsf{UNIV}}$ is a typed language, we have that the classes represented in $r[i]$ and $s[j]$ are compatible. Thus, by Proposition 1 there is a universal path between $r[i]$ and $s[j]$ that only goes through deds encoding UML schema constraints. Thus, we can build a cycle with no ded encoding OCL$_{\mathsf{UNIV}}$ by replacing such edges by their corresponding alternative universal-paths. So, since there is a cycle using the deds encoding the UML schema, there is a min cardinality cycle in the UML class diagram (see proof of Theorem 1). □

Now, we can finally state that reasoning with weakly acyclic UML class diagrams with OCL$_{\mathsf{UNIV}}$ constraints is decidable.

Theorem 2. *Reasoning on a weakly acyclic UML class diagram with OCL$_{\mathsf{UNIV}}$ constraints is decidable.*

Proof. Taking the contraposition of Proposition 2, we have that a UML schema with OCL$_{UNIV}$ constraints but no min cardinality cycle generates a weakly acyclic set of deds, which are known to be decidable [7,8]. □

4.3 Incorporating Acyclicity Constraints, Min Cardinalities Greater Than 1, and Incomplete Hierarchies

Our goal now is to show that weakly acyclic UML schemas with OCL$_{UNIV}$ constraints are still decidable when considering: (1) path acyclicity constraints, (2) minimum cardinalities greater than 1, and (3) incomplete hierarchies. In this way, the language we identify is able to deal with almost all identified frequent UML schema constraints [5].

Intuitively, a path is acyclic on a UML class diagram if and only if, given a class of the path, we can establish a stratification of the instances of such class. This can be emulated by means of considering a new fake attribute called *strata* in such class, and adding a new OCL$_{UNIV}$ constraint forcing that the strata of some instance of the class should be less than the strata that can be obtained through navigation by the cyclic path.

Theorem 3. *Reasoning on a weakly acyclic UML class diagram with OCL$_{UNIV}$ constraints and path acyclicity constraints is decidable.*

Proof. The proof is based on reducing the problem to reasoning on a UML class diagram with OCL$_{UNIV}$ constraints and no path acyclicity constraint.

Indeed, remove the acyclicity constraint and add some fake attribute *strata* in some class belonging to the acyclic path. Then, add a OCL$_{UNIV}$ constraint stating that each instance of such class should have a *strata* less or equal than the *strata* of the instances that can be obtained by navigating through the acyclic path. Clearly, the first schema is satisfiable iff the second one is satisfiable. Moreover, this transformation does not alter the existance/inexistance of a min cardinality cycle in the diagram (indeed, we are not altering the diagram), so, if the original UML diagram is weakly acyclic, the second one (the one with no acyclicity constraint) is weakly acyclic too, and thus, decidable. □

Consider now min cardinality constraints of n (n > 1). We now show that they can be emulated by considering *n* new associations of min cardinality one, and adding some constraints to ensure that each of these associations should retrieve a different object, and all *n* should be included in the original association. Note that, indeed, all these constraints can be written in OCL$_{UNIV}$. Formally:

Theorem 4. *Reasoning on a weakly acyclic UML class diagram with OCL$_{UNIV}$ constraints and general min cardinality constraints is decidable.*

Proof. The proof is based on reducing the problem to reasoning in a UML class diagram with OCL$_{UNIV}$ constraints and where all min cardinalities are of the kind "1" or "1..*".

Indeed, remove the min cardinality *n* and add *n* new associations with the same members, and a min cardinality 1 in all of them. Then, add *n* OCL$_{UNIV}$

constraints stating that each instance of such associations should be instance of the original association, and that all of them should be disjoint. Clearly, the first schema is satisfiable iff the second one is satisfiable. Moreover, this transformation does not alter the existance/inexistance of a min cardinality cycle in the UML class diagram (indeed, we are only adding min cardinalities between classes which already had min cardinalities), so, if the original UML class diagram is weakly acyclic, the second one (the one with no min cards greater than 1) is weakly acyclic too, and thus, decidable. □

Finally, we show that if a UML class diagram with OCL_{UNIV} constraints and incomplete hierarchies is weakly acyclic, then, it is also decidable.

Theorem 5. *Reasoning on a weakly acyclic UML class diagram with OCL_{UNIV} constraints and incomplete hierarchies is decidable.*

Proof. If the UML class diagram with OCL_{UNIV} constraints is weakly acyclic, then, its set of deds is weakly acyclic. Hence, the set of deds after removing the deds encoding *complete* constraints is still weakly acyclic. Thus, reasoning on a weakly acyclic UML class diagram with OCL_{UNIV} constraints and incomplete hierarchies is decidable. □

5 Expressiveness Study

OCL_{UNIV} is expressible enough to deal with the typical constraint patterns used in conceptual modeling that were identified in [5]. The unique exception is the path inclusion pattern (i.e., a constraint stating that the instances that can be reached navigating through some path in the UML diagram should be a subset of the instances that can be obtained following another path), which in OCL_{UNIV} is limited to paths of only one navigation step.

Such patterns are able to encode about the 60% of textual constraints in conceptual schemas [5]. Nevertheless, OCL_{UNIV} is able to encode expressions beyond such patterns, thus, a better coverage is expected.

To show the expressiveness of our fragment, we have evaluated how many constraints could we encode in our OCL_{UNIV} (i.e. the original OCL_{UNIV} with the extension we have proposed in this paper) in several typical UML/OCL case studies. In particular, we have used as case studies the schemas of osCommerce [10] (24 classes and 33 constraints), a Sudoku application [11] (10 classes, and 8 constraints), the DBLP schema [12] (17 classes, and 22 constraints), and the EU-rent fictional system [13] (33 classes, and 33 constraints). It is worth noting that two of them (osCommerce and DBLP) were obtained by reverse engineering of real systems.

For each case study, we have checked how many minimum cardinality constraints must be removed (if any) from the schema in order to ensure that the UML class diagram is *weakly acyclic*, and how many of their constraints may be encoded in OCL_{UNIV}. To be able to evaluate our results with regards to other decidable fragments of OCL, we have decided to compare our proposal with

OCL-Lite [3], which is, to our knowledge, the unique existing decidable and expressive fragment of OCL (appart form OCL$_{\text{UNIV}}$). To establish the comparison, we have counted how many cardinality constraints did we need to remove to ensure that the UML class diagram fulfilled the OCL-Lite requirements, and then, how many constraints could be written in OCL-Lite. Tables 1 and 2 summarize our results.

Table 1. Cardinalities removed to be compliant with OCL$_{\text{UNIV}}$ and OCL-Lite requirements

	OCL$_{\text{UNIV}}$	OCL-Lite
Sudoku	1	17
DBLP	0	14
EU-rent	0	24
osCommerce	0	14
Total	1	69

Table 2. OCL constraints encodable in our OCL$_{\text{UNIV}}$ vs OCL-Lite for our case studies

	OCL constraints	OCL$_{\text{UNIV}}$		OCL-Lite	
		Encodable	Non-encodable	Encodable	Non-encodable
Sudoku	8	8	0	7	1
DBLP	22	21	1	13	9
EU-rent	33	27	6	13	20
osCommerce	33	23	10	21	12
Total	96	79	17	54	42

As shown in Table 1, we only had to remove 1 minimum cardinality constraint from the Sudoku schema to ensure that the UML class diagrams were *weakly acyclic* in all cases, and thus, decidable under our OCL$_{\text{UNIV}}$ constraints. This is because the unique cycle found was between the relations *Sudoku has Rows*, *Rows have Cells*, *Cells are in Columns*, *Columns are in Sudokus*, which form a cycle with min cardinalities 1 in each association end. To break this cycle, it is only necessary to remove one of such min cardinality constraints. However, this does not entail with our approach a decrease in expressivity since the cardinality between *Column* and *Sudoku* could be replaced with an OCL$_{\text{UNIV}}$ constraint saying that each column has the sudoku of its cells (which entails the min cardinality one).

On the other hand, OCL-Lite required removing a total of 69 cardinalities considering all the schemas. This is because OCL-Lite cannot handle maximum cardinalities (which are pretty common in UML diagrams) and, hence, all of them must be removed.

In Table 2 we can see that OCL_{UNIV} can encode more constraints than OCL-Lite (82.3% against 56.3%). We believe that this is due to the lack of comparison operators (=, <, ≤, <>) in OCL-Lite, which made quite a lot of constraints encodable in OCL_{UNIV} not encodable in OCL-Lite. Conversely, only very few cases were encodable in OCL-Lite but not in OCL_{UNIV}. These cases were related to constraints forcing the existence of some object satisfying a particular condition (for instance, in the osCommerce, a constraint stating that there should exists an *enabled PaymentMethod* among the *PaymentMethods* in the system). Interestingly, neither OCL_{UNIV} nor OCL-Lite could deal with some constraints involving path inclusions (such as *the shopping cart atttributes should be included in the attributes of the products of the shopping cart*). OCL-Lite could not encode any of them because of the absence of equalities, and OCL_{UNIV} is limited to path inclusion constraints involving paths of only one navigation, which has been proven to be too limited in some of our case studies.

Given these results, we can state that the language we have identified in this paper is, up to now, the most expressive language for defining UML/OCL conceptual schemas while ensuring finite reasoning on them, with a substantial improvement with respect to the closest competitor found in the literature (OCL-Lite).

As a limitation of this experiment, we should point out that, due to the difficulties to find UML schemas with OCL constraints, only four schemas were used. In addition, it might be argued that evaluating expressiveness by means of counting encodable constraints might be insufficient since, subjectively, it could happen that OCL-Lite encoded constraints were more *interesting* than OCL_{UNIV} constraints. However, this notion is subjective and thus, out of the scope of the controlled experiment we have carried out.

6 Related Work

We analyze languages and approaches related to OCL_{UNIV}. We distinguish between UML/ER based, and tgd-based.

UML/ER Based. Reasoning the satisfiability of an ER diagram considering only association cardinalities is polynomial [14]. When, considering UML schemas with all features in exception of OCL constraints, the problem becomes EXPTIME-complete [2].

Adding OCL-Lite constraints in UML class diagrams maintains the EXPTIME-complete complexity (and thus, decidability), although it requires removing the maximum cardinality constraints [3]. This requirement is, in our opinion, too strong since most realistic UML class diagrams always have some kind of maximum cardinality. In addition, we have seen during our expressiveness study that this inability to encode constraints involving equalities/inequalities represents also a drawback in comparison to OCL_{UNIV}. However, OCL-Lite is not subsumed by OCL$_{\mathsf{UNIV}}$ since, for instance, OCL-Lite is capable of encoding the *exists* operator, which is forbidden in OCL$_{\mathsf{UNIV}}$.

Another option consists in using general UML/OCL constraints, and then, analyze whether that particular UML/OCL schema is decidable or not [1,6]. This approach subsumes OCL$_{\mathsf{UNIV}}$. Indeed, OCL$_{\mathsf{UNIV}}$ decidability relies in *weak acyclicity*, which is a condition subsumed by the previous decidability analysis [1]. However, we argue that it is quite difficult from the point of view of a conceptual modeller to write a UML/OCL schema that satisfies such decidability conditions. This is because such conditions are checked in the logic encoding of the UML/OCL schema, rather than the UML/OCL itself. In contrast, it is easy to check whether a UML/OCL schema satifies the decidabiilty requirements of our OCL$_{\mathsf{UNIV}}$ (i.e., *weak acyclicity* and the syntax of OCL$_{\mathsf{UNIV}}$).

Another interesting work is the one presented in [15]. In this work, UML/OCL constraints are written under the form of several constraint patterns, and such constraint patterns are analyzed to be consistent/inconsistent polynomially (through syntactic checks), which means that they not only guarantee decidability of reasoning, but also efficiency. However, this approach might bring false positives (i.e., it might say that some set of consistent constraints are inconsistent).

Finally, we have the approaches based in Armstrong tables [16]. An Armstrong table is, roughly speaking, an instantiation of the schema which exemplifies the satisfaction of the constraints entailed by the schema (and is a counterexample for anyone else). [16] shows how to build Armstrong tables for schemas considering min/max and not-null constraints. However, it does not target general constraints as we do.

TGD Based. Our approach is based on a logic encoding in deds of the UML/OCL schema, and the decidability of reasoning over such logic encoding. In particular, we have used the ded weak acyclicity property to ensure the termination of the chase algorithm to reason with such deds [7].

The weak acyclicity property of deds is subsumed by the stratification property stated in [8]. This means that we could potentially enlarge the subset of UML/OCL we can deal with if we based on stratification rather than weak acyclicity. However, we argue that this change is unfeasible. Indeed, checking whether a set of deds satisfy the weak acyclicity consists in a simple graph analysis, thus, we only needed to characterize which kind of UML/OCL expressions would bring an acyclic graph. In contrast, checking the stratification property requires solving a NP problem for each edge in the dependency graph. In our opinion, it is quite difficult to find some condition over the UML/OCL level that ensures that such NP condition is satisfied at the logic level.

Another family of decidable languages based on tgds is Datalog$^{+/-}$ [17]. The basic notion in Datalog$^{+/-}$ is *guardedness*. A ded is said to be guarded if there is some atom containing all its universal variables in a single atom in the left-hand side (called guard). Under this situation, reasoning over such set of deds is decidable. It is easy to see that OCL$_{\mathsf{UNIV}}$ is not subsumed by this language since ded 5 of our example is not guarded. It is also worth noting that $\mathsf{OCL_{UNIV}}$ does not subsume Datalog$^{+/-}$ since it does not offer existential variables (appart from the special min cardinality 1 case). So, both are languages with different expressiveness. However, we argue that it is quite difficult to realize an expressive OCL subset that ensures that its logic encoding is *guarded*.

7 Conclusions

We have seen that reasoning with UML schemas with no minimum cardinality cycles, path acycliclity constraints and $\mathsf{OCL_{UNIV}}$ constraints is decidable. This decidability result is guaranteed because, by construction, the logic encoding into deds of such schema is *weakly acyclic*, which guarantees that the chase algorithm terminates on such schema. Current UML/OCL reasoners such as [6] can benefit from this termination result.

We have compared the expressiveness of the decidable language we have identified with that of OCL-Lite [3], another decidable language based on OCL, and we have seen that $\mathsf{OCL_{UNIV}}$ is more expressive in all different UML/OCL case studies we have taken into account (while $\mathsf{OCL_{UNIV}}$ could handle about the 82% of constraints appearing in these schemas, OCL-Lite could only deal with around 56%).

As future work, we would like to extend our proposal to be able to admit more constraints involving existential variables. We understand that special attention should be put to inclusion path constraints. In addition, $\mathsf{OCL_{UNIV}}$ is designed only for ensuring decidability, so, a more sophisticated analysis should be done to bound its complexity.

Acknowledgements. This work is supported by the Ministerio de Economia y Competitividad, project TIN2014-52938-C2-2-R and by the Secretaria d'Universitats i Recerca de la Generalitat de Catalunya, project 2014 SGR 1534.

References

1. Queralt, A., Teniente, E.: Verification and validation of UML conceptual schemas with OCL constraints. ACM Trans. Softw. Eng. Methodol. **21**(2), 13 (2012)
2. Berardi, D., Calvanese, D., De Giacomo, G.: Reasoning on UML class diagrams. Artif. Intell. **168**(1–2), 70–118 (2005)
3. Queralt, A., Artale, A., Calvanese, D., Teniente, E.: OCL-Lite: finite reasoning on UML/OCL conceptual schemas. Data Knowl. Eng. **73**, 1–22 (2012)
4. Oriol, X., Teniente, E., Tort, A.: Computing repairs for constraint violations in UML/OCL conceptual schemas. Data Knowl. Eng. **99**, 39–58 (2015)
5. Costal, D., Gómez, C., Queralt, A., Raventós, R., Teniente, E.: Improving the definition of general constraints in UML. Softw. Syst. Model. **7**(4), 469–486 (2008)
6. Rull, G., Farré, C., Queralt, A., Teniente, E., Urpí, T.: AuRUS: explaining the validation of UML/OCL conceptual schemas. Softw. Syst. Model. **14**(2), 953–980 (2015)

7. Fagin, R., Kolaitis, P.G., Miller, R.J., Popa, L.: Data exchange: semantics and query answering. Theoret. Comput. Sci. **336**(1), 89–124 (2005)
8. Deutsch, A., Nash, A., Remmel, J.: The chase revisited. In: Proceedings of the 27th ACM SIGMOD-SIGACT-SIGART Symposium on Principles of Database Systems PODS 2008, pp. 149–158. ACM (2008)
9. Oriol, X., Teniente, E.: Incremental checking of OCL constraints through SQL queries. In: Proceedings of the 14th International Workshop on OCL and Textual Modelling, pp. 23–32 (2014)
10. Tort, A.: (The osCommerce case study). http://www-pagines.fib.upc.es/modeling/osCommerce_cs.pdf
11. Tort, A., Olivé, A.: (The sudoku case study). http://www.essi.upc.edu/atort/documents/Sudoku.pdf
12. Planas, E., Olivé, A.: The DBLP case study (2006). http://www-pagines.fib.upc.es/modeling/DBLP.pdf
13. Estañol, M., Queralt, A., Sancho, M.R., Teniente, E.: EU-rent car rentals specification. Technical report, Universitat Politècnica de Catalunya (2012). http://www.essi.upc.edu/estanyol/docs/artifacts_eu_rent.pdf
14. Hartmann, S.: On the consistency of int-cardinality constraints. In: Ling, T.-W., Ram, S., Lee, M.L. (eds.) ER 1998. LNCS, vol. 1507, pp. 150–163. Springer, Heidelberg (1998). doi:10.1007/978-3-540-49524-6_12
15. Wahler, M., Basin, D., Brucker, A.D., Koehler, J.: Efficient analysis of pattern-based constraint specifications. Softw. Syst. Model. **9**(2), 225–255 (2010)
16. Hartmann, S., Köhler, H., Leck, U., Link, S., Thalheim, B., Wang, J.: Constructing armstrong tables for general cardinality constraints and not-null constraints. Ann. Math. Artif. Intell. **73**(1–2), 139–165 (2015)
17. Calì, A., Gottlob, G., Lukasiewicz, T.: A general datalog-based framework for tractable query answering over ontologies. Web Semant.: Sci. Serv. Agents World Wide Web **14**, 57–83 (2012)

Conceptual Modeling and Business Processes

Goal Orchestrations: Modelling and Mining Flexible Business Processes

Metta Santipuri[1], Aditya Ghose[1(✉)], Hoa Khanh Dam[1], and Suman Roy[2]

[1] Decision Systems Lab, School of Computing and Information Technology, University of Wollongong, Wollongong, NSW 2522, Australia
{ms804,aditya,hoa}@uow.edu.au

[2] Infosys Ltd., #44 Electronics City, Hosur Road, Bangalore 560 100, India
Suman_Roy@infosys.com

Abstract. In many application domains, it is more natural to think of a process as a coordination model of goals to be achieved rather than of tasks or acitivities to be performed. Replacing tasks or activities with goals in process models allows us to enact processes in flexible, context-sensitive ways. We define a formal semantics for processes modeled in this manner (which we call *goal orchestrations*) and show how these enable flexible process execution. We also offer a simple means of mining goal orchestrations from readily available event logs, and present an evaluation with an event log consisting of 65000 entries from one of the world's largest IT companies.

1 Introduction

Business processes (and related conceptions, such as clinical processes or manufacturing processes) are typically specified in terms of *tasks that need to be executed.* This ignores an important alternative perspective on process modeling, in terms of *goals to be achieved.* Consider a physician preparing a patient for surgery. The treatment plan is typically conceived of as a sequence of goals to be achieved: *first we will lower the patient's blood pressure, then we will stabilize the patient's blood glucose levels, then treat the persistent chest infection before sending the patient into surgery.* Implicit in this treatment plan is a sequence of three goals to be achieved: "lower blood pressure", "stabilize blood glucose" and "treat chest infection". It is interesting to note (and this has been borne out by extensive interviews with physicians) that treatment plans do not involve task descriptions such as "administer drug X" or "treat with antibiotic Y". The key motivation behind conceiving these treatment plans as sequences of clinical goals/objectives to be achieved is to admit the possibility of achieving these goals in multiple different ways. Indeed clinicians often flesh out additional detail in such treatment plans by introducing what might be viewed as sub-processes of the form: *if medication X (for blood pressure) does not work, we'll try medication Y concurrent with hydration therapy.* Similar patterns of modeling can be

Suman Roy did this work when he was a visiting fellow at University of Wollongong on Infosys-CRC funded project of data-driven process discovery during July–Dec'14.

H.C. Mayr et al. (Eds.): ER 2017, LNCS 10650, pp. 373–387, 2017.
https://doi.org/10.1007/978-3-319-69904-2_29

found in a range of other settings (manufacturing, logistics as well as traditional "business" process application domains).

Our objective in this paper is to formalize this alternative approach to process modeling via *goal orchestrations*. As the name suggests, a goal orchestration is a coordination or orchestration model, where we describe the coordination of goals instead of the coordination of tasks. There are several reasons why these are of interest. First, goal orchestrations provide a more natural means of modeling behaviour (or processes) in many settings, as illustrated by the clinical example above. Second, goal orchestrations provide an easy means of achieving flexible process execution. The execution machinery for goal orchestrations is able to compute alternative task-level realizations of a goal if the initial attempt at realizing the goal fails to achieve the desired results (manifested by *events* or *effects* in the operating context). Third, goal orchestrations offer abstract, strategy-level views on processes, which can aid human understanding and ease process redesign (and other forms of analysis). More interestingly, as we will show below, goal orchestrations can be mined from readily available enterprise data in the form of *event logs*.

Goal orchestrations and their analysis involves considerable complexity (even though a superficial reading might suggest that all we are doing is replacing tasks in process models with goals). We need to consider temporal coordination of entities at three, progressively finer-grained, levels of abstraction: (1) the *goal level*, (2) the *task level* and (3) the *event level*. A given goal orchestration might admit multiple *conformant* task sequences. We need to use an important device from the reasoning about action literature, in the form of a *state update operator* to accumulate the persistent effects of tasks at the event level. The fact that state update, in general, leads to multiple non-deterministic outcomes means that the execution of a given task sequence might generate multiple event sequences (the non-determinism implies that we will be unable to specify at design time which of these event sequences will actually accrue when the task sequence is executed).

Of special interest are goal orchestrations that leverage an input *goal model* (in the form of an AND-OR goal graph). The input goal model can help identify alternative OR-refinements of a given goal, opening up a larger space of re-design alternatives in settings where the run-time monitoring machinery detects that the execution of a goal orchestration has not delivered the desired effects. The AND-refinements of a goal specified in a goal model can also be leveraged, but we do not formalize this in detail in this paper due to space constraints.

We note that much of the machinery we describe requires repeated use of the state update operator, and entailment checks. While space precludes a detailed empirical evaluation of computational cost of these, we can note that in the case of a propositional language for describing events/effects, fast SAT-solvers can execute these checks in near real-time. Well-known results about Horn clause theories also indicate that entailment checking can be executed in polynomial time.

In this paper, we provide a formal semantics of a goal orchestration model (in Sect. 2) by using abstractions spanning the goal level, the task level and finally the event level. We outline a machinery for executing goal orchestration models that achieves the flexibility discussed above (Sect. 3). We then outline an approach to mining goal orchestration models (Sect. 4) from event logs, leveraging in considerable detail the semantics described in Sect. 2. Finally, we present an empirical evaluation (Sect. 5), first with a synthetic dataset, and then with a dataset from one of the world's largest IT companies involving an event log with 65,000 distinct entries.

2 Goal Orchestration Models and Semantics

A goal can be represented in any truth-functional language that comes equipped with machinery for checking satisfiability (and hence entailment). In the following, we will only consider *achievement goals*. A *goal orchestration* (N, F) is best viewed as a process graph (as commonly used in the literature) with the tasks/activities replaced with goals, where $N = G \cup \Gamma \cup E$ (G is a set of goal assertions, Γ is a set of gateways, and $E = E_s \cup E_f$ is a set of special events (E_s represents start events and E_f denotes end events); $\mathrm{F} \subseteq (\mathrm{N}\backslash\mathrm{E} \times \mathrm{N}\backslash\mathrm{E}) \bigcup (E_s \times \mathrm{N}\backslash\mathrm{E}) \bigcup (\mathrm{N}\backslash\mathrm{E} \times E_f)$ corresponds to sequence flows connecting goal assertions with goal assertions, goal assertions with gateways, gateways with goal assertions, start events with goal assertions and goal assertions with end events. We will now describe the semantics by specifying under what circumstances an *event log* will be deemed to *satisfy* a goal orchestration. Recall that an event log is a set of pairs of the form $\langle event, timestamp \rangle$ (we ignore case IDs in the formulation, but if they are available, we can leverage these to cluster effects by process instance, if that granularity of analyisis is of interest). We order an event log from the earliest timestamp to the latest, obtaining a sequence $\langle e_1, e_2, \dots, e_n \rangle$, where each element is of the form $e_i = \langle \epsilon_i, \tau_i \rangle$ (ϵ_i is the i-th event, τ_i is its timestamp) and for every adjacent pair of elements in the sequence $\langle e_i, e_{i+1} \rangle$, $\tau_i \leq \tau_{i+1}$.

Every event involves one or more state transitions (a business object such as an insurance claim transitions from a *not-determined* state to an *accepted* state, or a task object transitions from an *incomplete* state to a *completed* state etc.). The effects of some events *persist* (an insurance claim once accepted remains in the accepted state) while others do not (a light that is initially switched on is eventually switched off). An event log describes the changes but not the non-changes. In other words, such a log describes new events as they occur but does not describe which prior events have persistent effects, so determining which effects hold at a given point requires specialized machinery. In the following, we will not distinguish between an event and its effects - thus the description of an event is also the description of its effects. To obtain a sequence of states or partial states (each denoted by a conjunction of *effect assertions*) from an event log, we *accumulate* effects using a *state update operator* in a manner similar to the approach adopted in [20,32]. A state update operator takes a state description and the effects of an action to generate one or more descriptions of the state that would accrue from executing this action in the input state. Some well-known state update operators are the Possible Worlds Approach (PWA) [15] and the

Possible Models Approach (PMA) [33] (other approaches based on the logic of theory change [3,12] and belief merging [23,24] can also apply, but we defer that discussion to future work). Given a set of accumulated effects (representing a possibly partial description of the state of the operating environment), and a new effect (representing the action just performed), we use the state update operator to determine what new set of accumulated effects should be (in our evaluation, we use the PWA operator, but others could be used without loss of generality). Applying the state update operator (denoted by $\oplus$) leads to non-deterministic outcomes. Thus, if s_1 and s_2 are states represented as conjunctions of event/effect assertions (we can think of the effects of an action being described, without loss of generality, as s_2), then $s_1 \oplus s_2$ is a set of states (the intuition being that any one of these could be the result of making s_2 true in state s_1.

The idea, now, is to generate from an event log a sequence of *sets of states* (we need sets of states and not single states because of the non-deterministic nature of the state update operator). Given a set of prior states and a set of posterior states (i.e., those obtained from the prior set via state update), it is important to note that a state in the posterior set can be arrived at only from some (but possibly not all) of the states in the prior set. Thus, there are predecessor-successor relationships connecting elements of temporally adjacent sets of states. We first extract from an event log a *state set sequence* consisting of pairs of states, where the first element is the predecessor and the second element is the successor. Given an event log $\langle e_1, e_2 \ldots, e_n \rangle$, we compute a *state set sequence* $\langle StateSet_1, StateSet_2, \ldots, StateSet_n \rangle$, where each $StateSet_i$ is of the form $\{StatePair_1, StatePair_2, \ldots, StatePair_k\}$ and each $StatePair_i$ is of the form $\langle state_{pred}, state_{succ} \rangle$ (i.e., these are predecesor-successor pairs) as follows:

- We set $StateSet_1 = \{\langle \emptyset, \epsilon_1 \rangle\}$ (where $\langle \epsilon_1, \tau_1 \rangle$ is the first entry in the temporally ordered event log).
- We set $StateSet_2 = \{\langle \epsilon_1, s \rangle \mid s \in \epsilon_1 \oplus \epsilon_2\}$ (where $\langle \epsilon_2, \tau_2 \rangle$ is the first entry in the temporally ordered event log).
- For $i = 3 \ldots n$, $StateSet_i = \{\langle s_{i-1}, s_i \rangle \mid s_{i-1} \in StateSet_{i-1}$ and $s_i \in s_{i-1} \oplus \epsilon_i\}$.

A *state sequence* $\langle s_1, s_2, \ldots, s_n \rangle$ is supported by a state set sequence $\langle StateSet_1, StateSet_2, \ldots, StateSet_n \rangle$, if and only if:

- $StateSet_1 = \{\langle \emptyset, s_1 \rangle\}$.
- Every adjacent pair $\langle s_{i-1}, s_i \rangle$ in the state sequence must be an element of $StateSet_i$ in the corresponding state set sequence.

Given a state sequence $\langle s_1, s_2, \ldots, s_n \rangle$ and a goal model with a goal set $\{g_1, g_2, \ldots, g_k\}$ (this represents our vocabulary of goals), we compute a *goal sequence* $\langle G_1, G_2, \ldots, G_n \rangle$ by setting each $G_i = \{g_i \mid s_i \models g_i\}$. Note that a goal sequence is a sequence of sets of goals. We define a *goal orchestration trace* as a sequence of goals $\langle g_1, \ldots, g_m \rangle$ satisfying the constraints of the corresponding goal orchestration model (much like a trace through a process model). Given a goal orhestration model and a trace $\langle g_1, \ldots, g_m \rangle$, we will say that the trace is *supported by* a goal sequence $\langle G_1, G_2, \ldots, G_n \rangle$ if it is the case that $n \geq m$ and every $g_i \in G_i$.

Given a goal model (and thence, the set of goals contained in it), an event log *satisfies* a goal orchestration model if and only if a goal sequence can be obtained from the event log and the goal model in the manner described above such that the goal sequence supports a trace for the goal orchestration model.

3 Executing Goal Orchestrations

For a goal orchestration approach to enable flexible process execution, we require tasks/activities or enterprise capabilities to be annotated with post-conditions, specified in the same ontology as the goals (as recent results in [27] show, post-conditions can be relatively reliably mined from readily available enterprise data). More generally, one can view this as an instance of a generic scheme that permits us to relate task execution to the functional outcomes that are used to specify goals. A number of recent proposals suggest that leveraging task post-condition annotations can be effective and practical [6–8, 10, 11, 13, 19, 20, 29, 32].

The first question we need to address is whether a goal orchestration is *feasible* with respect to an *enterprise capability library*. We shall view the latter as a repertoire of tasks or capabilities annotated with post-conditions. A goal orchestration is *strongly feasible* with respect to an enterprise capability library if and only if for every trace admitted by the orchestration, there exists a task/capability sequence $\langle t_1, \ldots, t_n \rangle$ with a corresponding sequence of post-conditions $\langle p_1, \ldots, p_n \rangle$ such that this latter, if viewed as an event log (this can be easily done by inserting time-stamps with each post-condition that respects the relative ordering), generates (given a goal model) a goal sequence that *supports* that trace. In the case of *weak feasibility*, we only require that there exist a task sequence that generates a goal sequence that supports at least one trace. The subsequent analyses will only be performed for goal orchestrations that are (strongly or weakly) feasible with respect to the available enterprise capability library.

Practical deployment of goal orchestrations must ideally be done with a goal model at hand. A goal model, typically an AND-OR goal tree, is critical in offering alternative means of arriving at the same outcome. We will refer to any goal related to a parent goal g in the goal model via an OR-link as an OR-refined child goal, and the OR-refined children of these and so on as the OR-refined descendants of g. We shall refer to the set of all OR-refined descendants of a goal g as the *OR-alternatives of g*. Given a goal orchestration model *GOM*, the set *OR-Alt(GOM)* of OR-alternatives of *GOM* consists of all goal orchestration models obtained by replacing at least one goal in *GOM* with an OR-alternative.

Executing a goal orchestration model consists of computing an *optimal suffix* for a partially executed task sequence (empty at the start of execution). By introducing a *current state* into the problem, one can deal with the problem of *semantic compensation* [17], where a process deviates from the functionality it is expected to deliver (manifested via events/effects) and where the challenge is to compute a new sequence of activities that will restore the process to *semantic conformance* (where it delivers the expected effects) and achieve the final goals.

Formally, given: (1) The current state S of the process and its environment, (2) a goal orchestration model and (3) The current sequence of goals achieved $\langle g_1, \ldots, g_i \rangle$, compute: a sequence of tasks $\langle t_j, \ldots, t_m \rangle$ drawn from the enterprise capability library such that the corresponding sequence of task post-conditions $\langle p_j, \ldots, p_m \rangle$, when concatenated with the achieved goal sequence $\langle g_1, \ldots, g_i \rangle$ generates a sequence of events $\langle g_1, \ldots, g_i, p_j, \ldots, p_m \rangle$ which can be viewed as an event log (with the appropriate insertion of sequence-maintaining time-stamps, as before) that generates a goal sequence that supports a goal trace through the input goal orchestration model.

Goal orchestrations serve to provide useful abstractions of underlying process models. Figure 2 shows a goal orchestration model for treating head injuries, providing an abstract view of a more detailed clinical process model in Fig. 1. A comparison of the 2 models reveals that the goal of administering IV bolus of dextrose is to maintain blood glucose level within the normal range, while giving extra dextrose helps achieve the goal of body fluid balance, and so on. 'Administer Paracetamol', 'Administer a bolus of IV morphine (50–100 µg/kg) and a morphine infusion (20–40 µg/kg/hr)', and 'Sedation' tasks are alternative ways of achieving the goal *Reduce patient's pain and stress.*

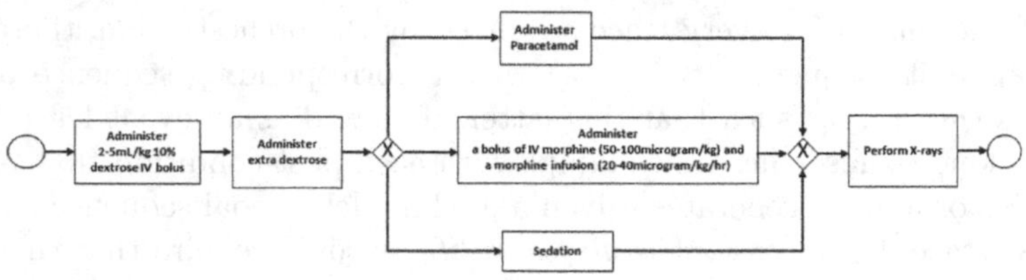

Fig. 1. Clinical process model fragment for treating head injuries

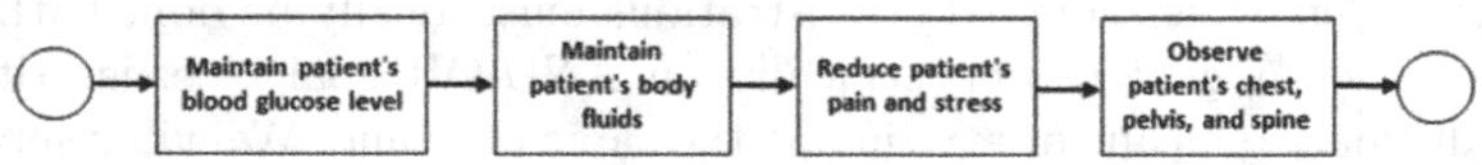

Fig. 2. Goal orchestrations for clinical process model in Fig. 1

4 Mining Goal Orchestrations

In this section, we show how goal orchestrations can be mined from event logs. A formal statement of the problem is as follows. Given: (1) An event log and (2) a goal model, compute: a goal orchestration that best explains the behaviour encoded in the event log. Recall that an event log records two kinds of events: events that flag the execution of a task and events that describe state transitions in objects impacted by a process. Our interest is in the latter kind of event (we shall refer to these as *effects*). It is useful to note that we do not need case IDs associated with effects. Given a set of effects, we are only interested in their temporal ordering, but not which process instance, or actor/agent, might have generated these effects. Our intent is to identify the sequence of goals achieved (and thence a goal orchestration model) from the sequence of effects manifested. The vocabulary of available goals (as provided in the input goal model) provides the lens through which we view the effects. If the goal model is specific to an actor or a process instance, then the goals we will recognize and mine will be specific to the process or actor in question.

Mining goal orchestrations from event logs involves a sequence of pre-processing steps, followed by the application of an off-the-shelf process mining tool (in the empirical evaluation presented in the next section, we use AlphaMiner from the ProM toolkit [31]). The steps involved are as follows:

- Processing an event log to obtain a *state set sequence*.
- Extracting a set of *state sequences* from the state set sequence.
- Extracting *goal sequences* from the state sequences.
- Extracting a set of ordering assertions from each goal sequence identified in the previous step (we do not elaborate this in any greater detail since this is the standard approach associated with the AlphaMiner tool).
- Running an off-the-shelf process mining tool (AlphaMiner) with the goals playing the role of tasks.

5 Evaluation

The purpose of the evaluation is to establish that our approach is capable of the following:

- Mining goal orchestrations from readily available data
- Identifying different alternatives to achieving a goal based on the execution history

We present two cases to perform our evaluation. The first case involve a synthetic dataset and the second evaluation using a real-life dataset from a ticket handling process.

Evaluation with Synthetic Process Models: We ran the first experiment with a synthetic semantically annotated process model (i.e., a process model where each task is associated with the events/effects that would be generated as a consequence of executing that task) using $T_1, T_2, \ldots$ etc., for task names and $p, q, \ldots$ for effects. The model consists of 12 tasks with an XOR-split leading to two alternative flows, one of which included a nested AND-split and the other a nested XOR-split. The semantic annotations were 2 or 3 literals long and involved a mix of conjunctions and disjunctions. We generated a large number of possible execution traces of this model, and obtained the synthetic log using BIMP (The Business Process Simulator)[1] (with a small process model, performing the execution by hand also produced similar logs). We also investigated the

[1] http://bimp.cs.ut.ee/.

effect of scaling up the complexity of the process model, by generating a second synthetic process model with 20 tasks with and XOR-split leading to four alternative flows, one flow included a nested AND-split, two included XOR-split (one leading to two alternative flows and the other leading to three alternative flows), and the other was a sequence.

We randomly assigned effects to tasks, then performed the pre-processing steps described in the previous sections to obtain goal sequences, and from there, mined the goal orchestration. We had access to the ground truth (by maintaining the original process models together with the effects associated with each task and the goal sequence of each trace in the process model) so that we were able to determine the fitness and precision values for the mined goal orchestration.

Table 1 below describes the results of the experiments with each of these two process models. We measure the fitness and precision of the goal orchestrations generated from the log. Fitness evaluates whether the observed process complies with the control flow specified by the process, while precision indicates how precisely the model describes the observed process. In both process model, the results shows that the goal orchestrations generated from the mining conform to the data. The results appear overly predictable, but serve to establish feasibility and provide a baseline.

Table 1. Evaluation result with synthetic data

# of instances	# of events	Fitness	Precision	Time (ms)
Process model 1				
100	1520	1.0	1.0	52
500	7540	1.0	1.0	160
1000	15094	1.0	1.0	257
5000	75640	1.0	1.0	548
10000	151080	0.99	1.0	1,149
Process model 2				
100	1810	1.0	1.0	95
500	9008	1.0	1.0	287
1000	18026	1.0	1.0	377
5000	90040	0.99	1.0	1,170
10000	180540	0.99	1.0	3,147

The synthetic effect logs used in these examples considered all possible flows. Real-life data might involve more imperfections (such as certain XOR flows never being executed, certain tasks never being executed and so on).

Evaluation with a Real-life Dataset: An important part of the evaluation of the feasibility of the overall approach to goal orchestration was to gain experience in using it in with a real-life dataset in a large complex practical setting. Our intent was to test several key elements of our proposal, including the processing (and pre-processing) of event logs, the identification of goals and goal sequences and the eventual use of process mining to obtain explicit goal orchestration models. Specifically, we looked at data from a team in one of the world's largest IT companies that supports IT infrastructure management as an outsourced service. Much of its activities involves the handling and resolution of *problem tickets* generated by customers. These can span the spectrum of complexity from a simple password reset to dealing with a complete ATM network that might have gone down. The dataset we analyzed described how 65000 distinct problem tickets were handled.

In the ticket handling process, when a member of a client firm faces IT-related problems or has queries about the IT systems whose management has been outsourced, they raise a ticket. The ticket handling system maintains records of ticket status from the opening of a ticket until the closing of it, responds with an acknowledgment to the user along with a notification to a system engineer who is assigned to handle the ticket. Also further input from the user may be requested. At this stage, if the problem can be resolved, the ticket is closed. In case the problem can not be resolved, the system checks to see whether there is any update from the user. If no update is provided and the ticket is not re-opened within a stipulated time, then the problem is considered as resolved and it is automatically closed. If the ticket is updated with new information then the system checks the nature of the ticket, whether it is incident or request, depending on which the ticket is serviced or resolved respectively.

The system records all events related to a ticket in the process. Each record represents all attributes of a ticket, such as incident number or ticket number to identify any particular ticket, the identity of the user or employee that raised the ticket, the timestamp of when the ticket is raised (`open date` attribute), when the problem is resolved (`resolve date` attribute), when the system sends a response to the user and the engineer (`respond date` attribute), when the ticket is closed (`close date` attribute), an attribute to signify if the ticket is reopened, etc. These attributes will be used to identify the current state of the ticket. For example, a ticket in the `Open` state signifies that the ticket has been received and currently at the start of the ticket handling process. Similarly, a ticket in `Close` or `Auto-close` state signifies that it is at the end of the process, etc. Based on these timestamps, we were able to identify 16 distinct event sequences, shown in Table 2.

We use the goal assertions in Table 3 to recognize goal sequences from event sequences (these goal assertions were provided by domain experts from the organization - the authors might have articulated these goals somewhat differently).

We extract a goal sequence for each event sequence in Table 2. Recall that a goal is recognized in an event if the formal representation of the event entails the formal assertion of the goal. The complete list of goal sequences thus obtained is presented in Table 4.

Table 2. Effect sequences identified in the log

Event sequence name	Event sequence	# of sequences
TR1	{open}, {open,respond}	1299
TR2	{open}, {open,respond,¬receive}	4546
TR3	{open}, {open,respond}, {open,respond,close}	2
TR4	{open}, {open,respond}, {open,respond,resolve}, {open,respond,resolve,close}	53296
TR5	{open}, {open,resolve}, {open,resolve,auto-close}	128
TR6	{open}, {open,approved}	70
TR7	{open}, {open,respond}, {open,respond,receive}, {open,respond,receive,¬reopen,auto-close}	25
TR8	{open}	296
TR9	{open}, {open,¬approved}	383
TR10	{open}, {open,respond}, {open,respond,rejected}, {open,respond,rejected,close}	1
TR11	{open}, {open,respond}, {open,respond,reopen,auto-close}	37
TR12	{open}, {open,respond}, {open,respond,receive}, {open,respond,receive,incident,resolve,auto-close}	1195
TR13	{open}, {open,respond}, {open,respond,receive}, {open,respond,receive,resolve,auto-close}	3169
TR14	{open}, {open,respond}, {open,respond,¬reopen,auto-close}	12
TR15	{open}, {open,respond}, {open,respond,receive}	531
TR16	{open}, {open,respond}, {open,respond,¬instock}	10

For this exercise, the first check is towards the end effect scenario of each trace where in all traces, the end effect must satisfy any one of the goal in the goal model. We can determine from Table 4 that among the 16 distinct traces, the end effect of `TR2`, `TR9` and `TR16` do not conform to any goal. Upon closer inspection, it reveals that some of these traces are not fault or error, but the process is not finished yet and the effects are simply some kind of intermediate state. For example in `TR2` where the end effect is `¬receive`, the state is to identify that the process is still waiting for user input and has not received any at the observed time.

For the 13 remaining traces, the next check would be whether any one of the effect in the trace conform to a goal. By annotating each effect, we discover that the effect `rejected` of `TR10` does not conform to any goal, therefore we annotate this trace as `exception`, while the 12 other traces are annotated as `normal`.

The last check is to examine whether in the normal trace, the goal precedence constraints in each trace is preserved. We perform the checking between any two consecutive goals (pair-wise) in the trace. From 12 normal traces, we found that all of them are preserving the goal precedence constraints.

Table 3. Goal assertions for the goal model

Goal	Goal assertion
Ticket handled (G0)	close ∨ auto-close
Ticket initiated (G1)	open
Ticket acknowledged and problem assigned (G2)	respond
Requirements provided (G3)	approved ∨ receive ∨ instock
DM approval acquired (G5)	approved
User input acquired (G6)	receive
Stock acquired (G7)	instock
Unresolved problem handled (G9)	auto-close
Problem resolved (G10)	resolve
Request fulfilled (G11)	request ∧ resolve
Incident resolved (G12)	incident ∧ resolve
New ticket created (G13)	reopen
Problem closed (G14)	¬reopen

Table 4. Goal sequence for effect trace

Event sequence name	Goal sequence
TR1	(G1),(G1,G2)
TR2	(G1),(G1,N/A)
TR3	(G1),(G1,G2),(G1,G2,G0)
TR4	(G1),(G1,G2),(G1,G2,G10),(G1,G2,G10,G0)
TR5	(G1),(G1,G10),(G1,G10,G9),(G1,G10,G9,G0)
TR6	(G1),(G1,G5)
TR7	(G1),(G1,G2),(G1,G2,G6,G3),(G1,G2,G6,G3,G14,G9,G0)
TR8	(G1)
TR9	(G1),(G1,N/A)
TR10	(G1),(G1,G2),(G1,G2,N/A),(G1,G2,N/A,G0)
TR11	(G1),(G1,G2),(G1,G2,G13,G9,G0)
TR12	(G1),(G1,G2),(G1,G2,G6,G3),(G1,G2,G6,G3,G12,G0)
TR13	(G1),(G1,G2),(G1,G2,G6,G3),(G1,G2,G6,G3,G11,G0)
TR14	(G1),(G1,G2),(G1,G2,G14,G9,G0)
TR15	(G1),(G1,G2),(G1,G2,G6,G3)
TR16	(G1),(G1,G2),(G1,G2,N/A)

We use these 12 normal traces to build the goal orchestrations model. However, we only use the complete trace, that is all traces that end in the highest goal (G0), therefore we omit TR1, TR6, TR8, and TR15 and left with eight traces to build the orchestrations. We utilize ProM [31] to mine the workflow net.

To determine the consistency between discovered the goal orchestrations with the goal model, we need to establish that all goals in the goal orchestrations

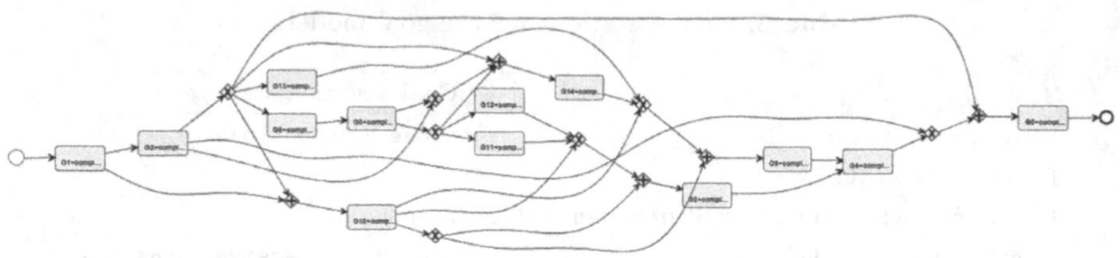

Fig. 3. Goal orchestrations for ticket handling process

presents in the goal model and all transitions preserves the goal precedence constraints in the goal model.

Looking at the goal orchestrations in Fig. 3, there are 13 goals in the goal orchestrations. We confirm that they are also goals in the goal model. The next checking compares the precedence constraints in our library with the transitions in the discovered model. There are 23 transitions between goals in the goal orchestration. Eight of the transitions have a precedence constraint related to them. The checking reveals that these transitions conform to the precedence constraints. The rest of the transitions do not have any constraints related to them. Take for instance, the transitions between G1 and G2. In the goal model, both are sub-goals of G0, thus both have precedence over their parent goal, but there is no constraint defined between G1 and G2. Since there is no violation of the goal precedence constraints, we conclude that the discovered goal orchestrations is consistent with the goal model.

6 Related Work

The nearest point of departure for our approach in the literature is the Azzurra framework [5], where business processes are modelled as social interactions between actors. A business process is seen as a coordination of actor's interactions to achieve the established goals. Interactions between actors are governed by commitments. While Azzurra focuses on inter-actor interactions in business processes and the realization of commitments, our work provides in addition a goal-oriented account of business process execution by individual actors.

Our work also builds on prior work on process mining [31] and the discovery of process designs from legacy artefacts [14]. It also builds on prior work on correlating goals with process designs [21].

There is a long history of work on checking goal realization in downstream artefacts, such as tracking goals through their lifecycle [18], management of changes and impact analysis [1], traces in and between requirements models [16,28], demonstrating compliance with some regulations [22], demonstration in real industrial settings [26], etc.

One of the main challenge highlighted by [28] is the need for presenting the traceability information in a clear and concise fashion. In our research, we represent our traceability problem by leveraging semantic annotation of business process using formal language in CNF.

To asses the goal realization, many frameworks make a comparison between goals with other system artefacts, such as comparison with testing cases [2,4], comparison with design [9], and comparison with code [25,30,34]. In comparison, our research also trace goal realization during or after system run-time, by comparing the task post-conditions defined during design-time with the result of the system execution.

7 Conclusion

In this paper we propose a representation of business process as a coordination of goals called goal orchestrations. This representation gives us a flexibe and context sensitive enactment of processes and convenient for a goal-driven and knowledge-intensive process. We also present a simple method of mining goal orchestrations from event logs. We illustrate this method using a real world setting of a ticket handling system. In our future work, we would like to further explore the mining of goal orchestrations and implement the concept in other application domains, more specifically in clinical setting.

References

1. Allehyani, B., Reiff-Marganiec, S.: Maintaining goals of business processes during runtime reconfigurations. In: Proceedings of the 8th ZEUS Workshop, pp. 21–28 (2016)
2. Arkley, P., Riddle, S.: Tailoring traceability information to business needs. In: Proceedings of the 14th IEEE International Conference Requirements Engineering, pp. 239–244. IEEE (2006)
3. Chopra, S., Ghose, A., Meyer, T.: Non-prioritized ranked belief change. J. Philos. Log. **32**(4), 417–443 (2003)
4. Cleland-Huang, J., Settimi, R., Duan, C., Zou, X.: Utilizing supporting evidence to improve dynamic requirements traceability. In: Proceedings of the 13th IEEE International Conference on Requirements Engineering, pp. 135–144. IEEE (2005)
5. Dalpiaz, F., Cardoso, E., Canobbio, G., Giorgini, P., Mylopoulos, J.: Social specifications of business processes with azzurra. In: 2015 IEEE 9th International Conference on Research Challenges in Information Science (RCIS), pp. 7–18, May 2015
6. Dasgupta, A., Ghose, A.K.: Implementing reactive BDI agents with user-given constraints and objectives. Int. J. Agent-Oriented Softw. Eng. **4**(2), 141–154 (2010)
7. Di Francescomarino, C., Ghidini, C., Rospocher, M., Serafini, L., Tonella, P.: Semantically-aided business process modeling. In: Bernstein, A., Karger, D.R., Heath, T., Feigenbaum, L., Maynard, D., Motta, E., Thirunarayan, K. (eds.) ISWC 2009. LNCS, vol. 5823, pp. 114–129. Springer, Heidelberg (2009). doi:10.1007/978-3-642-04930-9_8
8. Di Pietro, I., Pagliarecci, F., Spalazzi, L.: Model checking semantically annotated services. IEEE Trans. Softw. Eng. **38**, 592–608 (2012)
9. Ernst, N.A., Mylopoulos, J., Yu, Y., Nguyen, T.: Supporting requirements model evolution throughout the system life-cycle. In: Proceedings of the 16th IEEE International Requirements Engineering, RE 2008, pp. 321–322. IEEE (2008)

10. Fensel, D., Facca, F.M., Simperl, E., Toma, I.: Web service modeling ontology. Semantic Web Services, pp. 107–129. Springer, Heidelberg (2011). doi:10.1007/978-3-642-19193-0
11. Fensel, D., Lausen, H., Polleres, A., de Bruijn, J., Stollberg, M., Roman, D., Domingue, J.: Enabling Semantic Web Services: The Web Service Modeling Ontology. Springer, Heidelberg (2006). doi:10.1007/978-3-540-34520-6
12. Ghose, A., Goebel, R.: Belief states as default theories: studies in non-prioritized belief change. In: ECAI, vol. 98, pp. 8–12 (1998)
13. Ghose, A., Koliadis, G.: Auditing business process compliance. In: Krämer, B.J., Lin, K.-J., Narasimhan, P. (eds.) ICSOC 2007. LNCS, vol. 4749, pp. 169–180. Springer, Heidelberg (2007). doi:10.1007/978-3-540-74974-5_14
14. Ghose, A., Koliadis, G., Chueng, A.: Rapid business process discovery (R-BPD). In: Parent, C., Schewe, K.-D., Storey, V.C., Thalheim, B. (eds.) ER 2007. LNCS, vol. 4801, pp. 391–406. Springer, Heidelberg (2007). doi:10.1007/978-3-540-75563-0_27
15. Ginsberg, M.L., Smith, D.E.: Reasoning about action I: a possible world approach. Artif. Intell. **35**(2), 165–195 (1988)
16. Glorio, O., Pardillo, J., Mazon, J.N., Trujillo, J.: Dawara: an eclipse plugin for using i* on data warehouse requirement analysis. In: Proceedings of the 16th IEEE International Requirements Engineering, RE 2008, pp. 317–318. IEEE (2008)
17. Gou, Y., Ghose, A., Chang, C.-F., Dam, H.K., Miller, A.: Semantic monitoring and compensation in socio-technical processes. In: Indulska, M., Purao, S. (eds.) ER 2014. LNCS, vol. 8823, pp. 117–126. Springer, Cham (2014). doi:10.1007/978-3-319-12256-4_12
18. Hayes, J.H., Dekhtyar, A., Sundaram, S.K., Howard, S.: Helping analysts trace requirements: an objective look. In: Proceedings of the 12th IEEE International Requirements Engineering Conference, pp. 249–259. IEEE (2004)
19. Hepp, M., Leymann, F., Domingue, J., Wahler, A., Fensel, D.: Semantic business process management: a vision towards using semantic web services for business process management. In: IEEE International Conference on e-Business Engineering (ICEBE 2005), pp. 535–540. IEEE (2005)
20. Hinge, K., Ghose, A., Koliadis, G.: Process SEER: a tool for semantic effect annotation of business process models. In: Proceedings of the 13th IEEE International EDOC Conference (EDOC-2009). IEEE Computer Society Process (2009)
21. Koliadis, G., Ghose, A.: Relating business process models to goal-oriented requirements models in KAOS. In: Hoffmann, A., Kang, B., Richards, D., Tsumoto, S. (eds.) PKAW 2006. LNCS, vol. 4303, pp. 25–39. Springer, Heidelberg (2006). doi:10.1007/11961239_3
22. Aoki, T., Traichaiyaporn, K., Chiba, Y., Matsubara, M., Nishi, M., Narisawa, F.: Modeling safety requirements of ISO26262 using goal trees and patterns. In: Artho, C., Ölveczky, P.C. (eds.) FTSCS 2015. CCIS, vol. 596, pp. 206–221. Springer, Cham (2016). doi:10.1007/978-3-319-29510-7_12
23. Meyer, T., Ghose, A., Chopra, S.: Social choice, merging, and elections. In: Benferhat, S., Besnard, P. (eds.) ECSQARU 2001. LNCS, vol. 2143, pp. 466–477. Springer, Heidelberg (2001). doi:10.1007/3-540-44652-4_41
24. Meyer, T., Ghose, A., Chopra, S.: Syntactic representations of semantic merging operations. In: Ishizuka, M., Sattar, A. (eds.) PRICAI 2002. LNCS, vol. 2417, pp. 620–620. Springer, Heidelberg (2002). doi:10.1007/3-540-45683-X_88
25. Mirakhorli, M., Fakhry, A., Grechko, A., Wieloch, M., Cleland-Huang, J.: Archie: a tool for detecting, monitoring, and preserving architecturally significant code. In: Proceedings of the 22nd ACM SIGSOFT International Symposium on Foundations of Software Engineering, FSE 2014, New York, NY, USA, pp. 739–742. ACM (2014)

26. Panis, M.C.: Successful deployment of requirements traceability in a commercial engineering organization... really. In: Proceedings of the 18th IEEE International Requirements Engineering Conference (RE), pp. 303–307. IEEE (2010)
27. Santiputri, M., Ghose, A.K., Dam, H.K.: Mining task post-conditions: automating the acquisition of process semantics. Data Knowl. Eng. **109**, 112–125 (2017)
28. Siegl, S., Hielscher, K.S., German, R.: Model based requirements analysis and testing of automotive systems with timed usage models. In: Proceedings of the 18th IEEE International Requirements Engineering Conference (RE), pp. 345–350. IEEE (2010)
29. Smith, F., Proietti, M.: Rule-based behavioral reasoning on semantic business processes. In: ICAART, SciTePress, pp. 130–143 (2013)
30. Valderas, P., Pelecha, V., Pastor, O., et al.: Requirements engineering for pervasive systems. A transformational approach. In: Null, pp. 351–352. IEEE (2006)
31. Van der Aalst, W., Weijters, T., Maruster, L.: Workflow mining: discovering process models from event logs. IEEE Trans. Knowl. Data Eng. **16**(9), 1128–1142 (2004)
32. Weber, I., Hoffmann, J., Mendling, J.: Beyond soundness: on the verification of semantic business process models. Distrib. Parallel Databases **27**, 271–343 (2010)
33. Winslett, M.: Reasoning about action using a possible models approach. Urbana **51**, 61801 (1988)
34. Yu, Y., Wang, Y., Mylopoulos, J., Liaskos, S., Lapouchnian, A., do Prado Leite, J.C.S.: Reverse engineering goal models from legacy code. In: Proceedings of the 13th IEEE International Conference on Requirements Engineering, pp. 363–372. IEEE (2005)

Configurable and Executable Task Structures Supporting Knowledge-Intensive Processes

Nicolas Mundbrod(✉) and Manfred Reichert

Institute of Databases and Information Systems, Ulm University, Ulm, Germany
{nicolas.mundbrod,manfred.reichert}@uni-ulm.de
http://www.uni-ulm.de/dbis

Abstract. The operational support of knowledge-intensive processes (KiPs) constitutes a big challenge. As KiPs tend to be unpredictable and emergent, KiP execution is driven by knowledge workers utilizing their skills, experiences, and expertise. For coordination and synchronization, knowledge workers rely on simple task lists (e.g., to-do lists or checklists). Though these means are intuitive and prevalent, their current implementations are ineffective as well as error-prone: tasks are neither made explicit nor synchronized nor personalized. Furthermore, media disruptions frequently occur and no task lifecycle support is provided. Consequently, the effort knowledge workers invest in task management is not preserved for future KiPs. This work presents the proCollab approach, focusing on the generic concept of task trees. The latter enable to constitute digital task lists of any kind and to establish a task management lifecycle in the context of KiPs. Further, a configuration approach for reusable task lists (i.e., templates) is included to support knowledge workers in configuring task lists at both design and run time. proCollab is implemented as a proof-of-concept prototype and validated along a real-world use case from the healthcare domain. Overall, proCollab improves coordination and synchronization among knowledge workers, prevents media disruptions, and enables the reuse valuable coordination knowledge.

Keywords: Task management · Knowledge-intensive processes · Knowledge workers · Task lists · To-do lists · Checklists

1 Introduction

Residing in highly sensitive key business areas, such as research, engineering, or service management, knowledge-intensive processes (KiPs) have become the centerpiece for creating value in many companies in recent years [2,8]. Driving KiPs, knowledge workers make use of their distinguished skills, experiences, and expertise to cope with emerging tasks. Thus, the systematic and sustainable support of KiPs constitutes a prerequisite for achieving business goals. At the same time, a more sophisticated KiP support still poses one of the biggest challenges companies face today [3].

H.C. Mayr et al. (Eds.): ER 2017, LNCS 10650, pp. 388–402, 2017.
https://doi.org/10.1007/978-3-319-69904-2_30

KiPs can be characterized as *non-predictable*, *emergent*, *goal-oriented*, and *knowledge-creating* processes [8] whose elements (e.g., activities, artifacts, or resources) cannot be foreseen a priori. KiPs have not been fully supported by contemporary process-aware information systems at the operative level so far. Instead, knowledge workers, who aim to achieve common process goals, often rely on simple, paper-based task lists (e.g., to-do lists, checklists) to define and coordinate the various activities of a KiP (cf. Fig. 1) [1]. Though paper-based task lists are intuitive and prevalent on one hand, they are error-prone and ineffective on the other. Tasks are often managed based on paper, are not explicitly represented as coordination artifacts, and are spread over different localities [12]. Thus, knowledge workers suffer from media disruptions as well as the lack of a synchronized task lifecycle support. Due to this lack, knowledge workers cannot make use of existing artifacts (e.g., task lists) when facing comparable situations, i.e. in the context of other KiPs. If knowledge workers could reuse best practice task lists and combine them on demand, redundant efforts would be significantly reduced. Likely, in turn, work quality and productivity would be increased.

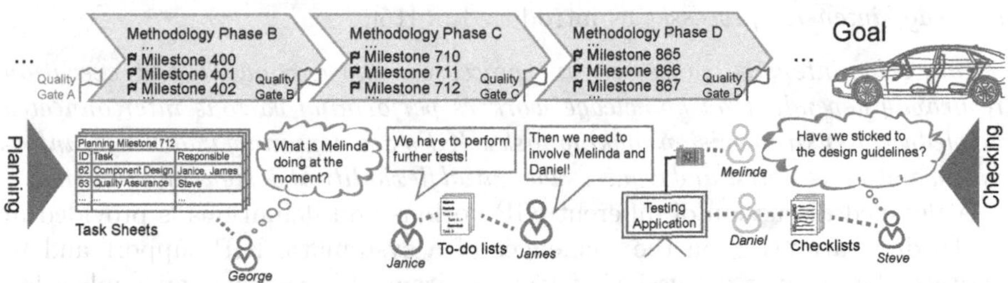

Fig. 1. Knowledge workers collaborating to achieve a goal (automotive domain)

In this work, we present fundamental aspects of the *proCollab*[1] approach, which aims at the systematic and sustainable support of KiPs. As tasks constitute the key entities for knowledge workers when it comes to coordination n the context of a particular KiP, but also across KiPs, proCollab provides the foundation for process- and lifecycle-based task management. In particular, it aims to empower knowledge workers to coordinate their activities among each other more effectively. To make use of best practices as well as knowledge gained in previous KiPs, proCollab encompasses the process-aware provision of *task list templates*, which knowledge workers may instantiate on demand. To foster the reuse of task list templates and to provide support for large sets of task list templates, a context-aware approach for configuring task list templates is included. This enables knowledge workers to easily configure task lists either at design or run time. Based on the proCollab approach, KiPs can be operationally supported through digital, synchronized and configurable task lists. Thereby, one can improve coordination and synchronization among knowledge workers,

[1] **Pro**cess-aware Support for **Collab**orative Knowledge Workers.

prevent media disruptions, and reuse valuable (process) knowledge. Finally, the feasibility of establishing an integrated task management lifecycle is demonstrated by a proof-of-concept prototype. Further, the configuration approach is evaluated by applying it to a real-world healthcare scenario.

The remainder of this paper is organized as follows: Sect. 2 presents fundamentals and discusses key requirements. Section 3 then introduces the proCollab approach, whereas Sect. 4 deals with generic task lists enabling the modeling of templates and instances of different types of task lists, e.g., to-do lists or checklists. Section 4 further sketches key operations on task tree structures. Referring to these operations, Sect. 5 describes a flexible approach for configuring task lists, which allows knowledge workers to easily compose pre-specified task list templates. Section 6 evaluates the approach and Sect. 7 discusses related work. Finally, Sect. 8 concludes the paper and gives an outlook on future work.

2 Fundamentals and Requirements

To establish a common understanding of KiPs, this paper uses the notion of *knowledge-intensive processes* as introduced in [15]:

"Knowledge-intensive processes are processes whose conduct and execution are heavily dependent on knowledge workers performing various interconnected knowledge-intensive decision making tasks. KiPs are genuinely knowledge, information and data-centric and require substantial flexibility at design- and run-time."

A detailed discussion of different KiP notions and definitions is provided in [2]. To draw attention on the challenges of a systematic KiP support and to facilitate the ensuing discussion of key requirements, we reuse an application scenario from prior work [9,14]:

Example 1. In development projects for electrical and electronic (E/E) car components, the involved knowledge workers aim at developing an E/E car component before a fixed release date. Hundreds of professionals (e.g., engineers) are involved in these projects for up to several years. To ensure effective E/E development, the knowledge workers follow a development methodology with sub-goals, e.g., *quality gates* or *milestones*. Each development phase, in turn, may comprise sub-phases, as well as concurrent development processes. Hence, the knowledge workers need to frequently communicate and synchronize with each other. To ensure compliance with regulations (e.g., ISO 26262), to foster the quality of engineering processes, and to track the engineering progress, a central project *checklist* with hundreds of *check items* is initially set up and continuously managed by one or more quality assurance officers. Usually, the currently relevant check items are regularly discussed during interview with the project members. Additionally, pro-active task lists (e.g., *to-do lists* and *task sheets*) are dynamically used by the knowledge workers to manage personal tasks as well as to coordinate with each other in smaller, more specialized teams.

The presented scenario constitutes a typical example of how knowledge workers follow a methodology to cooperatively achieve a common goal as well as to cope with the *emergent* and *unpredictable* nature of KiPs [8]. In general, respective methodologies, which are customized to a specific domain (e.g., the V model), can be abstracted by the Plan-Do-Study-Act (PDSA) cycle [8,9] (cf. Fig. 2). We want to emphasize that collaborating knowledge workers, who follow a methodology designed for KiPs, iteratively stride through the stages of planning work, performing work, studying work results, and optimizing plans. In particular, the planning and studying stages are utilized by knowledge workers to establish efficient coordination as well as to assure KiP quality and effectiveness.

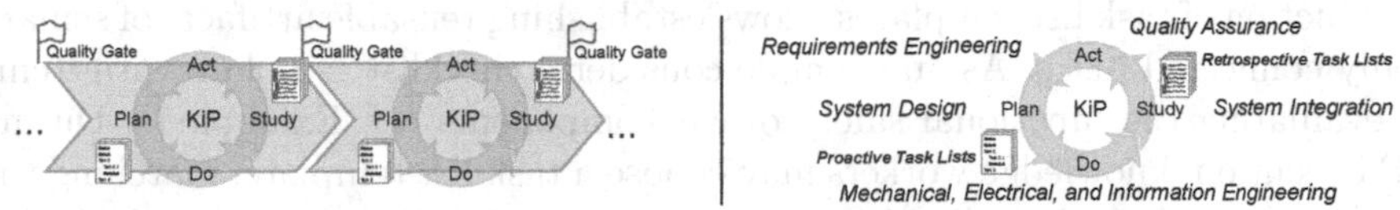

Fig. 2. PDSA-based methodology present in application scenario

In the planning and studying stages, knowledge workers rely on different types of task lists as their key artifacts in use. In this context, *proactive task lists*, e.g., to-do lists, are used to dynamically plan and coordinate the various tasks emerging in the context of a KiP, whereas *retrospective task lists*, e.g., checklists, are used for quality assurance. Furthermore, both types of task lists increase *work awareness* [4], i.e., the awareness of who is doing what in the considered KiP. In prior work [12], we could observe that checklists, in practice, are not changed frequently for the sake of quality assurance, whereas to-do lists, task sheets, and similar artifacts require frequent updates, especially, the insertion of new tasks or entire sub-lists. However, in all considered application scenarios, neither checklists nor to-do lists have been supported by a KiP-aware system in an integrated, synchronized, and lifecycle-oriented manner.

To support KiPs, like the one presented in Example 1, various challenges and requirements need to be addressed. In order to design an approach that systematically supports KiPs, we conducted several case studies primarily in healthcare (e.g., ward rounds and patient treatment) and in the automotive domain (e.g., E/E engineering) [6,8,12,14]. In these studies, we derived a set of key requirements [9]. In this paper, we focus on the *key requirements for enabling configurable and executable task lists* to properly support KiPs:

Meta Model (R1): A generic and expressive approach supporting KiPs must rely on a sound meta model that specifically allows for the representation of task lists of various types. Knowledge workers rely on task lists as key entities for planning, evaluating, and performing their work. Due to the emergent nature of KiPs, knowledge workers may continuously change task lists. For this use case, the meta model should provide change operations with a well-defined semantics that allow modifying a sound task list, ensuring soundness afterwards as well.

To further increase the knowledge workers' efficiency and convenience, a set of high-level change operations (e.g., to swap tasks) relying on the low-level ones, are required. Finally, the trade-off between expressiveness and comprehensibility of the meta model has to be well balanced to enable knowledge workers to seamlessly work with task lists.

Lifecycle Support (R2): In the context of a particular KiP, but also across KiPs, knowledge workers may want to use similar task lists when facing similar situations. For example, the engineering of an E/E car component requires checking functional safeness in a standardized way. To enable full lifecycle support of KiPs, therefore, the meta model needs to be enriched with an integrated and consistent support of *task list templates* and *instances* (cf. Fig. 3a). Thereby, the introduction of task list templates allows establishing reusable artifacts of semantically connected tasks. As an example consider a checklist template with items for evaluating the functional safety of car components (cf. Example 1). During KiP execution, knowledge workers may choose a task list template, matching the given goal, needs and application context, and create a corresponding instance. To cope with the emergent nature of KiPs, in-progress task list instances may be further enhanced on demand by knowledge workers, e.g., by selecting and instantiating task list templates as subordinated task list instances. Finally, a lifecycle-based meta model relying on templates and instances provides the necessary foundation for evolving templates over time [7].

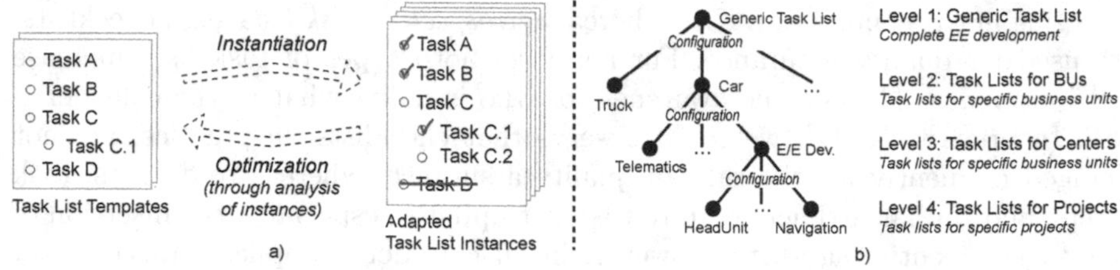

Fig. 3. Instantiation of task list templates and multi-level configuration

Configuration Support (R3): To facilitate the creation of task list templates, which may be reused in different contexts, as well as to decrease the efforts required to build up a task list, configuration support is needed. In particular, knowledge workers should be allows to configure a template in a way meeting the demands of the given application context. For example, the creation of new task list instances (e.g., checklists) may be performed by composing reusable task list templates. Additionally, configuration support necessitates the ability to remove and update existing tasks in a task list template before instantiating the latter. Generally, task list templates should be designed in a reusable and modular way to enable *multi-level configurations* (cf. Fig. 3b). This includes the use of a generic template and the stepwise (i.e. level-based) integration of more fine-grained (i.e. specialized) task list templates to finally create the overall task list template matching the present requirements. Based on this principle, the efforts needed for creating a specific *task list variant* can be minimized significantly.

3 The psroCollab Approach

The proCollab approach has been developed in the scope of a long-term research project to enable full lifecycle support for KiPs. In [8], we discussed the overall proCollab research vision, whereas [9] presented key challenges and requirements to be addressed by any KiP supporting approach. In turn, [7] introduced the key proCollab components focusing on an approach for optimizing and evolving task list templates based on the mining of existing task lists. This paper, in turn, focuses on the interplay of the key components of the proCollab meta model, its generic task trees and, in particular, an approach for configuring task lists.

To design the proCollab meta model, we specifically considered that knowledge workers repetitively perform the stages of planning work, performing work, studying work results, and optimizing plans (cf. Sect. 2). During these KiP stages, knowledge workers use widely established, task-based artifacts, e.g., checklists or to-do lists. Overall, proCollab relies on the key components of *processes*, *task trees*, and *tasks* to establish a framework with conceptual entities for representing KiPs as well as task-based artifacts used by knowledge workers during KiP execution (cf. Requirement R1). Moreover, to provide a lifecycle-based task management in the context of KiPs (cf. Requirement R2), processes and task trees are refined to *process templates* and *process instances* as well as *task tree templates* (with *task templates*) and *task tree instances* (with *task instances*) respectively (cf. Fig. 4).

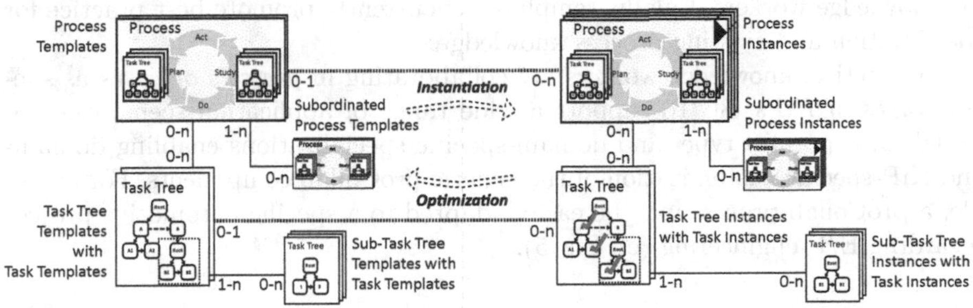

Fig. 4. Overview of the proCollab approach

Process templates and *task tree templates* shall enable knowledge workers to accelerate planning and coordination of their tasks based on best practices and standards. Before starting KiP execution, knowledge workers may retrieve a process template fitting best to their goals. Every process template may have an arbitrary number of subordinated process templates and feature various properties, conditions (e.g., a relative due date), and linked resources. Most importantly, every process template may be linked to an arbitrary number of task tree templates. A task tree template, in turn, contains *task templates* and, optionally, subordinated task tree templates. In particular, it reflects best practices for planning (to-do list) or quality assurance (checklist) in the context of KiPs. Hence, a task tree template refers to one or several goals addressed by the definition of a process template. For example, a standardized checklist for ensuring functional safety based on ISO26262 can be well deposited as a task tree template in proCollab.

At run time, knowledge workers may collaborate in the context of specific *process instances*. A process instance may represent a running *project*, a *case*, or another *type of collaboration*. Moreover, it has properties like start date, duration, goals, and resources (e.g., documents). A process instance may further refer to subordinated process instances enabling knowledge workers to focus on specialized sub-goals. It is also noteworthy that every process instance may comprise multiple *task tree instances* (with corresponding *task instances*). In turn, a task tree instance constitutes the generic representation of common task-based artifacts in use (e.g., a to-do list). For example, an automotive E/E engineering project with to-do lists for planning and checklists for quality assurance can be properly supported by a corresponding proCollab process instance with its linked task tree instances (of type "to-do list" and "checklist"). In general, knowledge workers may create a process instance based on a pre-specified process template or may start even without any pre-specified template. If a process template gets instantiated, all linked task tree templates are automatically instantiated as well. The generated task tree instances are then linked to the process instance. Furthermore, knowledge workers may instantiate further task tree templates or add blank task tree instances to process instances on demand. Based on this flexible approach, the initial setup for the support of planning in a KiP becomes easier for knowledge workers. Finally, template concurrently promote best practice for coordination and existing process knowledge.

In practice, knowledge workers are collaborating in *projects* or *cases* as specific *types of KiPs* [8]. To support a wide range of application scenarios, proCollab incorporates type- and domain-specific specializations enabling domain- and KiP-specific customization of the generic proCollab components. For example, a proCollab process may be easily adapted to a specific automotive project regarding E/E engineering (cf. Fig. 5).

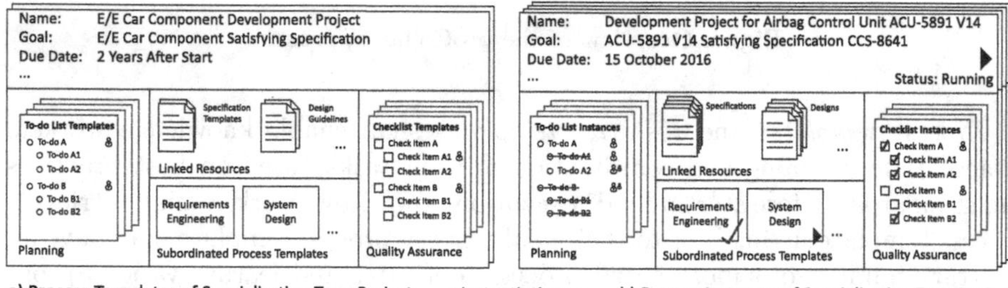

Fig. 5. Visualization of process templates and instances from the automotive domain

Moreover, proCollab task trees may be used as a basis for supporting checklists or to-do lists at the operative level. Depending on the chosen specializations, *proCollab processes* (e.g., projects) and *task trees* (e.g., to-do lists) may feature additional properties, conditions, constraints, or assignments. To realize respective specializations, in turn, proCollab employs *specialization types* enhancing the generic data structures of processes and task trees. For example, if a task tree template is linked to the specialization type "to-do list", it will be interpreted as a "to-do list template" with corresponding properties and an appropriate user interface representations (cf. Fig. 5). To ensure that certain specialization types are used coherently together, the specialization types can be interlinked. For example, the specialization types "to-do list" and "to-do item" may be interlinked and, hence, task trees of the type "to-do list" may only contain tasks of type "to-do item" (and none of the type "check item").

4 Task Trees

Enabling KiP support through process-related task lists and providing a solid meta model for representing the latter (cf. Requirement R1), proCollab employs the generic structure of *task trees*. In turn, a task tree includes *tasks* as well as *subordinated task trees* (cf. Fig. 6). The recommended order, in which tasks shall be processed, is specified through the *hierarchical* and *ordering edges* of a task tree. To be more precise, the pre-order traversal of any task tree directly provides its recommended sequence of tasks. To enable flexibility, however, knowledge workers may deviate from the recommended order, e.g., allowing them to deal with the current situation during KiP execution. Based on task lists relying on task trees, knowledge workers may iteratively refine coarse-grained tasks by defining more fine-grained sub-tasks. Thus, a particular task may refer to a set of subordinated tasks, which need to be completed to finish the task itself.

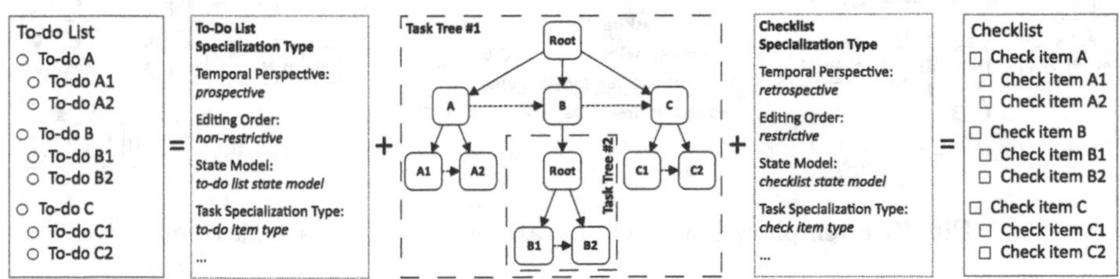

Fig. 6. Exemplary to-do list and checklist and their task tree representation

Every task tree exposes a root node with several ordered child nodes (cf. Fig. 6). The child nodes, in turn, themselves may comprise ordered child nodes. Except the root node, every task tree node either corresponds to a specific task or an embedded task tree (nesting). The root node does not correspond to a task, but may store task list properties (e.g., title, description, or purpose).

Using the conceptual model of a task tree yields several advantages. Task trees constitute an intuitive representation of common task lists. In particular, their generic and executable structure makes it possible to provide a powerful basis for both task list templates and instances as well as any concrete type of task lists, e.g., to-do lists or checklists. Furthermore, the data structure of a task tree provides a sound and common basis for defining required task tree operations (cf. Sect. 2). When using task lists, knowledge workers may add, update or remove tasks and subordinated task trees on demand. Hence, a task tree is manipulable through a set of low-level operations including the *insertion*, *update*, and *removal* of task tree nodes as well as an operation to *filter* node attributes. Note that the filter operation is useful to limit the number of attributes displayed to knowledge workers. Moreover, if the filter is applied to a task tree node with child nodes, the filtering is hierarchically applied. Due to lack of space, we omit a formalization of the sketched operations. Figure 7 illustrates the application of low-level operations to a task tree resulting in a new task tree version.

To add a task tree node to a task tree or to remove one, the respective parental node and the desired positions are required as parameters of the respective operations. As depicted in Fig. 7, a particular task tree may be inserted several times, which allows for the reuse of task trees in different contexts. Note that this option is useful for task tree templates. For example, a particular task tree template with several tasks assuring quality may be embedded and reused at different spots of a parental task tree template. Consequently, a particular task tree may have several parental task trees due to its use in different application contexts. The interconnected task trees then constitute a graph of task tree nodes. Especially when inserting a subordinated task tree into an existing one, this must be carefully considered to avoid recursive nesting.

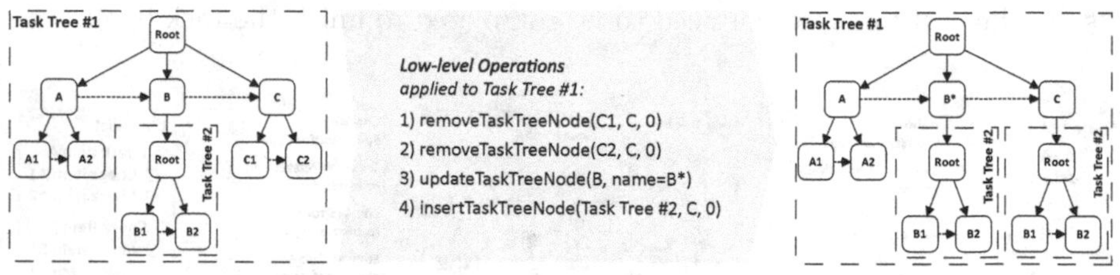

Fig. 7. Exemplary low-level operations applied to a task tree

To ease the management of task structures, a set of high-level task tree operations is provided by proCollab. Knowledge workers may *move*, *copy*, *split* or *merge* task tree nodes. Further, they may *filter* out nodes that match certain properties. Thereby, the high-level operations are mapped to one or several low-level task tree operations. For example, splitting a task tree node involves the insertion of task tree nodes as well as the removal of the node to be split. Figure 8 depicts the application of high-level operations on an exemplary task tree.

Relying on the conceptual model of task trees, all presented operations may be applied on both task tree templates and task tree instances no matter how they are refined by any specialization type. However, every task tree template solely consists of task templates and, optionally, subordinated task tree templates. Furthermore, every task tree template features additional template-specific properties, e.g., a specific state model. Analogously, task tree instances solely comprise task instances and subordinated task tree instances. Further, they may feature instance-specific properties and a dedicated state model, too. Based on this generic concept, proCollab supports the sound and integrated management of templates and instances of arbitrary task lists. In particular, knowledge workers may compose, configure, and instantiate arbitrary task tree templates when starting and executing proCollab process instances.

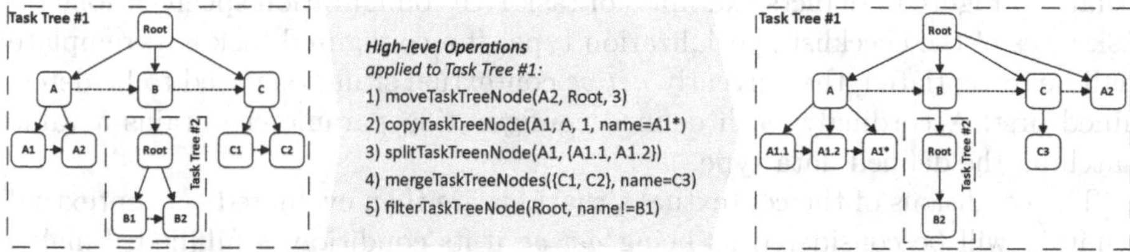

Fig. 8. Exemplary high-level operations applied to a task tree

5 Configurable Task Trees

To enable knowledge workers to efficiently configure task list templates in accordance to the given application context (cf. Requirement R3) or even to the given level of expertise involved knowledge workers expose, proCollab allows for the configuration of task tree templates. In this context, the sketched task tree operations provide the basis for a multi-level configuration of task tree templates. Furthermore, the operations enable both the combination of best practice task tree templates (e.g., inserting checklists for quality assurance) as well as the customization of task tree templates in accordance to knowledge workers' needs (e.g., filtering out non-relevant task templates).

To properly support the configuration of task tree templates, *contextual situations*, under which a task tree template might be instantiated, need to be explicitly defined. These contextual situations, in turn, may be utilized to define which operations shall be applied in which order to a task tree template during the configuration. To properly specify contextual situations, proCollab introduces *configuration parameters* each of which has a name, a pre-defined data type (*boolean*, *String*, etc.), and a value domain. Subsequently, *contextual situations* are defined by a name and a condition expressed in first-order logic relying on the set of pre-defined configuration parameters. Figure 9 illustrates exemplary configuration parameters and contextual situations in the scope of the automotive use case (cf. Example 1) and, especially, functional safeness requirements (ISO26262) regarding E/E car component engineering.

Configuration Parameters:

Name	Type	Domain
controllability (c)	ENUM	{C1, C2, C3}
exposure (e)	ENUM	{E1, E2, E3, E4}
severity (s)	ENUM	{S0, S1, S2, S3}
...	...	...

Contextual Situations:

Name	Condition
Safety Relevance Level D	c==C3 && e==E4 && s==S3
Safety Relevance Level C	(c==C2 && e==E4 && s==S3) || ...
Safety Relevance Level B	(c==C1 && e==E4 && s==S3) || ...
...	...

Fig. 9. Exemplary configuration parameters and contextual situations

Based on the defined contextual situations, one may provide one or more *configuration specifications* for a task tree template. A configuration specification contains a map data structure that allows assigning a sequence of *task tree operations* (applied on the respective task tree template) to every contextual situation. Figure 10 depicts examples of task tree configuration specifications for task trees of the checklist specialization type. If a configured task tree template shall be instantiated, the currently *active* contextual situations need to be determined first. Accordingly, each defined configuration parameter obtains a value matching the defined data type.

The conditions of the contextual situations are then evaluated—a contextual situation will be considered as being *active* if its condition is fulfilled. Finally, the configuration specifications are processed in the pre-defined order. For every active contextual situation, the defined sequence of operations is applied to the task tree template. As soon as the configuration process is successfully completed, the task tree template is finally instantiated, i.e., a new task tree instance is created as the final result of the configuration.

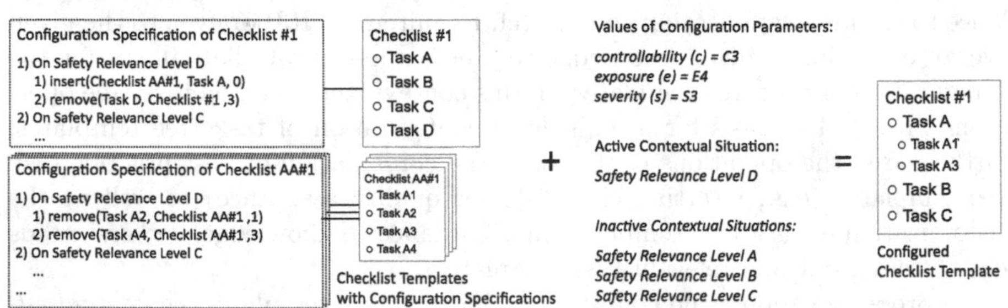

Fig. 10. Example of multi-level configuration specifications for checklists

Note that the application of task tree operations is not commutative. As a result, the order of the operations has to be carefully designed. For example, if a task tree node *A1* is inserted below an existing node *A*, the number of child nodes of *A* is consequently increased by one. Hence, one must consider this new fact for subsequent operations (e.g., more insert operations) accordingly. As a further consequence, sophisticated user interfaces are required to ensure the sound creation of configuration specifications at design time.

6 Evaluation

A mature proof-of-concept implementation is required to conduct empirical studies based on the proCollab approach. To prepare such studies and to validate the technical feasibility, we developed a sophisticated proof-of-concept prototype including the key concepts presented in this work. The prototype is realized with Java EE 7 and relies on a multi-layer architecture (cf. Fig. 11a) based on the Model–View–Controller design pattern. The application logic layer represents the core of the prototype realizing the key services of the proCollab approach and its key components. The RESTful interface enables web and mobile applications to communicate with the services. In particular, this includes the synchronized presentation of the proCollab components across connected clients. Hence, the user interface of the web application (cf. Fig. 11b) enables knowledge workers to collaboratively manage their projects or cases (i.e., proCollab processes) including task trees in the shape of to-do lists and checklists.

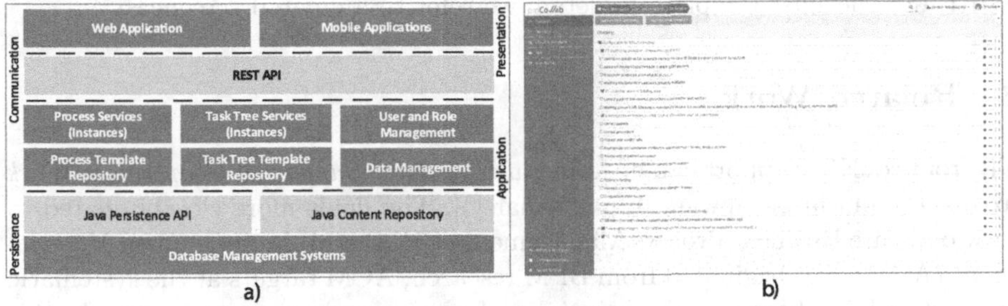

Fig. 11. Architecture and screenshot of the proCollab prototype

To validate the conceptual model of executable and configurable task structures, we applied proCollab to the SURPASS checklist[2] [16], which was designed for establishing a surgical patient safety system. The checklist is supposed to accompany a patient, who will get a surgery, during each step of the surgical pathway (cf. Fig. 12). In general, the checklist contains seven key parts (A0, A1,..., E), connected to the different stages of the pathway, and two additional parts dealing with the transfer of patients (T1, T2). The SURPASS checklist features three main variants: one for clinical surgeries, one for outpatient surgeries, and one for emergency surgeries. The variants mainly differ from each other in terms of contained parts (e.g., the emergency variant omits A0) and in the number of corresponding tasks. For example, in the context of part A of the outpatient variant, a surgeon has to process five check items, whereas in part A of the emergency variant, he has to process eleven items (three being identical).

Altogether, the variants of the checklists could be well supported by the proCollab tree template configuration approach. For this purpose, we first identified

[2] http://www.surpass-checklist.nl/.

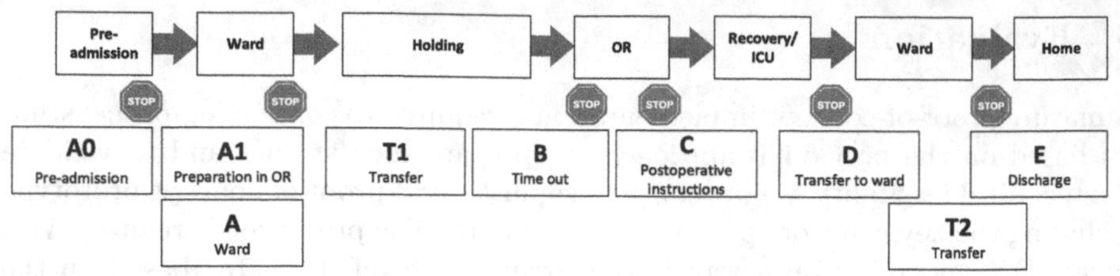

Fig. 12. SURPASS checklist parts in relation to surgical pathway

the common parts shared by all variants (e.g., A1, T1) and added them to a basic task tree template of the *checklist* specialization type. Then, we modelled the individual components of the SURPASS checklist variants as separated checklist templates and included them based on the contextual situations "clinical environment", "outpatient environment", and "case of emergency". To illustrate the entire configuration process and the proper instantiation of the configurable SURPASS checklist template in detail, we refer to a created screencast[3].

7 Related Work

The roots of KiP support can be found in *Computer Supported Cooperative Work* in general and in groupware in particular [4]. The fields more closely related to proCollab are Business Process Management (BPM) and *Adaptive Case Management* (ACM) [5]. Originated from BPM research, ACM targets at the systematic support of KiPs based on the principles of *case management* and *cases*. In this context, the Case Management Model and Notation (CMMN) was developed as modeling notation to create, deploy, and interchange case-based specifications for supporting KiPs [10]. As CMMN does not provide a dedicated representation for task trees and relies on various specialized case elements, proCollab does not implement CMMN. However, its components *process* and *task* may be related to the CMMN elements *case* and *task*. Another approach comparable to proCollab is *Cognoscenti* [13], which allows modeling and using projects with *goal lists* and corresponding *goals*. In this context, goals are comparable to tasks, but the approach lacks an integrated support of templates and, especially, the generic task tree meta model. [11] introduced a notation for task models to specify a wide range of temporal relationships among tasks. The notation, which also employs a tree-based approach, focuses on the relationship between tasks and discusses the implications of temporal relationships among tasks regarding their execution. However, operations on task trees, integrated lifecycle support and configurations of task trees are not discussed in [11].

[3] http://er2017.procollab.de.

8 Conclusion

Tasks and task lists constitute the key objects for knowledge workers when it comes to KiP coordination. Consequently, the proCollab approach aims at systematic and sustainable KiP support based on integrated task management. This paper focused on the generic representation of task-based artifacts, i.e., checklists and to-do lists, through corresponding task structures. Based on the latter, KiPs can be supported through digital, synchronized, and configurable task lists. To make use of best practices and knowledge gained in similar KiPs, proCollab enables the process-aware provision of *task list templates* to allow knowledge workers to instantiate these templates on demand. To provide a context-aware support for large sets of task list templates, a corresponding configuration approach was presented to enable knowledge workers to configure task list templates on demand. Finally, the feasibility of the approach was demonstrated by a proof-of-concept prototype and its application to a use case from the healthcare domain.

In future work, we will extend the proCollab approach and evaluate it in further case studies. Furthermore, the formal foundation of the proCollab meta model as well as constraints between proCollab components will be subject to future publications. Finally, we will consider the evolution of task tree templates and instances over time.

References

1. Bellotti, V., Dalal, B., Good, N., Flynn, P., Bobrow, D.G., Ducheneaut, N.: What a to-do: studies of task management towards the design of a personal task list manager. In: Proceedings of the CHI 2004, pp. 735–742 (2004)
2. Di Ciccio, C., Marrella, A., Russo, A.: Knowledge-intensive processes: characteristics, requirements and analysis of contemporary approaches. J. Data Semant. **4**(1), 29–57 (2014)
3. Drucker, P.F.: Knowledge-worker productivity: the biggest challenge. IEEE Eng. Manag. Rev. **34**(2), 29 (2006)
4. Gutwin, C., Greenberg, S.: A descriptive framework of workspace awareness for real-time groupware. CSCW **11**(3), 411–446 (2002)
5. Hauder, M., Pigat, S., Matthes, F.: Research challenges in adaptive case management: a literature review. In: Proceedings of the EDOCW 2014, pp. 98–107 (2014)
6. Lenz, R., Reichert, M.: IT support for healthcare processes - premises, challenges, perspectives. Data Knowl. Eng. **61**(1), 39–58 (2007)
7. Mundbrod, N., Beuter, F., Reichert, M.: Supporting knowledge-intensive processes through integrated task lifecycle support. In: Proceedings of the EDOC 2015, pp. 19–28 (2015)
8. Mundbrod, N., Kolb, J., Reichert, M.: Towards a system support of collaborative knowledge work. In: La Rosa, M., Soffer, P. (eds.) BPM 2012. LNBIP, vol. 132, pp. 31–42. Springer, Heidelberg (2013). doi:10.1007/978-3-642-36285-9_5
9. Mundbrod, N., Reichert, M.: Process-aware task management support for knowledge-intensive business processes: findings, challenges, requirements. In: Proceedings of the EDOCW 2014, pp. 116–125, September 2014

10. OMG: Case Management Modeling and Notation (CMMN) 1.1 (2016). http://www.omg.org/spec/CMMN/1.1/
11. Paternò, F., Mancini, C., Meniconi, S.: ConcurTaskTrees: a diagrammatic notation for specifying task models. In: INTERACT 1997, pp. 362–369 (1997)
12. Pryss, R., Mundbrod, N., Langer, D., Reichert, M.: Supporting medical ward rounds through mobile task and process management. Inf. Syst. e-Bus. Manag. **13**(1), 107–146 (2015)
13. Swenson, K.D.: Demo: cognoscenti open source software for experimentation on adaptive case management approaches. In: Proceedings of the EDOCW 2014, pp. 402–405 (2014)
14. Tiedeken, J., Reichert, M., Herbst, J.: On the integration of electrical/electronic product data in the automotive domain. Datenbank Spektrum **13**(3), 189–199 (2013)
15. Vaculin, R., Hull, R., Heath, T., Cochran, C., Nigam, A., Sukaviriya, P.: Declarative business artifact centric modeling of decision and knowledge intensive business processes. In: Proceedings of the EDOC 2011, pp. 151–160 (2011)
16. de Vries, E.N., Hollmann, M.W., Smorenburg, S.M., Gouma, D.J., Boermeester, M.A.: Development and validation of the SURgical PAtient Safety System (SURPASS) checklist. Qual. Saf. Health Care **18**(2), 121–126 (2009)

Various Notions of Soundness for Decision-Aware Business Processes

Kimon Batoulis(✉), Stephan Haarmann, and Mathias Weske

Hasso Plattner Institute, University of Potsdam, Potsdam, Germany
{kimon.batoulis,mathias.weske}@hpi.de, stephan.haarmann@student.hpi.de

Abstract. The Decision Model and Notation (DMN) specification enables process designers to represent the decision logic and requirements of business processes. When integrating DMN models into processes it needs to be assured that the correctness of the process is not impaired. The precise semantics for executing DMN models in the context of a business process permits to broaden existing soundness notions for workflow verification to encompass such decision-aware processes. This paper presents correctness notions for processes referring to DMN conform decision models and groups them in a manner that follows the intuition of the well established soundness notions for workflow nets. In doing so, we also make use of the different possible states the process can be in at the point at which a decision is made.

Keywords: DMN · BPMN · Soundness · Verification

1 Introduction

Business process management (BPM) is a technique widely used in industry to manage and support processes in organizations [19]. One of the most commonly used modeling languages for business processes is the Business Process Model and Notation (BPMN) standard [5]. Process models are not only used to capture and document workflows but also as a base for the processes' implementation and (partly) their automation.

With the increasing use of models in businesses' daily operations it becomes more and more important that these models are correct [2]. Soundness has been developed as a correctness criterion for workflows or processes specified by Petri nets [16]. In order for a process model to be sound, its structure must prevent certain (unwanted) situations such as dead transitions. Since soundness is a rather strict criterion and not all violations are harmful in every situation, different relaxations such as relaxed soundness and weak soundness have been proposed [8,16]. Still, all of these notions verify only the control-flow structure given in a process model.

However, many processes contain rather complex decision-making procedures and nowadays it is agreed that a separation of concerns of process and decision logic is necessary [3], leading to so called decision-aware processes [18]. In 2015

H.C. Mayr et al. (Eds.): ER 2017, LNCS 10650, pp. 403–418, 2017.
https://doi.org/10.1007/978-3-319-69904-2_31

the Decision Model and Notation (DMN) standard [7] has been published. DMN can be used complementary to BPMN to design and implement a process' decisions in a separate model. Also, by explicitly modeling decisions with a clear execution semantics in DMN and linking them to dedicated tasks in process models it becomes possible to extend the soundness considerations for traditional workflows to this class of decision-aware processes. Hence, process analysts would be able to verify process models containing DMN decisions.

In this paper, we define various notions of soundness for decision-aware processes and their relationships. These notions and their relationships are extensions of the existing soundness notions described in [16]. The extension of classical soundness defined in [1,2] has already been introduced in previous work [4]. This paper broadens the perspective of that work by defining other types of soundness in the context of processes associated with DMN decision models and giving illustrating examples along the way.

The remainder of the work is structured as follows: An overview of important related work is given for motivation and context in Sect. 2. Section 3 introduces necessary background knowledge, our running example and gives an outlook that emphasizes our contribution. In the main parts in Sects. 4 and 5 we extend the soundness notions to decision-aware processes. This paper concludes with a small summary and a discussion of our contribution in Sect. 6.

2 Related Work

Workflow nets are a prominent basis for formalizing and analyzing business processes [2], so that mappings for modeling notations such as BPMN to workflow nets have been proposed [9]. Different correctness criteria have been developed and grouped into different soundness notions, e.g. classical, relaxed, and weak soundness [2,8,14,15]. Each notion is tailored to different process models and scenarios, e.g., the initial purpose of weak soundness was the analysis of web services' compatibility [14,15]. Van der Aalst et al. organize different notions of soundness into a taxonomy and analyze the decidability of each in respect to extensions of workflow nets [16]. All of these notions are purely structural and do not consider decision logic.

Decisions and business rules are considered as another way to structure and organize operations in businesses. Expert systems and their underlying knowledge bases are methods to implement those rules. Vanthienen et al. analyze different problems that can occur in such systems [17,20]. Furthermore, isolated decision tables have been analyzed [12,13] and adapted for DMN conform decision tables [6].

Recently, the consistency between decisions and processes got increasing attention as DMN is a decision standard complementary to BPMN processes. Janssens et al. motivate the importance of consistent decisions and processes and they introduce different high-level categorizes [10]. Additionally, the notion of (classical) soundness [2] has been adopted to BPMN processes with complementary DMN decision logic [4]. Our work focuses on the adaptation of the soundness taxonomy [16] to decision-aware process models: we investigate different notions and extend them to decisions without changing their intuition or mutual relationships.

3 Prerequisites and Motivation

In this section we will introduce DMN as well as the different soundness notions for workflow nets. This will lay the foundations for applying these notions to decision-aware business processes. The description of a running example to illustrate the different notions as well as a figure summarizing our contribution conclude this section.

3.1 DMN and BPMN

Decision models in DMN can consist of two artifacts: On the one hand, decision requirements diagrams describe the dependencies between decisions and the necessary input data. On the other hand, the decision logic expresses the actual logic to make the decision. Since decision tables are standardized in DMN, we will illustrate our discussions using decision tables. Figure 1 shows an abstract decision model for illustration. In this figure, both rectangular decision elements reference a decision table. These tables consist of rows corresponding to rules and columns corresponding to inputs or outputs. Usually, there is only one output column, namely the rightmost one. The domain of each input/output column can be restricted by a list of possible values, displayed directly below the input/output name. The rules of a DMN table may be overlapping, meaning that for certain input values, more than one rule matches. For these cases, a *hit policy* can be defined to specify how such conflicts should be resolved. Since our soundness notions are independent of such matters, however, we will stick to the default policy *unique*. Finally, a DMN table is *complete* if and only if "it produces a result for every possible case" [7], i.e., for all possible input values at least one rule matches.

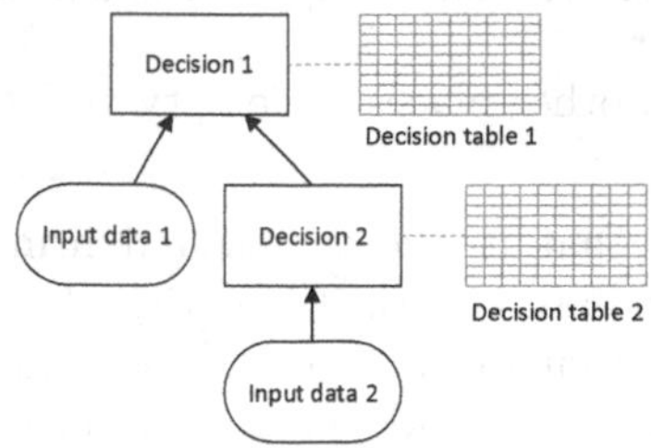

Fig. 1. An abstract decision model

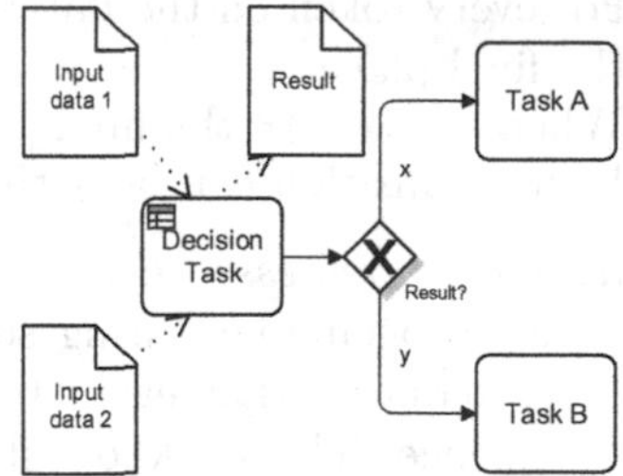

Fig. 2. An abstract decision fragment

A decision model is linked to a process by a business rule task, which we will call decision task in the following (cf. Fig. 2). Note that a decision model may be referenced by multiple decision tasks in multiple process models. When the control flow of a process instance reaches the decision task, the input data objects of that task are read and provided as input to the decision model. We assume that the decision model has a single top-level decision (such as *Decision 1* in the example), whose output will then be returned to the process, such that it is written into the output data object of the decision task. Hence, in the following, if a process model references a decision model that consists of only one decision table, we will disregard the requirements diagram and only show the table.

After the decision was made, the return value is subsequently evaluated to determine how the process proceeds. Thereby, we assume that a decision task is followed by a split-gateway with two or more outgoing branches, where each branch is annotated with a condition that refers to the output of the decision. We call such a process fragment a *decision fragment*. Finally, a process model that uses decision models to express the decisions necessary for executing the process is called a *decision-aware business process* [18].

3.2 Soundness of Workflow Nets

The verification of workflows has been the topic of many publications. The analysis is typically done by translating the workflow or process, expressed, for instance, in BPMN, to a workflow net [9]. A workflow net, introduced in [2] and [1], is a specific type of Petri net, with a distinguished initial place that has no incoming edge, and a distinguished final place that has no outgoing edge. Furthermore, every place and every transition is located on a path from the inital to the final place.

Based on such a workflow net, different notions of soundness can be investigated, which have been summarized in [16]. In the following, we will briefly explain each notion and provide exemplary workflow nets where appropriate. All kinds of soundness are based on the rather strict *classical soundness*, consisting of three criteria[1]:

(i) For every token on the initial place there will eventually appear a token on the final place.
(ii) When a token on the final place appears, all other places are empty.
(iii) Every transition can be activated.

Relaxed soundness "relaxes" this notion in that it allows unsound firing sequences to occur, i.e., firing sequences that violate criteria (i) or (ii). However, it is required that every transition can participate in at least one sound firing sequence. The workflow shown in Fig. 3 is not sound because the firing sequence $t1$, $t4$ leads to a remaining token on place $p2$. Yet, it is relaxed sound because all transitions can be activated in firing sequences that end with only a token in $p4$.

[1] We will refer to these criteria in the following with their given Roman numerals.

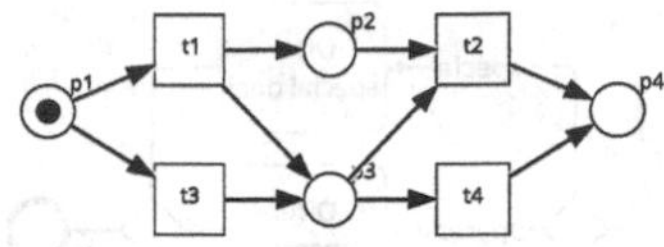

Fig. 3. A relaxed sound workflow net

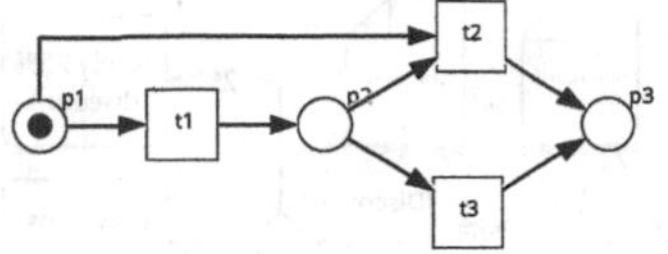

Fig. 4. A weak sound workflow net

Weak soundness is also less strict because it allows dead transitions. However, any transition that *can* fire must always lead to a proper termination. Therefore, only criterion (iii) may be violated. Figure 4 shows a workflow that is neither classically sound nor relaxed sound, because of the dead transition *t*2. Since the net without *t*2 fulfills all conditions (i)–(iii), however, the net is weak sound.

Weak soundness implies *lazy soundness* as well as *easy soundness.* Lazy soundness additionally allows the net to be lazy in the sense that there can be tokens left in the net after a token appeared on the final place. Therefore, also criterion (ii) may be violated. Still, the remaining tokens are not allowed to appear on the final place later on, i.e., they have to remain somewhere else in the net. The net in Fig. 5 is not weak sound because after a token on the end place *p*6 appears it will have a remaining token on place *p*2 or *p*4. Lastly, easy soundness extends weak and relaxed soundness by requiring criterion (i) to be fulfilled not for every token but only by at least one. An example for an easy sound net is given in Fig. 6. Only one firing sequence, *t*1, leads to the final place *p*2.

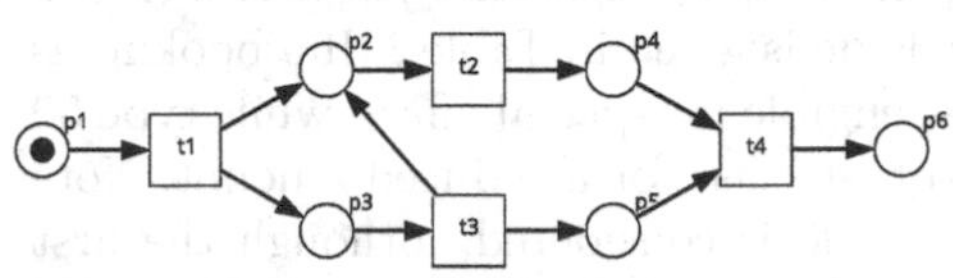

Fig. 5. A lazy sound workflow net

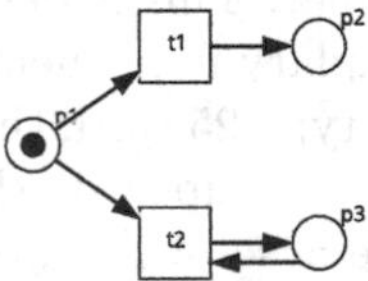

Fig. 6. An easy sound workflow net

3.3 Running Example

To illustrate the different notions of soundness of decision-aware business processes, we will use a discount handling process inferred from booking tickets from a German railway company. The corresponding process model is displayed in Fig. 7.[2] Customers can make discounted bookings with a discount card, called *BahnCard*, which exists in 3 different types: 25, 50, and 100. Each of these types correspond to a respective discount in percent. For example, a *BahnCard* of type 25 provides the customer with a discount of 25% on ticket prices. The decision

[2] For better readability, only the data objects of the decision tasks are modeled.

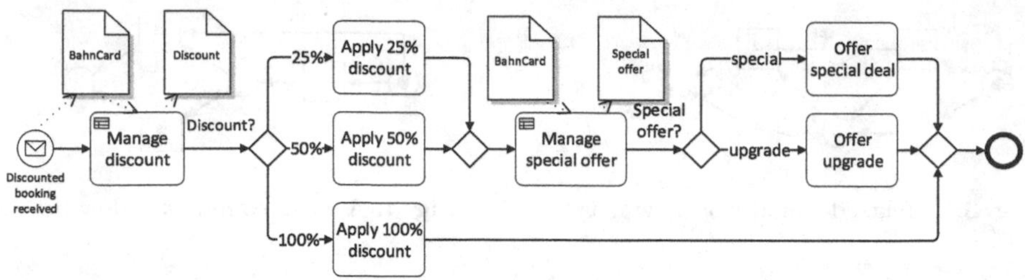

Fig. 7. Decision-aware business process for handling train ticket discounts

table implementing this is shown in Table 1 and is referenced by the *Manage discount* decision task.

Table 1. Decision table for the *Manage discount* decision task

U	Input	Output
	BahnCard.type	Discount
	25, 50, 100	*25%, 50%, 100%*
1	25	25%
2	50	50%
3	100	100%

Additionally, after the discount was applied, a special offer can be provided to the customer. This is decided during the *Manage special offer* decision task and an exemplary implementation of the logic is given in Table 2. If a booking is made with a type 25 card, the customer is eligible for special offers, while type 50 card holders may upgrade their ticket to first class for a reduced amount. Note that also the case of a *BahnCard* of type 100 is considered, although the first XOR-split gateway will prevent this case from actually occurring. This fact will become important during the discussions of the different notions of soundness in Sect. 5. Also, when showing different variants of the running example in the remainder of the paper, we will only show activities that are decision tasks, and leave out activities such as *Apply* 25% *discount* and data objects because they are not important for our considerations.

3.4 Outlook

Figure 8 summarizes the different notions of soundness and their relationships described in Sect. 3.2 as a directed graph where an arrow from a source to a target node can be interpreted as an implication [16]. In contrast, Fig. 9 shows the notions of decision-aware soundness that we derived for decision-aware business processes. As can be seen, the relationships are preserved and for each notion a corresponding definition is given in Sect. 5.

Table 2. Decision table for the *Manage special offer* decision task

U	Input	Output
	BahnCard.type	Special offer
	25, 50, 100	*None, special, upgrade*
1	25	Special
2	50	Upgrade
3	100	None

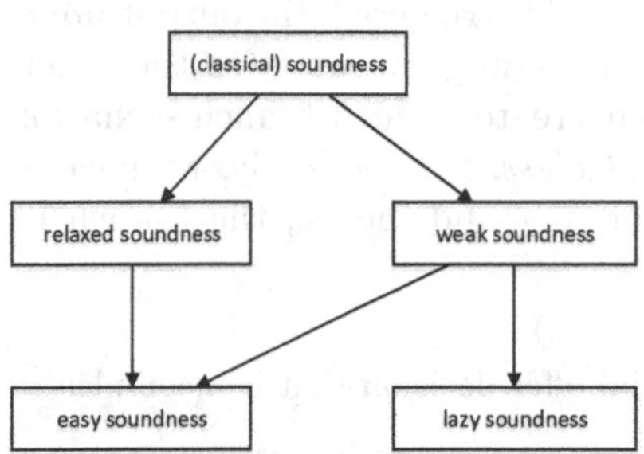

Fig. 8. Various notions of soundness

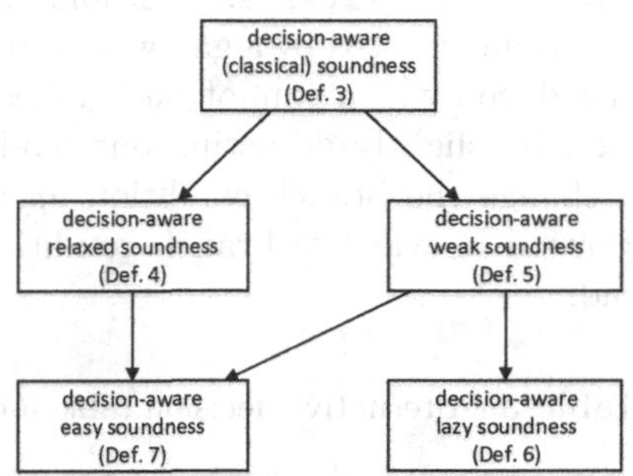

Fig. 9. Notions of decision-aware soundness

4 State-Based Soundness Criteria for Decision-Aware Processes

In this section we build on the soundness criteria defined in [4] and extend them by incorporating knowledge about the states of the process. This is first motivated in Sect. 4.1. In Sects. 4.2 and 4.3 we define the two extended criteria.

4.1 Using State Information for Soundness Checking

Whether or not a decision model causes soundness problems for a process model it is linked to, depends on the point of view of the analysis. We differentiate between two viewpoints. On the one hand, one can consider a decision fragment in isolation. On the other hand, one may additionally take the context of the decision fragment into account, or, put differently, the possible states of the process at the point when the decision is made. Both points of view agree on the criteria that need to be checked, but differ with respect to the method of checking them. The two criteria to be checked have already been introduced in [4]: *Decision deadlock freedom* makes sure that coupling a process model with a decision model does not lead to a deadlock. This requires all tables of the decision model to be complete, and that for every output of the decision there is a matching branch in the decision fragment of the process model, also known as *output coverage*. *Dead branch absence* demands that for every branch in the decision fragment there is an output of the decision model such that this branch is selected for execution.

We will illustrate these criteria as well as the two ways of checking them using the introduced example in Fig. 7. Let us first consider a decision fragment in isolation as in [4]. Table 3 shows a possible decision table for the *Manage special offer* decision task of the example. One can see that some input combinations, such as (25, 50%), are not covered. In a process instance where the decision is reached and (25, 50%) is provided as an input, no decision can be made because no respective rule exists. Additional problems can arise when the decision's outcome is interpreted by a gateway: If rule 3 of Table 3 is triggered, the output *none* is produced which cannot be handled by the succeeding gateway. On the other hand, by slightly adjusting our model, we can create a dead-branch-scenario: we change the branch condition *upgrade* to *1st class*. Consequently, we have a situation in which a branch condition is never met and, hence, the branch is dead.

Table 3. Alternative decision table for the special offer decision that is incomplete

U	Input		Output
	BahnCard.type	Discount	Special Offer
	25, 50, 100	*25%, 50%, 100%*	*None, upgrade, special*
1	25	25%	Special
2	50	–	Upgrade
3	–	100%	None

How does our analysis change if we analyze the possible states of the process at the point when the decision is made? Let us first motivate why this is a reasonable idea. DMN decision models are designed to be reused in different process models that deal with different aspects of a business but contain the same decisions [7]. Because of that, the decision model will not fit perfectly to every process model it is used in. For example, sometimes certain outputs of the decision are not relevant for a process, or the decision is made in a situation in which only a subset of the set of possible inputs of the decision could actually be provided as an input. Therefore, we extend the *decision deadlock freedom* as well as the *dead branch absence* criterion to also take state information into account. State information can be accessed in three ways, two of which we will illustrate in Sect. 4.2 and 4.3:

(1) The conditions of split gateway branches that led to the current state.
(2) The input and output values of the rules matched in previous decisions that led to the current state.
(3) The states of data objects.

4.2 State-Based Decision Deadlock Freedom

Table 3 was claimed to be incomplete because the input in which *BahnCard.type* = 25 and *discount* = 50% is not dealt with. Yet, by analyzing the state space of the process model, we can infer that such a state is unreachable when *Manage special offer* is enabled. The path on which this decision task lies is taken when $discount \in \{25\%, 50\%\}$, since these are the branch conditions of the preceding XOR split gateway. Moreover, by analyzing the decision table linked to the decision task preceding the gateway, Table 1, one can infer that $discount = 25\% \iff BahnCard.type = 25$ and $discount = 50\% \iff BahnCard.type = 50$. Therefore, the input combination (25, 50%) that was claimed to be missing in Table 3 can actually never occur. In conclusion, any input combination given by any state reachable before *Manage special offer* is covered and the decision table is *conditionally complete.*

The situation is similar for output coverage. As mentioned before, the output *none* is not covered by any branch condition of the succeeding gateway. But, this output will never be produced because it requires that *discount* = 100% (cf. rule 3 in Table 3). From our previous investigation we know that at the point when Table 3 is called, no such state is reachable. Hence, all outputs producible through any state reachable before *Manage special offer* are covered, i.e., all outputs of the decision model are *conditionally covered.* This leads to the definition of *state-based decision deadlock freedom*:

Definition 1 (Criterion: State-based decision deadlock freedom). *The state-based decision deadlock freedom* criterion is satisfied for a process *p associated with a set of decision models DM if and only if*

- *For all* $dm \in DM$*, every decision table of dm is conditionally complete.*
- *For all* $dm \in DM$*, all outputs of dm are conditionally covered.*

4.3 State-Based Dead Branch Absence

Let us now change the process model slightly to create a dead branch that cannot be detected by inspecting a decision fragment in isolation but also depends on the possible states of the process.[3] The process model is shown in Fig. 10. The second decision fragment now contains another branch with condition *none.* Considered in isolation, this fragment perfectly fits to Table 3. So, the usual dead branch absence criterion would be satisfied. However, we know from our state space analysis that the rule producing the output *none* cannot be triggered in this process. Hence, the newly added branch is actually dead. Therefore, a branch that cannot be reached by any output producible through any state reachable before the decision task is a *conditionally dead branch.* This leads to the definition of *state-based dead branch absence*:

[3] Note that we left out non-decision tasks for better readability.

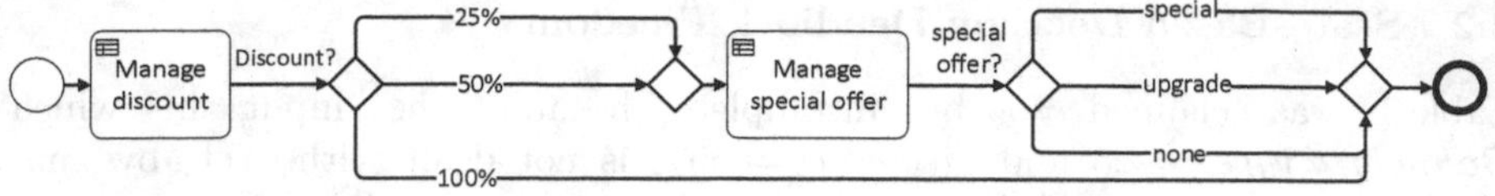

Fig. 10. Variant of the discount process with a conditionally dead branch

Definition 2 (Criterion: State-based dead branch absence). *The state-based dead branch absence* criterion is satisfied for a process *p associated with a set of decision models DM if and only if p does not contain any conditionally dead branches.*

Note that the state-based version of the dead branch absence criterion is stricter than the original one described in [4]. It is not sufficient to just check if there is a decision model output for every branch condition of the decision fragment. It also needs to be assured that this output can actually be produced by the decision model based on the possible states of the process.

5 Definition of Decision-Aware Soundness Notions

This section is dedicated to the definitions of the decision-aware soundness notions necessary when integrating DMN-based decisions into business processes. These extended soundness notions build on the notions described in [16] but additionally take into account decisions. Thereby, they allow or do not allow certain relaxations of the criteria defined in the previous section. We illustrate them with variants of the example introduced in Sect. 3.

5.1 Decision-Aware Soundness

This soundness criterion corresponds to the node *decision-aware (classical) soundness* in Fig. 9. Conforming to the relationship between the different soundness notions shown in Fig. 9, (classical) decision-aware soundness is supposed to be the strictest notion that implies relaxed and weak decision-aware soundness etc. Hence, we require the strictest criteria for this notion and define it as follows:

Definition 3 (Decision-aware soundness). *A decision-aware process model is decision-aware sound if and only if*

- *It is (classically) sound.*
- *It is decision deadlock free.*
- *It is state-based dead branch free.*

Consider the process in Fig. 11, which is the same as in Fig. 7, but without non-decision tasks to increase the readability of the model. Let the decision task of the second decision fragment be associated with Table 4, which is the same as

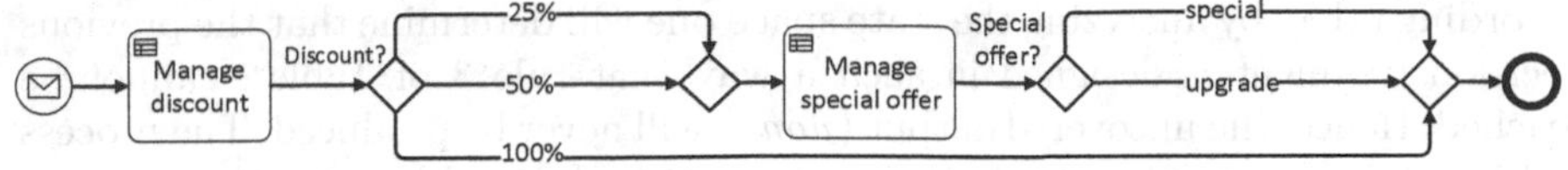

Fig. 11. Original discount handling process that is not decision-aware sound

Table 4. Decision table for the *Manage special offer* decision task, repeated for convenience

U	Input	Output
	BahnCard.type	Special offer
	25, 50, 100	*None, special, upgrade*
1	25	Special
2	50	Upgrade
3	100	None

Table 2, repeated for convenience. The process is not decision-aware sound: rule 3 of this table leads to an uncovered output. If we remove this rule, all outputs will be covered. However, note that then the table will be incomplete because no rule considers the input *BahnCard.type* = 100. Therefore, this value must be removed from the list of possible inputs as well. Lastly, notice that the third condition of decision-aware soundness requires *state-based* dead branch absence. Hence, the process in Fig. 10 would *not* be considered decision-aware sound, because the second decision fragment contains a conditionally dead branch.

5.2 Decision-Aware Relaxed Soundness

The notion of relaxed soundness [8] assumes an intelligent user or environment being responsible at runtime to perform decisions of which activity to execute next in such a way that only "good executions paths" occur [16]. When using DMN to explicitly model decision logic, this responsibility is transferred to design time. Hence, decision-aware relaxed soundness relaxes the deadlock considerations compared to the previous one: It does not allow deadlocks or dead branches *given the possible states* of the process at the point in which the decision is made, i.e.:

Definition 4 (Decision-aware relaxed soundness). *A decision-aware process model is decision-aware relaxed sound if and only if*

- *It is relaxed sound.*
- *It is state-based decision deadlock free.*
- *It is state-based dead branch free.*

The process in Fig. 11 is decision-aware relaxed sound: Although the decision fragment with the *Manage special offer* task does not cover all outputs of the according table, by analyzing the state space one will determine that the previous decision fragment is designed in such a way that rule 3 of Table 2 cannot be reached. Hence, the uncovered output (*none*) will never be produced. The process in Fig. 10, in contrast, is not decision-aware relaxed sound because it contains a conditionally dead branch and is therefore not state-based dead branch free.

5.3 Decision-Aware Weak Soundness

Weak soundness requires that every process instance will eventually complete properly [15]: the end event is reached without tokens left in the net. This, on the one hand, forbids all kinds of deadlocks—even on concurrent paths—and on the other hand, it allows dead parts. The mapping to decision-aware process models is straightforward:

Definition 5 (Decision-aware weak soundness). *A decision-aware process model is decision-aware weak sound if and only if*

- *It is weak sound.*
- *It is state-based decision deadlock free.*

Consequently, decision tables have to be complete to handle all possible inputs and some kind of output coverage must be fulfilled to prevent deadlocks caused by interpreting gateways. If certain outputs will never be produced, they cannot lead to a deadlock. Therefore, only conditional output coverage is required. The model in Fig. 12 violates the state-based dead branch absence criterion, but it is still decision-aware weak sound. In contrast, it is not decision-aware *relaxed* sound since it contains dead parts.

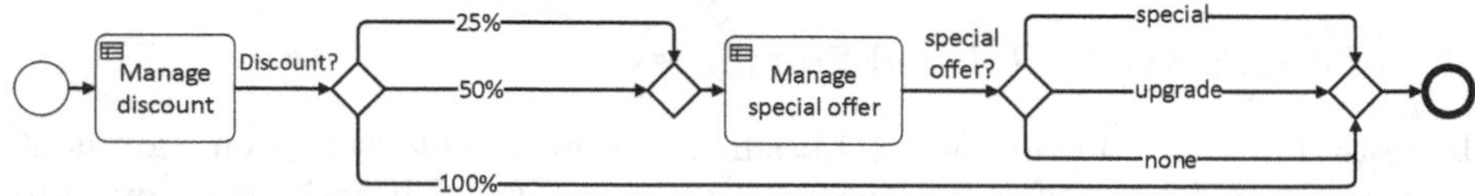

Fig. 12. Variant of the discount process that is decision-aware weak sound

5.4 Decision-Aware Lazy Soundness

A workflow net is considered lazy sound if from every reachable state the end event can be reached exactly once. This notion is similar to weak soundness: deadlocks are forbidden until the end is reached. In contrast, lazy sound nets may have tokens left in the net when the end event is reached and there can be transitions that are enabled or fire.

The production of tokens is not influenced by decision logic. However, decisions are fundamental for a process' branching behavior and, thus, can lead to deadlocks or unused tokens. In [4] it was motivated, that all outputs produced by decision should be consumed and used by the succeeding gateway. This is analogue to consuming all tokens in a Petri net before reaching the final place.

Definition 6 (Decision-aware lazy soundness). *A decision-aware process model is lazy sound if and only if each instance eventually reaches the end event exactly once.*

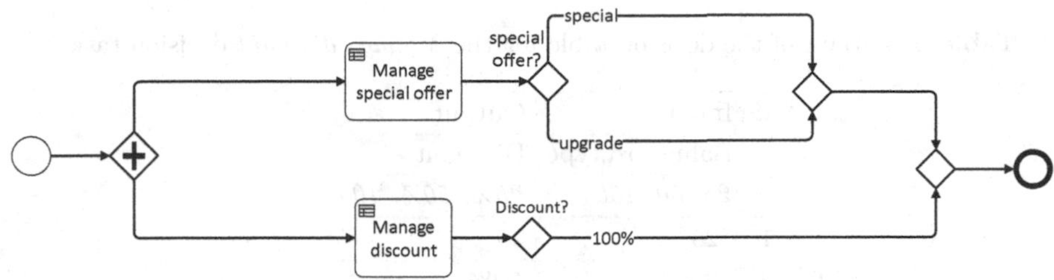

Fig. 13. Decision-aware business process that fulfils all criteria of decision-aware lazy soundness

This definition relaxes the criterion that enforces all tokens to be consumed. Additionally, processes can be decision-aware lazy sound but also contradict (classical) lazy soundness. If we look at the example process depicted in Fig. 13, we can see that it is not lazy sound: The parallel gateway spawns two concurrent paths which are later joined by an exclusive gateway right before the end event. Since the process model does not contain any structural deadlocks, each instance reaches the end event twice. Now let us take the decision logic into account (Tables 1 and 2). In every possible instance, exactly one of the concurrent branches contains a deadlock: if the *bahncard type* is *100* the upper branch stops at the gateway *special offer?*; if the type is *50* or *25* the lower branch stops at the gateway *discount*. Consequently, each process instance eventually reaches the end event and it does this exactly once. Hence, it is decision-aware lazy sound.

5.5 Decision-Aware Easy Soundness

A workflow net is considered easy sound if a state of proper completion can be reached at least once. Consider the process in Fig. 14, where the first decision task references Table 5 and the second references Table 6. Note that the second rule of the first decision table does not consider the case when $BahnCard.type =$ 50 anymore. This means it is incomplete and therefore violates (state-based) decision deadlock freedom. Furthermore, given that the *upgrade* branch of the second decision fragment can only be taken given that *BahnCard.type* is 50, this branch is conditionally dead.

Therefore, this process is neither decision-aware relaxed nor weak sound. Still, there is a path through the process and the decision tables that properly reaches the end event, namely in case $BahnCard.type = 25$. Therefore, the process is decision-aware easy sound, a notion that is defined as follows:

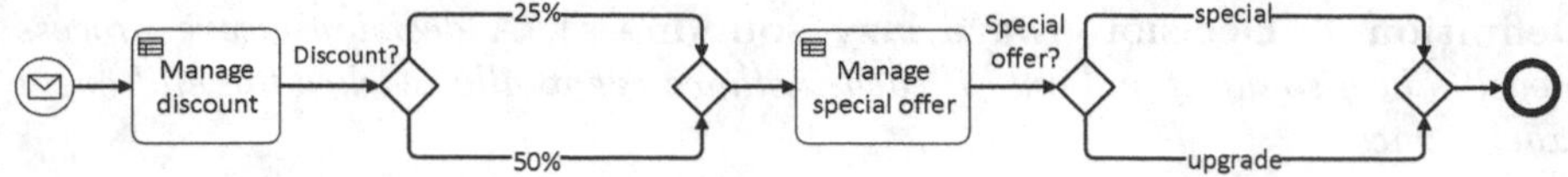

Fig. 14. Variant of the discount process that is decision-aware easy sound

Table 5. Variant of the decision table for the *Manage discount* decision task

U	Input	Output
	BahnCard.type	Discount
	25, 50, 100	*25%, 50%, 100%*
1	25	25
2	**25**	**50%**
3	100	100%

Table 6. Decision table for the *Manage special offer* decision task, repeated for convenience

U	Input	Output
	BahnCard.type	Special offer
	25, 50, 100	*None, special, upgrade*
1	25	Special
2	50	Upgrade
3	100	None

Definition 7 (Decision-aware easy soundness). *A decision-aware process model is decision-aware easy sound if and only if*

- *It is easy sound.*
- *It contains at least one path that is state-based decision deadlock free and state-based dead branch free.*

6 Discussion and Conclusion

Since DMN has been released, decision logic and requirements can be modeled in a standardized way complementary to process models and enterprises increasingly depend on the combination of both model types to document and support their operations. As a consequence, asserting a consistent and correct integration of decisions in process models becomes more important. We provided a set of notions and criteria to pursue this objective. Since analysts may have different requirements for the strictness of the verification, we presented different notions that are in line with the original taxonomy of soundness notions introduced by Van der Aalst et al. [16] offering various relaxations.

In real world scenarios enterprises can have hundreds of process models. Analyzing and checking them by hand is a time consuming task and, hence, automation becomes attractive. We can check the presented criteria by investigating the state space of the system described by our decision-aware process models. In the past, different approaches have been used, such as applying a mapping to Petri nets and extracting the reachability graph afterwards [19] or by extracting Kripke structures and describing properties in temporal logic [11]. These approaches can be applied to automatically extract state information as suggested in Sect. 4.1 and we intend to do so in future work.

Besides the notions discussed in this paper, [16] additionally considers *generalized*, *up-to-k* and *k-soundness*. We did not consider them for the following reasons. All of these notions analyze the behavior of workflow nets when there are multiple tokens in the initial place. If we map a BPMN model to a workflow net, such a token represents a process instance. Decisions are taken by a single business rule task, thus a single token is consumed during their execution. Furthermore, DMN decisions are functional and hence behave the same way each time they are called. So, neither do multiple instances affect decisions nor does a single execution of a decision impact multiple instances.

Our soundness notions consider both, decision logic and process structure. This paper focuses on decision tables, but DMN provides other concepts of expressing decision logic called literal expressions. Literal expressions need not be formal in which case using them for assessing the soundness of decision-aware processes requires manual effort of a domain expert. They can be formalized, however, using Friendly Enough Expression Language (FEEL) or some other expression/programming language [7]. In this case, in order to check the presented criteria for decision-aware processes, we need to be able to determine which inputs lead to which outputs and, along with it, which inputs can be processed and which outputs can be produced. If we look at FEEL, we can derive the sets of possible inputs and possible outputs from the *boxed context* which can be compared to method signatures in typed programming languages. In order to determine which input values lead to which output value, we must parse and analyze the expression itself—a complex task which is out of scope of this paper.

References

1. van der Aalst, W.M.P.: The application of petri nets to workflow management. J. Circuits Syst. Comput. **8**(1), 21–66 (1998)
2. van der Aalst, W.M.P.: Verification of workflow nets. In: Azéma, P., Balbo, G. (eds.) ICATPN 1997. LNCS, vol. 1248, pp. 407–426. Springer, Heidelberg (1997). doi:10.1007/3-540-63139-9_48
3. Batoulis, K., Meyer, A., Bazhenova, E., Decker, G., Weske, M.: Extracting decision logic from process models. In: Zdravkovic, J., Kirikova, M., Johannesson, P. (eds.) CAiSE 2015. LNCS, vol. 9097, pp. 349–366. Springer, Cham (2015). doi:10.1007/978-3-319-19069-3_22

4. Batoulis, K., Weske, M.: Soundness of decision-aware business processes. In: Carmona, J., Engels, G., Kumar, A. (eds.) BPM 2017. LNBIP, vol. 297, pp. 106–124. Springer, Cham (2017). doi:10.1007/978-3-319-65015-9_7
5. Business process model and notation, specification 2.0, version 2 (2011)
6. Calvanese, D., Dumas, M., Laurson, Ü., Maggi, F.M., Montali, M., Teinemaa, I.: Semantics and analysis of DMN decision tables. In: La Rosa, M., Loos, P., Pastor, O. (eds.) BPM 2016. LNCS, vol. 9850, pp. 217–233. Springer, Cham (2016). doi:10.1007/978-3-319-45348-4_13
7. Decision model and notation, specification 1.1, version 1.1 (2016)
8. Dehnert, J., Rittgen, P.: Relaxed soundness of business processes. In: Dittrich, K.R., Geppert, A., Norrie, M.C. (eds.) CAiSE 2001. LNCS, vol. 2068, pp. 157–170. Springer, Heidelberg (2001). doi:10.1007/3-540-45341-5_11
9. Dijkman, R.M., Dumas, M., Ouyang, C.: Semantics and analysis of business process models in BPMN. Inf. Softw. Technol. **50**(12), 1281–1294 (2008)
10. Janssens, L., Bazhenova, E., Smedt, J.D., Vanthienen, J., Denecker, M.: Consistent integration of decision (DMN) and process (BPMN) models. In: CAiSE 2016 Forum, pp. 121–128 (2016)
11. Kherbouche, O.M., Ahmad, A., Basson, H.: Using model checking to control the structural errors in BPMN models. In: 2013 IEEE Seventh International Conference on Research Challenges in Information Science (RCIS), pp. 1–12. IEEE (2013)
12. Kirk, H.: Use of decision tables in computer programming. Commun. ACM **8**(1), 41–43 (1965)
13. Lew, A.: Proof of correctness of decision table programs. Comput. J. **27**(3), 230–232 (1984)
14. Martens, A.: On compatibility of web services. Petri Net Newsl. **65**(12–20), 100 (2003)
15. Martens, A.: Consistency between executable and abstract processes. In: The 2005 IEEE International Conference on 2005 Proceedings e-Technology, e-Commerce and e-Service, pp. 60–67. IEEE (2005)
16. Van Der Aalst, W.M.P., van Hee, K.M., ter Hofstede, A.H., Sidorova, N., Verbeek, H., Voorhoeve, M., Wynn, M.T.: Soundness of workflow nets: classification, decidability, and analysis. Formal Aspects Comput. **23**(3), 333–363 (2011)
17. Vanthienen, J., Dries, E.: Developments in decision tables: Evolution, applications and a proposed standard. DTEW Research Report (1992)
18. Von Halle, B., Goldberg, L.: The Decision Model: A Business Logic Framework Linking Business and Technology. Taylor and Francis Group, Abingdon (2010)
19. Weske, M.: Business Process Management: Concepts, Languages, Architectures. Springer Publishing Company Incorporated, Heidelberg (2010)
20. Zaidi, A.K., Levis, A.H.: Validation and verification of decision making rules. Automatica **33**(2), 155–169 (1997)

Data, Control, and Process Flow Modeling for IoT Driven Smart Solutions

P. Radha Krishna[1(✉)] and Kamalakar Karlapalem[2]

[1] Infosys Limited, Hyderabad, India
radhakrishna_p@infosys.com

[2] Data Sciences and Analytics Centre, IIIT-Hyderabad, Hyderabad, India
kamal@iiit.ac.in

Abstract. Internet of Things (IoT) technologies advance physical objects capabilities regarding programmable, sensor-based and connected. Today's smart applications leverage IoT technologies that enable collaboration between different entities involved in the application. Further, smart applications provide local intelligence attached each device/physical object. The nature of an IoT application usually differs from time-to-time due to varied context and end-device sensing/response. The key issue is that of understanding the data and control flows which govern the processes that act on the sensed data all the way up to end user application. So, conceptually modeling of data, control and process flow for IoT-driven smart applications is more challenging, especially when further modeling the context and exceptions arise during the execution. In this paper, we discuss an architectural framework for IoT-driven smart applications that facilitate monitoring and managing data, control and process flows. We provide a vertically and horizontally integrated enactment of data modeling for smart solutions.

Keywords: IoT devices · Modeling · Workflows · Context

1 Introduction

Internet of Things (IoT) technologies advances physical objects capabilities regarding programmable, sensor based, and connected. IoT involves a lot of technologies such as a sensor, connectivity, embedded, mobility, and network. An entity instance is an object. An object is any physical entity that can communicate/connect with other objects. IoT connects different objects such as computing devices, sensors, actuators, people, vehicle, road and virtually any object that can be connected to other objects. Smart applications provide local intelligence (as information) attached to each device/physical object. These applications are connected to a variety of devices. Each device produces data that need to be shared and processed as per the process flow. Examples of smart applications include smart cities, smart home, smart meter, intelligent cars, health care monitoring, smart manufacturing plant, and real-time traffic monitoring. In this work, we assume that a smart solution is a composition of smart applications.

H.C. Mayr et al. (Eds.): ER 2017, LNCS 10650, pp. 419–433, 2017.
https://doi.org/10.1007/978-3-319-69904-2_32

The data from IoT devices are captured in two ways: push and pull. In the push scenario, the device/object send the data as and when it is created. The velocity of the data (the rate at which data is sent for processing) is dependent on the sensors and needs to be modeled. On the other hand, in the pull scenario, the application periodically polls the devices and capture the data from them. The application controls the level at which data is pulled. Hence the aggregating the data and buffering of the data needs to be modeled. In some applications, a hybrid scenario where both push and pull choices takes place. However, push scenario results in real-time data, whereas pull scenario there is a delay from the data generated time to data capturing (availability for the application to process) time. IoT applications are usually very short duration and highly specific purpose-built. Since the sensors built for the smart application are prone to energy-related issues, push choice is preferable as the pushed data can be stored and available immediately for down-stream processing.

Smart applications leverage IoT technologies that enable collaboration between different entities involved in the application. The nature of an IoT application usually differs from time-to-time due to varied context and end-device sensing/response. The devices that are part of smart applications are usually heterogeneous and possess a lot of autonomy while interacting/coordinating with the application. This nature of IoT devices limits the control and process flows. For instance, a mobile device goes out of sensing region and thereby communication/connection lost. Similarly, a computing device such as a server/laptop is shutdown. The owner of that device can shut down the system any time (since autonomy) irrespective of IoT applications that it involves. Events that are generated should be continuously monitored and perform their associated actions. In some cases, the devices may not respond due to failure, and exceptions may raise due to non-acceptance of the business process flow. Handling such failures necessitate (i) a seamless integration of data generated by the sensors to data processing and (ii) action at the end user level to support IoT-driven smart applications.

In this paper, we present an event, condition, and action driven conceptual modeling of data, control and process flow (supported by workflows) for IoT-driven smart applications. The main contributions of this work are:

- Developed a conceptual model for smart solutions (CM-SS)
- Views from IoT conceptual model to drive smart applications
- Presented an architectural framework for IoT-driven smart solutions
- Developed implementation mechanism for Event-Condition-Action (ECA) Rules to monitor data, control, and process flows in IoT applications
- Presented (a) vertically integrated modeling of data and control flow starting from IoT Sensors to Smart Application and (b) horizontally integrated modeling of a smart solution as a composition of smart applications.

The rest of the paper is organized as follows. Section 2 presents the related work. In Sect. 3, we discuss various issues that arise during modeling IoT-driven smart solutions and also present a conceptual model for smart solutions. In Sect. 4, an architecture for smart application is proposed, and in Sect. 5 we present a case study to show the applicability of proposed modeling for traffic movement solution. Section 6 concludes our paper.

2 Related Work

Chen [3] presented a four-layered architecture for IoT applications. The layers from top to bottom are (i) Object sensing and information gathering layer, (ii) Information delivering layer, (iii) Information handling layer and (iv) application and service layer. The first layers Object sensing and information gathering: The first layer enables smart services that collect contextual information about the environment, things and objects of interest. Wireless technologies such as sensor networks and mobile communication form Information delivery layer that is used to deliver the information. The third layer provides pervasive and autonomic services. The application and service layer represents network computing capability and energy efficiency features required for designing applications. Mervat et al. [7] discussed a data management framework for IoT that serves as a seed to build a comprehensive IoT data management solution. Their framework is a two-way publishing and querying of data and allows the system to respond to the immediate data and processing requests of the end users. This work mainly explores the integration of heterogeneous and distributed data sources and systems for IoT.

Zambonelli [10] presented a common set of features for IoT systems such as objects (including places and persons), Middleware, Services and Applications, and described software engineering concepts for developing complex IoT applications in a more systematic way. Zanella et al. [11] provided a comprehensive survey related to enabling technologies, protocols, and architecture for an urban IoT to support smart cities. They also proposed an architecture based on web service approach for the design of IoT services and discussed that can be used to interconnect the different parts of the IoT. Gaur et al. [4] described an architecture for Multi-Level Smart City using semantic web technologies and Dempster-Shafer uncertainty theory to inference rules to combine sensor information. Robles et al. [8] presented a smart water management model that combines IoT technologies with smart solution coordination and decision support systems using OPC UA (Object Linking and Embedding for Process Control Unified) standards.

All the above works focus is on providing architecture details that show functional and non-functional aspects of various components but lacks the conceptual modeling aspects for IoT applications. Though IoT-driven smart solutions are built over existing technologies, there is a need for understanding how the data, control, and process flow across the components. To the best of our knowledge, our work is the first attempt in conceptually modeling IoT-driven smart solutions along with a system oriented architectural framework.

3 Issues in Conceptual Modeling of IoTs Driven Smart Solutions

Sensors to IoT Store

Unlike traditional applications wherein the data is mostly captured from end users or points of interaction and stored in a database, IoT is a sensor that (i) captures the sensed data, (ii) may preprocess the data to store and load the data, or (iii) transfer the data to a database or a store. There is a data pipeline from IoTs to the IoT store. There are protocols such as HTTP, MQTT (Message Queue Telemetry Transport) [12], and CoAP (Constrained Application Protocol) [13] to format the sensed data and send it to the IoT store. For simplicity, we can consider that the IoT store is a central repository for all sensed data collected and preprocessed (to remove protocol specific tags) from all IoTs before any processing takes place.

Following are different aspects that need to be modeled for this part of the pipeline from IoTs to IoT store: (i) The metadata about the IoT-type such as the make, type, what do they sense, the unit of measurement and any constraints on the device. There can be many IoTs of the same IoT-type; (ii) The location of the deployed IoTs, if available; (iii) The rate at which the data is generated from the IoT, and whether the sensor supports push, pull or both ways of data transfer; and (iv) The health status information of the IoT device, if any.

The above information will be critical to be conceptually modeled so that the application designers can comprehend the IoTs that are the source of the data. For example, the solution architect can decide based on downstream processing requirements to replace one of the IoT types and to evaluate the impact of this replacement on the entire solution.

Extracting Entity Types and IoT Conceptual Model from IoT Store

The next aspect of modeling is the determination of entities that will be used for further processing in the IoT-driven solution. The key issue is how we model the entity, model the instances of the entity types, and how they are generated. There can be other entity types in the environment wherein IoTs are located (that need to be incorporated in the conceptual model) which are critical for the IoT solution. The key issues are: (i) The purpose of the entity type for downstream processing; (ii) The attributes of the entity types; and (iii) The relationships between these entity types and other non-IoT based entity types. At the end of this step, a conceptual model integrating the IoT sensed data with other related entity types is available. This model helps developers and solution architect to determine the interdependencies among the data collected as an available IoT conceptual model.

Determining Views from the IoT Conceptual Model

The main purpose of IoTs is to sense the environment to prepare data for controlling the environment. A given set of IoTs can sense different aspects of the environment. The smart application is driven by the events detected from the sensed data. For each aspect of control, a view is specified which determine the data that is part of the view, and the availability of this data for the downstream processing. The view is a bridge between the IoT conceptual model and the action layer where the event-condition-action processing is done. The key aspects to be modeled for the views are: (i) The implementation related specification of the view as a relational table, or as semi-structured XML object or JSON object; (ii) The refresh rate of the data in the view; and (iii) The predefined stored procedures that generate some aggregate attributes and values for downstream processing.

The views will model the necessary information for the developer and solution architect to identify the data relevant for action layer wherein the smart application takes its inputs for specific actions to be done.

Modeling the Action Layer and Its Interaction with Views

The action layer consists of processes (i) event detector, (ii) condition checker, and (iii) action generator. The specification of the events, conditions, and actions are done at this layer using the information got from the views. The key issues for this action layer modeling are (a) The event specification which can be (i) a predicate on the instances inserted in the view, (ii) output of execution of a stored procedure, (iii) external notifications or (iv) context related changes. Events themselves can be composite, that is, made up of other events. The event detector uses these specifications for event detection. (b) The conditions are modeled again as predicates or external checks to determine whether action needs to be taken. (c) The actions are either (i) notifications or (ii) processes or applications that are automatically executed. The purpose and output of these actions along with corresponding exceptions that may arise are also specified.

The above modeling can be done by ECA rules [1, 9], but in our case, the linkages to the views and the smart applications need to be modeled. The developer or the solution architect can understand the process flow and the control aspects of the smart application based this specification. At our modeling level, we can use ECA rules, but at the implementation level, the coding of these can be driven by the development environment used. In this case, the mapping from our model to the implantation artifacts needs to be provided.

Modelling Smart Application and Smart Solution

The main idea is that the smart application uses the IoT sensed information along with user preference level decisions to take actions based on their requirements. The key issues in modeling smart application are: (i) Mapping ECA rules to actions suggested to the end user. Some of the actions can be automatically performed based on user's prior approval, and other actions require user's explicit confirmation; (ii) Modeling exceptions and failures at the smart application level. The set of actions because of exceptions and failures need to be specified; (iii) The actions taken by the smart application can have external implications. So, need to model the data related to the applications which handle the implications; and (iv) The modeling of chaining of many smart applications orchestrated as a smart solution based on external implications.

The smart application can be modeled as a workflow and the smart solution as a loosely coupled integration of workflows of individual smart applications. The modeling from IoT to IoT store to IoT Conceptual Model to Views to Action layer to Smart Application is the enactment of vertically integrated data and control flow to the smart application from the IOT sensors. The modeling of smart solution from multiple smart applications is the enactment of the horizontally integrated modeling of a smart solution.

Discussion

Many of the issues listed above have been considered in various conceptual models, but the key issue is the systematic and comprehensive view of data, control and process flow that is required to be modeled for developer and solution architect. The storage and processing capabilities of IoT objects are restricted by the availability of resources (due to size, energy, and computational capability), and thus, the data need to be moved to a central store for downstream processing. IoT-driven smart applications are event-centric and context sensitive. Continuous generation of (complex) events raised by the IoT objects need to be stored, processed as they occur and to take appropriate action at real-time. These features of IoT-driven smart applications necessitate appropriate modeling of sensor data and events. Further, there is a need to streamline the design principles for data, control and process flow starting from sensors to smart applications. Therefore, the challenge is to provide a conceptual model that builds on an existing solution while providing an architectural framework for structuring the smart application and smart solution.

3.1 CM-SS: Conceptual Model for Smart Solutions

The conceptual model consists of following constructs as described below: (i) Sensors, (ii) IoT Store, (iii) Constraints, (iv) Entity types and relationship types, (v) ECA rules, and (vi) Workflows

Sensors

Most data generated in IoT-based smart solutions is through sensors, and this data is critical for deploying successful applications. Thus, it is necessary to understand the different characteristics of a sensor and its data. Figure 1 shows typical characteristics (but not exhaustive) of sensor data. The data is generated either continuously (stream data) or periodically. IoT devices suffer from a limited battery capability and high energy consumption. The life value information such as energy and signal range helps in determining the health of the sensor and usability of the data at a certain point in time. IoT applications can consider either all the generated data or a sample it for further processing. The devices associated with the sensor can be in the stationary position (ex. Camera sensor placed at a traffic junction, an on-the-road sensor that monitors pedestrians' traffic). Some devices have mobility when the data is captured (ex. GPS data while the car is in travel state).

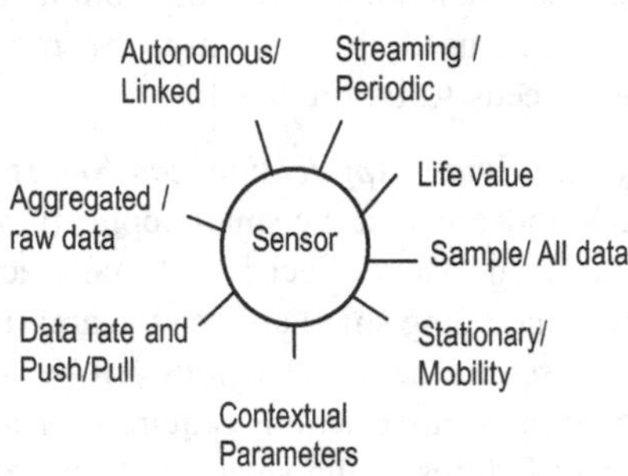

Fig. 1. Sensor data characteristics

The contextual parameters such as location and time of sensors possess distinctive characteristics that make the application as context-aware. The rate of the data at which the sensor generates provides applicability of either real-time or batch protocols to transmit data to IoT store to get processed as soon as it arrives at the IoT store. Applications consume the data either in the aggregated form or the raw data itself so that the devices can send the data accordingly. This characteristic has an impact on communication overheads as well as the delay in processing the data. Further, applications may consider data from each sensor without any dependence on other objects. Some applications may treat the data collectively (data fusion) from multiple sensors that are either physically or virtually connected. All these characteristics typically define the format (schema) and type of the data that need to be stored in a database management system. In our earlier work [5], we presented mechanisms to collect and analyze the context information during the enactment of workflows. A similar approach is followed in this work to analyze the context derived from IoT devices.

IoT Store

IoT store helps in capturing sensor data, communicate, store, access, and share data among the (physical) objects. For instance, IoT store stores RFID sensor data about the item to which RFID tag is attached. The data needs to be sensed and acted on when it arrives at the IoT store. Active databases [9] serve as IoT store. In addition to sensor data, the data related to other entities in the IoT solution are also captured in the IoT store. Views on IoT store can be created to facilitate monitoring and orchestrating a variety applications that constitute a specific solution.

Constraints

Constraints in the IoT solutions mainly show the dependence on the data that is shared among the objects and sensors. Constraints can be modeled using rules. Since IoT applications interact with the external entities, constraints can also include external entities.

Entity Types and Relationship Types

Figure 2 shows the ***CM-SS model***, an extended ER model, for the conceptual design of IoT-driven smart application. This model allows us to capture conceptual level details

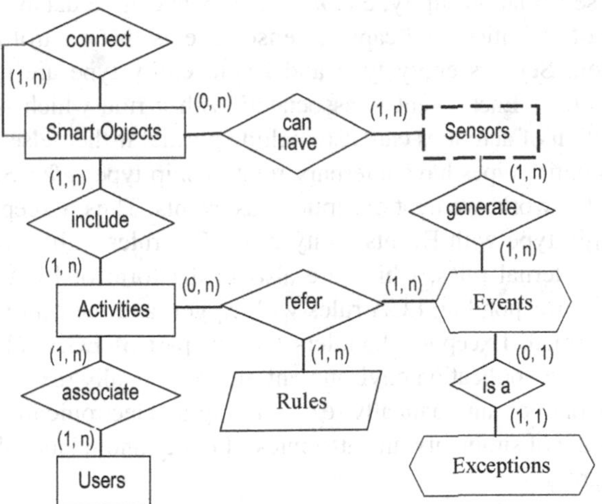

Fig. 2. CM-SS model for modeling IoT applications

required for such applications. This ER model serves as a meta-model template for building IoT applications and solutions.

Sensor data is mostly captured in the form of streams, and thus, there is a need of *stream type* to model sensor data. A stream represents an ordered, finite sequence of entities or values. Our model adds a stream type construct to model sensors data that models a sequence of instances *within* an entity. Similarly, events life span is very small and handled instantaneously. An event is a state transition in the application. When an event is detected, the variables are updated as per the actions in the ECA rule associated with that event. The states are typically implicit and are not explicitly defined in the traditional ER models. Smart objects, which serve as building blocks for IoTs, can understand and react to their environment. The events play a major role in the IoT applications as many smart objects are autonomous and at the same time connected with the other objects (i.e., entity instances) and exchange information among the applications. Due to the complexity in the IoT applications, events need to be modeled explicitly.

There are seven Entity types in IoT applications namely Activities, Smart Objects, Rules, Users, Sensors, Events, and Exceptions. Here, we introduce two new constructs to conceptually model *Sensors* and *Events* entity types which have special considerations in the IoT applications when compared to traditional applications. Sensors entity type represented by a dashed box to indicate the nature of data is a stream. The Events entity type is represented as hexagon box to indicate the nature of instantaneous handling. Further, *Exceptions* entity type is represented same as Events entity type. Also, we represented Rules entity type as parallelogram by following the ER-R model [9].

The IoT applications have pre-defined (system) activities that are executed at run-time. End users are actual beneficiaries in such applications and thus involve either directly or indirectly associated with the activities. So, Users entity type has a relationship type *associate* with Activities entity type. An activity consists of a set of tasks which need to be processed in a given order. Activities include smart objects which have sensors. Smart objects are connected to other smart objects, and thus Smart object entity type has a self-relationship type *connect*. Events can be database events (raised during execution of activities) and capture sensor events that control the execution of the IoT application. Sensors entity type and Event entity type are related to a relationship type *generate*. Each event is associated with a rule which is in the form of ECA rules. Execution of activities can also include normal if-then-else rules. Activities, Events and Rules entity types have a ternary relationship type *refer*. Some events lead to exceptions. In this work, we treat exceptions as events. Thus, Exceptions entity type has *is a* relationship type with Events entity type. The rules to handle exceptions are mostly treated as external rules, which are also in the form of ECA rules. When an exception occurs, corresponding ECA rules will trigger, and the action specified in the ECA rule is performed. Exception handlers (action part of ECA rules) are typically handled outside of the application environment either manually (ex., replacing a faulty sensor with a new one) or automatically (ex., sending an electronic message to external objects). For the sake of simplicity, the attributes of entity and relationship types are not shown in the diagram.

ECA Rules

Events handlers and Exceptions handlers are specified as ECA-rules. Execution of IoT applications is mostly event-driven. The actions taking place during the application execution is determined by the occurrence of various events. ECA rules facilitate the monitoring and execution of the application. Each rule consists of three components: an *event*, a *condition,* and an *action*. Rules can be specified on both primitive atomic events and composite events. An event can be specified by an event expression. Composite events, each of which in turn consists of a set of atomic events, are specified as event expressions, which are formed using event operators using SNOOP language [2]. Context-specific events can be specified using an event language developed for context-aware information push service (CAIPS) [1]. A composite event can be specified using the event operators. Events, either atomic or composite, happen instantaneously at specific points in time. Events are associated with activity transactions and specified to happen after a transaction begins and before a transaction commits/aborts. Examples of ECA rules are given below:

(i) *Event:* Abnormal behavior of Sensor
Condition: Sensor data is out of valid range
Action: Replace the sensor with a new one

(ii) For an IoT-driven smart application "Driver Assist Application", where smart vehicles can sense the health of passengers,

Event: Irregular eyelid movement
Condition: Driving for more than five hours
Action: Alert driver to take rest

Workflows

Workflows automate business logic for smart objects in the IoT applications. They can model both vertical integrations of data movement from sensors to the smart application, and among smart applications to form a smart solution. Usually, most of the IoT-driven smart applications involve business processes that span multiple organizations/entities. Workflows support cross-organizational workflows that are essential for the enactment of the application. Workflows can also be generated based on the situation. User workflows allow the users to create his/her workflow to process the incoming event from a specific device/sensor. The execution of specific workflows depends on the execution of previous workflows, transactions commit/rollback and the exceptions raised. However, in certain circumstances, human intervention is required to take a decision. An example workflows for a smart traffic solution is travel route finding workflow which includes tasks such as receive data from road sensors, estimation of traffic flow, traffic prediction and pathfinding.

4 Architectural Framework for IoT Driven Smart Applications

Figure 3 shows the architecture overview of IoT Applications. Smart applications can have either a dedicated infrastructure or subscribe to a cloud. The *infrastructure* usually includes data centers, networks, etc. The data from *IoT devices* can be captured either pushed into a data center or pulled from the IoT devices. Heterogeneous devices/ objects may have data of different data types, and a proper setting is needed which data needs to be stored or processed at data centers. *Business processes* of smart applications are automated using *workflows*. The workflow schema and rules about business process activity along with the data captured from IoT devices are stored in a *Database*.

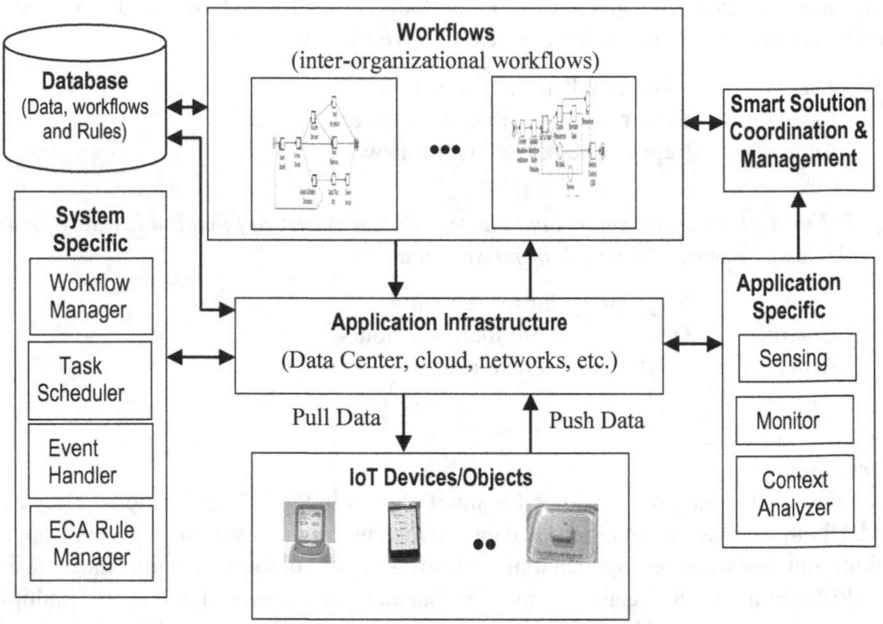

Fig. 3. Architectural framework for IoT smart applications

Smart Solution coordination and management component coordinates the overall execution of the application. Several applications can be developed using available IoT devices. *Workflow manager*, *task scheduler*, the *event handler* and *ECA (Event-Condition-Action) rule manager* represents the IoT ***system specific components***, whereas *sense*, *monitor* and *context analyzer* forms ***application specific components***. The events generated during the workflow execution are tracked by and handled *by the event handler*, which works with the *ECA rule manager* to trigger appropriate ECA rules.

The activities are scheduled by the *task scheduler*, whereas all the workflows and workflow instances are managed by the *workflow manager*. *Sensing* component analyzes the sensor data and their data types and allows the application to act based on the data. *Monitor* tracks the IoT devices and indicates whether there is any failure in the devices/objects. *Context analyzer* captures the context of the environment for the execution of application transactions (ex. Location, time, etc.) to determine the inference out of context. The three components namely *sensing*, *monitor* and *context analyzer* keep track of the health of the sensor attached to the IoT devices and generate necessary *workflows* in coordination with *Smart solution coordination and management.*

4.1 Implementation Mechanism

Figure 4 shows the implementation mechanism for IoT smart applications that are driven by ECA rules (adapted from [6]). The steps indicated in the figure are given below.

1. The smart application involves a set of business processes which automated using workflows. Appropriate workflow instances are initiated according to the application requirements. These requirements are mainly based on the current state of data, control, and process (DCP) flow.
2. Smart application captured the data either continuously or periodically and associated them with pre-defined control flows.
3. Further, the smart application consists of a variety of devices/physical objects which generate the data.
4. The devices (objects) uses context to access/control/process the data.
5. Devices monitor the rules, which can be specified in the application specification document.
6. Devices generate events at run-time and raise exceptions if there is any failure. Here, exceptions also treated as a specific class of events.
7. When an event occurs, it triggers some rules.
8. Next, the condition part of these rules will be evaluated.

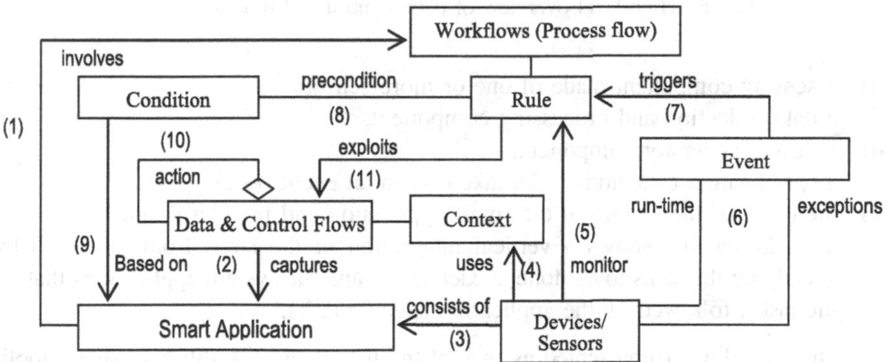

Fig. 4. ECA rules to monitor DCP flows in IoT applications

9. Data and constraints required for a business process are based on smart application.
10. Action in the rules may update the data or generate new data.
11. During the updating of data, other events may trigger. So, the workflow may exploit other rules for its update completeness.

Figure 5 shows the intuition behind modeling data, control and process flow for building smart applications/solutions. An IoT-driven smart solution consists of:

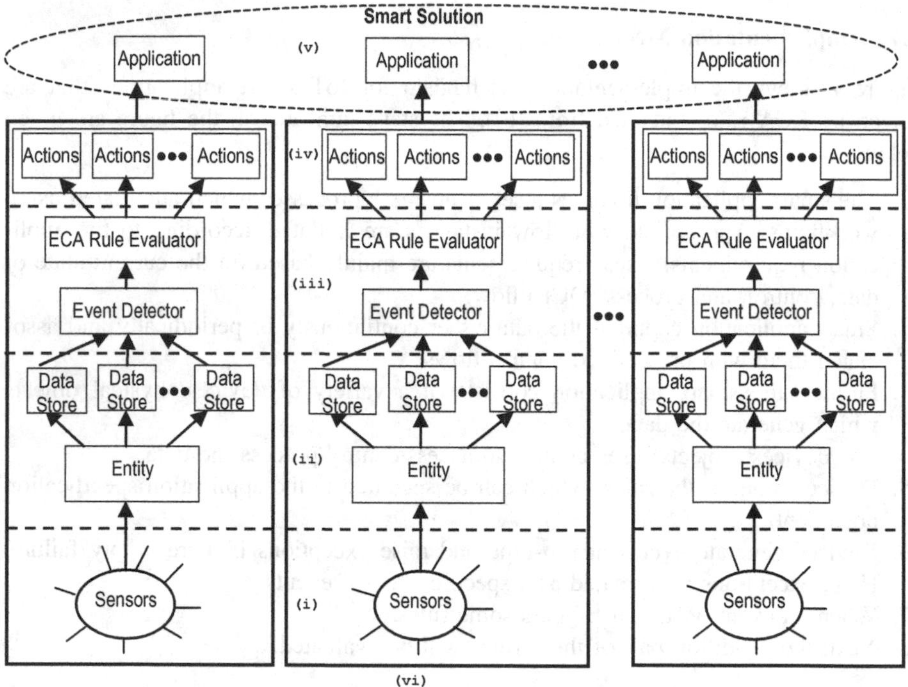

Fig. 5. High-level overview of data, control and process flows

(i) a sensing component made of one or more sensors,
(ii) a data collection and processing component,
(iii) an event generator component,
(iv) a specification of actions to be taken when an event occurs,
(v) the effect of the actions at the smart application end user level, and
(vi) a workflow that shows a vertical integration of the steps from (i) to (v) by specifying the tasks to be done at each level, and the system applications that do the tasks, followed by the application specific tasks.

At the other level (represented as oval at the top of Fig. 5), different smart applications can be horizontally coalesced to support a larger smart solution.

5 Traffic Advisor: A Case Study

Consider a smart traffic solution example provided to a city. The basic sensors are the vehicle detectors, the pedestrian detectors at different junctions, commuter detectors at bus stops and train stations, along with the flow of the public transport vehicles and trains. The vertical integration will consist of providing the number of pedestrians who are at a junction, and how many of them are coming from the bus stop and train station. Further, the time at which next bus will come at the bus stop or train at the train station based on sensors on the buses and trains. A simpler smart application will provide the density of the people at each junction and availability of space in next few trains or buses coming to that place. A horizontally integrated smart solution will use the data and events from each of the smart applications and develop a traffic movement solution for commuters to reduce the overall energy consumed by the city due to people mobility. Energy efficient transportation will involve dynamic management of traffic lights, bus and train frequencies, and pro-active guidance to the commuters on when to travel to reduce their costs and increase the comfort level of their trip.

The bottom level (see Fig. 5) mainly comprises sensors, which provides most of the data required for processing different activities in an IoT application. *An entity* can be sensors, computers, smartphones, mobile systems or any object that contains intelligent devices and/or connectedness with other entities. For instance, Vehicle with GPS is an Entity. Each entity is described regarding attributes. Examples of attributes for the use case include Road ID, Road Name, Time, Number of vehicles, etc.

Views are useful to serve as a data store and visualize the data specific to an application. They can capture data not only from sensors but also from other external entities. For instance, the direction of traffic movement at traffic signals is useful in assessing the traffic condition. Views can be further classified as control views or action views. *Control views* mainly relate to the control flows in the IoT application whereas *Action views* are about the specific actions to be carried out by executing smart solutions. Views for a smart traffic management application comprises data about (a) on-road sensors, cameras placed at traffic signals and GPS positioned on vehicles, (b) objects namely road, vehicles, pedestrians, and (c) flow of vehicles, weather conditions and road maps (ex., Google maps).

Event Detectors analyze the data to detect the events at runtime or patterns in the data. Some events dealt with (a) control the objects, (b) alter the business process (application) or (c) both. For instance, when traffic is heavy on a specific road, a congestion event raises which controls the traffic signals (such as on/off and adjust the time for traffic lights namely red, yellow and green). On the other hand, the smart vehicles sense a congestion event (by polling the traffic data at periodic intervals) to decide on a new route that has a less traffic for a vehicle. ECA rule evaluator reacts to events and chooses appropriate actions to control the objects/business processes. Actions correspond to the execution of ECA rules and coordinate with the smart environment. The application provides the information about specification of workflows, how to control workflows, what data is modeled, etc., and ensure the consistency while running entire application. It also provides necessary feedback on what additional data need to be captured and modeled, additional views to be created, exception handling, etc.

In this work, we modeled each of data flow, control flow, and process flow as workflows itself that are interdependent. For instance, for the above example, the tasks of control workflow include:

(a) capture the GPS data from vehicles,
(b) process time and vehicle location,
(c) find the distance between the vehicle and the current position of the end user,
(d) notify the user when the bus is fully occupied, and
(e) notify to end user the vehicle time to reach.

Each of such tasks can have separate exception handlers. This exception handler is also modeled as a workflow in our approach. Suppose, there is a long delay due to a vehicle breakdown, an exception handler initiates a workflow that consisting of tasks like arrange for another vehicle, move the passengers into the new bus, update the route if required, and inform the passengers who are waiting for the bus at designated stops. The integration of these workflows as part of a larger smart solution help us in adapting the smart applications for various (context related) scenarios, and at the same time, a specific IoT device data can be used in multiple applications. The core of any IoT-based applications is (a) localized intelligence and (b) contextual workflows. Making devices more intelligent enough facilitates appropriate communication with rest of the application. On the other hand, *contextual workflow instances* can be generated in order to serve a variety of application scenarios.

6 Conclusion

In this paper, we discussed the modeling aspects of data, control and process flow for IoT-driven smart solutions and presented an architecture that suits for entire data, control, and process flow of such solutions. We also presented a case study that illustrates our approach. The main objective of this work is to provide a conceptual model that drives the understanding of the vertical flow of data from sensors to the smart application, and loose composition of smart applications as a smart solution. Our CM-SS model along with the architectural framework aids the smart application/ solution developer and architect to understand the data, control and process flows. This provides discussion and modification of the existing solutions and development of newer solutions. In our ongoing work, we are working towards incorporating the formal specification of flows, and the service level constraints into our CM-SS model.

References

1. Beer, T., Rasinger, J., Höpken, W., Fuchs, M., Werthner, H.: Exploiting E-C-a rules for defining and processing context-aware push messages. In: Paschke, A., Biletskiy, Y. (eds.) RuleML 2007. LNCS, vol. 4824, pp. 199–206. Springer, Heidelberg (2007). doi:10.1007/978-3-540-75975-1_19
2. Chakravarthy, S., Krishnaprasad, V., Anwar, E., Kim, S.-K.: Composite events for active databases: semantics, contexts and detection. In: Proceedings of the 20th VLDB Conference Santiago, pp. 606–617 (1994)

3. Chen, M.: Towards smart city: M2M communications with software agent intelligence. Multimed. Tools Appl. **67**, 167–178 (2013)
4. Gaur, A., Scotney, B., Parr, G., McClean, S.: Smart city architecture and its applications based on IoT. Procedia Comput. Sci. **52**, 1089–1094 (2015). 5th International Symposium on Internet of Ubiquitous and Pervasive Things (IUPT 2015)
5. Jain, H., Radha Krishna, P., Karlapalem, K.: Context-aware workflow execution engine for e-contract enactment. In: Comyn-Wattiau, I., Tanaka, K., Song, I.-Y., Yamamoto, S., Saeki, M. (eds.) ER 2016. LNCS, vol. 9974, pp. 293–301. Springer, Cham (2016). doi:10.1007/978-3-319-46397-1_23
6. Krishna, P.R., Karlapalem, K.: A methodology for evolving e-contracts using templates. IEEE Trans. Serv. Comput. **6**(4), 497–510 (2013)
7. Mervat, A., Mohammad, H., Najah, A.: Data management for the internet of things: design primitives and solution. Sensors **13**, 15582–15612 (2013)
8. Robles, T., Alcarria, R., Martín, D., Navarro, M., Calero, R., Iglesias, S., López, M.: An IoT based reference architecture for smart water management processes. J. Wirel. Mob. Netw. Ubiquit. Comput. Dependable Appl. **6**(1), 4–23 (2015)
9. Tanaka, A.K., Navathe, S.B., Chakravarthy, S. Karlapalem, K.: ER-R: an enhanced ER model with situation-action rules to capture application semantics. In: Proceedings of International Conference on Conceptual Modeling (ER 1991), pp. 59–75 (1991)
10. Zambonelli, F.: Key abstractions for IoT-oriented software egnieering. IEEE Softw. **34**(1), 38–45 (2017)
11. Zanella, A., Bui, N., Castellani, A., Vangelista, L., Zorzi, M.: Internet of things for smart cities. IEEE Internet Things J. **1**(1), 22–32 (2014)
12. MQTT Version 3.1.1 Specification. http://docs.oasis-open.org/mqtt/mqtt/v3.1.1/os/mqtt-v3.1.1-os.html
13. The Constrained Application Protocol (CoAP) Specification RFC7252. https://tools.ietf.org/html/rfc7252

Model Efficiency

Determining the Preferred Representation of Temporal Constraints in Conceptual Models

C. Maria Keet(✉) and Sonia Berman

Department of Computer Science, University of Cape Town, Cape Town, South Africa
{mkeet,sonia}@cs.uct.ac.za

Abstract. The need for expressing temporal constraints in conceptual models is well-known, but it is unclear which representation is preferred and what would be easier to understand by modellers. We assessed five different modes of representing temporal constraints, being the formal semantics, Description logics notation, a coding-style notation, temporal EER diagrams, and (pseudo-)natural language sentences. The same information was presented to 15 participants in an experimental evaluation. Principally, it showed that (1) there was a clear preference for diagrams and natural language versus a dislike for other representations; (2) diagrams were preferred for simple constraints, but the natural language rendering was preferred for more complex temporal constraints; and (3) a multi-modal modelling tool will be needed for the data analysis stage to be effective.

1 Introduction

Modelling of temporal constraints for information systems has received attention since the mid-1990s and continues to do so (e.g., [9,15,16]), for it adds expressiveness to the model so as to ensure data integrity. For instance, to ensure that each Alumnus must have been a Student at that university before (*evolving object*), that a couple registered as divorcing in a census database must have been marrying before (an *evolving relation*), or that flex-workers may not always have an Office assigned (*temporal attribute*). This need has not subsided, and, perhaps, even increased with Big Data and the Internet of Things, for that data is inherently temporal. Capturing such information may be achieved with a temporal conceptual data modelling language. This adds a challenge during the data analysis stage, however, for modelling temporal aspects of the universe of discourse is non-trivial. This is due in part to the limited language options available to capture all these constraints. For instance, TimERplus [10] does not consider transition constraints for evolving entities, ER_{VT} [2] omits transition constraints for relationships and attributes (other than freezing), and TimeER [7], while including more on temporal attributes, has no specification for temporal relationships either. Another reason may be the graphical modelling languages, which have only recently been evaluated on whether the temporal adornments make sense to modellers, and which ones they prefer [21]. That evaluation [21] also demonstrated that graphical notations are not unambiguous and that there was a steep

H.C. Mayr et al. (Eds.): ER 2017, LNCS 10650, pp. 437–450, 2017.
https://doi.org/10.1007/978-3-319-69904-2_33

learning curve. An alternative is to *verbalise* information in natural language, as is common for the ORM language [12]. One also could present modellers with the more precise logic-based semantics. This smorgasbord of representation options raises the following main questions:

1. Which representation is preferred for representing temporal information: formal semantics, Description Logics (DL), a coding-style notation, diagrams, or (pseudo-)natural language sentences?
2. What would be easier to understand by modellers: a succinct logic-based notation, a graphical notation, or a 'coding style' notation?

The aim of this paper is to answer these questions. We conducted a survey of modeller preference and understanding of these representation modes. For the formal semantics, slightly more succinct DL notation, coding-style representation, and graphical notation, we use an extended version of ER_{VT} [2]. Because new temporal constraints have been added since ER_{VT} was proposed, and to ensure the, with current knowledge, 'best' graphical representation, we devised an updated and extended notation in line with findings of [21]. This extended and updated notation resulted in the **T**emporal information **R**epresentation in **En**tity-Relationship **D**iagrams, TREND language. Finally, verbalisations—or: (pseudo-)natural language sentences—of the temporal constraints were elucidated in a separate research activity [13], which were added as a fifth option to choose from. The evaluation with 15 modellers showed (1) a clear preference for graphical or verbalised temporal constraints over the other three representations (2) 'simple' temporal constraints were preferred graphically and complex temporal constraints preferred in natural language and (3) their English specification of temporal constraints was inadequate. This suggests the need for *multi-modal* modelling languages in the process of temporal conceptual model development, especially among graphical and verbalised temporal constraints.

The remainder of the paper is structured as follows. We describe the five modes of representation in Sect. 2 and the experiment and its results in Sect. 3. We discuss the results and related works in Sect. 4 and conclude in Sect. 5.

2 Representing the Same Information in Different Ways

This section provides a succinct overview of the different notations for temporal elements and constraints. Because we use the logic-based reconstruction into $\mathcal{DLR}_{\mathcal{US}}$ [1] as the foundation for both the semantics and DL notation, this will be introduced first. This is followed by the creation of the diagrammatic notation in the extended ER_{VT}, TREND, and finally basic information is provided for the verbalisation into natural language.

2.1 The Description Logic $\mathcal{DLR}_{\mathcal{US}}$: Syntax and Semantics

The temporal Description Logic $\mathcal{DLR}_{\mathcal{US}}$ [1] is an expressive fragment of first order logic that combines the propositional temporal logic with *Since* and *Until* operators with the (atemporal) DL $\mathcal{DLR}$ [6] so that the temporal operators can be used with relationships, entity types, and attributes. The syntax and semantics are included in Fig. 1. In short, as usual for DLs, there are concepts C (declared from atomic ones, CN), n-ary roles R (relationships, with $n \geq 2$, RN), binary attributes A between a class and a datatype, and DL role components (U, of which F denotes a role component in an attribute, $F \subseteq U$, and $F = \{\texttt{From}, \texttt{To}\}$). The selection expression $U_i/n : C$ denotes an n-ary relation whose i-th argument ($i \leq n$) is of type C and $[U_j]R$ denotes the j-th argument ($j \leq n$)—i.e., a DL role component, alike a projection over the role—in role R (we omit subscripts i and j if it is clear from the context). $\mathcal{U}$ntil and $\mathcal{S}$ince together with $\bot$ and $\top$ suffice to define the relevant temporal operators: $\Diamond^+$ (some time in the

$$
\begin{array}{rl}
C \rightarrow & \top \mid \bot \mid CN \mid \neg C \mid C_1 \sqcap C_2 \mid \exists^{\lessgtr k}[U_j]R \mid \exists[F]A \mid \\
& \Diamond^+ C \mid \Diamond^- C \mid \Box^+ C \mid \Box^- C \mid \oplus C \mid \ominus C \mid C_1 \,\mathcal{U}\, C_2 \mid C_1 \,\mathcal{S}\, C_2 \\
R \rightarrow & \top_n \mid RN \mid \neg R \mid R_1 \sqcap R_2 \mid U_i/n : C \mid \\
& \Diamond^+ R \mid \Diamond^- R \mid \Box^+ R \mid \Box^- R \mid \oplus R \mid \ominus R \mid R_1 \,\mathcal{U}\, R_2 \mid R_1 \,\mathcal{S}\, R_2 \\
A \rightarrow & \top_A \mid AN \mid \neg A \mid F : C \mid \\
& \Diamond^+ A \mid \Diamond^- A \mid \Box^+ A \mid \Box^- A \mid \oplus A \mid \ominus A \mid A_1 \,\mathcal{U}\, A_2 \mid A_1 \,\mathcal{S}\, A_2
\end{array}
$$

$$
\begin{array}{rl}
\top^{\mathcal{I}(t)} = & \Delta_O^{\mathcal{I}} \\
\bot^{\mathcal{I}(t)} = & \emptyset \\
CN^{\mathcal{I}(t)} \subseteq & \top^{\mathcal{I}(t)} \\
(\neg C)^{\mathcal{I}(t)} = & \top^{\mathcal{I}(t)} \setminus C^{\mathcal{I}(t)} \\
(C_1 \sqcap C_2)^{\mathcal{I}(t)} = & C_1^{\mathcal{I}(t)} \cap C_2^{\mathcal{I}(t)} \\
(\exists^{\lessgtr k}[U_j]R)^{\mathcal{I}(t)} = & \{ o \in \top^{\mathcal{I}(t)} \mid \sharp\{\langle o_1, \ldots, o_n \rangle \in R^{\mathcal{I}(t)} \mid o_j = o\} \lessgtr k\} \\
(\exists[F]A)^{\mathcal{I}(t)} = & \{ o \in \top^{\mathcal{I}(t)} \mid \sharp\{\langle o, d \rangle \in A^{\mathcal{I}(t)} \geq 1\}\} \\
(C_1 \,\mathcal{U}\, C_2)^{\mathcal{I}(t)} = & \{ o \in \top^{\mathcal{I}(t)} \mid \exists v > t.(o \in C_2^{\mathcal{I}(v)} \wedge \forall w \in (t, v).o \in C_1^{\mathcal{I}(w)})\} \\
(C_1 \,\mathcal{S}\, C_2)^{\mathcal{I}(t)} = & \{ o \in \top^{\mathcal{I}(t)} \mid \exists v < t.(o \in C_2^{\mathcal{I}(v)} \wedge \forall w \in (v, t).o \in C_1^{\mathcal{I}(w)})\} \\
(\top_n)^{\mathcal{I}(t)} = & (\Delta_O^{\mathcal{I}})^n \\
RN^{\mathcal{I}(t)} \subseteq & (\top_n)^{\mathcal{I}(t)} \\
(\neg R)^{\mathcal{I}(t)} = & (\top_n)^{\mathcal{I}(t)} \setminus R^{\mathcal{I}(t)} \\
(R_1 \sqcap R_2)^{\mathcal{I}(t)} = & R_1^{\mathcal{I}(t)} \cap R_2^{\mathcal{I}(t)} \\
(U_i/n : C)^{\mathcal{I}(t)} = & \{ \langle o_1, \ldots, o_n \rangle \in (\top_n)^{\mathcal{I}(t)} \mid o_i \in C^{\mathcal{I}(t)}\} \\
(R_1 \,\mathcal{U}\, R_2)^{\mathcal{I}(t)} = & \{ \langle o_1, \ldots, o_n \rangle \in (\top_n)^{\mathcal{I}(t)} \mid \exists v > t.(\langle o_1, \ldots, o_n \rangle \in R_2^{\mathcal{I}(v)} \wedge \\
& \quad \forall w \in (t, v).\, \langle o_1, \ldots, o_n \rangle \in R_1^{\mathcal{I}(w)})\} \\
(R_1 \,\mathcal{S}\, R_2)^{\mathcal{I}(t)} = & \{ \langle o_1, \ldots, o_n \rangle \in (\top_n)^{\mathcal{I}(t)} \mid \exists v < t.(\langle o_1, \ldots, o_n \rangle \in R_2^{\mathcal{I}(v)} \wedge \\
& \quad \forall w \in (v, t).\, \langle o_1, \ldots, o_n \rangle \in R_1^{\mathcal{I}(w)})\} \\
(\Diamond^+ R)^{\mathcal{I}(t)} = & \{\langle o_1, \ldots, o_n \rangle \in (\top_n)^{\mathcal{I}(t)} \mid \exists v > t.\, \langle o_1, \ldots, o_n \rangle \in R^{\mathcal{I}(v)}\} \\
(\oplus R)^{\mathcal{I}(t)} = & \{\langle o_1, \ldots, o_n \rangle \in (\top_n)^{\mathcal{I}(t)} \mid \langle o_1, \ldots, o_n \rangle \in R^{\mathcal{I}(t+1)}\} \\
(\Diamond^- R)^{\mathcal{I}(t)} = & \{\langle o_1, \ldots, o_n \rangle \in (\top_n)^{\mathcal{I}(t)} \mid \exists v < t.\, \langle o_1, \ldots, o_n \rangle \in R^{\mathcal{I}(v)}\} \\
(\ominus R)^{\mathcal{I}(t)} = & \{\langle o_1, \ldots, o_n \rangle \in (\top_n)^{\mathcal{I}(t)} \mid \langle o_1, \ldots, o_n \rangle \in R^{\mathcal{I}(t-1)}\} \\
(\top_A)^{\mathcal{I}(t)} = & \Delta_O^{\mathcal{I}} \times \Delta_D^{\mathcal{I}} \\
AN^{\mathcal{I}(t)} \subseteq & (\top_A)^{\mathcal{I}(t)} \\
(F : C)^{\mathcal{I}(t)} = & \{ \langle o, d \rangle \in (\top_A)^{\mathcal{I}(t)} \mid o \in C^{\mathcal{I}(t)}\} \\
(A_1 \,\mathcal{U}\, A_2)^{\mathcal{I}(t)} = & \{ \langle o, d \rangle \in (\top_A)^{\mathcal{I}(t)} \mid \exists v > t.(\langle o, d \rangle \in A_2 \wedge^{\mathcal{I}(v)} \forall w \in (t, v).\langle o, d \rangle \in A_1^{\mathcal{I}(w)})\} \\
(A_1 \,\mathcal{S}\, A_2)^{\mathcal{I}(t)} = & \{ \langle o, d \rangle \in (\top_A)^{\mathcal{I}(t)} \mid \exists v < t.(\langle o, d \rangle \in A_2^{\mathcal{I}(v)} \wedge \forall w \in (v, t).\langle o, d \rangle \in A_1^{\mathcal{I}(w)})\} \\
(\Diamond^+ A)^{\mathcal{I}(t)} = & \{\langle o, d \rangle \in (\top_A)^{\mathcal{I}(t)} \mid \exists v > t.\langle o, d \rangle \in A^{\mathcal{I}(v)}\} \\
(\oplus A)^{\mathcal{I}(t)} = & \{\langle o, d \rangle \in (\top_A)^{\mathcal{I}(t)} \mid \langle o, d \rangle \in A^{\mathcal{I}(t+1)}\} \\
(\Diamond^- A)^{\mathcal{I}(t)} = & \{\langle o, d \rangle \in (\top_A)^{\mathcal{I}(t)} \mid \exists v < t.\langle o, d \rangle \in A^{\mathcal{I}(v)}\} \\
(\ominus A)^{\mathcal{I}(t)} = & \{\langle o, d \rangle \in (\top_A)^{\mathcal{I}(t)} \mid \langle o, d \rangle \in A^{\mathcal{I}(t-1)}\}
\end{array}
$$

Fig. 1. Syntax and semantics of $\mathcal{DLR}_{\mathcal{US}}$; o denote objects, d domain values, $v, w, t \in \mathcal{T}_p$.

future) as $\Diamond^+ C \equiv \top \mathcal{U} C$, $\oplus$ (at the next moment) as $\oplus C \equiv \bot \mathcal{U} C$, and likewise for their past counterparts. Analogously, we have $\Box^+$ (always in the future) and $\Box^-$ (always in the past) are the duals of $\Diamond^+$ and $\Diamond^-$. The operators $\Diamond^*$(at some moment) and its dual $\Box^*$(at all moments) are defined as $\Diamond^* C \equiv C \sqcup \Diamond^+ C \sqcup \Diamond^- C$ and $\Box^* C \equiv C \sqcap \Box^+ C \sqcap \Box^- C$, respectively.

The model-theoretic semantics of $\mathcal{DLR}_{\mathcal{US}}$ assumes a linear flow of time $\mathcal{T} = \langle \mathcal{T}_p, < \rangle$, where $\mathcal{T}_p$ is a set of countably infinite time points (chronons) and $<$ is isomorphic to the usual ordering on the integers. The language of $\mathcal{DLR}_{\mathcal{US}}$ is interpreted in temporal models over $\mathcal{T}_p$, which are triples in the form $\mathcal{I} = \langle \mathcal{T}_p, \Delta^{\mathcal{I}}, \cdot^{\mathcal{I}(t)} \rangle$, where $\Delta^{\mathcal{I}}$ is the union of two non empty disjoint sets, the *domain of objects*, $\Delta^{\mathcal{I}}_O$, and *domain of values*, $\Delta^{\mathcal{I}}_D$, and $\cdot^{\mathcal{I}(t)}$ the interpretation function such that, for every $t \in \mathcal{T}_p$, every class C, and every n-ary relation R, we have $C^{\mathcal{I}(t)} \subseteq \Delta^{\mathcal{I}}_O$ and $R^{\mathcal{I}(t)} \subseteq (\Delta^{\mathcal{I}}_O)^n$; also, $(u, v) = \{w \in \mathcal{T}_p \mid u < w < v\}$. A *knowledge base* is a finite set Σ of $\mathcal{DLR}_{\mathcal{US}}$ axioms of the form $C_1 \sqsubseteq C_2$ and $R_1 \sqsubseteq R_2$, and with R_1 and R_2 being relations of the same arity. An interpretation $\mathcal{I}$ satisfies $C_1 \sqsubseteq C_2$ ($R_1 \sqsubseteq R_2$) if and only if the interpretation of C_1 (R_1) is included in the interpretation of C_2 (R_2) at all time, i.e. $C_1^{\mathcal{I}(t)} \subseteq C_2^{\mathcal{I}(t)}$ ($R_1^{\mathcal{I}(t)} \subseteq R_2^{\mathcal{I}(t)}$), for all $t \in \mathcal{T}_p$.

This enables one to capture not only temporal entity types, relationships, and attributes, but also transition constraints for them. One can use either the $\mathcal{DLR}_{\mathcal{US}}$ semantics notation directly, or its DL notation. For instance, the axiom $o \in Person^{\mathcal{I}(t)} \rightarrow \forall t'.o \in C^{\mathcal{I}(t')}$ (with $t, t' \in \mathcal{T}_p$) states that an object o is a member of the temporal interpretation (the "$\mathcal{I}(t)$") of the concept $Person$ at time t, and if that holds, then (the "$\rightarrow$") for all times t' in the set of time points $\mathcal{T}_p$, object o is still a member of $Person$; i.e, it holds at all time points in the past, present, and in the future. In $\mathcal{DLR}_{\mathcal{US}}$ notation, this is represented as $\mathsf{Person} \sqsubseteq \Box^* \mathsf{Person}$. In contrast, $o \in Student^{\mathcal{I}(t)} \rightarrow \exists t' \neq t.o \notin Student^{\mathcal{I}(t')}$ states there is a time t' that is different from time t where an object is not a student (whereas at time t it was, is, or will be). This is captured in $\mathcal{DLR}_{\mathcal{US}}$ as $\mathsf{Student} \sqsubseteq \Diamond^* \neg \mathsf{Student}$.

The core transition constraints are *dynamic extension* (Dex) and *dynamic evolution* (Dev). In an extension, the entity is *also* an instance of the other entity type whereas with evolution, the entity *ceases* to be an instance of the source entity type. An example of extension is $\mathsf{Employee} \sqcap \neg \mathsf{Manager} \sqcap \oplus \mathsf{Manager}$, and of evolution is $\mathsf{Caterpillar} \sqcap \neg \mathsf{Butterfly} \sqcap \oplus (\neg \mathsf{Caterpillar} \sqcap \mathsf{Butterfly})$. We use shorthand notation for these constraints, as in [2]: $\textsc{Dex}_{\mathsf{Employee,Manager}}$ and $\textsc{Dev}_{\mathsf{Caterpillar,Butterfly}}$, respectively.

2.2 ER_{VT}, EER^{++}_{VT}, and Further Extensions to TREND

The basic graphical and a textual version of ER_{VT} was introduced with $\mathcal{DLR}_{\mathcal{US}}$ as its logic-based reconstruction [1] and fully described as a temporal conceptual modelling language in [2]. ER_{VT} focused on temporalising classes, but $\mathcal{DLR}_{\mathcal{US}}$ is expressive enough to allow capturing temporal relationships and attributes, hence this was added by [14,15], respectively, and quantitative transition constraints, resulting EER_{VT}^{++}. The graphical notation, like with other temporal conceptual data modelling languages (e.g., [7,10,11,16,17,19]), was ad hoc. This was investigated systematically by [21], with the relevant outcome that clocks on temporal elements were preferred over any other icon and over ER_{VT}'s S and T, and arrows labeled with text for the transition constraints (DEV and DEX) were preferred over the icons tested.

In preparing the questions for the evaluation, especially in finding examples and the natural language generation (NLG) part for the pseudo-natural language sentences, it came afore that *mandatory* transition constraints are likely to be more interesting for conceptual modelling than optional ones. All prior versions did not address this distinction, so we devised our own notation for it, in line with ERD notation practices: maintaining the arrow notation, where a dashed shaft denotes an optional transition and a solid shaft denotes a mandatory transition. It appeared than none of the previous works had a sample diagram with quantitative transition constraints, so a notation was devised for that. To 'unclutter' the textual adornments, only DEV and DEX are used cf. EER_{VT}^{++}'s RDEX and ADEX etc. for the relationship and attribute transitions, for it can be easily deduced from the diagram (which elements are linked). A summary of the notation for temporal elements is listed in Fig. 2, with the other constraints following the same principles. Given that the primitives for the diagrammatic language are different from ER_{VT} and EER_{VT}^{++}, we refer to this language as TREND.

Icon	Name	Description
	Temporal entity type	**Entities of this type are *not always* entities of this type**
	Temporal relationship	**Relations of this relationship are *not always* relations of this type**
	Temporal attribute	**The entity does *not always* have a value for this attribute**
	Frozen attribute	**Once set, retains (drawing pin) its value in perpetuity (*forever*)**
DEX	**Mandatory dynamic extension in the future**	***Must* (solid shaft) in the future *also* be (dynamic extension/DEX) an instance of the target type**
DEV	**Optional dynamic evolution in the future**	***May* (dashed shaft) in future change *instead* (dynamic evolution/DEV) to the target type**
DEX⁻	**Optional dynamic extension in the past**	***May* in the past (-) *also* (DEX) have been a member of the source type**
DEX⁻4	**Mandatory quantitative extension in the past**	***Must* in the past (-) *also* (DEX) have been of the source type *4* time units earlier**
DEV4	**Optional quantitative dynamic evolution in future**	***May* in the future change *instead* (DEV) to the target type after *4* time units**

Fig. 2. Selection of the notation of the TREND diagram language.

An example of such a TREND diagram is shown in Fig. 3. Office is a temporal attribute, for with flex-work, employees may not always have an office. The mandatory transition DEX^- indicates that a manager must have been working for the company as a regular employee before being promoted to manager, and

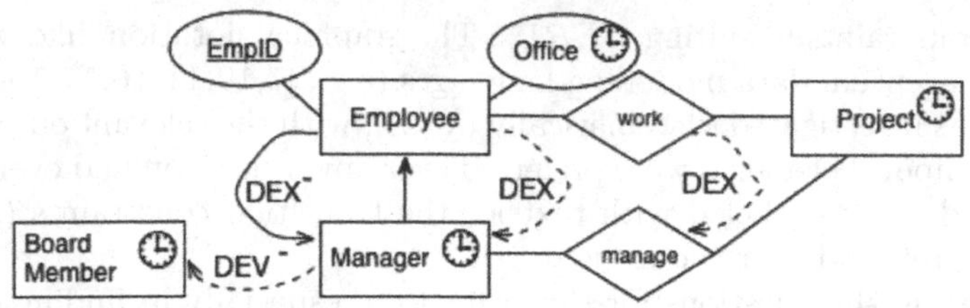

Fig. 3. Example of a temporally extended ER diagram in TREND notation.

thus that the transition from employee to manager happened in the past. Not all employees will be promoted to manager, hence, the optional DEX from employee to manager. Likewise, the transition from work to manage is optional.

2.3 Verbalising Temporal Conceptual Models

Verbalising atemporal conceptual data models is well established for the Object-Role Modeling (ORM) language [8,12], SBVR [18], and to some extent also for UML class diagrams [5]. These approaches are based on *templates*, where the natural language rendering of the constraint is the 'fixed' part of the sentence that then takes the vocabulary from the model with the constraints represented for it. A mandatory participation of an entity type in a relationship has a template like "*Each* <class1> <relationship1> *at least one* <class2>". Then if, say, <class1> = Professor, <relationship1> = teaches, and <class2> = Course in some conceptual model, it will generate the sentence *Each Professor teaches at least one Course*. The sentence planning stage of NLG [20] deals with which words to choose. For instance, the mandatory constraint also can be verbalised as "*Each* <class1> *must* <relationship1> *at least one* <class2>" to emphasise mandatory participation. Just like for atemporal constraints, it is possible to verbalise the temporal constraints and likewise decisions have to be taken on word choice. For instance, for a mandatory transition in the future, the 'nicer sounding' auxiliary verb "*will*" could be used, or a more strict auxiliary verb with a reference to the future, such as "*must be ... a later point in time*".

This has been investigated elsewhere [13], which we summarise here. For each of the relatively more interesting constraints (34 in total), 1–7 templates were designed and evaluated by three experts in temporal logic on whether each sentence captures the semantics adequately and which of the sentences were preferred. One of those questions is included in Fig. 4 for illustration. Observe here that with respect to the logic counterpart, often there is no literal 1:1 mapping between the axiom and the natural language sentences, but instead a 'free' rendering in natural language. For instance, consider the fairytale country where each non-tenured professor eventually will become a tenured professor, which can be formalised in $\mathcal{DLR}_{\mathcal{US}}$ as $\mathsf{NTProf} \sqsubseteq \Diamond^{+}\mathrm{DEV}_{\mathsf{NTProf},\mathsf{TProf}}$, but one would not want to read *Each NTProf is a subclass of some time in the future evolves from NTProf to TProf.* Instead, a sentence like *Each NTProf must evolve to*

(DEVM⁻) Mandatory dynamic evolution, past: $o \in \text{DEVM}^{-\mathcal{I}(t)}_{C_1,C_2} \rightarrow (o \in \text{C}_1{}^{\mathcal{I}(t)} \rightarrow \exists t' < t.o \in \text{DEV}^{\mathcal{I}(t')}_{C_1,C_2})$. For instance, Butterfly and the Caterpillar it used to be.
a. *Each ..C₁.. must have been a(n) ..C₂.. , but is not a(n) ..C₂.. anymore.*
b. *Each ..C₁.. was a(n) ..C₂.. before, but is not a(n) ..C₂.. now.*
c. *If ..C₁.. , then ..C₁.. was a(n) ..C₂.. before, but is not a(n) ..C₂.. anymore.*

Fig. 4. Verbalisation question for DEVM⁻ (mandatory dynamic evolution in the past) with three templates to choose from. The experts preferred option b.

TProf, ceasing to be NTProf sounds more natural. The outcome of this evaluation were the preferred sentences by majority voting, largely having chosen for the more natural-sounding templates. These selected sentences were used in the experiment that we will describe in Sect. 3.

3 Evaluation of Temporal CDMLs

The aim of the experimental evaluation is to find out which mode of representation 'regular modellers' prefer regarding temporal entities and constraints in temporal conceptual modelling languages. Regular modellers refers to the typical computer scientist who is conversant in conceptual modelling and has a basic understanding of logic. Because theoretical computer science and logic is not popular and the results on graphical notations not encouraging, the hypothesis to test is: *The natural language rendering of the temporal aspects is the preferred mode of representation among modellers.* We will test this by means of a questionnaire with a selection of elements and constraints that are represented in five different modes among which the participants have to choose, an extra question on whether they understand some of the representations, and auxiliary questions (such as their mother tongue).

3.1 Materials and Methods

Methods. The method followed a standard procedure for in-person questionnaires. In short, after purposive recruiting—honours or masters students who had attended either the Ontology Engineering or Logics for AI module—participants were informed about the aim of the experiment and given the consent form, and time to read the task and the provided background information on the notations. This was followed by about an hour in which to complete the questionnaire at their own pace. They did so in the same venue, with a researcher present at all times to answer any questions and to ensure that choices were given serious attention. All subjects volunteered for this experiment and were offered a small monetary incentive for participation.

After the experiment, submitted spreadsheets were combined with the typed-up paper-based data. Both researchers independently assessed the interpretations submitted for the $\mathcal{DLR}_{\mathcal{US}}$, coding-style, and TREND questions. Excel was used to analyse the data and chart results.

Materials. The materials consisted of a Consent Form to sign, a softcopy and printed copy of the questionnaire, and a spreadsheet for entering answers.

The questionnaire had some written explanation on the logic and diagram notations, which was kept to a minimum as they had seen similar logic notation and ER diagrams before, and because models should be sufficiently intuitive not to require lengthy explanations. Then 33 elements and constraints were presented where they had to indicate notation preferences. The 33 were ordered thus: 6 basic examples distinguishing snapshot from temporal classes, relationships and attributes; all 8 possible dynamic constraints for classes (DEV/DEX x optional/mandatory x past/future); 1 persistent class example (PDEX); all 8 quantitative dynamic constraints for classes; all 8 dynamic constraints for relationships; and 2 dynamic constraints for attributes (frozen, and quantitative evolution). Instructions required entering a value from 5 (most preferred) down to 1 (least preferred), or 0 if they disliked a notation's representation of a constraint. One of the questions is shown in Fig. 5.

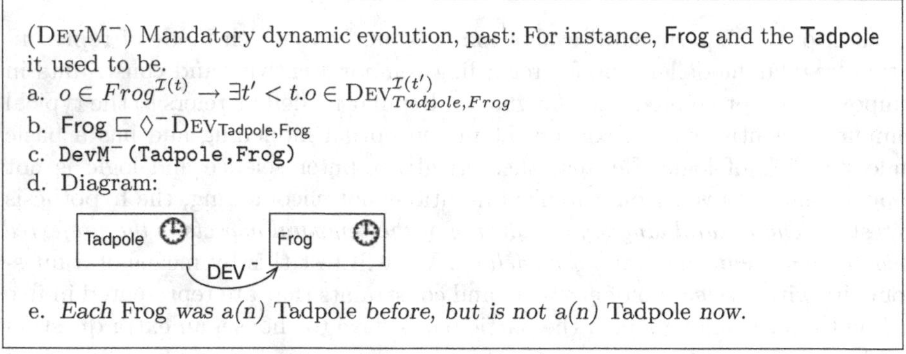

(DEVM$^-$) Mandatory dynamic evolution, past: For instance, Frog and the Tadpole it used to be.
a. $o \in Frog^{\mathcal{I}(t)} \rightarrow \exists t' < t.o \in \text{DEV}^{\mathcal{I}(t')}_{Tadpole,Frog}$
b. $\text{Frog} \sqsubseteq \Diamond^- \text{DEV}_{\text{Tadpole,Frog}}$
c. DevM⁻(Tadpole,Frog)
d. Diagram:
Tadpole
Frog
DEV⁻
e. *Each* Frog *was a(n)* Tadpole *before, but is not a(n)* Tadpole *now.*

Fig. 5. Question for DEVM$^-$, mandatory dynamic evolution in the past.

To ascertain how well they understood the notations, a question asked them to interpret 3 examples: one comprising 9 $\mathcal{DLR}_{\mathcal{US}}$ axioms, one comprising 8 coding-style statements, and one TREND diagram with 5 temporal aspects. In the final section of the questionnaire they indicated if English was their first (home) language, if they were 4th year or Masters students, which courses they had studied (ontologies, logic, both) and which notation they would prefer for modelling rather than understanding/reading temporal constraints. The questionnaire ended with an invitation to give any other comments. The questionnaire and data are available at http://www.meteck.org/files/ER17suppl.zip.

3.2 Results and Discussion

We first describe some pertinent details about the participants, which is followed by the quantitative results, the participants' comments, and finally the assessment on the participants' understanding of the models.

Participants. Fifteen students participated in the experiment, of which 10 were 4th year students and 5 Masters students. Most participants took a full hour to complete the questionnaire, with three finishing early and two running out of time due to other commitments and failing to finish the last section or two. Everyone completed the first section on choosing between the alternative representations and all had clearly devoted considerable time to the 33 examples.

Quantitative Results. Responses were analysed based on 3 metrics: responses calibrated to a standard competition ranking on a scale of 1–5, a favourite (highest ranked), and a dislike (0). Aggregating over the participants, the diagrams were the favourite for 10 constraints and the natural language sentence for 25 (there being two 'ties'); no other notation was chosen as favourite for any constraint. The overall rating totals are summarised in Table 1. Favourites and dislikes aggregated by group of constraints are shown in Fig. 6.

Zooming into details, a less straightforward picture of 'general winner' emerges; the two clearest of these results are shown Fig. 7: the 'simple' constraints of temporal elements (entity types, relationships, and attributes) were best represented in the diagram with the clock rather than as a sentence (option d; 57 favourites vs 28, and average rank 4.1 vs 3.5, respectively), whereas with transition (dynamic) constraints, the differences between diagrams and natural language were much smaller in favour of the sentence. For transition constraints for relationships on the future, the difference was smallest, with 26 vs 33 as favourite (average 3.9 vs 4.3), in favour of natural language sentences. The greatest difference was for class transitions on the past (19 vs 42 as favourite in favour of English), which was also their first encounter with arrows for transitions that

Table 1. Summary of the preference data. Percentages include 'tie' 1st/2nd choice, and 'tie' last choice.

	Rank total	Average	Favourite total	Dislikes	% Top 2	% Last
Formal semantics	785	1.6	49	136	15%	70%
$\mathcal{DLR}_{\mathcal{US}}$	1355	2.7	78	42	27%	16%
Coding-style	1406	2.8	77	45	31%	25%
TREND	1984	4.0	223	14	76%	7%
Natural language	2113	4.3	299	8	81%	3%

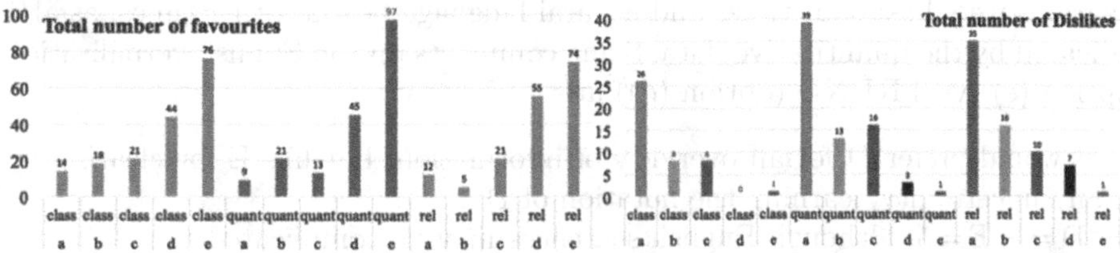

Fig. 6. The top-rated representation modes and 'dislike' ratings.

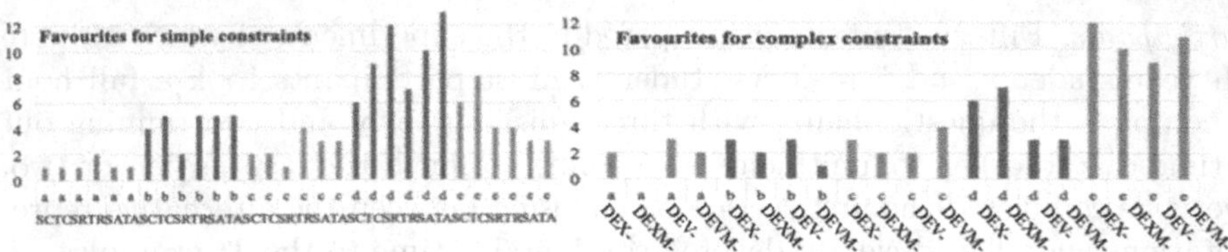

Fig. 7. Top choices by category of constraints, with a category A the 'simple' constraints—e.g., "C is a temporal class"—and category C one of the 'complex' set of constraints, being the transition constraints for classes in the past.

constrain the past. For the last examples of constraints on the past, the difference shrank to 29 vs 41 as favourite in favour of English, indicating that once familiar with those arrows, several participants favoured these as 'tie' best with English. Statistically, with a Kruskal-Wallis due to non-normal distribution of the data, the difference between graphical and natural language mode is significant for both the 'simple' ($p = 0.0003$) and 'complex' ($p = 0.0002$) constraints.

There is clear general *decrease* in preference from 'simple' temporal constraints in the DL representation in favour of natural language for the more complex (transition) constraints; that is, a natural language sentences such as "Person married-to Person *may be followed by* Person divorced-from Person, *ending* Person married-to Person." is deemed easier to understand than $\langle o, o' \rangle \in marriedTo^{\mathcal{I}(t)} \rightarrow \exists t' > t.\langle o, o' \rangle \in divorcedFrom^{\mathcal{I}(t')} \wedge \langle o, o' \rangle \notin marriedTo^{\mathcal{I}(t')}$ or $\Diamond^{+}\mathrm{RD}\textsc{ev}_{\mathsf{marriedTo},\mathsf{divorcedFrom}}$. However, $\mathsf{marriedTo} \sqsubseteq \Diamond^{*}\neg\mathsf{marriedTo}$ (a temporal relationship) was deemed easier to understand than the somewhat cumbersome sentence "*The objects participating in a fact in* Person married to Person *do* not *relate through* married-to *at some time*" (rank totals 54 and 49, respectively).

Preferences for class transitions were largely unaffected by the introduction of quantitative constraints (total rank changed by between 0.1% and 5% for the 5 notations). The distinction between dynamic extension (DEX) and dynamic evolution (DEV) similarly had negligible impact on preferences (total rank changes between 0.1% and 1.5%). This was also true for mandatory vs optional constraints (changes between 0.06% and 6%), and past vs future constraints (changes between 0.2% and 2%).

Respondent Comments. General comments made more than once were that the logic is "fine" for "simple" concepts but not "complex" examples. This is in agreement with the quantitative results (see Fig. 7). Also, it was noted that diagrams were best sometimes and natural language best at other times, as also indicated by the quantitative data. Some comments on the English verbalisation (option (e)) vs TREND (option (d)) are:

- "I would prefer D for an overview of information, but like E for clearing up any uncertainty/learning the notation of D";
- "D = 5; E = 5; although English sentences may be complicated";
- "it is quicker to interpret option (d) than most of the other options. Option (e) requires a lot of reading";

Feedback on individual examples included:

- "The +2, −1 are great ways to illustrate future and past";
- "the use of the clock in the diagrams for dynamic constraints is favoured";
- "(English) "since" confusing, I am not sure of meaning" (by an English home language speaker);
- "Perhaps Dev+6 so syntax matches the "-"";
- "option (c) and (d) are easier to write, however they require more interpretation they do not encode all the information";
- "(c) and (b) are prefered when having to write the relationship. Option (e) and (a) are prefered when reading.";
- "(c) would require memorization of the various "functions" such as "Sa"";
- "Since the source of the Dex is (clock) then the (clock) on the dest(ination) feels redundant", which indeed are redundant, because it can be inferred thanks to the logical implications proven in [2,14];
- "it is not clear why (DEV-) is not the same (as Dev) ... Can this not be achieved with Dev", indicating a lack of understanding, which is also evident from the questions on testing their understanding.
- "(c) has a favourable score because its function name (Freez) is clear";

Students twice noted that their preferences were changing as they progressed through the questionnaire due to repeated exposure improving their understanding of the new temporal concepts they were exposed to. One participant stated this for the diagrams only and another said this applied to (b), (c) and (d).

Interpretations and Testing Understanding Outside the Context of Individual Constraints. This was shown to be the hardest task. One student did not interpret any of the examples, and several tackled only some parts of some of the three notations, possibly through lack of time. Since this data is thus incomplete, we can state only that at least 3 students understood at least one notation well and at least 2 all notations. It was clear that precise and complete natural language description does not come naturally even to Computer Science postgraduates, as no student gave all and only the expected interpretation; they were frequently imprecise and generally failed to convey all the semantics.

The authors were like-minded in their evaluation of students' understanding. The values were calibrated on marks given for each constraint in the model and number of constraints in the model so as to compare the three fairly. The DL notation received a mark of 2.3, coding-style notation 2.7, and diagram notation 3.8. Thus, they understood the diagram best of the three notations.

The main source of fundamental errors were with the transition constraints—transition in the wrong direction and not distinguishing DEV from DEX—and with describing the distinction of mandatory versus optional constraints. In particular, $\mathsf{C} \sqsubseteq \Diamond^{+}\textsc{Dev}_{\mathsf{C,B}}$ and $\Diamond^{-}\textsc{Dev}_{\mathsf{C,B}}$ and similar were problematic[1]. Perhaps surprisingly, this question was answered somewhat better for option c (the

[1] "C *must* evolve into a B some time in the future" and "C evolved into a B in the past", with both ceasing to be a C, respectively.

coding-style notation) than either the DL notation or the TREND diagram. Some examples of imprecise English encountered were:

- "can evolve to" and "evolved from" without stating ceasing to be the original;
- "used to be and continues to be" instead of "must previously have been";
- "were not" instead of "may not have been";
- "is", "gets", "will" or "can" instead of "may" or "must"
- "immutable", which has a specific meaning that at least the ontology engineering students had been exposed to, instead of "snapshot"
- "can have" (attribute), without adding "at some time and not at other times".

That said, also three temporal logic experts did mostly not agree unanimously on a preferred natural language rendering of the semantics [13], so perhaps the general discourse about temporal constraints is not well developed.

The participants expect they prefer creating models in TREND most ($n = 7$), then in natural language ($n = 5$), and then in DL or coding-style notation ($n = 1$ each). The preference for the former may be explained by the fact that they seem to understand it best. That it may not be the natural language sentences as most preferred for modelling is also substantiated by the comments to the first part of the questionnaire (see previous section).

4 Discussion

To the best of our knowledge, this is the first attempt to evaluate different modes of representing temporal information to figure out what may be the 'best' way. Extant proposals for temporal conceptual modelling languages focus on inclusion of features rather than fitness for purpose, such as by [2,7,9,10,14–16,19] and on formal foundations [2,7,15,16]. However, they will receive broader uptake only if they are understandable and usable for modelling. Gianni et al. [9] do propose a multi-modal interface for ORM diagrams adorned with temporal information and verbalisations, but the verbalisations are for individuals only, rather than the information represented in the model, and also this proposal was not evaluated with modellers. This paper sought to fill this gap, with the hypothesis that the verbalisations would be preferred. The results show that verbalisations are preferred mainly for 'complex' constraints, but it is not a 'clear winner' in all cases. This may suggest that there is a need for a *multimodal interface*, alike in NORMA [8], that allows one to switch back and forth between, at least, the diagrams and natural language sentences.

Also, the (pseudo-)natural language renderings may be better for communication, especially with domain experts, but data suggests the diagrammatic representation is likely to be favoured most during the authoring stage of the model. The models were still small, however, so caution has to be exercised extrapolating from these results and it deserves further attention. We did not test the participants' understanding of the natural language sentences because we could not devise a satisfactory way: writing the sentences in different English seemed superfluous and, e.g., drawing the semantics may not test their understanding of the English but instead their abilities in the other representation model (be this TREND or the semantics with timelines).

One could perhaps argue that a particular verbalisation pattern was not optimal, or some graphical notation was not, and that others would have to be tested with. However, both the graphical notation and sentences have been evaluated with modellers and experts and found preferable [13,21], mitigating this argument. The (previously untested) graphical extension for quantitative transition constraints were deemed sufficiently clear by the participants. That said, these are currently limited when compared to natural language, in that they do not indicate if the given time units are a minimum, maximum or exact requirement, nor whether the previous state had to be retained continuously for that length of time or simply had to be true at some point that many time units ago. It would be useful to look into, especially since they are also easy to implement in temporal and atemporal databases with straight-forward triggers to provide easy integrity constraints.

Finally, the 33 constraints evaluated were a subset of the possible temporal constraints for conceptual models, and perhaps these are still too many. It may be of interest to constrain it further to those useful for temporal Ontology-Based Data Access only [3,4], for those temporal logics are fragments of $\mathcal{DLR}_{\mathcal{US}}$ and thus would constitute fragments of TREND as well.

5 Conclusion

In evaluating the mode of representing temporal constraints, the experimental evaluation made clear that there was a preference for diagrams and natural language, and a dislike for the formal semantics and coding-style notations. Diagrams were preferred for simple constraints, but transition constraints were best verbalised in natural language. The results demonstrated that a multi-modal modelling tool will be needed for the data analysis stage to be effective, due to the differing preferences and abilities of understanding and modelling temporal constraints. It also showed that transition constraints in the past were hardest to understand, but there was at least an increase observed in grasping the new temporal notions as the participants went along in the questionnaire.

Both the graphical TREND language proposed in this paper, and the natural language sentence are, with the current state of the art, optimal. This may facilitate broader uptake of temporal conceptual modelling and, with that, larger experiments may be conducted.

Acknowledgments. We thank all those who participated in the experiment.

References

1. Artale, A., Franconi, E., Wolter, F., Zakharyaschev, M.: A temporal description logic for reasoning over conceptual schemas and queries. In: Flesca, S., Greco, S., Ianni, G., Leone, N. (eds.) JELIA 2002. LNCS, vol. 2424, pp. 98–110. Springer, Heidelberg (2002). doi:10.1007/3-540-45757-7_9

2. Artale, A., Parent, C., Spaccapietra, S.: Evolving objects in temporal information systems. Ann. Math. Artif. Intell. **50**(1–2), 5–38 (2007)
3. Artale, A., Kontchakov, R., Wolter, F., Zakharyaschev, M.: Temporal description logic for ontology-based data access. In: Proceedings of IJCAI 2013 (2013)
4. Baader, F., Borgwardt, S., Lippmann, M.: Temporalizing ontology-based data access. In: Bonacina, M.P. (ed.) CADE 2013. LNCS (LNAI), vol. 7898, pp. 330–344. Springer, Heidelberg (2013). doi:10.1007/978-3-642-38574-2_23
5. Burden, H., Heldal, R.: Natural language generation from class diagrams. In: Proceedings of MoDeVVa 2011. ACM (2011)
6. Calvanese, D., De Giacomo, G.: Expressive description logics. In: The DL Handbook: Theory, Implementation and Applications, pp. 178–218. Cambridge University Press (2003)
7. Combi, C., Degani, S., Jensen, C.S.: Capturing temporal constraints in temporal ER models. In: Li, Q., Spaccapietra, S., Yu, E., Olivé, A. (eds.) ER 2008. LNCS, vol. 5231, pp. 397–411. Springer, Heidelberg (2008). doi:10.1007/978-3-540-87877-3_29
8. Curland, M., Halpin, T.: Model driven development with NORMA. In: Proceedings of HICSS-40, p. 286a. IEEE Computer Society (2007)
9. Gianni, D., Bocciarelli, P., D'Ambrogio, A.: Temporal capabilities in support of conceptual process modeling using object-role modeling. In: Proceedings of DEVS Integrative 2014 (2014)
10. Gregersen, H.: TimeER*plus*: a temporal EER model supporting schema changes. In: Jackson, M., Nelson, D., Stirk, S. (eds.) BNCOD 2005. LNCS, vol. 3567, pp. 41–59. Springer, Heidelberg (2005). doi:10.1007/11511854_4
11. Gregersen, H., Jensen, C.S.: Temporal entity-relationship models - a survey. IEEE Trans. Knowl. Data Eng. **11**(3), 464–497 (1999)
12. Halpin, T., Morgan, T.: Information Modeling and Relational Databases, 2nd edn. Morgan Kaufmann, Burlington (2008)
13. Keet, C.M.: Sentence planning for temporal conceptual models and their temporal constraints. Submitted to an International Conference. ACL (2017)
14. Keet, C.M., Artale, A.: A basic characterization of relation migration. In: Meersman, R., Dillon, T., Herrero, P. (eds.) OTM 2010. LNCS, vol. 6428, pp. 484–493. Springer, Heidelberg (2010). doi:10.1007/978-3-642-16961-8_70
15. Keet, C.M., Ongoma, E.A.N.: Temporal attributes: their status and subsumption. In: Proceedings of APCCM 2015, vol. 165, pp. 61–70. CRPIT (2015)
16. Khatri, V., Ram, S., Snodgrass, R.T., Terenziani, P.: Capturing telic/atelic temporal data semantics: generalizing conventional conceptual models. Trans. Knowl. Data Eng. **26**(3), 528–548 (2014)
17. McBrien, P.: Temporal constraints in non-temporal data modelling languages. In: Li, Q., Spaccapietra, S., Yu, E., Olivé, A. (eds.) ER 2008. LNCS, vol. 5231, pp. 412–425. Springer, Heidelberg (2008). doi:10.1007/978-3-540-87877-3_30
18. Object Management Group: Semantics of Business Vocabulary and Rules (SBVR) - OMG released versions of SBVR, formal/2008-01-02, January 2008. http://www.omg.org/spec/SBVR/1.0
19. Parent, C., Spaccapietra, S., Zimányi, E.: Conceptual Modeling for Traditional and Spatio-temporal Applications-the MADS Approach. Springer, Hedidelberg (2006). doi:10.1007/3-540-30326-X
20. Reiter, E., Dale, R.: Building applied natural language generation systems. Nat. Lang. Eng. **3**, 57–87 (1997)
21. Shunmugam, T.: Adoption of a visual model for temporal database representation. M. IT thesis, Department of CS, University of Cape Town, South Africa (2016)

User Perception of Numeric Contribution Semantics for Goal Models: An Exploratory Experiment

Norah Alothman, Mehrnaz Zhian, and Sotirios Liaskos(✉)

York University, Toronto, ON M3J 1P3, Canada
{norah,mehrnaz,liaskos}@yorku.ca

Abstract. Goal models have long been regarded to be an effective way for representing stakeholder goals and how they relate to one another during requirements engineering. One of the ways goals are connected in goal models is contribution relationships, which represent how satisfaction of one goal affects the satisfaction of another. There are several proposals in the literature on how contributions should be modelled and used, but little empirical evidence as to which one is more intuitive for users. We experimentally explore how users interpret numeric contribution labels in goal models. Experimental participants are exposed to a number of pre-constructed goal models and are asked what they believe the satisfaction degree of a goal is given the satisfaction degree of other goals in the model. We find that users tend to prefer specific aggregation rules over others, depending, also, on specific factors.

Keywords: Goal models · Model comprehension · Decision support

1 Introduction

Capturing and modeling stakeholder high-level objectives is an important part of the requirements analysis process. Prior to making any solution decisions analysts need to understand the general and vaguely defined goals that stakeholders consider important and use them as criteria for evaluating alternative solutions. Such high-level goals can be many, with various degrees of importance and interacting in various ways.

Goal models [1,20,25] have been suggested to be an effective way to represent goals and the complex interactions between them. Such models consist of various kinds of intentional elements and relationships between them. A particularly interesting type of intentional element used in many goal modeling languages is a goal for which there is no clear-cut criterion for deciding if it is satisfied or not [21,25]. Examples of such goals are “Happy Customer”, “Improve Patient’s Experience” or “Ensure Scheduling Fairness”. Such goals have traditionally been referred to as *soft-goals* or *quality goals* [16]. As analysts compare solution ideas for the elicited stakeholder problems, these goals serve as criteria to assess the fitness of various possibilities, the latter affecting the former in different degrees.

H.C. Mayr et al. (Eds.): ER 2017, LNCS 10650, pp. 451–465, 2017.
https://doi.org/10.1007/978-3-319-69904-2_34

In goal modeling languages, *contribution* relationships are used to show exactly how satisfaction of one such goal is believed to affect satisfaction of another.

Several approaches exist for modeling contribution links, both qualitative and quantitative. When devising an approach, language designers are confronted with the problem of defining what exactly the contribution links mean and how they can be used, most often in combinations, in order to calculate satisfaction of goals given the satisfaction status of other goals. Different such semantics have been proposed in the literature based on different satisfaction propagation and aggregation rules and techniques. However, given also the abstract nature of the subject matter that these models are meant to represent, how can one evaluate which one is best for adoption in practice?

In this paper, we focus on the intuitiveness of choices of contribution link semantics, understood here as the match between the intended meaning of the language, devised by its designers, and the meaning that the users of the language assign to it. We focus on numeric contribution links and distil from the literature four (4) different theories for contribution link semantics. Then, we perform an experiment with the following goals: (a) understand whether model users who are ignorant to any of the theories perceive contribution semantics in a way that tends to agree (or disagree) to one or more of the theories and (b) identify potential model- or user-related factors that affect such tenancies.

Specifically, we construct a number of goal models containing quality goals connected using numeric contribution links, fixing also the satisfaction level for some of the goals. We present the models to a number of experimental participants and ask them what they think is the most appropriate satisfaction value for a specific goal in the model whose satisfaction level is initially unknown. These are different numbers depending on what contribution semantics one adopts. We present the choices to the users and ask them which one they think is the most appropriate. We observe if there is any concentration of responses to any of the theories and, as such, whether the hypothesis that some semantics match user expectation better than others, is at all plausible. We do find such effects as well as some early indications of factors that can affect participant choices.

The paper is organized as follows. Section 2 presents goal models, contribution links and semantic possibilities thereof in more detail. In Sects. 3 and 4 we present the design and results of our experiment. Then in Sect. 5 we present related work and in Sect. 6 we offer our concluding remarks.

2 Background

2.1 Goal Models and Contribution Links

A goal model of the kind we consider in this research can be seen in Fig. 1 – adapted from Mylopoulos et al. [20]. The model represents a decision problem in the Meeting Scheduling domain. Design alternatives are represented through an AND/OR decomposition hierarchy of hard-goals (ovals), rooted in goal *Schedule Meeting*. The cloud-shaped elements represent *quality goals*, i.e., goals whose satisfaction is generally not defined in a clear-cut manner. Quality goals, written here in an unstructured way, form a separate hierarchy that acts as decision criteria: each alternative of the AND/OR decomposition implies different levels of satisfaction for each of the criteria. Modeling the level and quality of this satisfaction is possible through contribution links that originate from hard goals or quality goals and target (other) quality goals.

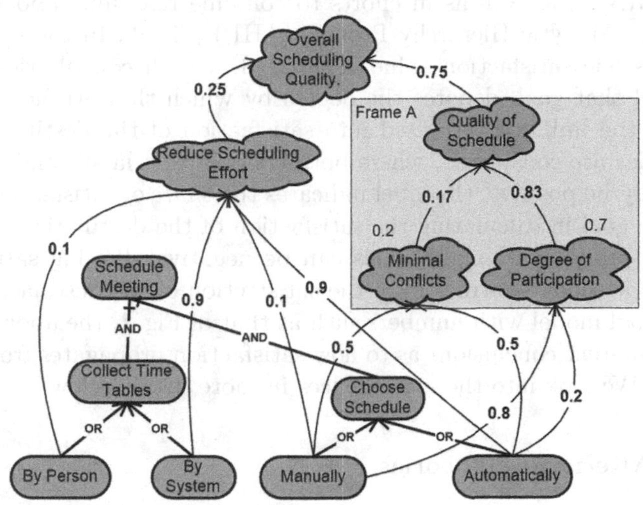

Fig. 1. A goal model represented as a diagram

Different approaches can be found in the literature on how contribution links can be labelled, and what such labels would mean. Most common are qualitative contribution labels, in which an ordinal scale such as {"– –", "–", "+", "++"} is used [2,25]. Elsewhere it is proposed that contribution labels can be values from a real interval such as [0, 1] (as in Fig. 1) or [−100,100] [1,9,17,19]. Most of these proposals come with concrete semantics as to how the contribution label is to be interpreted and used to infer satisfaction of goals from the satisfaction of other goals in the model. In this paper, we focus on quantitative contribution labels and different proposals for their semantics.

2.2 Quantitative Propagation Semantics

An established approach for modeling and reasoning about quantitative contribution links is offered by Giorgini et al. [9]. The framework they propose first assumes that each goal is associated with two variables, each representing the amount of evidence that the goal is satisfied or denied, respectively. The variables take values from the real interval [0, 1], 1.0 denoting maximum possible evidence and 0.0 denoting absence of evidence. When two goals are connected through a contribution link, the label of the link describes how the evidence of satisfaction and/or denial of the origin goal affects our belief of satisfaction and/or denial of the destination goal. Specifically the label is a number in the interval [0, 1], which denotes the degree of contribution, a subscript *S, D* or both (denoted through absence of subscript), denoting which of the two variables is considered and a sign "+" or "–" denoting that the contribution is positive or negative with respect to the involved variable.

A second approach to quantitative contribution has been proposed in the context of URN [1] as well as in efforts to combine reasoning about contributions with the Analytic Hierarchy Process (AHP) [17,19]. In these approaches each goal has one satisfaction value. The label of each contribution link that points toward that goal, denotes the degree by which the satisfaction value of the origin of the link is interpreted into satisfaction of the destination. When AHP semantics are considered, where both contribution labels and satisfaction values can only be positive, the label indicates the *share* of satisfaction influence of each origin goal in calculating the satisfaction of the destination goal. In the Amyot et al. proposal, though, labels can be negative allowing satisfaction of origin goal to actually subtract from the satisfaction of the destination [1].

Given a goal model with numbers such as that of Fig. 1, the above proposals can lead to different conclusions as to how satisfaction propagates from one goal to the other. We look into these differences in more detail below.

2.3 Four Alternative Theories

To allow for a comparison among the contribution modeling frameworks for our purposes here, we make certain assumptions and simplifications. Firstly, we consider simple acyclic hierarchies of quality goals such as the one seen in Fig. 1. Secondly, labels are a real number in the interval [0, 1] without any subscripts and signs (so assumed to be positive), rounded to two decimal places. Thirdly, only initial satisfaction values are considered, keeping initial denial values zero, when denial variables are defined by the theory at all. These restrictions take away much of the expressiveness of the examined frameworks, but make them comparable with respect to their core semantics, which is our interest here.

We may, thus, attempt a common formulation of satisfaction propagation, which will, in turn allow us to perform a comparison. Thus, let G be the set of all quality goals in the diagram and $s : G \mapsto [0, 1]$ denote the satisfaction value for each of them. Let further O_g be the set of goals g' for which there exists a contribution link from g' to g. Let also $S_g = \{s(g') : g' \in O_g\}$ be the set of satisfaction values of all these quality goals and $W_g = \{w : g' \overset{w}{\to} g; g' \in O_g\}$ the set of all labels of the corresponding contributions links. Then, the satisfaction of goal g is a function f of these two sets: $s(g) = f(S_g, W_g)$.

The literature proposals we discussed above, suggest four possible definitions for f. Three of them come directly from the label propagation framework proposed by Giorgini et al. [9]. According to the proposed algorithm the satisfaction/denial value of every node is always calculated by maximizing individual evidence values formed by the satisfaction/denial values of the origin nodes and the corresponding contribution weights. A generic operator $\otimes$ is used to denote that the two values (satisfaction values of origins and contribution link weights) are combined to produce a candidate value for the satisfaction of the destination: $s(g) = s(g') \otimes w(g', g)$. Note that given our assumptions of zero initial denial values and positive labels, the denial values are always zero and can, thus, be ignored. There are at least three ways to interpret $\otimes$, which will make for our first three possible definitions of f.

The fourth possible definition of f comes from interpreting how other literature [1,17,19] addresses combinations of incoming satisfaction evidence. While label propagation maximizes, these approaches sum-up individual incoming evidence, treating thereby contribution aggregation as a linear combination. Thus, our four possible definitions of f are as follows.

Bayesian, assumes that the satisfaction value of the origin is multiplied by the weight of the corresponding contribution link ($p_1 \otimes p_2 =_{def} p_1 \cdot p_2$). The function f is then defined as:

$$f_b(S_g, W_g) = \underset{g' \in O_g}{MAX}\{s(g') \times w(g', g)\}$$

Min-Max, assumes that $\otimes$ denotes the minimum of the satisfaction value of the origin and the weight of the corresponding contribution link ($p_1 \otimes p_2 =_{def} MIN(p_1, p_2)$). The function f is then:

$$f_m(S_g, W_g) = \underset{g' \in O_g}{MAX}\{MIN(s(g'), w(g', g))\}$$

Serial-Parallel, proposes that $\otimes$ combines the satisfaction value and the weight in a serial/parallel resistance model ($p_1 \otimes p_2 =_{def} p_1 \cdot p_2/(p_1 + p_2)$). The function f is then:

$$f_s(S_g, W_g) = \underset{g' \in O_g}{MAX}\{\frac{s(g') \times w(g', g)}{s(g') + w(g', g)}\}$$

Linear, is similar to the Bayesian with the difference that candidate values are not maximized but added up:

$$f_l(S_g, W_g) = \sum_{g' \in O_g} \{s(g') \times w(g', g)\}$$

Given the above four alternatives, it seems now inevitable to ask what criterion one should use to select a theory for a practical purpose.

2.4 Comparing Theories

We view visually represented conceptual models, such as goal models, as devices to be used by humans for comprehending and communicating domain knowledge. Designers of conceptual modeling languages have specific meanings in mind for the constructs they introduce, often in the form of formal semantics as in our case. Such semantics define, among other things, what are correct ways to perform inferences using the information represented in the visualized model. Users of the visualized models, however, may have their own way of interpreting the model constructs and perform inferences accordingly. In other words, users may develop a *mental model* on how the visualization device is supposed to be used [22,23]. This model can be due to a combination of factors: potentially partial and incomplete training, experience with similar models and tasks, educational or cultural background and, importantly, the way the model is visually represented – the "system image" according to Norman's discussion on mental models for user interface designs [22]. While in interface design designers strive to align their intent on how their devices are supposed to work with the corresponding perception that users develop, in our case, modeling language designers might likewise adjust either the semantics or the visual representation of the language so that the latter evokes correct perception of the former.

In our work we use "intuitiveness" as a working term for describing this level of a match between the designer's intended semantics and the user's assumed meaning. While the former can be drawn from the formal definitions above, the latter needs to be observed empirically. Thus, we measure the meaning users assign to contributions by observing how they perform inferences about goal satisfaction. We particularly perform a simple test: if we provide a decomposition such as that of Fig. 1, Frame A to (unsuspecting of any theories) users, how would they combine the numbers to decide a missing satisfaction value? The result of such a test is an assessment of users' expectation of how the numbers presented to them should be combined in order to perform inferences and, consequently, what the meaning of the contribution is.

3 Experimental Study

3.1 Study Design

The main objectives of the study are to: (a) assess whether model users who are oblivious to aggregation theories perceive contribution semantics in a way that tends to agree (resp. disagree) with one or more of the theories, supporting the hypothesis that such theories are more (resp. less) intuitive, (b) explore what factors related to the models or the users affect said agreement (resp. disagreement).

To fulfill these objectives, we first develop a number of goal models. The models consist exclusively of hierarchies of quality goals. We construct a total of nine (9) model structures. The structures are different in a number of ways, including the number of goals they contain, the depth of the hierarchy and the number of contributions they contain. Table 1 describes each structure in detail. As seen in the table, using depth as the primary size measure, we split the goals into three size levels: small, medium and large. The goals of all structures have "dummy" names, A, B, C, etc. For each structure we devise four (4) different concrete models. Each of the four models has a different *number-set*, i.e. set of labels for the contribution links and initial satisfaction values for the leaf level quality goals, the latter presented as an annotation next to the goal. The resulting models look like what is contained in Frame A of Fig. 1 (depth = 2,

Table 1. Structure characteristics

Size	Depth	# Goals	# Contributions
Small	1	3	2
	1	4	3
	1	5	4
Medium	2	5	4
	2	7	6
	2	6	5
Large	3	7	6
	3	9	8
	3	10	9

Table 2. Participant demographics

	Female	Male	Total
Business and econ.	8	5	**13**
Education	3	3	**6**
Fine arts	2	3	**5**
Health sciences	1	1	**2**
Humanities	8	3	**11**
Science and tech.	3	7	**10**
Social sciences	6	3	**9**
Total	**31**	**25**	**56**

num. of goals = 3, num. of contributions = 2). Given a complete model, one can calculate the satisfaction value of its root using each of the aggregation functions we introduced earlier (f_b, f_m, f_s and f_l), leading to four different corresponding values.

The choice of number-sets deserves further discussion. All values are randomly sampled, under the following conditions. Firstly, for two (2) out of the four (4) number-sets devised for each structure, labels of contributions pointing to the same goal are restricted to necessarily add up to exactly 1.0. For the other two (2) number-sets, such labels need to add up to more than 1.5. We refer to these as the two weighting styles: restricted (to 1.0) and unrestricted or free (to add up to any value above 1.5). Secondly, the four values that result from calculating the satisfaction value of the root goal using each of the four (4) aggregation functions must have a distance of at least 0.08 between each other – the number is the maximum we could achieve across all models. It is important to add that for a given number-set, the satisfaction values that result from applying each theory are ranked almost consistently, due to their mathematical structure. Serial-Parallel in all models gives the smallest number, followed by Bayesian which always is the second smallest. Linear is usually the largest number (~86% of times in our models) and MinMax is usually (~86% of times) the second largest.

In all, a total of (9 structures) × (2 weighting styles) × (2 number-sets per style) = 36 distinct models are constructed. The models are used to construct the experimental instrument. The instrument is a sequence of screens/tasks presented to the participants using an on-line survey tool (surveygizmo.com). On each screen the user is presented with one of the 36 models and the four (4) possible satisfaction values for the root goal that result from applying the four different aggregation functions; the values are presented in random order. Participants are asked to choose the "most appropriate satisfaction value" for the root goal. The 36 screens are presented in random order.

Prior to performing the tasks, the participants are also asked to provide demographic information and watch an instructional video. The video introduces goal models, explains what contributions are about and presents the idea that the more the contribution weight or the more the satisfaction of the origin, the more the satisfaction of the destination. It does not, however, provide any information of the precise method to calculate that value in a way that would bias the respondents in the subsequent tasks. Prior to beginning the tasks, participants are also instructed to not use calculator or pen and paper, and try to be quick, i.e. not spend more than half a minute in each screen. The reason for this request is to better simulate natural use of a goal model visualization.

A final question presents the participants with a small sample model and a list of formulae for calculating the satisfaction of the root goal, corresponding to the four theories under investigation. The participants are asked to choose the formula that describes the way they worked in the exercises or describe their own. In a second version of the instrument, this question is replaced with one in which the participants are asked whether they follow a specific calculation method, which they are asked to describe, or whether they *"just used [their] intuition"*.

Sixty (60) participants are recruited from Amazon's Mechanical Turk (AMT), an online crowdsourcing platform. In AMT the experiment is posted as a Human Intelligence Task (HIT) for members in the platform. Participants are screened to have at least a bachelor's degree and respond from North America. Half of them use the original instrument and the other half the instrument with the last question changed and at a later time. Data from a total of 56 participants are analyzed – four (4) are excluded for not passing a reliability test. Participants demographics can be seen in Table 2.

3.2 Results

More Preferred and Less Preferred Theories. As a first step of our analysis we test whether the participant responses deviate from the uniform distribution in each of the models. Thus, for each of the 36 models we collect all 56 responses. If, for a given model, participants pick each of the four theories randomly, we expect that the four choices will appear with equal likelihood in each of the 56 ratings. Reversely, if we observe substantial preference (or lack thereof) to one or more of the four categories, then we can suspect that participants do not respond randomly but exhibit preference toward (or against) one or more theories.

Running binomial tests for each model gives us this evidence. Figure 2 shows for how many of the 36 models there was at least one theory choice that was atypically high or low in preference; atypically meaning so high or low that the likelihood of it being due to a uniformly random process is very small $p < 0.05$. The figure organizes those numbers by model size and weighting style. In all cases, half or more of the models exhibit some deviation from the random and the effect is more pronounced for larger models. Figure 3 further shows for each of those factor configurations, how many times was each theory preferred more or less than uniformly randomly expected. For example, in large models with

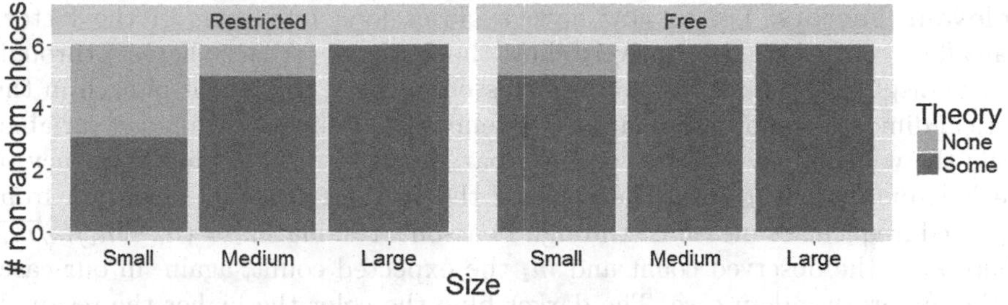

Fig. 2. Total occurrences of non-random preference to a theory

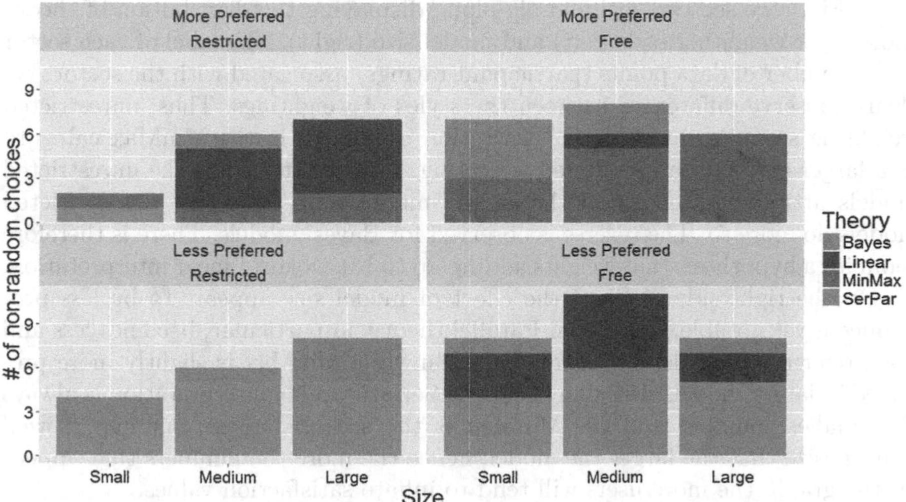

Fig. 3. More preferred and less preferred theories

free weighting, there were six (6) models in which the MinMax theory was chosen more frequently than expected under the uniform assumption (upper right chart), and five (5) models in which the Serial-Parallel theory was chosen less frequently than expected (lower right chart). Note that more than one occurrence of such statistically significant deviations may occur in one model.

We can apply the same logic within the responses of each participant to investigate whether each of them tends to "adopt" a specific theory by choosing it more frequently than expected – under a uniform randomness hypothesis. Indeed, out of the 56 participants only seven (7) seem to respond uniformly across the four (4) theories – i.e. they could be just selecting at random. All the other participant responses tend to concentrate on one or more theories. Thus, for 27, 13, 5 and 2 participants, there is a significant (Binomial test $p < 0.05$) concentration of their choices to MinMax, Linear, Bayes and the Serial-Parallel model, respectively; while for 35, 12, 9 and 4 participants Serial-Parallel, Linear, Bayes and MinMax theories were, respectively, significantly not chosen.

Relevant Factors. Let us now have a closer look into some of the factors that affect choice. We descriptively show these effects (or lack thereof) through mosaic displays [8]. Such displays are clusters of bars, the height of each in the vertical dimension show the relative frequency of the corresponding (y) variable, while the width of each sector within a bar shows the conditional frequency of the horizontal (x) variable. The color of the sector represents deviation from expected frequencies measured through Pearson's residuals $r_i = (n_i - m_i)/\sqrt{m_i}$, where n_i is the observed count and m_i the expected count, again, in our case, of the uniform random case. The darker blue the color the higher the residual, meaning that the observed count was higher than expected; the darker red the color the lower the residual, hence the observed count is lower than expected.

In Fig. 4 we see two such mosaic plots, displaying the distribution of theory choices per weighting style (left) and model size (right). The label of each sector is the number of data points (participant ratings) associated with the sector. We clearly observe differences between the styles of weightings. Thus, unrestricted weighting seems to induce a concentration of choices in the MinMax category to a larger extend than restricted weighting. Importantly while the unrestricted models attract less choice of the Linear model than expected, the restricted models do more so. The reverse is observed for Bayes' models. There is therefore room for a hypothesis that weights adding up to 1.0 evoke a Linear interpretation.

On the right side of Fig. 4 the effect of model size appears to be less pronounced, yet notable. The Serial-Parallel theory, in particular, becomes less and less preferred as model size increases. Meanwhile MinMax is slightly more preferred in larger models. Recalling that the Serial-Parallel interpretation is always the smallest number and the MinMax is the second largest, one can as well hypothesize that the larger the model, hence the more the numbers that appear on the graph, the more users will tend to inflate satisfaction values.

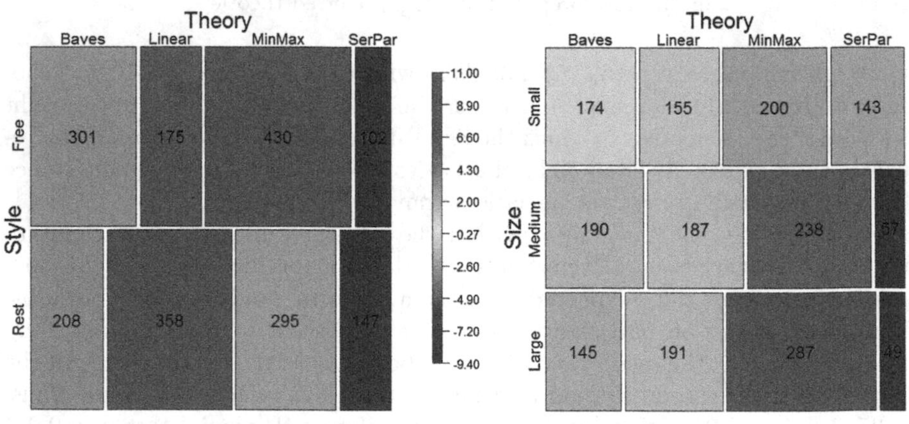

Fig. 4. The effect of style and size

A possible suspicion that mathematically-intensive academic background may affect the choice does not seem to be supported by these data. We omit a display for the interest of space.

Self Reporting. The results of the last question, in which participants self-report the method they think they used, strongly indicate that participants are not completely aware of the method they use. Only 20% of 35 participants who specified a concrete calculation method either forcedly (version 1 of instrument) or voluntarily (version 2), state that they use a method that also happens to be the one they actually used with statistically significant consistency. A higher 26% claim that they follow a theory which, in fact, they used unusually less in the exercises (chiefly Serial/Parallel). Importantly, of the participants who were asked if they used their intuition to respond (version 2), 81% states that they did, i.e., they did not use a specific calculation method.

4 Consequences and Validity Threats

Consequences. The general impression we get from the result is that untrained users of quantitative goal models may not come without expectations as to how numbers are supposed to be combined to infer goal satisfaction, and that such expectations may depend on aspects of the model. More specifically, we believe that our data seem to support further corroboration of at least four hypotheses. Firstly, for visual goal models as constructed in this experiment, participants tend to favour certain ways of inferring satisfaction of goals over others, particularly MinMax, Linear and, to a lesser extent, Bayesian. Secondly, the amount to which the weights of incoming contribution links to a goal sum up can affect the choice of interpretation of satisfaction propagation semantics; if the sum is 1.0 the Linear model becomes more popular. Thirdly, the larger the model is the more inflated the assessment of goal satisfaction appears to be. Finally, users do not appear to consciously follow a specific aggregation method but instead work intuitively.

There are, further, some important experimental validity points that deserve a closer look, particularly on construct and external validity.

Construct Validity. As we saw, to measure which theory users prefer we mainly rely on inference from how they use the models rather than on directly asking them (e.g., *"how would you combine these numbers?"*). This emphasis was in part due to practical reasons – on-line administration prevents meaningful open-ended interaction – but also due to our low confidence that users can provide valid data. The limited self-reporting we solicited (last questions of instrument) indeed revealed that participants have limited awareness of the process they themselves follow. Moreover, the input of those who volunteered to describe the method they followed in their own words proved difficult to interpret and was often plain incomprehensible. Thus, we remain unconvinced that there is a trivial interviewing protocol that can conclusively explain why participants work the way they do. It is, however, subject for future research.

Looking now at the observational measure, the substantial deviation from uniform randomness begs an explanation and supports, we believe, the validity of the endeavour: why are some theories preferred and some others avoided? One explanation is that the participants were asked to choose from a fixed set of values and, thus, naturally leaned toward those that were not extreme, choosing completely randomly one of them. This could explain why they avoided, for example, Serial-Parallel. But it would not completely explain why Linear was not avoided to the same extend, and why there was still concentration to MinMax versus the Bayesian theory – which both give values which are, generally, in the middle of the ranking. Future designs could allow for a more solid picture of the above by asking participants to freely specify satisfaction value that they find more appropriate, instead of offering a predefined inventory.

External Validity. We treat this study as exploratory, with no intent of making strong generalization arguments, about e.g. the universal suitability of a specific theory, our goal being to see if there is *any* effect. Keeping this in mind, in appreciating generalizability of the findings one should consider both the chosen participants and the chosen models. The former are users of MTurk, who are known to be a good enough proxy for random population samples [5], and might offer more variability than e.g. University students, especially when the latter are drawn from a specific department or course. More important is, we find, the level of representativeness of the models: different sizes, visual properties and goal contents (e.g. real domain concepts vs. A, B, C etc.) might certainly affect participants' reaction to them. Recall also that to enable comparability of the frameworks certain simplifications were made, such as for example not using negative contribution measures or not fully utilizing notions of satisfaction and denial values as defined in the Giorgini et al. framework. Generalizations should be predicated on these restrictions.

5 Related Work

There is a wealth of proposals for modeling partial goal satisfaction and influence thereof between goals in the literature, the semantics of which vary in intuitive meaning and their mathematical/algorithmic treatment (e.g. [3,7,10,14,15,18] in addition to ones discussed earlier; [12] for further survey). Such proposals are typically evaluated based on expressiveness standards, amenability to interesting and efficient reasoning or hypothesized ease of label acquisition.

Nonetheless, the idea of also empirically investigating the way a diagram elicits by its viewers a certain way of understanding its subject matter is not new to the conceptual modeling community, either. Several studies, for example, investigate the comprehensibility of diagrammatic notations such as UML state diagrams or ER diagrams [6,24]. Similar work has been done with goal models. Horkoff et al., for example, propose and evaluate an interactive evaluation technique for goal models [13]. The visual properties of goal modeling languages such as i^* vis-a-vis model comprehensibility have been the target of investigation as well. Moody et al. offer an assessment of the i^* visual syntax based on established rules ("Physics of Notations"). An empirical analysis was followed by Caire et al. [4] in which experimental participants evaluate visualization choices of the language's primitives. Elsewhere, Hadar et al. [11] compare goal diagrams with use case diagrams on a variety of user tasks, including reading and modifying.

The above efforts tell us that there is interest in the community in understanding how users interact with diagrams, and even have users define their visual properties of such, as e.g. Caire et al. demonstrate. Having users go beyond the visuals and evaluate the semantics of notations seems to be a natural next step. On that matter, although we could not find work in which interpretation of satisfaction contribution in goal models is empirically investigated the way we do here, we believe there is potential for much more research.

6 Concluding Remarks

We presented an exploratory experimental study aimed at assessing the intuitiveness of four theories of satisfaction propagation, operationalized through measuring the frequency by which inferences untrained users perform with the model match inferences that the theory prescribes. The results suggest that participants do not choose at random and tend to favour some theories over others. The way numbers are chosen as well as the size of the model also seem to affect selection of theory, a process which, moreover, appears to take place heuristically rather than through performance of precise calculations.

More investigation will be needed to fully understand how such results may affect the practice of goal modelers and goal modeling language designers. It is important to first consider that the results concern a specific diagrammatic way of visualizing goal models and the kinds of inferences the specific visualization evokes. If a modeler has compelling theoretical reasons to choose an "unintuitive" (vis-à-vis the visualization) propagation theory, e.g. Serial/Parallel if it eventually proves to be such, use of traditional goal diagrams may be problematic, as users will likely make goal satisfaction inferences that contravene the normative values, perhaps even if the latter are explicated in the diagram for the purpose of exactly preventing erroneous user inferences. We intuitively consider such situation sub-optimal compared to a situation in which the visualization and the theory are in alignment. Nevertheless, the impact of misalignment in practical model use needs to be explored in realistic model use scenarios (e.g. decision making), prior to elevating intuitiveness measurement to a priority for language designers.

References

1. Amyot, D., Ghanavati, S., Horkoff, J., Mussbacher, G., Peyton, L., Yu, E.S.K.: Evaluating goal models within the goal-oriented requirement language. Int. J. Intell. Syst. **25**(8), 841–877 (2010)
2. Amyot, D., Mussbacher, G.: User requirements notation: the first ten years, the next ten years. J. Softw. (JSW) **6**(5), 747–768 (2011)

3. Baresi, L., Pasquale, L., Spoletini, P.: Fuzzy goals for requirements-driven adaptation. In: Proceedings of the 18th IEEE International Requirements Engineering (RE 2010), Sydney, Australia, pp. 125–134 (2010)
4. Caire, P., Genon, N., Heymans, P., Moody, D.L.: Visual notation design 2.0: towards user comprehensible requirements engineering notations. In: Proceedings of the 21st IEEE International Requirements Engineering Conference (RE 2013), pp. 115–124 (2013)
5. Crump, M.J.C., McDonnell, J.V., Gureckis, T.M.: Evaluating Amazon's mechanical turk as a tool for experimental behavioral research. PLoS ONE **8**(3), 1–18 (2013)
6. Cruz-Lemus, J.A., Genero, M., Manso, M.E., Morasca, S., Piattini, M.: Assessing the understandability of UML statechart diagrams with composite states–a family of empirical studies. Empirical Softw. Eng. **14**(6), 685–719 (2009)
7. Elahi, G., Yu, E.S.K.: Requirements trade-offs analysis in the absence of quantitative measures: a heuristic method. In: Proceedings of the 2011 ACM Symposium on Applied Computing (SAC 2011), TaiChung, Taiwan, pp. 651–658 (2011)
8. Friendly, M., Meyer, D.: Discrete Data Analysis with R: Visualization and Modeling Techniques for Categorical and Count Data. Chapman Hall, New York (2015)
9. Giorgini, P., Mylopoulos, J., Nicchiarelli, E., Sebastiani, R.: Formal reasoning techniques for goal models. In: Spaccapietra, S., March, S., Aberer, K. (eds.) Journal on Data Semantics I. LNCS, vol. 2800, pp. 1–20. Springer, Heidelberg (2003). doi:10.1007/978-3-540-39733-5_1
10. Giorgini, P., Mylopoulos, J., Sebastiani, R.: Goal-oriented requirements analysis and reasoning in the Tropos methodology. Eng. Appl. Artif. Intell. **18**(2), 159–171 (2005)
11. Hadar, I., Reinhartz-Berger, I., Kuflik, T., Perini, A., Ricca, F., Susi, A.: Comparing the comprehensibility of requirements models expressed in use case and Tropos: results from a family of experiments. Inf. Softw. Technol. **55**(10), 1823–1843 (2013)
12. Horkoff, J., Yu, E.: Analyzing goal models: different approaches and how to choose among them. In: Proceedings of the 2011 ACM Symposium on Applied Computing (SAC 2011), TaiChung, Taiwan, pp. 675–682 (2011)
13. Horkoff, J., Yu, E.S.K.: Interactive goal model analysis for early requirements engineering. Requirements Eng. **21**(1), 29–61 (2016)
14. van Lamsweerde, A.: Reasoning about alternative requirements options. In: Borgida, A.T., Chaudhri, V.K., Giorgini, P., Yu, E.S. (eds.) Conceptual Modeling: Foundations and Applications. LNCS, vol. 5600, pp. 380–397. Springer, Heidelberg (2009). doi:10.1007/978-3-642-02463-4_20
15. Letier, E., van Lamsweerde, A.: Reasoning about partial goal satisfaction for requirements and design engineering. In: Proceedings of the 12th International Symposium on the Foundation of Software Engineering, FSE 2004, pp. 53–62 (2004)
16. Li, F.L., Horkoff, J., Mylopoulos, J., Guizzardi, R.S.S., Guizzardi, G., Borgida, A., Liu, L.: Non-functional requirements as qualities, with a spice of ontology. In: Proceedings of the 22nd International Requirements Engineering Conference (RE 2014), Karlskrona, Sweden, pp. 293–302 (2014)
17. Liaskos, S., Jalman, R., Aranda, J.: On eliciting preference and contribution measures in goal models. In: Proceedings of the 20th International Requirements Engineering Conference (RE 2012), Chicago, IL, pp. 221–230 (2012)

18. Liaskos, S., Khan, S.M., Soutchanski, M., Mylopoulos, J.: Modeling and reasoning with decision-theoretic goals. In: Ng, W., Storey, V.C., Trujillo, J.C. (eds.) ER 2013. LNCS, vol. 8217, pp. 19–32. Springer, Heidelberg (2013). doi:10.1007/978-3-642-41924-9_3
19. Maiden, N., Pavan, P., Gizikis, A., Clause, O., Kim, H., Zhu, X.: Making decisions with requirements: integrating i* goal modelling and the AHP. In: Proceedings of the 8th International Working Conference on Requirements Engineering: Foundation for Software Quality (REFSQ 2002), Essen, Germany (2002)
20. Mylopoulos, J., Chung, L., Liao, S., Wang, H., Yu, E.: Exploring alternatives during requirements analysis. IEEE Softw. **18**(1), 92–96 (2001)
21. Mylopoulos, J., Chung, L., Nixon, B.: Representing and using nonfunctional requirements: a process-oriented approach. IEEE Trans. Softw. Eng. **18**(6), 483–497 (1992)
22. Norman, D.: The Design of Everyday Things. Basic Books, New York (2013)
23. Payne, S.J.: A descriptive study of mental models. Behav. Inf. Technol. **10**(1), 3–21 (1991)
24. Purchase, H.C., Welland, R., McGill, M., Colpoys, L.: Comprehension of diagram syntax: an empirical study of entity relationship notations. Int. J. Hum. Comput. Stud. **61**(2), 187–203 (2004)
25. Yu, E.S.K.: Towards modelling and reasoning support for early-phase requirements engineering. In: Proceedings of the 3rd IEEE International Symposium on Requirements Engineering (RE 1997), Annapolis, MD, pp. 226–235 (1997)

On the Impact of the Model-Based Representation of Inconsistencies to Manual Reviews

Results from a Controlled Experiment

Marian Daun(✉), Jennifer Brings, and Thorsten Weyer

paluno – The Ruhr Institute for Software Technology, University of Duisburg-Essen, Essen, Germany
{marian.daun, jennifer.brings, thorsten.weyer}@paluno.uni-due.de

Abstract. To ensure fulfilling stakeholder wishes, it is crucial to validate the documented requirements. This is often complicated by the fact that the wishes and intentions of different stakeholders are somewhat contradictory, which manifests itself in inconsistent requirements. To aid requirements engineers in identifying and resolving inconsistent requirements, we investigated the usefulness for manual reviews of two different model-based representation formats for inconsistent requirements; one that represent the inconsistent requirements in separate diagrams and one that represents them integrated into one diagram using annotations. The results from a controlled experiment show that the use of such integrated review diagrams can significantly increase efficiency of manual reviews, without sacrificing effectiveness.

Keywords: Requirements validation · Inconsistencies · Controlled experiment

1 Motivation and Background

Model-based engineering has widely been adopted in the domain of embedded systems to cope with the growing complexity of such systems [1]. Model-based requirements engineering is often seen as an important part as it allows, among others, for full continuity across the entire engineering process [2]. As model-based documentation is often used from different requirements perspectives or to document the intentions of different stakeholders in different requirements models, inconsistencies between multiple requirements models can easily arise [3]. This particular challenge can often only be solved by manual validation, as automated approaches can only detect inconsistencies but not negotiate agreement between different stakeholders and thus, ensure the correctness of all requirements artifacts (cf. [4]).

An extended version containing supplemental experiment material can be found at: https://arxiv.org/abs/1707.02907.

H.C. Mayr et al. (Eds.): ER 2017, LNCS 10650, pp. 466–473, 2017.
https://doi.org/10.1007/978-3-319-69904-2_35

Message sequence charts like languages are commonly used in requirements engineering. While message sequence charts have shown to be an effective and efficient language to be used in manual reviews (cf. [5]), the validation of different inconsistent requirements models is challenging because it involves investigating a potentially vast number of diagrams containing identical parts, alternative parts, and contradictory parts. To reduce the number of diagrams to be reviewed, existing automated model merging techniques (e.g., [6]) can create diagrams that represent inconsistent properties integrated in just one diagram.

Figure 1 illustrates a very simple merge of just two separate basic message sequence charts (bMSCs) ((a1) and (a2) in Fig. 1). Both bMSCs show the same excerpt of a specification of an automotive lane keeping support system (LKS). Diagram (a1) shows how the system shall handle lane departures from the perspective of one stakeholder and diagram (a2) shows how this functionality is specified from another stakeholder's perspective. As can be seen, these two diagrams differ in just one message that the LKS either receives the current steering angle from the electronic stability support (ESS) or not. Diagram (b) shows the merged behavior in a corresponding bMSC, which displays both interaction sequences specified by the originating bMSC. In the following, we will refer to the original bMSCs as the separate and the merged bMSC as the integrated representation.

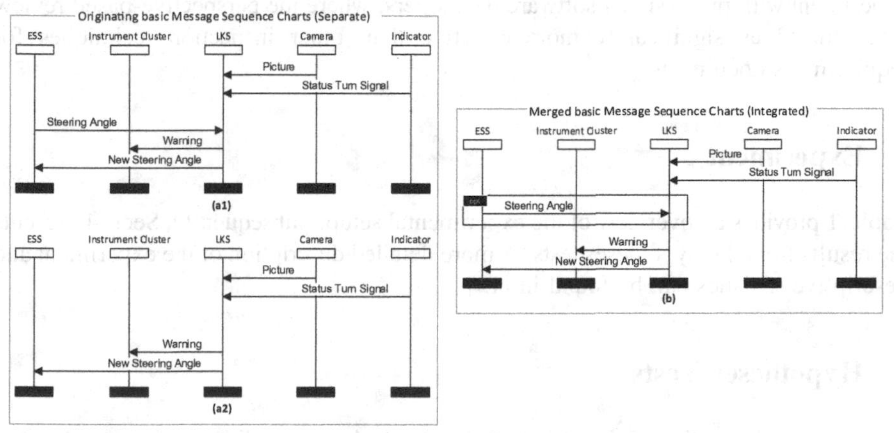

Fig. 1. Exemplary model merging of bMSCs

This paper reports on a controlled experiment to investigate whether model merging can be used to improve effectiveness and efficiency of reviews. Therefore, the experiment compares the two representations of inconsistencies. Results show that the representation of inconsistencies has no significant impact on the review's effectiveness; but for diagrams with few inconsistencies, it is significantly more efficient to use the integrated representation.

Section 2 gives an overview of the related work. Section 3 defines the experimental setup and Sect. 4 reports on the results of the experiment. Finally, Sect. 5 concludes the paper.

2 Related Work

Several approaches exist to support the manual review of model-based specifications. In [7], *Denger and Ciolkowski* describe a defect taxonomy to apply a perspective-based inspection technique to statecharts. In addition, *Binder* defines a checklist to validate statecharts from a testing perspective in [8]. A more general approach to validate model-based specifications is presented by *Travassos et al.* [9]. The approach addresses the consistency between UML diagrams of different types. For this purpose, perspective-based reviews of scenarios from different perspectives are suggested.

In previous work, we proposed the use of dedicated review models to support the validation of embedded systems' functional design and behavioral requirements [10]. Among others, we found that the use of ITU message sequence charts as review artifact is more effective, efficient, and subjectively supportive compared to the use of the original specification of the embedded systems' functional design (cf. [5]).

Several studies already investigated effectiveness and efficiency of different review types. Therefore, the experiment design presented in this paper is based on the experiment design of these reported experiments. For example, *Miller et al.* [11] report on a student experiment with 50 trained students, finding that perspective-based reviews are more effective than checklist-based approaches for error detection in natural language requirements specifications. *Basili et al.* [12] report on a controlled experiment with professional software developers, where the perspective-based review is evaluated as significantly more effective than other inspection techniques for requirements documents.

3 Experiment

Table 1 provides an overview of the experimental setup. Subsequently, Sect. 4 presents the results from the hypotheses tests. A more detailed description of the experiment and descriptive statistics can be found in [13].

4 Hypotheses Tests

This section shows the results of hypotheses tests. As preconditions of parametric test were satisfied, we conducted two-way repeated measures ANOVAs and followed up significant interaction effects using t tests.

Effectiveness. The results of a two-way repeated measures ANOVA indicate no significant main effect of the representation. $F(1, 35) = 0.001$, $p > .05$, d = 0.01, Power: .92. There was, however, a highly significant main effect of degree of consistency. $F(1, 35) = 34.86$, $p < .01$, $d = 0.99$, Power: 1. As there was no significant interaction effect $F(1, 35) = 0.46$, $p > .05$, $d = 0.11$, Power: .18 between representation and degree of consistency, the significant main effect of degree of consistency can be interpreted globally. Since effectiveness is higher when reviewing diagrams with a high degree of consistency (*H*) we accept **HEff2-1a**. However, we cannot reject **HEff1-0** and **HEff3-0**.

Table 1. Experiment planning

Goals	Investigate, whether the integrated representation (i.e. the merged diagram) is advantageous compared to the separate representation (i.e. the original bMSC diagrams) for reviews with respect to their *effectiveness*, and efficiency
Participants	The experiment was conducted with 41 graduate students. We filtered some of the participants' data sets from the final data set. This was necessary, since some of the participants did obviously not perform serious reviews, since these participants finished the review of all four tasks (consisting of the validation of 34 natural language stakeholder intentions) in less than five minutes. In total, we used 36 data sets for further analysis
Experiment material	An industrial sample specification of an avionics collision avoidance system and a set of natural language stakeholder intentions
Independent variables	Representation format: *Integrated (short: I):* The participants reviewed a diagram using the integrated representation, which displays inconsistencies in the same bMSC *Separate (short: S):* The participants reviewed diagrams using the separate representation, which displays inconsistencies in two separate bMSCs Degree of consistency: *High (short: H):* The participants reviewed diagrams, which are highly consistent, i.e., that have only few inconsistencies between each other *Low (short: L):* The participants reviewed diagrams in I or S, which are highly inconsistent, i.e., have many inconsistencies between each other
Dependent variables	*Effectiveness:* the ratio of correct review decisions made *Efficiency:* the average time spent per correct review decision
Hypotheses	**H_{Eff}1-0:** The review is equally effective no matter the representation **H_{Eff}1-1a:** The review is more effective in *I* **H_{Eff}1-1b:** The review is more effective in *S* **H_{Eff}2-0:** The review is equally effective no matter the degree of consistency **H_{Eff}2-1a:** The review is more effective for *H* **H_{Eff}2-1b:** The review is more effective for *L* **H_{Eff}3-0:** There is no interaction effect between the representation and the degree of consistency in terms of effectiveness **H_{Eff}3-1: NOT** H_{Eff}3-0 **H_{Efy}1-0:** The review is equally efficient no matter the representation **H_{Efy}1-1a:** The review is more efficient in *I* **H_{Efy}1-1b:** The review is more efficient in *S* **H_{Efy}2-0:** The review is equally efficient no matter the degrees of consistency **H_{Efy}2-1a:** The review is more efficient for *H* **H_{Efy}2-1b:** The review is more efficient for *L* **H_{Efy}3-0:** There is no interaction effect between the representation and the degree of consistency in terms of efficiency **H_{Efy}3-1: NOT** H_{Efy}3-0
Experiment design	The study was conducted as an experiment using an online questionnaire. The experiment was designed to last about 30 min. The experiment used a within-subject design. Each participant conducted a review of an excerpt from the specifications of the avionics collision avoidance system in both representations (I and S). The order of the reviews using the different representations was randomized

Efficiency. The results of the two way repeated measures ANOVA show a significant main effect of representation $F(1, 35) = 4.83$, $p < .05$, $d = 0.38$, Power: .97, and a significant main effect of degree of consistency $F(1, 35) = 5.18$, $p < .05$, $d = 0.39$, Power: .98. There was also a highly significant interaction effect between representation and degree of consistency $F(1, 35) = 9.36$, $p < .01$, $d = 0.52$, Power: .99. This indicates that the representation had different effects on the participants' efficiency depending on the degree of consistency between the reviewed diagrams. We therefore accept **HEfy3-1**.

As the interaction diagrams (cf. Fig. 2) show a disordinal interaction between representation and degree of consistency, the significant main effects cannot be interpreted globally.

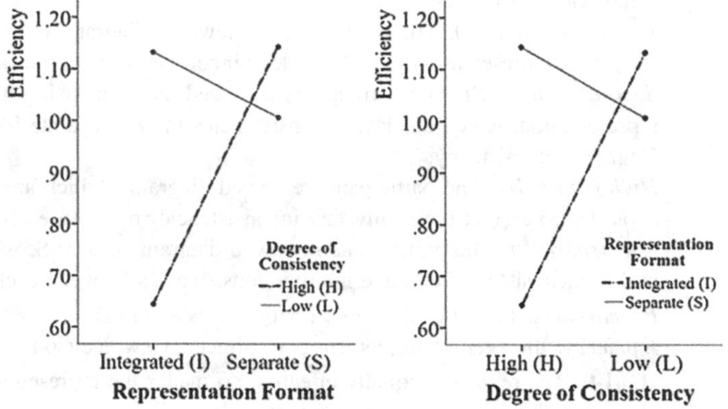

Fig. 2. Interaction diagrams – efficiency

To investigate the interaction effect, we conducted t tests, where we kept one of the factors constant. On average, participants reviewed diagrams with a high degree of consistency (*H*) (M = 0.65, σ = 0.39) significantly more efficiently than diagrams with a low degree of consistency (*L*) (M = 1.13, σ = 0.58) when using the integrated representation (*I*) t(34) = −5.30, p < .05, d = 0.89, Power: .99.

When using the separate representation (*S*), the participants' efficiency was not significantly higher when reviewing diagrams with a low degree of consistency (*L*) (M = 1.04, σ = 0.60) than when reviewing diagrams with a high degree of consistency (*H*) (M = 1.13, σ = 0.87) t(35) = −0.548, p > .05, d = 0.09, Power: .08.

When reviewing diagrams with a high degree of consistency (*H*), participants were highly significantly more efficient when using the integrated representation (*I*) (M = 0.65, σ = 0.39) than when using the separate representation (*S*) (M = 1.14, σ = 0.88), t(34) = −3.08, p < .01, d = 0.52, Power: .63.

When reviewing diagrams with a low degree of consistency (*L*), participants were not significantly more efficient when using the separate representation (*S*) (M = 1.04, σ = 0.60) than when using the integrated representation (*I*) (M = 1.12, σ = 0.58), t (35) = −0.68, p > .05, d = 0.11, Power: .10.

5 Discussion and Conclusion

5.1 Evaluation of Results and Implications

Regarding *effectiveness*, the representation format itself had no significant impact. When reviewing diagrams with a low degree of consistency the readability of the integrated representation seems to decrease. Additionally, effectiveness is considerably higher when reviewing diagrams with a high degree of consistency than with a low degree of consistency, regardless of the representation.

Regarding *efficiency*, it depends on the degree of consistency whether an integrated or a separate representation is more advantageous when reviewing inconsistent behavioral properties. As the results show, when reviewing diagrams with a high degree of consistency, efficiency is highly significantly higher when using the integrated representation. Since there is no significant difference in effectiveness, we conclude that diagrams with a high degree of consistency can be more efficiently reviewed using the integrated representation without sacrificing accuracy. The fact that there is no statistically significant difference between the representation formats when reviewing diagrams with a low degree of consistency might be due to low statistical power in this case. Surprisingly, participants using the separate representation were more efficient when reviewing diagrams with a low degree of consistency than when reviewing diagrams with a high degree of consistency.

5.2 Threats to Validity

To address threats to validity, which exist for this type of study, we have employed certain mitigation strategies [14]. While the detailed mitigation strategies applied can be found in [13], in this paper we limit the discussion to the remaining threats:

Construct Validity. In case of efficiency, we must discuss some threats to validity arising from the experiment setup. As we used an online questionnaire, which does not measure the time usage for a single decision but for the review of a whole diagram, we can make no statements about the exact time used for reviewing each single stakeholder intention. Since the experiment participation was done online, we have no knowledge about time-consuming activities participants might have done during their experiment participation. In a short briefing, we stressed the need for focused work on the experiment. In addition, we designed the experiment in such a way that the experiment could be completed in less than 30 min to minimize the number of participants losing focus. While we removed outliers indicating large irregularities, we cannot eliminate the issue that smaller activities (e.g., chatting or answering phone calls) could have influenced our measurements.

Internal Validity. We designed the experiment as an online questionnaire to be conducted within about 30 min and gave the participants a time frame of 5 days to participate. Thus, we assume that internal threats to history, maturation, or mortality do not exist. However, it must be noted that allowing a time frame to participate and to allow participation online also relates to losing control over participants' behavior regarding experiment participation.

External Validity. The participants were mostly graduate students except for a few undergraduates in their senior year. As the participants were students, the question of generalizability to an industrial setting arises. Since studies (cf. [15, 16]) showed that graduate students can serve as an adequate replacement for industry professionals in experiments, and we discussed experiment material, experiment tasks and experiment results with our industry partners, we are confident that the findings can be generalized.

5.3 Inferences

Regarding the question, whether it is beneficial for manual reviews to first merge inconsistent behavioral properties into one integrated diagram compared to the review of inconsistent properties in separate diagrams, the experiment shows that such a model merging seems to have only limited impact on the effectiveness of the review. In contrast to previous work that has shown that the use of model transformations and model merging for consistent behavioral properties does significantly impact effectiveness of the review (cf. [5]), no such overall advantages (or any disadvantages) for inconsistencies were recognizable in this experiment. However, two major findings remain and may provide a starting point for future work:

First, when reviewing models with minor inconsistencies a merging of the inconsistent parts into one diagram can significantly improve the reviews efficiency. Since minor inconsistencies easily occur in model-based engineering (e.g., due to simple misnaming errors), this effect might significantly impact the overall review of an entire specification. Consequently, future work should deal with determining the maximal ratio of inconsistent and consistent parts that should be merged to allow for efficient reviews of the merged diagram.

Second, the results show that regardless of the representation format (i.e. two separate diagrams or one merged diagram) the effectiveness of the review is considerably higher when reviewing diagrams with a high degree of consistency than when reviewing diagrams with a low degree of consistency. Therefore, for manual validation, it might be beneficial to determine the degree of consistency between different views beforehand. Based on the degree of consistency it can then be decided, which representation format should be chosen for the review. Therefore, future work should deal with the question, how best to determine the degree of consistency and what the preferable review format for a certain degree of consistency is. Furthermore, it might also be interesting to investigate the tradeoff between more reviews in shorter time and fewer reviews far between. Hence, the question arises whether shorter reviewing cycles are advantageous to longer review cycles, as inconsistencies are removed earlier and, in conclusion, larger inconsistencies are less likely to occur.

Acknowledgment. This research was partly funded by the German Federal Ministry of Education and Research (grant no. 01IS16043V and grant no. 01IS12005C). We thank Stefan Beck and Arnaud Boyer (Airbus Defence and Space), Jens Höfflinger (Bosch), and Karsten Albers (inchron) for their support regarding the adoption of industrial specifications to fit as experiment material.

References

1. France, R., Rumpe, B.: Model-driven development of complex software: a research roadmap. In: 2007 Future of Software Engineering, pp. 37–54. IEEE Computer Society, Washington, DC (2007)
2. Loniewski, G., Insfran, E., Abrahão, S.: A systematic review of the use of requirements engineering techniques in model-driven development. In: Petriu, D.C., Rouquette, N., Haugen, Ø. (eds.) MODELS 2010. LNCS, vol. 6395, pp. 213–227. Springer, Heidelberg (2010). doi:10.1007/978-3-642-16129-2_16
3. Finkelstein, A., Goedicke, M., Kramer, J., Niskier, C.: ViewPoint oriented software development: methods and viewpoints in requirements engineering. In: Bergstra, J.A., Feijs, L.M.G. (eds.) Algebraic Methods II: Theory, Tools and Applications. LNCS, vol. 490, pp. 29–54. Springer, Heidelberg (1991). doi:10.1007/3-540-53912-3_17
4. ISO/IEC/IEEE: ISO/IEC/IEEE 29148:2011 - Systems and software engineering – Life cycle processes – Requirements engineering (2011)
5. Daun, M., Salmon, A., Weyer, T., Pohl, K.: The impact of students' skills and experiences on empirical results: a controlled experiment with undergraduate and graduate students. In: Proceedings of International Conference on Evaluation and Assessment in Software Engineering, pp. 29:1–29:6. ACM (2015)
6. Klein, J., Caillaud, B., Hélouët, L.: Merging scenarios. Electron. Notes Theor. Comput. Sci. **133**, 193–215 (2005)
7. Denger, C., Ciolkowski, M.: High quality statecharts through tailored, perspective-based inspections. In: 29th EUROMICRO Conference 2003, New Waves in System Architecture, pp. 316–325. IEEE Computer Society (2003)
8. Binder, R.V.: Testing Object-Oriented Systems: Models, Patterns, and Tools. Addison-Wesley, Reading (1999)
9. Travassos, G., Shull, F., Fredericks, M., Basili, V.R.: Detecting defects in object-oriented designs: using reading techniques to increase software quality. In: Proceedings of the 1999 ACM SIGPLAN Conference on Object-Oriented Programming Systems, Languages & Applications (OOPSLA 1999), pp. 47–56. ACM (1999)
10. Daun, M., Weyer, T., Pohl, K.: Detecting and correcting outdated requirements in function-centered engineering of embedded systems. In: Fricker, S.A., Schneider, K. (eds.) REFSQ 2015. LNCS, vol. 9013, pp. 65–80. Springer, Cham (2015). doi:10.1007/978-3-319-16101-3_5
11. Miller, J., Wood, M., Roper, M.: Further experiences with scenarios and checklists. Empir. Softw. Eng. **3**, 37–64 (1998)
12. Basili, V.R., Green, S., Laitenberger, O., Lanubile, F., Shull, F., Sørumgård, S., Zelkowitz, M.V.: The empirical investigation of perspective-based reading. Empir. Softw. Eng. **1**, 133–164 (1996)
13. Daun, M., Brings, J., Weyer, T.: On the impact of the model-based representation of inconsistencies to manual reviews: results from a controlled experiment - extended version. arXiv:1707.02907 Cs (2017)
14. Daun, M., Salmon, A., Bandyszak, T., Weyer, T.: Common threats and mitigation strategies in requirements engineering experiments with student participants. In: Daneva, M., Pastor, O. (eds.) REFSQ 2016. LNCS, vol. 9619, pp. 269–285. Springer, Cham (2016). doi:10.1007/978-3-319-30282-9_19
15. Höst, M., Regnell, B., Wohlin, C.: Using students as subjects-a comparative study of students and professionals in lead-time impact assessment. Empir. Softw. Eng. **5**, 201–214 (2000)
16. Svahnberg, M., Aurum, A., Wohlin, C.: Using students as subjects an empirical evaluation. In: Proceedings of the 2nd International Symposium on Empirical Software Engineering and Measurement, ESEM 2008, pp. 288–290. ACM (2008)

Ontologies

On the Semantics of Ongoing and Future Occurrence Identifiers

Nicola Guarino(✉)

ISTC-CNR Laboratory for Applied Ontology, Trento, Italy
nicola.guarino@cnr.it

Abstract. According to the standard wisdom, all temporal occurrences are considered as "frozen in time". This means that all their properties are fully determined, and they can't change. This is certainly true for historical occurrences, but, at least in the ordinary language, ongoing and future occurrences seem to admit the possibility of change: the score of an ongoing match may change in time, and a future trip may be delayed. But if ongoing and future events can change in time, what are their identifiers? In this paper I propose a *tensed* ontological account (contrasted with the dominant *tenseless* tradition) that provides an answer to this question.

Keywords: Event · Process · Occurrence · Identifier · Ontology · Time · Tense · Change

1 Introduction

References to ongoing and future temporal occurrences appear very often in our everyday discourse. The ongoing football match, Mary's next medical appointment, her next trip to Rome, her coming birthday, the writing of this paper... These expressions are considered as denoting unique, well-defined individuals, although some of their properties are not completely fixed, so that they may change in time. Indeed, many software systems consider these entities as first-class citizens, since they need to handle crucial information about them. This means that, as Scheer puts it, we do have some *knowledge of the future*, "in spite of the truism that there is always the possibility that something will turn up to prevent the event whose occurrence we supposedly have knowledge of" [20, p. 212]. In particular, in sharp contrast with events that are necessarily unknown (like the outcome of a future football match), there is an important class of future events we *must* have knowledge of, namely those that are customarily scheduled (like the match itself) or anyway *expected*, as those dealt with in the following examples:

- A flight reservation system may associate properties such as (possibly changing) expected departure and actual departure to the same flight identifier;
- A football match management system may have a variable standing for 'the present score' associated to the match identifier;

H.C. Mayr et al. (Eds.): ER 2017, LNCS 10650, pp. 477–490, 2017.
https://doi.org/10.1007/978-3-319-69904-2_36

- A news management system may assign unique event identifiers to news appearing in different media, and dynamically classify them as describing future/ongoing/past events;
- A business process management system may assign a unique identifier to each ongoing process instance;
- A financial risk management system may assign a unique identifier to each loan instalment.

But what is the semantics of these identifiers? What is the ontological nature of ongoing and future temporal occurrences? In a recent paper with Guizzardi and Almeida [11], we pointed out to a serious problem concerning them, resulting from two established premises in conceptual modeling and in formal ontology:

(1) Instances of classes used in conceptual modeling should be denoted by *rigid* Object Identifiers (OIDs) referring to exactly one element of the domain of discourse, whose identity remains the same across different states of the world [23];
(2) According to the mainstream philosophical view [4,15], temporal occurrences are "frozen in time", in the sense that their temporal parts and their temporal location are essential to them. This means that they can't have modal properties and can't genuinely change in time.

If we accept these premises, the result is that we can only have past occurrences in our domain of discourse, since occurrence identifiers cannot denote entities having different temporal locations and temporal parts at different times. For example, we cannot state that a process instance is incomplete at a certain time and complete at a later time, since its temporal location can't change. To talk of ongoing and future occurrences in the way we want, it seems that we have to either reject (1), adopting a non-classical semantics for OIDs and admitting that occurrence identifiers may have a variable reference, or reject (2), adopting a non-classical ontological accounts of temporal occurrences.

Of course, there is still the possibility of ignoring the distinction between past and future occurrences, adopting an *eternalist* view according to which all occurrences are assumed to be already fully determined, although possibly unknown. This is indeed the position adopted in the DOLCE ontology [3] and in most foundational ontologies. Modeling occurrences in this way may be useful to express general constraints about them (saying for instance that all air flights involve an airplane), but, as we have seen, doesn't offer a clear semantics for an identifier such as 'The AZ1490 flight of December 30, 2017', whose exact temporal location is presently indeterminate. What we need in practice is a way to account for a crucial aspect of ongoing and future occurrences, that is their possibility to change, depending on how the actual future will be: that flight may be postponed or even canceled, the present game's scores may change, and so on.

A possible solution to this problem is offered in the paper cited above [11], where a modeling alternative that accepts both premises (1) and (2) is described. The essence of the idea is rather simple, and is based on Lombard's view [15] that temporal occurrences (events, in the original text[1]) are manifestations of *qualities* of their participants. So, the subject of an (apparent) event's change is not the event itself, but rather those qualities of its participants that are *manifested* by the event, which are defined in [10] as the event's *focal qualities.* Assuming that a flight event has an airline company as a participant, and the company's *commitment* to run that flight is a quality of the company, the flight itself can be seen as a manifestation of the company's commitment. So, saying that a flight has been postponed means that the commitment to run that flight has changed. We rely in the paper on the notion of quality introduced in the DOLCE ontology [16], further discussed by Borgo and Masolo [3] and recently revisited by Guarino and Guizzardi [10]. Since qualities so understood are considered as (dependent) *objects* and not as events, no problem for them to undergo genuine changes, and to have modal properties. This is a very powerful technique, since pointing to specific focal qualities gives us the possibility to talk of fine-grained aspects of an event, but still it is only a partial solution to our problems, since in some cases we have to talk of properties concerning the events themselves, and not their participants' qualities. In particular, there are at least four kinds of properties of events that can't be reduced to properties of their participants' qualities:

1. *Local properties* such as a flight's instantaneous speed, ascribed to the whole event but actually depending just on what happens at a given time. These can be hardly understood as concerning a participant's quality, such as the plane's spatial location: instantaneous speed is actually the average speed of a (suitably short) event, considered as a whole.
2. *Cumulative properties* depending on an event's past history, such as the distance covered so far by an ongoing flight, the present score of a football match, or the total number of changes in the present paper's writing. These appear to be as global properties of the event, and not of its participants.
3. *Contextual properties* depending on the broader event's context, i.e. whatever happens in the scene where the event occurs without involving the focal qualities (for example, the weather during the flight, which may be expected to be nice and may actually turn out to be bad), or even beyond the scene (e.g., a delay due to the late arrival of the aircraft).
4. *Modal properties* depending on the future parts of the event, such as the possibility, for an ongoing trip, to miss the next connection, or for a match to be interrupted before the end.

So, going back to our flight example, in *some cases* we can avoid referring to ongoing and future flights by just talking of the airline's commitments and the flight schedule, but to talk of the properties described above a direct reference to ongoing or future flight occurrences seems to be unavoidable.

[1] We have a serious terminological issue here. In philosophy, multiple terms (e.g., *perdurant, occurrent, event, eventuality...*) have been used to denote what I have been calling so far an 'occurrence'. Although the latter term is probably the least ambiguous, 'event' seems to be the most common, so, to better reflect the literature I will be citing, I will use it as a synonym of 'occurrence' from now on, ignoring that 'event' is also used in a stricter sense, in contraposition to *states* and *processes.*

A further way of dealing with the problem of (apparent) change for ongoing events is the approach pursued by Antony Galton (and Riichiro Mizoguchi) in several papers [7–9], inspired by Stout's idea [21] of processes as *continuants* (that is, objects instead of events). According to Galton's view, the dynamic behavior of an ongoing event concerns not the event itself, but rather the *process* that constitutes it, considered as an object (depending on the event's participants) that is fully present in the thin temporal window where we experience things happening at the present time and moves forward as time passes by, assuming different properties at different times. As we shall see, this approach has several interesting features that contributed to inspire the solution proposed in this paper, but in a sense it has the same problems as the previous solution, since, restricting the subject of change to a specific object (the process), is not able to fully describe what's happening while an event goes on, and does not take future events into account.

In conclusion, describing ongoing and future events in terms of their local qualities or in terms of their constituting processes is only a partial solution to our problem, so we have to face the challenge: giving up either (1) or (2). In this paper I will argue in favor of rejecting (2), namely the view that events are "frozen in time", by proposing a *tensed* ontological account (contrasted with the dominant *tenseless* tradition) according to which only past events are frozen in time, while ongoing and future events may have modal properties concerning their actual occurrence. At the core of this proposal there is a radical thesis: from the *experiential* point of view (that is, if we take tense seriously), ongoing events *do* change. They change by *embodying* temporal parts as time passes by, which *accumulate* with the previous parts. As a new temporal part is embodied, the event's properties and its elapsed duration may change accordingly. Hence, the final temporal location of ongoing events is not an essential property of them—that is, they can (literally!) *take place* at different time intervals, although their starting time is fixed. As a generalization of this approach, future events are conceived as *empty embodiments* at the time we refer to them, being free to take place at any future time interval.

In the following, I will defend and illustrate this thesis by first discussing some DOLCE-core axioms [3] concerning time-indexed parthood and the notion of 'being present at t' in the light of a tensed approach. I will then define ongoing and future events as variable embodiments, introducing a difference between *processes* and *episodes* and providing a minimal axiomatic characterization that shows how we can account for their temporal, cumulative, contextual and modal properties. Finally, I will discuss the practical consequences of this approach, its relationships with other approaches, and the future work.

2 The Need for Tensed Properties and Tensed Parthood

As mentioned above, most upper-level ontologies (including in particular DOLCE [16] and BFO [2]) adopt an *eternalist* view about the ontological nature of time, which means that all points in time are considered as real, and it is perfectly plausible to quantify over past, present or future entities. This position is technically very simple, and does not impact on our problem. More subtle is the choice concerning the way properties hold in time, that is, the interpretation of formulas of the form $F(x,t)$. Under the (dominant) *tenseless* view, properties may vary in time not differently from the way they may vary in space, independently of what the present time is. On the contrary, under the *tensed* view, whether or not a property holds depends on the present time.

In their re-visitation of DOLCE's foundational choices resulting in DOLCE-core, Borgo and Masolo [3] suggest a way to account for these formulas that they borrow from Merricks:

(3) $F(x,t)$ can be read as follows: "x exists at t and it has the property F when t is (was, will be) present" [17]

This interpretation seems very natural, and apparently shows an attitude to take tense seriously. However, I think there is delicate issue concerning the proviso 'x exists at t', which Borgo and Masolo interpret (in the strong ontological sense) as 'x is present at t', assuming the following axiom scheme:

(4) $F(x,t) \rightarrow Pre(x,t)$.

In the formula above, we shall assume that t denotes a time interval, and $F(x,t)$ stands for a generic property holding for x in the interval t, while $Pre(x,t)$ is a primitive standing for 'x is present in the interval t'[2]. The problem with this assumption is that it leaves no room for *tensed* properties of x that may hold at t when x is not present at t. Properties of this kind are rather common, especially for events. For instance, if x is an event that occurs at t_0 (say, a person's birthday), it may be *expected* at a time $t_1 < t_0$ only if x is *not* present at t_1, and *remembered* at a time $t_2 > t_0$ only if x is *not* present at t_2, since we can't expect nor remember something that is present. Similarly, a person can have various properties, such as being admired or being the mother of somebody, also when she is not present anymore since she is died. So, presumably, (4) is valid for *intrinsic* properties, but cannot be generalized to all kinds of properties. In conclusion, I suggest that we should reject it, and just rely on the logical existence of x while quantifying on x in $F(x,t)$. This means that we are free to ascribe a *tensed* property, holding when t is present, to every entity that exists somehow in our domain[3], independently on whether it is present at t. Note that, otherwise, (4) would be interpreted in *tenseless* way, since, needing that x is

[2] 'Being present' is taken here as a primitive notion, which we can roughly understand as 'being *perceivable*'. When we say that a time is present we assume to have some kind of perceivable clock that shows us what the present time is. A time interval is assumed to be present if it contains the present time.

[3] I will be deliberately vague on this point. While a person may exist after her death without being present, arguably she does not exist before her conception. Similarly, a future medical appointment does not exist before it is decided. To account for these issues, a temporalized existence predicate might be introduced in addition to the temporalized presence predicate. Here I assume to quantify on things that exist.

present when t is present, it just describes *where* F holds in time, independently of what the present time is.

Adopting a tensed interpretation for $F(x,t)$ is of crucial importance for our argument, since it has a direct impact on describing how events accumulate temporal parts as time passes by. The point is the interpretation of the time-indexed parthood relation $P(x,y,t)$, which in DOLCE-core is constrained by the following axiom (besides the usual ones of extensional mereology):

(5) $P(x,y,t) \rightarrow Pre(x,t) \wedge Pre(y,t)$

Note that, in the original version of DOLCE, time-indexed parthood was restricted to objects only, since, following Hawley [13], one of the distinctions between objects and events was exactly that only objects require a time-indexed parthood relation. Intuitively, the rationale of this choice was that "...a statement like 'this keyboard is part of my computer' is incomplete unless you specify a particular time, while 'my youth is part of my life' does not require such specification". In DOLCE-core, in an attempt for generality, the argument restrictions on x and y were removed, so that (5) holds both for objects and events. This axiom can be seen as a direct consequence of the scheme (4), since it implies that, if x has the property of being a part of some y at t, then x has to be present at t, and, viceversa, if y has the property of having some x as a part at t, then y has to be present at t. The problems we have seen for (4) have therefore an impact on accepting (5).

The crucial issue is that, if we assume that (5) holds also for events, and not just for objects, we over-constrain the notion of part of an event, imposing it a tenseless reading that violates its tensed nature. Indeed, a characteristic of events, as we shall see, is exactly the fact that their temporal parts become past as time passes by. So, the property of being a part of an event needs to hold also when the part is not present. The reason why this is so can be explained intuitively by observing that, at each time an event is present, it has some *cumulative* properties (say, the elapsed duration or the actual score of the football match) that are influenced by *all* previous parts. So, an event *grows* in time like a glacier[4], by having a present part (the "moving front") that is constantly changing, and keeping memory—so to speak—of the parts that are not present any more. In my view, this behavior seems indeed at the core of the established view that events "unfold in time", in the sense that

(6) Whenever a (non-instantaneous) event is present, it is not *wholly* present, since some of its parts are not present.

To account for such behavior, we clearly have to reject (5) as a general axiom, reserving it only for objects. Of course, getting rid of (5) for events is not enough, since we need to suitably constrain the notion of presence and the temporal behavior of parthood in order to avoid non-intended models. As we shall see, such behavior comes in two main kinds, marking the difference between *episodes* and *processes*.

[4] The 'glacier' or 'growing block' metaphor is used in the philosophical literature to illustrate a position concerning the tensed theory of time [24].

3 Episodes and Processes

Before continuing, it is time to introduce episodes and processes as particular kinds of events. I define an episode as an event that requires a completion. It is therefore a *telic* event, while processes are *atelic*[5] [14]. A football match, a run to the station, running for an hour or just being sitting for an hour are all examples of episodes (some static, some dynamic). On the contrary, processes are events that do not require a completion. A walk is a typical example of a process, while a walk from home to the station is an episode. Pouring water in a container or preparing the coffee are also considered as processes, but only if we think of them as occurring independently of their result.

This is established wisdom, but a crucial aspect of the novel view I am presenting is that processes become present as soon as their first temporal part is present[6], and they remain present for an extended interval by *embodying* new temporal parts that *accumulate* with the previous ones, so that processes are bearers of *cumulative properties* that may change over time. This accumulation phenomenon is such that, when a process is present, most of its parts are past, while only the part located at the present time (the moving front) is present. So, under the glacier metaphor, our processes are similar to *growing blocks*, while Galton's processes resemble *moving fronts*, or, more exactly, to the "dynamo" that drives their move [8, p. 334]. So, with the due adjustments, the two approaches may be coexist, with the latter being more suitable to *explain* why the block grows, and the former to *describe* what happens to the whole growing block.

A further characteristic of processes is that they can finish anytime, with no need of completion, so that they are open-ended, but not open-started. Suppose for instance that a bicycle run started at 9, and was still continuing at 9:30 and at 10. If somebody starts observing the run at 9:30, she may ascribe cumulative properties to the process that started at 9:30, which is different from the one that started 9, as indeed the former is a proper part of the latter.

Episodes behave in a very different way. While processes keep accumulating parts that are genuinely new, parts of episodes are somehow *predefined a priori*, since, while still being able of later changes, they are conceptualised as parts before being perceived (and therefore becoming present). Like processes, episodes become present as soon as their first temporal part is present, but they remain only *partially* present until becoming *fully* present when their culminating part becomes present. On the contrary, processes are always fully present, since, whenever they are present, they have no parts that are not present yet. Note that being *fully/partially* present is very different from being *wholly/partly* present. Being wholly present means that all the parts are present, while being

[5] In DOLCE, telic events are called *accomplishments*, while atelic events are distinguished into *states* and *processes*. Here, for the sake of simplicity, states are considered as a particular case of processes.

[6] I will not discuss granularity issues here. Anyway, I am sympathetic with Galton's position according to which a walking process would be present even at a time when the first step is still in the air, assuming that the intention to run remains constant.

fully present means that there are no parts yet to be present (although some parts may be past). Wholly presence implies fully presence, but not viceversa.

This means that episodes have *essential parts* that have to become present, sooner or later, in order for the episode to be fully present[7]. For an episode, being partially present means that there is a part that is not present *yet*. We are then in the position to define the meaning of *ongoing* precisely: for processes, being ongoing is just synonym of being present. For episodes, it means being partially present. Although they are very different from each other, there is an important relationship between episodes and processes: for an episode to be present at t, there must be a corresponding *realization* process present at t. We shall say that an episode is *gradually embodied* by a process. When the embodiment is complete, the episode becomes fully present, so we may say it is *constituted* by a process that is temporally co-located with it[8].

Before explaining the embodiment notion more in detail, let me illustrate the temporal behavior of processes and episodes by means of Fig. 1. Suppose e is a football match episode, consisting of two parts, the first half ($e1$) and the second half ($e2$). The figure shows that, when $t1$ is present (situation a), the process p

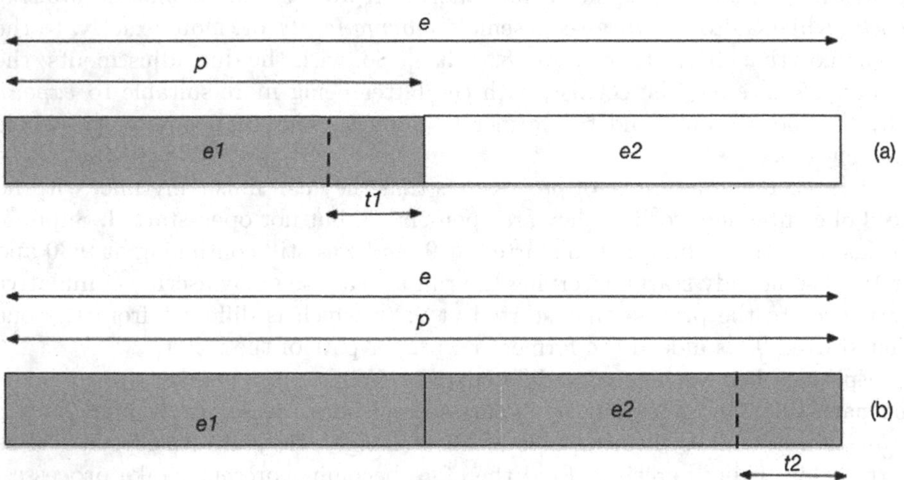

Fig. 1. Episode e being *gradually embodied* by process p. (a) describes the situation where $t1$ is present, and (b) the situation when $t2$ is present. For the sake of generality, reference times $t1$ and $t2$ are assumed as intervals and not as instants.

[7] Of course, a *past* episode must have been fully present previously. Once an episode of a given kind is aborted, it is not "registered" as an episode of that kind.

[8] The fact that an episode and its realizing process are temporally co-located does not mean that they have the same temporal parts. For instance, a process of walking that happens to stop at the station is different from an episode of walking from home to the station, since the focal qualities [10] of the two events are different: some qualities of the station (its location) are in the focus of the latter, but not of the former.

has been ongoing until then (its part located at $t1$ being the "moving front"), embodying therefore $e1$, which has just become fully present. e is however only partially present, since $e2$ is not present yet (it is still *unembodied*). When $t2$ is present (situation b), since p has been continuing, $e2$ is now fully present as an *embodied* part, and since it completes e, e is also fully present. $e1$ is not present any more, still being an (embodied) part of e.

4 Ongoing and Future Events as Variable Embodiments

Let us now discuss in more detail what it means to consider events as variable embodiments, and what are the practical consequences of this approach. The notion of variable embodiment has been introduced by Fine [6], and then refined, notably, by Moltmann [18,19]. Using Moltmann's words,

> "A variable embodiment, according to Fine, is an entity that allows for the replacement of constituting material and thus may have different material manifestations in different circumstances. Organisms and artifacts, in particular, are variable embodiments. They allow for a replacement of constituting matter and thus may have different material manifestations at different times. Variable embodiments are not identical with their constituting matter, but rather are entities associated with a function mapping a time to their material manifestation at the time. Variable embodiments differ from 'rigid embodiments', which are entities that do not allow for a replacement of their immediate parts" [19, p. 4].

A classic example of variable embodiment is a river, but for our purposes the example of a lake is more appropriate. Of course, a lake may be filled with different quantities of water at different times, and yet we say it remains the same lake. According to Fine, the referent of 'the water in the lake' (in its *de dicto* interpretation) is a variable embodiment. But also the lake itself, including its basin, is a variable embodiment: using Fine's words, we have therefore two variable embodiments: a *content* (the water), and a *container-cum-content* (the lake). Now we may admit that a lake is temporarily empty of water, and still it is the same lake. This means that the content may lack its manifestation—the water, but still the container-cum-content exhibits the properties necessary for its identification, e.g., its geographical location. Another example closer to our goals is 'the book John needs to write', which according to Moltmann [19] is a variable embodiment that does not have a manifestation in the actual circumstances, but only in those circumstances in which John's needs are fulfilled. She uses here the variable embodiment mechanism to explain a reference to a future object. The idea described in this paper is to use the same approach to also explain references to future events. The possibility to consider temporal entities as variable embodiments was briefly suggested by Kit Fine, but never exploited in practice, as far as I know:

> "A process—such as the erosion of a cliff, for example—may be taken to be a variable embodiment whose manifestations are the different states of erosion of the cliff." [6, p. 72]

In terms of their behavior as variable embodiments, there is a striking analogy, in my opinion, between a lake and the water that fills it, on one hand, and an episode and the process that embodies it, on the other hand. A future episode is like a dried lake: from the shape and the position of its basin we know—roughly—where the lake is located, and similarly, on the basis of our previsions and expectations, we know—roughly—where the future episode is (will be?) located. The water that comes in is like the time that comes: the lake becomes gradually "alive" (fully perceivable in all its aspects), being filled (embodied) by water, while the episode becomes gradually present (fully perceivable in all its aspects), being embodied by actual events. There are several differences, of course. One is that the lake—at least at the beginning of the filling process—embodies its parts synchronically, since when a new amount of water arrives the previous one is still there, so all the embodied parts are present at each time the lake is present. The episode, on the contrary, embodies its parts diachronically, since when a part becomes present the previous one is not present any more, so the embodied parts are spread out in time. This is a consequence of the fact that the lake is an object, while the episode is an event[9]. A further difference is that an episode may be embodied only once: because of the irreversibility of time, once a part is embodied, it "freezes".

On the other hand, it is easy to see that the water that gradually fills the lake is analogous to the process that gradually embodies the episode. While the lake, as a container-cum-content, exists without being embodied by the content, the content exists only if it is embodied. Similarly, a future episode exists (at least in the mind of somebody) as soon as its characteristics are uniquely determined, but the process embodying it only exists when it becomes present.

In the light of this discussion, let us now consider the different properties episodes and processes may have, how they are related to those of their embodiments, and why we can claim that events may be subjects of genuine change. Following Moltmann [19, p. 5], a generic event, understood as a variable embodiment, will have, at a time t, some *local* properties (if any) inherited from those of its embodiment at t, as well as *global* properties cumulatively depending on previous embodiments. They will be both *dynamic* properties, since they may change during the embodiment process. In addition, if the variable embodiment is not just a content, but a container-cum-content, it will also have some properties that are specific of the container (say, specific of the lake's size and location). Although these properties may change in time, their truth does not depend on what the actual embodiment is. They will be therefore *static* properties. Note that a process has only dynamic properties, while an episode may have both

[9] Indeed, a popular distinction between objects and events is based on the fact that an object is wholly present whenever it is present, while an event is always partially present. These notions are notoriously difficult to formalize [5], while they are unproblematic under the present approach.

dynamic and static properties. In particular, the *expected* starting and ending times of a future episode (or its temporal location) may be considered as static properties. The *actual* starting time will be the starting time of the process that embodies the episode. Also, the mereological properties of an episode (having or not a particular part, or a part of a certain kind) can be considered as static properties. An important consequence of having such static properties is that among them there are those that are *essential* for an episode, contributing in this way to endow it with a rigid identifier (OID).

Let us consider now the properties mentioned in the introduction:

1. *Local properties:* the speed of a process, at a time t, can be defined as the average speed of its moving front at t (speed is therefore understood as a quality of an event). The speed of an ongoing event will be just the speed of its realization process.
2. *Cumulative properties:* the score of a football match, at a time t, is a global property of its embodying process at t.
3. *Contextual properties:* these are local properties of (the moving front of) the realization process, which are inherited by the ongoing episode. For instance, a football match may have the property of being under the sunshine at time $t1$, and under the rain at time $t2$.
4. *Modal properties:* because of the way they have been defined, both processes and episodes are perfect bearers of modal properties, as long as they are ongoing or future. So, an ongoing process may evolve in one way or another, a future flight may change its starting and ending times, and an ongoing match may end with a tie or not. On the contrary, past episodes and processes are considered as "frozen", and for them the standard assumptions concerning events still apply.

In conclusion, let me recap the reasons why I claim that events—so conceived—may be subjects of genuine change. In the view I have presented, an event's change is not just a variation concerning two different temporal parts that have different properties. The presence of cumulative properties is perhaps the most vivid example why this is not so. A cumulative property is a global property of an event, reflecting at a given time the contribution of multiple past temporal parts. If the same event (say, the football match) has the cumulative property P at time $t1$ and P' at time $t2$, then we can say it has genuinely changed.

5 A Preliminary Axiomatization

In the following, I will adopt a standard tenseless parthood relation $P(x, y)$ for intervals of time, and a tensed version $P(x, y, t)$ to express the dynamic mereological behavior of events. Both of them will be assumed to satisfy the axioms of standard extensional mereology, which I will omit here for the sake of space (note that, differently from [3], these axioms are not constrained to hold only when the arguments of P are present).

I will also rely on Allen's interval logic [1] to express some useful temporal relations holding between temporal entities each of which can be either an event of a time interval. Since, on the basis of previous discussion, I am assuming that events' temporal location may change in time, I will add a temporal index to express the time interval that is assumed to be present when the temporal relation holds. For the sake of simplicity, I will consider these relations as primitives, omitting their axiomatization (notice that they are mutually exclusive):

(D1) $Sts(x, y, t)$ *(when t is present, x starts y)*
(D2) $Fin(x, y, t)$ *(when t is present, x finishes y)*
(D3) $Drn(x, y, t)$ *(when t is present, x is during y)*
(D4) $Ovl(x, y, t)$ *(when t is present, x overlays y)*
(D5) $Cloc(x, y, t)$ *(when t is present, x and y are colocated in time)*
(D6) $Ins(x, y, t) \triangleq Sts(x, y, t) \vee Drn(x, y, t) \vee Fin(x, y, t) \vee Cloc(x, y, t)$

Note that, according to (D6), being inside an event means just happening while the event is ongoing, without necessarily being a temporal part of it. We shall define the notion of *temporal part* as follows:

(D7) $TP(x, y, t) \triangleq Ins(x, y, t) \wedge P(x, y, t) \wedge \neg\exists z(Ins(x, y, t) \wedge \neg P(z, x, t))$

So the temporal part of an event includes all the parts (such as spatial parts) that are co-located in certain interval of the event's time span. Now we can characterize the mereological behavior of presence in time as follows:

(A1) $Pre(x, t) \wedge P(t, t') \rightarrow Pre(x, t')$
(A2) $Pre(x, t) \rightarrow \exists y(TP(y, x, t) \wedge Pre(y, t))$
(A3) $Pre(x, t) \wedge Ins(x, y, t) \rightarrow Pre(y, t)$
(A4) $P(x, y, t) \wedge Pre(x, t) \wedge t' > t \rightarrow P(x, y, t')$
(D8) $FP(x, t) \triangleq Pre(x, t) \wedge \forall y(P(y, x, t) \rightarrow Pre(y, t) \vee \exists t'(Pre(y, t') \wedge t' < t))$

Note that, according to (A2), if an event is present at t, then it is not necessarily wholly present at t. The interpretation of the presence predicate is therefore different from [3], since it does not admit presence dissectivity. Axiom (A3) links the presence of an event with the presence of a co-located event. (A4) states that, as soon as a part of an event becomes present, it keeps being a part at any future time; this means that past events, but not future or ongoing events, cannot change their parts in time. Finally, (D8) defines the notion of *full presence*.

After these general axioms, let us now constrain the specific behavior of processes (Pr) and episodes (Ep):

(A5) $Pr(x) \rightarrow (Pre(x, t) \leftrightarrow Ovl(x, t, t) \vee Fin(t, x, t))$
(A6) $Ep(x) \rightarrow (Pre(x, t) \leftrightarrow \exists yz(Pr(y) \wedge TP(z, x, t) \wedge Sts(z, x, t) \wedge Rlz(y, z, t))$
(A7) $Rlz(x, y, t) \rightarrow (Pr(x) \wedge Ep(y) \wedge Pre(y, t) \wedge Cloc(x, y))$

Axiom (A5) conveys the essence of the approach I presented. In practice, a process is an event with a *moving front*, since whenever it is present at t it must be such that the interval t overlaps or coincides with its ending part. All the other parts except the moving front are located in the past. In other words, a part of a process is present only if it is present at the front. On the other hand, according to (A2), if a process is present at t, then it has always a part "at its front".

Axiom (A6) constrains the way episodes are present. For an episode, to be present means that there is an ongoing process that has just realized an initial part of it. $Rlz(x, y, t)$ is a primitive standing for 'x is a realization of y at time t', which is only constrained by axiom (A7). Clearly this notion may deserve to be analyzed more in detail, as it implies some notion of causality, but this is outside the scope of the present paper.

6 Related Work and Conclusions: Let's Defrost Events!

I am well aware that the views expressed here may be seen as rather unconventional, so it is a bit difficult to compare them properly with previous approaches to conceptual modeling, besides the few I mentioned already [7–9,11]. Most of the work in temporal databases deals with temporal aspects of objects without including events explicitly in the domain, and those who consider events typically see them as instantaneous. An exception is the work by Terenziani *et al.* [14,22], who admit events as extended in time and explicitly account for the difference between telic events (episodes) and atelic ones (processes and states), although they (obviously) limit themselves to historical events. Another paper addressing the ontological foundations of events in conceptual modeling in the framework of the UFO ontology is the one by Guizzardi *et al.* [12], which presents some modeling patterns to account for complex events and temporal relationships, again limited to the case of historical events. Of course this is a preliminary work, whose main relevance—independently of the ontological details discussed here—would be to show that ongoing and future events *can* actually be endowed with rigid identifiers, and hence be considered as first-class citizens, without the restrictions coming from the view that considers them as frozen in time.

In the future, I plan to integrate this approach with the general theory of events, scenes, and relationships presented in [10], hopefully finding a way to harmonize it with the notion of process developed by Galton and Mizoguchi. On the application side, I plan to consider specific practical cases, especially those involving business processes and service systems, which seem to rely on a notion of *activity* poorly formalized so far.

Acknowledgements. I am grateful to Giancarlo Guizzardi and Tiago Prince Sales for some interesting discussions that motivated the need for this approach. I am also very grateful to Antony Galton and the anonymous reviewers for their constructive comments. Part of this work has been done in the framework of project 'KAOS: Knowledge-Aware Operational Support', funded by the Euregio Tirol-Südtirol-Trentino.

References

1. Allen, J.F.: Maintaining knowledge about temporal intervals. Commun. ACM **26**(11), 832–843 (1983)

2. Arp, R., Smith, B., Spear, A.D.: Building Ontologies with Basic Formal Ontology. MIT Press, Cambridge (2015)
3. Borgo, S., Masolo, C.: Foundational choices in DOLCE. In: Staab, S., Studer, R. (eds.) Handbook on Ontologies. IHIS, pp. 361–381. Springer, Heidelberg (2009). doi:10.1007/978-3-540-92673-3_16
4. Casati, R., Varzi, A.C.: Events. In: Stanford Encyclopedia of Philosophy (2014)
5. Crisp, T.M., Smith, D.P.: 'Wholly present' defined. Philos. Phenomenol. Res. **71**(2), 318–344 (2005)
6. Fine, K.: Things and their parts. Midwest Stud. Philos. **23**(1), 61–74 (1999)
7. Galton, A.: On what goes on: the ontology of processes and events. In: Bennett, B., Fellbaum, C. (eds.) Formal Ontology in Information Systems, pp. 3–11 (2006)
8. Galton, A.: Experience and history: processes and their relation to events. J. Logic Comput. **18**(3), 323–340 (2007)
9. Galton, A., Mizoguchi, R.: The water falls but the waterfall does not fall: new perspectives on objects, processes and events. Appl. Ontol. **4**(2), 71–107 (2009)
10. Guarino, N., Guizzardi, G.: Relationships and events: towards a general theory of reification and truthmaking. In: Adorni, G., Cagnoni, S., Gori, M., Maratea, M. (eds.) AI*IA 2016. LNCS, vol. 10037, pp. 237–249. Springer, Cham (2016). doi:10.1007/978-3-319-49130-1_18
11. Guizzardi, G., Guarino, N., Almeida, J.P.A.: Ontological considerations about the representation of events and endurants in business models. In: La Rosa, M., Loos, P., Pastor, O. (eds.) BPM 2016. LNCS, vol. 9850, pp. 20–36. Springer, Cham (2016). doi:10.1007/978-3-319-45348-4_2
12. Guizzardi, G., Wagner, G., de Almeida Falbo, R., Guizzardi, R.S.S., Almeida, J.P.A.: Towards ontological foundations for the conceptual modeling of events. In: Ng, W., Storey, V.C., Trujillo, J.C. (eds.) ER 2013. LNCS, vol. 8217, pp. 327–341. Springer, Heidelberg (2013). doi:10.1007/978-3-642-41924-9_27
13. Hawley, K.: How Things Persist. Clarendon Press, Oxford (2001)
14. Khatri, V., Ram, S., Snodgrass, R.T., Terenziani, P.: Capturing telic/atelic temporal data semantics: generalizing conventional conceptual models. IEEE Trans. Knowl. Data Eng. **26**(3), 528–548 (2015)
15. Lombard, L.B.: Events. A Metaphysical Study. International Library of Philosophy. Routledge and Kegan Paul, London (1986)
16. Masolo, C., Borgo, S., Gangemi, A., Guarino, N., Oltramari, A.: The DOLCE ontology. Technical report Deliverable D18, European Community, IST Project 2001–33052 "WonderWeb: Ontology Infrastructure for the Semantic Web" (2003)
17. Merricks, T.: Endurance and indiscernibility. J. Philos. **91**(4), 165–184 (1994)
18. Moltmann, F.: Abstract Objects and the Semantics of Natural Language. Oxford University Press, Oxford (2013)
19. Moltmann, F.: Variable objects and truthmaking. In: Dumitru, M. (ed.) Metaphysics, Meaning, and Modality. Oxford University Press, Oxford (2014)
20. Scheer, R.K.: Knowledge of the future. Mind **80**(318), 212–226 (1971)
21. Stout, R.: Processes. Philosophy **72**(279), 19–27 (1997)
22. Terenziani, P.: Coping with events in temporal relational databases. IEEE Trans. Knowl. Data Eng. **25**(5), 1181–1185 (2013)
23. Wieringa, R.J., De Jonge, W.: Object identifiers, keys, and surrogates: object identifiers revisited. Theory Pract. Object Syst. **1**(2), 1–18 (1995)
24. Zimmerman, D.W.: The a-theory of time, the b-theory of time, and "taking tense seriously". Dialectica **59**(4), 401–457 (2005)

Ontological Evolutionary Encoding to Bridge Machine Learning and Conceptual Models: Approach and Industrial Evaluation

Ana C. Marcén[1,2(✉)], Francisca Pérez[2], and Carlos Cetina[2]

[1] Centro de Investigación en Métodos de Producción de Software, Universitat Politècnica de València, Camino de Vera, s/n, 46022 Valencia, Spain
acmarcen@usj.es

[2] SVIT Research Group, Universidad San Jorge, Autovía A-23 Zaragoza-Huesca Km. 299, 50830 Zaragoza, Spain
{mfperez,ccetina}@usj.es

Abstract. In this work, we propose an evolutionary ontological encoding approach to enable Machine Learning techniques to be used to perform Software Engineering tasks in models. The approach is based on a domain ontology to encode a model and on an Evolutionary Algorithm to optimize the encoding. As a result, the encoded model that is returned by the approach can then be used by Machine Learning techniques to perform Software Engineering tasks such as concept location, traceability link retrieval, reuse, impact analysis, etc. We have evaluated the approach with an industrial case study to recover the traceability link between the requirements and the models through a Machine Learning technique (RankBoost). Our results in terms of recall, precision, and the combination of both (F-measure) show that our approach outperforms the baseline (Latent Semantic Indexing). We also performed a statistical analysis to assess the magnitude of the improvement.

Keywords: Machine learning · Traceability link recovery · Evolutionary computation · Model driven engineering

1 Introduction

Machine Learning (ML) is known as the branch of artificial intelligence that gathers statistical, probabilistic, and optimization algorithms, which learn empirically. ML has a wide range of applications, including search engines, medical diagnosis, text and handwriting recognition, image screening, load forecasting, marketing and sales diagnosis, etc. Even though the research on ML has been applied in Software Engineering tasks that target source code artifacts [7,33], other software artifacts such as conceptual models have been neglected.

Most of the ML techniques are designed to process feature vectors as inputs [8]. Feature vectors are known as the ordered enumeration of features that characterize the object being observed [10]. Therefore, to apply ML techniques in

H.C. Mayr et al. (Eds.): ER 2017, LNCS 10650, pp. 491–505, 2017.
https://doi.org/10.1007/978-3-319-69904-2_37

models, the first challenge consists in identifying the features from models and selecting the most suitable ones to encode the models in feature vectors.

In this work, we propose the Ontological Evolutionary Encoding (OnEvEn) approach, which allows models to be encoded in feature vectors. The approach is based on a domain ontology to transform each model to a feature vector and on Evolutionary Computation to perform the selection of the most relevant features. Once the most relevant features have been selected, the approach generates as output the feature vectors from the models according to the selected features. Then the ML techniques can make use of these feature vectors to perform Software Engineering tasks.

The presented approach was evaluated in CAF[1], a worldwide provider of railway solutions. Thanks to our OnEvEn approach, their models were encoded, making it possible for a ML technique (RankBoost [16] that belongs to the family of Learning to Rank) to take advantage of these encoded models to recover the traceability between the requirements and the models. The outcome shows that our approach provides the best results, and proves that the approach can be applied in a real world environment. The statistical analysis of the results assesses the magnitude of the improvement.

The contribution of this paper is twofold. First, we show how to encode models by means of our OnEvEn approach in order to be able to apply ML in models. Second, we provide evidence that by using our OnEvEn approach, ML techniques are applicable to Software Engineering tasks such as traceability link recovery between the requirements and the models.

The remainder of this paper is structured as follows: Sect. 2 presents our OnEvEn approach. Section 3 provides the evaluation carried out. Section 4 describes the threats to validity. Section 5 presents the related work, and Sect. 6 concludes the paper.

2 The OnEvEn Approach

The objective of the OnEvEn approach is to provide the encoding of a model in the form of a feature vector. To do this, the approach consists of three phases (see Fig. 1): Ontological Encoding, Evolutionary Encoding, and Feature Selection. In the first phase, the approach encodes the model based on a domain ontology. In the second phase, the approach generates a mask, taking advantage of a knowledge base. In the third phase, the approach applies the mask to the feature vector that is the result of the Ontological Encoding. As output, the approach generates a feature vector, which is the encoding of the model.

The input of the approach consists of a model, a domain ontology, and the knowledge base that is provided by domain experts. Specifically, the knowledge base consists in a set of triplets that are generated using the domain experts' experience, results, and documentation. In Fig. 1, each triplet of the knowledge base is composed of a requirement description, a model whose fragment is marked by a dashed square with different background, and an assessment.

[1] www.caf.net/en.

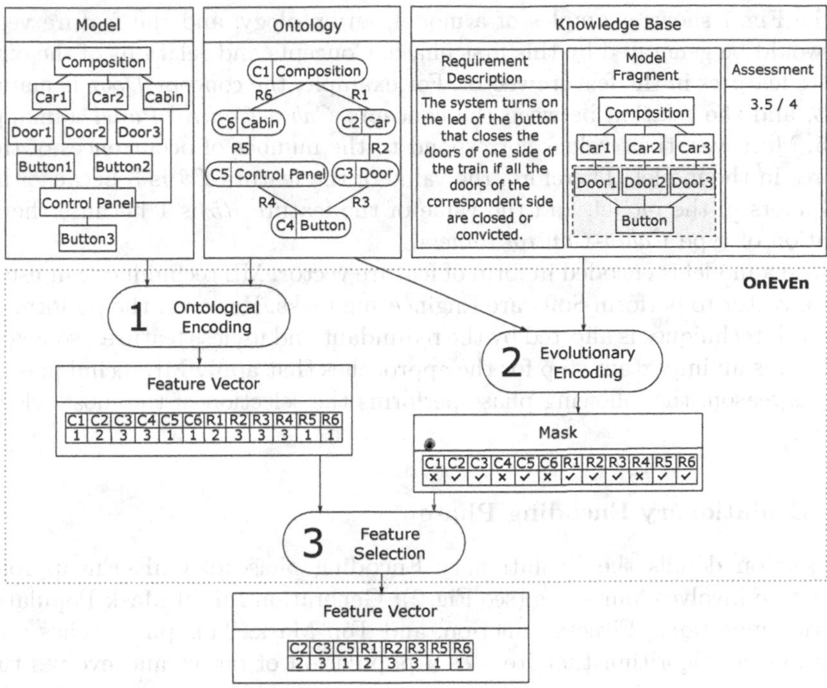

Fig. 1. Overview of our OnEvEn approach.

The requirement description uses natural language to define the requirement. The model fragment consists of an element or a set of elements that belongs to a model. To formalize these model fragments, we use the Common Variability Language (CVL) [27]. The assessment determines if the model fragment realizes the requirement to a greater or lesser extent. That is, the assessment determines the similarity between the requirement description and the model fragment.

Figure 1 shows an example of the knowledge base to perform requirement traceability. However, if we plan to perform concept location [21], the knowledge base would be composed of concept descriptions, model fragments, and assessments. Therefore, the knowledge base depends on the Software Engineering task that is going to be performed.

2.1 Ontological Encoding Phase

In this first phase, the model is turned into a feature vector based on the domain ontology. We consider each concept and relation in the ontology as a feature in the feature vector. The value of each feature is computed as the frequency of the concept or the relation in the model. Therefore, the output of this phase is a feature vector that represents the model, taking into account the concepts and the relations of the ontology.

The Fig. 1 shows examples of a model, an ontology, and the feature vector that would be generated by this first phase. Concepts and relations of the ontology are features in the feature vector. For example, the concept *Door* is mapped as *C3*, and the relation between the concepts *Cabin-Control Panel* is mapped as R5. Moreover, their values correspond to the number of occurrences of these features in the model. Therefore, the value of the feature *C3* is 3 because there are 3 doors in the model, and the value of the feature *R5* is 1 because there is 1 relation of type *Cabin-Control Panel*.

Once a model is encoded in form of feature vector, ML techniques can use the feature vector to perform Software Engineering tasks. However, the performance of the ML techniques is affected by the redundant and useless features, so Feature Selection is an important step for the approaches that apply ML techniques [23]. For this reason, the following phase performs the selection of the most relevant features.

2.2 Evolutionary Encoding Phase

This section details the Evolutionary Encoding phase of OnEvEn approach. This phase involves four steps (see Fig. 2): Generation Initial Mask Population, Genetic Operations, Fitness Function, and Top Mask. This phase relies on an Evolutionary Algorithm that iterates a population of masks and evolves them using genetic operations. As output, the phase provides the top mask, which enables only the features that optimize the model encoding.

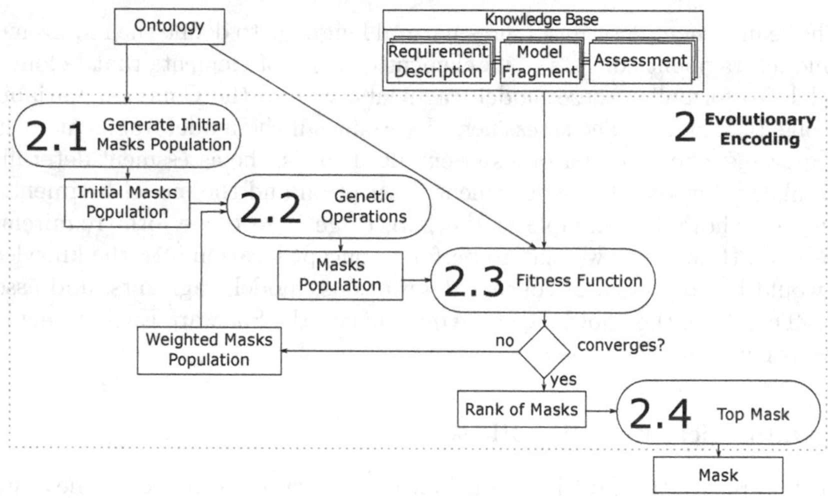

Fig. 2. Details of the evolutionary encoding phase of the OnEvEn approach.

Generate Initial Masks Population. The first step is to generate randomly a population of masks. Figure 1 shows an example of a mask. Each position of the mask indicates if a concept or relation that belongs to the ontology is enabled or disabled. In order words, if the concept or the relation should be used or not for the encoding.

Genetic Operations. The second step is to generate a set of masks that could optimize the model encoding. The generation of masks is done by applying genetic operators that are adapted to work on masks. In other words, new masks that are based on the existing ones are generated through the use of two genetic operators: the mutation and the crossover.

I. The crossover operator is used to imitate the sexual reproduction that is followed by some living beings in nature to breed new individuals. In other words, two individuals mix their genomic information to give birth to a new individual that holds some genetic information from one parent and some from the other one. This could make that the new individual adapt better (or worse) to its living environment depending on the genetic information inherited from its parents. Following this idea, our crossover operator that is applied to masks takes two masks as input and combines them into two new individuals.

II. The mutation operator is used to imitate the mutations that randomly occur in nature when new individuals are born. In other words, a new individual has a small difference with respect to its parents that could make it adapt better (or worse) to its living environment. Following this idea, the mutation operator that is applied to masks takes a mask as input and mutates it into a new one that is produced as output. Specifically, the mutation operator can perform randomly two kinds of modifications based on the features, to enable a feature that is disabled in the mask, or vice versa, to disable a feature that is enabled in the mask.

Fitness Function. The third step of the process consists of the assessment of each candidate mask that is produced according to a fitness function. The fitness score of each mask in the population is calculated as follows:

I. Knowledge Base Encoding generates a set of feature vectors, which correspond to the triplets of the knowledge base. To encode a triplet, the main terms of the requirement description and the model fragment are extracted using well-established Information Retrieval (IR) techniques: tokenizer, Parts-of-Speech (POS) tagging technique, and stemming techniques. Then, these terms are used to generate the feature vector as the Sect. 2.1 describes.

II. Training and Testing are performed by means of cross-validation [20]. Cross-validation consists of randomly dividing the knowledge base into k-independent partitions. Then, $k-1$ of the partitions are used to train a classifier, which consists in a rule-set that is learnt from a given knowledge base [26]. Then, this classifier is used to test the partition that is left out. This procedure is repeated k times, each time leaving out another partition. This produces k estimations of the classifier, allowing assessment of its central tendency and variance [18].

III. Assignment of the Fitness Score is performed according to the central tendency and variance that are obtained for the classifier. Therefore, the fitness score assesses the relevance of each mask candidate based on how much the results are optimized by using this mask.

IV. Loop At this point, if the stop condition is met, the process will stop returning the rank of the masks. If the stop condition has not been met yet, the Evolutionary Algorithm will keep its execution one generation more.

Top Mask. The mask with the highest fitness score will be the top mask. This step returns the top mask as output, which allows the model encoding to be optimized by selecting only the most relevant features.

2.3 Feature Selection Phase

In the third phase, we apply feature selection on the feature vector that is obtained in the first phase. To do so, the mask that is generated in the second phase is used to reduce the features of the feature vector. As the Fig. 1 shows, each disabled feature in the mask is discarded in the feature vector. Therefore, the feature vector is only composed by the features that are enabled in the mask. As output, our OnEvEn approach returns this feature vector as encoding of the model. In fact, taking into account that the mask is generated to select the most relevant features and avoid the useless and redundant features, the feature vector obtained is able to optimize the performance of ML technique that is used to perform Software Engineering tasks in models.

3 Evaluation

This section presents the evaluation of our approach: the experimental setup, a description of the case study where we applied the evaluation, the implementation details, the obtained results, and the statistical analysis.

3.1 Experimental Setup

The goal of this experiment is to determine if our OnEvEn approach can be used to encode models so that the ML techniques can take advantage of the encoding to perform Software Engineering tasks. In addition, we compare the OnEvEn approach with a baseline.

Figure 3 shows an overview of the process that was followed to evaluate the baseline and our OnEvEn approach. The top part shows the documentation provided by our industrial partner: the requirements, the product models, and the approved traceability between requirements and product models. The Test Cases are prepared from the documentation provided by our industrial partner, and each test case comprises a requirement and a model fragment of each product model that might be relevant for that requirement. The ontology and the knowledge base that our approach uses as input are provided by a domain expert.

On the one hand, the baseline approach (see the dotted red elements of Fig. 3) uses Latent Semantic Indexing (LSI) to analyze the relevance between requirements provided in Test Cases and the model fragments. There are many Information Retrieval techniques, but most research efforts show better results when applying LSI [24]. On the other hand, our approach (see the solid blue elements of Fig. 3) encodes the models in both the Test Cases and the knowledge base in order to enable the application of ML techniques to models. In this evaluation, we use RankBoost [16] for the ML classifier. RankBoost belongs to the family of Learning to Rank (LETOR) ML algorithms that automatically address ranking tasks [31]. LETOR has been successfully applied in a lot of fields [9] like document retrieval, collaborative filtering, expert finding, anti web spam, sentiment analysis, product rating, and feature location. Our OnEvEn approach enables the application of LETOR to models.

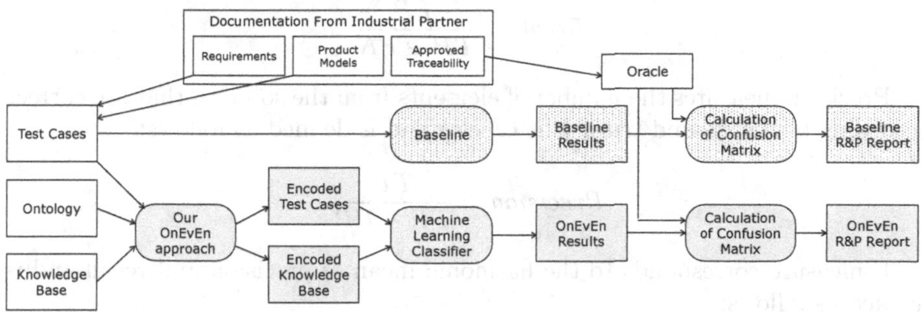

Fig. 3. Experimental setup

We run the baseline and OnEvEn to obtain as results a ranking of relevant model fragments for each requirement of the Test Cases. Next, we first take the best solution of the ranking of the baseline approach, and then we take the best solution of the ranking of the OnEvEn approach. These best solutions are then compared with an oracle, which is the ground truth. The oracle is prepared using the approved traceability provided by our industrial partner. Once the comparison is performed, a confusion matrix for each approach is calculated.

A confusion matrix is a table that is often used to describe the performance of a classification model (in this case both the baseline and OnEvEn) on a set of test data (the best solutions) for which the true values are known (from the oracle). In our case, each solution outputted by the approaches is a model fragment composed of a subset of the model elements that are part of the product model. Since the granularity is at the level of model elements, each model element presence or absence is considered as a classification. The confusion matrix distinguishes between the predicted values and the real values classifying them into four categories:

- True Positive (TP): values that are predicted as true (in the solution) and are true in the real scenario (the oracle).
- False Positive (FP): values that are predicted as true (in the solution) but are false in the real scenario (the oracle).
- True Negative (TN): values that are predicted as false (in the solution) and are false in the real scenario (the oracle).
- False Negative (FN): values that are predicted as false (in the solution) but are true in the real scenario (the oracle).

Then, some performance measurements are derived from the values in the confusion matrix. In particular, we create a report including three performance measurements (recall, precision, and F-measure), for each of the test cases for both the baseline and OnEvEn.

Recall measures the number of elements of the solution that are correctly retrieved by the proposed solution and is defined as follows:

$$Recall = \frac{TP}{TP + FN}$$

Precision measures the number of elements from the solution that are correct according to the ground truth (the oracle) and is defined as follows:

$$Precision = \frac{TP}{TP + FP}$$

F-measure corresponds to the harmonic mean of precision and recall and is defined as follows:

$$F - measure = 2 * \frac{Precision * Recall}{Precision + Recall} = \frac{2 * TP}{2TP + FP + FN}$$

Recall values can range between 0% (which means that no single model element from the realization of the requirement obtained from the oracle is present in any of the model fragments of the solution) to 100% (which means that all the model elements from the oracle are present in the solution). Precision values can range between 0% (which means that no single model fragment from the solution is present in the realization of the requirement obtained from the oracle) to 100% (which means that all the model fragments from the solution are present in the requirement realization from the oracle). A value of 100% precision and 100% recall implies that both the solution and the requirement realization from the oracle are the same.

3.2 CAF Case Study

The case study where we applied our approach was CAF, a worldwide provider of railway solutions. Their trains can be found all over the world and in different forms (regular trains, subway, light rail, monorail, etc.). A train unit is furnished with multiple pieces of equipment through its vehicles and cabins. These pieces of equipment are often designed and manufactured by different providers, and their aim is to carry out specific tasks for the train. Some examples of these devices are: the traction equipment, the compressors that feed the brakes, the pantograph that harvests power from the overhead wires, and the circuit breaker that isolates or connects the electrical circuits of the train. The control software of the train unit is in charge of making all the equipment cooperate to achieve the train functionality, while guaranteeing compliance with the specific regulations of each country.

Our evaluation is made up of 29 test cases, 247 concepts and 161 relationships in the ontology, and 102 triplet in the knowledge base. It is important to highlight that the requirements and the models of the knowledge base are different from the requirements and models of the test cases. The requirements have about 50 words and the models have about 1200 elements. For each test case, we followed the experimental setup described in Fig. 4. Finally, each test case was run 30 times. As suggested by [6], given the stochastic nature of OnEvEn approach, several repetitions are needed to obtain reliable results.

3.3 Implementation Details

We have used the Eclipse Modeling Framework to manipulate the models and CVL to manage the model fragments. The IR techniques used to process the language have been implemented using OpenNLP [1] for the POSTagger and the English (Porter 2) [3] stemming algorithm. LSI has been implemented using the Efficient Java Matrix Library (EJML [2]). The genetic operations are built upon the Watchmaker Framework for Evolutionary Computation [13]. Finally, RankBoost has been implemented using the library RankLib [11].

For the settings of the evolutionary algorithm of OnEvEn, we have mainly chosen values that are commonly used in the literature [25]. As suggested by [6], tuned parameters can outperform default values generally, but they are far from optimal in individual problem instances. Therefore, the objective of this paper is not to tune the values to improve the performance of our algorithm.

3.4 Results

This subsection presents the results obtained for each of the Test Cases by both the baseline and OnEvEn. Figure 4 shows the charts with the recall and precision results for the baseline (in the left side of the figure) and OnEvEn (in the right side of the figure). A dot in the graph represents the average result of precision and recall for each of the 29 Test Cases for the 30 repetitions.

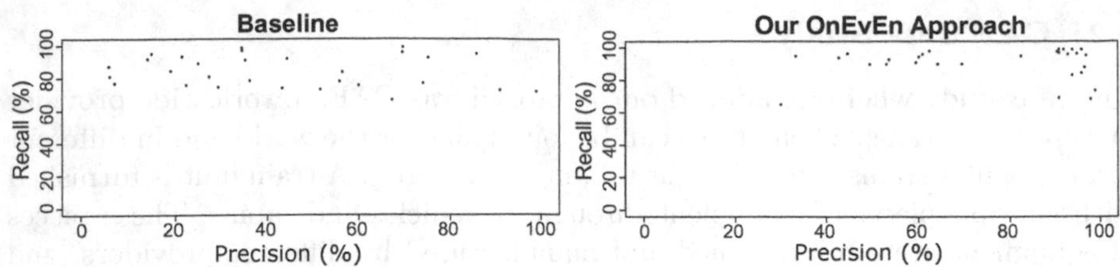

Fig. 4. Mean recall and precision values for baseline and OnEvEn approaches

Table 1 shows the mean values of recall, precision and F-measure of the graphs for both the baseline and OnEvEn. OnEvEn obtains the best results in recall and precision, providing an average value of 90.47% in recall and 75.19% in precision. The baseline obtains an average value of 84.22% in recall and 43.97% in precision. Hence, OnEvEn outperforms the baseline.

Table 1. Mean Values and Standard Deviations for Precision, Recall, and the F-Measure for Baseline and OnEvEn

	Recall $\pm$ (σ)	Precision $\pm$ (σ)	F-measure $\pm$ (σ)
Baseline	84.22 ± 9.58	43.97 ± 26.81	52.61 ± 23.35
OnEvEn	90.47 ± 9.68	75.19 ± 22.37	79.99 ± 15.33

3.5 Statistical Analysis

Statistically significant differences can be obtained even if they are so small as to be of no practical value [5]. Then it is important to assess if an approach is statistically better than another and to assess the magnitude of the improvement. *Effect size* measures are needed to analyze this.

For a non-parametric effect size measure, we use Vargha and Delaney's $\hat{A}_{12}$ [28]. $\hat{A}_{12}$ measures the probability that running one approach yields higher values than running another approach. If the two approaches are equivalent, then $\hat{A}_{12}$ will be 0.5.

The $\hat{A}_{12}$ value for recall between our OnEvEn approach and the baseline is 0.6938, which means that we would obtain better results for recall in 69.38% of the runs with OnEvEn. With regard to the precision, the $\hat{A}_{12}$ value between OnEvEn and the baseline is 0.8056, which shows a superiority of OnEvEn since its results are better in 80.56% of the runs. Hence, these results confirm that the use of our OnEvEn approach has impact on the results, specially on the results for precision.

4 Threats to Validity

In this section, we use the classification of threats of validity of [29] to acknowledge the limitations of our approach.

Construct validity: This aspect of validity reflects the extent to which the operational measures that are studied represent what the researchers have in mind. To minimize this risk, our evaluation is performed using three measures: precision, recall, and the F-measure. These measures are widely accepted in the software engineering research community.

Internal Validity: This aspect of validity is of concern when causal relations are examined. There is a risk that the factor being investigated may be affected by other neglected factors. RankBoost tend to overfit when the dataset is not large enough and there are many features [30]. Therefore, the number of triplets in our knowledge base may look small. However, Feature Selection in ML enables to avoid overfitting [19] so this threat has been reduced by Feature Selection through the Evolutionary Algorithm.

External Validity: This aspect of validity is concerned with to what extent it is possible to generalize the finding, and to what extent the findings are of relevance for other cases. Our OnEvEn approach is designed to encode models for using ML techniques, but there must be an ontology and a knowledge base. If these conditions are satisfied, the models of any domain could be encoded using this approach. Nonetheless, OnEvEn should be applied to other domains before assuring its generalization.

Reliability: This aspect is concerned with to what extent the data and the analysis are dependent on the specific researchers. To reduce this threat, the creation of the ontology and the knowledge were performed by a domain expert who was not involved in the research. Moreover, the requirements descriptions and the product models were provided by our industrial partner.

5 Related Work

In this section, we present the related works, which are divided into two parts. First, we overview research on Feature Selection. Second, we overview research papers on Requirements Traceability.

5.1 Feature Selection

Haiduc et al. [17] perform feature selection among 21 measures using the gain ratio technique during the retrieval of software artifacts. Ye et al. [34] apply feature selection in mapping bug reports to identify the features that have the most impact on the ranking performance. However, our approach makes use of models instead of other software artifacts such as source code and of a domain ontology as a basis for identifying the features.

Evolutionary Computation techniques have also recently been applied in Feature Selection. Xue et al. [32] present a survey of the state-of-art work on Evolutionary Computation for feature selection in different fields such as image analysis, text mining, and gene analysis. Our approach also takes advantage of Evolutionary Computation to perform feature selection, but it focuses on a domain ontology to encode models and on these encoded models to perform Software Engineering tasks.

5.2 Requirements Traceability

CERBERUS [15] provides a hybrid technique that combines information retrieval, execution tracing, and prune dependency analysis allowing to trace requirements to source code. Eaddy et al. [14] presents a systematic methodology for identifying which code is related to which requirement, and a suite of metrics for quantifying the amount of crosscutting code. Antoniol et al. [4] propose a method based on information retrieval to recover traceability links between source code and free text documents, such as, requirement specifications, design documents, manual pages, system development journals, error logs, and related maintenance reports. Zisman et al. [35] automate the generation of traceability relations between textual requirement artifacts and object models using heuristic rules. These approaches recover the traceability between source code and requirements. In contrast, our work recovers the traceability between requirements and models instead of source code.

Some works rely on models as the software artifacts to perform traceability. De Lucia et al. [12] present a traceability recovery method and tool based on LSI in the context of an artifact management system. Marcus and Maletic [22] use LSI for recovering the traceability relations between source code and documentation (manual, design documentation, requirement documents, test suites, etc.). Our approach makes it possible for a ML technique (Rank Boost) to take advantage of encoded models to recover traceability links between the requirements and the models. Our results show that Rank Boost significantly outperforms LSI in traceability link recovery between the requirements and the models of our industrial partner.

6 Conclusion

Machine Learning (ML) has a wide range of successful applications but current research efforts have neglected the application of ML to models. In this paper, we propose OnEvEn approach that encodes models in order to enable the application of ML techniques to models. We also show that by using our OnEvEn approach, ML techniques are applicable to Software Engineering tasks such as traceability link recovery between the requirements and the models.

We evaluate our OnEvEn approach in terms of precision, recall and F-measure. To do so, we compared it to a baseline in an industrial domain (firmware of train PLCS with CAF). We report our evaluation, including: experimental setup, results, statistical analysis, and threats to validity.

The results show that enabling the application of ML techniques by means of OnEvEn pays off for traceability link recovery. Results also show that our approach can be applied in real world environments. The statistical analysis of the results assesses the magnitude of the improvement of our approach.

Acknowledgments. This work has been developed with the financial support of the Spanish Ministry of Economy and Competitiveness under the project TIN2016-80811-P and co-financed with ERDF. We also thank both ITEA3 15010 REVaMP[2] Project and MINECO TIN2015-64397-R VARIAMOS Project.

References

1. Apache opennlp: Toolkit for the processing of natural language text. https://opennlp.apache.org/. Accessed Apr 2017
2. Efficient Java matrix library. http://ejml.org/. Accessed Apr 2017
3. The English (porter2) stemming algorithm. http://snowball.tartarus.org/algorithms/english/stemmer.html. Accessed Apr 2017
4. Antoniol, G., Canfora, G., Casazza, G., De Lucia, A., Merlo, E.: Recovering traceability links between code and documentation. IEEE Trans. Softw. Eng. **28**(10), 970–983 (2002)
5. Arcuri, A., Briand, L.: A hitchhiker's guide to statistical tests for assessing randomized algorithms in software engineering. Softw. Test. Verif. Reliab. **24**(3), 219–250 (2014)
6. Arcuri, A., Fraser, G.: Parameter tuning or default values? An empirical investigation in search-based software engineering. Empirical Softw. Eng. **18**(3), 594–623 (2013)
7. B Le, T.D., Lo, D., Le Goues, C., Grunske, L.: A learning-to-rank based fault localization approach using likely invariants. In: Proceedings of the 25th International Symposium on Software Testing and Analysis, pp. 177–188. ACM (2016)
8. Bianchini, M., Maggini, M., Jain, L.C.: Handbook on Neural Information Processing. Springer, Heidelberg (2013). doi:10.1007/978-3-642-36657-4
9. Cao, Z., Qin, T., Liu, T.Y., Tsai, M.F., Li, H.: Learning to rank: from pairwise approach to listwise approach. In: Proceedings of the 24th International Conference on Machine Learning, ICML 2007, pp. 129–136. ACM, New York (2007)
10. Chandrashekar, G., Sahin, F.: A survey on feature selection methods. Comput. Electr. Eng. **40**(1), 16–28 (2014)
11. Dang, V.: The lemur project - wiki - ranklib (2013). http://sourceforge.net/p/lemur/wiki/RankLib/. Accessed Apr 2017
12. De Lucia, A., Fasano, F., Oliveto, R., Tortora, G.: Enhancing an artefact management system with traceability recovery features. In: Proceedings of 20th IEEE International Conference on Software Maintenance, pp. 306–315. IEEE (2004)
13. Dyer, D.: The watchmaker framework for evolutionary computation (evolutionary/genetic algorithms for Java). http://watchmaker.uncommons.org/. Accessed Apr 2017
14. Eaddy, M., Aho, A., Murphy, G.C.: Identifying, assigning, and quantifying crosscutting concerns. In: Proceedings of the First International Workshop on Assessment of Contemporary Modularization Techniques, p. 2 (2007)

15. Eaddy, M., Aho, A.V., Antoniol, G., Guéhéneuc, Y.G.: Cerberus: tracing requirements to source code using information retrieval, dynamic analysis, and program analysis. In: ICPC 2008 Conference, pp. 53–62. IEEE (2008)
16. Freund, Y., Iyer, R., Schapire, R.E., Singer, Y.: An efficient boosting algorithm for combining preferences. J. Mach. Learn. Res. **4**(Nov), 933–969 (2003)
17. Haiduc, S., Bavota, G., Oliveto, R., De Lucia, A., Marcus, A.: Automatic query performance assessment during the retrieval of software artifacts. In: International Conference on Automated Software Engineering, pp. 90–99. ACM (2012)
18. Hirzel, A.H., Le Lay, G., Helfer, V., Randin, C., Guisan, A.: Evaluating the ability of habitat suitability models to predict species presences. Ecol. Model. **199**(2), 142–152 (2006)
19. Joachims, T.: Text categorization with support vector machines: learning with many relevant features. In: Nédellec, C., Rouveirol, C. (eds.) ECML 1998. LNCS, vol. 1398, pp. 137–142. Springer, Heidelberg (1998). doi:10.1007/BFb0026683
20. Kohavi, R., et al.: A study of cross-validation and bootstrap for accuracy estimation and model selection. In: IJCAI, Stanford, CA, vol. 14, pp. 1137–1145 (1995)
21. Marcus, A., Sergeyev, A., Rajlich, V., Maletic, J.: An information retrieval approach to concept location in source code. In: Proceedings of the 11th Working Conference on Reverse Engineering, pp. 214–223, November 2004
22. Marcus, A., Maletic, J.I.: Recovering documentation-to-source-code traceability links using latent semantic indexing. In: Proceedings of 25th International Conference on Software Engineering, pp. 125–135. IEEE (2003)
23. Navot, A., Shpigelman, L., Tishby, N., Vaadia, E.: Nearest neighbor based feature selection for regression and its application to neural activity. Adv. Neural Inf. Process. Syst. **18**, 995 (2006)
24. Poshyvanyk, D., Gueheneuc, Y.G., Marcus, A., Antoniol, G., Rajlich, V.: Feature location using probabilistic ranking of methods based on execution scenarios and information retrieval. IEEE Trans. Softw. Eng. **33**(6), 420–432 (2007)
25. Sayyad, A.S., Ingram, J., Menzies, T., Ammar, H.: Scalable product line configuration: a straw to break the camel's back. In: 2013 IEEE/ACM 28th International Conference on Automated Software Engineering (ASE), pp. 465–474, November 2013
26. Shabtai, A., Moskovitch, R., Elovici, Y., Glezer, C.: Detection of malicious code by applying machine learning classifiers on static features: a state-of-the-art survey. Inf. Secur. Tech. Rep. **14**(1), 16–29 (2009)
27. Svendsen, A., Zhang, X., Lind-Tviberg, R., Fleurey, F., Haugen, Ø., Møller-Pedersen, B., Olsen, G.K.: Developing a software product line for train control: a case study of CVL. In: Bosch, J., Lee, J. (eds.) SPLC 2010. LNCS, vol. 6287, pp. 106–120. Springer, Heidelberg (2010). doi:10.1007/978-3-642-15579-6_8
28. Vargha, A., Delaney, H.D.: A critique and improvement of the CL common language effect size statistics of McGraw and Wong. J. Educ. Behav. Stat. **25**(2), 101–132 (2000)
29. Wohlin, C., Runeson, P., Höst, M., Ohlsson, M.C., Regnell, B., Wesslén, A.: Experimentation in Software Engineering. Springer Science & Business Media, Heidelberg (2012). doi:10.1007/978-3-642-29044-2
30. Wolf, L., Martin, I.: Robust boosting for learning from few examples. In: Computer Vision and Pattern Recognition, vol. 1, pp. 359–364. IEEE (2005)
31. Xuan, J., Monperrus, M.: Learning to combine multiple ranking metrics for fault localization. In: Proceedings of the 30th International Conference on Software Maintenance and Evolution (2014)

32. Xue, B., Zhang, M., Browne, W.N., Yao, X.: A survey on evolutionary computation approaches to feature selection. IEEE Trans. Evol. Comput. **20**(4), 606–626 (2016)
33. Ye, X., Bunescu, R., Liu, C.: Learning to rank relevant files for bug reports using domain knowledge. In: Proceedings of the 22nd ACM SIGSOFT International Symposium on Foundations of Software Engineering, pp. 689–699. ACM (2014)
34. Ye, X., Bunescu, R., Liu, C.: Mapping bug reports to relevant files: a ranking model, a fine-grained benchmark, and feature evaluation. IEEE Trans. Softw. Eng. **42**(4), 379–402 (2016)
35. Zisman, A., Spanoudakis, G., Pérez-Miñana, E., Krause, P.: Tracing software requirements artifacts. In: Software Engineering Research and Practice, pp. 448–455 (2003)

The OntoREA© Accounting and Finance Model: Ontological Conceptualization of the Accounting and Finance Domain

Christian Fischer-Pauzenberger and Walter S.A. Schwaiger(✉)

Institute of Management Science – TU Wien, Vienna, Austria
{christian.fischer-pauzenberger, walter.schwaiger}@tuwien.ac.at

Abstract. Geerts and McCarthy [1, 2] extended McCarthy's [3] Resource-Event-Agent (REA) accounting model with a forward-looking perspective by including commitments and economic contracts. Schwaiger [4] investigated the extended REA accounting model with respect to accounting and finance requirements and developed the REA-based Asset-Liability-Equity (ALE) accounting model. Due to the ontological neutrality of UML class diagrams [5], financial instruments are not concisely conceptualized. This holds true especially for derivative instruments which have very special temporal modal and identity-related peculiarities. For modeling them the OntoUML language developed by Guizzardi [6] provides a solid foundation. In this article ontological meta-properties of OntoUML are used to specify these peculiarities and to derive the *OntoREA© Accounting and Finance Model*, which constitutes a valid ontology-based conceptualization of the accounting and finance domain. This model should be beneficial especially for business analysts who have to understand and develop conceptual models for up-to-date enterprise and accounting information systems.

Keywords: Accounting · Finance · REA accounting model · OntoUML · Unified Foundational Ontology · Ontology-driven conceptual modeling · Design patterns

1 Introduction

Geerts and McCarthy [1, 2] extend McCarthy's *Resource-Event-Agent (REA) accounting model* to the REAC accounting model by introducing the concept of commitments (C). The REAC model goes beyond the accounting domain as it allows the modeling of future events. Furthermore the definition of economic contracts as bundling of commitments opens the model for mapping more complex situations. The REAC accounting model evolved to the *REA business ontology* as well as the *Accounting and economic ontology* and was promoted as such as industry standard in (ISO 15944-4, [7]). Schwaiger [4] investigates the REAC accounting model with respect to the traditional Asset-Liability-Equity (ALE) accounting logic. He extends the model by including debit and credit events to address changes in the ALE-categorized economic resources. This semantic extension provides the foundation for modeling

H.C. Mayr et al. (Eds.): ER 2017, LNCS 10650, pp. 506–519, 2017.
https://doi.org/10.1007/978-3-319-69904-2_38

non-derivative financial instruments as well and consequently can be understood as an important step for integrating the finance within the accounting domain.

One substantial drawback, however, is substantiated within the modeling language of all aforementioned models. The Unified Modeling Language (UML) class diagrams bear several deficiencies for modeling derivative instruments due to their special nature and behavior over time. Unlike tangible resources and non-derivative financial instruments, they can have a value of zero and are likely to change their ALE-status over time. Such meronymic (part-whole) and temporal modal properties can explicitly be specified in the Unified Foundational Ontology (UFO), which was established by Guizzardi [6]. Accordingly, it seems worthwhile to conceptualize the finance domain in the UFO-based OntoUML language. Furthermore the usage of OntoUML as conceptual modeling language should allow an even deeper integration of the finance domain into the accounting domain, as this language was already used for modeling the REA accounting context. Gailly et al. [8] use the OntoUML language to classify the endurant primitives in the REA enterprise domain ontology (REA-EO) in terms of the metaphysical UFO upper-level ontology. Fischer-Pauzenberger and Schwaiger [9] deepen the anchoring of REA-based accounting models in the accounting domain by developing the OntoREA accounting model which represents the REA-based Asset-Liabiliy-Equity (ALE) accounting model in terms of the OntoUML language.

The deeper integration of the finance into the accounting domain by using the OntoUML language for the ontological conceptualization constitutes the primary research objective of this article. This objective is guided by two principal research questions: What are the special temporal modal and meronymic properties of derivative instruments? Can these properties be modeled within the OntoREA accounting model or is an extension of the model needed?

To address the research objective and to answer the two questions, the special properties of derivative instruments are identified and specified according to OntoUML's ontological meta-properties and they are integrated into the REA accounting model. The resulting *OntoREA© Accounting and Finance Model* is derived in two steps. Firstly, the REAC accounting model is transformed into the REA©-based ALE accounting model by modeling the duality as well as the reciprocity relationship in a *balanced* version that includes the (present) value constraints of business transactions. Secondly, the OntoREA accounting model is extended by incorporating the future related commitment and balanced reciprocity concepts as well as an adequate conceptualization of derivative instruments.

The OntoREA© accounting and finance model goes substantially beyond the OntoREA accounting model by modeling the meronymic nature and the temporal modal behavior of derivative instruments with OntoUML's *Collective*, *Role* and *Phase* classes. Especially the definition of derivative instruments with the *Collective* class makes the OntoREA© model very distinct from the OntoREA accounting model which considers such instruments simply as economic resources. Finally, the development of the OntoREA© model is based on the ontology-driven conceptual modeling methodology introduced by Guizzardi et al. [10] and elaborated by Verdonck et al. [11], and its syntactical validity with respect to the UFO axioms is proven by verifying the correct application of the OntoUML design patterns in the OntoUML class diagram representing the OntoREA© accounting and finance model.

The remainder of this article is structured as follows. In the next chapter, the *REA©* accounting model is developed. Its characteristic compared to the REA accounting model is the inclusion of the commitment entity and the reification of the balanced reciprocity relationship. This relationship acts as *truthmaker* for the relationship between economic commitments, it refers to the promises of two *economic agents* to transfer *economic resources* in the future and it includes the present value constraint. In the following section, the *OntoREA Accounting Model* is presented and discussed in more detail with respect to its ontological meta-properties. In Sect. 4 the *OntoREA© Accounting and Finance Model* is developed by modeling the REA©-based ALE accounting model in terms of OntoUML's ontological meta-properties. The final section concludes the paper and gives directions for future research.

2 REA© Accounting Model: Additional Reification of the Balanced Reciprocity Relationship

Geerts and McCarthy [1] analyzed the REAC accounting model *ontologically* and introduced some new components and concepts as commitments and reciprocity as analogue to the duality principle. The same authors [2] extended the model further by integrating policy-level definitions specifying *"what should, could or must be"*. The ISO standard *ISO 15944-4, Business transaction scenarios - Accounting and economic ontology* [7] describes economic contracts as economic bundles of economic commitments which fulfill the reciprocity principle. The publication also promotes the *REA business ontology* as recognized international industry standard.

Before going into ontological details the integration of economic contracts (C) into the REAC accounting model is addressed. This model adds the economic commitments to the already existent notion of economic exchange. *Commitments do not occur in isolation because partners simply do not agree to value exchanges without reciprocation.* ISO/IEC 15944:2007(E) [7]. The specific extensions in the REAC model compared to the REA accounting model are defined as follows [7]:

- *An Economic Commitment is a promise to execute an Economic Event at some point in the future.*
- *A fulfillment relationship is an association between an Economic Commitment and the Economic Event that executes that commitment.*
- *A reciprocal relationship is an association between Economic Commitments that each in turn individually fulfills compensating economic events.*
- *An Economic Contract is a bundle of reciprocating commitments wherein two Parties agree to a future schedule of exchanges with compensating economic events. An Agreement is similar to an economic contract, but it is not legally enforceable.*
- *An economic bundle relationship is an association between an Economic Contract and its pair of reciprocal Economic Commitments.*

The REAC accounting model as stated in the ISO/IEC 15944:2007(E) standard is shown in Fig. 1 in form of an UML class diagram. The commitments are modeled on top of the economic events, connected by a fulfillment relationship and bundled to

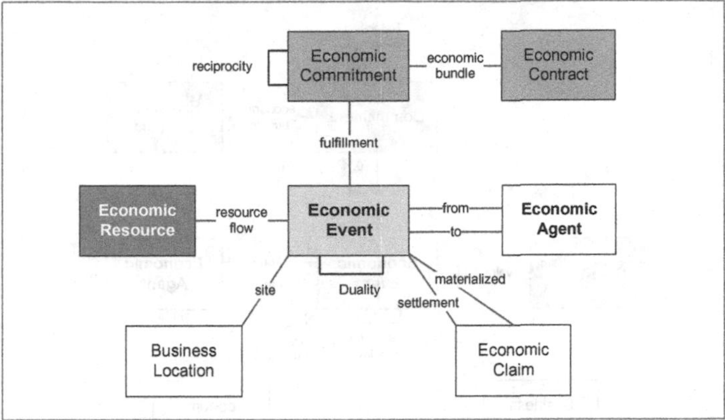

Fig. 1. REAC accounting model – UML class diagram

economic contracts. By using this approach, the REA accounting framework becomes capable of modeling future events, especially future commitments associated with financial instruments.

Although the REAC accounting model is intended to specify the accounting domain as well, it does not cover essential accounting requirements. Schwaiger identified several deficiencies concerning the traditional Asset-Liability-Equity (ALE) accounting logic [12]. In the REAC accounting model, there is no reference to debits, credits and accounts. This however is essential for modeling traditional accounting logic. McCarthy explicitly avoided those classic double-entry bookkeeping elements in his initial design of the REA accounting model to be able to establish a generic framework. However, debit and credit linguistics are essential to give the increment and decrement events of assets, liabilities and equity a consistent interpretation within the ALE-based accounting system.

Schwaiger [4] extends the REAC accounting model by introducing the ALE typification of economic resources, i.e. the inclusion of liabilities and equity next to assets. By integrating this typification the model is suitable for ALE accounting applications as well as modeling future events. Fischer-Pauzenberger and Schwaiger [9] eliminate the business transaction class from Schwaiger's model by putting the value constraint associated with these transactions into the duality relationship. To indicate this integration the relationship is called *balanced duality relationship*. This can be seen in Fig. 2 in the reflexive relationship under the Economic Event class. Next to that the figure contains the *balanced reciprocity relationship* on top of the Commitment class. This relationship expresses the combined occurrence of future in- and outflowing events that underlie the debited and credited commitments and it includes – like the balanced duality relationship – a value constraint. Due to the future fulfillment of the commitments the reciprocity relationship includes the commitments' present values. Finally the Economic Contract class is defined with respect to one or more commitments.

Due to the different extensions the model shown in Fig. 2 is called *REA©-based ALE Accounting Model*. The © sign is used in order to explicitly indicate its distinction from other REAC model versions. Its conceptualization can be summarized as follows:

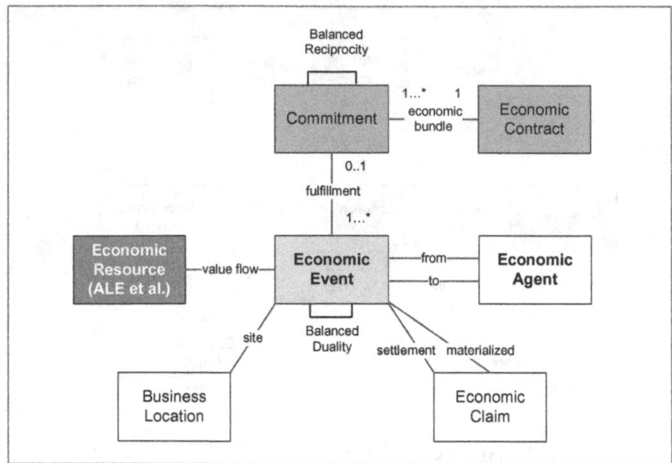

Fig. 2. REA©-based ALE accounting model – UML class diagram

REA©-based ALE accounting model covers all resources related to assets, liabilities and equity instead of tangible assets and cash only. Furthermore, it features the value flow relationship related to debit and credit events instead of relying on stock flow relationships related to increment and decrement events.

The balanced relationships include the value constraints. In the duality context the constraint requires the equality of the values of the debited and credited events. In the reciprocity context the constraint requires the equality of the commitments' present values. For illustrative purposes, the balanced reciprocity of a *stock forward instrument* (for further details see e.g. Hull [13]) is taken: At the day of the contract setting the forward only consists of commitments. The buyer of the forward is committed to receive the stock in the future (debit commitment) and to pay the forward price (credit commitment). The forward seller takes exactly the opposite commitment positions so that the contracting of a forward constitutes a zero sum game.

The balanced reciprocity only requires the equality of the commitment values, but it does not show the specific values of the different commitments involved in the derivative instruments. Consequently for the forward instrument with net value of zero no insights into the different commitments' values are given and the forward does not appear on the balance sheet. As enterprises – especially banks – often trade huge volumes in derivative instruments the net values are not sufficient. Consequently concepts from finance are integrated to solve this deficiency.

3 OntoREA Accounting Model: Ontological Meta-Properties – Stereotypes in OntoUML Class Diagrams

Ontology is a philosophical discipline (metaphysics) that addresses existential properties of things. The ontological analysis of Geerts and McCarthy [1] relate to Sowa's ontology definition [14]. But there are other definitions as well. According to the research questions the focus of this article refers to the OntoUML language. This language is based on the Unified Foundational Ontology (UFO) which is influenced by the Four-Category-Ontology from Lowe [15]. UFO covers different scopes, namely UFO-A for the ontology of endurants, UFO-B for the ontology of perdurants and UFO-C covering the ontology of social concepts.

It is important to note that this article only uses endurant constructs and thus UFO-A in order to be in line with the OntoUML-based REA accounting research. In the following the OntoREA accounting model developed by Fischer-Pauzenberger and Schwaiger [9] is presented. It will serve in the subsequent chapter as basis for the deeper integration of finance into the accounting domain.

Before the OntoREA accounting model is presented some propaedeutic UFO considerations seem appropriate. A very important UFO meta-property is *rigidity*. Rigidity in the modal sense regards the necessity of individuals to instantiate given universals throughout time. Anti-rigid universals however, are the ones whose instances contingently instantiate them [16]. Ruy et al. summarizes the ontological meta-properties by giving illustrative examples [17]: *By referring to a number of formal and ontological meta-properties, UFO proposes a number of distinctions among object types. Within these, sortal types are types that either provide or carry a uniform principle of identity for their instances. Within sortal types, we have the distinction between rigid and anti-rigid sortals. A rigid type is a type that classifies its instances necessarily (in the modal sense), i.e., the instances of that type cannot cease to be an instance of that type without ceasing to exist. Anti-rigidity, in contrast, characterizes a type whose instances can move in and out of the extension of that type without altering their identity. For instance, contrast the rigid type Person with the anti-rigid types Student or Husband. While the same individual John never ceases to be instance of Person, he can move in and out of the extension of Student or Husband, once he enrolls in/finishes college or marries/divorces, respectively.*

In conceptual modeling entity types and relationship types are the most fundamental constructs [18]. Taken from [9] the following entity types (subsequently marked in bolded letters), which are derived from the UFO typification tree (marked in italic letters) are of importance for the OntoREA accounting model:

- **Kinds** are *rigid substance sortals* and they provide their own identity principle (rather than just carrying it). *Kinds* are also considered as an OntoUML model's backbone [19] and they are used to model resources, events and agents as endurants.
- **SubKinds** are *rigid sortals* and do not provide their own identity principle, they are merely inheriting the principle from another *Substance Sortal.*
- **Roles** are *anti-rigid sortals* and therefore can change their instantiation in a modal sense according to an extrinsic generalization condition. Furthermore, Roles are relational-dependent, they have to rely on at least one other universal. Roles get their identity principle through the generalization relation from the instance of its parent universal.
- **Phases** are *anti-rigid sortals* as well with a significant distinction to Roles. Phases are relational (i.e. external) independent. Due to the predetermined disjoint and complete generalization sets, instances of Phases, in contrast to instances of Roles,

can change according to their intrinsic (and not extrinsic) generalization condition. As Roles, Phases also get their identity principle through the generalization relation.

Next to the above mentioned entity types the following relationship types will be important for the OntoREA accounting model to be developed:

- **Relator Universals**, are *moment universals* which represent the objectification of a relational property. Relator Universals are existentially dependent on a multitude of individuals, thus, mediating them. Relators are the foundation of the so-called **Material Relations** [20] and act as truth-makers of the relation.
- **Formal Relations** hold directly between entities without requiring any intervening individual.

The remaining entity types and relationship types of UFO are not needed for the OntoREA accounting model. The current and complete version of UFO is specified in the UFO reference [21].

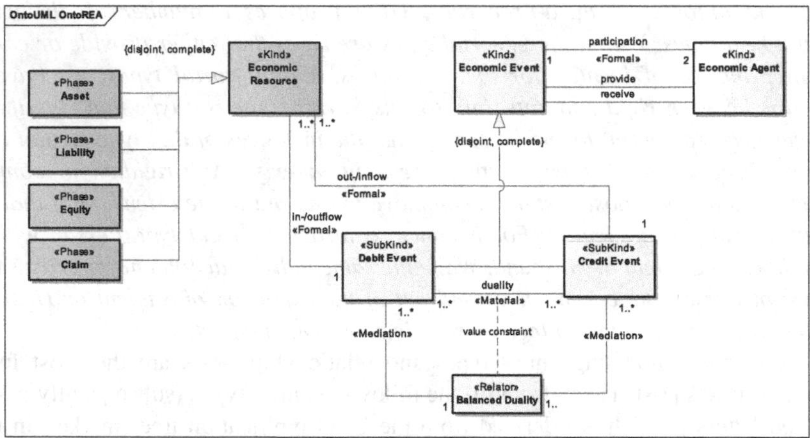

Fig. 3. OntoREA accounting model – OntoUML class diagram

These UFO-based entity types and relationship types are the definitions of the stereotypes used in OntoUML class diagrams. In Fig. 3 the OntoREA accounting model is presented in the OntoUML language. It features special modeling characteristics [9], which are briefly elaborated:

- The endurant backbone in the OntoREA model are the rigid *Kind* classes Economic Resource, Economic Event and Economic Agent.
- The typification relationship of the Economic Event into the two *SubKind* classes Debit Event and Credit Event is modeled by a disjoint and complete generalization set. Thus, an event can only be either a debit event or a credit event. This typification is needed for handling changes in the ALE resource types. An increase in liabilities and equity is related to a credit event, whereas an increase of assets relates to a debit event.

- The (*Material*) balanced duality relationship is modeled via the *Relator* class Balanced Duality. It acts as truthmaker and reifies the relationship between the endurant debit event and the endurant credit event. The balanced duality relationship incorporates the value constraint so that the debit and credit events have the equal values. Furthermore the duality relationship is not only referring to the value constraint for keeping the balance in the fundamental ALE-equation (*classificational* double entry), but it also describes a REA-based cause-effect relationship (*causal* double entry).
- The use of *Phase* classes for modeling the typification of the *Kind* class Economic Resources introduces the modal meta-property into the OntoREA model. The *Phase* class is an anti-rigid, non-identity providing sortal which receives its identity from its superclass in the inheritance relationship. The anti-rigidity allows the economic resources to change *Phases* over time without losing identity.
- The modal meta-property is used for conceptualizing the temporal modal behavior of claims [9]. Claims are defined as imbalances in the balanced duality relationship that are neither assets nor liabilities or equity. When claims materialize, they convert to their corresponding resource types.

4 OntoREA© Accounting and Finance Model: Collectives Beyond ALE Phases

After defining the balanced reciprocity relationship in Sect. 2 and illustrating the OntoREA accounting model in Sect. 3, both parts can be integrated. Before that, the balanced reciprocity relationship is conceptualized in the OntoUML language. All subsequent OntoUML models are implemented in the open-source tool *Menthor Editor* [22] as well as the proprietary *Enterprise Architect* from *Sparkx*. An important benefit of these modeling support tools lies in their built-in quality control functions. According to this support function the syntactic correctness of the developed OntoUML class diagram is assured. This validation tool is used throughout the paper so that the syntactic validity of all developed OntoUML models is proven.

Figure 4 contains the balanced reciprocity relationship. The *Kind* class Commitment is like the *Kind* class Economic Event typified by two disjoint subsets in form of *SubKind* classes for the Debit and Credit Commitment. Both classes are related in the balanced reciprocity relationship. In this *Material* relationship the balanced reciprocity is reified by the *Relator* class. Furthermore the balanced reciprocity relationship includes the present value constraint. This ensures that the (present) value of the debit commitments has to be equal to the (present) value of credit commitments. Finally the *Kind* classes Commitment and Economic Event are in a *Formal* fulfillment association. Its cardinalities indicate that a commitment relates to at least one economic event, whereas an economic event can but must not have a commitment.

Now the dynamic modal behavior of a derivative instrument is elaborated in the context of a *stock forward instrument*. The value of the forward is derived from the price of its underlying stock. Initially the forward price is set in such a way that the forward value has a value of zero. Over time the value of the stock forward changes

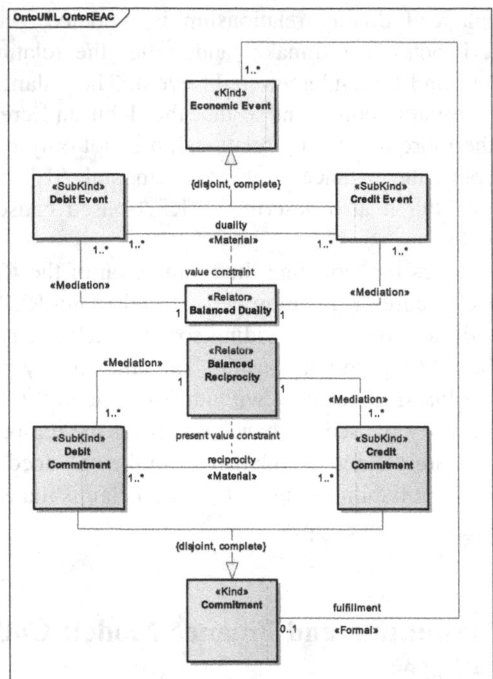

Fig. 4. Balanced reciprocity relationship – OntoUML class diagram

according to changes in the prices of its underlying stock. For the buyer of the forward the value of the forward becomes ceteris paribus negative (positive) if the stock price goes up (down). At a subsequent measurement date a positive (negative) value of the forward is recorded as an asset (liability) in the balance sheet. In the double-entry bookkeeping accounting system the recognition as asset is recorded by debiting the financial asset account and by crediting the financial revenue account. A liability is recorded by debiting the financial expense account and crediting the liability account.

From the finance perspective these value changes of the stock forward can be explained by the *no-arbitrage pricing theory* which was introduced by the Nobel laureates Merton [23] and Black/Scholes [24]. An easier accessible approach to this theory is the discrete time approach introduced by Cox, Ross and Rubinstein. Applied to the stock forward instrument it can be shown that the forward value is equal to the sum of the values of the assets (A) and liabilities (L) in the forward *hedging portfolio* [25, p. 233]. The A/L hedging portfolio representation underlying the no-arbitrage pricing proposition explains the meronymic peculiarity of derivative instruments. On the one side, the derivative instrument class is a rigid sortal universal that provides the identity principle to its instantiations. On the other side, the identity principle cannot be related to the ALE typification of the economic resources as derivative instruments can change their ALE-status quite easily and often over time. The changes between on- and off-balance sheet as well as asset and liability position make the derivative instruments even very distinct from claims. Claims can only change from off- to on-balance positions but not from assets to liability or vice versa. Hence the ALE-based typification of the economic resources is not sufficient for derivative instruments.

The ontological foundation of OntoUML shows very beneficial for solving this problem. Of importance are the meronymic meta-properties which address the different types of parthood relationships and define the special rigid and identity principle providing universal, i.e. the *Collective* universal. The *Collective* universal has the same ontological meta-properties as the *Kind* universal. The difference lies in the scope of the universals. The *Kind* universal specifies individual universals whereas the *Collective* universal goes beyond individual universals by specifying collections. The *Beatles* are an example for such a collection. Seen as an instantiation of a *Collective* universal the Beatles as a group has its own identity. The members of the Beatles as persons are instantiations of a *Kind* universal and consequently have their personal identity. It is important not to confuse the personal identity with the identity of the group. In OntoUML this distinction relates to the meronymic meta-property of a *MemberOf* parthood-relationship. Due to the different identities of the group as a whole and its individual members it is possible that group member leave or join the group without changing the group identity. Applied to the Beatles example this happened when Pete Best left the group and Ringo Starr joint it.

In the light of the *no-arbitrage A/L hedging portfolio representation* a derivative instrument is a collective and its members are assets and liabilities composing the A/L hedging portfolio. Hence the first research question can now be answered: Financial derivatives are a *Collective* universal with a *MemberOf* parthood-relationship to its members that are economic resources in form of assets and liabilities. With this answer also the second question can be answered: The existing REA-based ALE accounting framework has no Collective universals included so that it has to be extended in order to include the meronymic peculiarities of derivative instruments.

The needed extension of the REA-based ALE accounting framework can be seen in the top-left corner of Fig. 5. It shows the *Collective* class Derivative Instrument. This class has a *MemberOf* relationship to the *Kind* class Economic Resource. The cardinality says that derivative instruments have two economic resource members, i.e. one asset and one liability. Furthermore the *Collective* class Derivative Instrument is typified via a *Phase* partition that consists of the *Phase* classes Asset, Liability and Null. According to this the derivate instruments can change the phases over time without losing its identity by switching from the *Phase* Null, i.e. an off-balance position, into an on-balance position either to the *Phase* Asset or the *Phase* Liability and so on.

The overall conceptualization in Fig. 5 represents the *OntoREA© Accounting and Finance Model*. By modeling the derivative instrument as a *Collective* class this model goes substantially beyond the REA-based ALE accounting. Derivative instruments are no longer seen as economic resources related to a *Kind* class. Instead they are seen by their no-arbitrage representation as a collection (hedging portfolio) of asset and liability resources which have their own identity principles. The big advantage of explicitly including the derivative instruments in form of their no-arbitrage A/L hedging portfolio lies in the added flexibility: Depending on the purpose the derivate instruments can be shown on a net basis for financial reporting purposes or on an un-consolidated basis for strategic and management control purposes.

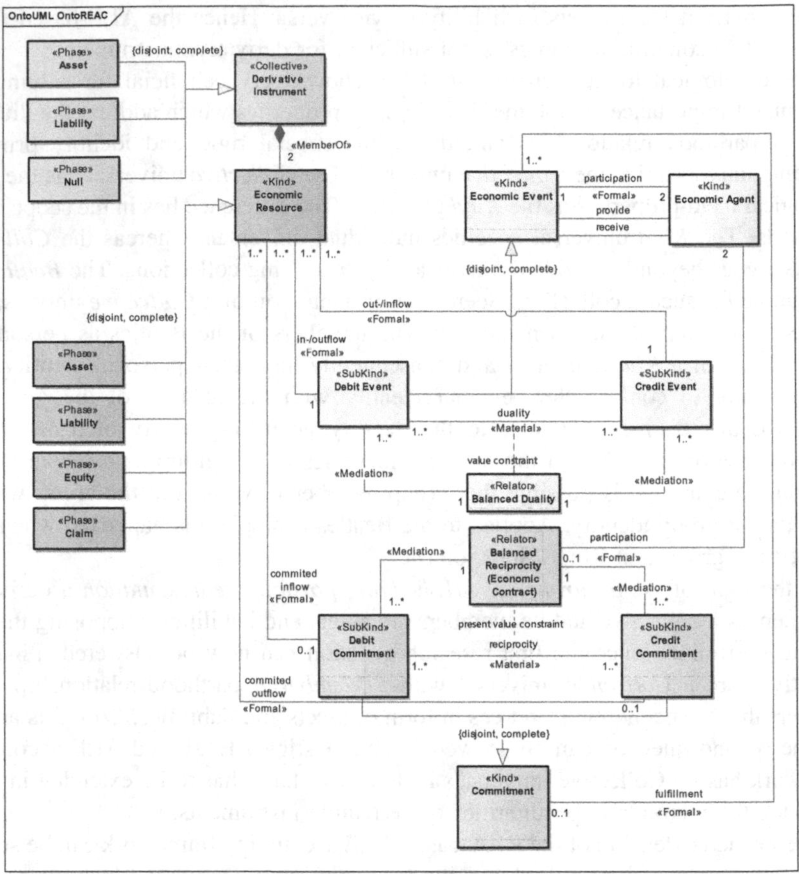

Fig. 5. OntoREA© accounting and finance model – OntoUML class diagram

Finally the double nature of the balanced reciprocity relationship has to be mentioned. In Fig. 5 this can be seen by the additional term *Economic Contract* set in parenthesis. The reason for the double nature is due to the fact that actually the economic contract is the truthmaker in the *Relator* class Balanced Reciprocity by which the debit and credit commitments between the two involved agents are contractually determined. Hence derivative instruments are special economic contracts for which the temporal modal peculiarities are explicitly specified.

5 Conclusions

The primary research objective addressed in this article relates to the deeper anchoring of the finance domain into the accounting domain. In order to achieve this the temporal modal and meronymic properties of derivative instruments had to be identified, specified and integrated into the REA-based ALE accounting framework. For this purpose the UFO-ontological foundation of Guizzardi's OntoUML language showed to be the key as this foundation provides a precise understanding for investigating existence, identity and rigidity related topics. This foundation was used to specify the derivative instruments according to the no-arbitrage A/L hedging portfolio representation as a *Collective* universal with *MemberOf* parthood relationships to economic resources in form of assets and liabilities. Their temporal modal behavior, where derivative instruments – what especially relates to forward contracts – can switch between asset, liability and off-balance position, was captured by *Phase* universals. These universals allow anti-rigidity what underlies the temporal modal behavior and that cannot be modeled in the ontologically neutral UML class diagrams.

Equipped with these ontological meta-properties Geerts and McCarthy's REAC accounting model was extended. In the first step the balanced reciprocity relationship was defined. Then the OntoREA accounting model [9] was presented. Finally the OntoREA© accounting and finance model was developed by integrating the collective conceptualization of the derivative instrument and the balanced reciprocity relationship with the economic contract as truthmaker into the OntoREA model.

The syntactical validity of the OntoREA© accounting and finance model with respect to OntoUML modeling rules is assured by applying a reactive validation strategy specified in the ontology-driven conceptual modeling methodology [10, 11]. This validation strategy is implemented by using the open-source tool *Menthor Editor* [22] as well as the proprietary *Enterprise Architect* from *Sparkx* where the compliance with the ontological distinctions and UFO axioms underlying the OntoUML language is continuously checked during the subsequent combinations of the pre-defined ontological design patterns within the conceptual modeling process. In order to provide a deeper validation next to the current validation two additional steps will be taken in the future: A model simulation in the logic-based Alloy language for detecting possible misspecifications and the usage of real derivative instrument cases for demonstrating and assessing the model's adequacy.

The resulting model can be used for different purposes. One possibility is its usage in the accounting (AIS – see Steinbart and Romney [26]) as well as enterprise information systems (EIS – see Dunn et al. [27]) research by establishing ontology-based accounting and enterprise information systems. Such systems could be designed and implemented e.g. within a model-driven software development approach (see e.g. Brambilla et al. [28], Stahl and Völter [29] or Rybola et al. [30]) by establishing the OntoREA© model first and subsequently transforming it into a software application.

Finally, an interesting idea for future research relates to the used UFO ontology. Instead of only using enduring entities from UFO-A for all REA primitives, it seems worthwhile to model economic events via perduring entities from UFO-B and economic agents via agents as described in UFO-C. By doing this, enterprise models can be developed that cover a much broader scope compared to the narrow compliance requirements within the ALE accounting domain. This would require a complete redesign and would contribute to the ongoing discussions [31].

References

1. Geerts, G.L., McCarthy, W.E.: An ontological analysis of the economic primitives of the extended-REA enterprise information architecture. Int. J. Account. Inf. Syst. **3**, 1–16 (2002)
2. Geerts, G.L., McCarthy, W.E.: Policy level specifications in REA enterprise information systems. J. Inf. Syst. **20**, 37–63 (2006)
3. McCarthy, W.E.: The REA accounting model: a generalized framework for accounting systems in a shared data environment. Account. Rev. 554–578 (1982)
4. Schwaiger, W.S.A.: The REA accounting model: enhancing understandability and applicability. In: Johannesson, P., Lee, M.L., Liddle, S.W., Opdahl, A.L., López, Ó. P. (eds.) ER 2015. LNCS, vol. 9381, pp. 566–573. Springer, Cham (2015). doi:10.1007/978-3-319-25264-3_43
5. Karlsson, F., Linander, F., von Schéele, F.: A conceptual framework for time distortion analysis in method components. In: Bider, I., Gaaloul, K., Krogstie, J., Nurcan, S., Proper, H.A., Schmidt, R., Soffer, P. (eds.) BPMDS/EMMSAD-2014. LNBIP, vol. 175, pp. 454–463. Springer, Heidelberg (2014). doi:10.1007/978-3-662-43745-2_31
6. Guizzardi, G.: Ontological foundations for structural conceptual model. http://doc.utwente.nl/50826 (2005)
7. Standardization/International, E.C.I.O. for: Information Technology—Business Operational View—Part 4: Business Transactions Scenarios—Accounting and Economic Ontology. ISO/IEC FDIS. 15944 (2007)
8. Gailly, F., Geerts, G., Poels, G.: Ontological reengineering of the REA-EO using UFO. In: OOPSLA Workshop on Ontological Software Engineering (2009)
9. Fischer-Pauzenberger, C., Schwaiger, W.S.A.: The OntoREA accounting model: ontology-based modeling of the accounting domain. Complex Syst. Inform. Model. Q. **54**, 20–37 (2017)
10. Guizzardi, G., Das Graças, A.P., Guizzardi, R.S.S.: Design patterns and inductive modeling rules to support the construction of ontologically well-founded conceptual models in OntoUML. In: Salinesi, C., Pastor, O. (eds.) CAiSE 2011. LNBIP, vol. 83, pp. 402–413. Springer, Heidelberg (2011). doi:10.1007/978-3-642-22056-2_44
11. Verdonck, M., Gailly, F., De Cesare, S., Poels, G.: Ontology-driven conceptual modeling: a systematic literature mapping and review. Appl. Ontol. **10**, 197–227 (2015)
12. Horngren, C., Harrison, W., Oliver, S., Best, P., Fraser, D., Tan, R., Willett, R.: Accounting. Pearson Higher Education AU, New York (2012)
13. Hull, J.C.: Options, Futures, and Other Derivatives. Pearson Education, London (2009)
14. Sowa, J.F.: Knowledge Representation: Logical, Philosophical, and Computational Foundations. Brooks/Cole Publishing, Pacific Grove (2000)
15. Lowe, E.J.: The Four-Category Ontology: A Metaphysical Foundation for Natural Science. Oxford University Press (2006)
16. Sales, T.P.: Ontology Validation for Managers (2014)
17. Ruy, F.B., Reginato, C.C., Santos, V.A., Falbo, R.A., Guizzardi, G.: Ontology engineering by combining ontology patterns. In: Johannesson, P., Lee, M.L., Liddle, S.W., Opdahl, A.L., López, Ó.P. (eds.) ER 2015. LNCS, vol. 9381, pp. 173–186. Springer, Cham (2015). doi:10.1007/978-3-319-25264-3_13
18. Guizzardi, G., Wagner, G., Almeida, J.P.A., Guizzardi, R.S.S.: Towards ontological foundations for conceptual modeling: the unified foundational ontology (UFO) story. Appl. Ontol. **10**, 259–271 (2015)

19. Rybola, Z., Pergl, R.: Towards OntoUML for software engineering: introduction to the transformation of OntoUML into relational databases. In: Pergl, R., Molhanec, M., Babkin, E., Fosso Wamba, S. (eds.) EOMAS 2016. LNBIP, vol. 272, pp. 67–83. Springer, Cham (2016). doi:10.1007/978-3-319-49454-8_5
20. Sales, T., Barcelos, P., Guizzardi, G.: Identification of semantic anti-patterns in ontology-driven conceptual modeling via visual simulation. In: 4th International Workshop on Ontology Information System (ODISE 2012), Graz, Austria (2012)
21. Ontology Project: UFO-A Specification. http://ontology.com.br/ufo-a/spec/
22. Menthor Editor on github. https://github.com/MenthorTools/menthor-editor
23. Merton, R.C.: Theory of rational theory option pricing. Bell J. Econ. **4**, 141–183 (1973)
24. Black, F., Scholes, M.: The pricing of options and corporate liabilities. J. Polit. Econ. **81**, 637 (1973)
25. Cox, J.C., Ross, S.A., Rubinstein, M.: Option pricing: a simplified approach. J. Financ. Econ. **7**, 229–263 (1979)
26. Romney, M., Steinbart, P., Mula, J., McNamara, R., Tonkin, T.: Accounting Information Systems. Pearson Higher Education AU, New York (2012)
27. Dunn, C.L., Hollander, A.S., Cherrington, J.O.: Enterprise Information Systems: A Pattern-Based Approach. McGraw-Hill/Irwin, New York (2005)
28. Brambilla, M., Cabot, J., Wimmer, M.: Model-driven software engineering in practice. Synth. Lect. Softw. Eng. **1**(1), 1–182 (2012)
29. Völter, M., Stahl, T., Bettin, J., Haase, A., Helsen, S.: Model-Driven Software Development: Technology, Engineering, Management. Wiley, Hoboken (2013)
30. Pergl, R., Sales, T.P., Rybola, Z.: Towards OntoUML for software engineering: from domain ontology to implementation model. In: Cuzzocrea, A., Maabout, S. (eds.) MEDI 2013. LNCS, vol. 8216, pp. 249–263. Springer, Heidelberg (2013). doi:10.1007/978-3-642-41366-7_21
31. Guizzardi, G., Guarino, N., Almeida, J.P.A.: Ontological considerations about the representation of events and endurants in business models, pp. 1–16 (2016)

Teleologies: Objects, Actions and *Functions*

Fausto Giunchiglia and Mattia Fumagalli(✉)

Department of Information Engineering and Computer Science (DISI), University of Trento, Via Sommarive 9, 38123 Povo, Trento, Italy
{Fausto.Giunchiglia,Mattia.Fumagalli}@Unitn.it

Abstract. We start from the observation that the notion of concept, as it is used in perception, is distinct and different from the notion of concept, as it is used in knowledge representation. In earlier work we called the first notion, *substance concept* and the second, *classification concept.* In this paper we integrate these two notions into a general theory of concepts that organizes them into a hierarchy of increasing abstraction from what is perceived. Thus, at the first level, we have *objects* (which roughly correspond to substance concepts), which *represent what is perceived* (e.g., a car); at the second level we have *actions*, which *represent how objects change in time* (e.g., move); while, at the third level, we have *functions* (which roughly correspond to classification concepts), which represent *the expected behavior of objects* as it is manifested in terms of "an object performing a certain set of actions" (e.g., a vehicle). The main outcome is the notion of *Teleology,* where teleologies provide the basis for a solution to the problem of the integration of perception and reasoning and, more in general, to the problem of managing the *diversity of knowledge.*

Keywords: Conceptual modeling · Perception · Knowledge

1 Introduction

A crucial characteristic of humans is their ability to build and exploit representations of what they perceive, what we usually call *the world.* Such representations usually consist of complex combinations of *concepts*, where we take a concept to be *an abstract idea generalized from particular instances*. However, the very notion of concept is controversial [1]. Thus, for instance, on one side, we have the *Biosemantics* approach, which takes a concept to be a device and a representation supporting certain biological processes, in particular, perception (e.g., human vision) [2, 3], while, on the other side, we have the so-called *Descriptionist* approach which takes a concept to be a class, namely a set of instances characterized by some shared set of properties, as the basic construct enabling knowledge representation, classification and reasoning [4]. The former and latter notions of concept underlie the work in Computer Vision (CV) [5] and in Knowledge Representation (KR) [6], respectively.

This work has been supported by QROWD (http://qrowd-project.eu), a Horizon 2020 project, under Grant Agreement No. 732194.

H.C. Mayr et al. (Eds.): ER 2017, LNCS 10650, pp. 520–534, 2017.
https://doi.org/10.1007/978-3-319-69904-2_39

The work in [1] shows how the two notions above have different characteristics and calls them *substance concepts* (as from Millikan [4]) and *classification concepts*, respectively. Substance concepts represent what we perceive and, therefore, are characterized by a notion of *perceptual identity* (and diversity) while classification concepts represent what we reason about and, therefore, are characterized by a notion of *reasoning identity* (and diversity). *While perceptual identity captures invariance over the occurrences of what we perceive, reasoning identity captures invariance over the occurrences of what we reason about*. Thus, for instance, we recognize a *rock* as being such depending on what we perceive, while we reason about the same rock as an *obstacle* when it is in our way, or as a kind of *weapon* when throwing it at someone.

In this paper we show how to integrate substance and classification concepts into a hierarchy of increasing abstraction from what is perceived. Thus, at the first level, we have *objects* (which roughly correspond to substance concepts), which are *representations of what is perceived* (e.g., *a car*); at the second level we have *actions*, which *represent how objects change in time* (e.g., *move*, where, among others, cars can move); while, at the third level, we have *functions* (which roughly correspond to classification concepts), which represent *the expected behavior of objects* as it is manifested in terms of "an object performing a certain set of actions" (e.g., *a vehicle,* where vehicles, e.g., cars, can perform many actions, e.g., move and stop). The intuition is that, by performing *actions*, *objects interfere* with other objects, this being the basic mechanism by which the world evolves. In this perspective, *functions model the expected interference among objects*. Object interference, and therefore function, is captured via the notions of *producer* and *consumer*, where an object is a producer when it performs an action affecting another object and a consumer when it is affected by it.

The patterns by which producers affect consumers provide the basis for the construction of *Teleologies.*[1] *Ontologies*[2] are defined as explicit formal specifications of the terms in a domain [7]. The same definition can be applied for teleologies but with the proviso that teleologies focus on function and on how a chosen representation fits a certain purpose, this being the basis for a general model for the *diversity of knowledge* [8]. In this respect, the distinction between objects and their multiple functions is the *first source of heterogeneity*, modeling the diversity between the representation of what we *perceive* and the representation of what we *reason about*. The *second source of heterogeneity* is our ability to represent and reason about what we perceive at different levels of abstraction, as function of the problem to be solved. Thus, for instance, I can describe a person as *moving her legs*, as *walking*, or as *moving*, depending on my focus.

This work is a first step towards a solution to the problem of managing knowledge diversity not in the sense that we are able to define the ultimate teleology which can be reused in general (which is impossible), but, rather, in the sense that we provide the basis for a general methodology for the construction, integration and/or adaptation of data and knowledge coming from multiple heterogeneous sources. We organize the

---

[1] The word teleology builds on the Greek words *telos* (meaning "end, purpose") and *logia*, (meaning "a branch of learning").

[2] The word *ontology* builds on the Greek words *ont* (meaning "being") and *logia*, (meaning "a branch of learning").

paper as follows. In Sect. 2, we introduce objects, actions and functions. In Sect. 3 we introduce producers, consumers and producer – consumer (PC) patterns. In Sect. 4 we introduce the three PC pattern transformations which can be used to *reduce* one pattern to another pattern, *preserving the pattern intended meaning*. In Sect. 5, we provide a small example of how to build and how to adapt a teleology, using the pattern transformations from Sect. 4, *adaptation* being they key for handling diversity in knowledge. Finally, in Sect. 6, we provide the related work.

2 Object, Action and Function

We live immersed in a *spatio-temporal continuum* where space and time are the *a-priori* forms of perception [9]. We do not perceive space or time, but anything we perceive is *part* of a precise spatial or temporal ordering, and fills it. We perceive these parts through *encounters*, namely events during which such parts *manifest* themselves to an observer. We call such parts, *substances*, where, as from [4], "... *substances are those things about which you can learn from one encounter something of what to expect on other encounters, where this is no accident but the result of a real connection*".

People represent substances as *concepts*. However, the mapping between substances and concepts is not one-to-one [1]. Thus, I may perceive a substance as a cat that I am trying to avoid hitting, as *my* cat, as an animal, or as an obstacle. Even more, there are substances for which we do not have a concept. One such example, the part of the mountain that I can see from the window of my office. *Concepts represent those parts of the spatio-temporal continuum that are relevant to us, in the way which is most convenient for us,*[3] *as the world where we live.*[4] But if the world, as we perceive it, *is* representation, and if there is a certain degree of freedom in what we represent and in how we represent it, is there a general principle to which we all adhere and that allows us to live in the same world, or at least in worlds which are very similar?

Our answer to the above questions is based on a distinction among three types of concepts, namely *objects*, *actions*, and *functions*, which represent what is perceived, across encounters, at increasing levels of abstraction (see Fig. 1).

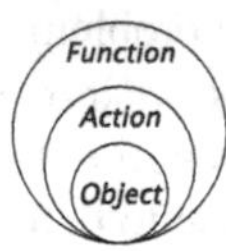

Fig. 1. Object, action and function.

[3] The concepts we use are also largely influenced by our language, culture, history, place where we live, and many other contextual factors, see, e.g., [10].

[4] Interestingly enough, the ancient Latin word for world is *mundus*, meaning "clean, elegant", itself a translation of the Greek word cosmos, meaning "orderly arrangement".

We take *Objects* to be those concepts that *represent substances, i.e., what is perceived* across encounters. Examples of objects are: cats, cars, rivers. As from [1], an object can be thought as the set of all of the representations of how the same substance "fills" space, any time we encounter it. Objects can be *individuals* (what in KR we call instances, e.g., my cat Garfield) or *kinds* (i.e., generic instances of what in KR we call classes, e.g., any cat that I can encounter while walking). Objects are *first level abstract representations* in the sense that they abstract over multiple occurrences of the same substance (as recognized during encounters) and collect them in clusters (one cluster per object). An object, e.g., "a cat", is nothing else but the set of representations of all the times we have perceived (e.g., seen) it.

We take *Actions* to be those concepts that *represent how objects change in time.* Examples of actions are: running (performed by, e.g., cats), carrying (performed by, e.g., cars) and flowing (performed by, e.g., rivers). As with objects, actions are generated any time we encounter a substance. Actions are *second level abstract representations* in the sense that they abstract over multiple occurrences of changes in time of a substance (as recognized during encounters) and collect them in clusters (one cluster per action). An action, e.g., "running", is taken to be the set of representations of all times we have perceived a running object, e.g., "a cat" (or "a dog"), where the representation of "a running cat" or ("a running dog"), is a temporal sequence of "cat" ("dog") occurrences. Notice how actions are independent of the specific object carrying them out; objects are abstracted away to keep track only of what changes.

We say that *a certain object O performs a certain action A* when we perceive O subject to the change described by A. Notice that there are only so many actions that can be performed by an object. For instance a car cannot be used to fly. We capture this intuition by saying that any object O is associated to *a set of admissible actions* $\{A\}_{a:O}$, where A is an action and "a:O" stands for "admissible for O". We have the following:

$$\mathrm{AaO(O)} = \{\mathrm{A}\,|\,\textit{for any}\,\mathrm{A} \in \{\mathrm{A}\}_{\mathrm{a:O}}\}$$
$$\mathrm{OaA(A)} = \{\mathrm{O}\,|\,\textit{for any}\,\mathrm{O}\,\textit{such that}\,\mathrm{A} \in \{\mathrm{A}\}_{\mathrm{a:O}}\}$$

where AaO and OaA are to be read, respectively, *(admissible) Actions of (Object)* and *Objects of (admissible Action).* Thus, for instance we have AaO(car) = {move, transport, trap, …} and OaA(move) = {car, bus, person, table, …}. For any object, its set of admissible actions, as well as its set of not admissible *(inadmissible)* actions, is infinite, as infinite are the ways in which an object can evolve in time. At the same time, an admissible action can be performed only under certain contextual conditions. For instance, a car needs gas to run its engine and move around. Admissible actions are similar in spirit to Millikan's *abilities* [4] and somewhat related to the notion of *affordance,* as formalized by Gibson [11] and then taken up in various contexts, see, e.g., [12, 13]. The crucial difference is that affordances are related to what an environment enables an object to do, more than what an object is, by itself, able to do.

Certain admissible actions occur quite rarely. For instance, a car can be used as a trap for certain animals, but this is rather unusual. Many admissible actions are instead quite common. Thus for instance, a car usually moves around and transports people, while a person usually eats, sleeps and walks. Similarly, at school, quite often an older person (that we call “a teacher”) explains some topic to a younger person (that we call “a student”), she gives homework, she grades it, and so on. The fact that certain sets of actions are repeatedly performed by the same object allows humans to make predictions about the future behaviour of objects and to reason about this. We formalize this fact through the notion of *function*. *The function of an object formalizes the behavior that an object is expected to have.* This expected behavior may be due to the object's *purpose* (as it is the case with artifacts, e.g., a car) or to its *role*, for instance in the world and society (as it is the case with living organisms, e.g., a cat, a tree or a person). Sometimes the word used to denote a function is the same used to denote the object performing it (e.g., car, cat); in many cases language provides dedicated words (e.g., teacher, parent) possibly with a negative connotation (e.g., obstacle, enemy, garbage).

We capture this intuition by saying that *an object can perform one or more functions*, where a *function is defined as a set of actions*. Let O be an object and $\{F_O\}_{p:O}$ a set of *proper functions* F_O (where *proper* emphasizes the fact that these are functions which are “expected”). Then we have the following (“p:O/p:F_O” stands for “proper for O/F_O”):

$$FpO(O) = \{F_O \,|\, \textit{for any}\, F_O \in \{F_O\}_{p:O}\}$$
$$OpF(F_O) = \{O \,|\, \textit{for any}\, O\, \textit{such that}\, F_O \in \{F_O\}_{p:O}\}$$

with:

$$ApF(F_O) = \{A \,|\, \textit{for any}\, A \in \{A\}_{p:F_O}\}$$
$$FpA(A) = \{F_O \,|\, \textit{for any}\, F_O\, \textit{such that}\, A \in \{A\}_{p:F_O}\}$$

where: FpO and OpF are to be read *(proper) Functions of (Object)* and *Objects of (proper) Function*, respectively, and ApF and FpA are to be read *(proper) Actions of (Function)* and *Functions of (proper Action)*, respectively. Thus, for instance, we have ApF(vehicle) = {move, transport, …} and FpA(move) = {vehicle, person, …}. Obviously, $\{A\}_{p:F_O} \subset \{A\}_{a:O}$. $\{F_O\}_{p:O}$ is assumed to be finite. The finiteness of $\{F_O\}_{p:O}$, in the case of artifacts follows from the fact that we build artifacts with a specific *purpose* in mind. The finite functionality of living beings is not connected to the fact that we know their purpose but to the fact that they have shape and behavior which comes from nature and is replicated through reproduction, and from the fact that we model it as their *role* [14]. It is a fact that (the functions of) living beings are more easily recognized and perceived than (those of) artifacts [15]. At the same time, *$ApF(F_O)$ contains (again) a possibly infinite number of actions*, this meaning, in practice, that there is always the possibility to characterize a specific change of an object/function as a new action. If language allows us to precisely denote an object or a function with a word, a precise characterization in terms of its possible actions is impossible [1, 4].

As from Fig. 1, functions are *third level abstract representations* in the sense that they abstract over multiple occurrences of objects performing actions (as recognized during encounters) and collect them in clusters (one cluster per function). A function, e.g., “mover”, consists of the set of representations of all the times we have perceived an object performing a certain expected action, e.g., “a running cat” or “a walking person”.

3 Producer – Consumer Patterns

We model the interaction between objects, actions and functions using patterns like the one in Fig. 2. More precisely, the pattern in Fig. 2, is a specific instance of what we call an *OAO (for Object-Action-Object) pattern.* In OAO patterns, round boxes represent objects, arrow boxes represent actions and square boxes represent functions. t_1 and t_2 define start and end of the action. The specific pattern in Fig. 2 instantiates what in natural language we would describe as *'a car transporting a person'*. In Fig. 2, *Transport* is the action, *Car* is the producer object, *Person* is the consumer object, *Vehicle* is the function performed by the producer while *Passenger* is the function performed by the consumer. The intuition is that *an object plays the function of a producer when it performs an action affecting another object, possibly itself, and that the function of consumer is played by the object being affected by this action.* The intuition of what *"an action affecting another object"* means is that an object is associated with a *state* and that this state changes any time an object is a consumer. The state of an object includes its physical properties (e.g., position, shape, beauty), the actions it performs (a subset of the set AaO(O)), namely the patterns where it is a producer and the state of its functions (being, e.g., active, idle, malfunctioning, sick, in love, angry, …).

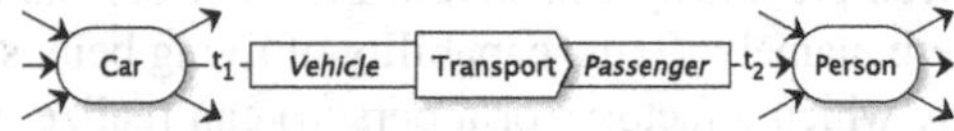

Fig. 2. 'OAO pattern – A car transporting a person'.

In Fig. 2, the arrows from/to objects represent two crucial aspects of the model:

1. an object is *always* both a producer and a consumer, being embedded in the continuous evolution of the world;
2. an object may occur in multiple OAO patterns while an action may occur only inside a single OAO pattern.

OAO patterns have the form of the pattern in Fig. 2 with three possible variations: *(i)* producer and consumer may be dropped when the relevant concept is not lexicalized or it is lexicalized with the same term as the object, *(ii)* the producer and the consumer may be the same object (as in, e.g., *"a person walking"*), in which case the pattern forms a cycle, and *(iii)* the action may be in passive form (as in, e.g., *"a person transported by a car")*, this being useful to compose OAO patterns, as described below.

OAO patterns model the world evolution. Clearly there are infinitely many such patterns. However, that there are only *four primitive OAO patterns* and corresponding *primitive functions*, which model *the world evolution basic modalities*. These patterns model *(i)* how new objects are conceived, *(ii)* how they are realized and *(iii)* how they are destroyed, and *(iv)* how they affect the state of other objects. The first such pattern, called *Conception,* or *OCO pattern,* defines the function *conceiver.* See Fig. 3.

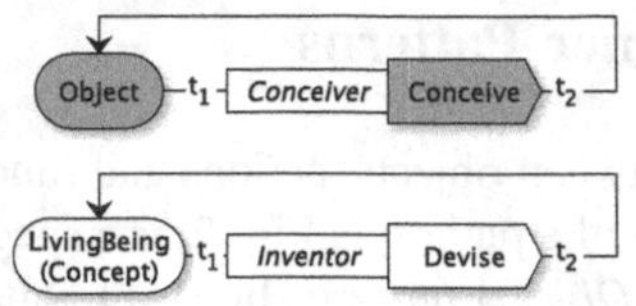

Fig. 3. 'OCO - object conception pattern'.

Conception represents the process by which a concept, which was not lexicalized before, is conceived. Concept conception amounts not only to the creation of the new concept in the mind of a living being, e.g., a person, but also to the creation, via perception, of the causal relation between the concept and the substance being perceived. For instance, Johannes Gutenberg in 1439 conceived the first printing press. Notice that living beings are the only objects which can conceive new functions and that they do this by reflexively "enriching" their state with a new concept, where the word in parenthesis in Fig. 3 represents the concept being conceived.

The second primitive pattern, that we call *Realization*, or *ORO pattern*, defines the function *maker*. See Fig. 4. The realization of an object coincides with the moment when an object assumes its (recognizable) identity in the world. For instance, my car was realized in 2014, 15 days before I bought it. For an object to be realized, its defining functions must have been previously conceived. Figure 4 depicts three important specializations of the pattern, namely: *(i)* the capability of living beings to procreate, *(ii)* the manufacturing skills by which a factory (or a person) can realize objects, e.g., a press, and *(iii)* the ability of "intelligent" machines to assemble new objects.

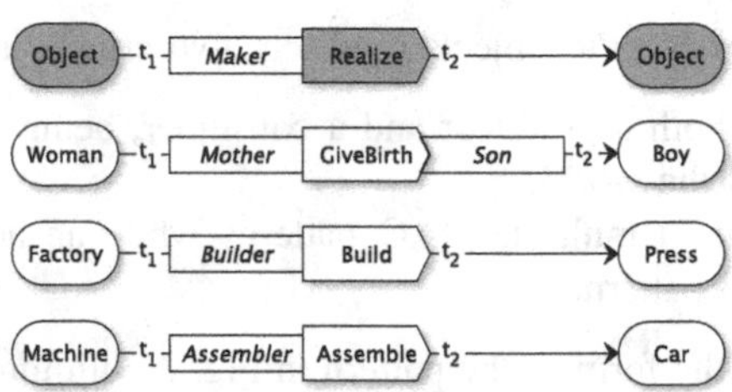

Fig. 4. 'ORO - object realization pattern'.

The third primitive pattern, called *Destruction,* or *ODO pattern*, defines the function *destroyer*. See Fig. 5.

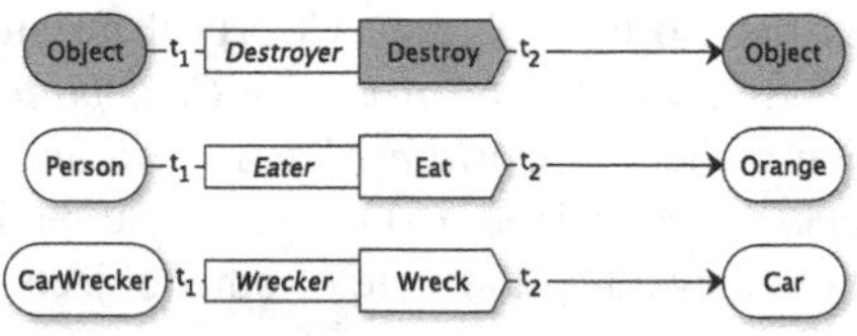

Fig. 5. 'ODO - object destruction pattern'.

ODO patterns represent the process by which an object "disappears" because losing its identity. This is the inverse pattern of realization. Thus, eating an orange and a car wrecker destroying my car are both instantiations of this pattern.

The last primitive pattern, called *Service Provision,* or *OSO pattern*, defines the functions *provider* and *receiver*. See Fig. 6.

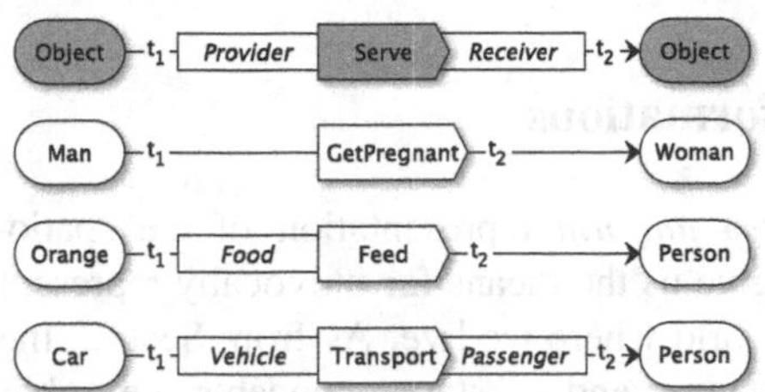

Fig. 6. 'OSO - object service pattern'.

This is the pattern that models the process by which any two objects may affect one another. The specialization patterns represent some important specializations, namely: *(i)* the inception of a living being (it is a "service" in the sense that the state of the consumer is changed), *(ii)* a living being acquiring the energy needed to live by eating, and *(iii)* an object affecting the state, e.g., the position, of another object.

The key observation is that *the world evolution can be modeled by suitably specializing/generalizing and/or by composing OAO patters to produce complex patterns.* We call the patterns obtained in this way, *Producer – Consumer (PC) patterns*. The figures above provide examples of specializations. PC patterns compose OAO patterns by making the consumer of a former pattern coincide with the producer of a latter pattern. PC patterns can produce graphs of arbitrary complexity. The simplest versions of PC patterns are OAOAO patterns. These patterns are of particular relevance since they represent how the application of the function in the first OAO pattern provides input to the function applied in the second OAO pattern. Examples of relevant OAOAO patterns are: *reproduction,* which models how something is constructed as a copy of some object, *transformation* which models how objects change their function (e.g., a car transformed into a cage or a rock into a chair); *undo* by which the second function, under certain conditions, cancels the effects of the first function, this allowing to define the *inverse* function; *service composition*, which models how complex services are provided, online or in the world, and so on. As an example of OAOAO pattern, Fig. 7 depicts *Creation.*

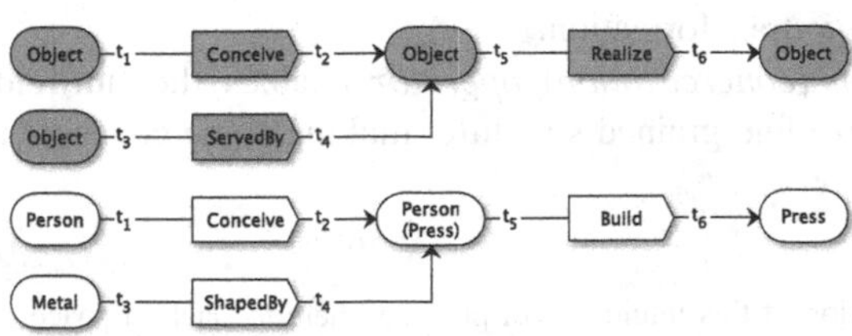

Fig. 7. 'Creation compound pattern'.

Creation allows for the construction of a new type of object (e.g., presses, in the case of Gutenberg's press). Notice that the central object has two inputs which may occur at different times. The first observation is that the double input captures the fact that nothing can be created but can only be "transformed" from something else. The second is that what we represent is always an approximation, e.g., we could further complicate the above pattern to consider more materials, human effort, and so on.

4 Pattern Transformations

PC patterns allow for a *uniform* representation of the spatio-temporal continuum. However, they do not give us the means for univocally representing this continuum as (the evolution of) the world where we live. As from Sect. 2, there is a many-to-many mapping between substances and substance concepts (i.e., objects) and, as from [1], there is a many-to-many mapping between substance concepts and classification concepts, this latter intuition being captured by the two relations FpO and OpF introduced in Sect. 2. These two mappings are at the core of the phenomenon of knowledge diversity and formalize two levels of freedom in the representation of the spatio-temporal continuum. The first, from substances to objects, corresponds to the many possible ways in which the same substance can be *perceived* as a certain object. The second, from objects to functions, corresponds to the many possible ways in which the same object can be *reasoned about* in terms of the function it performs.

Our solution to the problem of managing diversity in knowledge is to exploit the uniform representation provided by PC patterns and define a set of *PC pattern transformation operators* that allow, given any two PC patterns, to reduce one to the other, *preserving their intended meaning*. The intuition is that the existence of such a reduction will be evidence that the two PC patterns represent the same or similar configurations of substances, and the contrary when this is not the case. Notice how this *does not avoid* the possibility of multiple descriptions of the same (set of) substances, but it *does provide* a systematic approach for absorbing diversity.

We have identified three PC pattern transformation operators, that we call *Granularity*, *Abstraction* and *Partiality,* where the combined effects of these three operators allow to transform patterns, still preserving the underlying semantics.[5]

The *Granularity operator* allows for two types of transformation: *(i)* substituting *parts* with *wholes* or vice versa, and *(ii)* substituting *more specific* concepts with *more general* concepts or vice versa. The examples in the previous section are all applications of this operator. Figure 8 provides a further example where the pattern at the bottom is obtained from the one at the top via a *whole-part* transformation and a *more general-more specific* transformation.

The *Abstraction (concretization) operator* enables the (un)folding of concepts, towards a less (more) fine-grained structure; making some concepts implicit (explicit).

[5] A general formalization of this intuition, not provided here for lack of space, will be provided in a follow-up paper and will be based on the work described in [16], which provides a formalization of the problem of theory transformation in terms of abstraction operators.

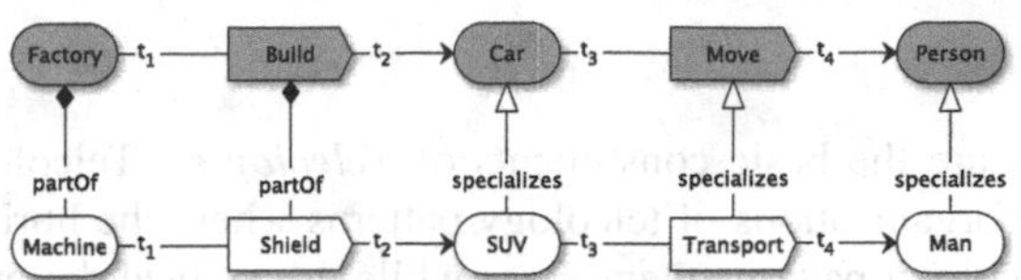

Fig. 8. 'Granularity operator'.

Figure 9 provides an example of abstraction (top) and one of concretization (bottom). Notice how an Action Object Action pattern gets reduced to a single action and vice versa.

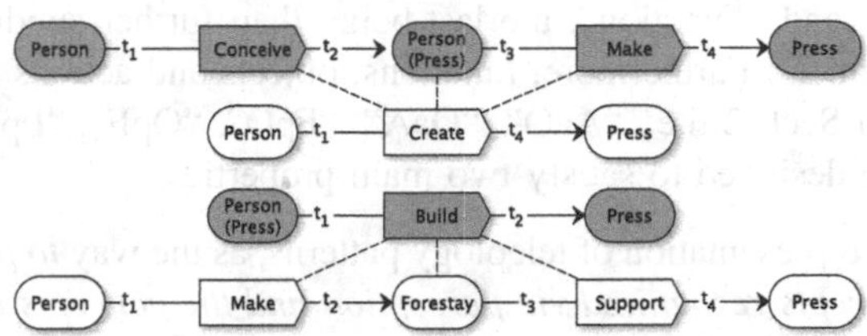

Fig. 9. 'Abstraction/concretization operator'.

The granularity and the abstraction operators output PC patterns. This is not the case for the *Partiality operator* which outputs two patterns, namely *(i)* patterns containing only actions and functions, that we call *AA patterns*, and *(ii)* patterns containing only objects and functions, that we call *OO patterns*. The *Partiality operator* achieves this result by dropping all elements of certain kinds (O or A). Consider for instance Fig. 10, where the top pattern is obtained from the middle one by dropping objects (and functions) and where the bottom pattern is obtained from the middle one by dropping actions. Notice how AA patterns focus *on the process*, as it is done, e.g., in planning and activity recognition (see, e.g., [17–19]) while OO patterns focus *on objects and their functions*, as it is done, e.g., in *Schema.org* [20]. The choice of where to focus depends on the purpose of the modeling. We call the union of PC patterns, OO patterns and AA patterns, *teleology patterns*, to capture the idea that any representation is chosen to best fit the problem to be solved.

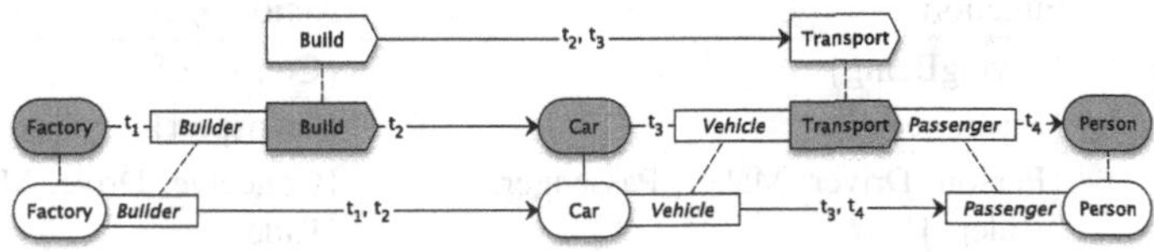

Fig. 10. 'Partiality operator'.

5 Teleologies

Teleology patterns are the basic constituents of *Teleologies*. Teleologies are nothing else but structured organizations of teleology patterns where the horizontal dimension is given by the teleology patterns themselves while the vertical dimension follows the "usual" more/less general hierarchy. In this respect the name "teleology" has a double motivation as, on one side, teleologies allow for the explicit representation of function, while, on the other side, are organized as needed for the problem to be solved.

The top part of teleologies is organized in two levels. The root is "Concept", meaning that the focus is on representation rather than on what is the case, as it happens in (upper level) ontologies (where, for instance, the root of *DOLCE* is "Thing" [21] and the root of *SUMO* is "Entity" [22]). In turn, the root has three children, namely "Object", "Action" and "Function", the last being then further subdivided into "Producer" and "Consumer". Furthermore, functions, objects and actions are linked by the relations defined in Sect. 2, i.e., "AaO", "OaA", "FpO", "OpF", "FpA" and "ApF".

Teleologies are designed to satisfy two main properties:

1. to allow for the representation of teleology patterns, as the way *to provide a uniform view of the concepts recognized via perception and the concepts used and derived via reasoning*;
2. to allow for their continuous modification, via pattern transformation operators, as the way by which a teleology can be *adapted to integrate new inputs*, e.g., new concepts needed to represent a new input from perception or from a heterogeneous dataset, or concepts coming from another teleology.

Let us start with the first property. For the sake of argumentation, as an example, we can assume that we have, as initial set of "relevant" concepts, those which are reported in Table 1 and are not tagged with "*". Notice that in Table 1 we have "Person" and "Car" but also "LivingBeing" and "Machine", with the latter two concepts being more general than the former two. It is in general a good practice to use a set of high level concepts as collectors of functions and actions. Thus, for instance, the functions and actions of "LivingBeing" can be inherited by, e.g., "Cat". The idea is to avoid unnecessary diversity as the more general concepts drive the instantiation of their more specific concepts.

Table 1. An example of relevant concepts.

Object	Function	Action
LivingBeing	{LivingBeing}	{Conceive}
Machine	{Machine}	{Transport}
Person	{Person, Driver, Maker, Passenger, *Rider*}	{Conceive, Drive, Make, *Ride*}
Car	{Car, Vehicle, Transportation}	{Transport}
Motorcycle	{*Motorcycle*, Vehicle}	{Transport}

A snapshot of the resulting teleology is reported in Fig. 11.

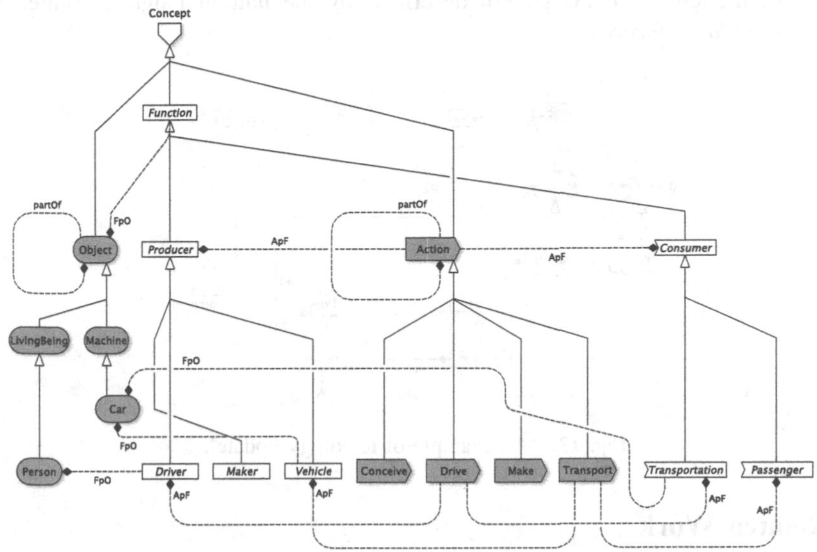

Fig. 11. 'A small example of teleology'.

The white arrows represent *more/less general* relations, the black diamonds represent *associative* relations, e.g., "partOf", "FpO" and "ApF". The "ApF" links in Fig. 11 must be read as follows: producers enable the actions in ApF(producer) while consumers are affected by the actions in ApF(consumer). Notice how the PC pattern in Fig. 2 is reconstructed via the associative relations linking "Car", "Person", "Vehicle", "Transport" and "Passenger". Notice also how *roles* such as, e.g., "driverOf" or vehicleOf", not represented in Fig. 11 for lack of space, are more specific concepts than the relation resulting from the composition of FpO and ApF. Roles are crucial for the representation of OO patterns like the one represented in Fig. 10 (bottom).

Let us now see how we can use the same process as above to adapt, e.g., extend/change, the current teleology in the presence of a new concept (for instance coming from another vocabulary). Consider, for instance, the concept "Car", classified in *Schema.org*[6] as a "Product" and as a "Vehicle". This concept is perfectly aligned with that with the same name in the teleology in Fig. 11. The only (optional) addition is to add "Product" (as a function, more precisely as a consumer). Consider now the more complex situation of updating the teleology in Fig. 11 by adding the object "Motorcycle", as defined in *Schema.org*[7], as a specialization of "Machine". "Motorcycle" is not present in Fig. 11 nor is there any PC pattern to which it can be connected. The relevant PC pattern(s) can be added by applying the granularity operator, more specifically by specializing the function "Driver" with "Rider" and the action "Drive"

6 http://schema.org/Car .

7 https://auto.schema.org/Motorcycle .

with "Ride". Figure 12 represents a focus on the relevant part of Fig. 11 where the new concepts (marked with "*" in Table 1) are added. The resulting teleology is now capable of modeling the PC pattern described by the natural language sentence *'a person riding a motorcycle'*.

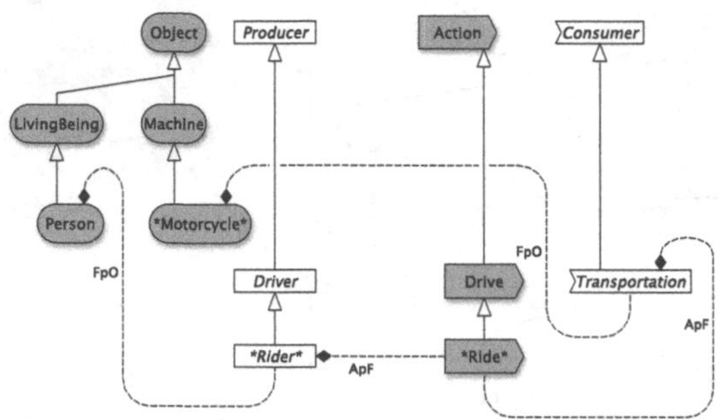

Fig. 12. 'An example of teleology update'.

6 Related Work

Our work is coherent and shares some intuitions with some recent work on the *theories of intentionality* (see, e.g., [23]), where the central focus is on *how* minds are able to *represent* and *be about* objects, as the basis for understanding *what* minds represent. Of direct relevance to our notion of function are Searle's notions of *status function* and *function imposition* and how they contribute to the construction of *social reality* [24].

From a methodological point of view, the work which is closer in spirit to ours is that on *upper ontologies*. However, we can articulate two main differences. The first is connected to what they are modeling, as well represented by the different roots (see the previous section). The second, which is a direct consequence of the first, is in how teleologies are built. Ontologies are designed on the basis of a thorough analysis of how the world appears to us. As a consequence, the problem reduces to finding the most suitable more general classes from which an entity can be derived by specialization. This approach cannot be used in the definition of teleologies. With teleologies the general idea is to *build* the most suitable teleology and to *adapt* it as needed following the evolution of the world (see Sect. 6). What is defined a priori is not teleologies but the process by which they are built starting from their top level concepts.

The approach presented in this paper has some important commonalities with the work on biosemantics [25], and was initially inspired by Millikan's work, as cited throughout the paper. In particular Millikan was the first to introduce the notions of *producer* and *consumer*, with the goal of explaining the process by which meaning gets transferred [14]. Millikan's notions are a particular case of the corresponding notions introduced in this paper. Figure 13 (top) reports one of Millikan's most famous producer and consumer examples describing how bees communicate to other bees, via a specific dance, where the nectar is.

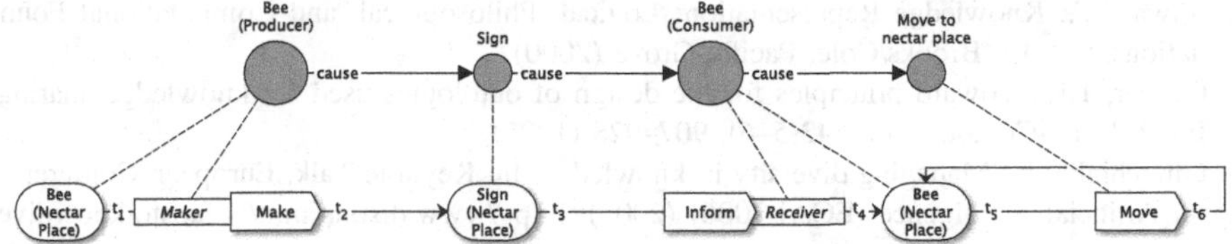

Fig. 13. ‘A bee telling another bee where the nectar is’.

Figure 13 shows how the bee example is an instance of an OROSOSO pattern where *sign* is meant to be a “word” in the bee language, and *inform* is a service by which the sign, by being seen, *informs* the second bee about the location where the nectar is.

Last but not least, PC patterns can be seen as a formalism for modeling *causality*. This fact was not intended when we started this work and came out completely unexpected. At this point in time we are not ready for a thorough discussion on this issue. The only two observations that we are able to make is that certain argumentations on *causal factors*, see, e.g., [26], can be modeled as suitable PC patterns and that, at the same time, Millikan’s notion of causal factor [4], as also discussed in [1], relates to the notion of function, as introduced in this paper.

7 Conclusion

In this paper we have shown how the world is modeled in terms of three concepts at three increasing levels of abstractions: *objects*, *actions* and *functions*. These three notions have allowed us to introduce *PC patterns* and *teleologies* as a first step towards a general solution of the problem of *managing knowledge diversity*. To this extent, we have briefly described how teleologies can be tuned to the specific problem and later adapted as needed, following a precise methodology. The future work will consist in the development of large scale teleologies (including a full formalization of *schema.org*) and a detailed mapping to the work done in biosemantics.

References

1. Giunchiglia, F., Mattia F.: Concepts as (recognition) abilities. In: Proceedings of the 9th International Conference Formal Ontology in Information Systems (FOIS 2016), vol. 283, p. 153. IOS Press (2016)
2. Millikan, R.G.: Biosemantics. J. Philos. **86**(6), 281–297 (1989)
3. Prinz, J.: Beyond appearances: the content of sensation and perception. In: Perceptual Experience, pp. 434–460 (2006)
4. Millikan, R.G.: On Clear and Confused Ideas: An Essay About Substance Concepts. Cambridge University Press, Cambridge (2000)
5. Forsyth, D.A., Jean, P.: Computer Vision: A Modern Approach. Prentice Hall, Upper Saddle River (2011)

6. Sowa, J.F.: Knowledge Representation: Logical, Philosophical, and Computational Foundations, vol. 13. Brooks/Cole, Pacific Grove (2000)
7. Gruber, T.R.: Toward principles for the design of ontologies used for knowledge sharing. Int. J. Hum.-Comput. Stud. **43**(5–6), 907–928 (1995)
8. Giunchiglia, F.: Managing diversity in knowledge. In: Keynote Talk, European Conference on Artificial Intelligence (ECAI-2006) (2006). http://www.disi.unitn.it/~fausto/knowdive.ppt
9. Bird, G.: Kant's Theory of Knowledge: An Outline of One Central Argument in the 'Critique of Pure Reason, vol. 1. Routledge, Abingdon (2016)
10. Giunchiglia, F., Khuyagbaatar B., Gabor, B.: Understanding and exploiting language diversity. In: IJCAI (2017)
11. Gibson, J.J.: The theory of affordances. In: Perceiving, Acting, and Knowing: Toward an Ecological Psychology, pp. 67–82 (1977)
12. Şahin, E., Çakmak, M., Doğar, M.R., Uğur, E., Üçoluk, G.: To afford or not to afford: a new formalization of affordances toward affordance-based robot control. Adapt. Behav. **15**(4), 447–472 (2007)
13. Ortmann, J., Kuhn, W.: Affordances as qualities. In: FOIS, pp. 117–130 (2010)
14. Millikan, R.G.: Language, Thought, and Other Biological Categories: New Foundations for Realism. MIT press, Cambridge (1984)
15. Rosch, E., Mervis, C.B., Gray, W.D., Johnson, D.M., Boyes-Braem, P.: Basic objects in natural categories. Cogn. Psychol. **8**(3), 382–439 (1976)
16. Giunchiglia, F., Walsh, T.: A theory of abstraction. Artif. Intell. **57**(2–3), 323–389 (1992)
17. Chen, L., Nugent, C.D., Wang, H.: A knowledge-driven approach to activity recognition in smart homes. IEEE Trans. Knowl. Data Eng. **24**(6), 961–974 (2012)
18. Rodríguez, N.D., Cuéllar, M.P., Lilius, J., Calvo-Flores, M.D.: A survey on ontologies for human behavior recognition. ACM Comput. Surv. (CSUR) **46**(4), 43 (2014)
19. Ni, Q., Pau de la Cruz, I., García Hernando, A.B.: A foundational ontology-based model for human activity representation in smart homes. J. Ambient Intell. Smart Environ. **8**(1), 47–61 (2016)
20. Barker, P., Campbell, L.M.: What is schema.org? LRMI (2015). Accessed 21 Apr 2014
21. Masolo, C., Borgo, S., Gangemi, A., Guarino, N., Oltramari, A., Oltramari, R., Schneider, L.: Lead Partner ISTC-CNR, Ian Horrocks. WonderWeb Deliverable D17. The WonderWeb Library of Foundational Ontologies and the DOLCE ontology (2002)
22. Niles, I., Pease, A.: Towards a standard upper ontology. In: Proceedings of the International Conference on Formal Ontology in Information Systems, vol. 2001, pp. 2–9. ACM (2001)
23. Millikan, R.G.: Varieties of Meaning: The 2002 Jean Nicod Lectures. MIT Press, Cambridge (2004)
24. Searle, J.R.: Social ontology and political power. In: Friederick, S.F. (ed.) Socializing Metaphysics: The Nature of Social Reality, pp. 195–210 (2003)
25. Macdonald, G., Papineau, D. (eds.): Teleosemantics. Clarendon Press, Wotton-under-Edge (2006)
26. Sober, E., Papineau, D.: Causal factors, causal inference, causal explanation. Proc. Aristot. Soc. Suppl. Vol. **60**, 97–136 (1986)

Author Index

Printed in the United States
By Bookmasters